Do I Want to Be a Teacher?

1

Do I Want to Be a Teacher?

Chapter Outline

Rewards and Challenges in Teaching
> Rewards in Teaching • Challenges in Teaching

The Teaching Profession
> Characteristics of Professionalism • Are Teachers Professionals? • Putting Teacher Professionalism into Perspective

Diversity: The Changing Face of U.S. Classrooms

The Modern Reform Movement in Education
> Changes in Teacher Preparation • INTASC: Standards in Teacher Education • Teaching in an Era of Reform

Learning Objectives

After you have completed your study of this chapter, you should be able to:

1. Describe the major rewards and challenges of teaching.

2. Describe the different characteristics of professionalism, and explain how they relate to teaching.

3. Identify the different dimensions of learner diversity, and explain why understanding different teaching and learning environments is important for beginning teachers.

4. Explain how the current reform movement in education is changing the teaching profession.

Case Studies

 Elementary

 Middle

 Secondary

"Do I want to be a teacher?" In this chapter, we hope to help you begin answering this question by providing you with information about the teaching profession. As you read the following case studies, think about each teacher's experiences and how they compare to your own.

I always liked working with kids. I enjoyed watching my little brother when my mom ran errands, and I often helped out with summer youth programs. In high school I started thinking about being a music teacher, since I enjoyed playing the piano and singing in choral groups.

Then, I went to college and one of my courses required us to be a high school teacher's aide. I worked with a music teacher but never felt like I really fit in. Luckily, in a second course I had a chance to work in an elementary school. I went home after the first day and thought, "Yes, this is it."

There have been ups and downs, of course. My first job was in an urban second-grade classroom with 26 kids. Fortunately, I had an aide who spoke Spanish, and she was a huge help, since several of my students were still struggling to learn English.

Now here I am, 10 years later, married with a family of my own, and I still love teaching. The first few years were a bit of a struggle, but I learned so much. Now I've got my own student teacher and am eager to help her figure it all out. (Amy Carson, first-grade teacher in an urban elementary school)

Before I became a teacher, I worked for 20 years in the pharmaceutical industry, first in a research lab and then as a project manager. It was challenging, and I made a good salary, but I began to feel that there was more to life than making money for some big company.

A couple years ago I read a book in which the author described the difference between a person's "job" and a person's "work." Your job is how you make money; your work is how you contribute to the world. It began to crystallize everything for me. Business, for me, was a job, but I didn't really have any "work."

Then, I thought about my high school chemistry teacher, and I remembered how much he loved that stuff. I began to think about teaching, and, to make a long story short, I went back to school, and this time I did what I've always wanted to do. Of course it's tough some days. The kids can be "off the wall," and I periodically feel like I'm drowning in paperwork. But, when you see the lightbulb go on for someone, it's all worth it. Now, my job and my work are the same thing. (Matt Shepard, high school science teacher in a suburban high school and recent entry into teaching)

Some of you probably have characteristics similar to both Amy and Matt. You're intelligent and introspective, and you've had a number of life experiences. You've thought about teaching but aren't sure if it's for you or where you might fit in the profession. Others of you are less certain, still in the process of deciding what you want to do with your life. You enjoyed your school experiences, and most of your ideas about teaching are based on them. The idea of working with young people is attractive, but you're still not sure.

To begin answering the question "Do I want to be a teacher?" let's consider some reasons people go into teaching by responding to the survey on the following page.

We gave the same survey to other prospective teachers, averaged their responses, and ranked them from most (1) to least (9) important reasons for becoming a teacher. Table 1.1 summarizes the results. Let's see how yours compare.

We see from Table 1.1 that the desire to work with young people (Item 5) and wanting to contribute to society (Item 6) were survey participants' two most important reasons for considering teaching. These reasons are consistent with Amy's and Matt's thinking, and they're also consistent with polls of teachers over a nearly 25-year period (National Education Association, 1997).

A Public Agenda poll of new teachers found similar results, with 86 percent of new teachers viewing teaching as "a true sense of calling," 75 percent considering teaching a lifelong choice, and 68 percent reporting teaching as very satisfying. In addition, an amazing 96 percent of beginning teachers reported that teaching is work they love to do (Wadsworth, 2001).

Let's look more closely at the reasons people go into teaching.

Rewards and Challenges in Teaching

People go into teaching because it's rewarding, and, as with any occupation, it can also be challenging. We examine both in this section.

Rewards in Teaching

Intrinsic rewards. Rewards that come from within oneself and are personally satisfying for emotional or intellectual reasons.

Extrinsic rewards. Rewards that come from outside oneself, such as job security and vacations.

The rewards in teaching can be either **intrinsic**, those that come within oneself and are personally satisfying for emotional or intellectual reasons, or **extrinsic**, those that come from the outside, such as job security and vacations. Let's look at each.

Intrinsic Rewards

Many people become teachers because of intrinsic rewards, which fall into two broad categories—emotional and intellectual.

professional knowledge: test yourself!

For each item, circle the number that best represents your thinking. Use the following scale as a guide.

1 = Strongly disagree
2 = Disagree
3 = Uncertain
4 = Agree
5 = Strongly agree

1. Job security is a major reason I'm considering becoming a teacher.

    1   2   3   4   5

2. My family has strongly influenced my decision to teach.

    1   2   3   4   5

3. Long summer vacations are important to me as I consider teaching as a career.

    1   2   3   4   5

4. I've never really considered any other occupation besides teaching.

    1   2   3   4   5

5. My desire to work with young people is an important reason I'm considering becoming a teacher.

    1   2   3   4   5

6. I'm thinking of teaching because I'd like to contribute to our society.

    1   2   3   4   5

7. My interest in a subject matter field is a major reason I'm thinking about becoming a teacher.

    1   2   3   4   5

8. I'm considering entering teaching because of the influence of a former elementary or secondary teacher.

    1   2   3   4   5

9. I'm considering teaching because of the opportunity for a lifetime of self-growth.

    1   2   3   4   5

This is available in a downloadable format on the Companion Website for personal portfolio use.

TABLE 1.1 Responses to Interest in Teaching Inventory

Survey Rank	Item Focus	Average Response of Students	Item
1	Work with youth	4.6	5
2	Value to society	4.5	6
3	Self-growth	3.9	9
4	Content interest	3.8	7
5	Influence of teachers	3.6	8
6	Job security	3.1	1
7	Summer vacations	2.9	3
8	Family influence	2.8	2
9	Other careers not considered	1.9	4

Emotional Rewards. To begin this section, let's look at some true stories that teachers have shared.

Kasia, 23, calls her boyfriend, Jeff. It's "Teacher Appreciation Week" at her middle school, and she has just received a dozen roses from a group of her seventh-grade science students.

"I was always on them about whispering too," she excitedly tells Jeff. "I maybe would have expected this from my fifth-period class, but never from this bunch.

"Let me read the note I got from them," she continues. She reads,

"Thank you for all that you've done for us and for all the wonderful things that you've teached [sic] us. You are truly an amazing teacher. Thank you again."

Happy Teacher Appreciation Week,
Sincerely, Alicia, Rosa, Shannon, Tina, Stephanie, Melissa, Jessica, and Becca

"That's wonderful," Jeff laughs. "Good thing you're not their English teacher."
"I know. I showed Isabel [the students' English teacher] the note, and she broke up. 'So much for grammar,' she said."

Miguel Rodriguez, 42, another middle school teacher, received the following note from one of his students.

Mr. Rodriguez,

I wanted to think of some creative way to thank you for being the best teacher I ever had. (But I couldn't).

Even though all the geography skills I'll ever use in my life I learned in second grade, I just wanted to say thanks for teaching me how to really prepare for life in the years to come.

Every day I looked forward to coming to your class (and not just because of Mike [a boy in the class]). I always enjoyed your class, because there was a hidden message about life in there somewhere.

Your [sic] my very favorite teacher and you've taught me some of the best lessons in life I could ever learn. Thank you so much.

A grateful student,
Erica Jacobs

P.S. No, I didn't write this to raise my grade.

6

These notes and the flowers Kasia received symbolize some of the emotional rewards in teaching. "They're what keep you going," Miguel commented matter-of-factly while discussing his enjoyment of his work.

Sharon, a veteran first-grade teacher, also describes emotional rewards in her work. "The beginning of the day gets me going," she said, smiling, when she described her continued commitment to her career. "I stand at the door, and the kids give me a hug, a high five, or a handshake when they come in the room. Even if the previous day was a bad one, all those little faces are enough to get me started all over again."

Sometimes students show their affection in strange ways, as this middle school teacher experienced:

Joanne, a first-year teacher, entered her classroom first thing in the morning on her birthday. Her students had arranged with the custodian to gain access to her room and had moved all the desks to the center of the room and had wrapped them with tape and toilet paper. How would you react?

Joanne was delighted. "I called [the perpetrators] out of class and had them come down and [another teacher] took a picture of them standing out in the middle of it all. I left it here all day. I made them sit on the floor. It was really fun. It was really a fun day." (Bullough, 1989, p. 86)

It helps to have a sense of humor when you teach. All teachers reap emotional rewards from their work with students, whether they are wide-eyed first graders, middle school students like Erica Jacobs, or high school seniors struggling to become adults.

Intellectual Rewards. While emotional rewards motivate them as well, many people choose to teach because they are interested in a certain content area and want to share their interest and excitement with others (Liston, 2004).

David Ling, a high school physics teacher, enthusiastically begins his class: "Think about these questions and try to figure out what they have in common," and he then writes the following on the board:

Why do we have seatbelts in our cars?
Why does an automatic washer have holes in the drum?
How does a dog shake the water off itself when it comes out of a pond?

The students look at the list, and after several seconds David continues, "Now, what have we been studying?"

"Inertia," Taneka responds after hesitating briefly.

"Exactly," David says, smiling. "So let's review for a minute. What is inertia? . . . Go ahead, Dana."

"The tendency . . . of something moving to keep on moving . . . straight."

"Or something not moving to remain still," Jamal adds.

"Excellent," David responds with a nod. "Now, let's answer the questions on the board using the idea of inertia."

With David's guidance, the students conclude that if their cars suddenly stop, their bodies tend to keep moving because of inertia, and seatbelts stop them, so they don't get hurt. They also decide that inertia separates water from clothes in the washer because the water goes straight out through the holes in the drum, but the clothes are kept in it. Finally, they determine that as the dog shakes one way, and then stops, the water keeps moving, and the same thing happens when it shakes the other way. So the dog uses the principle of inertia to shake the water from itself.

"Neat," Rebecca says. "Where'd you get that stuff, Mr. Ling?"

Teachers' interactions with their students provide a major source of intrinsic rewards. (Tom Watson/Merrill)

"Oh, I thought up the questions over time," David replies. "The more I study, the more examples I find. . . . That's what we're here for. We study science so we can learn how the world around us works."

Our survey, discussed earlier (Table 1.1), found that "the opportunity for a lifetime of self-growth" and "interest in a subject matter field" were reasons for considering teaching, ranking 3 and 4 out of 9. Learning more about the world and seeing students get excited about the same things we do are some of the intellectual rewards of teaching. One teacher candidate commented, "I would like to think that contact with me would . . . deepen their confidence in their own thinking and make them more curious about the world" (Richardson & Watt, 2005, p. 485). Not surprisingly, these intellectual rewards also help keep veteran teachers in the field. One researcher studying exemplary veteran teachers concluded, "Without exception, intellectual stimulation is a burning need of the teachers I interviewed" (Williams, 2003, p. 72).

Extrinsic Rewards

Extrinsic rewards also attract people to teaching. For example, job security and summer vacations ranked sixth and seventh, respectively, in the survey.

The job security found in teaching is greater than in most other occupations. For example, after a short probation period—usually about 3 years—teachers are typically awarded tenure. Originally designed to attract good people and protect them from political pressures, tenure provides teachers with job security.

For some, working in a profession with long vacations is rewarding. According to an old joke, a student asked to identify three reasons for going into teaching responded, "June, July, and August." In addition, teachers have vacations throughout the year at times when vacations are most attractive—the Friday after Thanksgiving, the winter holiday season, and spring break, for example.

In addition to job security and desirable vacations, teachers enjoy convenient work schedules and occupational status. Teachers' schedules are similar to those of students, so, for example, teachers' own children don't go home to empty houses after school. Additionally, despite perceptions to the contrary, the teaching profession enjoys considerable occupational status (National Education Association, 2002). If you have doubts, consider how parents feel as they approach a parent–teacher conference. They want nothing more than to hear that everything is okay in school and that their child is growing academically and socially. Into no other profession's hands is so much care of young people placed.

Teachers' salaries are another extrinsic reward that both motivate teachers to enter and to leave the profession. While low compared to other professions, teacher salaries, when combined with benefits and favorable work schedules, provide a major extrinsic reward for entering the profession. However, low salaries are often cited as a major reason for leaving the profession after several years of teaching (Ingersoll & Smith, 2003). Salaries are improving, however. For instance, the average teacher salary in the United States for 2003–2004 was $46,597, ranging from a high of $56,516 in Connecticut to a low of $33,236 in South Dakota. In the same year, the average beginning salary was almost $32,000. Table 1.2 lists the average and beginning teacher salaries for each state in 2003–2004.

Union officials call the salary picture a "mixed bag" (American Federation of Teachers, 2004). While teacher salaries have risen an average of 3 percent the last 5 years, they still fall well below the starting salaries of other occupations such as engineering ($50,033) and accounting ($40,779).

Your beginning salary will depend on a number of factors, such as the local cost of living and the location of the school district. Local property taxes are the major funding source for schools, so teachers' salaries depend, in large part, on property values. Also, urban districts typically have higher salaries than their rural counterparts because of a higher cost of living. Though money isn't everything, research shows that higher salaries are related to

TABLE 1.2   Beginning and Average Teacher Salaries for U.S. States in 2003–2004

State	Average Salary	Beginning Salary
Alabama	$38,282	$30,973
Alaska	51,136	40,027
Arizona	42,324	28,236
Arkansas	39,226	26,129
California	56,444	35,135
Colorado	43,318	31,296
Connecticut	56,516	34,462
Delaware	51,112	34,566
Florida	40,598	30,696
Georgia	45,848	35,116
Hawaii	45,456	37,615
Idaho	40,111	25,908
Illinois	53,820	35,114
Indiana	45,791	29,784
Iowa	38,381	26,967
Kansas	38,622	28,530
Kentucky	39,831	28,416
Louisiana	37,123	29,655
Maine	39,864	25,901
Maryland	50,303	33,760
Massachusetts	53,274	34,041
Michigan	54,474	34,377
Minnesota	45,010	30,772
Mississippi	36,217	28,106
Missouri	38,247	28,938
Montana	37,184	24,032
Nebraska	39,635	28,527
Nevada	43,211	27,942
New Hampshire	42,689	27,367
New Jersey	53,663	37,061
New Mexico	38,469	31,920
New York	55,181	36,400

(continued)

TABLE 1.2   Beginning and Average Teacher Salaries for U.S. States in 2003–2004 (continued)

State	Average Salary	Beginning Salary
North Carolina	43,211	27,572
North Dakota	35,411	24,108
Ohio	47,791	28,692
Oklahoma	35,061	29,473
Oregon	47,829	33,396
Pennsylvania	52,640	34,140
Rhode Island	54,809	32,902
South Carolina	41,162	27,883
South Dakota	33,236	25,504
Tennessee	40,318	30,449
Texas	40,476	32,741
Utah	38,976	26,130
Vermont	43,009	25,819
Virginia	43,936	32,437
Washington	45,437	30,159
West Virginia	38,496	26,692
Wisconsin	41,687	23,952
Wyoming	39,537	28,900
U.S. AVERAGE	$46,597	$31,704

Source: American Federation of Teachers (2004).

teachers' staying longer in the profession in general, as well as remaining in a particular district or location (Guarino, Santibañez, & Daley, 2006).

Other economic factors also influence the attractiveness of teaching. For example, annual salary increases are virtually guaranteed, and, as we said earlier in the chapter, vacation periods are ideal. Medical, dental, and retirement benefits are usually provided, and job security is high. In addition, teachers are often paid supplements for extra duties, such as club sponsorships, coaching, chairing departments (e.g., chairing the English department in a middle school), and mentoring beginning teachers. In schools with year-round schedules, teachers work 11 months of the year versus 9 or 10 and are paid accordingly.

Challenges in Teaching

Teaching can be rewarding, but it is also challenging. The complexities of classrooms and the multiple roles that teachers perform are two of those challenges.

Complexities of Classrooms

"Classrooms are complex" is an understatement. Teachers make literally hundreds of decisions every day, and many must be made with nearly split-second timing (Kennedy, 2006). What does it feel like to actually teach and make these decisions? Let's look at different teachers' experiences.

Ken, an elementary teacher, shares the following incident in his teaching journal:

March 3: My class is sitting in a circle. I look up and notice one of the girls, Sylvia, is crying. Joey, she claims, has called her a fat jerk. The rest of the students all look at me to watch my response. I consider the alternatives: send Joey to hallway and talk to him in a few minutes; have Joey sit next to me; ask Joey to apologize; direct Sylvia to get a thick skin; ask Sylvia, "How can you solve this problem?"; send Joey to principal; have Joey write an apology letter; ask Joey, "Why did you do this?"; ignore the situation completely; keep Sylvia and Joey in for recess for dialogue; put Joey's name on the board; yell at Joey; send Sylvia and Joey to hallway to work out problem; tell them to return to their seats and write in journals about problem.

It took me about 10 seconds to run through these alternatives, and after each one I thought of reasons why it wasn't a good idea. By the time I look up at Sylvia after this brief introspection, she had stopped crying and was chattering away with a friend about something else. On surface, the problem had gone away. (Winograd, 1998, p. 296)

Joanne, a first-year middle school English teacher, has the following experience the first day back after a 4-day holiday. The students are excited and difficult to settle down. They talk about their weekends, some wander in late, and others are listless as she tries to get class started.

Finally, she can begin, but keeping them on task is a struggle. They don't listen to her directions, and their questions, complaints, and requests for help seem never-ending.

Joanne limps through the day, and as the end appears in sight, she nearly explodes. While her back is turned, one student throws a sponge ball across the room, another jumps up to catch it and knocks his desk over with a clatter. The rest of the class erupts into laughter, and Joanne says loudly, "Everyone settle down this instant, or there will be after-school detention." This seems to work. "If every day was like this, I'm not sure I would make it," she sighs after her students have finally left for the day.

Two high school student teachers discuss their frustrations in taking attendance on the day of a special school dance held during regular class hours:

Cheryl: One boy comes in, he's dressed up. He says, "I have to go to the dance." Comes in early and tells me. Good kid. I'm like, "OK, that's fine Aaron." Then, Kent comes in five minutes late. This is tall Kent, has his own band and never lets me mark him tardy even though he's always tardy, "I'm going to the dance!" After I've already started class! "Ahem. Thank you, Kent. Please sit down." So he's wanting to leave but I can't let him go because he just interrupted my class and . . . I was so mad at him. So I say, "Do you have a ticket?" And he's like, "Well, yeah," and pulls out a ticket that goes to the movie he went to on Friday night and I say, "No, that's not the right ticket."

Dani: What color was it?

Cheryl: Pink.

Dani: What was the color for the . . . ?

Cheryl: The other guy who was legit had a gray one. But then, then, I don't know. And I mean WHO KNOWS! I said, "You're not on my excused list" but neither was the other guy and I'm like . . .

Dani: I didn't even get an excused list! I didn't even know this dance was—I kind of heard something over the intercom. (Dulude-Lay, 2000, p. 4)

11

Figure 1.1 Characteristics of Classrooms

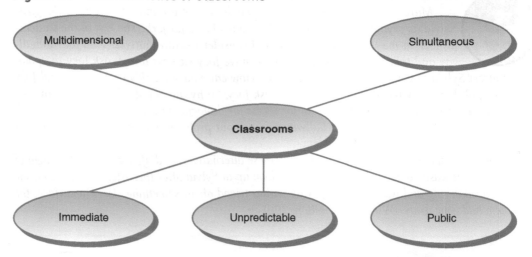

Each of these vignettes illustrates the challenging and sometimes frustrating world of teaching. Researchers have identified several characteristics of classrooms that contribute to this complexity (W. Doyle, 1986):

- Classrooms are multidimensional. Large numbers of events and tasks take place because so many people are in a classroom.
- Classroom events are simultaneous. The events and tasks happen at the same time.
- Classroom events are immediate. Events occur rapidly, sometimes too rapidly.
- Classrooms are unpredictable. Events often take unexpected turns.
- Classrooms are public. Teachers do their jobs in "fishbowls" with people constantly observing their actions.

These characteristics are outlined in Figure 1.1 and discussed in the following sections.

Classrooms Are Multidimensional.   Think about all the different roles you'll perform today. You're a student, a friend, a coworker, and perhaps even a parent. Your life is multidimensional. A classroom is as well; when you teach, you'll need to attend to a number of different events and perform various roles. For instance, while working with one group of students, you'll need to monitor other groups working on assignments. Students will request permission for routine activities, such as going to the bathroom, and learners with special needs may be pulled out of your classroom for extra help. Some students will be attentive and involved in your learning activities, whereas others will drift off and may even be disruptive. Ken found this out when he tried to begin his lesson.

Announcements, assemblies, and other school functions also add to the complexity. For example, Cheryl and Dani had to adjust their plans because of the dance. "If I only had time to teach," is a common teacher lament.

Classroom Events Are Simultaneous.   Many classroom events occur at the same time. For example, while Ken and Joanne were trying to teach, management problems arose. And, as Cheryl and Dani were trying to take roll and begin class, students came in needing immediate attention, asking questions, showing hall passes, and presenting admission slips. Knowing which problem to attend to first can be challenging, if not bewildering.

Classroom Events Are Immediate.   Experts estimate that teachers make somewhere between 800 and 1,500 decisions every day (Jackson, 1968; Murray, 1986). Beyond the sheer numbers, the need to make decisions *right now* adds to the demands on a teacher. Sylvia was crying; Ken needed to decide whether or not to intervene. Kent came in with a bogus hall pass; Cheryl needed to decide whether or not to honor it. And they needed to decide "*right*

now." The immediacy of classroom life requires challenging, split-second decision making.

 Classrooms Are Unpredictable. *One first-grade teacher, attempting to involve students in a lesson about a story they had read about shoes, brought a shoe into class. Pulling it out of a bag, she began, "What can you tell me about this shoe?"*
"It's red," Mike responded.
The shoe was black—there was no sign of red on it anywhere!

Effective teachers plan carefully, but even this may not be enough. Planning for this child's response was impossible. Similarly, Ken couldn't anticipate the incident between Joey and Sylvia, and the same is true for many of the events in Joanne's, Cheryl's, and Dani's classrooms. Often, teachers have little time for thoughtful analysis and consideration of alternatives. After the fact, it is often easy to see what should have been done, but in the heat of the moment, a teacher must respond immediately to unanticipated events. Classrooms are exciting, unpredictable places—a major reason people find teaching both exhilarating and challenging.

Classrooms are complex learning environments in which many events occur simultaneously. (© Ellen B. Senisi/Ellen Senisi)

Classrooms Are Public. The fact that we teach in front of people is obvious. In a sense, we're on stage, and our triumphs and mistakes occur in public for all to see. As we work with students, we are bound to make mistakes, and our actions can have unintended consequences. Ken ignored Joey's (allegedly) calling Sylvia a "fat jerk." Did he unintentionally communicate that verbal abuse is acceptable? Cheryl considered allowing one student to slip out of her class with a bogus pass. If she had, would other students try the same thing? A "fishbowl" is an apt metaphor for teaching; as we swim through our day, both students and other teachers watch us and form judgments about our actions.

Will your first year of teaching necessarily consist of a series of unpredictable situations? Probably. Learning to teach is a journey filled with unanticipated events, and your first year will be exhausting, at times overwhelming, and frequently exhilarating. One book about the experiences of first-year teachers is aptly named *The Roller Coaster Year* (K. Ryan, 1992). It may help to remember, however, that thousands of other beginning teachers have not only survived but flourished.

The Multiple Roles of Teaching

The multiple professional roles that teachers perform is a second factor that makes teaching so challenging. Three of the most important include:

- Creating productive learning environments
- Working with parents and other caregivers
- Collaborating with colleagues

Creating Productive Learning Environments. Creating a productive learning environment is a teacher's most essential role. A productive learning environment is one that is safe and inviting, focuses on learning, and provides opportunities for social and personal growth. In productive learning environments, students feel safe, both physically and emotionally, and the day-to-day routines—including the values, expectations, learning experiences, and both spoken and unspoken rules and conventions—are designed to help students learn and grow (Weinstein, 2007).

Working with Parents and Other Caregivers. Learning should be a cooperative venture, with teachers, students, and parents/caregivers working together. Because the home environment has such a powerful influence on learning, teachers need to develop strategies to increase parental involvement in their children's academic life. These strategies should go beyond traditional once-a-year parent–teacher conferences and should actively involve parents, encouraging them to monitor and help with homework, limit television viewing, and read to their young children (Epstein, 2001; Marzano, 2003).

Students benefit from home–school cooperation in several ways:

- Greater willingness to do homework
- Higher long-term achievement
- More positive attitudes and behaviors
- Better attendance and graduation rates
- Greater enrollment in postsecondary education (Garcia, 2004; Hong & Ho, 2005)

These outcomes result from parents' increased participation in school activities, higher expectations for their children's achievement, and teachers' increased understanding of learners' home environments. Deciding how to respond to a student's disruptive behavior is easier, for example, when his teachers know that his mother or father has lost a job, his parents are going through a divorce, or a family member is ill.

Parent–teacher collaboration can also have long-term benefits for teachers. Teachers who encourage parental involvement have more positive feelings about teaching and their school, and they also have higher expectations for parents and rate them as being more helpful and more likely to follow through on teacher requests (Epstein, 2001).

Virtually all schools have formal communication channels, such as open houses (usually occurring within the first 2 weeks of the school year when teachers introduce themselves and describe general guidelines); interim progress reports, which tell parents about their youngsters' achievements at the midpoint of each grading period; parent–teacher conferences; and, of course, report cards.

Making Connections:
To deepen your CW understanding of the topics in this section of the chapter and integrate them with topics you've already studied, go to the *Making Connections* module for Chapter 1 at **www.prenhall.com/kauchak.** Respond to questions 1–3.

Collaborating with Colleagues. A third major teacher role is collaborating with colleagues. Teachers spend considerable time and effort collaborating with their colleagues, during which effective teachers make cooperative decisions about topics such as curriculum, assessment, grading, and teaching strategies. Administrators assess teachers' ability and inclination to collaborate in the initial job interview, and many principals view collaboration as one of the most essential characteristics of effective teachers.

At the beginning of the chapter, we said that our goal in writing it was to help you decide whether or not you want to be a teacher. Being aware of the rewards and challenges in teaching and teachers' multiple roles can help you make this decision.

IN TODAY'S CLASSROOMS: VIDEO

The Multiple Roles of Teachers

Having read about the multiple roles that teachers perform, you now can see one teacher immersed in these roles. The episode focuses on a middle school teacher involved in instruction, collaborating with colleagues in a team meeting, and working with parents during a parent–teacher conference.

To view this video, go to the *Becoming a Professional* DVD included with this text, click on *In Today's Classrooms,* and then this chapter's video: *The Multiple Roles of Teachers.*

To answer questions about the video online and receive immediate feedback, go to the Companion Website at www.prenhall.com/kauchak, then to the In Today's Classroom *module for Chapter 1.*

Check Your Understanding

1.1 What are the major rewards in teaching?

1.2 What are the major challenges in teaching?

1.3 Identify the four most often cited reasons to enter teaching.

 For feedback, go to Check Your Understanding *at the end of this chapter.*

The Teaching Profession

What does it mean to be a professional? Are teachers professionals? In the last 20 years, attempts to answer these questions have increased (Labaree, 2004, 2006; Neville, Sherman, & Cohen, 2005). Advocates contend that developing teaching into a true profession comparable to medicine and law would benefit teachers, students, and their parents. For teachers it would mean better preparation programs and higher standards for performance and ethics. For students and their parents, increased professionalism could result in parents more fully trusting teachers to help their children grow and develop. We believe in the potential of professionalization to transform teaching in many positive ways and have made it a major theme of this text. But let's examine the issue further.

Characteristics of Professionalism

Why are occupations such as medicine and law considered professions? Researchers examining these and other established professions have identified the following characteristics of **professionalism**:

- A specialized body of knowledge
- Autonomy
- Emphasis on decision making and reflection
- Ethical standards for conduct (Labaree, 2004; Neville et al., 2005)

These characteristics are discussed in the following sections.

A Specialized Body of Knowledge

Professionals understand and utilize a specialized body of knowledge in serving their clients (see Figure 1.2). A physician, for example, understands and can recognize symptoms of diseases and other ailments and can prescribe medications, surgical procedures, or other forms of therapy to eliminate both the symptoms and their causes. People seek the advice and help of physicians because of their specialized knowledge.

Do teachers possess specialized knowledge? Researchers believe the answer is yes and suggest that this knowledge exists in four forms (Borko & Putnam, 1996):

- *Knowledge of content:* A thorough understanding of the content they will be teaching such as math, science, geography, or literature. Research shows that content knowledge influences both what and how teachers teach (T. Smith, Desimone, & Ueno, 2005).
- *Pedagogical content knowledge:* The ability to illustrate abstract concepts, such as equivalent fractions in math or nationalism in history, in ways that are understandable to students.

Professionalism. An occupation characterized by a specialized body of knowledge with emphasis on autonomy, decision making, reflection, and ethical standards for conduct.

Figure 1.2   Professionalism Requires a Specialized Body of Knowledge

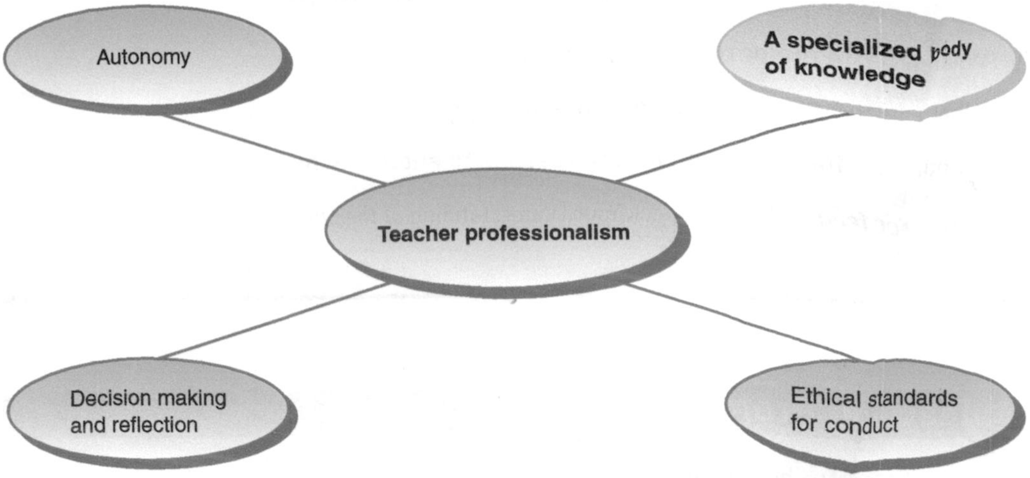

- *General pedagogical knowledge:* Knowledge of general principles of teaching and learning, such as the ability to maintain an orderly and learning-focused classroom or to guide student learning with questions.
- *Knowledge of learners and learning:* Knowledge of theories of development and learning, such as understanding that learners, even in high school, tend to be egocentric, seeing the world from their own perspectives and ignoring the views of others.

To these we add knowledge of the profession, which includes an understanding of the social, historical and philosophical, and organizational and legal aspects of teaching, together with the ability and inclination to continue learning. These different dimensions of knowledge allow teachers to make professional decisions in complex, ill-defined situations.

The ability and inclination to continue learning is also essential for professionals. Just as physicians must continually upgrade their knowledge of medications, surgical procedures, and therapies, teachers must stay abreast of research in their field. For instance, intuition suggests that we encourage students who aren't successful to work harder, but research indicates that this can be counterproductive. Young children generally believe they are already working hard, so they're bewildered by the suggestion, and older students often believe that an admonition to work hard is an indicator of low ability (Brophy, 2004; Pintrich & Schunk, 2002). Teachers who are aware of this research encourage students to change the *way* they study instead of the *amount* they study. Without this professional knowledge, teachers wouldn't be able to adapt their instruction to best meet students' needs. Much of this text is designed to help you develop your knowledge of the profession.

Extended Training for Licensure.   Extended training for licensure is required to develop these different forms of professional knowledge. As with physicians, lawyers, and engineers, teachers must earn a license that allows them to practice their profession. The license is intended to certify that the teacher is competent, and, as with other professions, teachers must periodically renew their license to confirm that they are staying current in their fields. Teachers need at least a bachelor's degree before licensure, and in many states they must complete the degree in a content area, such as math or English, before they begin teacher-preparation experiences (Darling-Hammond & Bransford, 2005). Licensure also requires clinical experiences, such as internships, which are designed to ensure that teachers can apply the professional knowledge they have acquired in the real world of schools.

Autonomy. The capacity to control one's own professional life.

Autonomy

With knowledge also comes **autonomy**, the capacity to control one's own professional life. Professionals have the authority to make decisions based on their specialized knowledge

Figure 1.3 Professionalism Requires Autonomy

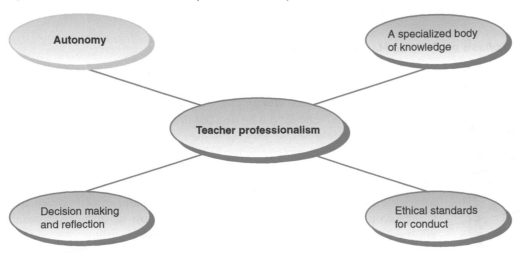

(see Figure 1.3). When a person sees a physician because of stomach pains, for example, no set of standards mandates specific treatments or medications; doctors have the authority to treat patients as they see fit. Some researchers suggest that teaching isn't a profession because states and districts, instead of teachers, prescribe what teachers teach (the **curriculum**) as well as how student understanding is measured (**assessment**) (van den Berg, 2002).

Indeed, states and districts prescribe **standards**, statements specifying what students should know and what skills they should have upon completing an area of study, and districts often require students to meet these standards before allowing them to move from one grade to another or graduate from high school (McCombs, 2005). However, in spite of these mandates, teachers still have a great deal of control over what is taught, how they teach it,

Teacher autonomy to design and implement instruction comes with teacher professionalism. (Hope Madden/Merrill)

Curriculum. What teachers teach.

Assessment. How student understanding is measured.

Standards. Statements specifying what students should know and what skills they should have upon completing an area of study.

and how students are assessed. Autonomy gives teachers the freedom to make professional decisions in their classrooms.

Emphasis on Decision Making and Reflection

As we saw earlier in the chapter, classrooms are complex, and teachers must make an enormous number of decisions in ill-defined situations. For example, Ken had to decide if he should ignore the incident when Sylvia accused Joey of calling her a fat jerk, or if he should intervene. And if he decided to intervene, what should this intervention be? Should he take Joey out of the classroom and talk to him? Make him apologize? Write a note to Sylvia? Call his parents? And, what if Sylvia wasn't telling the truth, or misunderstood what Joey said?

David Ling, in his lesson on inertia, had to decide how to begin his lesson, what examples to use, what students to call on and in what order, how long he would give them to answer, what kind of follow-up question he would ask if they were unable to answer, and a host of other decisions.

Making decisions in situations such as these is one of the differences between a professional and a **technician**, a person who uses specific skills to complete well-defined tasks, such as an electrician wiring an outlet (Sandholtz & Reilly, 2004). **Decision making**, by contrast, involves problem solving in ill-defined situations and is based on professional knowledge. This text attempts to help you develop your professional decision-making abilities by providing a "Decision Making: Defining Yourself as a Professional" exercise at the end of this chapter.

But how do teachers know if they have made good decisions? They receive little feedback about the effectiveness of their work. They are observed by administrators a few times a year at most, and they receive only vague, sketchy, and uncertain feedback from students and parents. In addition, they get virtually no feedback from their colleagues, unless the school has a peer coaching or mentoring program (Gilbert, 2005; Wayne, Youngs, & Fleischman, 2005). To develop as a professional, teachers must be able to continually assess their own classroom actions.

Reflection provides teachers with opportunities to think about and improve their practice. (Mary Kate Denny/PhotoEdit Inc.)

The ability to conduct this self-assessment requires that teachers develop a disposition for continually and critically examining their work. This is the essence of a simple, yet powerful idea called **reflection** (Lee, 2004; Schon, 1983), the act of thinking about and analyzing your actions. Reflective teachers are thoughtful, analytical, even self-critical about their teaching. They plan lessons thoughtfully and take the time to analyze and critique them afterward.

Reflection is important in teaching not only because it improves our effectiveness but also because it helps us develop as professionals (Bransford et al., 2005; Hammerness, Darling-Hammond, & Bransford, 2005). By analyzing their work, reflective professionals develop a coherent philosophy of teaching that helps them integrate theory and practice and continually refine their teaching (Rodgers, 2002) (see Figure 1.4).

Professional Ethics

Professionals also have ethical standards for conduct. To understand what this means, consider the following scenarios:

An ardent advocate of gun control, you believe that access to guns should be strictly regulated, and you have said so in class. Eric, one of your students, brings a newspaper editorial to school that makes a compelling argument against gun control. Because of your beliefs, you don't allow the student to share the editorial with the class.

Technician. A person who uses specific skills to complete well-defined tasks.

Decision making. Problem solving in ill-defined situations, based on professional knowledge.

Reflection. The process of teachers' thinking about and analyzing their work to assess its effectiveness.

Figure 1.4 Professionalism Requires Decision Making and Reflection

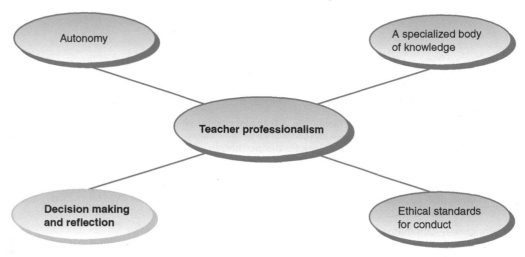

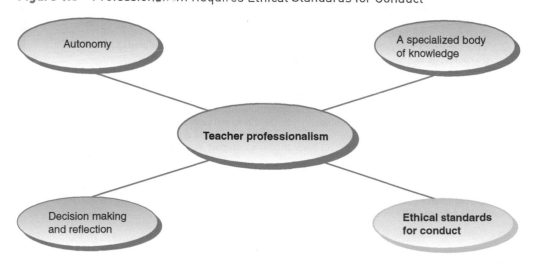

Greg is a very difficult student in one of your classes. He is continually disruptive and periodically shouts insults at other students and sometimes even at you. You've tried everything you know to control his behavior, but you've been unsuccessful. Finally, in exasperation one day, you walk up to him while he is talking, clap your hands together, and say angrily, "Greg, I've had it with you! You can't keep your mouth closed for more than 1 minute, and you're an embarrassment to yourself and the other students in this class. I don't want to hear another sound out of you the rest of the period." Surprisingly, Greg sits quietly for the remainder of the period. Now, finding that anger seems to be the only way to keep Greg from being disruptive, you sometimes use it to manage his behavior.

Have you behaved "ethically" in these examples? How do you know? **Ethics** are sets of moral standards for acceptable professional behavior, and all professions have codes of ethics intended to guide professionals as they make decisions about how to act (see Figure 1.5). In its code of ethics, the National Education Association (NEA), the largest professional organization in education, addresses the behavior of teachers working with their students (see Figure 1.6).

Figure 1.5 Professionalism Requires Ethical Standards for Conduct

Ethics. Sets of moral standards for acceptable professional behavior.

Figure 1.6   National Education Association Code of Ethics

Preamble

The educator, believing in the worth and dignity of each human being, recognizes the supreme importance of the pursuit of truth, devotion to excellence, and the nurture of democratic principle. Essential to these goals is the protection of freedom to learn and to teach and the guarantee of equal educational opportunity for all. The educator accepts the responsibility to adhere to the highest ethical standards.

The educator recognizes the magnitude of the responsibility inherent in the teaching process. The desire for the respect and confidence of one's colleagues, of students, of parents, and the members of the community provides the incentive to attain and maintain the highest possible degree of ethical conduct. The Code of Ethics of the Education Profession indicates the aspiration of all educators and provides standards by which to judge conduct.

The remedies specified by the NEA and/or its affiliates for the violation of any provision of this Code shall be exclusive and no such provision shall be enforceable in any form other than one specifically designated by the NEA or its affiliates.

Principle I—Commitment to the Student

The educator strives to help each student realize his or her potential as a worthy and effective member of society. The educator therefore works to stimulate the spirit of inquiry, the acquisition of knowledge and understanding, and the thoughtful formulation of worthy goals.

In fulfillment of the obligation to the student, the educator—

1. Shall not unreasonably restrain the student from independent action in the pursuit of learning.
2. Shall not unreasonably deny the student access to varying points of view.
3. Shall not deliberately suppress or distort subject matter relevant to the student's progress.
4. Shall make reasonable effort to protect the student from conditions harmful to learning or to health and safety.
5. Shall not intentionally expose the student to embarrassment or disparagement.
6. Shall not on the basis of race, color, creed, sex, national origin, marital status, political or religious beliefs, family, social or cultural background, or sexual orientation unfairly:
   a. Exclude any student from participation in any program;
   b. Deny benefits to any student;
   c. Grant any advantage to any student.
7. Shall not use professional relationships with students for private advantage.
8. Shall not disclose information about students obtained in the course of professional service, unless disclosure serves a compelling professional purpose or is required by law.

Principle II—Commitment to the Profession

The education profession is vested by the public with a trust and responsibility requiring the highest ideals of professional service.

In the belief that the quality of the services of the education profession directly influences the nation and its citizens, the educator shall exert every effort to raise professional standards, to promote a climate that encourages the exercise of professional judgment, to achieve conditions which attract persons worthy of the trust to careers in education, and to assist in preventing the practice of the profession by unqualified persons.

In fulfillment of the obligation to the profession, the educator—

1. Shall not in an application for a professional position deliberately make a false statement or fail to disclose a material fact related to competency and qualifications.
2. Shall not misrepresent his/her professional qualifications.
3. Shall not assist entry into the profession of a person known to be unqualified in respect to character, education, or other relevant attribute.
4. Shall not knowingly make a false statement concerning the qualifications of a candidate for a professional position.
5. Shall not assist a noneducator in the unauthorized practice of teaching.
6. Shall not disclose information about colleagues obtained in the course of professional service unless disclosure serves a compelling professional purpose or is required by law.
7. Shall not knowingly make a false or malicious statement about a colleague.
8. Shall not accept any gratuity, gift, or favor that might impair or appear to influence professional decisions or actions.

Source: From National Education Association. (1995). Code of Ethics of the Education Profession, NEA Representative Assembly. Reprinted by permission.

Let's evaluate your actions based on the information in the NEA Code of Ethics. Item 2 of Principle I, Commitment to the Student, states that a teacher "shall not unreasonably deny the student access to varying points of view." In our first example, you didn't let Eric share the editorial with the other students, so you have denied them access to a view that differs from your own. Whether or not your denial was "unreasonable" is open to interpretation, as is the case with ethical standards in any profession.

In the second example, you were desperately searching for a way to manage Greg's behavior, and by chance you found that anger (and possibly intimidation) was the only thing that seemed to work. However, Item 5 of Principle I says, a teacher "shall not intentionally expose the student to embarrassment or disparagement." This case is clear; in your desperation and frustration, you intentionally used anger and disparagement as a strategy with Greg, so you are in violation of the ethical code.

Other examples of ethical lapses sometimes seen in teaching include retaliating against students for alleged slights or offenses by grading unfairly or making unfair placement decisions, accepting fees for tutoring one's own students, and cheating on state tests by giving students more than the prescribed time or by giving them clues and/or answers (Raths & Lynman, 2003). Ethical standards are so important to professionals that they are often written into employment contracts. These standards are also important because they can provide an important basis for your own professional decision making.

Professional ethics guide teachers in their interactions with students, parents and caregivers, and colleagues. (Laura Bolesta/Merrill)

Are Teachers Professionals?

Not everyone believes that teachers are professionals. Critics' arguments include lack of rigorous training and lack of autonomy (Labaree, 2004, 2006).

Lack of Rigorous Training

The academic rigor of teachers' professional training has historically been criticized (Neville, Sherman, & Cohen, 2005). Entrance into teaching isn't as competitive as entrance into professions such as medicine or law, and many proposed reforms suggest that pedagogical content knowledge, general pedagogical knowledge, and knowledge of learners and learning be de-emphasized in favor of knowledge of content (Berry, Hoke, & Hirsch, 2004). The argument is often made, though not supported by research, that the only thing that teachers need is knowledge of the subjects they teach (Darling-Hammond & Bransford, 2005). The extended training for licensure that we discussed earlier suggests that teaching is a demanding profession that requires several forms of knowledge together with firsthand experience with students and classrooms.

Lack of Autonomy

In the last section we argued that teachers have a great deal of autonomy. Although we maintain this position, we also acknowledge that teachers have less autonomy than other professionals. For example, unlike physicians and lawyers, teachers are supervised and evaluated by their immediate school administrators, and states or districts mandate a substantial portion of the curriculum. Teachers have little to say about the standards for licensure, and many teachers even have to sign in at the beginning of the day and sign out at the end. The extent to which this detracts from them being true professionals continues to be debated.

Putting Teacher Professionalism into Perspective

The issue of whether teaching is a profession is controversial and won't be resolved in the near future. Without question, the training required for professions such as medicine and law is more extensive and rigorous than the training required for teaching, although rigor in teacher education is on the rise (Darling-Hammond & Bransford, 2005). Prospective teachers are expected to know and do more, and their professional knowledge is now more commonly assessed with tests that measure their understanding of the content they teach as well as their understanding of how to help students learn. We discuss these tests later in the chapter.

With respect to autonomy, a battle is currently being fought on both sides of the issue (Meier, 2002). Some would curtail teachers' autonomy by mandating what and how to teach and how to assess student learning. Others argue that this technical view of teaching is not feasible, because teaching requires too many split-second decisions to be reduced to mandates, and attempts to do so discourage creative people from considering teaching as a career (Kohn, 2000).

It is clear that teachers share many of the characteristics that describe members of established professions: They possess a specialized body of knowledge, they make many important decisions as they work, and they have a significant amount of autonomy. Effective teachers take time to reflect on their actions and take care to follow the ethical standards established by educational leaders. Are teachers professionals? At this time, many educational commentators seem to be saying "not quite" (Labaree, 2004, 2006; Neville et al., 2005). To truly "professionalize" teaching, researchers believe a number of reforms are necessary. We discuss these in the next section.

> **Making Connections:**
> To deepen your understanding of the topics in this section of the chapter and integrate them with topics you've already studied, go to the *Making Connections* module for Chapter 1 at **www.prenhall.com/kauchak**. Respond to questions 4–5.

Check Your Understanding

2.1 What are the essential characteristics of professionalism?

2.2 What are the primary arguments for teaching being a profession?

2.3 What are the major arguments against teaching being a profession?

2.4 How do the arguments for and against teacher professionalism balance each other?

For feedback, go to Check Your Understanding *at the end of chapter.*

Diversity: The Changing Face of U.S. Classrooms

When we walk into classrooms around the United States, one fact quickly becomes clear; our students are amazingly diverse. For example, experts in California predict the following:

- By 2010, the number of Latino and white California residents will be equal, each comprising nearly 40 percent of the population.
- By 2014, half of the children in California public schools will be Hispanic, and many will have limited English language skills.
- By 2020, 43 percent of the state's residents will be Latino, 34 percent will be white, 13 percent will be Asian, and the remaining 10 percent will be African American and Native American (Coleman, 2005).

While one of the more extreme examples, California's experience is not unique; every state in our country is becoming more culturally and ethnically diverse, and in the 25 largest U.S. cities, students of color compose at least half of the student population (Ladson-Billings, 2005).

When you begin teaching, you will have students who come from a variety of cultural, ethnic, and religious backgrounds (Gray & Fleischman, 2005). Along with cultural and ethnic diversity, you will also encounter many students who speak a native language other than English. Their **socioeconomic status**—the amount of money their parents make, their parents' level of education, and the kinds of jobs their parents have—will also differ. These differences can have a powerful influence on children's learning. For example, some parents can afford annual trips to other states and even countries; other parents struggle to provide even a decent place to live and enough food to eat. Some students will have many school-related experiences such as trips to zoos and museums that make learning nearly effortless, whereas others' school-related experiences will be severely limited. These differences translate into dramatic differences when the teacher asks questions during a lesson that require students to use their background knowledge about the world.

In a single grade you will have learners who are mature for their age and others who are slower in developing. Some will be poised and self-confident; others, shy and hesitant. You will certainly have a mix of boys and girls, their preferred ways of learning will vary, and you're likely to have some students with learning problems that will require extra help. Some of these students with special needs and/or talents will be served by a team of instructors in a program formalized through an individualized education program (IEP).

Each of these sources of diversity can strongly influence students' classroom behaviors and academic performance. How you respond to these differences will influence how much students learn, how they feel about school, and your own enjoyment of teaching.

Making Connections:
To deepen your understanding of the topics in this section of the chapter and integrate them with topics you've already studied, go to the *Making Connections* module for Chapter 1 at **www.prenhall.com/kauchak**. Respond to questions 6–7.

Check Your Understanding

3.1 Identify the different dimensions of student diversity. Explain how these dimensions will influence your work as a teacher.

3.2 Why is an understanding of different teaching and learning environments important for beginning teachers?

 For feedback, go to Check Your Understanding *at the end of this chapter.*

The Modern Reform Movement in Education

You're considering teaching in one of the most tumultuous periods in the history of American education. Critics, both inside and outside the profession, are calling for **reforms**, suggested changes in teaching and teacher preparation intended to increase the amount students learn. To implement these reforms, teachers must be well prepared, and states and districts often hold teachers accountable for their performance in classrooms. The current reform movement has already changed teaching and will continue to do so as you enter the profession. To prepare you for these changes, we have made reform the third major theme for this text, following professionalism and learner diversity.

To place recent reform efforts into perspective, we should point out that the process of change and reform has been a part of education throughout American history (Cuban, 2005).

Socioeconomic status. The amount of money students' parents make, their parents' level of education, and the kinds of jobs their parents have.

Reforms. Suggested changes in teaching and teacher preparation intended to increase the amount students learn.

exploring diversity

Teaching in Rural, Suburban, and Urban Environments

Because of its powerful influence on teaching, we have made diversity a second theme of this text, along with professionalism. In this section of the chapter, we focus on teaching in rural, suburban, and urban environments. Teaching in these three types of schools differs significantly, influenced not only by the social context, but also by the students themselves.

Teaching in Rural Schools

Researchers are engaged in an ongoing debate about the relative advantages of smaller versus larger schools (Bloomfield, 2006; Robelen, 2006). Small-school advocates need look no further than the approximately 350 remaining one-teacher schools in rural areas (Swidler, 2004). While not all rural districts have schools such as these, they are smaller in comparison to their urban and suburban counterparts. The smallest rural districts had an average of 126 students in the 2001–2002 school year, compared to 4,015 students in suburban and urban districts (U.S. Government Accounting Office, 2006). Rural schools in these smallest districts are also small, enrolling an average of 77 students, versus 560 students in nonrural schools. Small size also translates into lower numbers of students per teacher, with the smallest rural schools averaging 11 students per class versus 17 for their counterparts in larger districts (U.S. Government Accounting Office, 2006).

The students in rural districts tend to be less culturally diverse than those in urban and suburban districts, though this is slowly changing (Lichter & Johnson, 2006). Recent immigrants from Latin America and Asia are slowly finding their way into rural America, seeking jobs in construction, meat-packing, and other food-processing industries, slowing an earlier trend of general population decrease in rural areas (Macionis, 2006). Poverty is also an issue in rural districts, particularly in the South and Southwest (Hardy, 2005). For example, 42 percent of students in rural districts qualify for free or reduced lunch programs versus 36 percent in nonrural schools (U.S. Government Accounting Office, 2006).

Teaching in rural districts has both advantages and disadvantages. Because they are smaller, they have a greater sense of community, with schools often serving as the social center for the community (Brooke, 2003). Class sizes are smaller, and communication with parents is often easier. In addition, innovation and change may be easier because of rural districts' small size (Reeves & Bylund, 2005).

Teaching in Suburban Schools

The latter half of the 20th century resulted in unprecedented growth in the suburbs. At the turn of the 21st century, most of the U.S. population lived in suburbs, resulting from shifts from both urban and rural populations (Macionis, 2006). With respect to diversity, suburban schools are more culturally diverse than rural schools, with much of the diversity coming from well-educated professionals working in high-tech industries (Macionis, 2006). However, they tend to be less culturally diverse than urban schools. In addition, average household incomes tend to be higher than in rural or urban areas.

Most of the highest achieving school districts in the United States are found in suburban areas, and many suburban families select neighborhoods based on the quality of the school districts (Brimley & Garfield, 2005; Spring, 2006). The exodus to the suburbs also brought with it a growing tax base, which resulted in greater expenditures on suburban schools (Macionis & Parillo, 2007; Spring, 2006). Because of a solid tax base, suburban districts can spend more per student than either rural or urban districts, and this often shows up in smaller class sizes and greater access to resources such as science labs and technology.

New and veteran teachers alike seek jobs in suburban schools, so competition for existing jobs is the primary challenge for new teachers wanting to work in a suburban district.

Teaching in Urban Schools

With respect to jobs, urban schools are "where the action is." Consider the following statistics (Hoffman, 2003; Young, 2002):

The modern reform movement is often traced to 1983, when the National Commission on Excellence in Education published *A Nation at Risk: The Imperative for Educational Reform*. This widely read document suggested that America was "at risk" of being unable to compete in the world economic marketplace because our system of education was inadequate. The terms "at-risk students" and more recently "students placed at-risk" grew out of this book, and educators use them to refer to students who are unlikely to acquire the knowledge and skills needed for success in our modern, tech-

Urban schools provide job openings and opportunities for personal and professional growth. (Scott Cunningham/Merrill)

- The nation's 100 largest school districts represent less than 1 percent of the districts, but they are responsible for the education of nearly one-fourth of all students. For example, the New York City Public Schools and the Los Angeles Unified School District, the two largest in the nation, each have enrollments greater than the total enrollments of 27 states.
- The 100 largest districts employ more than a fifth of the nation's teachers.

Nearly 70 percent of urban students are cultural minorities, and some urban schools have enrollments that are more than 95 percent minority (Macionis & Parillo, 2007). More than half of all urban students are eligible for free or reduced-price lunch.

Unquestionably, teaching in urban schools differs from teaching in other settings. Urban schools are large, and most of their students come from culturally diverse backgrounds. Research also indicates that in urban schools, "Children are often taught by teachers who are the least prepared; children are less likely to be enrolled in academically challenging courses; they are too often treated differently in what they are expected to do and the kinds of assignments they are given and teachers often lack the resources they need to teach well" (Armour-Thomas, 2004, p. 113).

Unfortunately, a number of negative stereotypes about urban students exist, ranging from "All urban kids are in gangs" to "Urban children are mostly from poor, dysfunctional homes, homeless shelters, or foster homes and come to school 'just to grow up' and then drop out" (Goldstein, 2004, pp. 43–44). These stereotypes tend to create fear in people not familiar with the situation. This fear can then lead to actions that are damaging to everyone. One urban student reported,

When I was in high school, we had the chance to host a group of students from the suburbs. . . . So, this girl comes with her friends, and they pair us up. Later on I find that they [the students from the suburbs] were told not to wear any jewelry or nice clothes or bring any money with them so they wouldn't get robbed. . . . All they saw when they visited us were people who might rob them. (Goldstein, 2004, p. 47)

How is this information relevant to you as a prospective teacher, and how might it help you answer the question, "Do I want to be a teacher?" First, many of the stereotypes of urban students are untrue. These students want to succeed and learn and grow just as other students do. In many cases their access to educational experiences has been lacking, so they come to schools with greater needs than do more advantaged students (Armour-Thomas, 2004; Rubinson, 2004). Second, many job opportunities exist in urban environments, so your first job offer likely will be in an urban setting. Many school districts now offer special incentives, such as salary bonuses, support for housing, and moving expenses, in an effort to encourage highly qualified professionals to work in urban settings (Herszenhorn, 2006). Finally, while urban environments pose special challenges, they can also be immensely rewarding, providing opportunities for you to grow in a number of dimensions (Weiner, 2006). Now is the time to begin thinking about the opportunities that working in an urban environment might afford.

nological society. Since 1983 many other suggestions have been made for improving our nation's schools and the teachers who work in them.

To help you understand the scope of reforms in education, we examine two of the most prominent: *changes in teacher preparation* and *accountability and high-stakes testing*. These reforms are occurring at both the national and state levels, and we close this section with an example from Kentucky to illustrate a state-level reform.

Changes in Teacher Preparation

Increased emphasis on professionalism and criticisms suggesting that too many underqualified teachers enter the field have resulted in a number of reforms in teacher education, most enacted at the state level (Raths & Lynman, 2003). These reforms include

- Raising standards for admission into teacher training programs
- Requiring teachers to take more rigorous courses than in the past
- Requiring higher standards for licensure, including teacher-competency tests
- Expanding teacher preparation programs from 4 to 5 years
- Requiring experienced teachers to take more rigorous professional development courses (Cochran-Smith, 2005)

The emphasis on professionalism is further reinforced through the No Child Left Behind (NCLB) Act of 2001, a federal law that includes a call for improved teacher quality as a major provision. (We discuss the NCLB Act later in the chapter.) NCLB required that, by 2005–2006, all teachers were to be fully qualified, and paraprofessionals working in schools should have 2 years of college or demonstrate equivalent knowledge on a competency test (Popham, 2004b; Dillon, 2006). This provision of the law is a direct result of research indicating that teachers have a powerful effect on student learning (Milanowski & Kimball, 2005) and that many poor, minority, and urban children are frequently taught by underqualified teachers (Rhee & Levin, 2006).

Competency Testing

States and districts are increasingly assessing teacher quality through competency testing, which means it is likely that you will be required to pass a test to be admitted to the profession. Currently, most states require some type of standardized test for licensure; in addition, most colleges of education also require tests for admission into teacher-education programs (Wayne & Youngs, 2003).

Praxis: Comprehensive Teacher Testing.   The most common form of teacher testing is the Praxis Series, published by the Educational Testing Service. The Praxis Series (*praxis* refers to putting theory into practice) is currently being used in 35 states and exists at three levels (Educational Testing Service, 2006):

- Praxis I: Academic Skills Assessments. These tests are designed to measure the basic skills in reading, writing, and math that all teachers need.
- Praxis II: Subject Assessments. The subject assessments are intended to measure teachers' knowledge of the subjects they will teach. In addition to 70 content-specific tests, Praxis II also includes the Principles of Learning and Teaching (PLT) tests, which measure professional knowledge.
- Praxis III: Classroom Performance Assessments. These tests use classroom observations and work samples to assess beginning teachers' ability to plan, instruct, manage, and understand professional responsibilities. In addition, Praxis III assesses the teacher's sensitivity to learners' developmental and cultural differences.

You are most likely to encounter Praxis I before being admitted to a teacher licensure program, Praxis II after its completion, and Praxis III during your first years of teaching.

The Principles of Learning and Teaching (PLT) tests, four tests specifically designed for teachers seeking licensure in Early Childhood, or grades K–6, 5–9, and 7–12, are an important part of the Praxis Series. Each of the grade-level tests has two parts (Educational Testing Service, 2006). The first consists of 24 multiple-choice questions similar to those in the self-assessment quizzes on the Companion Website (*www.prenhall.com/kauchak*). The second part presents case histories that you read and analyze with short-answer questions. The PLT case histories are similar to the case studies you'll find in this text. We have designed this text to help you pass your licensure exam, whether it is a Praxis PLT or an exam created by your state, by including case-based formats in the "Preparing for Your Licensure Exam" exercises at the end of this chapter. In addition, the Teacher Prep Website (*www.prenhall.com/teacherprep*) contains additional information that will help you prepare for these tests.

Portfolios: Individual Teacher Accountability

Testing can provide valuable information about teachers' knowledge and skills, but test content is often removed from the day-to-day challenges that teachers face (Berliner, 2006). A **professional portfolio**, or collection of materials representative of one's work, provides an alternate way to document teacher competence. Just as a portfolio of artwork is prepared by an artist, a professional portfolio is produced by a prospective teacher to document developing knowledge and skills. **Digital portfolios** allow you to compress large amounts of information onto a computer file, making it easy to edit and burn to a CD to share with prospective employers.

As you proceed through your teacher-preparation program, you will likely be required to prepare a portfolio to document your developing professional competence, and it will be a tool you can use during job interviews to demonstrate your capabilities as a teacher. We provide "Online Portfolio Activities" and "Guidelines for Beginning a Professional Portfolio" at the end of this chapter.

Whether reforms such as teacher testing and the use of portfolios to document competency will result in the hoped-for improvements in education remains to be seen and will continue to be debated. One thing is certain, however; efforts to reform schools, teachers, and the way teachers are prepared will continue, and you will begin your career in the midst of these changes. One of the most significant of these changes are the INTASC standards described in the next section.

INTASC: Standards in Teacher Education

In addition to testing and portfolios, school districts are also using standards to increase the quality and rigor of teacher preparation programs. A rapidly expanding body of research consistently demonstrates that teaching now requires professionals who are highly knowledgeable and skilled (Berliner, 2006; Darling-Hammond & Bransford, 2005).

The profession is responding. Created in 1987, the Interstate New Teacher Assessment and Support Consortium (INTASC) was designed to help states develop better teachers through coordinated efforts of support and assessment. INTASC (1993) has raised the bar by setting rigorous standards for new teachers in important areas such as planning, instruction, and increasing student motivation. These standards describe what you should know and be able to do when you first walk into a classroom.

To date, INTASC has prepared general, or "core," standards organized around 10 principles (see Table 1.3) and is preparing standards for various subject-matter areas and specific student populations. INTASC is also developing a Test for Teaching Knowledge (TTK) linked to the core principles. The "Online Portfolio Activities" found at the end of the chapter is linked to the INTASC core standards.

The INTASC standards are demanding, but this is as it should be. If you expect to be treated as a professional, you should have the knowledge and skills that allow you to make the decisions expected of a professional. Being able to meet the INTASC standards is a good beginning.

Teaching in an Era of Reform

To involve you in examining prominent reforms, we include a feature called "Teaching in an Era of Reform." We introduce the feature and illustrate how you can use it to increase your understanding of educational reforms in the United States.

Professional portfolio. A collection of representative work materials to document developing knowledge and skills.

Digital portfolio. A collection of materials contained in an electronic file that makes the information accessible to potential viewers.

TABLE 1.3 The INTASC Principles

Principle	Description
1. Knowledge of subject	The teacher understands the central concepts, tools of inquiry, and structures of the discipline(s) he or she teaches and can create learning experiences that make these aspects of subject matter meaningful for students.
2. Learning and human development	The teacher understands how children learn and develop, and can provide learning opportunities that support their intellectual, social and personal development.
3. Adapting instruction	The teacher understands how students differ in their approaches to learning and creates instructional opportunities that are adapted to diverse learners.
4. Strategies	The teacher understands and uses a variety of instructional strategies to encourage students' development of critical thinking, problem solving, and performance skills.
5. Motivation and management	The teacher uses an understanding of individual and group motivation and behavior to create a learning environment that encourages positive social interaction, active engagement in learning, and self-motivation.
6. Communication skills	The teacher uses knowledge of effective verbal, nonverbal, and media communication techniques to foster active inquiry, collaboration, and supportive interaction in the classroom.
7. Planning	The teacher plans instruction based upon knowledge of subject matter, students, the community, and curriculum goals.
8. Assessment	The teacher understands and uses formal and informal assessment strategies to evaluate and ensure the continuous intellectual, social and physical development of the learner.
9. Commitment	The teacher is a reflective practitioner who continually evaluates the effects of his/her choices and actions on others (students, parents, and other professionals in the learning community) and who actively seeks out opportunities to grow professionally.
10. Partnership	The teacher fosters relationships with school colleagues, parents, and agencies in the larger community to support students' learning and well-being.

Source: From Interstate New Teacher Assessment and Support Consortium (1993). *Model standards for beginning teacher licensing and development: A resource for state dialogues.* Washington, D.C.: Council of Chief State School Officers. Reprinted by permission.

Accountability. The process of requiring students to demonstrate understanding of the topics they study as measured by standardized tests, as well as holding educators at all levels responsible for students' performance.

High-stakes tests. Assessments that states and districts use to determine whether or not students will advance from one grade to another, graduate from high school, or have access to specific fields of study.

The feature includes the following elements:

- Discussion of a reform issue.
- Arguments on both sides of the issue.
- We ask you to take a position by responding to the issue.

We illustrate this process in the following section, discussing accountability and high-stakes testing as the reform issue. **Accountability** is the process of requiring students to demonstrate understanding of the topics they study as measured by standardized tests, as well as holding educators at all levels responsible for students' performance. Accountability often occurs along with **high-stakes tests**, which are assessments that states and districts use to determine whether or not students will advanced from one grade to another, graduate from high school, or have access to specific fields of study.

VIDEO PERSPECTIVES

The Test

 To view this video, go to the *Becoming a Professional* DVD included with this text, click on ABC News, and then this chapter's video: *The Test*. This ABC News video examines high-stakes testing in Florida from multiple perspectives. Interviews with students, parents, and administrators help us understand the implications of high stakes for a variety of people.

Think About This

1. What are the advantages and disadvantages of high-stakes testing?
2. What types of students are most adversely affected by high-stakes testing?
3. What can schools do to minimize the negative effects of high-stakes testing?

 To answer these questions online and receive immediate feedback, go to the Companion Website at **www.prenhall.com/kauchak**, *then to the* ABC News *Video Perspectives module for Chapter 1.*

Analyzing One Statewide Reform: The Kentucky Education Reform Act

Will reform efforts produce the hoped-for results? One of the most ambitious and well-known state reform efforts, the Kentucky Education Reform Act (KERA), was precipitated by a 1989 Kentucky Supreme Court ruling that declared that the state's system of funding public schools was unconstitutional (Flanagan & Murray, 2004). Funding disparities between rich and poor school districts had resulted in a system that was inequitable and inefficient. The state legislature responded with a comprehensive educational reform bill that attempted to address several of the issues. The major components of the effort, and the changes that resulted, are found in Table 1.4.

As you can see from Table 1.4, KERA affected every student and every teacher in the state. To fund these reforms, the Kentucky legislature approved a $1.3 billion tax increase, and public school expenditures increased 50 percent over the first 5 years of implementation ("Will KERA?", 2003).

TABLE 1.4   Major Provisions of Kentucky Education Reform Act

Reform Component	Result
Curriculum guides established	Clearly defined student learning goals for key areas such as math, reading, and social studies.
Assessment and accountability systems	Created a statewide testing system that held schools accountable for student learning.
Ungraded primary program for K–3	Eliminated grade levels and used multiage grouping to educate primary students.
Extended school services for students placed at-risk	Provided extra instruction after school and in the summer for students placed at-risk.
School-based decision making	Created school level councils consisting of parents and teachers to provide input on how schools were run.
Pre-school program for children placed at-risk	Students who were eligible for free or reduced lunches or those who were developmentally delayed received developmentally appropriate preschool programs.
Family and youth resource centers	Provided links between schools and families and offered information on other government agencies.

teaching in an era of reform

Accountability and High-Stakes Testing

In response to concerns about students graduating from high school without the skills needed to succeed either in college or the workplace, reformers have called for greater accountability for both students and teachers. Calls for accountability were prompted by evidence indicating that students were being promoted from grade to grade without mastering essential content; some students were graduating from high school without basic skills in reading, writing, and math; and even more had limited scientific literacy and a general lack of understanding of our world. For example, in a recent survey of 18- to 24-year-olds, 6 in 10 respondents couldn't find Iraq on a map of the Middle East and about half couldn't locate New York State (Manzo, 2006).

No Child Left Behind

One of the most far-reaching accountability reforms is the No Child Left Behind (NCLB) Act of 2001, which one expert called "the most significant change in federal regulation of public schools in three decades" (Hardy, 2002, p. 201). Researchers evaluating it described it as "comprehensive in its impact, affecting who teaches, what is taught, how learning is assessed and the consequences for poor performance" (Debray, McDermott, & Wohlstetter, 2005, p. 15).

Signed by President George W. Bush in 2002, NCLB officially reauthorized the Elementary and Secondary Education Act, which began in 1965 and resulted in billions of dollars be-ing spent on compensatory education programs for disadvantaged students. Several key provisions of NCLB address teacher preparation, standards, accountability, and testing, and these provisions will influence teachers' professional lives in the years to come (Popham, 2004b).

Accountability is the most important provision of NCLB, and it calls for accountability at several levels. For example, NCLB requires states to create standards for what every child should know and learn for all grades. States were to develop standards for math, reading, and science by the 2005–2006 school year, and states must implement these standards in order to receive continued federal funding. Responsibility for implementing the standards and gathering information about their attainment exists at the district level. Individual schools are held accountable for ensuring that every child in that school has achieved satisfactory progress toward the standards. Schools, districts, and states must keep records of performance to document achievement of different groups of students by race, ethnicity, gender, and English proficiency.

If a school fails to make adequate yearly progress with any of these student subgroups for 2 consecutive years, students may transfer to another school. After 3 years of sub-par performance by a school, students within underachieving schools are entitled to outside tutoring at district expense. After 4 years, the state will place the school on probation and take corrective measures. States, districts, individual schools, and teachers are already feeling the pressures of accountability (Christie, 2005).

Testing is the key to NCLB accountability. Beginning in the 2005–2006 school year, districts will test each child in grades 3 through 8 every year in math and reading and will test children at least once more in grades 10–12. By 2007–2008, districts will assess students in science at least once in their academic career. States and districts will use these test scores to hold schools accountable for student achievement.

Often, accountability is accomplished through high-stakes testing. When students aren't allowed to graduate from high school because they fail a test, for example, the "stakes" are very high, thus, the term *high-stakes tests.* In a similar way, when districts and specific schools within them are singled out as failing or "leaving children behind," the stakes are also very high.

A major element of many current reform efforts, including No Child Left Behind, is increased emphasis on testing in schools. (Anthony/Magnacca/Merrill)

The Issue

As you might expect, accountability through high-stakes testing is very controversial. Critics argue that—faced with pressures to help students achieve in math, reading, and science—teachers will underemphasize other subjects like social studies, art, music, health, and physical education (Nichols & Berliner, 2005). This narrowing of the curriculum deprives students of a well-rounded education, critics assert, and it also stifles teacher creativity because they spend too much time teaching only test content and helping students practice for the tests.

Teachers also report that testing programs have forced them to teach in ways that contradict sound instructional practices. For example, despite knowing that computers can be an effective tool for teaching writing, teachers have abandoned technology because a state writing test is hand written (Pedulla et al., 2003).

The pressure for students to perform well on the tests can also produce unintended consequences. To avoid test-related sanctions, teachers in states with high-stakes tests frequently request transfers out of grades that are tested, and experts fear that veteran teachers will transfer out of urban schools where students often underachieve, depriving students of the expert teachers they need (Guarino et al., 2006; Lynn, 2003). In addition, research suggests that high school exit examinations, in use in 23 states in 2006, have contributed to the dropout problem, and the adverse effects are greater for low socioeconomic status and cultural minority students (Warren, Jenkins, & Kulick, 2006).

Critics also contend that current tests are not adequate for crucial decisions about students' lives (Neill, 2003; Popham, 2004) and that cutoff scores are often arbitrary. For example, when the state of Virginia lowered the cutoff score for its test by 1 point, 5,625 failing scores turned into passing scores (Bracey, 2003b). Deciding student grade promotion or graduation on the basis of one score is being increasingly criticized by a number of professional organizations, both within and outside education, including the American Educational Research Association (2006) and the American Psychological Association (2006). In addition, other experts assert that high-stakes tests can have negative side effects, including decreased motivation and higher dropout rates (Amrein & Berliner, 2003).

Finally, questions related to high-stakes testing with minority students remain unanswered. One involves test bias and whether or not existing tests can provide an accurate picture of minority achievement, and particularly the achievement of students who are not native English speakers (Abedi, Hofstetter, & Lord, 2004; Popham, 2004b).

Advocates of testing, while conceding that teacher preparation, instructional resources, and the tests themselves need to be improved, argue that these tests are the fairest and most effective means of achieving the aims of successful learning for all students (Steches, Hamilton, & Scott-Naflet, 2005). Further, they assert, evidence indicates that educational systems that require content standards and use tests that thoroughly measure the extent to which the standards are met greatly improve the achievement for all students, including those from disadvantaged backgrounds.

For too long, the poor achievement of our most vulnerable students has been lost in unrepresentative averages. African American, Hispanic, special education, limited English proficient, and many other students were left behind because schools were not held accountable for their individual progress. Now all students count. (U.S. Department of Education, 2004, p. 18)

Some advocates are even promoting national standards and tests, claiming that those coming from different states vary too much and result in inequalities between states (Olson, 2005b). Hirsch (2000) summarized the testing advocates' position: "They [standards and tests that measure achievement of the standards] are the most promising educational development in half a century" (p. 64).

Polls indicate that the public and most parents support the general goals of No Child Left Behind (Olson, 2005a). Ninety-five percent of respondents in a national poll said that it is important to close the achievement gap between minority students and their peers who are not members of minorities, and 58 percent of respondents said it is the responsibility of the schools to do so (Rose & Gallup, 2005). However, more than two-thirds say that a single test cannot give a fair picture of student achievement. This suggests that, while believing that schools should do more to help all students learn, the public isn't sure about how it should be accomplished.

You Take a Position

Now it's your turn to take a position on the issue. State in writing whether you feel that accountability and high-stakes testing will improve the quality of education or harm it, and provide a two-page rationale for your position.

For additional references and resources, go to the Companion Website at www.prenhall.com/kauchak, then to the Teaching in an Era of Reform module for Chapter 1. You can respond online or submit your response to your instructor.

How successful was this "most sweeping statewide education reform plan ever enacted" (Rothman, 1997)? Evaluations range from "success beyond all expectations" to "dismal failure" (Petroska, Lindle, & Pankratz, 2000). Research suggests that this reform did improve student performance; between 1992 and 1996, 92 percent of Kentucky's schools showed improvements in achievement (Rothman, 1997). These increases were especially evident at the elementary level in math, reading, and social studies (Petroska et al., 2000). In addition, the preschool programs for students placed at-risk appeared to have long-lasting benefits for young students.

As with all reforms, however, the Kentucky plan was not without its critics. Conservatives argued that it cost too much, and as often happens with education reforms, funding for the program significantly decreased over time (D. Hoff, 2003b). In addition, teachers now question whether the emphasis on accountability narrows the curriculum and forces teachers to "teach to the test," a common complaint about accountability through testing. In many respects KERA, with its emphasis on systemic reform and accountability, was a precursor to the No Child Left Behind Act, the federal reform effort.

But the Kentucky Education Reform Act differs from No Child Left Behind in several important respects. First, it is a state versus a federal effort, which gives the people in the state more control over it. Second, it doesn't rely solely on testing and accountability to improve education. Instead, it provides extra funding for the reform, something that critics of No Child Left Behind feel hampers federal efforts to improve student performance. This extra money provides extra services to both students and their families, something experts feel is necessary for long-term change in the education of students placed at-risk (Mathis, 2005).

Making Connections:
To deepen your understanding of the topics in this section of the chapter and integrate them with topics you've already studied, go to the *Making Connections* module for Chapter 1 at **www.prenhall.com/kauchak.** Respond to questions 8 and 9.

Check Your Understanding

4.1 How is the current reform movement in education changing the teaching profession?

4.2 Describe the major changes in teacher preparation that have resulted from the reform movement in education.

4.3 What is INTASC? How has it influenced teacher preparation?

For feedback, go to Check Your Understanding *at the end of this chapter.*

decision making

Defining Yourself as a Professional

You are a sophomore in college taking your first education course and trying to decide whether you want to be an elementary or secondary teacher. Fortunately, your class provides clinical experiences at both levels, so you can observe teachers working with both younger and older students.

Your first experience is with a third-grade teacher. At times, the classroom seems bewildering, with small groups of students working on a number of different projects at the same time. After awhile, you start to make sense of the schedule Mrs. Ortiz puts on the board each morning, and you're beginning to learn students' names.

Then you move to a high school math classroom. The students seem really old, and they are, compared to the third graders and even you. Some are only two or three years younger than you are. At first, you're intimidated, but then after you start working with

students one-on-one, you realize they share many of the same characteristics as third graders. They come to school to learn, but having friends and being respected by others is really important to them. You also become aware that you know more math than you realized and that it's fun helping others understand how to solve problems.

At the end of the term, you find that you still haven't firmly decided on a grade level but that you know a lot more than you did before the term started. To help you decide, you reread the section "Rewards and Challenges in Teaching."

What level would you choose?

To respond to this question online and receive immediate feedback, go to the Decision Making *module of Chapter 1 on the Companion Website at www.prenhall.com/kauchak.*

Meeting Your Learning Objectives

1. **Describe the major rewards and challenges of teaching.**
   - Rewards in teaching include both intrinsic and extrinsic benefits. Intrinsic rewards come from within oneself and are personally satisfying for emotional or intellectual reasons. Intrinsic rewards for teaching include helping young people grow emotionally, socially, and academically. They also include opportunities for a lifetime of intellectual growth. Extrinsic rewards come from outside oneself and include desirable vacation times, convenient work schedules, occupational status, and salaries. The unique configuration of these in teaching provides attractive incentives to a number of people considering the profession.
   - Research indicates that people most commonly choose to teach because they desire to work with young people and make contributions to society. Other reasons to enter teaching include intellectual growth and interest in a content area.
   - Challenges in teaching include the complexities of classrooms as well as the multiple roles that teachers perform. Classrooms are multidimensional, and the events that occur in classrooms are simultaneous, immediate, unpredictable, and public. In terms of roles, teachers create productive learning environments, are ambassadors to the public, and work with other professionals as collaborative colleagues.

2. **Describe the different characteristics of professionalism, and explain how they relate to teaching.**
   - Characteristics of professionalism include a specialized body of knowledge, autonomy to make decisions, the ability to make decisions in ill-defined situations as well as to engage in reflection to assess one's own performance, and ethical standards that guide professional conduct.
   - Some argue that teachers are not professionals, suggesting their training isn't rigorous and they lack autonomy. Others contend that teaching is a developing profession that is still evolving.
   - Though teachers possess many of the characteristics of a profession, including a specialized body of knowledge, autonomy, decision making and reflection, and ethical standards, the future status of teaching will be largely determined by current reform efforts.

3. **Identify the different dimensions of learner diversity, and explain why understanding different teaching and learning environments is important for beginning teachers.**
   - Student diversity is a fact of life in today's classrooms and comes in various forms. Culture and ethnicity, religion, socioeconomic status, academic ability, physical and emotional maturity, gender, and learner exceptionalities are all dimensions of diversity than can influence student learning.
   - Understanding different learning and teaching environments can be significant for beginning teachers because these environments present different opportunities and challenges to beginning teachers. Rural districts tend to be smaller and more homogeneous in terms of diversity. Suburban districts are intermediate in size and funded better than other districts, but competition for teaching jobs is greater there. Urban districts are more culturally diverse and also offer the greatest number of teaching opportunities for first-year teachers. Urban environments also present unique challenges and opportunities, and school districts often offer incentives to encourage teachers to take jobs in urban classrooms.

4. **Explain how the current reform movement in education is changing the teaching profession.**
   - The current reform movement in education has resulted in a number of changes in teacher education. Prospective teachers will encounter reforms calling for higher standards, more rigorous training, and increased testing. In addition to increased use of licensure exams, beginning teachers will also be asked to demonstrate their competence through professional portfolios.

(continued)

- INTASC, the Interstate New Teacher Assessment and Support Consortium, was designed to help states develop better teachers. It outlines 10 basic principles that guide the preparation of new teachers. The "Online Portfolio Activities" at the end of the chapter are linked to these principles.
- Increasingly, students and their teachers are being held accountable for learning progress. New federal legislation in the form of the No Child Left Behind Act makes educators accountable for the learning progress of the children they teach. This accountability often occurs in the form of standardized tests designed to measure acquisition of essential content. When the test results have important consequences for either students or teachers, such as nonpromotion or sanctions, then these are termed *high-stakes tests*.
- The Kentucky Education Reform Act created a statewide system of comprehensive reform. It includes curriculum standards, accountability systems, extended school services for students placed at-risk, school-based decision making, and school-based resource centers. Because of its scope, many compare this state's act to the federal No Child Left Behind Act.

Important Concepts

accountability
assessment
autonomy
curriculum
decision making
digital portfolio
ethics
extrinsic rewards
high-stakes tests

intrinsic rewards
professionalism
professional portfolio
reflection
reforms
socioeconomic status
standards
technician

Developing as a Professional

Preparing for Your Licensure Exam

This exercise will provide you with practice answering questions similar to the Praxis™ Principles of Learning and Teaching exam as well as your state-specific licensure exam.

Read the following case study, and then answer the questions that follow.

Marissa Anderson enters the teacher's lounge and collapses in a large overstuffed chair.

"I'm bushed," she comments, smiling at her friend, Anthony, another third-year teacher at her school.

"Late night partying?" he asks, examining a brown paper bag for the remains of his lunch.

"Don't I wish. Those evening classes are killing me, but I almost have my ELL [English language learner] endorsement. If I weren't learning so much, I'd start to wonder."

"Anything good that I can use?" Anthony asks.

"Well, we talked last night about the importance of verbal language in learning to read and how important it is to provide lots of opportunities for kids to practice their developing English skills."

"Hmm. That makes sense, but it doesn't sound much like the reading program our district wants us to use. It has a lot of individual worksheets and stresses teacher-centered instruction."

"I know. I've been thinking about that. Our reading program probably works for students who speak English, but how can my kids do worksheets when they can't even read the directions? So I've

got a dilemma—do what the district says, or do what I know and what research shows is best for my kids. For now I'm just going to shut my door and do the right thing. Down the line I need to talk with Jan [the school principal] and see if she can help me resolve this dilemma."

Analyze this case in terms of the following dimensions of professionalism. In your analysis, identify specific parts of the case that relate to professionalism and explain the connection.

1. Specialized body of knowledge

2. Extended training for licensure

3. Decision making and reflection

4. Autonomy

5. Ethical standards of conduct

 To receive feedback on your responses to these exercises, go to the Companion Website at www.prenhall.com/kauchak, then to the Preparing for Your Licensure Exam module for Chapter 1.

Discussion Questions

1. Do the reasons cited in the chapter for becoming a teacher change with the grade level or content area targeted by teachers? Why?

2. Do you believe teaching is more or less rewarding than it was in the past? Is it more or less difficult? Why do you think so?

3. Which of the intrinsic and extrinsic rewards in teaching are likely to become more important in the future? Less important?

4. For which group of teachers—teachers of elementary school students (grades K–5), middle school students (grades 6–8), or secondary students (grades 9–12)—are emotional rewards likely to be the greatest? Why?

5. For which group of teachers—elementary school, middle school, or secondary school teachers—are intellectual rewards likely to be the greatest? Why?

6. Is teaching a profession? If not, what would be necessary to make it one?

7. Will the move toward teacher professionalism be beneficial for teachers? Why or why not?

Developing as a Professional: Online Activities

Going into Schools

Go to the Companion Website at *www.prenhall.com/kauchak,* and click on the *Going into Schools* module for Chapter 1. You will find a number of school-based activities that will help you link chapter content to the schools in which you work.

Virtual Field Experience: Using Teacher Prep to Explore the Profession

If you would like to participate in a Virtual Field Experience, access the Teacher Prep Website at *www.prenhall.com/teacherprep*. After logging in, complete the following steps:

1. Click on "Video Classroom" on the left panel of the screen.
2. Go to "Foundations and Introduction to Education."

3. Finally, select "Module 1: Why Become a Teacher?" This video allows you to explore the teaching profession at three different levels. Answer the questions that follow the video clip.

Online Portfolio Activities

To develop your professional portfolio, further apply your understanding of chapter content, and address the INTASC standards, go to the Companion Website, then to this chapter's *Online Portfolio Activities*. Complete the suggested activities.

Guidelines for Beginning a Professional Portfolio

Preparing a professional portfolio involves five steps (Bullock & Hawk, 2005; Campbell et al., 2007).

Step 1. *Specify a goal.* For example, you're probably taking this course because you've either decided that you want to teach, or you're at least considering teaching. Finding a satisfying teaching job would be a likely goal.

Step 2. *Determine how both past and future experiences relate to the goal.* You might choose to tutor a student with a reading problem, for example, to get professional experience that will make you more marketable.

Step 3. *Collect items that provide evidence of your developing knowledge and skill.* In addition to your résumé, which is always included in a portfolio, you might consider the following types of entries typically found in a teaching portfolio:

- Unit and lesson plans
- Samples of your work as a student
- Philosophy of education paper
- Description of your management system, including rules and procedures
- Grading policies
- Videotapes of you interacting with students (e.g., a clip of you working with the student you are tutoring)
- Transcripts

The Online Portfolio Activities you will complete are designed to get you thinking about several of these components. In fact, any number of the activity products would make excellent entries for your portfolio. Other suggestions for portfolio components can be found in Bullock and Hawk (2005).

As you gather and create items, you should date each potential entry. The dates will help you later when you are organizing your portfolio.

Step 4. *Decide what items among your collection best illustrate your knowledge and skills.* A prospective employer is unlikely to view a bulky collection or series of videotapes, so you need to be selective; a videotaped lesson is likely a better entry than is a clip from a tutoring session.

Although you want to be selective when initially planning your portfolio, we suggest that you err on the side of including too much in your portfolio at first. If you think you might use an item, include it now. You can always remove an item, but recovering something that's been discarded earlier is often difficult.

Step 5. *Determine how to best present the items to the person or people connected to your goal.* You may be presenting your portfolio to the principal of the school in which you want to teach, for example.

You will want to organize your portfolio to make it accessible to an evaluator. The portfolio should open with a title page, followed by a table of contents. The most impressive entries go first to highlight your accomplishments. Work samples and evidence of performance, such as video clips, should always be displayed more prominently than, say, testimonial letters, which an evaluator often disregards. A chronological arrangement would provide viewers with some idea of your progress during the program.

To help you organize, put yourself in the evaluator's shoes. Remember, the evaluator knows little about you, and your portfolio is a way of introducing yourself. You're trying to convince a prospective employer that you're knowledgeable, skilled, and committed to the profession. Let communication and ease of access be your guide for arranging the information in your portfolio. If the portfolio is well organized, it will create a positive impression; the opposite will occur if it is disorganized or if items are inaccessible.

As we move further into the information age, many preservice teachers are developing electronic portfolios (Kilbane & Milman, 2003). They include everything a paper-based portfolio includes, but they do it more efficiently. For example, one CD-ROM can hold the equivalent of 300,000 text pages. Typed documents can be scanned into word processing files and stored on floppy disks or CD-ROMs, and video can be digitized and also stored on CD-ROMs. This saves both time and energy. Evaluators who want to view a video episode in a paper-based portfolio must find a VCR, review the tape, and put it back into the correct portfolio container. In contrast, video footage in an electronic portfolio can be augmented with text and graphics, which reviewers can access with the click of a mouse.

To create an electronic portfolio, you'll need to have the proper computer equipment and software and be skilled in their use. If these are obstacles for you, you can certainly create a traditional portfolio. However, you will also want to hone your computer skills and educate yourself about electronic portfolios. With the expansion of technology into more and more areas of teaching, it is likely that paper-based portfolios will eventually become obsolete.

Regardless of whether your portfolio is paper-based or electronic, it should provide your prospective employer with an overview of your experience and qualifications and offer an inviting snapshot of you as a developing professional in the field of teaching. For a detailed discussion of professional portfolios, see Bullock and Hawk (2005) and Campbell, Cignetti, Melenyzer, Nettles, and Wyman (2007).

Check Your Understanding

1.1   What are the major rewards in teaching?

The major rewards in teaching can be divided into two main categories, intrinsic and extrinsic. In terms of intrinsic benefits, emotional rewards such as getting to know students on a personal level and helping young people grow and develop are important, as well as the intellectual rewards of learning new content and playing with ideas.

Extrinsic rewards include job security, frequent vacations, convenient work schedules, and the relatively high occupational status of teaching.

1.2   What are the major challenges in teaching?

The major challenges in teaching include the complexities of classrooms, which make professional decision making so difficult, as well as the multiple roles that teachers perform.

The first challenge—the complexity of classrooms—is described by five interrelated characteristics of teaching: It is (1) multidimensional and (2) simultaneous, meaning a number of things are going on in classrooms at the same time. (3) Classroom events are also pressing, requiring immediate attention from the teacher. (4) Classroom events, being human, are unpredictable. (5) Finally, classrooms are also public, making the decisions a teacher makes visible to students, and even parents and other professionals.

A second challenge facing teachers is their performance of multiple roles. Teachers are expected to create productive learning environments, work as partners with parents and caregivers, and collaborate with colleagues.

1.3 **Identify the four most often cited reasons to enter teaching.**

Results from a national poll, as well as our own informal surveys, indicate that wanting to work with young people and wanting to contribute to society are the two major reasons that people go into teaching. Our results showed that opportunities for personal growth and learning more about a content area were also important.

2.1 **What are the essential characteristics of professionalism?**

A specialized body of knowledge that sets the professional apart from the lay public is perhaps the most important characteristic of professionalism. Autonomy, which provides the freedom to make important decisions, is a second characteristic. A specialized body of knowledge together with autonomy allow the professional to make decisions in ill-defined situations, and reflection helps professionals improve their decisions. Finally, ethical standards provide sets of principles that guide professionals as they work with students and caregivers.

2.2 **What are the primary arguments for teaching being a profession?**

Proponents of teaching as a profession point to the growing body of research on teaching that shows that effective teaching requires several different kinds of knowledge and requires an extended period of training for licensure. In addition, teaching professionals engage in continuous decision making in their classrooms and reflect on the effectiveness of these decisions. Teachers also have considerable autonomy in their classrooms and are guided by ethical standards for conduct.

2.3 **What are the major arguments against teaching being a profession?**

Critics who claim that teaching isn't a true profession base their claims on two major points. First, they point out that teaching often doesn't require rigorous training before licensure. Second, they point out that teacher autonomy is limited by curricular standards and assessment procedures.

2.4 **How do the arguments for and against teacher professionalism balance each other?**

Though the rigor required for teaching isn't as great as other professions, it is increasing. In addition, though their current autonomy is restricted by standards and testing, teachers still have a considerable amount of autonomy in the classroom. The future of the professionalization movement in teaching will be significantly influenced by current reform efforts.

3.1 **Identify the different dimensions of student diversity. Explain how these dimensions will influence your work as a teacher.**

Culture and ethnicity, language, religion, socioeconomic status, academic ability, physical and emotional maturity, gender, and learner exceptionalities are all sources of diversity. These different dimensions of diversity provide both challenges and opportunities to teachers. Diverse classrooms are more challenging to work in because they increase the number of decisions that teachers have to make. They also provide opportunities for both teacher and student growth. By working with diverse students, teachers learn about themselves and also have opportunities to enrich the lives of their students by helping them understand commonalities and differences in all people.

3.2 **Why is an understanding of different teaching and learning environments important for beginning teachers?**

Each of the different teaching and learning environments offers both opportunities and challenges to beginning teachers. Rural districts are smaller and tend to be more culturally homogeneous. Suburban districts are intermediate in size and tend to be better funded. Urban districts are larger and more culturally diverse. The number of jobs available in urban settings is increasing, and many urban districts target beginning teachers for job offers. They do this by offering a number of incentives to work in their classrooms.

4.1 How is the current reform movement in education changing the teaching profession?

The current reform movement in education is changing the profession in at least two ways. First, changes are occurring in teacher preparation, with teachers being held to higher academic standards and having their competency measured through state licensure exams.

Second, standards, specifying what students should know and be able to do after a course of study, and accountability, the process of holding students and their teachers responsible for demonstrating that they have met specified standards, are at the heart of the reform movement. Standards and accountability are influencing the curriculum—what teachers teach—and in some cases even how they teach, meaning that they teach in ways that maximize the likelihood of students doing well on the tests. In addition, high-stakes testing is often used to determine whether students can progress from one grade to the next or graduate.

4.2 Describe the major changes in teacher preparation that have resulted from the reform movement in education.

Major changes in teacher preparation primarily target higher standards for admission and higher academic standards within the programs themselves. Candidates are required to take more rigorous courses both before they enter and within teacher preparation programs. Prospective teachers also face higher licensure requirements for entering the profession, including teacher-competency tests. Many teacher-preparation programs are being expanded from 4 to 5 years, and experienced teachers are being asked to take more rigorous professional development courses.

4.3 What is INTASC? How has it influenced teacher preparation?

The Interstate New Teacher Assessment and Support Consortium (INTASC) was created in 1987 to help states develop better teachers through coordinated interstate cooperation. It created core standards for teacher preparation organized around 10 principles. These include knowledge of subject, knowledge of learners and human development, planning and instructional strategies as well as ways to work with parents and colleagues. These standards have improved the quality of teacher education and brought about greater uniformity in programs across states.

Developing as a Professional

2

Developing as a Professional

Chapter Outline

Beliefs of Preservice and Beginning Teachers

Entering the Profession
  Traditional and Alternative Licensure
  Developing a Professional Reputation
  Making Yourself Marketable
  Finding a Job

Your First Year of Teaching
  Survival Skills for the First Year
  Induction and Mentoring Programs
  Teacher Evaluation

Career-Long Professional Development
  Membership in Professional Organizations
  Becoming a Teacher-Leader
  Attaining Certification: The National Board for
    Professional Teaching Standards

Learning Objectives

After you have completed your study of this chapter, you should be able to:

1. Describe the beliefs of beginning teachers.

2. Explain differences between traditional and alternative licensure and the essential factors involved in finding a desirable job.

3. Identify factors that contribute to a successful first year of teaching.

4. Describe career-long professional development opportunities available to teachers.

Case Studies

 Elementary

 Middle

 Secondary

In this chapter we examine the beliefs of beginning teachers as well as the processes involved in developing as a professional and finding your first job. Let's begin by looking at one beginning teacher's experience as she recalls her first faculty meeting.

My first faculty meeting. Very interesting. Mrs. Zellner [the principal] seems really nice. She went on and on about what a great job the teachers did last year and how test scores were way up compared to the year before. She also extended a special welcome to those of us who are new.

Speaking of new teachers, there sure are a lot of us. I wonder if they're all as scared as I am. I'm not sure what I would have done if Mrs. Landsdorp [the teacher in the room next door] hadn't taken me under her wing. She made me feel much better about starting in an urban school. So many of the kids come from low-income homes, and English isn't the first language for several of them. She said that some of the teachers tend to "write them off" and assume that they can't learn, but that isn't true at all. In fact, many of them are quite bright. They just need a lot of help and support. She's wonderful. She's sort of gruff, but Andrea [a new friend and second-year teacher] say's she's a softy underneath, and she really loves the kids.

I can't believe how much there is to do—IEPs, progress reports, CPR training, being responsible for spotting signs of abuse. When do I teach? I hope I can cut it. (Shelley, a new third-grade teacher, reflecting on her first faculty meeting)

When you finish your program, and if you choose to teach, you'll be joining people like Shelley. To see how the Shelleys of the world view themselves and teaching, please respond to the following survey. We examine each of these items below as the chapter unfolds.

professional knowledge: test yourself!

For each item, circle the number that best represents your thinking. Use the following scale as a guide.

1 = Strongly disagree
2 = Disagree
3 = Uncertain
4 = Agree
5 = Strongly agree

1. When I begin teaching, I will be a better teacher than most of the teachers now in the field.

   1   2   3   4   5

2. As I gain experience in teaching, I expect to become more confident in my ability to help children learn.

   1   2   3   4   5

3. The most effective teachers are those best able to clearly explain the content they teach their students.

   1   2   3   4   5

4. I will learn about most of the important aspects of teaching when I get into a classroom.

   1   2   3   4   5

5. If I thoroughly understand the content I'm teaching, I'll be able to figure out a way of getting it across to students.

   1   2   3   4   5

 This is available in a downloadable format on the Companion Website for personal portfolio use.

Beliefs of Preservice and Beginning Teachers

The course for which this book is used is likely one of the first you'll take in your teacher preparation program. One of the goals of the course is to help you begin the process of learning to teach.

Teachers' beliefs have a strong influence on their teaching and the process of learning to teach (Richardson, 2003). Our goal in this section is to help you examine your own beliefs and the impact they can have on your professional growth.

Let's begin by returning to the survey you just completed. If you either agreed or strongly agreed with each of the statements, your beliefs are consistent with those commonly held by other students in teacher preparation programs. Let's see what research tells us about these beliefs.

Item 1: When I begin teaching, I will be a better teacher than most of the teachers now in the field. Preservice teachers are optimistic and idealistic: "Prospective teachers report being confident and self-assured in their teaching ability," but they "may be unrealistically optimistic about their future teaching performance" (Borko & Putnam, 1996, p. 678). The danger occurs when the realities of classrooms shock beginning teachers, who then feel as though "nobody prepared me for this" (Feiman-Nemser, 2001). Optimism wanes, and they may question their career choice; about 1 in 4 quits after the second year, and 4 in 10 leave the profession within the first 5 years (Grant, 2006).

Item 2: As I gain experience in teaching, I expect to become more confident in my ability to help children learn. As with Item 1, most preservice teachers expect to become increasingly confident in their ability to help children learn. However, the opposite often occurs. During the first few years of teaching, many tend to become less democratic in their work with students and less confident in their ability to overcome the limitations of home environments and family background (Bransford, Darling-Hammond, & LePage, 2005). We emphasize this point so that you might avoid this trap that ensnares many beginning teachers.

Item 3: The most effective teachers are those best able to clearly explain the content they teach their students. Many preservice teachers believe that teaching is essentially a process of "telling" or explaining content to students, probably because most of their own teachers simply lectured to them (van den Berg, 2002; J. Wang & Odell, 2002). However, research suggests that lecturing to students, especially young or unmotivated ones, is quite ineffective (Eggen & Kauchak, 2007).

Let's look at one intern's experience.

My first lesson with the kids. Chris [her supervising teacher] said I was on my own, sink or swim. I hardly slept last night, but today I feel like celebrating. The kids were so into it. I brought my Styrofoam ball and had the kids compare the latitude and longitude lines I had drawn on it and then look at the globe. I thought the first period was supposed to be Chris's lowest, but they did the best. He was impressed.

Now I understand the stuff Dr. Martinez [one of her professors] stressed so much when he was always after us to use concrete examples and question, question, question. I know I have a lot to learn. I thought I could just explain everything to them, but they got confused and drifted off so fast I couldn't believe it. As soon as I started asking questions about the lines on the Styrofoam ball, though, they perked right up. I think I can do this. It was actually a heady experience. (Gabriel, an intern in a seventh-grade geography class)

As Gabriel quickly discovered, teaching is much more complex than simply explaining (Donovan & Bransford, 2005). Research indicates that explaining, by itself, is often ineffective for helping students understand topics in depth.

Item 4: I will learn about most of the important aspects of teaching when I get into a classroom. This is another common preservice teacher belief. Many preservice teachers believe that experience is the only way they can learn to teach, and they also believe that their teacher education classes are little more than hoops they must jump through before getting into their own classrooms (Faject, Bello, & Leftwich, 2005).

Experience in classrooms *is* essential in learning to teach, but it isn't sufficient by itself. Unfortunately, in many cases, experience results in using the same procedures and techniques year after year, even when they're ineffective. Research also consistently indicates that students who go through traditional teacher preparation programs (such as the one you're in) are more successful and satisfied in their work than those who just jump into classrooms without prior classes (Darling-Hammond, 2000). Research and theory, combined

Making Connections:
To deepen your understanding of the topics in this section of the chapter and integrate them with topics you've already studied, go to the *Making Connections* module for Chapter 2 at **www.prenhall.com/kauchak.** Respond to questions 1 and 2.

with experience, help beginning teachers make sense of the often bewildering classrooms and students they'll encounter. This is one of the reasons you're studying this text.

Item 5: If I thoroughly understand the content I'm teaching, I'll be able to figure out a way of getting it across to students. One of the most pervasive myths in teaching is that knowledge of subject matter is all that is necessary to teach it effectively. Knowledge of content is essential, of course, but learning to teach requires a great deal of additional knowledge—knowledge you'll acquire in your teacher-preparation program (Darling-Hammond & Baratz-Snowdon, 2005).

Check Your Understanding

1.1 How effective do beginning teachers believe they will be compared to teachers already in the field?

1.2 Describe beginning teachers' beliefs about what makes a teacher effective.

1.3 Describe how beginning teachers' confidence in their ability to help students learn changes as they gain experience.

For feedback, go to Check Your Understanding *at the end of this chapter.*

Entering the Profession

Having examined the beliefs of preservice and beginning teachers, let's look now at the processes involved in entering the teaching profession.

Traditional and Alternative Licensure

All professionals—physicians, lawyers, and psychologists, for example—must be "licensed" in order to work in their occupations, and this applies to teachers as well. This process of licensure is designed to protect the public and ensure competence in each profession. In this section, we examine the processes involved in earning a license and what you can do to make yourself marketable.

Traditional Licensure

All K–12 teachers are required by law (in all 50 states plus the District of Columbia) to be licensed by a state department of education before they can teach in public schools. **Licensure** is the process by which a state evaluates the credentials of prospective teachers. By awarding a license, the state certifies that a teacher is competent in subject-area content, teaching skills, and classroom management, and is morally fit to work with youth.

You're likely taking this course in a traditional licensure program through which you'll earn a bachelor's degree. The program consists of a general education component that includes courses in history, English, math, and science, as well as education courses designed to help you develop your professional knowledge—the pedagogical content knowledge, general pedagogical knowledge, and knowledge of learners and learning. If you're planning to become a high school teacher, you are also required to accumulate a specified number of course hours in the subject area (e.g., math) in which you plan to teach (36 states have this requirement) (McCabe, 2006).

Increasingly, teachers are also being asked to pass competency tests that measure their basic skills in reading, writing, and mathematics (37 states had this requirement in 2006); high school teachers' background in an academic area such as chemistry or English (43 states

Licensure. The process by which a state evaluates the credentials of prospective teachers to ensure that they have achieved satisfactory levels of teaching competence and are morally fit to work with youth.

require this); and their understanding of learning and teaching (25 states require this) (McCabe, 2006). The Praxis™ Series, which consists of all three of these types of components, is currently being used in 35 states (Educational Testing Service, 2005).

The specific requirements for licensure vary from state to state, and the student advising office in your college or university can help you access them. If you're planning to move to another state, your education library may have books that describe the licensure requirements for all the states. If it doesn't, you can write or call the state certification office directly. The addresses and phone numbers of these offices can be found on this text's Companion Website at *www.prenhall.com/kauchak*.

During the process of licensure, teachers are increasingly being asked to demonstrate their competence through portfolios, interviews, tests, and on-the-job performance. (Will Hart/PhotoEdit Inc.)

Alternative Licensure

To meet the demand for more teachers, many states are developing alternative routes to licensure, and some of you taking this course may be involved in one of these programs. Currently, 45 states have alternative-route programs, and more than 75 percent of college or university teacher-education programs run one or collaborate with them. About a third of the teachers hired each year are licensed in this way (Blair, 2003; McCabe, 2006).

A person seeking alternative licensure must hold a bachelor's degree in the content area to be taught, such as math or English; pass a licensure test; complete a brief, intensive teacher training experience; and complete a supervised teaching internship.

Alternative licensure is controversial. Proponents make several arguments supporting this teacher-preparation route. Most alternative licensure candidates are older than students in undergraduate education programs, so they've had more life experiences; they have already earned bachelor's degrees, so they are more focused on learning to teach than are undergraduates who must combine classes in their content areas with courses in professional education (Dill & Stafford-Johnson, 2002). Also, alternative programs are shorter and tend to attract members of cultural minorities and talented and experienced people in areas of critical need, such as math and science (Blair, 2003). Proponents also argue that students in these programs are more academically talented than those in traditional programs.

Critics, however, point to the limited training in pedagogy that alternative licensure candidates receive (e.g., acquiring the pedagogical content knowledge, general pedagogical knowledge, and knowledge of learners and learning). Critics argue that this limited training results in instruction that is not responsive to students' needs (Darling-Hammond, Chung, & Frelow, 2002). Further, the intensive mentoring and supervision during the first few months of full-time teaching that is supposed to compensate for the new teachers' lack of formal course work often doesn't exist (Ansell & McCabe, 2003). Consequently, the first year of teaching becomes a sink-or-swim situation, with many teachers (and their students) failing (Darling-Hammond et al., 2002).

Finally, critics cite statistics indicating that the 2-year dropout rate for alternative licensure candidates is more than three times greater than the national average for new teachers (Darling-Hammond, 2000), though other research suggests the opposite (Guarino et al., 2006). This negative statistic may be skewed, however, because alternative licensure teachers are disproportionately assigned to the most demanding teaching situations, such as urban schools with high numbers of cultural minorities from low-income households (Blair, 2003). It is paradoxical that the students who need experienced teachers the most are often least likely to have them (Archer, 2003; Blair, 2003).

Conclusive assessments of alternative licensure are difficult to make because so much variation exists among programs (Johnson & Birkeland, 2006). High-quality alternative licensure programs are both time-consuming and costly. Research examining the performance of students taught by teachers from alternative licensure programs is also mixed. Some data suggest students fare as well as those taught by traditionally prepared teachers; however, most data do not (Darling-Hammond et al., 2001; Laczko-Kerr & Berliner, 2003).

Developing a Professional Reputation

Since you're at the beginning of your teacher-preparation program, it might appear that preparing for a job is well into the future. This isn't true. The time to begin developing a professional reputation is now. Let's look at one student's experience.

Developing a professional reputation begins with the college courses you are currently taking. (Michael Newman/PhotoEdit Inc.)

I really wish someone had reminded me of these things sooner. When I started, like a lot of others, I didn't take it all too seriously. I'd blow class off now and then, and I didn't always get there on time. I actually did study, but I guess not as hard as I should have.

When I asked Dr. Laslow for a letter of recommendation, he refused. Actually, he said he didn't know me well enough to write a good one. I couldn't believe it. He was nice about it, but he wouldn't write one, advising me to find someone who knew me better and was more familiar with my work. And a couple others were sort of lukewarm, especially in my major. I guess the classes were just too large for them to get to know me. Now it's too late. My record is a little spotty and I feel bad about it now, but I can't go back. I used to wonder why Brad and Kelly always seemed to get all the breaks. Now I get it. (Jeremy, a recent graduate without a job)

Do you know people who seem to get a lot of breaks? Do you get your share? Do your instructors know you, and do they respect and value your work? Students who get breaks do so for a reason. They attend all their classes, turn their work in on time, and attempt to learn as much as possible from their experiences. The quality of their work is consistently high. In other words, they behave professionally. Just as teachers in the field demonstrate professional behaviors, students are expected to as well. Professors value conscientiousness, and students like Jeremy trouble them. It's easy to understand why Brad and Kelly got breaks while Jeremy didn't.

What can you do to develop a professional reputation? Here are some suggestions:

- Attend all classes, and be on time. If you must miss, see your professor in advance or explain afterward.
- Turn in required assignments on time, and follow the established guidelines or criteria.
- Study conscientiously, and try to learn as much as possible in all your classes.
- Participate in class. Offer comments and ask questions. You will enjoy your classes more and also learn more from them.
- Extend your classroom behavior to your life. Take every opportunity to learn something new. For example, travel, especially to other countries, provides opportunities to learn about other cultures and the ways they approach education. Trips like these also make valuable entries on your résumé (which we'll discuss shortly).
- Read and try to be well informed. Learn for its own sake.
- Set yourself the goal to be the best student you can.

If you sincerely attempt to learn and grow, your professional reputation will take care of itself. But you must begin now.

TABLE 2.1 Making Yourself Marketable

Suggested Experience	Example	Professional Benefits
Develop a minor area of study in a high-need area.	If you're a French major, consider a minor in Spanish. If you're a biology major, consider a minor in chemistry.	You'll have more versatility in the jobs you apply for.
Join professional organizations.	Join your university's chapter of the National Education Association or a student chapter of another professional organization. (Professional organizations are listed on the Companion Website and in Table 2.3.)	You'll stay up-to-date on issues in your field and expand your network of professional contacts.
Tutor a child.	Become a reading tutor at a local school. Most schools welcome volunteer tutors and may also share your name with parents interested in a private tutor.	You'll gain direct experience working with children and may earn some extra money.
Seek leadership positions.	Run for a student government office.	Leadership experience on a résumé tells potential employers that you have effective human relations skills and the desire to be a lifelong learner.
Do volunteer work.	Spend a few hours each weekend helping out at the local food pantry.	Volunteer work can be enriching, and it indicates your desire to contribute to society.
Become an aide.	Ask your local school district about job openings for part-time classroom aides.	Working as an aide will give you valuable classroom experience and a part-time job.

Making Yourself Marketable

The most effective way to make yourself marketable is to acquire as much professional knowledge and experience as possible. The knowledge component will be addressed in the courses you'll take in your program; your professional experiences will complement this knowledge by applying it in varied contexts. Some suggestions for potential professional experiences are included in Table 2.1. If you pursue any of these experiences, you can write about them in your portfolio and include them in the résumé you construct to summarize your qualifications.

Building a Portfolio and Résumé

The interview was going okay, but I was uneasy. The principal I was interviewing with was cordial, but she certainly wasn't enthusiastic. "I've had it," I thought to myself. She even quit asking me questions after about 20 minutes. I really wanted the job, too.

As I was about to leave, I happened to mention, "Would you like to see my portfolio?" She looked at it for a couple minutes, and then she started asking some probing questions. When she stuck my DVD in her computer and saw me teaching, she really lit up. I got the job! (Shelley, the new teacher at the beginning of the chapter)

Activities are suggested at the end of the chapter to help you develop your professional portfolio.

The first item that appears in your portfolio should be a résumé summarizing your strengths and accomplishments as a teacher. A **résumé** is a document that provides an overview of an individual's job qualifications and work experience. It typically is the first thing a prospective employer sees and should make a clear and persuasive statement about your qualifications.

> **Résumé.** A document that provides an overview of an individual's job qualifications and work experience.

When constructing your résumé, clarity and simplicity should be guiding principles. People reading your résumé want to be able to easily find personal information, such as your address and phone number, as well as information about your education, work experience, and interests. They'll expect you to list references or be willing to provide them later. An effective résumé has the following components:

- Personal data
- Professional objectives
- Education
- Teaching experience
- Work experience
- Extracurricular activities
- Honors and awards
- References

The office of career planning and placement at your college or university will be able to help you in preparing your own résumé. A sample résumé containing these components is shown in Figure 2.1.

Creating a Credentials File

Your college or university will have a placement center designed to help graduates find jobs. An essential service of this center, in addition to providing information about job openings, is to serve as a repository for your credentials file. A **credentials file** is a collection of important documents teachers submit when they apply for teaching positions. It typically includes background information about you, your résumé, type of position sought, courses taken, performance evaluations by your internship-cooperating teacher and college or university supervisor, and letters of recommendation (usually three or more). When you apply for a job, you notify the placement center, which then sends your credentials file to the prospective employer. If, after reviewing this file, the district feels there is a potential match, you'll be contacted for an interview.

Writing a Successful Letter of Application

You have written a résumé and constructed a portfolio showcasing your skills and experiences. Now it is time to actually apply for a teaching position. School districts typically have a number of positions open before the start of the school year, so your letter of application, which will serve as a cover letter for your résumé, should clearly state the kind of position for which you are applying. In addition, it should highlight key elements of your résumé that you'd like to emphasize to a potential employer. And, finally, it should close with a statement detailing your availability for an interview, the topic of the next section. (See Figure 2.2 for a sample letter of application.)

Finding a Job

To this point we have discussed factors that will make you more effective once you get a teaching position. But when and how do you get started in the process of finding a job? The answer to *when* is now. We address the question of how in this section.

Where Are the Jobs?

Your ultimate goal is to locate a teaching position that will allow you to utilize your skills and develop as a professional, but such a position may not be easy to find. Several factors influence teacher supply and demand.

Geography is one factor. Student growth patterns vary by geographic area and grade level, mirroring demographic trends in the country. The greatest student enrollment increases are

Credentials file. A collection of important documents teachers need to submit when they apply for teaching positions.

Figure 2.1 A Sample Résumé

Melinda Garcia

Personal Data
Address:
2647 Bay Meadows Road
Jacksonville, FL 32224

Home phone: 904-267-5943
Work phone: 904-620-6743
E-mail: mgarcia@msn.com

Professional Objectives:
Elementary Teaching Position, K–6
Elementary Title I Reading Teacher, K–6

Education:
B.A. Elementary Education, University of North Florida, June 2007
Major Area: Elementary Education, K–8
Endorsements: Reading, K–8

Teaching Experience:
Student Teaching: Paxon Elementary, Duval County School District.
    Cooperating Teacher: Mrs. Nola Wright.
    Worked in a first-grade urban classroom with seven students who were English Language Learners; assumed full control of classroom for one eight-week grading period. Also worked with Mrs. Althea Walkman, First Grade Title I Coordinator. Administered reading diagnostic tests and developed specialized reading programs for groups of students.

Math and Reading Clinical Experience: Mathew Gilbert Elementary, Duval County School District.
    Cooperating Teacher: Ms. Linda Gonzalez
    Served as a teacher aide in a fifth-grade, self-contained classroom. Taught both small-group and whole-class lessons in reading and math.

Elementary Tutoring: Sandalwood Elementary, Duval County School District.
    Cooperating Teacher: Mrs. Alice Watkins
    Observed and tutored third-grade students in all subject matter areas. Tutored students in reading and math one-on-one and in small groups.

Work Experience:
Counselor and Tutor: YWCA After-school Activities Program. June 2006 to present. Worked with elementary students in both academic and recreation areas.

Lifeguard, Duval County Recreation Program. Summers, 2006, 2007. Full-time summer lifeguard; also provided swimming lessons for young students (4–6 years old).

Extracurricular Activities and Interests:
Vice President, University of North Florida, Student International Reading Association.
Senator, University of North Florida, Student Government Association.
Member, University of North Florida Swim Team.

Honors and Awards:
B. A. with Honors, University of North Florida.
Florida UTEACH Scholarship Recipient, 2005–2007.

References:
References and credentials file available upon request.

Figure 2.2 Letter of Application

Melinda Garcia
2647 Bay Meadows Road
Jacksonville, FL 32224

June 20, 2007

Dr. Robert Allington
Personnel Director
Duval County School District
2341 Prudential Drive
Jacksonville, FL 32215

Dear Dr. Allington,

I am writing this letter to apply for an elementary teaching position in your district beginning this fall. I recently graduated with honors from the University of North Florida, with a degree in elementary education and an endorsement in reading.

As my enclosed résumé indicates, I have had a number of rewarding experiences working with students in your district. Early in my elementary education program, I observed and tutored students in a third-grade classroom at Sandalwood Elementary School. I then did extensive clinical experiences in fifth-grade math and reading classes at Matthew Gilbert Elementary. During my internship at Paxon Elementary School, I was assigned to a first-grade classroom with significant numbers of Title I students and English Language Learners. During this experience, I learned a great deal about helping culturally diverse first-graders become skilled readers.

As I worked toward my degree, I focused on reading as my major area of endorsement. Reading is the key to success in all other subjects, and I believe I have the knowledge and skills to help young children become successful readers. Through my extensive experiences in classrooms at different levels, I have seen how effective reading programs build on the background knowledge and skills of developing readers. Please note that I have had formal course work in reading diagnosis as well as hands-on experiences implementing different diagnostic tests. I would like to utilize this expertise in a teaching position in your district.

I have arranged for my credentials file to be sent to you from the Placement Office at the University of North Florida. Please feel free to contact me at the telephone numbers listed on my résumé for any additional information. I am available for an interview at any time this summer.

Thank you for considering my application.

Sincerely,

Melinda Garcia

Melinda Garcia

occurring in the South and West and where general population growths are also occurring. These regions will have the greatest demand for teachers (Kober, 2006).

Within geographic areas, specific locations also influence teacher supply and demand. Job opportunities are much greater in rural and urban schools than they are in the suburbs, and these districts employ a number of recruiting strategies to attract competent new teachers, such as offering signing bonuses, financial help for professional development courses, and even housing incentives (Archer, 2003). For example, New York City recently offered housing subsidies of up to $14,600 to attract math, science, and special education teachers (Herszenhorn, 2006). Shelley, our new teacher at the beginning of the chapter, experienced these patterns:

At first I looked for jobs in two suburban schools, but there were no openings. However, I received offers from three different urban schools. I was a little hesitant at first because I had read about the challenges of working in urban settings, especially for first-year teachers. But one of the assistant principals was great. She talked to me about the job, what it entailed, and the kind of help I'd receive in an induction program at that school. I was paired with a wonderful mentor (Mrs. Landsdorp), and I'm having a challenging but great year. I love these kids and think I'm going to make it.

The specific teaching position you seek will also affect your chances of finding a job. Areas such as special education, English language learning (including bilingual education and English as a second language), foreign languages (especially Spanish), technology, math, physics, and chemistry need teachers more than others such as English, history, or physical education (Murphy, DeArmond, & Guin, 2003).

What implications do these job patterns have for you? First, if you haven't already decided on a major, don't select one based on job availability alone. To be effective, you must want to teach in the area you select. Don't major in chemistry, for example, if you dislike chemistry. However, if you want to teach chemistry, you now know that there is a high probability of getting a job in the area. Second, try to become knowledgeable about where teaching jobs exist. The career placement center at your college or university can help you. You'll increase your chances of finding a job if you're flexible about where you'll teach. Your first teaching position may not be in an ideal location, but you can use it to gain experience and as a stepping stone to other positions.

Interviewing Effectively

Professional behavior in an interview is essential. This is the setting that almost certainly will determine whether or not you get a job. Some guidelines for interviewing effectively are outlined in Table 2.2.

What are some things schools look for in new teachers during an interview? Research suggests the following:

- Knowledge of a content area(s) as well as knowledge of how to help students learn
- An understanding of how to organize and manage a classroom
- A sincere interest in making a difference in students' lives
- A variety of life experiences that can contribute to your classroom
- The ability to work with others
- Adaptability and flexibility

Interviews provide opportunities for teaching candidates to explain their qualifications as well as find out about the positions they're applying for. (Michael Newman/PhotoEdit, Inc.)

TABLE 2.2 Guidelines for Interviewing Effectively

Guideline	Rationale
Be on time.	Nothing creates a worse impression than being late for an interview.
Dress appropriately.	Wear an outfit appropriate for an interview, and be well-groomed. Shorts, jeans, and T-shirts are inappropriate, as is an eyebrow ring. You have the right to dress and groom yourself in any way you choose, but if you are serious about getting' a job, you won't demostrate your freedom of expression during a job interview.
Speak clearly, and use standard English and grammar.	Clear language is correlated with effective teaching, and your verbal ability creates an impression of professional ability.
Sit comfortably and calmly.	Fidgeting—or worse, glancing at your watch—suggests that you're either nervous or you'd rather be somewhere else.
Communicate empathy for children and a desire to work with them.	Communicating an understanding of learning, learner development, and instruction demonstrates that you have a professional knowledge base.

If you are genuinely interested in working with young people, and if you've been conscientious in your teacher-preparation program, the interview will largely take care of itself. Nothing communicates more effectively than a sincere desire to do the job for which you're interviewing.

Additional preparation can increase the positive impression you make, however. For example, how would you respond to the following questions, all of which are frequently asked in teacher interviews?

- Why do you want to teach?
- Why do you want to work in this school?
- What is your philosophy of education?
- How would you motivate unmotivated learners?
- How would you plan for classroom management?
- How would you handle an incident of misbehavior?
- How would you organize a unit on a topic in your area?
- How would you involve parents or caregivers in their children's education?

The more specific and concrete your response to each of the questions, the more positive an impression you will make. We suggest that you keep these questions in mind and begin to form answers to them as you go through your teacher-preparation program. If you are prepared, you will also be more at ease during the interview.

For instance, here is a specific response to the question about teaching philosophy:

"I believe that all children can learn, and I would try my best to make that happen by ensuring that all students are involved in the lessons I teach. Research suggests that active involvement is essential for learning. I would get them involved by calling on each of them as often as possible and using group work to develop content knowledge as well as develop social skills."

The answer communicates that you're clear about what you would try to do and why. Also, citing research suggests that you are knowledgeable, something all school districts value (Strong & Hindman, 2003). In contrast, a vague response, such as "I am a humanistic and learner-centered teacher," leaves the interviewer with the impression that you're just saying abstract words you learned in a class, which is much less persuasive.

Assessing Prospective Schools

The interview process is a two-way street. Not only are you being interviewed, but you are also interviewing the school. You want a job, but you also want to determine if the school is the kind of place in which you want to work. Research suggests that the upkeep and condition of the school as well as its culture have a powerful influence on teachers' satisfaction on the job (Buckley, Schneider, & Shang, 2005). When you interview, you should ask questions of the principal and other people you would work with. Doing so helps you learn about the position and communicates that you are thoughtful and serious about the job.

Some factors to consider when evaluating a school as a potential workplace include:

- *Commitment and leadership of the principal.* The principal's leadership sets the tone for the school (S. Johnson & Birkeland, 2003; Ubben, Hughes, & Norris, 2004). When teachers leave a school because of adverse conditions, dissatisfaction with support from administrators was the number one reason (Luekens, Lyter, & Fox, 2004). Does the principal demonstrate caring for students and support for teachers? The answers to these questions are highly inferential, but you can look for evidence in the principal's manner and comments.
- *School mission.* Does the principal communicate a clear mission for the school? If you have a chance to talk to other teachers, ask them if the teachers feel as if they're a team, all working for the benefit of students. The collective beliefs of teachers in a school that they can positively influence students' lives have a powerful influence on teacher morale and even student achievement (Goddard, Hoy, & Hoy, 2004).
- *School climate.* Does the emotional climate of the school seem positive? How do office personnel treat students? Does the support staff, such as custodians and cafeteria workers, feel like part of the team? Do school employees communicate a positive and upbeat attitude? Workplace conditions, both emotional and physical, are major factors influencing whether teachers leave or remain in a school (Luekens et al., 2004).
- *The physical plant.* Are student work products such as art and woodshop projects displayed in cases and on the walls? Do signs and notices suggest that the school is a positive environment for learning? Are the classrooms, halls, and restrooms generally clean and free of debris and graffiti?
- *The behavior of students.* Are students generally orderly and polite to one another and to the teachers? Do they seem happy to be at school?
- *Community support.* Do people in the community value education and support the school? How does the school involve parents in their children's education, and do they support school functions?
- *An induction program for teachers.* Does the school have a mentoring program for first-year teachers? First-year teachers who participate in mentoring programs are more likely to succeed and stay in teaching than those who don't (Darling-Hammond & Baratz-Snowdon, 2005). (We examine induction and mentoring programs in more detail later in the chapter.)

These questions are difficult to answer in one visit to a school, but they are important for your future development and satisfaction with the job. Working conditions in schools vary dramatically, and they can make the difference between a rewarding first year of teaching and one that makes you reconsider your decision to teach (S. Johnson & Birkeland, 2003). In addition, the support of parents and the community is important because it makes a huge difference in the attitudes, behaviors, and work habits of students (Marzano, 2003).

Private School Employment

You might also consider teaching in a private school; approximately 12 percent of all students attend private schools (Kober, 2006). There were 29,273 private K–12 schools in the United States in 2001, an increase of 7 percent over 1999 (National Center for Education Statistics, 2004). Most (76 percent) are religiously oriented, with Catholic schools being the most common (37 percent) of private schools. You are most likely to find private school employment in the South and in urban areas or large towns.

Average starting salaries for private school teachers are about 30 percent lower than those in public schools, however, and the difference increases to more than 40 percent for maximum salaries. In addition, private schools typically don't provide the same insurance benefits offered in public schools. Because of these adverse financial conditions, private school teachers in 2000–2001 were almost twice as likely to leave teaching as their public school counterparts (Luekens et al., 2004). When they left private schools, more than half (53 percent) transferred to public schools.

exploring diversity

The Competition for Minority Teachers

Nearly a third of school-age children in the United States are members of cultural minorities, and in two states, California and Texas, less than 50 percent of the school population is White. In the 25 largest cities, students of color compose at least half of the student population (Ladson-Billings, 2005; National Education Association, 2003). At the same time, the percentage of teachers who are members of minority groups remains fixed at about 12 percent, and in some areas is as low as 1 percent (Ladson-Billings, 2005). Projections indicate that before the mid 21st century, more than half of the nation's students will be members of cultural minorities (U.S. Bureau of Census, 2003).

Concern over these changing demographics has resulted in greater efforts to recruit minority teachers. Although no evidence suggests that nonminority teachers cannot work effectively with minority students, many educators believe that minority teachers bring valuable and unique perspectives to the classroom. Students need role models who share their cultural backgrounds, and minority role models may more effectively motivate students, because students can identify more closely with them (Pintrich & Schunk, 2002). Minority teachers can also provide more culturally relevant instruction by helping bridge differences between minority students' homes and cultures and schools. In addition, they can enrich a school's faculty by providing alternate perspectives on effective teaching and learning practices for minority students (Ladson-Billings, 2005; Yan & Gong, 2003).

To attract minority candidates to teaching, recruiters in many states have developed scholarships and loan-forgiveness programs. Alternative licensure programs often interest older people interested in a career change and are promising avenues for bringing minorities into the profession.

However, difficulties with these programs exist. For example, the recruitment strategies sometimes conflict with current reforms attempting to raise academic standards for teachers. Recruiters are attempting to attract teachers, whereas reformers are calling for more rigid academic standards, usually measured by standardized tests. This practice has a history of negatively and disproportionately affecting minorities (Guarino, Santibañez, & Daley, 2006).

School districts have also used alternative licensure to attract minorities to teaching; for example, nearly half of the candidates who went through California's alternative program in

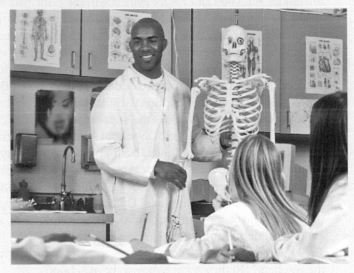

Minority teachers act as role models for minority students and help bridge gaps between homes and schools. (Getty Images, Inc—Image 100 Royalty Free)

1998–1999 were members of minority groups, as were 41 percent of those who went through the Texas program in 1998 (National Center for Education Information, 2000). However, as we saw earlier in the chapter, a much higher percentage of teachers who go through alternative licensure programs leave teaching than do those who complete traditional programs.

There is some room for optimism. The enrollment of African-American students in colleges of education increased from 6 percent to 9 percent in the 1990s, suggesting that the downward trend in the number of African-American teachers might be reversing (Archer, 2000a). Surveys indicate that African-American, Native American, and Hispanic college graduates are more likely to become teachers than are White graduates. However, the current bottleneck in K–12 schools limits the number of minority teachers who go on to college and become teachers; students in these groups are less likely to succeed in and ultimately graduate from high school (Barton, 2006; Swanson, 2004). Leaders suggest that a nation wanting the teaching force to more nearly reflect the composition of society must first focus its educational efforts on today's K–12 students.

Teachers often choose to work in private schools because these schools often waive the licensing requirements that public school teachers are required by law to meet. In addition, teachers sometimes choose private school employment because the school is dedicated to religious or intellectual principles consistent with the teacher's beliefs, communication between administrators and teachers is easier because these schools are often smaller, and parents whose children attend private schools tend to be more involved in school activities than those in public schools. Deciding to teach in a public or private school is ultimately an individual decision, influenced by your values and needs.

Making Connections:
To deepen your understanding of the topics in this section of the chapter and integrate them with topics you've already studied, go to the *Making Connections* module for Chapter 2 at www.prenhall.com/kauchak. Respond to questions 3–5.

Check Your Understanding

2.1 What are two differences between traditional and alternative licensure?

2.2 What are the two most essential factors involved in finding a desirable job?

2.3 In which areas are teaching jobs most plentiful?

 For feedback, go to Check Your Understanding *at the end of this chapter.*

Your First Year of Teaching

What will your first year of teaching be like? Unfortunately, a significant number of beginning teachers drop out in the first few years on the job. About 6 percent of all public school teachers leave the profession each year, but the number of new teachers who leave after their first year is much higher—about 15 percent. In addition, another 15 percent leave after their second year, and still another 10 percent after their third (Ingersoll & Smith, 2004). After the fifth year of teaching, a discouraging 46 percent of new teachers have left the profession (Kober, 2006).

The following comments help explain why some beginning teachers leave the profession:

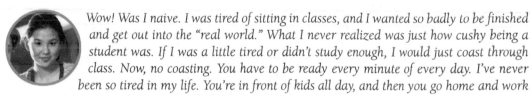 *Wow! Was I naive. I was tired of sitting in classes, and I wanted so badly to be finished and get out into the "real world." What I never realized was just how cushy being a student was. If I was a little tired or didn't study enough, I would just coast through class. Now, no coasting. You have to be ready every minute of every day. I've never been so tired in my life. You're in front of kids all day, and then you go home and work late into the night to get ready for the next day. They have us filling out reports, doing surveys, and everything other than teaching, so I don't get a chance to plan during the day. I can't even make a phone call unless it's during my lunch break or planning period.*

And then there's my fourth period. They come in from lunch just wired. It takes me half the period to get them settled down, and that's on a good day.

Sometimes I just need someone to talk to, but we're all so busy. Everybody thinks they're an expert on teaching, because they've been a student. They don't have a clue. Let them try it for 2 days, and they'd be singing a different tune. (Antonio, a first-year middle school math teacher)

New teachers face the following problems:

- Working conditions that require teachers to spend too much time on nonteaching duties and offer them too little time for planning and no time for themselves
- Unruly students and a disorderly teaching environment
- Loneliness and alienation (S. Johnson & Birkeland, 2003)

The stress of the first year is reduced, however, when teachers have someone to turn to for help, as Shelley did ("I'm not sure what I would have done if Mrs. Landsdorp hadn't taken me under her wing"). Beginning teachers without mentors and support are nearly twice as likely to leave as those with programs designed to help them make the transition from the university to the K–12 classroom (Horn, 2005).

The first year can also be rewarding. Let's look at another of Antonio's experiences:

Wow, what a day. We've been working so hard on solving equations, and all of a sudden Jeremy [one of Antonio's weaker students] bursts out right in the middle of our discussion, "Hey, I get this. It ain't all that bad." What a rush. When you see the light bulb finally come on in a kid's head, it keeps you going for another month. And, yesterday, Natalia [another struggling student] came up and said, "Mr. Martinez, I used to really, really hate math, but now I actually look forward to coming to algebra." I didn't drive home after school yesterday; I flew.

It is, indeed, a heady experience to see students understand something new and know that you helped make it happen.

Survival Skills for the First Year

You can also prepare for your first year of teaching by developing what we call "survival skills." They include

- Organization
- Classroom management
- Knowing your students
- Teaching effectively

Let's look at these skills.

Organization

Organization can help teachers maximize the time they have for the numerous professional roles they perform. (Anthony Magnacca/Merrill)

One of the first experiences you'll have as a beginning teacher will be lack of time. You'll feel as though you don't have a second to yourself. As Antonio said earlier, "I've never been so tired in my life. You're in front of kids all day, and then you go home and work late into the night to get ready for the next day." And at the beginning of the chapter, Shelley commented, "I can't believe how much there is to do—IEPs, progress reports, CPR training, responsibility to look for signs of abuse. When do I teach?"

Although a simple solution to this problem doesn't exist, careful organization is essential (Mandel, 2006). A large body of research, dating back to the 1970s, indicates that effective teachers are better organized (S. Bennett, 1978; Rutter et al., 1979). A student in one of our classes made the following observation of a first-year teacher he had visited: "His desk was a mess. Books and papers piled everywhere. He couldn't find anything, and he was always shuffling through papers looking for something." If he couldn't find "anything," you can bet that he wasted time looking for lesson plans and student papers. If you frequently or even occasionally lament that "I must get organized," now is a good time to start changing your habits. Having your instructional materials stored and readily accessible, creating procedures for routine tasks (e.g., turning in, scoring, and returning papers), and establishing policies for absences and making up missed work are all essential for using time effectively. For expert teachers, these organizational skills have become automatic; for beginning teachers, they must be learned (Weinstein, 2007).

Classroom Management

Classroom management has historically been the primary concern of beginning teachers, and disruptive students are an important source of stress for beginners and veterans alike (Bohn, Roehrig, & Pressley, 2004; Public Agenda, 2004). It is a major reason that teachers leave the profession during their first 3 years (L. Weiner, 2002). New teachers often feel ill-equipped to deal with management, and this dimension of effective teaching is one of the most important skills you'll learn in your teacher education program.

Teaching Effectively

Even though classroom management is the primary concern of beginning teachers, it is virtually impossible to maintain an orderly classroom without effective teaching strategies (Good & Brophy, 2003). If instruction is boring or if students don't understand what they're supposed to be learning and why, the likelihood of having classroom management problems increases dramatically.

Knowing Your Students

Knowing your students is an essential survival skill. It communicates that you care about them as people, which is crucial both for effective teaching and for classroom management. Commit yourself to knowing all your students' first names within the first week of school.

Again, watch your professors and teachers out in the field. See how they use students' names in their instruction. You will notice a striking difference between teachers who know and address students by name and those who do not.

Knowing students' names is important, but it's only a first step. Knowing them as people provides you with insights into their needs and interests as well as the kinds of experiences they bring into your classroom. Experienced teachers often begin the school year by having students fill out a questionnaire. The following are some examples of questions that might be included:

- What do you want to learn from this class?
- What are your favorite topics?
- How do you like to learn?
- What kinds of learning activities do you enjoy?
- Describe three important things about yourself as a person.

More important than the actual questions is the fact that the teacher cares enough to ask them. It makes students feel as if they and the teacher are "in this together," which is important for maximizing student learning.

Being well organized, developing an effective classroom management system, teaching effectively, and knowing your students are essential for a successful first year. This is why we call them survival skills. But what other actions can beginning teachers take to make their first year of teaching productive? We discuss induction and mentoring programs in the next section.

Induction and Mentoring Programs

Mrs. Landsdorp is wonderful. She is so supportive, and she is the person I always go to when I want a straight answer about what's really going on in the school and the district. She's also been very helpful in giving suggestions about how to deal with difficult parents and how I should handle myself in situations where I'm uncertain. She hasn't helped me a whole lot with nitty-gritty stuff, like planning lessons or watching me teach, but that's not her fault. She has a full teaching load too, so she really doesn't have time. I guess what it really amounts to is that she's been a real source of emotional support, and this year is going better than I could have hoped for. (Shelley, a first-year third-grade teacher talking about her mentor)

Effective induction and mentoring programs can help ease the transition into the teaching profession. (Jonathan Nourok/ PhotoEdit Inc.)

The transition to teaching is rarely as smooth as Shelley experienced. Teachers are sometimes hired at the last moment, left isolated in their classrooms, and given little help—examples of the sink-or-swim experience of many beginning teachers. As you saw at the beginning of this section, nearly a third of new teachers leave the profession within the first 2 years (Ingersoll & Smith, 2004), and isolation and lack of support are reasons why.

To address this problem, schools are increasing emphasis on induction and mentoring programs. **Induction programs** are professional experiences for beginning teachers that provide systematic and sustained assistance to ease the transition into teaching. These programs may include structured staff-development activities (e.g., workshops focusing on problems commonly experienced by first-year teachers), procedures for providing new teachers with crucial information, and mentors. **Mentors** are experienced teachers who provide guidance and support for beginning teachers (Bartell, 2005). Ideally, mentors provide not only emotional support, as Shelley reported, but also technical support in planning and conducting lessons and assessing student learning. Induction and mentoring programs can reduce first-year attrition by almost one third (Ingersoll & Smith, 2004).

Successful induction programs have the following elements (Gilbert, 2005; Wayne, Youngs, & Fleischman, 2005; Wong, Britton, & Ganser, 2005):

- A systematic attempt to help beginning teachers with both classes and opportunities to observe and dialogue with experienced teachers.
- Special help in the beginning years of their career to help them link their instruction to state and district standards.
- Professional development activities designed to increase mentors' effectiveness and compensation for mentors.
- Mentor support with everyday problems and encouragement for developing a reflective professional attitude.
- Feedback to new teachers based on classroom observation.

Actual classroom observations with feedback are essential; beginning teachers provided with this help significantly improved in organizing and managing instruction, and their students were better behaved and more engaged during lessons (Evertson & Smithey, 2000).

Many beginning teachers, however, do not participate in anything more than perfunctory school orientations, and many of the mentoring programs that do exist are like the one Shelley described; they provide emotional support but little specific help in the process of learning to teach (Olson, 2003). As we said earlier, the existence of an effective mentoring program is one of the factors you should consider when looking for your first job. Ask the principal and talk to teachers—and especially those who are new—about the availability of induction and mentoring programs.

Induction programs. Professional experiences for beginning teachers that provide systematic and sustained assistance to ease the transition into teaching.

Mentors. Experienced teachers who provide guidance and support for beginning teachers.

Teacher Evaluation

Teacher testing and accountability have become facts of professional life, and you likely will be required to pass competency tests before you're licensed. You will also be evaluated during your first years of teaching. Teacher evaluation has two primary purposes: **formative**, which is the process of gathering information and providing feedback that teachers can use to improve their practice, and **summative**, which is the process of gathering information about a teacher's competence, usually for the purpose of making decisions about retention and promotion (Ubben et al., 2004). You will likely encounter both in your first years of teaching.

Evaluation processes vary, so you should check to see how they are handled in your state and district. Typically, however, they are based on research about learning and teaching, and combine theory and research studies that examine the relationships between teacher actions and student learning (Borman & Kimball, 2005; Odden, Borman, & Fermanich, 2004). Research from a variety of sources is gathered and compiled, and observation instruments are created based on the literature (Pecheone & Chung, 2006). For example, research indicates that effective teachers have well-established classroom routines, use instructional strategies that produce high levels of student involvement, and quickly identify and eliminate sources of disruption (Emmer et al., 2006; Evertson et al., 2006).

Observation instruments used to evaluate teachers' effectiveness skills then ask the observer to

- Assess whether or not routines are in place and used effectively.
- Evaluate the extent to which students are attentive and involved in the lesson.
- Decide whether the teacher correctly identifies sources of misbehavior and deals with them quickly.

Observers use the same process to evaluate skills in other domains.

Before being observed, you should ask to see the instrument that will be used. If any of the categories are unclear, ask either the principal or an experienced teacher to explain. It always helps to know how you'll be evaluated, and knowing this also helps reduce the stress and anxiety that are always there when someone observes your teaching.

Some states (e.g., North Carolina) use existing standards, such as the INTASC principles, as frameworks for designing evaluation systems. Teachers compile portfolios of lesson plans, videotapes, student artifacts, and reflections that address each of these principles, and trained experts then evaluate these portfolios (Lashley, 2001). Portfolio-based teacher evaluation systems are likely to become more prominent in the future, which is another reason for you to learn how to develop an effective portfolio as early in your program as possible.

Making Connections:
To deepen your understanding of the topics in this section of the chapter and integrate them with topics you've already studied, go to the *Making Connections* module for Chapter 2 at **www.prenhall.com/kauchak**. Respond to questions 6–8.

Formative evaluation. The process of gathering information and providing feedback that teachers can use to improve their practice.

Summative evaluation. The process of gathering information about a teacher's competence, often for the purpose of making administrative decisions about retention and promotion.

IN TODAY'S CLASSROOMS: VIDEO

Succeeding in Your First Year of Teaching

In this video episode, a middle school teacher, near the end of the first year of teaching, describes her experiences, including the rewards and challenges that she experienced during that year.

To view this video, go to the *Becoming a Professional* DVD included with this text, click on *In Today's Classrooms*, and then this chapter's video: *Succeeding in Your First Year of Teaching.*

To answer the questions about the video online and receive immediate feedback, go to the Companion Website at **www.prenhall.com/kauchak**, *then the* In Today's Classrooms *module for Chapter 2.*

teaching in an era of reform

Merit Pay

One of the first questions you'll want to know as a beginning teacher is how much you'll be paid and what you'll need to do to receive pay increases over the years. Currently, most teacher salary increases are based on the number of years of experience and the number of graduate and in-service credit hours that teachers have earned. However, one aspect of the teaching profession that is receiving increased attention is the issue of merit pay, a supplement to a teacher's base salary intended to reward superior performance or work in a high-need area such as special education or teaching in urban schools.

Merit pay takes several forms. Some merit systems reward individual teachers based on their students' performance on tests. Others reward teachers based on principals' observations or teaching artifacts such as exemplary lessons or student work. A third type of merit pay rewards entire schools for student test performance, and a fourth provides teachers with extra salary for teaching in high-need areas such as math and science or at challenging sites such as high-poverty, low-performing urban schools (Keller, 2002; Odden, 2003). Some advocates suggest complex systems that include elements of each of the forms of payment (Koppich, 2005).

Because many policy makers want some form of pay-for-performance for teachers, and many school districts are considering merit pay, it is likely that you will encounter the issue early in your career (Drevitch, 2006). In 2006, at least 30 states were offering incentives, such as housing benefits or loan forgiveness, to address teacher shortages in certain subjects and geographical areas (Jacobson, 2006).

The Issue

Merit pay is highly controversial. Proponents argue that exemplary teaching performance should be rewarded and that money can provide incentives for teacher excellence (Odden, 2003). The superintendent of the Houston, Texas, district, the largest one to experiment with merit pay, comments, "It simply doesn't make sense any more. The system that pays the worst teacher the same that it pays the best teacher is not working" (Cook, 2006, p. 4). Others assert that simple economics suggest teachers in certain areas, such as math and science, should receive higher salaries, because they enjoy better job prospects outside education than do those in fields such as history or English. They further argue that higher salaries are essential for attracting skilled professionals willing to work in underperforming, urban schools (Ritter & Lucas, 2005).

The majority (more than 60 percent) of teachers are in favor of higher pay for teachers who work in tough neighborhoods with low-performing students, or for those who work harder and put in longer hours, or for those who consistently receive high evaluations by their principals (Public Agenda, 2003). But teachers' support for merit pay drops to 42 percent for paying teachers in high-demand areas, and 38 percent when the system is based on student test scores.

Critics contend that merit pay is divisive, damages morale, and make teachers less likely to cooperate with each other (Ramirez, 2001). Other critics argue that the systems are often too complex and fail to address the need for higher base salaries for all teachers (Cook, 2006).

Critics also contend that merit pay systems are often put into place without establishing agreed-upon and objective measures of teacher performance, without creating effective processes for identifying high-performing teachers, or without designing mechanisms for evaluating the effectiveness of the systems (Guthrie & Springer, 2006).

Tying merit pay to student performance on high-stakes tests is one way to simplify merit systems, and a number of states are considering this approach, but research indicates that these systems are generally ineffective because of a number of problems, including the students being taught (Gratz, 2005). Students in high socioeconomic status (SES) schools are more likely to score higher and have higher achievement gains than low-SES students. Consequently, teachers who work in low-SES schools would have less opportunity to receive merit increases. This would then discourage teachers from working in these schools, the exact opposite of what some proponents of merit pay intend.

You Take a Position

Now it's your turn to take a position on the issue. State in writing whether you favor or oppose merit pay, and provide a two-page rationale for your position.

For additional references and resources, go to the Companion Website at www.prenhall.com/kauchak, then to the Teaching in an Era of Reform module for Chapter 2. You can respond online or submit your response to your instructor.

Check Your Understanding

3.1 What are four factors that will determine whether or not your first year of teaching will be successful?

3.2 Describe the characteristics of successful induction programs.

3.3 How are teacher-evaluation systems created and used?

 For feedback, go to Check Your Understanding *at the end of this chapter.*

Career-Long Professional Development

To this point, we have discussed finding your first job and how to succeed in your first year of teaching. Now is also the time to begin thinking about your career 3 to 5 or more years down the road, because long-term professional goals can guide you during your teacher-preparation program. In this section, we examine three aspects of career-long professional development:

- Membership in professional organizations
- Becoming a teacher-leader
- Attaining certification through the National Board for Professional Teaching Standards

Membership in Professional Organizations

One of the first steps in your professional growth should be involvement in the professional organizations in education. These organizations support a variety of activities designed to improve teaching and schools, such as the following:

- Disseminating professional publications that provide up-to-date research and information on trends in the profession
- Providing professional development activities for teachers
- Holding yearly conferences that present research about recent professional advances
- Providing resources where teachers can find answers to questions about professional issues and problems
- Providing politicians and policy makers with information about important issues facing education

Table 2.3 includes a list of prominent professional organizations, their Website addresses, and descriptions of their missions or goals. We recommend that you join at least one professional organization as an integral part of your professional growth. Many organizations have student memberships that allow you to become involved while still in school.

Two of the largest professional organizations are the National Education Association (NEA) and the American Federation of Teachers (AFT). Founded in 1857, the NEA is the largest professional organization, enrolling approximately two thirds of the teachers in this country (National Education Association, 2006a). Most (78 percent) of the members are teachers, but NEA also includes guidance counselors, librarians, and administrators. AFT was founded in 1916 and has over 1.3 million members who primarily teach in urban areas (American Federation of Teachers, 2006). AFT does not allow administrators to join and has gained notoriety for its emphasis on better pay and better working conditions. You are likely to encounter representatives from at least one, if not both, of these organizations in your first year on the job. Talk with experienced teachers in your school about the pros and cons of each.

> **Merit pay.** A supplement to a teacher's base salary intended to reward superior performance or work in a high-need area.

TABLE 2.3 Professional Organizations for Educators

Organization and Web Address	Organization Mission or Goal
American Council on the Teaching of Foreign Languages *http://www.actfl.org*	To promote and foster the study of languages and cultures as an integral component of American education and society
American Federation of Teachers *http://www.aft.org*	To improve the lives of our members and their families, to give voice to their legitimate professional, economic, and social aspirations
Association for Supervision and Curriculum Development *http://www.ascd.org*	To enhance all aspects of effective teaching and learning, including professional development, educational leadership, and capacity building
Council for Exceptional Children *http://www.cec.sped.org*	To improve educational outcomes for individuals with exceptionalities, students with disabilities, and/or the gifted
International Reading Association *http://www.reading.org*	To promote high levels of literacy for all by improving reading instruction, disseminating research and information about reading, and encouraging the lifetime reading habit
Music Teachers National Association *http://www.mtna.org/flash.html*	To advance the value of music study and music making to society and to support the professionalism of music teachers
National Art Education Association *http://www.naea-reston.org*	To promote art education through professional development, service, advancement of knowledge, and leadership
National Education Association *http://www.nea.org*	To fulfill the promise of a democratic society, NEA shall promote the cause of quality public education and advance the profession of education
National Science Teachers Association *http://www.nsta.org*	To promote excellence and innovation in science teaching and learning for all
National Council for the Social Studies *http://www.ncss.org*	To provide leadership, service, and support for all social studies educators
National Council of Teachers of English *http://www.ncte.org*	To promote the development of literacy, the use of language to construct personal and public worlds and to achieve full participation in society, through the learning and teaching of English and the related arts and sciences of language.
National Council of Teachers of Mathematics *http://www.nctm.org*	To provide broad national leadership in matters related to mathematics education
National Association for Bilingual Education *http://www.nabe.org*	To recognize, promote, and publicize bilingual education
Phi Delta Kappa *http://www.pdkintl.org*	To promote quality education as essential to the development and maintenance of a democratic way of life by providing innovative programs, relevant research, visionary leadership, and dedicated service
Teachers of English to Speakers of Other Languages *http://www.tesol.org*	To improve the teaching of English as a second language by promoting research, disseminating information, developing guidelines and promoting certification, and serving as a clearinghouse for the field

Becoming a Teacher-Leader

At this point in your career, you may react to becoming a teacher-leader with, "Teacher-leader! I'm just trying to become a *teacher* first." Expectations for teachers have risen significantly since the beginning of the 1990s, and teachers' roles are also changing. For example, teachers now have much more input into decisions about teacher preparation, certification, and staff development than they had in the past. This has thrust teachers into new leadership roles, and the term *teacher-leader* has become part of the language of educational reform. Becoming a teacher-leader also creates a tangible goal for your growth as a professional educator.

Teachers can develop leadership skills in a number of ways:

- Serving on school-level or districtwide curriculum committees
- Helping establish school-level or districtwide policies on issues such as grading, dress codes, and attendance policies
- Writing grant proposals for student- or teacher-development projects
- Proposing and facilitating staff-development projects
- Arranging school–business partnerships
- Initiating and facilitating school-to-work activities
- Conducting action research

Because of its emphasis on research and the development of professional knowledge and its potential for developing teachers as professionals, we examine action research in more detail next.

Designing and Conducting Action Research

Understanding and critically examining others' research is one way for teachers to increase their professional knowledge. Another is for teachers to conduct research in their own classrooms. **Action research** is a form of applied research designed to answer a specific school- or classroom-related question (Gall, Gall, & Borg, 2003; Wiersma & Jurs, 2005). Teachers, school administrators, or other education professionals can conduct action research, using a variety of methods. The primary intent in action research is to improve practice within a specific classroom or school (McMillan, 2004).

Four steps guide teachers as they plan and conduct action research studies (B. Johnson & Christensen, 2004):

1. Identify a problem.
2. Plan and conduct a research study.
3. Implement the findings.
4. Use the results to generate additional research.

Let's see how Tyra Forcine, an eighth-grade English teacher, attempted to implement these steps in her classroom.

Action research provides opportunities for teachers to build upon their professional knowledge by dialoguing with other teachers about important issues. (Robin Sachs/PhotoEdit Inc.)

Tyra and a group of her colleagues are discussing the problems they are having with homework. Kim Brown complains that her students often "blow off assignments," and Bill McClendon reports he has so much trouble getting his students to do homework that he has stopped assigning it.

"I've heard teachers say that homework doesn't help that much in terms of learning, anyway," Selena Cross adds.

"That doesn't make sense to me," Tyra counters, shaking her head. "It has to help. The more kids work on something, the better they have to get at it."

Tyra consistently gives her students homework and checks to see if they have done it, but because of the conversation, she decides to take a more systematic look at its effects. She can't find a satisfactory answer on the Internet or in any of her college textbooks, so she decides to find out for herself.

Tyra begins her study at the start of the third grading period. She collects homework every day and gives the students 2 points for having done it fully, 1 point for partial completion, and 0 points

Action research. A form of applied research designed to answer a specific school- or classroom-related question.

for minimal effort or not turning it in. Each day she discusses some of the most troublesome items on the homework. On Fridays she quizzes students on the content covered Monday through Thursday, and she also gives a midterm test and a final exam. She then tries to see if a relationship exists between students' homework averages and their performance on the quizzes and tests.

At the end of the grading period, each student has a homework score, a quiz average, and an average on the two tests. Tyra calls the district office to ask for help in summarizing the information, and together they find a positive but fairly low correlation between homework and test averages.

"Why isn't the correlation higher?" she wonders in another lounge conversation.

"Well," Kim responds. "You're only giving the kids a 2, 1, or 0 on the homework—you're still not actually grading it. So I suspect that some of the kids are simply doing the work to finish it, and they aren't really thinking about it."

"On the other hand," Bill acknowledges, "homework and tests are correlated, so maybe I'd better rethink my stand on no homework. . . . Maybe I'll change what I do next grading period."

"Good points," Tyra responds. "I'm going to keep on giving homework, but I think I need to change what I'm doing, too. . . . It's going to be a ton of work, but I'm going to do two things. . . . I'm going to repeat my study next grading period to see if I get similar results, and then, starting in the fall, I'm going to redesign my homework, so it's easier to grade. I'll grade every assignment, and we'll see if the correlation goes up."

"Great idea," Kim replies. "If the kids see how important it is for their learning, maybe they'll take their homework more seriously, and some of the not-doing-it problem will also get better. . . . I'm going to look at that in the fall." (Adapted from Eggen & Kauchak, 2007)

Let's see how Tyra attempted to apply the four steps for action research in her classroom. First, she identified a problem: To what extent does homework contribute to my students' performance on quizzes and tests? This personalized approach increases teachers' motivation to do action research, because it answers questions that are important to them (Mills, 2002; Quiocho & Ulanoff, 2002).

Second, she systematically designed and conducted her study, and third, Tyra and her colleagues implemented the results of her project immediately. Bill, for example, planned to give homework during the next grading period. Action research is rewarding because it can address issues and problems that teachers really care about.

Finally, like most research, her project led to further studies (Hyland & Noffke, 2005). Tyra planned another study to see if scoring the homework more carefully would increase the correlation between homework and tests, and Kim planned to investigate the question of whether or not more careful scoring would lead to students' more conscientiously doing their homework.

In addition to answering questions about real classroom issues, conducting action research increases teachers' feelings of professionalism. Contributing to a body of knowledge and making decisions based on reflection helps teachers grow both personally and professionally (Darling-Hammond & Hammerness, 2005). Engaging in action research projects also contributes to teachers' perceptions of their own autonomy. These factors are outlined in Figure 2.3.

The results of well-designed studies can often be presented at professional conferences and published in professional journals. This allows the knowledge gained to be made public and integrated with other research, two important steps in the development of a professional body of knowledge (J. Hiebert, Gallimore, & Stigler, 2002).

Attaining Certification: The National Board for Professional Teaching Standards

Certification. Special recognition by a professional organization indicating that an individual has met certain requirements specified by the organization.

Earlier, we saw that licensure is the process states use to ensure that teachers meet professional standards. In comparison, **certification** is special recognition by a professional organization indicating that an individual has met certain requirements specified by the organization.

Figure 2.3   Conducting Action Research Enhances Professionalism

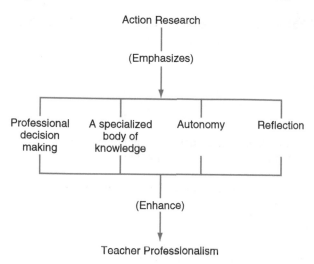

One important form of certification is offered by the National Board for Professional Teaching Standards (NBPTS). Created in 1987 as an outgrowth of the Carnegie Forum report, *A Nation Prepared: Teachers for the 21st Century* (Carnegie Forum on Education and the Economy, 1986), the board is composed mostly of K–12 teachers but also includes union and business leaders and university faculty (NBPTS, 2006). NBPTS seeks to strengthen teaching as a profession and raise the quality of education by recognizing the contributions of exemplary teachers, compensating them financially, giving them increased responsibility, and increasing their role in decision making.

National Board certification is based on standards that grew out of the board's policy statement *What Teachers Should Know and Be Able to Do*. The NBPTS summarized the professional standards contained in this report into five core propositions about what professional educators should know and be able to do. These propositions and descriptions of how they play out in practice are outlined in Table 2.4.

National Board certification has five important features:

- It is designed for experienced teachers. Applicants must have graduated from an accredited college or university and must have taught at least 3 years.
- Applying for National Board certification is strictly voluntary and independent of any state's licensure. It is intended to indicate a high level of skill and professionalism.
- Acquiring National Board certification requires that teachers pass a set of exams in their area of specialty, such as math, science, early childhood, or physical education and health.
- Additional evidence, such as videotapes of teaching and a personal portfolio, are used in the assessment process.
- The primary control of the NBPTS is in the hands of practicing teachers, which increases the professionalism of teaching.

Certification by the NBPTS is for veterans, so you may be wondering why we are providing information about it to preservice teachers early in their programs. There are three reasons. First, professionalism is a major theme of this book, and the NBPTS is a national effort to professionalize teaching. The propositions in Table 2.4 emphasize the pedagogical content knowledge, general pedagogical knowledge, and knowledge of

TABLE 2.4 Propositions of the National Board for Professional Teaching Standards

Proposition	Description
1. Teachers are committed to to students and their learning.	• Accomplished teachers believe that all students can learn, and they treat students equitably. • Accomplished teachers understand how students develop, and they use accepted learning theory as the basis for their teaching. • Accomplished teachers are aware of the influence of context and culture on behavior, and they foster students' self-esteem, motivation, and character.
2. Teachers know the subjects they teach and how to teach those subjects to students.	• Accomplished teachers have a rich understanding of the subject(s) they teach, and they appreciate how knowledge in their subject is linked to other disciplines and applied to real-world settings. • Accomplished teachers know how to make subject matter understandable to students, and they are able to modify their instruction when difficulties arise. • Accomplished teachers demonstrate critical and analytic capacities in their teaching, and they develop those capacities in their students.
3. Teachers are responsible for managing and monitoring student learning.	• Accomplished teachers capture and sustain the interest of their students and use their time effectively. • Accomplished teachers are able to use a variety of effective instructional techniques, and they use the techniques appropriately. • Accomplished teachers can use multiple methods to assess the progress of students, and they effectively communicate this progress to parents.
4. Teachers think systematically about their practice and learn from experience.	• Accomplished teachers are models for intellectual curiosity, and they display virtues—honestly, fairness, and respect for diversity—that they seek to inspire in their students. • Accomplished teachers use their understanding of students, learning, and instruction to make principled judgments about sound practice, and they are lifelong learners. • Accomplished teachers critically examine their practice, and they seek continual professional growth.
5. Teachers are members of learning communities.	• Accomplished teachers contribute to the effectiveness of the school, and they work collaboratively with their colleagues. • Accomplished teachers evaluate school progress, and they utilize community resources. • Accomplished teachers work collaboratively with parents, and they involve parents in school activities.

learners and learning. The NBPTS recognizes that increasing professionalism requires teachers who are both highly knowledgeable and skilled in their areas of specialization.

Second, National Board certification can be a long-term career goal for which there is also a financial incentive. As of 2003, an estimated $316 million had been spent on this venture at the national level, and 39 states and nearly 200 school districts had spent millions of additional dollars to reward teachers who successfully completed the process (Lustick, 2002; Thirunarayanan, 2004). For example, the state of Florida appropriated $69 million during 2003–2004 to provide board-certified teachers and mentors for future board-certified teachers with a 10 percent salary raise (Thirunarayanan, 2004). In addition, in 2003–2004 the state of Washington rewarded board-certified teachers with a $3,500 bonus (Margolis, 2004). As of 2005, there were 47,356 board-certified teachers nationwide, and this number is likely to increase (McCabe, 2006).

Finally, some evidence indicates that National Board certification makes a difference in teacher quality. In a study comparing teachers who had successfully completed the process to those who had attempted but failed to achieve certification, the nationally certified teachers scored higher on nearly all measures of teaching expertise. The study involved at least 75 hours of observation of each teacher, along with interviews and samples of student work (Blair, 2000). However, a more recent study found no achievement gains for students taught by National Board–certified teachers (Keller, 2006). And another study found that the certification process encouraged teachers to become more reflective about their work and their relationships with other professionals (Lustick, 2002). National Board certification is well worth pursuing, and we encourage you to keep it in mind as you begin your career.

> **Making Connections:**
> To deepen your understanding of the topics in this section  of the chapter and integrate them with topics you've already studied, go to the *Making Connections* module for Chapter 2 at **www.prenhall.com/kauchak**. Respond to questions 9 and 10.

Check Your Understanding

4.1 What are three career-long professional development opportunities that are available to you as a teacher?

4.2 What are five different activities designed to improve teaching and schools that professional organizations support?

4.3 What are the two primary assessment processes involved in attaining National Board certification?

 For feedback, go to Check Your Understanding *at the end of this chapter.*

decision making

Defining Yourself as a Professional

You're interviewing for a position in a large, urban middle school. The leadership team of the school is composed of the school principal, a vice principal, and two assistant principals. Both the principal and vice principal are involved in the interview, which is scheduled for 1 hour.

You've been asked a number of probing questions, such as, "What is the biggest problem you faced in your internship?" "How would you motivate a class of unmotivated learners?" and "How would you enforce rules with students who are disruptive in your class?"

As you respond, the vice principal appears to listen attentively, but the principal appears distracted. He nods and responds in general terms to your answers but doesn't follow up on any of the questions.

After 45 minutes have passed, the interview seems to be winding down, so you attempt to ask some questions about the school. The principal cuts you off, saying he has a meeting he

must attend. He cordially thanks you for coming and quickly leaves the office, 10 minutes before the scheduled end of the interview. The vice principal, on the other hand, asks you to come into his office and says he is willing to try to answer any questions you have. You spend another half hour with him, and he takes you on a tour of the school, during which the discussion of the school and students continues. The principal's name doesn't come up in the discussion, but the physical plant is clean and attractive, the students are orderly as they move between classes, and one who accidentally bumps you says, "Oh, excuse me."

If it was offered, would you take a job at this school? Explain why you would or would not.

To respond to this question online and receive immediate feedback, go to the Decision Making module for Chapter 2 on the Companion Website at www.prenhall.com/kauchak.

Meeting Your Learning Objectives

1. Describe the beliefs of beginning teachers.
   - Beginning teachers are idealistic and optimistic. They generally believe that they will be effective, and they often believe that they will be more effective than teachers now in the field.
   - Beginning teachers expect to become more confident about their ability to promote learning as they acquire experience. Unfortunately, the opposite often occurs.
   - Beginning teachers believe that effective teachers are those who are best able to clearly explain content to students, and if they understand their content, they will be able to teach it effectively.
   - Beginning teachers tend to believe that they will learn most of what they need to know to be an effective teacher from their experiences in classrooms.

2. Explain differences between traditional and alternative licensure and the essential factors involved in finding a desirable job.
   - Traditional licensure consists of a general education component, as well as education courses designed to help teachers develop professional knowledge. Secondary majors are also required to take a specified number of course hours in the subject area (e.g., math) in which they plan to teach.
   - In alternative licensure programs, people who have bachelor's degrees in areas other than education complete a short, intensive training program with a clinical component.
   - Finding a desirable job requires developing a professional reputation, building a portfolio and résumé, and creating a credentials file. The more quickly students in preservice programs begin to develop a professional portfolio, gathering experiences that make them marketable and building their professional reputation, the better equipped they will be to find a job when they graduate.

3. Identify factors that contribute to a successful first year of teaching.
   - Lack of time and classroom management are the most common problems beginning teachers face. Getting organized, becoming well-informed, getting to know their students, and developing effective instructional strategies are teachers' most effective ways to prepare for both their internship and their first year of teaching.
   - Induction and mentoring programs help beginning teachers make the transition from being students to being effective teachers. The best mentoring programs provide systematic help for beginning teachers, help teachers link their instruction to state and district standards, provide teachers with support in dealing with everyday problems, encourage teachers to develop a reflective professional attitude, and provide feedback based on classroom observation.
   - Evaluation is also a part of a beginning teacher's experience. Formative evaluation is designed to provide helpful feedback to teachers; summative evaluation is designed to ensure adequate performance by teachers. Teacher evaluation based on research and standards-based evaluation are two approaches that schools commonly use throughout the United States.

4. Describe career-long professional development opportunities available to teachers.
   - Professional organizations provide a variety of services for teachers throughout their careers. These include publications with current research, professional development activities, annual conferences, and resources for teachers' questions and concerns.
   - Teachers can develop professionally by becoming teacher-leaders, such as by serving on district- and state-level committees; writing grants; designing and facilitating staff development activities; and conducting action research, research designed to address an immediate school-level problem.
   - The National Board for Professional Teaching Standards (NBPTS), in an attempt to professionalize teaching, has established rigorous standards and assessments for teachers who have completed at least 3 years of successful service. Substantive financial rewards exist in most states for teachers who have successfully completed National Board certification.

Important Concepts

action research
certification
credentials file
formative evaluation
induction programs

licensure
mentors
merit pay
résumé
summative evaluation

Developing as a Professional

Preparing for Your Licensure Exam

This exercise will provide you with practice answering questions similar to the Praxis™ Principles of Learning and Teaching exam as well as your state-specific licensure exam.

In this chapter, we discussed use of time, classroom management, knowing your students, and teaching effectively as factors that will help you succeed in your first year of teaching. Keep these factors in mind as you read the case study below, and then answer the questions that follow.

Kaycee Vess is a first-year geography teacher in a large, urban middle school. With 29 students, her classroom is crowded. This morning, in homeroom, Shiana comes through the classroom doorway just as the tardy bell rings.

"Take your seat quickly, Shiana," Kaycee directs. "You're just about late. All right. Listen up, everyone," she continues. "Ali?"

"Here."

"Gaelen?"

"Here."

"Chu?"

"Here."

Kaycee finishes taking the roll and then walks around the room, handing back a set of papers.

"You did quite well on the assignment," she comments. "Let's keep up the good work. . . . Howard and Manny, please stop talking while I'm returning papers. Can't you just sit quietly for 1 minute?"

The boys, who were whispering, turn back to the front of the room.

"Now," Kaycee continues, returning to the front of the room, "we've been studying the Middle East, so let's review for a moment. . . . Look at the map, and identify the longitude and latitude of Cairo. Take a minute and figure it out right now."

The students begin as Kaycee goes to her file cabinet to get out some transparencies.

"Stop it, Damon," she hears Leila blurt out behind her.

"Leila," Kaycee responds sternly, "we don't talk out like that in class."

"He's poking me, Miss Vess."

"Are you poking her, Damon?"

"Uhh . . . ."

"Well?"

"Not really."

"You did, too," Leila complains.

"Both of you stop it," Kaycee warns. "Another outburst like that, Leila, and your name goes on the board."

As the students are finishing the problem, Kaycee looks up from the materials on her desk to check an example on the overhead. She hears Howard and Manny talking and laughing at the back of the room.

"Are you boys finished?"

"Yes," Manny answers.

"Well, be quiet then until everyone is done," Kaycee directs and goes back to rearranging her materials.

"Quiet, everyone," she again directs, looking up in response to a hum of voices around the room. "Is everyone finished? . . . Good. Pass your papers forward. . . . Remember, put your paper on the top of the stack. . . . Roberto, wait until the papers come from behind you before you pass yours forward."

Kaycee collects the papers, puts them on her desk, and then begins, "We've talked about the geography of the Middle East, and now we want to look at the climate a bit more. It varies somewhat. For example, Syria is extremely hot in the summer but is actually quite cool in the winter. In fact, it snows in some parts.

"Now, what did we find for the latitude of Cairo?"

"Thirty," Miguel volunteers.

"North or south, Miguel? . . . Wait a minute. Howard? . . . Manny? . . . This is the third time this period that I've had to say something to you about your talking, and the period isn't even 20 minutes old yet. Get out your rules and read me the rule about talking without permission. . . . Howard?"

"Uhh . . . ."

"It's supposed to be in the front of your notebook."

"Uhh . . . ."

"Manny?"

"'No speaking without permission of the teacher,'" Manny reads from the front page of his notebook.

"Howard, where are your rules?"

"I don't know."

"Move up here," Kaycee directs, pointing to an empty desk at the front of the room. "You've been bothering me all week. If you can't learn to be quiet, you will be up here for the rest of the year."

Howard gets up and slowly moves to the desk Kaycee has pointed out. After Howard is seated, Kaycee begins again, "Where were we before we were rudely interrupted? . . . Oh yes. What did you get for the latitude of Cairo?"

"Thirty north," Miguel responds.

"Okay, good. . . . Now, Egypt also has a hot climate in the summer—in fact, very hot. The summer temperatures often go over 100 Fahrenheit. Egypt is also mostly desert, so the people have trouble making a living. Their primary source of subsistence is the Nile River, which floods frequently. Most of the agriculture of the country is near the river."

Kaycee continues presenting information to the students for the next several minutes.

"Andrew, are you listening to this?" Kaycee interjects when she sees Andrew poke Jacinta with a ruler.

"Yes," he responds, turning to the front.

"I get frustrated when I see people not paying attention. When you don't pay attention, you can't learn, and that frustrates me because I'm here to help you learn."

Kaycee continues with her presentation.

1. How effective was Kaycee's organization? Provide evidence from the case study to support your assessment.

2. Did Kaycee know her students? How do you know?

3. How effective was Kaycee's classroom management? Provide evidence from the case study to support your analysis.

4. How effective was Kaycee's teaching? Again, provide evidence from the case study to support your evaluation.

To receive feedback on your responses to these exercises, go to the Companion Website at www.prenhall.com/kauchak, then to the Preparing for Your Licensure Exam *module for Chapter 2.*

Discussion Questions

1. What can preservice teachers do to decrease the likelihood that they will leave the profession? What can school leaders do?

2. The National Board for Professional Teaching Standards is attempting to increase the professionalism of teaching. How successful is it likely to be? Explain your thinking.

3. Some critics suggest that teaching isn't a profession, because it doesn't have a body of knowledge on which to base its decisions. How would you respond to these critics?

4. In this chapter, we suggested that you attempt to establish a professional reputation by being conscientious in your classes. What are some other ways students can develop a professional reputation?

5. We offered several suggestions for making yourself marketable in this chapter. Is it reasonable to expect that preservice teachers involve themselves in these activities? Explain your thinking.

6. What are some professional qualities beginning teachers should look for in a mentor? What are some personal qualities?

Developing as a Professional: Online Activities

Going Into Schools

Go to the Companion Website at *www.prenhall.com/kauchak*, and click on the *Going Into Schools* module for Chapter 2. You will find a number of school-based activities that will help you link chapter content to the schools in which you work.

Virtual Field Experience: Using the Internet to Explore the Profession

If you would like to participate in a Virtual Field Experience, access the following website: *http://www.rnt.org*. This site contains a number of different perspectives on recruiting and retaining new teachers as well as information on areas of high teacher demand.

Online Portfolio Activities

To develop your professional portfolio, further apply your understanding of chapter content, and address the INTASC standards, go the Companion Website at *www.prenhall.com/kauchak*, then to the *Online Portfolio Activities* for Chapter 2. Complete the suggested activities.

Check Your Understanding

1.1   How effective do beginning teachers believe they will be compared to teachers already in the field?

Beginning teachers are idealistic and believe they will be very effective. They further believe that they will be more effective than teachers who are now in the field, and they believe that their confidence in their ability to promote student learning will increase as they gain experience.

1.2   Describe beginning teachers' beliefs about what makes a teacher effective.

Beginning teachers believe that the most effective teachers are those best able to clearly explain the content they teach to their students, and they also believe that if they thoroughly understand their content, they will figure out a way of helping students learn it.

1.3 **Describe how beginning teachers' confidence in their ability to help students learn changes as they gain experience.**

Unfortunately, as beginning teachers acquire experience in their first few years of teaching, their confidence in their ability to help students learn tends to decrease, and they often feel as if "No one prepared me for this."

2.1 **What are two differences between traditional and alternative licensure?**

First, students in traditional licensure programs take professional training courses in education while working toward their bachelor's degree. Alternative licensure students have already earned a bachelor's degree in some field other than education.

Second, traditional licensure people get much more professional training in education than do alternative licensure candidates. Typically, alternative licensure candidates take short intensive training in education, and they are supposed to receive extensive mentoring when they get out on the job. This mentoring is commonly missing, however.

2.2 **What are the two most essential factors involved in finding a desirable job?**

The two most essential factors involved in finding a desirable job are developing a positive professional reputation and interviewing effectively. If you have developed a positive professional reputation, you will earn supportive letters of recommendation, which make you more marketable.

Interviewers assess a variety of factors during an interview, such as your professional knowledge, personality characteristics, dress, use of language, and enthusiasm for teaching. How you come across in each of these areas will be significant in whether or not you're offered a job.

2.3 **In which areas are teaching jobs most plentiful?**

Two categories of plentiful jobs exist. The first is related to content area. For example, jobs are plentiful in areas such as math, science (particularly chemistry and physics), special education, and foreign languages, and particularly Spanish.

Many jobs also exist in challenging teaching situations, such as underperforming urban schools with high percentages of minority students and students whose native language is other than English.

3.1 **What are four factors that will determine whether or not your first year of teaching will be successful?**

Organization, classroom management, effective instruction, and knowing your students are four factors that will influence how successful your first year will be. For this reason, we describe them as "survival skills" for your first year of teaching. Each is important, but classroom management is one of the most essential. More beginning teachers leave the profession because of their inability to manage students than for any other reason.

3.2 **Describe the characteristics of successful induction programs.**

Effective induction programs include systematic efforts that are designed to help beginning teachers and give special attention to new teachers to help them link their instruction to state and district standards. They also include professional development activities designed to increase mentors' effectiveness and compensation for mentors, offer support with everyday problems, and encourage teachers to develop a reflective professional attitude. In addition, new teachers in effective induction programs are observed, and they're given detailed feedback and support with planning and instruction.

3.3   How are teacher-evaluation systems created and used?

Educators base the design of teacher-evaluation systems on research and theory that describes connections between teaching and learning. Educators gather and compile findings from a variety of sources and create observation instruments based on research. Administrators or supervising teachers then observe and evaluate teachers using the observation instruments as a guide.

4.1   What are three career-long professional development opportunities that are available to you as a teacher?

Involving yourself in professional organizations, becoming a teacher-leader, and attaining National Board certification are all long-term professional development opportunities.

4.2   What are five different activities designed to improve teaching and schools that professional organizations support?

Professional organizations attempt to improve teaching and schools by (1) producing and disseminating professional publications that provide up-to-date research and information on trends in the profession, (2) providing professional development activities for teachers, (3) holding yearly conferences that present theory and research about recent professional advances, (4) providing resources where teachers can find answers to questions about professional issues and problems, and (5) providing politicians and policy makers with information about important issues facing education.

4.3   What are the two primary assessment processes involved in attaining National Board certification?

The two primary assessment processes involved in acquiring National Board certification are passing a set of exams in an area of specialty, such as math, science, early childhood, or physical education and health, and submitting evidence of teaching ability, such as videotapes of classroom instruction and a personal portfolio that demonstrates expertise.

The Organization
of American Schools

3

The Organization of American Schools

Chapter Outline

What Is a School?

The Organization of Schools
Personnel
The Physical Plant
Organization of the Curriculum

School Levels
Early Childhood Programs
Elementary Schools
Junior High and Middle Schools
High Schools

What Is an Effective School?
Research on Effective Schools
Parents' and Other Taxpayers' Perceptions of
Effective Schools

Learning Objectives

*After you have completed your study of this chapter,
you should be able to:*

1. Describe different meanings of the
concept school.

2. Identify the components of a typical school
organization.

3. Describe important differences among
schools at different levels.

4. Identify the characteristics of an effective
school.

Case Studies

 Elementary

 Middle

 Secondary

Myrleen Ferguson Cate/PhotoEdit Inc.

Most of you are seriously considering becoming a teacher, but many of you haven't determined which level you want to teach. Fortunately, we've all attended schools and experienced them as students, so we're familiar with the basic ways in which they're organized. But what do schools look like from a teacher's perspective? The answer to this question could help you decide whether to become an elementary, middle school, or high school teacher. Let's take a look at one teacher's experience.

"Wow, noon. I need to get going," Chris Lucio says to his colleague April Jackson as he finishes the last bite of his lunch and jumps up from the couch in the teacher's lounge. "My kids will be chomping at the bit trying to get into the room."

Chris hurriedly leaves the lounge, stops by the main office to check his box, and then walks across the courtyard to his building.

The courtyard sits at the center of the campus of Lakeside Junior High. Created 30 years earlier as a middle school for grades 6–9, Lakeside is now one of three junior high schools housing seventh and eighth graders in Orange Park, a suburb of a large eastern city. Four main buildings surround the courtyard: one for administration and three for classrooms. The administration building houses the principal's and other administrators' offices, a cafeteria—with a stage at one end—that doubles as an auditorium, and a media center and computer lab holding 30 computers. A gymnasium and fine arts building, built 10 years ago when Lakeside became a junior high, and athletic facilities (tennis courts and baseball, softball, and soccer fields) are positioned outside the main buildings.

Chris walks briskly to the room where he teaches seventh-grade geography.

"Okay everyone, the bell is going to ring in a couple minutes. . . . Find your seats quickly," Chris calls out, unlocking the door to his room.

"Mr. Lucio, can I go to the bathroom?" Armondo asks as he heads through the open door.

"Hurry—you don't want to be tardy," Chris answers as he smiles at him.

"Are you going to come to our track meet this afternoon?" Devon, another of Chris's students asks as he enters the room. "We're going to kick butt on Ridgeview."

"Wouldn't miss it," Chris replies and thinks to himself, "Yikes, I almost forgot. . . . I promised Joe and Karen [the boys' and girls' track coaches] that I'd be a timer for the 100- and 200-meter races."

"What time does it start?" Chris asks Devon.

"Right after school—4 o'clock, I think."

As the bell signals the start of the period, Chris moves to the front of the room and starts taking roll as the students begin working on a warmup exercise that Chris has displayed on the overhead.

If you're in your mid-20s or younger, you've spent more than half of your life in school. But exactly what is a school, and what does it mean to teach and learn in one? We consider these questions in this section, but before we continue, please respond to the following survey.

---

professional knowledge: test yourself!

For each item, circle the number that best represents your thinking. Use the following scale as a guide.

1 = Strongly disagree
2 = Disagree
3 = Uncertain
4 = Agree
5 = Strongly agree

1. Teachers are the people in schools who have the ultimate responsibility for the successful operation of the school.

    1   2   3   4   5

2. A major tension in the organization of elementary schools is between the dual goals of meeting the developmental needs of students and content acquisition.

    1   2   3   4   5

3. Middle and junior high schools are essentially the same but are given different labels.

    1   2   3   4   5

4. In general, larger schools provide students with a better-quality education, because they have better facilities and a wider variety of programs

    1   2   3   4   5

5. The assessment program in a school is a major factor influencing the school's effectiveness.

    1   2   3   4   5

This is available in a downloadable format on the Companion Website for personal portfolio use.

We address each of the survey items as the chapter develops.

What Is a School?

As a concept, a *school* can be described as a place where young people go to learn and develop intellectually, personally, and socially. Whether or not this is the "best" definition, however, can be debated. Churches have vacation Bible *school,* and we've all heard of students being *homeschooled.* At a simpler level, a school is a physical place—a building or set of buildings where teachers and students spend considerable amounts of time.

At a third level, school is a **social institution**, an organization with established structures and rules designed to promote certain goals. Schools are social institutions whose goals are to promote both students' growth and development and the well-being of a country and its citizens. Other social institutions include churches, religions, and governments. They all are designed to make society a better place in which to live.

We use *social institution* as the framework for our discussion in this chapter, as we examine the ways in which schools are organized and how this organization is designed to help meet their goals. Some ways of organizing schools are better than others, and these differences influence how much students learn and how they develop. These differences will also influence your life as a teacher.

Every school operates as a relatively independent unit within a **school district**, an administrative unit within a state, defined by geographical boundaries and legally responsible for the public education of children within those boundaries. A school district may encompass an entire county, or large counties may be divided into more than one district.

Districts are important because schools are embedded within them, and their rules and policies affect teachers' and students' lives. Some districts are quite bureaucratic and hierarchical, controlling major elements of curriculum and instruction. Others give more of the decisions about what and how to teach to individual schools and teachers. When you interview for a job, you will want to talk to teachers about their perceptions of the district and how its administrators treat teachers.

Let's turn now to the organization of individual schools, but before we do, check your understanding of the ideas in this section.

> **Making Connections:**
> To deepen your understanding of the topics in this section of the chapter and integrate them with topics you've already studied, go to the *Making Connections* module for Chapter 7 at www.prenhall.com/kauchak. Respond to questions 1 and 2.

Check Your Understanding

1.1 What are three different meanings of the concept school?

1.2 Explain how a school and a school district differ.

1.3 Is the family a social institution? Explain why it is or is not.

For feedback, go to Check Your Understanding *at the end of this chapter.*

> **Social institution.** An organization with established structures and rules designed to promote certain goals.
>
> **School district.** An administrative unit within a state, defined by geographical boundaries, and legally responsible for the public education of children within those boundaries.

The Organization of Schools

Think about the schools you attended as a student. If the organization was typical of schools in the United States, you first went to an elementary school, which began with kindergarten, or even prekindergarten, followed by first grade, second grade, and so on. You then went to a middle school or junior high, and finally to a high school. As we look at how these schools are organized and why, we'll examine the following:

- Personnel
- The physical plant
- The organization of the curriculum

Personnel

No school is better than the people who work there. School personnel include all the people—the administrators, the support staff, and the teachers—who help make a school an effective social institution.

The central office is the school's nerve center; the office staff plays an important role in greeting guests and assisting both teachers and students. (Will Hart/PhotoEdit Inc.)

Administrators and Support Staff

Elementary, middle, junior high, and high schools all have **administrators**, individuals responsible for the day-to-day operation of a school. Administrators include a **principal**, the individual given ultimate administrative responsibility for the school's operation, and this definition addresses the first item on our survey at the beginning of the chapter, "Teachers are the people in schools who have the ultimate responsibility for the successful operation of the school." This ultimate responsibility lies with the principal, and, as with expert teachers, the most effective principals possess a great deal of professional knowledge (Saha & Biddle, 2006).

If the school is large, a vice principal, assistant principal, or both support the principal in his or her work and are also part of the administration. Lakeside Junior High, the school in the case study at the beginning of the chapter, has a principal, vice principal, and two assistant principals. The vice principals' responsibilities typically include scheduling, collecting student records (e.g., grade reports) from teachers, keeping master records for the school, and maintaining communication with district-level administrators and parents. One of the assistant principals manages the physical plant, arranging the distribution of lockers to students, co-ordinating the duties of the custodial staff, and overseeing all maintenance and construction. The other assistant principal is in charge of discipline—including referrals made by teachers and both in-school and out-of-school suspension of students, ordering and distributing textbooks to department heads, and maintaining in-service records for teachers.

Depending on the size of the school and the financial status and organization of the school district, schools may also have guidance counselors, school psychologists, and health-care providers, such as school nurses. Lakeside Junior High also has two full-time guidance counselors and a school psychologist it shares with other schools. The guidance counselors schedule and coordinate the statewide assessment tests and provide information to students about course offerings and career options. The school psychologist administers individual-ized intelligence tests and other tests used in making decisions about whether students qual-ify for special education or programs for the gifted and talented. The school psychologist also provides individual counseling for students having emotional problems and makes recom-mendations for further mental health assistance.

Administrators. Individuals responsible for the day-to-day operation of a school.

Principal. The individual who has the ultimate administrative responsibility for the school's operation.

Lakeside also has a full-time licensed practical nurse; she maintains all student health records, is trained in administering CPR, supervises medical evacuations, and dispenses all medications to students. Nationally, 33 percent of schools have nurses (Kober, 2006). Students at Lakeside are not allowed to take even an over-the-counter painkiller, such as aspirin, on their own, and teachers may not give students any form of medication.

In addition, all schools have support staff, such as the following:

- Secretaries and receptionists, who greet visitors to the school
- Administrative and instructional support staff, who complete paperwork for the principal and other administrators, duplicate tests and handouts for teachers, maintain payroll records, and perform other functions
- Media center specialists, who manage books and different forms of technology
- Physical plant staff, such as custodians who clean the rooms and buildings and cafeteria workers who prepare school lunches

Schools vary in the way they assign duties to administrators, so the duties of the administrators and support staff in schools that you visit, or the school in which you take your first job, may differ from those we described here.

Why do you need to know about different school personnel and their roles? A school is a complex social institution, and all the people working in a school contribute to making it run smoothly. As a professional, your ability to work with the other personnel will influence how effective you and the school will be. For example, if you have a student who is so unruly that you can't work with him or her in your classroom, you will need the support of the assistant principal and perhaps the advice of the school psychologist to help you address the problem. Although you may be alone in your classroom when you teach, your effectiveness will depend on your ability to coordinate your efforts with many different people in your school.

A common adage suggests that you can tell a great deal about a school by observing the way a school receptionist greets students and visitors when they enter the main office. Likewise, the way you treat support staff also helps set the tone for a positive school climate. For example, requesting—instead of demanding—services, such as having a test duplicated, communicates to support staff that you value their contributions to the overall functioning of the school. The most effective schools are those in which all personnel work together for the benefit of students.

Teachers

While school principals have ultimate administrative responsibility for the school's operation, teachers are at the heart of any effective school. A huge body of literature consistently indicates that students taught by expert teachers learn more than those taught by teachers with less expertise (Bransford, Darling-Hammond, & LePage, 2005; Darling-Hammond & Baratz-Snowdon, 2005). "Supportive teachers and clear and high expectations are key to ensuring that students feel

IN TODAY'S CLASSROOMS: VIDEO

The Principal's View of Professionalism

To view this video, go to the *Becoming a Professional* DVD included with this text, click on *In Today's Classrooms*, and then this chapter's video: *The Principal's Role in Instructional Leadership*. Answer the questions you'll find on the DVD.

In this video episode, a school principal describes his role as an instructional leader.

To answer questions about the video online and receive immediate feedback, go to the Companion Website at **www.prenhall.com/kauchak**, *then the* In Today's Classrooms *module for Chapter 7.*

in control and confident about their ability to learn" (Lewis, 2006, p. 565). Helping you develop into an expert teacher who can support student learning is a major goal of this text.

The Physical Plant

One definition of a school that we considered was a physical place. Schools have classrooms, hallways that allow students to move from one room to another, a central administrative office, and one or more large rooms, such as auditoriums, gymnasiums, music rooms, and cafeterias. Many schools have a simple boxlike structure, with hall upon hall of separate cells, which critics argue isolates teachers and fragments the curriculum. Classrooms also offer teacher privacy and sanctuary from the hectic pace of school life. When teachers retreat into their classrooms and close their doors, no one else knows what goes on in there. Open classrooms with large movable walls have gone in and out of popularity and are usually resisted by teachers because of noise and lack of privacy (Bolkan, Roland, & Smith, 2006).

An elementary school usually includes a staff parking area, playground, and driveway used for dropping off and picking up students. Middle, junior high, and high schools also have athletic facilities, such as playing fields, stadiums, and sometimes swimming pools. In some middle schools, however, the design intentionally omitted gyms or other facilities that support competitive activities. High schools also have parking spaces available for students who drive their own cars to school.

School enrollments often increase so rapidly that physical plants can't keep up (Ortiz, 2004). As a result, many schools have "temporaries" or "modulars," individual buildings on the perimeter of school campuses that provide additional classroom space.

What will the physical arrangement of schools mean for you as a teacher? Positively, your own classroom will be your own domain where you can define yourself as a teacher. But it will also separate you from your colleagues. When you're in your classroom and you shut the door (as many teachers do), you'll be on your own. You'll be responsible for 20 to 30 second graders, for example, all day, every day. If you teach in middle or high school, you'll spend most of your workday in the confines of your classroom, where you'll be responsible for the education and safety of five or six different classes of students.

Second, although your primary responsibility will be to teach students in your classroom, you'll also be expected to carry out noninstructional activities in other areas of the school .If you teach in an elementary school, you may need to escort your students to and from the cafeteria or the media center, for example. If you're a middle or secondary teacher, you'll be expected to monitor students as they move through the corridors and attend auditorium assemblies. You may also be asked to sell tickets at football games, attend track meets, and go to band concerts. A teacher's responsibilities result, in part, from the way schools are physically organized.

Organization of the Curriculum

Schools are social institutions designed to help young people grow, develop, and prepare to function effectively in today's (and tomorrow's) world. To function effectively in today's technologically oriented and fast-changing world, students need to acquire essential knowledge and skills. Our task as educators is to organize the curriculum in a way that maximizes students' opportunities for learning and development. Theorists offer a variety of definitions of curriculum, and no single one is generally accepted (Armstrong, 2003). For our purposes in this chapter, however, we'll define **curriculum** simply as what teachers teach and what students learn.

A curriculum is typically organized around learning goals, such as the following:

- Students will recognize the letters of the alphabet.
- Students will write short paragraphs using correct paragraph structure.
- Students will use the correct order of operations to simplify expresions such as $9 + 4(7 - 3)/2$
- Students will understand the concepts *mass* and *inertia*.

Curriculum. The knowledge and skills that teachers teach and students are supposed to learn.

Historically, educators have decided that the most efficient way of helping students reach goals such as these is to organize instruction according to different grade levels, ages of students, and subject areas. For instance, children in kindergarten are expected to reach the first goal, third graders the second, seventh-grade pre-algebra students the third, and eleventh-grade physics students the fourth. Learning goals for different grade levels and subject areas are part of a school's general curriculum, and these goals provide teachers with direction as they make decisions about what to teach.

School Organization and the Curriculum

How should teachers and students be grouped to help students most effectively learn the content of the curriculum? For example, does it make sense to have 6-year-olds in the same building and walking the same halls as 17- or 18-year-olds? Safety, as well as seemingly mundane concerns such as the height of drinking fountains and toilets, suggests no.

Most school systems are organized into three levels: elementary schools for younger children, middle or junior high schools for young adolescents, and high schools for later adolescents. The grades included at each level vary from place to place, however, and as a teacher you may encounter various organizational patterns. Table 7.1 outlines some of the most common.

What factors do educators consider when making decisions about organizing schools? For example, why do middle schools typically include grades 6–8 or grades 7 and 8? Two factors are most powerful: (1) the developmental characteristics of students and (2) economics and politics.

Developmental Characteristics of Students

Development refers to the physical changes in children as well as changes in the way they think and relate to their peers that result from maturation and experience. For example, fifth graders are bigger, stronger, and more coordinated than first graders; that is, they are physically more developed. Similarly, fifth graders think differently than do first graders. When shown the drawing on page 220, for example, typical first graders conclude that Block A is heavier than Block B, because their thinking tends to focus on size—the most obvious aspect of the balance and blocks. Fifth graders, on the other hand, are more likely to conclude that the blocks have the same weight, because they recognize that the beam is balanced (level). Their thinking is more developed (Eggen & Kauchak, 2007).

TABLE 7.1 Common Ways to Organize Schools

School Level	Grade Ranges
Elementary school	K–2 K–3 K–5 K–6
Middle school	5–8 6–8 7–8
Junior high school	7–8 7–9 8–9
High school	9–12 10–12

Development. The physical, intellectual, and social changes in children that occur as a result of experience.

Differences in social development also exist. For example, when faced with a disagreement about who in a group gets to report on which topic, a fifth grader is more likely to step back, recognize the others' perspectives, and compromise. Socially, fifth graders are often capable of considering where a classmate is "coming from," whereas first graders tend to be more self-centered in their thinking (Berk, 2006; McDevitt & Ormrod, 2007). Advances in social development allow teachers to use instructional strategies, such as cooperative learning, that are more effective with older children than with those who are younger or less developed socially (Brophy, 2006).

Similar differences can be found between fifth graders and high school students. Many older students are physically young men and women, some think quite abstractly, and they can be socially skilled.

These developmental differences influence the ways in which schools are organized. For example, students in elementary schools are typically assigned to one teacher who monitors the cognitive, social, and emotional growth of students in that classroom. In some schools **looping**, the practice of keeping a teacher with one group of students for more than a year, is used to help individual teachers better nurture the development of individual students. Older students are more capable of learning on their own and fending for themselves, so they are assigned to a number of teachers who also serve as subject-matter specialists.

Economics and Politics

Economics and politics are also factors that influence decisions about school organization. For example, both influenced the development of Lakeside, Chris Lucio's school, first in its creation as a middle school and later in its conversion to a junior high.

At the time Lakeside was developed, the elementary schools in Orange Park had become overcrowded because of rapid population increases in the city, and the process of building additional elementary schools couldn't keep up with demand. Creating middle schools temporarily solved the problem, because sixth graders could be moved into the middle schools. This was a decision based on economics.

Also, the middle school movement was gathering momentum at this same time, and Mary Zellner, Lakeside's first principal, was an outspoken proponent of middle schools. She was a respected leader in district politics, and because of her influence, Lakeside was built according to middle school philosophy. This philosophy de-emphasized competition among students, and as a result, the school didn't have competitive athletics, which was the reason the school didn't originally have a gymnasium. Although Mary Zellner's advocacy of middle schools was grounded in research, the district-level decision to avoid competitive activities at Lakeside was a result of her political influence.

Issues then became further complicated. Coaches at Orange Park High complained that potential athletes came to them from the middle schools without the athletic experiences students attending competing schools enjoyed. (These pressures are not unusual; many middle-level schools in the United States offer organized competitive sports.) The fact that Orange Park High, the only high school in the district, had become overcrowded presented a bigger problem. District officials solved both problems by converting the middle schools into junior highs, moving ninth graders from the high school to the junior highs, and sending sixth graders back to elementary schools. By

Looping. The practice of keeping a teacher with one group of students for more than a year.

86

this time, the elementary schools were able to accept the additional students, because a number of new elementary schools had recently been built in the city. The decision to convert middle schools to junior highs was based on both economics and politics; it had little to do with the developmental needs of students.

Unfortunately, organizational changes such as these are not uncommon in education. Keep these factors—developmental, economic, and political—in mind as we look at schools at different levels in more depth in the next section.

Making Connections:
To deepen your understanding of the topics in this section of the chapter and integrate them with topics you've already studied, go to the *Making Connections* module for Chapter 7 at **www.prenhall.com/kauchak.** Respond to questions 3 and 4.

Check Your Understanding

2.1 What are the major components of a typical school organization?

2.2 Most school systems are organized into three levels. Describe each of the three.

2.3 What are two factors that influence the way school curriculum is organized?

For feedback, go to Check Your Understanding, *at the end of this chapter.*

School Levels

In the previous section, we saw that schools are typically organized into elementary, middle or junior high, and high school levels. In this section, we take a closer look at how schools are organized to meet the developmental needs of students and how different organizational patterns influence the lives of teachers. Let's begin our examination of different levels of schools with a look at early childhood programs.

Early Childhood Programs

Visitors to Sharon Broderick's preschool classroom at first are struck by the seeming chaos. Students around her classroom are working on a number of different and unconnected tasks. Sharon and her aide, Carmen Sanchez, circulate among the groups, asking questions and offering suggestions.

Closer examination of the room reveals several clusters of activity organized around centers. One center has a tub of water where students measure water in different-sized cups and also determine which kinds of objects sink and float. Another has a table with an assortment of plastic geometric blocks and shapes that children are using to construct things. A third has different costumes and clothing along with two telephones that students use for pretend conversations and dialogues. A fourth contains a variety of picture books that require different amounts of expertise with letters and words. Children circulate among these different centers, and the teacher and her aide keep track of who has been to which center and completed different tasks.

Most of you reading this probably attended kindergarten, and some of you may have even attended a prekindergarten program. However, one of your authors, educated in a small town in a rural area, attended neither, because they weren't offered there at the time.

Early childhood education is a general term encompassing a range of educational programs for young children, including infant intervention and enrichment programs, nursery schools, public and private prekindergartens and kindergartens, and federally funded Head Start programs. Early childhood education is a mid–20th-century development in the United

Early childhood education. A general term encompassing a range of educational programs for young children, including infant intervention and enrichment programs, nursery schools, public and private prekindergartens and kindergartens, and federally funded Head Start programs.

States, although its philosophical roots go back 250 years. The French philosopher Rousseau, for example, gave this advice about educating young children:

Do not treat the child to discourses which he cannot understand. No descriptions, no eloquence, no figures of speech. . . . In general, let us never substitute the sign for the thing, except when it is impossible for us to show the thing. . . . Things! Things! I shall never tire of saying that we ascribe too much importance to words. (Rousseall, quoted in Compayre, 1888)

Rousseau was arguing that young children need to play and work with concrete objects ("Things! Things!") rather than being taught with abstract words. This idea is consistent with the need for concrete experiences that the famous developmental psychologist Jean Piaget (1952, 1970) emphasized, and it is at the core of developmentally appropriate early childhood programs.

Developmental programs accommodate differences in children's development by allowing them to acquire skills and abilities at their own pace through direct experiences. Visitors in a developmental classroom are likely to see learning centers around the room such as those in Sharon Broderick's class. Unlike traditional teacher-centered instruction, the teacher's role is to provide experiences for children and encourage exploration.

The need for learning-related experiences early in life is well recognized (Berk, 2006; McDevitt & Ormrod, 2007), and the benefits of early intervention programs are long-lasting. For example, the Perry Preschool study compared the experiences of 123 poor African-American children who either attended 3 years of preschool or did not (the program did not have room for all applicants) (Bracey, 2003a). Dramatic differences were found between the preschool students and students in the control group. By the time these students turned 27, 71 percent of the preschool group had attained a high school diploma or GED, compared to only 54 percent of the control group. Forty-two percent of the males in the preschool group reported making more than $24,000 a year, compared to only 6 percent of the males in the control group. Thirty-six percent of the preschool group, but only 13 percent of the control group, owned their own homes. Control group members had twice as many arrests as those who attended the preschool, and five times as many of the control group had been arrested five or more times. Clearly, the Perry Preschool program had long-lasting beneficial effects on the children it served.

A more ambitious program in North Carolina provided nutritional help and social services from birth, as well as parenting lessons and a language-oriented preschool program (Bracey, 2003a; Jacobsen, 2003). Follow-up studies revealed that, compared to nonparticipants, participants scored higher on intelligence and achievement tests, were twice as likely to attend postsecondary education, and delayed having children by 2 years. Early childhood education programs pay off, both in immediate school and also later in life. David Broder, a prominent *Washington Post* columnist, observed: "The evidence that high-quality education beginning at age 3 or 4 will pay lifetime dividends is overwhelming. The only question is whether we will make the needed investment" (quoted in Bracey, 2003a, p. 32).

In the early 1970s, only 23 percent of 4-year-olds were enrolled in early childhood programs; by 2001, this figure had increased to 66 percent (Magnuson, Meyers, Ruhm, & Waldfogel, 2004). Much greater emphasis is now being placed on high-quality early intervention programs in all settings. As full-time pre-K programs become increasingly common, job opportunities in these areas will continue to grow.

Elementary Schools

To begin our examination of the organization of elementary schools, let's look at the schedules of two elementary teachers. Examine the schedules in Table 7.2, and see what you notice.

Your observations might include the following:

- Both teachers are responsible for all the content areas, such as reading, language arts, math, science, and social studies.

Developmental programs. Programs that accommodate differences in children's development by allowing them to acquire skills and abilities at their own pace through direct experiences.

TABLE 7.2 Schedules for Two Elementary School Teachers

Sharon's First-Grade Schedule		Susie's Third-Grade Schedule	
8:30 AM	School begins	8:30 AM	School begins
8:30–8:45	Morning announcements	8:30–9:15	Independent work (practice previous day's language arts and math)
8:45–10:30	Language arts (including reading and writing)	9:15–10:20	Language arts (including reading and writing)
10:30–11:20	Math	10:20–10:45	Snack/independent reading
11:20–11:50	Lunch	10:45–11:15	Physical education
11:50–12:20	Read story	11:15–12:15	Language arts/social studies/science
12:20–1:15	Center time (practice on language arts and math)	12:15–12:45	Lunch
		12:45–2:00	Math
1:15–1:45	Physical education	2:00–2:30	Spelling/catch up on material not covered earlier
1:45–2:30	Social studies/science		
2:30–2:45	Class meeting	2:30–2:45	Read story
2:45–3:00	Call buses/dismissal	2:45–3:00	Clean up/prepare for dismissal

- The schedules are quite different. Although both teachers teach young children, Sharon begins with language arts, for example, while Susie begins by having the children practice their previous day's math and language arts.
- The amount of time the teachers allocate to each of the content areas is a personal decision. Sharon, for example, devotes 50 minutes to math, whereas Susie teaches math for 75 minutes a day.

In conversation, both teachers noted that the schedules in Table 7.2 were approximate and often changed depending on their perception of students' needs and the day of the week. For example, if students were having trouble with a math topic, they might devote more time to math on a given day (S. Mittelstadt, personal communication, August 15, 2006; S. Van Horn, personal communication, August 16, 2006).

If you observe in elementary classrooms, you're likely to see a schedule that varies from those in Table 7.2. This level of individual teacher freedom and autonomy is characteristic of elementary school organization and is a major reason that people become elementary teachers.

Why are elementary schools organized this way? In the first elementary-level schools in early America, a single teacher was typically responsible for all of the content areas. Until about the mid-1800s, elementary schools weren't even organized into grade levels. In many rural, one-room schools, a single teacher was responsible

Self-contained elementary classrooms attempt to meet young students' developmental needs. (Scott Cunningham/Merrill)

for all the grade levels and content areas. In some rural areas, one-room school houses still exist today (Swidler, 2004). So, history has influenced the way elementary schools are organized.

The developmental characteristics of students have also influenced the organization of elementary schools. We saw earlier that young children look, think, and interact with their peers in ways that are different from older students. Educators have historically believed that young children need the stability of one teacher and a single classroom to function most effectively in school. Schools can be frightening places for little children, and self-contained classrooms provide emotional security. Further, simply moving from room to room, as middle and secondary students do, can be challenging for young children. Imagine, for example, a first grader going to Room 101 for math, 108 for language arts, and so on. Rotating schedules, which are becoming increasingly popular under block scheduling, would be even more confusing.

Many educators question the idea of a single classroom and teacher. Expecting one teacher to be sufficiently knowledgeable to effectively teach reading, language arts, math, science, and social studies is asking the impossible, they say. As a result, teachers commonly de-emphasize some content areas, such as science, social studies, art, and music. Both Sharon and Susie acknowledged that they strongly emphasized reading, language arts, and math, and de-emphasized the other areas, even though these other content areas appear on their schedules (see Table 7.2).

So educators, teachers, and parents face a dilemma: Are social and emotional well-being more important than content for elementary students? Historically, the answer has been yes. This section provides us with an answer to the second item on our survey, "A major tension in the organization of elementary schools is between the dual goals of meeting the developmental needs of students and content acquisition." The answer is yes, and this tension will continue to grow as efforts to document student academic growth through testing continue to grow.

Junior High and Middle Schools

To see differences between elementary schools and middle, junior high, and high schools, we need only compare Chris's experiences (in the chapter's opening case) to Susie's and Sharon's (in Table 7.2). Elementary teachers typically teach all the content areas and set their own schedules. In contrast, as a middle school teacher, Chris teaches only one subject (geography), and he (along with all the other teachers in his school) follows a specific, predetermined schedule. The lengths of class periods are uniform for all the content areas, and the beginnings and endings are signaled by a bell. Also, Chris is not responsible for monitoring his students as they move from place to place on the Lakeside campus as elementary teachers are, but he is involved in extracurricular activities (e.g., the track meet), which are part of middle schools, junior highs, and high schools.

Why are upper-level schools organized in this way? To answer this question, think back to our description of school as a social institution designed to promote the development of children and the welfare of society. Also, views about educational goals have changed over time. For instance, in colonial times, people felt that society would benefit most from having students learn to read and understand the Bible. Much later (near the end of the 19th century), educators felt that having both college-bound and non-college-bound students take the same curriculum would serve the needs of society. This view was based on the belief that mental discipline was the most important function of education. Also, schools were organized to accommodate the large influx of immigrants to help them assimilate into American society.

As educational thinking evolved, leaders felt that society needed citizens well schooled in a variety of academic subjects. This emphasis on the mastery of subject matter resulted in the departmentalization found in the middle schools, junior highs, and high schools that you most likely attended. But a tension exists between this emphasis on content and meeting the development needs of students. Let's look at how this tension affected the organization of middle and junior high schools.

Historically, schools in the early 20th century were organized into eight elementary and four high school grades. This 8–4 organization changed when emphasis shifted away from basic skills, such as reading and math, and toward the more intensive study of specific content areas, such as history, literature, and science. This intensive study required teachers who were subject-matter experts. In addition, educators began to recognize the unique needs of early adolescents. The result was the development of the "junior" high school.

Most junior high schools today have a variety of offerings, although not as comprehensive as those in high schools, and they also include competitive athletics and other extracurricular activities. Although initially designed to help students make the transition between elementary and high schools, they are in every sense of the word "junior" high schools.

However, early adolescence is characterized by considerable variability in students' development. Think back to the friends you knew when you were in the sixth, seventh, or eighth grades. Some of the girls were young women, fully developed physically, whereas others were still little girls. Some boys needed to shave, but others looked like fifth graders. Boys and girls were becoming physically attracted to each other, and in many cases they didn't know why. This was the transitional period of early adolescence.

Because of these rapid physical, emotional, and intellectual changes, early adolescence is a unique period in a child's development. At no other time in a person's life, except infancy, is change so rapid or profound. As a result, many educators believe that schools for young adolescents should be organized to meet the unique needs of these students (Jackson & Davis, 2000).

This thinking, and the fact that junior highs weren't meeting early adolescents' developmental needs, led to the formation of **middle schools**. Typically for grades 6–8, middle schools are specifically designed to help students through the rapid social, emotional, and intellectual changes characteristic of early adolescence.

What is teaching in a middle school like? Let's look at one teacher's experience.

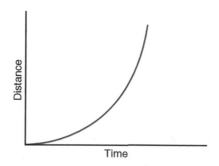

Robin West is an eighth-grade teacher in an urban middle school. She teaches physical science, and she and her team members have a common planning period. They teach the same group of students and often spend their planning period discussing the students and the topics they are teaching. Many of their students are not native English speakers, and their discussions often center on what can be done to help those who struggle with language. In addition, Robin has four students with learning disabilities in her classroom. The teachers try to integrate topics across as many of the four areas as often as possible.

"Can you help me out with anything on graphing?" Mary, the math teacher, asks the others one Monday. "The kids just see graphs as some meaningless lines. I explain the heck out of them, but it doesn't seem to help all that much."

"I know what I can do," Robin offers, after thinking for a few seconds. "I'll do some simple demonstrations and then have them link the demonstration to a graph. . . . Here, look."

She holds out her pen and drops it. She then draws a graph on a piece of paper:

(graph: vertical axis labeled "Distance", horizontal axis labeled "Time", showing an upward curving line)

> Middle schools. Schools, typically for grades 6–8, specifically designed to help students through the rapid social, emotional, and intellectual changes characteristic of early adolescence.

"The graph represents the relationship between the distance the pen falls and the time it takes to fall," she explains. "Time is on the horizontal axis, and distance is on the vertical axis. . . . I'll do

this with the kids, and you can refer to what I did when you do your work on graphs," she adds, nodding to Mary.

"Great. Thanks. . . . When will you do it?"

"We're between units now, so I can do it tomorrow. . . . Then you and I can talk about it after school for a few minutes, and I'll let you know how it went. . . . By the way, how is Lorraine Williams doing in math?"

"Not so good," Mary responds. "In fact, I was going to ask you all about her. She hasn't been turning in her homework, and she seems only 'half there' in class."

"Same thing in history," Keith, the history teacher and Lorraine's homeroom teacher, adds. "We'd better see what's going on. . . . I'll call her parents tonight."

The first middle school was created in Bay City, Michigan, in 1950, and from their inception, as this episode suggests, middle schools have tried to do things differently than junior highs (Manning, 2000). Effective middle schools make the following adaptations (Weiss & Kipnes, 2006):

- *They organize teachers and students into interdisciplinary teams.* For example, a team composed of a math, science, English, and social studies teacher instructs the same group of students and works together to coordinate topics.
- *They attempt to create and maintain long-term teacher–student relationships with attention to emotional development.* In many middle schools, a period is set aside to allow teachers to carefully track their students' academic progress and discuss nonacademic topics.
- *They use interactive teaching strategies.* Teachers are encouraged to move away from the lecture-dominated instruction so common in high schools and toward instruction based on questioning and student involvement. In addition, teachers place greater emphasis on study strategies, such as note taking and time management.
- *They eliminate activities that emphasize developmental differences, such as competitive sports.* In middle schools everyone is invited to participate in intramural sports and clubs.

When done well, the preceding adaptations have a positive influence on students (Weiss & Kipnes, 2006). For instance, interdisciplinary teams allow teachers to efficiently plan for the integration of topics across different content areas, as Robin and Mary did with math and science. Also, when teachers have the same students, they can more carefully monitor students' progress, as the team did with Lorraine. Forming relationships with students helps them adjust to an atmosphere less personal than that in their elementary schools. And eliminating competitive sports encourages greater participation in athletic activities and minimizes the advantages early-maturing students have over their later-developing classmates.

Interactive teaching strategies are particularly important in middle school. These strategies actively involve students in learning activities that can also develop their thinking and social interaction skills. Research indicates that motivation often drops during the early adolescent years, and some researchers believe that this drop is due to increased use of lecture as a teaching strategy, which places students in passive roles (Pintrich & Schunk, 2002; Stipek, 2002).

The number of middle schools continues to increase. By the start of the 21st century, middle schools outnumbered junior highs by a ratio of 4 to 1 (National Center for Education Statistics, 2002). However, middle schools are currently being criticized from several perspectives. A comprehensive report by the Rand Corporation critical of existing middle schools contributed to the controversy (Juvonen et al., 2004). Advocates of a greater emphasis on academics question the emphasis on development and growth; instead, they recommend a return to basics, with greater attention to reading and math. One proposal receiving increased attention and actually implemented in a number of large cities, including Baltimore, Cincinnati, and Philadelphia, suggests returning to a K–8 organization model where academics are stressed (Yecke, 2006). Defenders of the middle school concept claim that the problem isn't the idea itself, but the fact that it never has been effectively implemented (Swaim, 2004). The emphasis that the No Child Left Behind (NCLB) legislation places on testing, accountability, and subject matter mastery (discussed in Chapter 1) is likely to fuel this controversy.

This section addresses the third item in our beginning-of-chapter survey, which said, "Middle and junior high schools are essentially the same but are given different labels." If middle schools are designed according to their original conceptions, the statement is false.

High Schools

Each of you attended high school, and some of you have graduated only within the last year or two. Most of you probably graduated from a **comprehensive high school**, a secondary school that attempts to meet the needs of all students. Let's examine the comprehensive high school more closely.

The Comprehensive High School

In *The American High School*, James Conant (1959) argued persuasively that the most effective high schools are those large enough to offer diverse academic courses and facilities for all students (Hammack, 2004). In attempting to do this, most high schools organize students into tracks (Oakes, 2005). For example, students in the college-preparatory track take courses designed to prepare them for college-level work. A college-prep track might include honors or advanced placement classes in core subject areas. **Advanced placement classes** are courses taken in high school that allow students to earn college credit, making college less time-consuming and expensive. A general track composed of "standard" classes is designed for students of average ability who may or may not go on to college. Students in this track may take some vocational courses, such as word processing, designed to provide them with practical skills they can use immediately after graduating. A vocational track specifically targets students not going to college, preparing them for careers in such areas as automobile repair or technology.

Extracurricular activities provide valuable learning opportunities not typically tapped by traditional classrooms.
(Scott Cunningham/Merrill).

A comprehensive high school also offers extracurricular activities (e.g., band, chorus, and theater) and athletics (e.g., football, swimming, soccer, and tennis). These options are intended to integrate students from different tracks, allowing them to mix and learn about other students, and to help all students develop personally, socially, and intellectually.

Criticisms of the Comprehensive High School. Can a comprehensive high school be all things to all students? Critics say no and focus on four factors: tracking, size, departmentalization, and lack of academic rigor.

A paradox of the comprehensive high school is that different tracks, designed to present quality alternatives, often produce exactly the opposite. Instead of providing freedom and choice, tracking limits choices and segregates students, often leaving many with substandard educational experiences (Oakes, 2005). Lower-ability, minority, and low-socioeconomic status (SES) students are often steered into vocational or lower-level tracks, where the curriculum is less challenging and instruction is often poor. Instead of effectively preparing students for the world of work, lower tracks often segregate students from their college-bound peers and communicate that challenge and deep understanding are not for them. Some critics charge that tracking should be eliminated completely and that all students should be prepared, to the extent possible, for college work (Vander Ark, 2003).

Comprehensive high school. A secondary school that attempts to meet the needs of all students.

Advanced placement classes. Courses taken in high school that allow students to earn college credit.

A second criticism of high schools relates to school size, which exceeds 1,000 students in many U.S. high schools (Feldman, López, & Simon, 2006; Howley & Howley, 2004). As schools become larger, they also tend to become more impersonal and bureaucratic. They virtually become shopping malls in which students mill around looking for entertainment and educational bargains. Like smart shoppers, the brighter students (or their parents) know what they want and quickly find the more challenging, college-preparatory courses. Lower achievers get lost in the shuffle, spending time but not receiving a quality education (Howley & Howley, 2004). One critic remarked that because of their unwieldy size, "our high schools are the least effective part of the American education system" (Vander Ark, 2003, p. 52).

According to critics, departmentalization, or the organization of teachers and classes into separate academic areas, is a third problem of the comprehensive high school. Departmentalization fragments the curriculum and interferes with learning:

While the adults organize as separate departmental entities isolated from one another, however, their teenage students seek interconnectedness and relevancy in their school experience. What they get instead is math with no relationship to social studies, science without any connection to literature, and so forth. This relevancy-starved approach continues year in, year out with no alternatives, and any "reforms" seen in public education are invariably found at the elementary or middle school level. (Cooperman, 2003, p. 30)

To prevent such fragmentation, some educators suggest that schools cluster teachers and classes into interdisciplinary teams, as in effective middle schools, where connections between disciplines are emphasized.

A fourth criticism of comprehensive high schools relates to academic rigor; in attempting to be all things to all students, high schools fail to challenge students and provide them with the necessary job skills needed for a technologically oriented modern society (Botstein, 2006; Perkins-Gough, 2005a). Bill Gates, president of Microsoft, claimed U.S. high schools are "obsolete" and ruin the lives of millions of Americans every year because they fail to prepare students for the modern world of work (Hammack, 2005). Others decry the lack of academic challenge and the failure of high schools to engage the minds of teenage youth (Botstein, 2006). Solutions to these problems range from more rigorous graduation requirements, especially in core areas such as math, science, and English, to high school exit exams (Perkins-Gough, 2005b).

Alternatives to Comprehensive High Schools. One concrete solution to the problem of large high schools is the creation of "smaller learning communities" within large schools, allowing students to keep the same guidance counselor throughout high school, and offering specific opportunities for students and teachers to get to know one another. These ideas are discussed further in the section on school size later in the chapter.

A second alternative to large, comprehensive high schools is the creation of **career technical** schools designed to provide students with education and job skills that will enable them to get a job immediately after graduating from high school (Lynch, 2000). In more than 1,000 vocational centers nationwide, students attend part of the day or evening in specialized programs. They then attend their "home" high school for academic or general education courses during the other part of the day. In addition, about 250 career or specialty high schools in the United States focus on preparing students for work in a particular occupation or industry but also offer the academic and general courses at that school. Students attend these career technical schools full time (Lynch, 2000).

Career technical, or vocational education as it was called earlier, got its beginning in the early 1900s to better meet the need of working class children who were, for the first time, attending high schools in large numbers but were not headed for professional careers. Early vocational programs were designed to prepare students with practical skills for the nation's farms, factories, and homes. Currently, programs have evolved, with more emphasis on technology-related careers.

Career technical. A term used to identify programs designed to provide students with education and job skills that will enable them to get a job immediately after graduating from high school.

As with many other aspects of education, career technical education is going through a process of reform. Most of the reforms are aimed at increasing academic standards and related general educational knowledge together with teaching students all aspects of an industry rather than focusing on a specific job skill. The federal government currently contributes an annual $1.3 billion to these programs to encourage modernizing and focusing academic programs on essential job skills (Cavanagh, 2006a). However, interest in these programs continues to decline as more and more students opt for college-prep programs (Newman, 2006).

> **Making Connections:**
> To deepen your understanding of the topics in this section of the chapter and integrate them with topics you've already studied, go to the *Making Connections* module for Chapter 7 at **www.prenhall.com/kauchak.** Respond to questions 5–9.
>
>

teaching in an era of reform

Grade Retention

Because it makes sense to expose students to increasingly complex ideas as they develop, U.S. schools are organized so that children progress from grade to grade as they grow older. But what should happen when a student can't master course content at a specific grade level?

The United States has shown an increased interest in grade retention, the practice of having students repeat a grade if they don't meet certain criteria. An important plank in current reform efforts is the elimination of "social promotion"—that is, promoting low-achieving students to the next grade so they can be with their age-similar peers.

Grade retention is not new, but its popularity as a reform tool has grown over the years; in the 2000–2001 school year, 11 percent of Texas third graders were retained (Bali, Anagnostopoulos, & Roberts, 2005). In 2005, 7 other states linked retention to test scores, typically in grades 3, 5, and 8, and Florida even considered grade-retention policies based on test scores for all grade levels (Richard, 2005).

The Issue

Proponents of grade retention argue that retaining students in a grade until they've acquired the knowledge and skills for that level makes sense (Greene & Winters, 2006). For example, allowing students to move from the fourth to the fifth grade when they haven't mastered the content and abilities expected of typical fourth graders is counterproductive because students are less likely to succeed in the fifth grade. Spending a second year in a grade gives learners another chance to acquire the necessary understanding and skills and sends the message that schoolwork is important.

Opponents of grade retention argue that holding students back does not improve their academic performance, and they further argue that the costs don't justify any benefits that might result (Eide & Goldhaber, 2005). They also point to studies indicating that students retained in grade tend to perform lower on subsequent achievement tests than their nonretained classmates (Jimerson, Pletcher, & Graydon, 2006) and are also more likely to later drop out of school (Holmes, 2006). Opponents note that school dropouts are five times more likely to have repeated a grade than students who complete high school and that the probability of dropping out for students who repeat two grades is nearly 100 percent. They further note that minorities and low-SES children are much more likely to be retained than are their White, wealthier counterparts (Anagnostopoulos, 2006).

Opponents also argue that grade retention causes emotional problems. In one study children rated the prospect of repeating a grade as more stressful than "wetting in class" or being caught stealing. Going blind or losing a parent were the only two life events that children said would be more stressful than being retained (Shepard & Smith, 1990). Opponents note that the psychological effects of grade retention are especially acute in adolescence, where physical size differences and peer awareness exacerbate the problem (G. Anderson, Jimerson, & Whipple, 2002).

Finally, opponents suggest, better alternatives to social promotion are available. Before- and after-school programs, summer school programs with reduced class sizes, instructional aides who work with low-achieving children, and peer tutoring are all alternatives. Each is less expensive than the thousands of dollars spent on having children repeat what they have already experienced, and students in these alternative programs are more likely to meet standards than those who have repeated grades (Jimerson, Pletcher, & Graydon, 2006).

You Take a Position

Now it's your turn to take a position on the issue. State in writing whether you do or do not believe that grade retention is beneficial and is likely to increase student learning, and provide a two-page rationale for your position.

For additional references and resources, go to the Companion Website at www.prenhall.com/kauchak, then to the Teaching in an Era of Reform module for Chapter 7. You can respond online or submit your response to your instructor.

Check Your Understanding

3.1 What are two ways in which teaching in an elementary school differs from teaching in a middle school, junior high, or high school?

3.2 What are four differences between effective middle schools and junior highs?

3.3 Describe a comprehensive high school. How does a comprehensive high school differ from a vocational high school?

 For feedback, go to Check Your Understanding, *at the end of this chapter.*

What Is an Effective School?

You're either thinking about teaching or are actually planning to teach; this is the reason you're taking this course. A major factor that will influence your satisfaction in teaching will be the effectiveness of that school in promoting student learning and development. But what is an effective school, and what is it like to teach in one? We try to answer these questions in this section.

Although the public commonly refers to schools as good or not so good, as in "Woodrow Wilson is a very good elementary school," researchers use the term *effective* instead. An **effective school** is one in which learning for all students is maximized. But how does a school do this? Researchers attempting to answer this question identified schools that, despite challenging circumstances, produced more learning in their students than comparable ones that weren't as successful (Marzano, 2003). They also looked at poor-performing schools as counterexamples. Let's see what these researchers found.

Research on Effective Schools

Research has identified several characteristics of schools that maximize learning for all students (Bransford, Brown, & Cocking, 2000; Taylor, Pressley, & Pearson, 2002). They are outlined in Figure 7.1 and discussed in the sections that follow.

Figure 7.1 Characteristics of Effective Schools

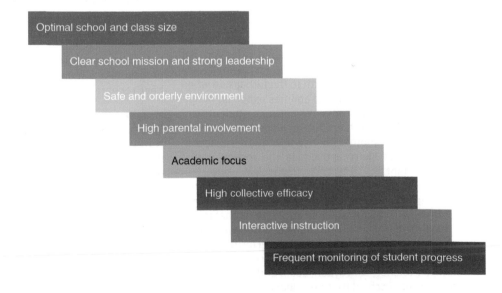

Optimal school and class size

Clear school mission and strong leadership

Safe and orderly environment

High parental involvement

Academic focus

High collective efficacy

Interactive instruction

Frequent monitoring of student progress

Effective school. A school in which learning for all students is maximized.

Optimal School and Class Size

This chapter focuses on school organization, and the way schools are organized has a significant effect on learning. An important dimension of this organization is size—both the size of the school and the size of classes.

School Size. Are small schools better than big ones, or is the reverse true? As it turns out, the relationship between size and quality isn't simple or direct. Schools must be large enough to provide the varied curricular offerings needed to help students learn in different content areas, but not so large that students get lost (Ready, Lee, & Welner, 2004).

How big is too big? The largest high school on record, DeWitt Clinton High School in the Bronx, boasted 12,000 students in 1934 (Allen, 2002). (Can you imagine what it must have been like to be a ninth grader walking into that school on the first day of the school year?) One-room elementary schools are at the other end of the spectrum; for example, one K–4 elementary school in Grantville, Vermont, had 18 students in 2002 (Shelley, 2003). School size also relates to level, with elementary schools being the smallest and high schools the largest. In the 2000–2001 school year, the average elementary school in the United States had 482 students, and the average secondary school had 795 students (National Center for Education Statistics, 2002). More than 70 percent of U.S. high school students, however, attend schools of 1,000 students or more, and a number of urban districts have high schools of over 5,000 students (Allen, 2002).

Research suggests the ideal size for a high school is considerably less than this, somewhere between 600 and 900 students (Lee, 2000). This research suggests that the fourth item on our beginning-of-chapter survey, which said, "In general, larger schools provide a better-quality education, because they have better facilities and a wider variety of programs," is not true. Schools must be large enough to provide adequate facilities and resources, but not so large that they lose the human, personal dimension.

School size affects low- and high-SES students differently. For example, the decrease in learning in very large or very small high schools is greater for low-SES than it is for high-SES students (Howley & Howley, 2004). The only schools not fitting this pattern are elite private schools that enroll students with similar backgrounds and provide extensive resources, such as well-equipped science and computer labs. Unfortunately, a disproportionate number of low-SES students attend either very small or very large high schools. Examples include small rural schools in sparsely populated states, such as Wyoming or Montana, and large, urban schools in major cities such as New York or Los Angeles.

How does school size influence student learning? Researchers suggest that school size, in itself, doesn't cause students to learn less than they would in an ideally sized school. Rather, size influences other factors (Feldman et al., 2006; Ready et al., 2004). As schools become larger, for example, it becomes more difficult to create learning environments that promote a sense of physical and emotional safety in students. In large schools, education is less personal, and it is harder for teachers and students to get to know one another and to work together.

Both parents and teachers want smaller schools, but the cost of building them deters taxpayers. In a national survey, parents said they felt their children received a more rigorous and personalized education in smaller schools, and teachers said that smaller schools prevented students from "falling through the cracks" (Public Agenda, 2002). Research also supports smaller schools, indicating that they have significantly higher graduation and college attendance rates and fewer discipline and safety issues than do large schools (Vander Ark, 2002).

One solution to the problem of large schools is to create schools within schools, smaller learning communities where both teachers and students feel more comfortable. For example, Kernan Middle School in Jacksonville, Florida, has over 1,200 students, more than experts recommend for any school, in particular for a middle school.

To address the issue of school size, Kernan students are placed within "houses" of approximately 400 students at the start of 6th grade. The students then stay in their houses through 8th grade, enabling them to get to know and recognize the adults in their building. They deal with a small front office managed by an assistant principal, who, for all intents and purposes, is the principal of this mini school. The students get to know all the teachers in the hallway as well as the other students who are part of their houses. The goal is for each student to be well known by at least one adult. Students are at ease in making the transition to the next grade level because of the feeling of familiarity with the house and all its components (people, rules, procedures). Typically, when asked, a student will identify himself or herself as a "house B student." At the end of the middle school experience, this student will hopefully have formed meaningful, personal relationships with more people than they would if they were in a school of 1,200 students with less of an identity (Desiree DiFabio, Personal Communication, September 11, 2006).

Class-size reduction can be an effective tool to increase achievement. (Scott Cunningham/Merrill)

Class Size. Class size also influences a school's effectiveness. Classes of 20 or fewer students are considered optimal, but many classes are much larger, especially in middle, junior high, and high schools. One of your authors recently taught a high school health teacher who had 47 students assigned to her class. If all the students showed up for class, there weren't enough desks. Although critics argue either that class size doesn't matter or that reducing class size isn't worth the cost, research consistently indicates that reducing class size does, indeed, increase learning for all students, and the effects are particularly pronounced in the lower grades and for students placed at-risk (Gilman & Kiger, 2003; Peevely, Hedges, & Nye, 2005).

Reductions in class size can have both short- and long-term positive effects (Finn, Gerber, & Boyd-Zaharias, 2005; Nye, Hedges, & Konstantopoulos, 2001). In Tennessee, where average class sizes were reduced from 25 to 15 students, researchers found immediate gains in reading and math scores. Follow-up studies revealed that the positive effects lasted through 12th grade; low-SES students who participated in the program for 4 years were twice as likely to graduate from high school as their large-class-size counterparts. Students in the smaller classes also took more challenging courses later on in school, and were more likely to attend college than their counterparts in larger classes. These positive effects were especially strong for low-SES and African-American students.

Smaller class sizes also positively affect teachers' lives; when class sizes are reduced, teachers' morale and job satisfaction increase (Muñoz & Portes, 2002). In smaller classes, teachers spend less time on discipline and more time on small-group work and diagnostic assessment. Researchers caution, however, that these positive changes don't occur automatically; teachers need to learn how to adjust their instruction to take advantage of the smaller number of students in their classrooms (Peevely, Hedges, & Nye, 2005).

Clear School Mission and Strong Leadership

In effective schools, a clearly stated mission exists, and it remains at the forefront of the thinking of the entire school staff. For example, if developing literacy is emphasized in the mission of an elementary school, evidence of this theme appears in teachers' instruction. Teachers focus on reading comprehension in all classes, not simply when they are explicitly teaching reading, and children are given extensive practice in putting their understanding of math, science, and other content into words. The same is true for other aspects of the school mission. In effective schools, teachers share an understanding of and commitment to instructional goals, priorities, and assessment procedures, and they accept responsibility for students' meeting the school's curricular goals.

Strong leadership is essential to the success of a school. In effective schools, the principal understands learning and teaching and acts as an instructional leader who can advise staff and serve as a resource to parents and students (Mosenthal et al., 2004; Sergiovanni, 2004, 2006). Faculty meetings focus on instructional issues, and learning and effective teaching are continually discussed topics.

Safe and Orderly Environment

Students are concerned about school safety issues, such as fighting, bullying, and other students who are disruptive in class. Schools, which should be sheltered communities for learning, often mirror the problems of society. Marzano (2003) noted, "If teachers and students do not feel safe, they will not have the necessary psychological energy for teaching and learning" (p. 53).

The need for safe and orderly schools is supported by both research and theory. Researchers found effective schools to be places of trust, order, cooperation, and high morale (Marzano, 2003; Rutter, Maughan, Mortimore, Ouston, & Smith, 1979). Students need to feel emotionally safe in schools for learning to occur.

One essential characteristic of an effective school is hallways that are safe and orderly. (Getty Images, Inc.–PhotoDisc)

Theories of learner development, which we briefly discussed earlier in the chapter, suggest that people are born with a desire to live in an orderly rather than chaotic world (Piaget 1952, 1970). In addition, the psychologist Abraham Maslow (1968), who described a hierarchy of human needs, argued that only the need for survival is more basic than the need for safety. Studies of classroom management also confirm the need for order; orderly classrooms promote both learning and student motivation (Emmer, Evertson, & Worsham, 2006; Evertson, Emmer, & Worsham, 2006).

Strong Parental Involvement

Schools, no matter how well they're organized, can't be effective if parents aren't involved in their children's education (Marzano, 2003). Learning is a cooperative venture, in which teachers, students, and parents are in it together.

Research indicates that students benefit from home–school cooperation in a number of ways, including the following:

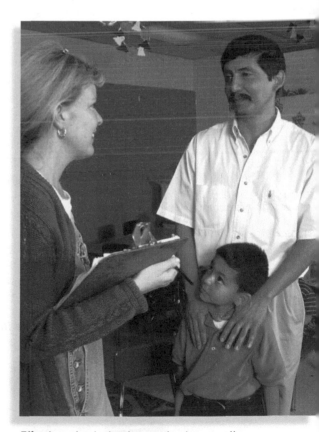

- Students achieve more, regardless of SES, ethnic/racial background, or the parents' levels of education. The more extensive the parental involvement, the higher the student achievement.
- Students earn higher grades and test scores, attend school more regularly, and complete homework more consistently.
- Students exhibit more positive attitudes and behavior.
- Student alcohol use, violence, and antisocial behaviors decrease as parental involvement increases.
- Educators hold higher expectations for students whose parents collaborate with teachers. They also hold higher opinions of those parents (U.S. Department of Education, 2001).

Effective schools develop mechanisms to allow parents and teachers to work together. (Michael Newman/PhotoEdit Inc.)

These outcomes likely result from parents' increased participation in school activities, their more positive attitudes about schooling, and teachers' increased understanding of students' home environments.

Academic Focus

Promoting learning is the central mission of effective schools, and as we saw earlier, this mission is clear to the teachers in the school, and the tone is set by the school principal and other administrators. In academically focused schools, teachers have high expectations, and they maximize the time available for instruction. Students are directly involved in learning activities for as much of the day as possible, and instruction remains focused on essential content and skills. An array of clubs, sports, and other extracurricular offerings exist and are important, but they don't take precedence over learning. In effective schools, for example, classes are not canceled so students can attend sporting events, and class time isn't used for club meetings.

One study investigating the effects of academic focus on learning concluded, "Students learn more in schools that set high standards for academic performance, that use their instructional time wisely, and that use student learning as a criterion for making decisions" (Lee & Smith, 1999, p. 941). Schools with an academic focus are also more positive places in which to work because both students and teachers feel that learning is occurring. You will want to look for signs that academic focus is present in the schools in which you're considering working.

High Collective Efficacy

Contributing to a school's academic focus is **high collective efficacy**, the belief by teachers that their school can make a difference in students' lives (Goddard, Hoy, & Hoy, 2004). High collective efficacy begins with **personal teaching efficacy**, each teacher's belief that he or she can promote learning in all students, regardless of their backgrounds. High-efficacy teachers take responsibility for the success of their own instruction (Bruning, Schraw, Norby, & Ronning, 2004). In other words, if students aren't learning as much as they should be, rather than blaming students' lack of intelligence, poor home environments, uncooperative administrators, or some other cause, high-efficacy teachers conclude that they could be doing a better job and look for ways to increase student learning.

Three aspects of high-collective-efficacy schools are important. First, students from all socioeconomic levels—high, middle, and low—learn more in them than they do in schools where collective efficacy is lower. This, in itself, isn't surprising; it makes sense that the more teachers strive for student learning, the more students will learn. Second, and more important, low-SES students in high-collective-efficacy schools have achievement levels nearly as high as high-SES students in low-collective-efficacy schools. Third, differences in achievement levels among low-, middle-, and high-SES students in high-collective-efficacy schools are smaller than they are in low-collective-efficacy schools (Lee, 2000). In other words, high-collective-efficacy schools help reduce achievement differences between groups of students who typically benefit quite differently from schooling.

How do high-efficacy teachers and high-collective-efficacy schools accomplish these results? A number of factors contribute, but two are essential: (1) interactive instruction and (2) frequent monitoring of student progress.

High collective efficacy. The belief by teachers that their school can make a difference in students' lives.

Personal teaching efficacy. Each teacher's belief that he or she can promote learning in all students, regardless of their backgrounds.

Interactive Instruction

Cassie Jones walks through the halls of the inner-city middle school where she is the principal and listens to the sounds coming from the different classrooms. As she walks by Ben Carlson's social studies class, she hears him say, "Yesterday we talked about the stengths and weaknesses of the North and South at the outbreak of the Civil War. Who remembers one of these?"

As Cassie proceeds down the hall, she stops in front of Sarah McCarthy's science class. Sarah is at the front of the room swinging a set of keys from a piece of string. "Hmmm," Cassie thinks, "no wonder her class is so quiet—she's got them hypnotized." As she listens further, she hears Sarah ask,

"Class, this is a simple pendulum, just like the one we find in grandfather clocks. Who can tell me what factors influence the rate at which a pendulum swings?"

"Good question," thinks Cassie. "Maybe that's why her kids are so quiet."

When Cassie turns the corner, she is greeted by a steady stream of student voices arguing about something.

"I don't care what you say, stealing is wrong."

"But his family didn't have enough to eat. They were hungry—he couldn't let them starve!"

"What's Hector up to today?" Cassie thinks as she listens more closely to Hector Sanchez's English class.

"Class," Hector breaks in with a booming voice, "it's not enough just to disagree with your partners. You have to explain why. Remember, one of the reasons we read books like Sounder *is to help us understand our own lives. So, you have three more minutes in your discussion groups to explain why the father was right or wrong to steal food for his family."*

Cassie chuckles as she hears Hector's class rejoin the battle. "He's sure got them stirred up today. I guess I'm lucky to have such a talented teaching staff that has so many different strengths" (adapted from Jacobsen, Eggen, & Kauchak, 2006, pp. 194–195).

Imagine that you're walking through the hallways of a school, the doors of classrooms are open, and you glance inside. Can you determine anything about the effectiveness of the school with a simple glance? The answer is *yes.* If the prevailing pattern is one in which teachers are asking large numbers of questions and students are involved in discussions, the likelihood that the school is effective increases. In contrast, if you see teachers primarily lecturing or students spending most of their time working alone and doing seat work, the school is less likely to be effective. Evaluating schools in this way is admittedly simplistic, and many additional factors influence how much students learn. Nevertheless, interaction between teacher and students and students with one another is an essential ingredient for learning (Eggen & Kauchak, 2007).

Not only is interactive teaching essential for learning, it is also important for motivation (Pintrich & Schunk, 2002). Students at all levels prefer challenging and interactive activities to ones that require them to sit passively, listening to teacher lectures (Brophy, 2004). Effective schools provide opportunities for students to become actively involved in their learning.

Frequent Monitoring of Student Progress

The extent to which teachers frequently assess learning and provide students with feedback is another essential factor differentiating more- from less-effective schools. Experts suggest that effective learning environments are assessment centered (Bransford, Brown, & Cocking, 2000). In other words, assessment isn't tacked on at the end of an instructional period, such as teachers' giving a test once a month or at the end of a unit; rather, it is an integral part of the entire teaching–learning process. Teachers in effective schools continually collect information about students' learning progress. They regularly collect work samples and give frequent quizzes and tests, and the assessments measure more than recall of facts. Teachers return assessments, such as quizzes and assignments, shortly after they're given, and the teachers thoroughly discuss test items to provide students with feedback about their responses (Bransford et al., 2000; Marzano, 2003). The need for assessment-centered classrooms also helps us understand why interactive instruction is so essential. Teachers gather a great deal of information about students' understanding by listening to their attempts to describe their thinking.

So, now we have an answer to the fifth item on our introductory survey, "The assessment program in a school is a major factor influencing the school's effectiveness." Students, parents, and teachers all use assessment data to determine whether school learning is taking place.

Parents' and Other Taxpayers' Perceptions of Effective Schools

How do parents and taxpayers view effective schools? On what do they base their perceptions? What do they most commonly look for in judging a school? Let's take a look.

School Organization and the Achievement of Cultural Minorities

Emphasis on higher standards and increased accountability is the most prominent reform in education today. Change, however, can have unintended outcomes, and one outcome of this reform has been a widening gap between the achievement of cultural minorities—particularly African-American and Hispanic students—and the achievement of their White and Asian counterparts (Hoff, 2000). Between 1970, when the National Assessment of Educational Progress first began systematically measuring students' achievement, and 1980, African-American and Hispanic students made great progress in narrowing the achievement gap that had separated them from their White peers. This progress stopped abruptly in the late 1980s, however, and since then the gap has either remained constant or widened (Fairchild, 2006; Jencks & Phillips, 1998). Dropout rates for minority students have followed a similar pattern, either flattening out or even increasing (Olson, 2006b). Similarly, recent data on schools found lacking under NCLB rules found a preponderance of failing schools with high proportions of minority students and students of poverty (Archer, 2006a).

Researchers have cited numerous factors to explain these differences in achievement between White and minority students, including poverty, peer pressure, and parental values (Byrnes, 2003; Ogbu, 2003). These are all likely candidates, but research has also identified two aspects of school organization that are believed to influence the achievement of minority students: tracking and class size.

Cultural Minorities and Tracking

Earlier in the chapter, we mentioned that comprehensive high schools have been criticized for the practice of tracking, because evidence indicates that educational experiences on lower-level

tracks are often substandard (Oakes, 2005). This evidence is particularly relevant for cultural minorities, because they tend to be underrepresented in higher-level tracks and overrepresented in lower-level tracks. The problem is exacerbated by the fact that minority students tend not to enroll in more demanding classes. As shown in Table 7.3, the students least likely to enroll in such classes are also least likely to graduate from college (Viadero, 2000).

Tracking and minority achievement have a form of negative synergy; that is, student achievement in low-level classes is reduced compared to the achievement of students of comparable ability in high-level classes. Because decisions about tracking are based on students' records of past achievement, minority students continue to be placed in lower-level tracks, and the negative relationship between achievement and tracking is magnified. Unfortunately, school leaders haven't identified a satisfactory solution to this problem.

Cultural Minorities and Class Size

The relationship between class size and minority achievement is more encouraging. Earlier we said that research supports the contention that student achievement is higher in smaller classes. This research is important, because the beneficial effects of reducing class size are greater for cultural minorities than for nonminorities (Gewertz, 2000; Smith, Molnar, & Zahorik, 2003).

Two studies are particularly significant. First, assessments of a major class-size-reduction project in Tennessee found the following (Finn et al., 2005; Illig, 1996):

- Children in small classes (about 15 students per class) consistently outperformed children in larger classes.
- Inner-city children (about 97 percent of whom were minorities) in small classes closed some of the achievement gap between themselves and nonminority children in large classes.
- Children in small classes outperformed children in larger classes, even when teachers in the large classes had support from aides.

In the second study, a 4-year experiment with class-size-reduction in Wisconsin, researchers found that the achievement gap between minorities and nonminorities shrank by 19 percent in smaller classes, whereas in comparable regular classrooms it grew by 58 percent (Molnar, Percy, Smith, & Zahorik, 1998; Smith, Molnar, & Zahorik, 2003). In addition to narrowing the achievement gap between minority and nonminority students in first grade, the program also prevented it from widening when class-size-reduction students progressed to second- and third-grade classrooms. Researchers have found that when class sizes are reduced, teachers have more personal contacts with individual students and can design more effective learning activ-

Tracking can result in the segregation of cultural minorities into low-level classes where instruction tends to be less challenging. (AP Wide World Photos)

TABLE 7.3 **Percentages of Students Taking Advanced Math Courses and Graduating from Four-Year Colleges**

Race/Ethnicity	1992 High School Graduates Who Completed Algebra 2 and Geometry (%)	Freshmen at Four-Year Colleges Who Graduate Within Six Years (%)
Asian-American	55.5	65
White	53.1	59
Hispanic American	41.9	46
Native American	35.7	37
African-American	35	40

Source: Data from Johnston & Viadero (2000).

ities to engage students (Blatchford, Bassett, & Brown, 2005). The results of the class-size-reduction experiment were so compelling that the Wisconsin legislature appropriated $59 million beginning in 2000 to expand the program to 400 schools (Gewertz, 2000).

If the other characteristics of an effective school don't exist, however, reducing the number of students in classes, by itself, won't increase achievement. Narrowing the achievement gap requires the systematic implementation of all the effective school characteristics.

The results of research examining parents' and other taxpayers' perceptions of effective schools are not surprising. As would be expected, people react most strongly to factors that are concrete and observable. For example, as a result of highly publicized incidents of school violence, school safety is a primary concern, and both parents and other taxpayers rank creating orderly classrooms as one of the most important problems teachers face (L. Rose & Gallup, 2004).

Parents and other taxpayers also look for qualified teachers and test results as indicators of student and school performance (Olson, 1999a). The desire for qualified teachers isn't surprising, because teachers represent schools and are the people who work most directly with parents' sons and daughters. To determine how children and schools are doing, parents also turn to standardized test scores and school report cards. Currently, under the federal NCLB, all states are required to test students annually and publish report cards on their schools; in accordance with NCLB, in 2006, all 50 states were regularly testing students and publishing annual report cards on individual schools (Archer, 2006a). Olson (1999b) summarized parents' views of effective schools: "In short, parents and taxpayers view school safety and the presence of qualified teachers as two essential ingredients of education. Once those basic conditions are met, they want results" (p. 34).

These results are consistent with the characteristics of effective schools discussed earlier. For instance, we saw school safety on both lists. Other factors, such as teaching efficacy, interactive instruction, and frequent monitoring of student progress, are more complex and harder to understand for people outside the profession.

Making Connections:
To deepen your understanding of the topics in this section of the chapter and integrate them with topics you've already studied, go to the *Making Connections* module for Chapter 7 at **www.prenhall.com/kauchak.** Respond to questions 10–13.

Check Your Understanding

4.1 Describe the characteristics of an effective school.

4.2 What is the most distinguishing characteristic of effective instruction in effective schools?

4.3 Why is frequent monitoring of student progress essential for an effective school?

 *For feedback, go to* Check Your Understanding *at the end of this chapter.*

decision making

Defining Yourself as a Professional

You're sitting in the teacher workroom about a month into a new school year, and one of your colleagues comes in and comments, "I just don't know what's wrong with these kids. I explained everything so carefully yesterday, and when they came in today it was as if they hadn't heard a word I said.

"On the other hand, these kids come from the worst backgrounds, so there isn't all that much we can do about them anyway. They won't pay attention, they don't give a rip about what we're studying, and they won't take a lick of responsibility for their own learning.

"Their parents, if they even are living with their parents, don't care either, so what's the use. If I can gut it out until the end of this year, I'm going to try for all I'm worth to get a transfer at the end the year."

What would you say to your colleague?

To respond to this question online and receive immediate *feedback, go to the* Decision Making *module for Chapter 7 on the Companion Website at www.prenhall.com/kauchak.*

Meeting Your Learning Objectives

1. **Describe different meanings of the concept** *school.*
   - One definition describes schools as places where young people go to learn and develop intellectually, personally, and socially. And schools exist in other places such as vacation bible school or students being homeschooled. Another definition describes a school as a physical place—a building or set of buildings.
   - This chapter describes a school as a social institution, organized to promote student growth and development, as well as the welfare of society. All societies have a number of social institutions in addition to schools, such as churches and governments.
   - Schools are organized within districts, administrative units with the responsibility of educating children within geographic areas.

2. **Identify the components of a typical school organization.**
   - Personnel make up one component of the total school organization, and personnel include the school principal and other administrators, support staff (e.g., administrative assistants, custodians, and cafeteria workers), and teachers.
   - The physical plant, another component, includes the buildings that house classrooms, the library, computer labs, the cafeteria, and the administration. In addition, junior highs and high schools usually have gymnasiums, playing fields, sometimes swimming pools, and may even have buildings devoted to fine arts.
   - The curriculum, what is taught in school, is a third component, and it is typically organized into grade levels, and content is intended to be taught to students of different ages.

3. **Describe important differences between schools at different levels.**
   - Educators have come to realize the importance of early learning experiences—at home and in programs such as preschools and kindergartens—for long-term school success.

Developmentally appropriate programs attempt to match classroom instruction to the learning needs of young children.

- Elementary schools are organized so that a single teacher is responsible for all, or most, of the instruction in the different content areas. Elementary teachers arrange their own schedules, and the amount of time they allocate to different content areas can vary widely. Typically, elementary teachers emphasize reading, language arts, and math in their instruction, and they de-emphasize content areas such as science, social studies, and the arts.

- High schools, junior highs, and middle schools are organized very differently than elementary schools. Teachers in these schools have content specialties, they teach only in these specialty areas, and class schedules are fixed schoolwide.

4. Identify the characteristics of an effective school.
   - Effective schools promote learning for all students. Size is important. Effective elementary schools keep class sizes below 20 students per class, and effective high schools have enrollments in the 600–900 range.
   - Effective schools are safe and orderly, academically focused, and involve parents. Teachers in effective schools take responsibility for student learning, maintain high levels of interaction with students, and continually monitor student progress.
   - Polls indicate that parents and other taxpayers emphasize school safety and order, highly qualified teachers, and student scores on standardized tests as indicators of an effective school.

Important Concepts

administrators
advanced placement classes
career technical
comprehensive high school
curriculum
development
developmental programs
early childhood education

effective school
high collective efficacy
looping
middle schools
personal teaching efficacy
principal
school district
social institution

Developing as a Professional

Preparing for Your Licensure Exam

This exercise will provide you with practice answering questions similar to the Praxis™ Principles of Learning and Teaching Exam as well as your state-specific licensure exam. Read the following case study, and answer the questions that follow.

Donna Barber, an eighth-grade teacher at Lincoln Middle School, a school of about 1,200 students, teaches three sections of standard physical science and two sections of earth science. Donna's schedule is as follows:

Period 1 (Earth Science)	7:45–8:40
Period 2 (Standard)	8:45–9:40
Period 3 (Earth Science)	9:45–10:40
Period 4 (Standard)	10:45–11:40
Lunch	11:45–12:40
Period 5 (Standard)	12:45–1:40
Period 6 (Planning)	1:45–2:40

Her fifth-period class has been studying the make-up of the atom and now is moving to a discussion of static electricity.

"C'mon," Susan says to a group of students at 12:43 as they're standing outside the classroom. "The bell is going to ring, and we'll be late."

"Did you finish your homework?" Jay asks Patricia as they walk in.

"Are you kidding? You miss a homework assignment in this class, and you're a dead duck," Amy interjects.

"Yeah," Chris nods. "You don't dare come without it. You know how Mrs. Barber is constantly saying that she wants to find out how well we understand this stuff."

As he enters the classroom, Ken comments, "Boy, Mrs. Barber, you had my whole family on the ropes last night. I had both my Mom and Dad helping me find examples of the elements you assigned us."

"That's great," Donna smiles back. "I know it was a tough assignment, but it makes you think. And besides, it was designed to be practical. It will get easier the more you work at it."

Danielle, who had been standing in front of the room taking roll, hands the roll slip to Donna as the bell rings.

"Thanks, Danielle," Donna smiles, taking the slip and moving to the front of the room. "Class, just a reminder," she continues, "we're having a notebook check tomorrow, and your last test with your parents' signature on it must be in the notebook. I want to be sure your parents know what we've been studying. . . . Also, tell them to e-mail or call me if they have any questions about your score. . . . What are we in school for?"

"Learning!" the students nearly shout in unison, repeating a theme they hear from Donna on a regular basis.

"Yes," Donna smiles at their response. "And Mrs. Garnett, our principal, commented on that again in our last assembly when she emphasized that all of you can understand what you're studying and you can all be successful if you're willing to work. All the teachers in our school feel the same way."

At 12:47 Donna begins, "We've been talking about elements. Let's see what we remember. Look at the model. What element does this represent? . . . Allen?"

"Lithium," Allen responds.

"Good, and how do we know? . . . Kathleen?"

"There are three protons in there."

"All right! Very good. Now let's switch gears. We've been dealing with the nucleus of the atom, but now we're going to focus on the electrons. . . . What do we know about them? . . . Armondo?"

"They're out around the nucleus."

"Yes, good. We've said that the numbers of electrons and protons are equal, and the electrons are in orbit around the nucleus. Are they tightly or loosely attracted to the nucleus? Janice?"

"Sort of loosely, I think."

"Yes, good. We can 'scrape' electrons off," Donna continues, "so we think of them as being loosely attached. Now keep that in mind, because it's important. We can get electrons off the atoms fairly easily with heat or even by simply rubbing them, but the nucleus is very hard to break up."

"Now let's take a look," Donna says as she steps quickly over to her file cabinet and takes out an inflated balloon and a wool sweater. "Watch." She rubs the balloon vigorously with the sweater, steps over to Michelle, and holds the balloon over her hair. "What do you notice here? . . . Vicki?"

"The balloon is making Michelle's hair stick up," Vicki responds to the giggles of the class.

Donna explains that their goal for the day is to understand why the balloon makes Michelle's hair stick up. She then takes another inflated balloon, holds it against the chalkboard, and lets it go. "What happened here? Joe?"

"It just fell down," Joe shrugs.

"Let's try it again," Donna continues and rubs the balloon on the sweater and again holds it against the board.

"Now what? . . . Melody?"

"It's stuck up there now."

Donna uses a series of questions to guide the students into concluding that some of the electrons were rubbed off the sweater and collected on the balloon, so the balloon had more electrons than protons and the extra electrons attracted the protons in Michelle's hair and the board.

106

Donna explains to students that this is called static electricity, and she continues, "Two everyday examples of static electricity are clothes sticking together in the dryer and getting a shock after you walk across a carpet and touch a doorknob.

"For tomorrow," she says in conclusion, "I want you to write a one-paragraph explanation for each of these using the ideas we've discussed here today."

At 1:38 she says, "OK, everyone. It's time to head for your next class. Collect any paper or other scraps around your desk and get ready to go. We'll start right where we left off tomorrow."

1. Identify at least four characteristics of Lincoln Middle School that are also characteristics of an effective school. Support each of your descriptions with evidence taken directly from the case study.

2. Identify one characteristic of Lincoln Middle School that is not consistent with an effective school.

3. Identify one characteristic of an effective school for which direct evidence doesn't exist in the case study.

To receive feedback on your responses to these exercises, go to the Companion Website at www.prenhall.com/kauchak , then to the Preparing for Your Licensure Exam *module for Chapter 7.*

Discussion Questions

1. Based on the organization of typical elementary schools, what are the primary advantages and disadvantages of teaching in an elementary school? How could elementary schools be organized differently to improve the education of all students?

2. Based on the organization of typical middle schools, what are the primary advantages and disadvantages of teaching in a middle school? How could middle schools be organized differently to improve the education of all students?

3. Based on the organization of typical high schools, what are the primary advantages and disadvantages of teaching in a high school? How could high schools be organized differently to improve the education of all students?

4. In which kind of school—elementary, middle, junior high, or high school—do teachers have the most autonomy? The least autonomy? What implications does this have for you as a prospective teacher?

5. Consider what you know about the organization of elementary, middle, junior high, and high schools. Which type of school is best suited to your academic and personal characteristics? Why do you think so?

Developing as a Professional: Online Activities

Going Into Schools

Go to the Companion Website at *www.prenhall.com/kauchak*, and click on the *Going Into Schools* module for Chapter 7. You will find a number of school-based activities that will help you link chapter content to the schools in which you work.

Virtual Field Experience: Using the Internet to Explore the Profession

If you would like to participate in a Virtual Field Experience, access the following Website: *http://www.rand.org/pubs/monographs/2004/RANDMG138.pdf* and *http:www.Indiana.edu/~soenews/news/news1151614366.html* . These sites contain perspectives and opinions about reform efforts in middle and high schools.

Online Portfolio Activities

To develop your professional portfolio, further apply your understanding of chapter content, and address the INTASC standards, go the Companion Website at *www.prenhall.com/kauchak*, then to the *Online Portfolio Activities* for Chapter 7. Complete the suggested activities.

Check Your Understanding

1.1   What are three different meanings of the concept *school*?

One definition describes a school as a place where students go to learn and develop; a second describes a school as a physical place—a building or set of buildings. A social institution, an organization with established structures and rules designed to promote certain goals is the third definition and will serve as the framework for this chapter.

1.2   Explain how a *school* and a *school district* differ.

A school is a social institution that exists with the goal of promoting students' growth and development, whereas a school district is a larger administrative unit designed to help schools reach their goals.

1.3   Is the *family* a social institution? Explain why it is or is not.

The family is widely considered to be a social institution. It has a structure that has historically been viewed as composed of a father, mother, and one or more children, with the goal of promoting the well-being of the entire family. (Some of the politics surrounding social issues, such as gay marriage, center on controversies about what the family's "established structure" should be.)

2.1   What are the major components of a typical school organization?

The components of a typical school include personnel, the physical plant, and the organization of the curriculum. The administrative staff, which includes the principal, vice principal, and one or more assistant principals in large schools; support staff, such as clerical workers, receptionists, and custodians; and teachers make up the personnel of a school.

The physical plant often includes several buildings, such as an administrative building, classroom buildings, a cafeteria, and in most middle, junior high, and high schools, sports facilities, such as a gymnasium, football and baseball fields, and perhaps a running track.

The curriculum is designed to teach content that is appropriate for students at different ages, which is the reason that schools are usually organized into elementary, middle or junior high, and high school levels.

2.2   Most school systems are organized into three levels. Describe each of the three.

As you saw in the feedback for exercise 2.1, schools are typically organized into elementary, middle or junior high, and high school levels. Elementary schools usually house students from kindergarten, or pre-K, through the fifth or sixth grade. Middle schools usually involve some combination of fifth through eighth grades, with 6–8 being the most common. Junior highs most commonly include some combination of grades 7–9, and high schools typically consist of grades 9–12 or 10–12.

2.3   What are two factors that influence the way school curriculum is organized?

The developmental characteristics of students and economics–politics are the two factors that most commonly influence the way the curriculum is organized. Since a typical first grader thinks differently than does a typical fifth grader, for example, the curriculum is organized to accommodate those developmental differences.

Economic factors, such as school overcrowding, and political factors, such as high school coaches' wanting potential athletes to be prepared for high school teams, also influence the way schools are organized.

3.1   What are two ways in which teaching in an elementary school differs from teaching in a middle, junior high, or high school?

Elementary teachers are responsible for teaching all the content areas, such as reading, math, science, social studies, art, and music, whereas teachers at the upper levels are re-

108

sponsible for teaching only one area, such as math (or sometimes two, such as a combination of math and science classes). This is one important difference.

In addition, teachers in elementary schools set their own schedule; that is, they decide how many minutes per day that they will allocate to each of the content areas. At the upper levels, the time allocated for each class period is preset by schoolwide schedules and bells.

3.2 **What are four differences between effective middle schools and junior highs?**

First, effective middle schools organize teachers and students into interdisciplinary teams, so that all the teachers on a team have the same group of students and instruction emphasizes connections between different curriculum areas. This isn't the case in junior highs. Second, middle schools more strongly emphasize long-term teacher–student relationships with greater attention to students' emotional development than do junior highs. Third, teachers in effective middle schools more strongly emphasize interactive teaching strategies than do teachers in junior highs. Finally, middle schools eliminate activities in which developmental differences among students become apparent, such as competitive athletics.

3.3 **Describe a comprehensive high school. How does a comprehensive high school differ from a vocational high school?**

A comprehensive high school is a school that attempts to meet the needs of all students. This means that it attempts to provide offerings for students who are likely to attend college, but at the same time meet the needs of students who will be entering the job market after graduating from high school.

Vocational high schools are more likely to offer a curriculum designed to provide students with education and job skills that will enable them to get a job immediately after graduating from high school.

4.1 **Describe the characteristics of an effective school.**

Research indicates that effective schools are optimal in size—neither too small nor too large; they have a clear school mission and strong leadership; their environments are safe and orderly; parental involvement is strong; and they maintain a solid academic focus.

4.2 **What is the most distinguishing characteristic of effective instruction in effective schools?**

The most distinguishing characteristic of effective instruction is interactive teaching. Instead of lecturing and giving students extensive seat work, effective teachers design learning activities that actively involve students in the content they are learning.

4.3 **Why is frequent monitoring of student progress essential for an effective school?**

Frequent monitoring of student progress performs several important functions. First, and most important, it tells students whether they are learning important ideas and skills. It also informs teachers of learning gains, allowing them to adjust instruction to meet learning gaps. Finally, it provides helpful information to administrators and parents about children's learning progress.

Helping Diverse Learners Succeed in Today's Classrooms

4

From *Introduction to Teaching: Becoming a Professional*, Third Edition. Donald Kauchak, Paul Eggen. Copyright © 2008 Pearson Education, Inc. Published by Merrill Prentice Hall. All rights reserved.

Helping Diverse Learners Succeed in Today's Classrooms

Learning Objectives

After you have completed your study of this chapter, you should be able to

1. Explain how cultural diversity influences learning and how effective teachers respond to this diversity.

2. Describe the major approaches to dealing with language diversity.

3. Explain how gender differences influence school success and how effective teachers respond to these differences.

4. Explain different views of ability differences, and describe how schools respond to ability differences.

5. Explain how schools have changed the ways they deal with exceptionalities, and describe the major categories of exceptionalities found in classrooms.

Case Studies

 Elementary

 Middle

 Secondary

Bonnie Kamin/PhotoEdit Inc.

Teachers begin their careers expecting to find classrooms like the ones they experienced when they were students, and in some ways they are the same. Students go to school to study and learn, but they also want to have fun and be with their friends. They expect to work but often need encouragement from their teachers. They're typical kids.

Classrooms are changing, however; an increasing number of students now come from different cultures and speak different languages at home. And other types of diversity, including differences between boys and girls, are receiving increased attention. As you read the following case study, think about these differences and how they will influence your life as a teacher.

Carla Jackson, a first-grade teacher in an urban elementary school, watches as her students stream into her room on the first day of school. Though she has read the class rolls, she can't believe the different shapes, colors, and sizes before her eyes. Some are tall and well developed—looking almost like second graders—whereas others look like they should be in preschool. She also notices differences in the way they learn and behave. Some are bright and eager, while others look sleep deprived.

Several know how to print and read their names, but books appear almost strange to a few. Some use their fingers to add or even count, and others suck their thumbs when they become tired or discouraged.

And the names—she hopes she'll be able to remember and pronounce them all correctly. There is Jones and Lee and Wong and Hassad and Trang and Jamal. Because she is in a large, urban school, Carla knew in advance that her students would be diverse, but she wasn't prepared for this—eleven different cultures and six different languages. She jokingly refers to her class as her "Little United Nations."

A field trip to a local zoo gives Carla a chance to see her students in a different setting. She can't believe how differently they act on the field trip. Some are active and lead the way in exploring while others hang back, clinging to her for emotional support. Some eagerly ask questions while others listen shyly. She knows that this diversity can make learning experiences richer for the students, but she hasn't quite figured out how.

When you begin teaching, the students in your classes are likely to come from a variety of backgrounds, primarily because the diversity in today's schools is rapidly increasing and also because new teachers are likely to find jobs in schools that serve diverse populations (Olson, 2003). This diversity has several dimensions (Figure 3.1), and it presents both challenges and opportunities for you as a beginning teacher.

Figure 3.1 Dimensions of Diversity

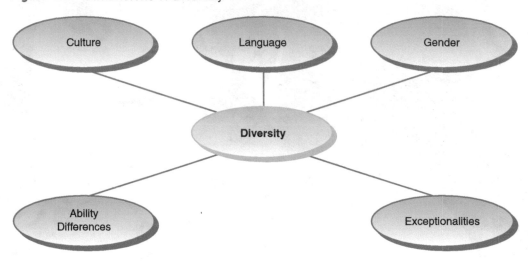

To meet these challenges, teachers need a deep understanding of diversity and teaching strategies that address the learning needs of students from varying backgrounds. Before continuing, take a few minutes to complete the questionnaire on the following page designed to assess your thinking about different aspects of diversity in our schools.

We address each of the questions as the chapter unfolds. Let's turn now to *culture*, one of the most important sources of learner diversity.

Cultural Diversity

Think about the clothes you wear, the kind of music you like, and even the food you eat. Your clothing, music, and foods, along with other dimensions such as religion and family structure are all part of your **culture**, the knowledge, attitudes, values, customs, and behavior patterns that characterize a social group (Banks, 2006b). **Cultural diversity** refers to the different cultures that you'll encounter in classrooms and how these cultural differences influence learning. As shown in Figure 3.2, culture is one of the most important dimensions of diversity in classrooms.

Culture influences many important dimensions of our lives. For instance, take eating. Culture influences when we eat; when do you typically eat dinner? In some cultures, dinner occurs after 8:00 in the evening, while in others 6:00 is the standard dinner time. Culture also influences who we eat with. Again, does your whole family sit down together, or does everyone "eat on the run"? It also influences how we eat; do you eat with a knife and fork or chopsticks, and when you cut a piece of meat, do you then transfer the fork back to your right hand or leave it in your left hand? And, of course, culture influences what we eat, as evidenced by the growing number of ethnic restaurants around the country.

Culture. The knowledge, attitudes, values, customs, and behavior patterns that characterize a social group.

Cultural diversity. The different cultures that you'll encounter in classrooms and how these cultural differences influence learning.

professional knowledge: test yourself!

For each item, circle the number that best represents your thinking. Use the following scale as a guide:

1 = Strongly disagree
2 = Disagree
3 = Uncertain
4 = Agree
5 = Strongly agree

1. While students from different cultures have varying attitudes and values, these variations have little impact on the amount they learn.

       1   2   3   4   5

2. Students who are not native English speakers learn English most effectively if they are required to speak only English in school.

       1   2   3   4   5

3. Boys generally get better grades in school than girls.

       1   2   3   4   5

4. Students who are talented in one area of school are generally talented in all the others.

       1   2   3   4   5

5. Most students with exceptionalities require help and assistance in special classrooms designed to meet their needs.

       1   2   3   4   5

 This is available in a downloadable format on the Companion Website for personal portfolio use.

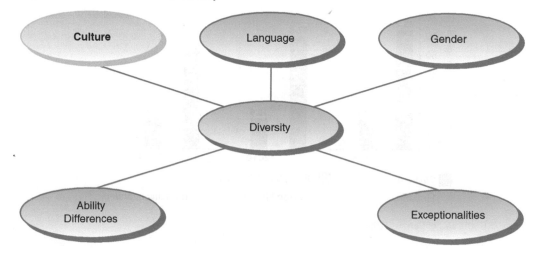

Figure 3.2 Culture and Diversity

Ethnicity, which refers to a person's ancestry—the way individuals identify themselves with the nation from which they or their ancestors came—is an important part of culture (Gollnick & Chinn, 2006). Members of an ethnic group share a common identity defined by their history, language (although sometimes not spoken), customs, and traditions. Experts estimate that nearly 300 distinct ethnic groups currently reside in the United States (Gollnick & Chinn, 2006).

Immigration and other demographic shifts have resulted in dramatic changes in our country's school population. Congress passed the Immigration Act of 1965, which ended quotas based on national origin. This law resulted in more immigrants coming to the United States and also in changes in their point of origin. While most immigrants during the early 1900s came from Europe, more recent immigrants come from Central America (37%), Asia (25%), and the Caribbean (10%), with only 14 percent of recent immigrants having Europe as their point of origin (U.S. Census Bureau, 2004). This has resulted in a dramatic increase in the proportion of students who are members of cultural minorities (U.S. Department of Education, 2005b), and it helps us understand why the backgrounds of Carla's students are so diverse.

By the year 2020, the U.S. school-age population will see many more changes (see Figure 3.3). Experts predict considerable increases in the percentages of all groups of students except White, non-Hispanic. During this span of time, the percentage of White students will decrease from over 63 percent to a little more than half of the total school population (U.S. Census Bureau, 2003). By 2050, no one group will be a majority among adults.

Urban Schools and Diversity

The term *cultural minority* is often used to refer to various non-White cultural groups. Based on sheer numbers, this term may soon be obsolete and is already a misnomer in many parts of the country, especially in urban areas. For example, Hispanics, African-Americans, and Asians—when combined—now make up the majority of the population in 48 of the 100 largest U.S. cities (Macionis, 2006). In addition, children of color make up the majority of public school enrollments in six states and over 90 percent of the students in Detroit, the District of Columbia, Chicago, Houston, and Los Angeles (Kober, 2006).

The growth of minority student populations in urban areas is the result of immigration coupled with higher birth rates. For example, between 1990 and 2000, Hispanic populations increased 43 percent and Asian populations surged 40 percent in urban areas (Lichter & Johnson, 2006). Experts estimate that almost one in five students is a child of immigrants

Ethnicity. A person's ancestry; the way individuals identify themselves with the nation from which they or their ancestors came.

Figure 3.3   Changes in School-Age Population, 2000–2020

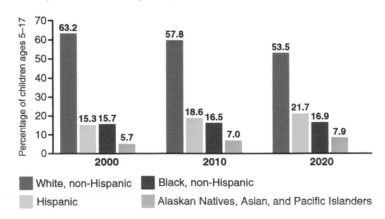

Source: U.S. Bureau of Census (2003).

(Kober, 2006). Urban centers are often called "gateway cities" for recently arriving immigrants (Lichter & Johnson, 2006), and these population increases are reflected in urban schools. In Adlai Stevenson High School in New York City, for example, African-Americans and Hispanics make up 97 percent of the student population; only five tenths of 1 percent of students are White (Kozol, 2005). Many of these recent immigrants do not speak English as their first language, which poses challenges for schools and teachers. Teachers skilled in helping students simultaneously learn English and the content of their classes are sorely needed.

Knowledge of the cultural attitudes and values these students bring to school is also essential. This is the topic of the next section.

The cultural diversity in urban schools provides teachers with both opportunities and challenges. [Mary Kate Denny/PhotoEdit Inc.]

Cultural Attitudes and Values

Our students come to school with a long learning history. Cultural influences exist in their dress, family configurations, interactions with parents and peers, and attitudes and values. When they enter our classrooms, they bring these attitudes and values with them. Some complement school learning; others do not. This suggests that the first statement in our beginning-of-chapter survey, "While students from different cultures have varying attitudes and values, these variations have little impact on the amount they learn," is not true. Let's see why.

Language is an example. Students are sometimes hesitant to drop the use of nonstandard English dialects in favor of "school English" because doing so might alienate their peers (Ogbu, 1999). The same problem occurs in classrooms where students are asked to learn English and quit using the languages of their homes. Programs encouraging students to drop their native languages can also distance students from their parents, many of whom cannot speak English.

Even school success can be an issue. Succeeding in school is sometimes interpreted by members of minorities as rejecting their native culture; to become a good student is to become "White"—to embrace and uphold only White cultural values. Members of minorities who study and succeed academically risk losing the friendship of their peers. John Ogbu, an anthropologist who studied the achievement of minority students, believes that in many schools peer values either don't support school learning or actually oppose it; students form what he called "resistance cultures" (Ogbu & Simons, 1998). Low grades, management and motivation problems, truancy, and high dropout rates are symptoms of this conflict.

Cultural attitudes and values can also complement learning. For instance, researchers studying the amazing academic success of Vietnamese and other Asian-American students found that hard work, perseverance, and pride were heavily emphasized in the home (Kristoff, 2006). In 2005, Asian-American students scored highest (1091) on the Math–Verbal parts of the SAT test, outscoring Whites by 23 points and other cultural minorities by an average of 168 points. Willingness to take challenging courses was also a factor in academic success; research showed that 40 percent of Asian-American students took calculus in high school versus 28 percent of the general population. One Vietnamese student who became the valedictorian at her high school after only 7 years in the United States commented, "Anybody can be smart, can do great on standardized tests. But unless you work hard, you're not going to do well" (Kristoff, 2006, p. 13).

Research on Indian students' success in U.S. national spelling bees found a similar emphasis on hard work and study (Bracey, 2005b). Children of Indian descent consistently place high in these academic contests, winning much more often than other ethnic groups.

Cultural Interaction Patterns

Because our students learn to interact with others at home, cultural conflict can occur when they enter our classrooms. Let's look at an example:

A second-grade class in Albuquerque, New Mexico, was reading The Boxcar Children *and was about to start a new chapter. The teacher said, "Look at the illustration at the beginning of the chapter and tell me what you think is going to happen." A few students raised their hands. The teacher called on a boy in the back row.*

He said, "I think the boy is going to meet his grandfather."

The teacher asked, "Based on what you know, how does the boy feel about meeting his grandfather?"

Trying to involve the whole class, the teacher called on another student—one of four Native Americans in the group—even though she had not raised her hand. When she didn't answer, the teacher tried rephrasing the question, but again the student sat in silence.

Feeling exasperated, the teacher wondered if there was something in the way the lesson was being conducted that made it difficult for the student to respond. She sensed that the student she had called on understood the story and was enjoying it. Why, then, wouldn't she answer what appeared to be a simple question?

The teacher recalled that this was not the first time this had happened, and that, in fact, the other Native American students in the class rarely answered questions in class discussions. She wanted to involve them, wanted them to participate in class, but could not think of ways to get them to talk. (Villegas, 1991, p. 3)

Why do you think this problem occurred? One explanation suggests that Native American children are not used to the fast-paced, give-and-take patterns that characterize many American classrooms (Starnes, 2006). When involved in discussions such as the one just described, they are uncomfortable and, as a result, reluctant to participate (Banks, 2006b).

Studies comparing the interaction patterns of White and African-American students have also found cultural differences (Heath, 1989, 1982). For instance, researchers looked at students' responses to teacher directives such as "Let's put the scissors away now." Accustomed to this indirect way of speaking, White students interpreted it as a command; African-Americans, used to more direct statements such as "Put your scissors away now," did not (Heath, 1982). Teachers viewed a student's failure to comply as either a management or a motivation problem when instead, a mismatch between home and school cultures existed.

Made aware of these differences, teachers worded their requests more directly, "Begin your homework now" (Heath, 1982). They also encouraged all students to actively participate in learning activities and liberally praised their efforts to do so. In this way, the teacher built bridges between the students' and the school's cultural learning styles.

Educational Responses to Cultural Diversity

Historically, social commentators have used different metaphors to describe the relationships among the diverse cultures in the United States. A "melting pot" was one of the first. Those who saw the United States as a melting pot emphasized **assimilation**, a process of socializing people so that they adopt dominant social norms and patterns of behavior. Assimilation attempted to make members of minority cultural groups "similar" to those belonging to the dominant cultural group, typically Whites of northern European descent.

The melting pot metaphor was especially popular in the early 1900s, when large numbers of immigrants from southern and eastern Europe came to the United States. Society assigned schools the task of teaching immigrants how "Americans" were supposed to think, talk, and behave. Immigrants, eager to become "American" and share in this country's economic wealth, generally accepted efforts to assimilate them.

About the middle of the 20th century, a shift in thinking occurred. People realized that assimilation had never totally worked and that there was no "melting pot," as indicated by

> **Assimilation.** A process of socializing people so that they adopt dominant social norms and patterns of behavior.

neighborhoods and groups that continued to speak their home languages, celebrate their unique cultural holidays, and maintain their cultural habits, such as eating ethnic foods. The contributions of different cultural and ethnic groups were increasingly recognized, and leaders began to realize that some educational practices aimed at assimilation were actually counterproductive. For example, in an effort to encourage English language acquisition, schools in the Southwest didn't allow students to speak Spanish, even on playgrounds. Schools became hostile places where students had to choose between family and friends, and school. The policy probably did as much to alienate Hispanic youth as it did to encourage English language development (Spring, 2006).

Multicultural Education

To remedy these problems, educators began developing new approaches to addressing cultural diversity. **Multicultural education** is a general term that describes a variety of strategies schools use to accommodate cultural differences in teaching and learning. We discuss some of these strategies in the following section "Culturally Responsive Teaching." Instead of trying to create a melting pot, these approaches align with new metaphors that describe America as a "mosaic" or "tossed salad" in which society recognizes and values each culture's unique contributions.

Multicultural education is highly controversial. Critics contend that it is divisive because it places too much emphasis on differences between cultural groups and not enough on our commonalities (Schlesinger, 1992). Textbooks have been scrutinized; in 2000, a spokesperson for the *American Textbook Council* criticized modern history textbooks as emphasizing multicultural themes at the expense of basic information about U.S. history (Sewall, 2000). Recently, a major controversy erupted over singing the national anthem in Spanish (Goldstein, 2006). Critics claimed that the national anthem is a symbol of unity for a diverse people united by common values and our country's Constitution. Criticism became so widespread that bills were submitted in Congress mandating that the anthem never be recited or sung in a foreign language (despite the fact that the national anthem has historically been translated and sung in a number of different languages, including French, Polish, and Italian).

Proponents of multicultural education assert that building on students' cultures is nothing more than sound teaching; by recognizing, valuing, and utilizing students' cultures and languages in their instruction, teachers help students link the topics they're studying to what they already know, a process consistent with effective teaching (Eggen & Kauchak, 2007; Ormrod, 2006). In addition, proponents of multicultural education point out that the United States has always been a nation of immigrants and this diversity has long been recognized. For example, our society embraces the music, holidays (e.g., St. Patrick's Day, Cinco De Mayo, Hanukkah, and the Chinese New Year), and foods of many cultures. Good multicultural education continues this tradition by recognizing and building on students' cultural heritages, proponents argue.

Like all approaches, multicultural education will undoubtedly evolve as educators decide what works and what doesn't. One promising approach to working with diverse student populations is called culturally responsive teaching.

Culturally Responsive Teaching

Shannon Wilson, a fifth-grade teacher in a large urban elementary school, walks around her classroom, helping students as they work on a social studies project. A number of hands are raised, and she feels relieved that she has Maria Arguelas, her special education resource teacher, to help her. Shannon has 27 students, seven of whom are not native English speakers. Five are Hispanic, and fortunately, Maria can help them with language-related problems. Shannon often spends extra time with Kwan and Abdul, the other two non-English speakers. Maria also assists Shannon by working with four of her students who have learning disabilities.

Multicultural education. A general term that describes a variety of strategies schools use to accommodate cultural differences in teaching and learning.

119

Culturally responsive teaching builds on students' cultural backgrounds, accepting and valuing differences and accommodating different cultural learning styles. [Bob Daemmrich/The Image Works]

Shannon's class is preparing for Parents' Day, an afternoon when parents and other caregivers join the class in celebrating the students' ancestral countries. The students present information about the countries' history, geography, and cultures in their projects. The class has already prepared a large world map with pins marking the students' countries of origin. While several of the pins are clustered in Mexico and Central and South America, the map shows that students also come from many other parts of the world. Each student is encouraged to invite a family member to come and share a part of the family's native culture. The parents can bring food, music, and native dress from their different homelands.

Culturally responsive teaching is instruction that acknowledges and accommodates cultural diversity (Gay, 2000, 2005). It attempts to accomplish this goal in three ways:

- Accepting and valuing cultural differences
- Accommodating different cultural interaction patterns
- Building on students' cultural backgrounds

Accepting and Valuing Cultural Differences. By recognizing and accepting student diversity, teachers communicate that all students are welcome and valued. This is particularly important for members of cultural minorities, who sometimes feel alienated from school. As a simple example, Shannon had her students identify their ethnic homelands on the map. This showed an interest in each student and helped them feel accepted and valued.

Genuine caring is an essential element in making students feel part of the classroom. Teachers communicate caring in several ways, including the following:

- Devote time to students—for example, be available before and after school to help with schoolwork and discuss students' personal concerns.
- Demonstrate interest in students' lives—for example, ask about Jewish, Muslim, Latin-American, and African-American festivals.
- Involve all students in learning activities—for example, call on all students as equally as possible.

Each of these suggestions communicates that the teacher welcomes and values all students.

Accommodating Cultural Interaction Patterns. Teachers who are sensitive to possible differences between home and school interaction patterns adapt their instruction to best meet their students' needs. For example, we saw earlier that the communication patterns of Native Americans may clash with typical classroom practices (Starnes, 2006). Recognizing that these students may not be comfortable in teacher-centered question-and-answer activities, teachers can use additional strategies, such as cooperative learning, to complement teacher-centered approaches. Similarly, knowing that White and African-American students sometimes have different communication patterns, teachers can word instructions more directly, such as, "Open your books to page 53 now."

As another example, when a teacher learned that her Asian-American students were overwhelmed by the bustle of American schools, she tried to keep her classroom quiet and orderly and encouraged shy students to participate with open-ended questioning, giving

Culturally responsive teaching. Instruction that acknowledges and accommodates cultural diversity.

them extra time to respond, and gently reminding them to speak a bit louder (C. Park, 1997). Another teacher noticed this about her Vietnamese students:

> *I traditionally end every day with the students lining up and receiving a hug before they leave. My Vietnamese kids were always the stiff huggers until October. Through my understanding of their cultures, I now give all students the choice of a hug, handshake, or high five. This simple act may make children feel more comfortable interacting with me.* (McAllister & Irvine, 2002, p. 440)

Through increased sensitivity to each cultural group's learning needs, teachers can make their classrooms safe and inviting learning environments for all students.

Accommodating different cultural interaction patterns can result in minority students' adapting to the dominant culture (including that of schools) without losing their cultural identities, a process called "accommodation without assimilation" (Ogbu, 1992, 1999, 2003). Accommodation without assimilation helps students function comfortably in both cultures, including using different language patterns in school compared to the home or other social environments (DeMeulenaere, 2001). The challenge for teachers is to help students learn about the "culture of schooling," the norms, procedures, and expectations necessary for success in school, while honoring and valuing students' home cultures.

Building on Students' Backgrounds. Effective teachers also learn about their students' cultures and use this information to promote personal pride and motivation, as we saw in Shannon's class and as we see in the following example:

> *Jack Seltzer, a high school biology teacher on the Navajo Nation Reservation, uses his students' background experiences to illustrate hard-to-understand science concepts. He uses Churro sheep, a local breed that Navajos use for food and wool, to illustrate genetic principles. When they study plants, he focuses on local varieties of squash and corn that have been grown by students' ancestors for centuries. He uses geologic formations in nearby Monument Valley to illustrate igneous, sedimentary and metamorphic rocks. (Baker, 2006).*

Making Connections:
To deepen your understanding of the topics in this section of the chapter and integrate them with topics you've already studied, go to the *Making Connections* module for Chapter 3 at **www.prenhall.com/kauchak.** Respond to questions 1–5.

Both students and their parents benefit from building on students' cultural backgrounds. Student achievement increases, and parents become more positive about school, both of which enhance student motivation. Shannon recognized this when she invited parents and other caregivers to share their cultural heritages with her class. Jack also capitalized on this idea by providing examples with which the students could personally identify.

IN TODAY'S CLASSROOMS: VIDEO

Culturally Responsive Teaching

In this video episode, a teacher describes the adjustments she made to accommodate the religious beliefs of a fourth-grade Muslim girl and make her feel welcome in school. We also see how willingly the other students support the teacher's efforts.

To view this video, go to the *Becoming a Professional* DVD, included with this text, click on *In Today's Classrooms*, and then this chapter's video: *Culturally Responsive Teaching*.

To answer the questions online and receive immediate feedback, go to the Companion Website at **www.prenhall.com/kauchak,** *then to the* In Today's Classroom *module for Chapter 3.*

Check Your Understanding

1.1 How do cultural attitudes, values, and interaction patterns influence learning?

1.2 What are three ways in which effective teachers respond to cultural diversity in their classrooms?

1.3 What is the relationship between urban schools and cultural diversity?

 For feedback, go to Check Your Understanding *at the end of this chapter.*

Language Diversity

Ellie Barton, a language arts teacher at Northeast Middle School, is the school's English Language Learner (ELL) Coordinator. She teaches ELL classes, and she is also in charge of the school's testing and placement program.

Her job is challenging, as her students vary considerably in their knowledge of English. For instance, one group of Somali-Bantu children just arrived from a refugee camp in Kenya. They cannot read or write, because there is no written language for their native tongue, Mai-Mai. Language isn't their only challenge; many had never been in a building with more than one floor, and others found urinals and other aspects of indoor plumbing a mystery. At the other end of the continuum is a young girl from India who can read and write in four languages: Hindi, the national language of India; Urdu, the language of her Persian ancestors; Telegu, a regional language in India; and Arabic.

To sort out this language diversity, the district uses a placement test that categorizes students into three levels: newcomer classrooms for students who have little or no expertise with English; self-contained ELL classrooms, where a primary emphasis is on learning to read and write English; and sheltered English, where students receive structured help in learning academic subjects such as science and social studies. However, the placement process is not foolproof, since English skills are sometimes nonexistent, and some parents don't know the exact ages of their children. Ellie's principal deals with this information void in creative ways; he recently asked a dentist friend to look at a student's teeth to estimate the child's age (adapted from Romboy & Kinkead, 2005).

Imagine trying to help someone understand something if they don't understand the words you are saying. Further, imagine trying to help them when you can't understand what they are saying to you. This is the daunting task many teachers in today's schools face.

Language is one of the most important parts of any culture. Because language diversity has such a powerful influence on learning (see Figure 3.4), and responses to this diversity are so controversial, we devote this section of the chapter to the topic.

As we saw earlier, immigration has brought increasing numbers of students with limited backgrounds in English to our country's classrooms. The number of English language learners (ELLs) in the United States increased by 95 percent between 1991 and 2002 (Gollnick & Chinn, 2006).

Educational responses to language diversity differ in the degree to which they built upon and attempt to maintain students' first language. [Bob Daemmrich/The Image Works]

Figure 3.4 Language and Diversity

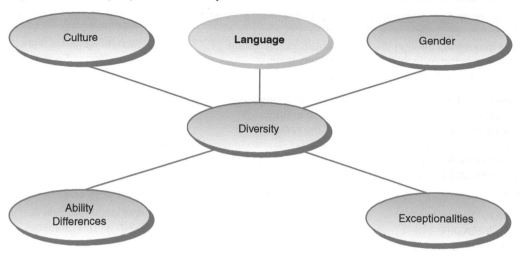

English language learners (ELLs) are students whose first language is not English and who need help in learning to speak, read, and write in English. In the 2003–2004 school year, 10 percent of U.S. students' first language was not English, and in many cities and states, these students now make up a significant proportion of the student body (Kober, 2006). Currently, 329 different languages are spoken in the United States, with the most common language groups being Spanish, Vietnamese, Hmong, Chinese, and Korean (OELA, 2004).

Language Diversity: The Government's Response

The federal government, through legislation and court rulings, initially attempted to address the needs of ELL students through bilingual approaches, approaches that attempt to maintain the first language while students learn English. For example, in 1968 Congress passed the Bilingual Education Act, which provided federal funds for educating non-native English speakers. In 1974 the Supreme Court ruled unanimously, in the controversial *Lau v. Nichols* case, that the San Francisco School District unlawfully discriminated by failing to address children's language problems (Bennett, 2007). More recently, the English Acquisition component of the No Child Left Behind (NCLB) Act of 2001 mandated that the primary objective of U.S. schools should be the teaching of English without any attempt to preserve minority languages (No Child Left Behind Act, 2001). Accordingly, the previous Office of Bilingual Education became the Office of English Language Acquisition (OELA). In 2006, during a debate on immigration reform, the U.S. Senate voted to designate English as the national language (Hulse, 2006). Each of these government actions has changed our schools, as we'll see in the next section.

Language Diversity: Schools' Responses

Schools across the country have responded to the challenge of language diversity in very different ways, outlined in Table 3.1. Although all of the programs are designed to ultimately teach English, they differ in how fast English is introduced and to what extent the first language is used and maintained.

    Maintenance language programs place the greatest emphasis on using and sustaining the first language. For example, in one bilingual program in Houston, students initially received 90 percent of instruction in Spanish and 10 percent in English (Zehr, 2002a). The emphasis on English then increased in each grade. The future of maintenance programs is uncertain given the English Acquisition component of the NCLB Act, which discourages such programs.

    At the opposite end of the continuum, **immersion** and **English as a second language (ESL) programs** emphasize rapid transition to English. Halfway between the two ends of the continuum, **transition programs** maintain the first language until students acquire sufficient English to proceed in that language.

English language learners (ELLs). Students whose first language is not English and who need help in learning to speak, read, and write in English.

Maintenance language programs. Language programs that place the greatest emphasis on using and sustaining the first language.

Immersion program. Language program that emphasizes rapid transition to English.

English as a second language (ESL) program. Language program that emphasizes rapid transition to English.

Transition programs. Language programs that maintain the first language until students acquire sufficient English.

123

TABLE 3.1 Different Programs for ELL Students

Type of Program	Description	Advantages	Disadvantages
Maintenance	First language maintained through reading and writing activities in first language while English introduced.	Students become literate in two languages.	Requires teachers trained in first language. Acquisition of English may not be as fast.
Transition	Students learn to read in first language and are given supplementary instruction in English as a Second Language. Once English is mastered, students are placed in regular classrooms and first language discontinued.	Maintains first language. Transition to English is eased by gradual approach.	Requires teachers trained in first language. Acquisition of English may not be as fast. First language is dropped.
Immersion	Students learn English by being "immersed" in classrooms where English is the only language spoken.	When effective, quick transition to English. Does not require teachers trained in second language.	Loss of native language. Sink-or-swim approach hard on students.
English as a Second Language (ESL) Programs	Pull-out programs where students are provided with supplementary English instruction or modified instruction in content areas (also called Sheltered English programs).	Easier to administer when dealing with diverse language backgrounds.	Students may not be ready to benefit from content instruction in English. Pull-out programs segregate students.

Logistics are often a factor when schools consider which type of program to use. For example, transition programs can be effective when classes are composed of large numbers of ELL students who speak the same language (such as Spanish-speaking students in Los Angeles), because one teacher who speaks the students' native language can be hired. This isn't possible when several different first languages exist. For example, in 2001, 79 percent of the U.S. ELL population spoke Spanish, but the remaining 21 percent spoke a wide variety of other languages, making it virtually impossible to find a teacher who spoke all the different languages in one classroom (Girard, 2005). This happened at Northeast Middle School and is a major reason why Ellie Barton teaches in an ELL program that places minimal emphasis on students' first language.

teaching in an era of reform

Bilingual Education

Bilingual education has been the focus of several reform efforts. Through the Bilingual Education Act of 1968 and guidelines drafted as a result of *Lau v. Nichols* in 1974, the federal government signalled its commitment to providing services for non-native English speakers.

A counter reform occurred in California in 1998, when voters passed Proposition 227, a ballot initiative that sharply reduced bilingual education programs, replacing them with English-only immersion programs for ELL students. Similar measures were passed in Arizona and 25 other states (Garcia, 2006). These initiatives have sharply curtailed the use of bilingual education in these states. For example, before the initiatives occurred in Arizona and California, about one third of ELL students were taking bilingual education classes; after the initiatives, the numbers plummeted to 11 percent in both states (Zehr, 2002b). In addition, 26 states have passed laws making English the official language (U.S. English, Inc., 2006). (See Figure 3.5.) Although these laws are mostly symbolic, they are influencing state government publications,

Figure 3.5 States with Official Language Legislation

☐ Official English law (26)
☐ No official English law (24)

Alabama	(1990)	Mississippi	(1987)
Alaska	(1998)	Missouri	(1998)
Arkansas	(1987)	Montana	(1995)
California	(1986)	Nebraska	(1920)
Colorado	(1988)	New Hampshire	(1995)
Florida	(1988)	North Carolina	(1987)
Georgia	(1986 & 1996)	North Dakota	(1987)
Illinois	(1969)	South Carolina	(1987)
Indiana	(1984)	South Dakota	(1995)
Iowa	(2002)	Tennessee	(1984)
Kentucky	(1984)	Utah	(2000)
Louisiana	(1811)	Virginia	(1981 & 1996)
Massachusetts	(1975)	Wyoming	(1996)

Source: U.S. English, Inc. (2002). Washington, DC.

and they illustrate growing public sentiment in favor of English and fears about losing English as a common cultural bond.

In addition, in 2002 Congress failed to renew the Bilingual Education Act, instead packaging funds for English language learners into the NCLB Act, which requires students to attain "English fluency" in 3 years and requires schools to teach students in English after that time period.

The Issue

The essence of bilingual programs is an attempt to maintain and build on students' native languages while they learn English. Proponents make several arguments in support of bilingual education. First, they contend that the programs make sense with respect to learning because they provide a smooth and humane transition to English by building on students' first languages. They also argue that being able to speak two languages has practical benefits; a bilingual person can live and communicate in two worlds, which can increase economic and career opportunities. They also cite research. One review concluded that exist-

ing evidence favors bilingual approaches versus English immersion approaches in terms of helping students learn to read (Slavin & Cheung, 2005). Further research indicates that knowledge and skills acquired in a native language—literacy in particular—are "transferable" to the second language, providing students with a better understanding of the role of language in communication and how language works (K. Gutiérrez et al., 2002; Krashen, 1996).

Proponents of bilingual education also contend that immersion programs place unrealistic language demands on learners. They note that conversational English, such as that spoken on the playground, is learned quite quickly, but the cognitively demanding language needed for academic success is learned much more slowly (Peregoy & Boyle, 2005).

Critics of bilingual education attack it on several grounds. They contend that it is

- Divisive, encouraging groups of non-native English speakers to remain separate from mainstream American culture

- Ineffective, slowing the process of acquiring English for ELL students

- Inefficient, requiring expenditures for the training of bilingual teachers and materials that could be better spent on quality monolingual programs (English Only, 2006; Schlesinger, 1992).

Critics also cite their own research. For instance, one California school district reported that standardized test scores for students in the early grades—those most affected by the move from bilingual to immersion programs—improved from the 35th to the 45th percentile after students spent just 1 year in an immersion program, and additional research found similar positive results across California (Barone, 2000).

This issue addresses the second statement in our beginning-of-chapter survey, "Students who are not native English speakers learn English most effectively if they are required to speak only English in school." As you see from our discussion of this issue, the truth of the statement depends on whom you ask. Proponents of bilingual education would argue that the statement is false, whereas critics take the opposite position.

You Take a Position

Now it's your turn to take a position on the issue. State in writing whether you feel that schools should make efforts to retain students' native languages or whether it makes more sense to move students into English as quickly as possible, and provide a two-page rationale for your position.

For additional references and resources, go to the Companion Website at www.prenhall.com/kauchak, then to the Teaching in an Era of Reform module for Chapter 3. You can respond online or submit your response to your instructor.

Language Diversity in the Classroom

How will language diversity affect you as a teacher? First, although bilingual programs have been reduced, the need for teachers with ELL expertise will only increase. Experts estimate that U.S. schools will need an additional 290,000 teachers with ELL certification to meet the demands of these students (Zhao, 2002). In addition, 73 percent of urban school districts identified bilingual teachers as an immediate hiring need (Recruiting New Teachers, 2006). Teaching candidates who speak two languages, especially Spanish, are in high demand across the country.

Second, you will almost certainly have non-native English speakers in your classroom, and your ability to make informed professional decisions will be essential to help them learn. In working with students from diverse language backgrounds, your professional knowledge will be tested perhaps more than in any other area of your work.

Research offers the following suggestions for working with these students:

- Attempt to create a warm and inviting classroom environment by taking a personal interest in all students and involving everyone in learning activities.

- Avoid situations that draw attention to students' lack of English skills. One student commented:

  I think it is a bad strategy to make [ELLs] read aloud in front of other kids when they really can't. Teachers should give them time and make them more welcome by talking to them in Spanish first and later in English. They shouldn't expect them right away to do everything in English. (Thompson, 2000, p. 85)

- Mix teacher-centered instruction with learner-centered approaches, such as group work and cooperative learning, to allow students to interact informally and practice their developing language skills with the topics they study.

- Use concrete examples to provide reference points for new ideas and vocabulary (Echevarria & Graves, 2007; Peregoy & Boyle, 2005). For example, a middle school science teacher who was teaching the concept *bilateral symmetry* had a student come up to the front of the room and hold out his hands and feet to illustrate how both sides of his body were mirror images of each other.

These strategies represent good instructional practice for all students; for ELL students, they are essential.

Check Your Understanding

2.1 What has been the government's response to language diversity in our nation's schools?

2.2 What are the primary differences in the two major approaches schools use in working with English Language Learners?

2.3 What are the major ways that teachers can adapt their instruction to meet the needs of students with varying language backgrounds?

For feedback, go to Check Your Understanding *at the end of this chapter.*

Making Connections:
To deepen your understanding of the topics in this section of the chapter and integrate them with topics you've already studied, go to the *Making Connections* module for Chapter 3 at **www.prenhall.com/kauchak**. Respond to Question 6.

Gender

What Geri Peterson saw on her first day of teaching advanced-placement calculus was both surprising and disturbing. Of the 26 students watching her, only 4 were girls, and they sat quietly in class, responding only when she asked them direct questions. One reason that Geri had gone into teaching was to share her interest in math with other females, but this situation gave her little chance to do so.

Lori Anderson, the school counselor at an urban middle school, looked up from the desk where she was working on her annual report to the faculty. From her course work at the university and her internship, she knew that boys traditionally outnumber girls with respect to behavioral problems, but the numbers she was seeing were disturbing. In every category—referrals by teachers, absenteeism, tardies, and fights—boys out-numbered girls by a more than 2 to 1 margin. In addition, the number of boys referred to her for special education testing far exceeded referrals for girls.

Gender and Society

The fact that males and females are different is so obvious that we often don't think about it, but research has uncovered some important differences. Researchers have found, for example, that fe-males generally are more extroverted, anxious, and trusting; they're less assertive and have slightly lower self-esteem than males of the same age and background; and their verbal and motor skills tend to develop faster than do boys' (Berk, 2005, 2007; Gurian & Stevens, 2005). In addition, the play habits of boys and girls differ, with boys typically preferring more "rough and tumble" play. Gender differences make a significant contribution to diversity in the classroom (Figure 3.6).

Why do these gender differences exist? As with most other student differences, research suggests the causes are a combination of genetics and environment (Berk, 2005, 2007). Genetics result in physical differences such as size and growth rate and may also influence temperament, aggressiveness, and early verbal and exploratory behaviors. And some researchers now believe that boys' and girls' brains are wired differently for learning. For example, components of the brain that build word centers and fine motor skills are developmentally a year ahead in girls, which gives them an advantage in reading, use of pencils, cursive writing, and other small-motor tasks. Emotive centers in the brain are also more advanced for girls, making them calmer and more able to sit still for the long periods that classrooms often require. These researchers argue that schools, as they currently exist, may be more compatible with girls' innate genetic makeup (Gurian & Stevens, 2005).

Environment also plays an important role in shaping gender differences. From the day they're born, boys and girls are treated differently (Berk, 2005, 2007; McDevitt & Ormrod, 2007). Girls are given pink blankets, are called cute and pretty, and are handled delicately. Boys are dressed in blue, are regarded as handsome, and are seen as tougher, better coordinated, and hardier. Fathers are tougher with their sons and involve them in more physical stimulation and play; they tend to be gentler with their daughters and offer more sex-stereotyped toys, such as dolls and stuffed animals. Not surprisingly, boys and girls grow up looking and acting differently.

Figure 3.6 Gender and Diversity

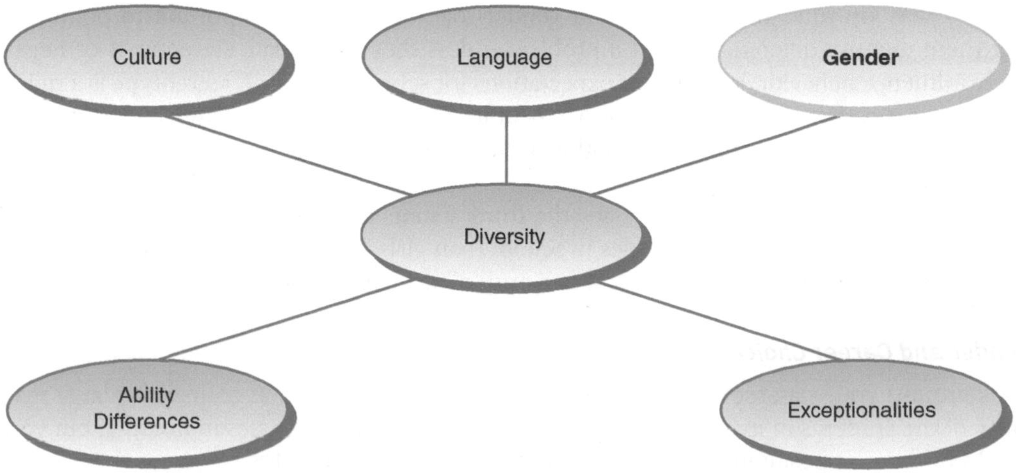

Gender and Schooling

Differences between boys and girls should generally be celebrated, but they become problems when societal or school forces limit the growth and academic potential of students—either male or female, as occurred in Geri Peterson's AP calculus class. For example, in high school, girls score lower than boys on the math sections of the SAT and ACT, two tests that are essential for college admission, and women score lower on all sections of the Graduate Record Exam, the Medical College Admissions Test, and admissions tests for law, dental, and optometry schools (Alperstein, 2005; Coley, 2001). These tests are important because they serve as gatekeepers to prestigious and high-paying professions.

Boys have their own problems. They outnumber girls in remedial English and math classes, are held back in grade more often, and are more than twice as likely to be placed in special education classes. Boys receive not only lower grades but also the majority of failing grades, and they drop out of school 4 times more often than girls. They are also cited for disciplinary infractions as much as ten times more frequently than girls (Gurian & Stevens, 2005; Hunsader, 2002).

So, what we have is an uneven picture of male and female strengths and weaknesses. But historically, concerns about girls received the most attention. For instance, in 1992's *How Schools Shortchange Girls,* the American Association of University Women (AAUW) argued that different treatment of boys and girls by both teachers and society seriously hampered the educational progress, self-esteem, and career choices of girls, with girls lagging well behind boys, particularly in math and science. In the 1998 *Gender Gaps: Where Schools Still Fail Our Children,* the AAUW reiterated many of its earlier claims.

These assertions have been controversial. For example, Christina Sommers (2000), author of *The War Against Boys: How Misguided Feminism Is Harming Our Young Men,* outlined many of the problems boys encounter in school that we described here. Yet it's the myth of the fragile girl that continues to receive the lion's share of attention, Sommers argued.

More recently, male problems in school have been receiving increased attention. For example, the January 30, 2006, issue of *Newsweek* focused on "The Trouble With Boys" as their lead story, and male educational problems extend into college. A *New York Times* article on the subject proclaimed, "At college women are leaving men in the dust" (Lewin, 2006, p. A1). As evidence, the article noted that women are more likely to attend college, earn a degree, get higher grades, and earn a master's degree.

As with gender differences in general, a combination of genetics and the environment probably explains the relative strengths and weaknesses of boys and girls in school. Because little can be done about genetics, more attention has been given to the environment, particularly **gender-role identity** differences, expectations and beliefs about appropriate roles and behaviors of the two sexes. Society as a whole treats boys and girls differently and expects them to develop fundamentally different gender-role identities. It's important to point out that these identity differences aren't a problem unless they perpetuate stereotypes or negatively influence behavior, learning, or expectations for school success. A **stereotype** is a rigid, simplistic caricature of a particular group of people. For example, women aren't good at math and men don't make good nurses are both inaccurate and damaging stereotypes because they limit career choices.

The preceding discussion addresses the third statement in our introductory questionnaire, "Boys generally get better grades in school than girls." As it turns out, quite the opposite is true; girls outperform boys on the majority of academic measures.

Gender and Career Choices

Look around your classroom for this course. If it's a typical education course, the large majority of the students in it are women. The same would be true in classes in nursing, but you would find the opposite in math, science, and computer-related fields.

Gender-role identity. Differences in expectations and beliefs about appropriate roles and behaviors of the two sexes.

Stereotype. A rigid, simplistic caricature of a particular group of people.

Where do stereotypes of "appropriate" careers for boys and girls originate? Society and the media perpetuate stereotypes, but ironically, parents—and particularly mothers—are often the most powerful sources. For instance, one study found that mothers who held negative gender-stereotyped attitudes about girls' ability in math adversely influenced their daughters' achievement in, and their attitudes toward, math (J. Campbell & Beaudry, 1998). When mothers believed that math was a male domain, their daughters took fewer math classes, got lower grades in them, and were less likely to pursue math-related fields such as computer science and statistics.

Parents can also have powerful positive influences on their children. One female software developer reported:

Role models are effective in preventing students from forming gender-stereotypic views about appropriate careers. [Geri Engberg/Geri Engberg Photography]

My mother always engendered in me the attitude that I could do absolutely anything I ever want to do. So she really gave me the confidence that is a big part of success in academics and maybe in other things—sometimes you get to a point where you don't have that much either skill or knowledge, and you have to just go on your guts or your confidence. You have to just kind of push your way through something until you have the time to accumulate the knowledge. And I think that that's something she engendered in me just by always being herself so confident of my abilities, rightly or wrongly. And my father certainly never detracted from that. He always portrayed her as being the smarter of the two. So I was raised in an environment where women were not only capable but were even potentially very well and highly regarded. (Zeldin & Pajares, 2000, p. 229)

Gender-stereotypic views can also negatively influence career decisions (Francis & Skelton, 2005; Wessel, 2005). Girls are less than half as likely as boys to pursue careers in engineering and physical and computer sciences (AAUW, 1998). At the high school level, only 11 percent of students taking the College Board advanced placement test in computer science in 2001 were women (Stabiner, 2003). The percentages of female physicians (26 percent), lawyers (27 percent), and engineers (8 percent), as well as new doctorates in science-related fields (38 percent), remain low as well (Wessel, 2005). The problem of gender-stereotypic views of math, science, and computer science careers is especially acute for minority females (Dance, 2002; Ginsberg, Shapiro, & Brown, 2004).

Similar problems exist for men. Go to any elementary or middle school, and you'll see that the faculties are overwhelmingly female, and, while more men are choosing nursing as a career, they remain in a distinct minority.

Single-Gender Classrooms and Schools

One response to gender-related problems has been the creation of **single-gender classes and schools**, where boys and girls are segregated for part or all of the day (Vail, 2002; Weaver-Hightower, 2005). The number of single-gender classrooms in the United States has increased ten-fold, from less than a dozen in 2000 to 211 in 2006 (Thiers, 2006).

Some research indicates that both girls and boys benefit in single-gender schools. Girls in these schools are more apt to assume leadership roles, take more math and science courses, have higher self-esteem, and have firmer beliefs that they are in control of their destinies (Datnow, Hubbard, & Conchas, 2001). Advocates of all-male schools claim that they promote male character development and are especially effective with males from low-income and minority families.

Single-gender classes and schools. Classes and schools where boys and girls are segregated for part or all of the day.

Effective teachers are sensitive to gender differences in the classroom and make a conscious effort to involve all students.
[David Young-Wolff/PhotoEdit Inc.]

This research raises other issues, however (Datnow et al., 2001; Vail, 2002). For example, because boys and girls are isolated from one another, single-gender schools and classes can exacerbate stereotypic views of the opposite sex and fail to prepare students for the "real world" in which males and females must work together (Datnow et al., 2001). In addition, some critics question the legality of single-gender schools and classrooms based on Title IX, the federal law that prohibits discrimination on the basis of gender (Fischer, Schimmel, & Stellman, 2006; Thiers, 2006). More research is needed to determine whether or not these experiments are effective for helping students learn and develop.

Gender and Schooling: Implications for Teachers

What can you do to prevent gender inequities in your classroom? To begin, you should be aware that you may have stereotypical attitudes of your own that can influence the way you interact with boys and girls. Research indicates that teachers interact with boys more often, ask them more questions, and those questions are more conceptual and abstract. In addition, boys are more likely to ask questions and volunteer comments about ideas being discussed in class (Good & Brophy, 2003). These differences increase as students move through school. In the extreme, these patterns can result in girls becoming less involved in learning activities and ultimately lowered achievement.

The following suggestions can help make your classroom more gender friendly for all students:

- Communicate openly with students about gender issues and concerns. Simply telling your students that teachers often treat boys and girls differently and that you're going to try to treat them equally is a positive first step.
- Encourage equal participation in all classes. One demanding but extremely effective technique is to call on everyone in your classes individually and by name, regardless of whether or not their hands are raised (Kauchak & Eggen, 2007).
- Make an effort to present cases of men and women in nonstereotypical roles, such as women who are engineers and men who are first-grade teachers.
- Encourage girls to pursue science-related careers and boys to consider careers in non-traditional male fields such as nursing or teaching (Francis & Skelton, 2005; Ginsberg et al., 2004).

The powerful influence that teachers can have on students is captured in the following remembrance from a 42-year-old female math professor:

It was the first time I had algebra, and I loved it. And then, all of a sudden, I excelled in it. And the teacher said, "Oh no, you should be in the honors course," or something like that. So, there's somebody who definitely influenced me because I don't think I ever even noticed. I mean, I didn't care one way or the other about mathematics. It was just something you had to do. I remember she used to run up and down the aisle. She was real excited. . . . She said, "Oh, you gotta go in this other class. You gotta." And she kind of pushed a little bit, and I was willing to be pushed. (Zeldin & Pajares, 2000, p. 232)

The student ended up majoring in math and ultimately became a math professor. When teachers believe in their students, students start believing in themselves. No one is suggesting that boys and girls are, or should be, the same. Teachers should, however, attempt to provide the same academic opportunities and encouragement for all students.

Making Connections:
To deepen your understanding of the topics in this section of the chapter and integrate them with topics you've already studied, go to the *Making Connections* module for Chapter 3 at www.prenhall.com/kauchak. Respond to questions 7 and 8.

Check Your Understanding

3.1   Explain how society influences gender differences in our students.

3.2   How should teachers respond to gender differences?

For feedback, go to Check Your Understanding *at the end of this chapter.*

Ability Differences

Melanie Parker, an intern from a nearby university, is ready to teach her first lesson in Mrs. Jenkins's middle school math class. The topic is the decimal system, including a review of place value, such as identifying 3,154 as composed of 3 "thousands," 1 "hundred," 5 "tens," and 4 "ones." Though nervous at the beginning, everything goes smoothly as she explains the concept and uses concrete materials to illustrate it. As she passes out practice worksheets, Mrs. Jenkins walks over to Melanie and whispers, "You're doing great. I need to run down to the office. I'll be right back." The students quickly begin to work, and Melanie's nervousness calms as she circulates among the students, periodically making comments. She notices that some are galloping through the assignment, others need minor help, and a few are totally confused. As she works with students, she notices that the quiet of the classroom is turning into a low buzz.

"Joel, why aren't you working?" Melanie asks as she turns to a student near her.

"I'm done."

"Hmm?" she thinks as she looks around the room.

"Beth, finish your assignment and stop talking," Melanie says, turning to another student visiting with her neighbor.

"I can't do this stuff!"

Melanie looks at the clock and sees that there are still 10 minutes to the bell, and, from the fidgeting and talking, it appears that several of the students have completed their assignment, while others have barely begun. Now what? (Adapted from Kauchak & Eggen, 2007.)

As experienced teachers know, and Melanie discovered, some students simply learn faster than others (Marzano, 2003), and this fact of classroom life makes instruction much more demanding. (Figure 3.7). In this section, we examine ability differences and describe how schools attempt to deal with these differences.

What Is Intelligence?

To begin this section, try to answer the following questions, and then decide what they have in common.

1. On what continent is Brazil?
2. A coat priced $45 is marked 1/3 off. When it still doesn't sell, the sale price is reduced by half. What is the price after the second discount?
3. Who was Albert Einstein?
4. In terms of size, what are the largest and smallest states in the United States?
5. How are a mountain and a plateau alike?

Figure 3.7 Ability Differences and Diversity

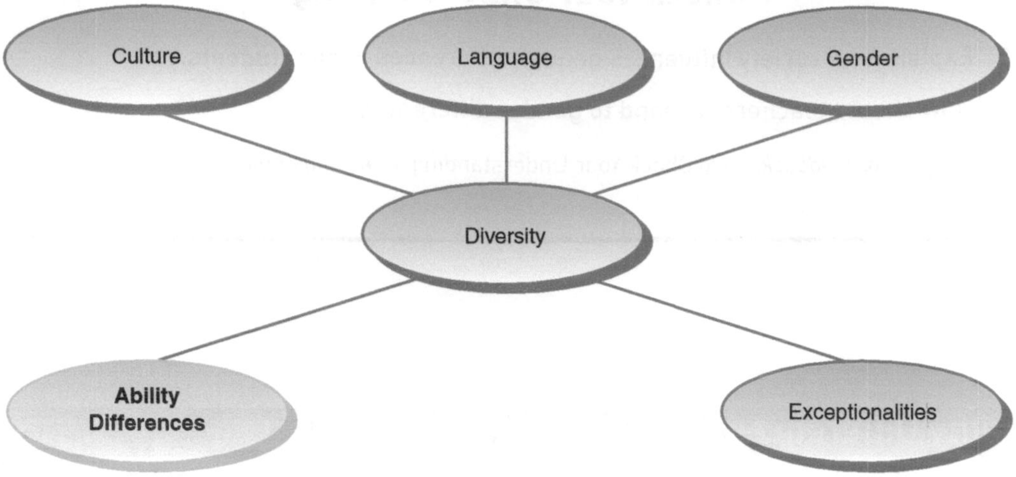

The common feature of these questions may surprise you. Each is similar to an item found on the Wechsler Intelligence Scale for Children—Third Edition (Wechsler, 2003), one of the most widely used intelligence tests in the United States. In other words, experts believe that the ability to answer questions such as these is an indicator of a person's intelligence, or ability to learn new information.

We all have intuitive notions of intelligence; it's how "sharp" people are, how much they know, how quickly and easily they learn, and how perceptive and sensitive they are. Researchers, however, more precisely define **intelligence** as the capacity to acquire knowledge, the ability to think and reason in the abstract, and the ability to solve problems (Louis et al., 2000; Sattler, 2001). It is these three dimensions that intelligence tests attempt to measure. These three dimensions also play a powerful role in determining learning ability and school success.

Changes in Views of Intelligence

Historically, researchers believed that intelligence was a unitary trait and that all people could be classified along a single continuum of "general" intelligence. Thinking has changed, however, and some researchers now believe that intelligence is composed of several distinct dimensions that may occur alone or in various combinations in different individuals.

Howard Gardner (1983, 1999), a Harvard psychologist who did groundbreaking work in this area, is one of the most well-known proponents of this idea. He proposed a theory of **multiple intelligences**, which suggests that overall intelligence is composed of eight relatively independent dimensions (Table 3.2).

Gardner's theory makes intuitive sense. For example, we all know people who don't seem particularly "sharp" analytically but who excel in getting along with others. This ability serves them well in a number of jobs requiring "people" skills such as sales and even teaching, and in some instances they're more successful than their "brighter" peers. Other people seem very self-aware and can capitalize on their personal strengths and minimize their weaknesses. Gardner would describe these people as high in *interpersonal* and *intrapersonal* intelligence, respectively.

While popular with educators, Gardner's theory also has its critics. Some caution that the theory and its applications have not been validated by research (Corno et al., 2002). Others disagree with the assertion that abilities in specific domains, such as naturalist or musical, qualify as separate forms of intelligence (McMahon et al., 2004; Sattler, 2001).

Despite the theory's popularity with teachers, most classrooms focus heavily on the linguistic and logical-mathematical dimensions and virtually ignore the others (Viadero, 2003b). If the other dimensions are to develop, however, students need experiences with them. For example, cooperative learning activities can help students develop interpersonal intelligence, participation in sports or dance can improve bodily-kinesthetic abilities, and playing in a band or singing in choral groups can improve musical intelligence.

Intelligence. The capacity to acquire knowledge, the ability to think and reason in the abstract, and the ability to solve problems.

Multiple intelligences. A theory that suggests that overall intelligence is composed of eight relatively independent dimensions.

132

TABLE 3.2   Gardner's Eight Intelligences

Dimension	Description	Example of an Individual Who Might Be High in This Dimension
Linguistic intelligence	Sensitivity to the meaning and order of words and the varied uses of language	Poet, journalist
Logical-mathematical intelligence	The ability to handle long chains of reasoning and to recognize patterns and order in the world	Scientist, mathematician
Musical intelligence	Sensitivity to pitch, melody, and tone	Composer, violinist
Spatial intelligence	The ability to perceive the visual world accurately and to re-create, transform, or modify aspects of the world on the basis of one's perceptions	Sculptor, navigator
Bodily-kinesthetic intelligence	A fine-tuned ability to use the body and to handle objects	Dancer, athlete
Interpersonal Intelligence	An understanding of interpersonal relations and the ability to make distinctions among others	Therapist, salesperson
Intrapersonal intelligence	Access to one's own "feeling life"	Self-aware individual
Naturalist intelligence	The ability to recognize similarities and differences in the physical world	Biologist, anthropologist

Source: Adapted from H. Gardner and Hatch (1989) and Chekles (1997).

This section provides one perspective related to the fourth statement in our introductory questionnaire, "Students who are talented in one area of school are generally talented in all the others." A unitary view of intelligence would agree with the statement, but Gardner's theory of multiple intelligences suggests that intelligence is multifaceted and that students can excel in different ways in different areas.

Now, let's see how schools respond to differences in students' abilities to learn.

Ability Grouping and Tracking: Schools' Responses to Differences in Ability

The most common way schools respond to differences in students' abilities is by **ability grouping**, the practice of placing students of similar aptitude and achievement histories together in an attempt to match instruction to the needs of different groups (Holloway, 2001; Lou, Abrami, & Spence, 2000).

Ability grouping is popular in elementary schools and typically exists in two forms. **Between-class ability grouping** divides all students in a given grade into groups, such as high, medium, and low, whereas **within-class ability grouping** divides students within one classroom into ability groups. Most elementary teachers endorse ability grouping, particularly in reading and math.

In middle, junior high, and high schools, ability grouping goes further, with high-ability students studying advanced and college preparatory courses and lower-ability classmates receiving vocational or work-related instruction. In some schools, students are grouped only in certain areas, such as English or math. In others, the grouping exists across all content areas, a practice called **tracking**, which places students in a series of different classes or curricula on the basis of ability and career goals. Some form of tracking exists in most middle, junior high, and high schools (Oakes, 2005).

Why is ability grouping so common? Advocates claim that it increases learning because it allows teachers to adjust methods, materials, and instructional pace to better meet students' needs (Gladden, 2003). Because lesson components and assessments are similar for students in a particular group, instruction is also easier for the teacher, they argue.

Ability grouping. The practice of placing students of similar aptitude and achievement histories together in an attempt to match instruction to the needs of different groups.

Between-class ability grouping. Grouping that divides all students in a given grade into high, medium, and low groups.

Within-class ability grouping. Grouping that divides students within one classroom into ability groups.

Tracking. The practice of ability grouping that places students in a series of different classes or curricula on the basis of ability and career goals.

However, research has uncovered several serious problems with tracking:

- Homogeneously grouped low-ability students achieve less than heterogeneously grouped students of similar ability (Good & Brophy, 2003).
- Within-class grouping creates logistical problems for teachers, because different lessons and assignments are required, and monitoring students in different tasks is difficult (Good & Brophy, 2003).
- Improper placements occur, and placement tends to become permanent. Cultural minorities are underrepresented in high-ability classes and overrepresented in those with lower-ability students (Oakes, 2005).
- Low groups are stigmatized, and the self-esteem and motivation of students in these groups decrease (Stipek, 2002).

In addition, absentee rates, delinquency, truancy, and dropping out of school are much higher for students in low groups than for students in general (Slavin, 2006). Tracking also often results in racial or cultural segregation of students, which impedes social development and the ability to form friendships across cultural groups (Oakes & Wells, 2002).

Teachers can avoid many of the problems associated with ability grouping and tracking by having appropriately high expectations for all students and working with them in heterogeneous groups whenever possible. Instructional adaptations will be needed, however, to ensure the success of students of varying abilities. Some effective strategies include the following:

Effective teachers accommodate ability differences in a number of ways including group work, peer tutoring, and assignment options. [Scott Cunningham/Merrill]

- Break long assignments into shorter ones, and provide additional scaffolding and support for those who need it.
- Give students who need it more time to complete assignments.
- Provide peer tutors for students requiring extra help.
- Use small-group work in which students help each other learn.
- Provide options on some assignments, such as giving students the choice of presenting a report orally or in writing (Tomlinson, 2003; Tomlinson & Callahan, 2001).

Effective teachers adapt instruction to meet the needs of all students; these adaptations are essential for low-ability students.

Learning Styles

One thing Chris Burnette remembers from his methods classes is the need for variety. He has been primarily using large-group discussions in his middle school social studies classes, and most of the students seem to respond okay. But others seem disinterested, and their attention often drifts.

Today, Chris decides to try a small-group activity involving problem solving. The class has been studying the growth of American cities, and he wants the students to think about solutions to some of the problems of big cities. As he watches the groups interact, he is surprised at what he sees. Some of the students who are most withdrawn in whole-class discussions are leaders in the groups.

"Great!" he thinks. But at the same time, he notes that some of his more active students are sitting back and not getting involved.

How do you like to study? Do you learn most effectively with others or alone? Do you prefer teacher presentations or reading a textbook? Your answers to these questions reflect your unique **learning style**, or your preferred way of learning, problem solving, or processing information (Denig, 2003).

One approach to learning styles distinguishes between deep and surface approaches to processing information (Evans, Kirby, & Fabrigar, 2003). For instance, when you study a new idea, do you ask yourself how it relates to other ideas, what examples of the idea exist, and how it might apply in a different context? If so, you were using a deep-processing approach. On the other hand, if you simply memorized the definition, you were using a surface approach.

As you might expect, deep-processing approaches result in higher achievement if tests focus on understanding and application, but surface approaches can be successful if tests emphasize fact learning and memorization. Students who use deep-processing approaches also tend to be more intrinsically motivated, whereas those who use surface approaches tend to be more motivated by high grades and their performance compared to others (Pintrich & Schunk, 2002).

Learning Styles: Research Results

The idea of *learning styles* is popular in education, and many consultants use this label when they conduct in-service workshops for teachers. These practices are controversial, however. Advocates claim matching learning environments to learner preference results in increased achievement and improved attitudes (Carbo, 1997; Farkas, 2003). Critics counter by questioning the validity of the tests used to measure learning styles (Stahl, 1999), and they also cite research indicating that attempts to match learning environments to learning preferences have resulted in no increases and, in some cases, even decreases in learning (Brophy, 2004; Klein, 2003).

Learning Styles: Implications for Teachers

The concept of *learning style* has three implications for teachers. First, it reminds us of the need to vary instruction, since no instructional approach will be preferred by all students (Brophy, 2004). Chris Burnette discovered this when he tried to implement a one-size-fits-all approach to his teaching. Effective teachers use a variety of instructional strategies. Second, awareness of learning styles can increase our sensitivity to differences in our students, making it more likely that we will respond to our students as individuals. Third, it suggests that teachers should encourage students to think about their own learning, that is, to develop their metacognition.

Metacognition refers to students' awareness of the ways they learn most effectively and their ability to control these factors. For example, a student who realizes that studying with a stereo on reduces her ability to concentrate, and then turns the stereo off, is demonstrating metacognition. Students who are metacognitive can adjust strategies to match learning tasks better than their less metacognitive peers can and, as a result, their achievement is higher (Eggen & Kauchak, 2007). By encouraging students to think about how they learn best, teachers provide students with a powerful learning tool they can use throughout their lives.

> **Making Connections:** To deepen your understanding of the topics in this section of the chapter and integrate them with topics you've already studied, go to the *Making Connections* module for Chapter 3 at **www.prenhall.com/kauchak**. Respond to questions 9–13.

Check Your Understanding

4.1 Explain the differences in current definitions of intelligence.

4.2 How do schools respond to differences in ability? What does research suggest about its application in classrooms?

4.3 What are learning styles? What are the implications of learning styles for teachers?

 For feedback, go to Check Your Understanding *at the end of this chapter.*

> **Learning styles.** Students' personal approaches to learning, problem solving, and processing information.
>
> **Metacognition.** Students' awareness of the ways they learn most effectively and their ability to control these factors.

Students With Exceptionalities

Celina Curtis, a beginning first-grade teacher in a large urban elementary school, has survived her hectic first weeks. She is beginning to feel comfortable, but at the same time, some things are bothering her.

"It's kind of frustrating," she admits, as she shares her half-hour lunch break with Clarisse, a "veteran" of 3 years who has become her friend and confidant. "I think I'm teaching, but some of the kids just don't seem to get it."

"Maybe you're being too hard on yourself," Clarisse responds. "Students are different. Remember some of the stuff you studied in college? One thing the professors emphasized was that we should be trying our best to treat students as individuals."

"Well, . . . yes, I understand that, but that seems too simple. I still have this feeling. For instance, there's Rodney. You've seen him on the playground. He's cute, but his engine is stuck on fast. I can barely get him to sit in his seat, much less work.

"When he sits down to do a reading assignment, he really struggles. In math and science he's just fine, except when he has to read something. And he seems like a bright kid.

"Then there's Amelia; she's so sweet, but she simply doesn't get it. I've tried everything under the sun with her. I explain it, and the next time, it's as if it's all brand new. I feel sorry for her, because I know she gets frustrated when she can't keep up with the other kids. When I work with her one-on-one, it seems to help, but I don't have enough time to spend with her. She's falling farther and farther behind."

"Maybe it's not your fault. You're supposed to be bright and energetic and do your best, but you're going to burn yourself out if you keep this up," Clarisse cautions "Check with the Teacher Assistance Team. Maybe these students need some extra help."

As Celina discovered, students differ in several important ways, and effective teachers consider these differences when they plan and teach (see Figure 3.8). **Students with exceptionalities** are learners who need special help and resources to reach their full potential. Exceptionalities include **disabilities**, functional limitations or an inability to perform a certain act, such as hear or walk, as well as **giftedness**, abilities at the upper end of the continuum that require support beyond regular classroom instruction to reach full potential. Extra help and resources can include special educators, special schools, self-contained classrooms designed especially for these students, resource rooms where students can go to receive supplemental instruction, and inclusion in regular classrooms with the support of specially trained professionals.

Figure 3.8 Exceptionalities and Diversity

Students with exceptionalities. Learners who need special help and resources to reach their full potential.

Disabilities. Functional limitations or an inability to perform a certain act, such as hear or walk.

Giftedness. Abilities at the upper end of the continuum that require support beyond regular classroom instruction to reach full potential.

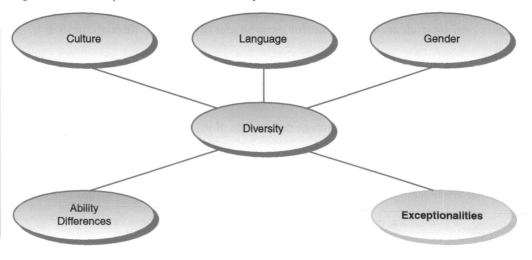

Special education refers to instruction designed to meet the unique needs of students with exceptionalities. The terms *children with exceptionalities, students with special needs,* and *individuals with disabilities* have all been used to describe students needing additional help to reach their full potential. Note that in all of these terms, *children, students,* and *individuals* come first. This "people-first" practice emphasizes that, foremost, these individuals are people like you and other students, and they deserve to be treated with the same care and respect.

Federal Laws Change the Way Schools and Teachers Help Students With Exceptionalities

In the past, students with exceptionalities were separated from their peers and placed in segregated classrooms or schools. However, instruction in these settings was often inferior, achievement was no better than in regular education classrooms, and students didn't learn the social and life skills they needed to function well in the real world (Karten, 2005; T. Smith et al., 2004). Educators and lawmakers looked for other ways to help these students.

In 1975 the U.S. Congress passed Public Law 94-142, the Individuals with Disabilities Education Act (IDEA). A central component of IDEA was the Free and Public Education (FAPE) provision, which guarantees a free public education for all students with exceptionalities. This law helped ensure consistency in how different states addressed the needs of these students. IDEA, combined with recent amendments, provides the following guidelines for working with students having exceptionalities. Schools should

- Guarantee an appropriate education for all students with exceptionalities.
- Identify the needs of students with exceptionalities through nondiscriminatory assessment.
- Involve parents in developing each child's educational program.
- Create an environment that is the least restrictive possible for promoting learning.
- Develop an individualized education program (IEP) of study for each student.
- Guarantee the opportunity for schools and families to hold each other accountable for a students' education.

Since 1975, Congress has amended IDEA five times in attempts to ensure that all children with disabilities are protected and provided with a free and appropriate public education (Howard, 2006). For example, amendments in 1986 extended the rights and protections of IDEA to children aged 3 through 5 and held states accountable for locating young children who need special education services. That provision is sometimes called Child Find.

Amendment 1997, known as IDEA 97, clarified and extended the quality of services to students with disabilities. This amendment helped ensure protection against discrimination in testing, and it provided due process and an IEP to meet the specific learning needs of each student. This amendment also requires districts to keep confidential records of each child and share them with parents on request.

More recently, Congress enacted another change called IDEA 2004 that has the following elements (Council for Exceptional Children, 2005):

- Methods will be established to reduce the number of students from culturally and linguistically diverse backgrounds who are inappropriately placed in special education.
- Discipline procedures will be put in place that allow districts to remove students from the classroom who "inflict serious bodily injury" on others.
- Students with disabilities will be included in accountability systems, but districts will be provided with more flexibility in meeting the highly qualified teacher requirements of the NCLB legislation of 2001.
- The special education paperwork burden will be reduced by deleting short-term objectives and benchmarks from IEPs (except for students who take alternative assessments).

The effectiveness of these legislative changes will be determined over the next few years.

Special education. Instruction designed to meet the unique needs of students with exceptionalities.

Inclusion attempts to integrate students with special needs into the regular classroom through instructional adaptations that meet their special needs. [Scott Cunningham/Merrill]

The Evolution Toward Inclusion

As educators realized that segregated classes and services were not meeting the needs of students with exceptionalities, they searched for alternatives. The first was **mainstreaming**, the practice of moving students with exceptionalities from segregated settings into regular education classrooms, often for selected activities only. Popular in the 1970s, mainstreaming began the move away from segregated services. Mainstreaming had problems, however, as one student's experience documents:

> *When I got to sixth grade, they put me in regular ed. classes. The work was way too hard, and the teachers did not try to help me. They went way too fast, and I got confused. I got scared and angry. I needed the help, but none of the teachers seemed to care. They didn't pay attention to me. No one ever noticed that I couldn't keep up with the work they were giving me. They were too busy teaching. (Schrimpf, 2006, p. 87)*

Students with exceptionalities were often mainstreamed into regular classrooms without adequate support and services, and the results were unsatisfactory (Hardman et al., 2005).

In attempting to solve these problems, educators developed the concept of the **least restrictive environment (LRE,)** one that places students in as normal an educational setting as possible while still meeting their special academic, social, and physical needs. Broader than the concept of mainstreaming, the LRE allows a greater range of placement options, from full-time placement in the regular classroom to placement in a separate facility, if parents and educators decide that this environment best meets the child's needs (see Figure 3.9).

As educators considered mainstreaming and the LRE, they gradually developed the concept of **inclusion**, a comprehensive approach to educating students with exceptionalities that includes a total, systematic, and coordinated web of services. Inclusion has three components:

- Include students with special needs in a regular school campus.
- Place students with special needs in age- and grade-appropriate classrooms.
- Provide special education support within the regular classroom.

Mainstreaming. The practice of moving students with exceptionalities from segregated settings into regular education classrooms.

Least restrictive environment (LRE). The placement of students in as normal an educational setting as possible while still meeting their special academic, social, and physical needs.

Inclusion. A comprehensive approach to educating students with exceptionalities that advocates a total, systematic, and coordinated web of services.

138

Figure 3.9 Educational Service Options for Implementing the LRE

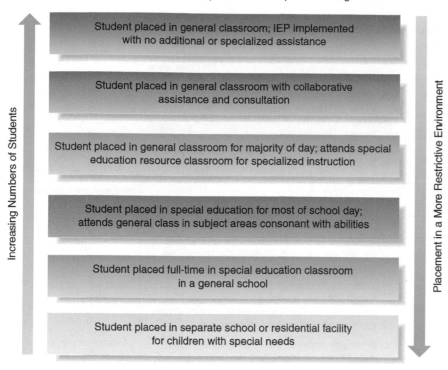

Source: U.S. Department of Education, 2007.

Individualized Education Program

To ensure that inclusion works and learners with exceptionalities don't get lost in the regular classroom, a team of educators prepares an **individualized education program (IEP)**. Special education and general education teachers, resource professionals, parents, and sometimes the student collaborate to devise this individually prescribed instructional plan. The IEP specifies the following:

- An assessment of the student's current level of performance
- Long- and short-term objectives
- Services or strategies to be used to ensure the student's academic progress
- Schedules for implementing the plan
- Criteria to be used in evaluating the plan's success

A sample IEP is illustrated in Figure 3.10. It has three important features. First, the initials of all participants indicate that its development is a cooperative effort. Second, the information in Sections 3–7 is specific enough to guide the classroom teacher and special education personnel as they implement the plan. Classroom teachers play an integral role in helping to create and implement IEPs. Third, the mother's signature indicates that a parent was involved in developing the plan and agrees with its provisions.

Inclusion and No Child Left Behind

No Child Left Behind (NCLB) has had a major influence on education. It also is affecting the education of students with exceptionalities. In an attempt to clarify how the NCLB Act would influence these students, the U.S. Department of Education issued regulations requiring students with exceptionalities to be tested as part of NCLB's comprehensive testing program (U.S. Department of Education, 2003b). Although states are allowed to create alternative tests and standards for these students, the test scores are used in determining whether a school has made adequate yearly progress.

Individualized education program (IEP) An individually prescribed instructional plan devised by special education and general education teachers, resource professionals, and parents (and sometimes the student).

Figure 3.10 Individualized Education Program (IEP)

INDIVIDUALIZED EDUCATION PROGRAM

Date _____ 3-1-07 _____

(1) Student	(2) Committee	Initial
Name: Joe S.	Mrs. Wrens — Principal	D.Q.W.
School: Adams	Mrs. Snow — Regular Teacher	A.S.
Grade: 5	Mr. LaJoie — Counselor	S.L.J.
Current Placement: Regular Class/Resource Room	Mr. Thomas — Resource Teacher	M.T.
	Mr. Ryan — School Psychologist	H.R.R.
	Mrs. S. — Parent	J.S.
Date of Birth: 10-1-95 Age: 11-5	Joe S. — Student	Joe L. EP from 3-15-07 to 3-15-08

(3) Present Level of Educational Functioning	(4) Annual Goal Statements	(5) Instructional Objectives	(6) Objective Criteria and Evaluation
MATH Strengths 1. Can successfully compute addition and subtraction problems to two places with regrouping and zeros. 2. Knows 100 basic multiplication facts. Weaknesses 1. Frequently makes computational errors on problems with which he has had experience. 2. Does not complete seatwork. Key Math total score of 2.1 Grade Equivalent.	Joe will apply knowledge of regrouping in addition and renaming in subtraction to four-digit numbers.	1. When presented with 20 addition problems of 3-digit numbers requiring two renamings, the student will compute answers at a rate of one problem per minute and an accuracy of 90%. 2. When presented with 20 subtraction problems of 3-digit numbers requiring two renamings, the student will compute answers at the rate of one problem per minute with 90% accuracy. 3. When presented with 20 addition problems of 4-digit numbers requiring three renamings, the student will compute answers at a rate of one problem per minute and an accuracy of 90%. 4. When presented with 20 subtraction problems of 4-digit numbers requiring three renamings, the student will compute answers at a rate of one problem per minute with 90% accuracy.	Teacher-made tests (weekly) Teacher-made tests (weekly) Teacher-made tests (weekly)

(7) Educational Services to be provided

Services Required	Date initiated	Duration of Service	Individual Responsible for the Service
Regular reading-adapted	3-15-07	3-15-08	Reading Improvement Specialist and Special Education Teacher
Resource room	3-15-07	3-15-08	Special Education Teacher
Counselor consultant	3-15-07	3-15-08	Counselor
Monitoring diet and general health	3-15-07	3-15-08	School Health Nurse

Extent of time in the regular education program: 60% increasing to 80%
Justification of the educational placement:
It is felt that the structure of the resource room can best meet the goals stated for Joe, especially when coordinated with the regular classroom.
It is also felt that Joe could profit enormously from talking with a counselor. He needs someone with whom to talk and with whom he can share his feelings.

(8) I have had the opportunity to participate in the development of the Individualized Education Program.
   I agree with the Individualized Education Program   (✓)
   I disagree with the Individualized Education Program   ( )
Parents Signature _____ Mrs S. _____

Source: Adapted from *Developing and Implementing Individualized Education Programs* (3rd ed., pp. 308, 316) by B. B. Strickland and A. P. Tumbull, 1990, Upper Soddle River, NJ: Merrill/Prentice Hall.

Advocates of this testing requirement claim that teachers will expect more of students and work harder at teaching students with exceptionalities if they know these students will be tested (Samuels, 2006a). The logistics of how to implement these new guidelines are still being worked out.

Categories of Special Education Students

About 6 million students in the United States are enrolled in special education programs, two thirds of them for relatively minor problems (Heward, 2006). Approximately 14 percent of students in a typical school receive special education services; 78 percent are in a regular classroom for a significant portion of the school day (Kober, 2006).

Federal legislation has created categories to identify students eligible for special education services, and educators use these categories in developing programs to meet students' specific needs. The use of categories is controversial, however. Advocates argue that categories provide a common language for professionals and encourage specialized instruction that meets the specific needs of students (Heward, 2006). Opponents claim that categories are arbitrary, many differences exist within them, and categorizing encourages educators to treat students as labels rather than as people. Despite the controversy, these categories are widely used, so they should be part of your professional knowledge base.

The federal law describing the educational rights of students with disabilities, the IDEA, discussed earlier in this chapter, lists 13 categories of disability. These are listed by order of frequency in Table 3.3.

TABLE 3.3 Number of Students Ages 6–21 Who Received Special Education Services Under the Federal Government's Disability Categories (2003–2004 School Year)

Disability Category	Number	Percentage of Total
Specific learning disabilities	2,816,361	47.2
Speech or language impairments	1,118,543	18.8
Mental retardation	570,643	9.6
Emotional disturbance	482,597	8.1
Other health impairments	449,093	7.5
Autism	140,473	2.3
Multiple disabilities	131,225	2.2
Hearing impairments	71,188	1.2
Orthopedic impairments	67,772	1.1
Developmental delay	65,878	1.1
Visual impairments	25,294	0.4
Traumatic brain injury	22,459	0.4
Deaf-blindness	1,603	<0.1
All disabilities	5,963,129	100.0

Source: U.S. Department of Education. (2004b). Individuals with Disabilities Education Act (IDEA) data (Table AA3). Washington, DC: Author. Available at http://www.ideadata.org/PartBdata.asp.

Note that the top four categories in Table 3.3 make up more than three fourths of the exceptional student population. They are

- Students who have specific learning disabilities (47 percent)
- Students with communication disorders (19 percent)
- Students with mental retardation (10 percent)
- Student with emotional disturbance or behavior disorders (8 percent)

We focus on these four main categories in the sections that follow.

Learning Disabilities

Students with **learning disabilities** have exceptionalities that involve difficulties in acquiring and using listening, speaking, reading, writing, reasoning, or mathematical abilities (National Joint Committee on Learning Disabilities, 1994). Problems with reading, writing, and listening are most common. Rodney, in the case study that began this section, probably had a learning disability; he did fine in subjects that didn't require a lot of reading but struggled in those that did.

Students with learning disabilities make up the largest group of students with exceptionalities—almost half of the special education population and 4.4 percent of the total school population (U.S. Department of Education, 2004b). The category first became widely used in the early 1960s, and the number of school-age children diagnosed as learning disabled has continually increased since then.

Students with learning disabilities have the following problems:

- Uneven performance (e.g., capabilities in one area, extreme weaknesses in others)
- Hyperactivity and difficulty in concentrating
- Lack of follow-through in completion of assignments
- Disorganization and tendency toward distraction

Students with learning disabilities don't necessarily have all of these problems, and some are typical of general learning problems or immaturity. Unlike developmental lags, however, problems associated with learning disabilities, instead of disappearing, tend to increase over time. Students fall further behind in achievement, behavior problems increase, and self-esteem declines (Hardman et al., 2005; Heward, 2006). Lowered achievement and reduced self-esteem interact, and significant learning problems often result.

Identification is the first and perhaps the most important step in dealing with a learning disability. Classroom teachers are crucial in this process, because they collect work samples and keep records of the specific areas where students are experiencing problems with classroom work. This information is also valuable in preparing an IEP for the student.

Traditionally, educators used a discrepancy model to identify learning disabilities (Turnbull et al., 2007). For example, if differences between students' scores on intelligence tests and their performance on specific areas of the curriculum, like math or reading, exist, then educators suspect a learning disability (Shaywitz & Shaywitz, 2004). However, experts caution that language-intensive intelligence tests may not adequately identify learning disabilities in students who are ELLs (Gunderson & Siegel, 2001). This is where the classroom teacher's input and documentation are so essential.

Communication Disorders

Communication disorders are exceptionalities that interfere with students' abilities to receive and understand information from others and express their own ideas. They exist in two forms: speech and language disorders (Bernstein & Tiegerman-Farber, 2002). **Speech disorders** (sometimes called *expressive disorders*) involve problems in forming and sequencing sounds. Stuttering and mispronouncing words, such as saying, "I taw it" for "I saw it," are examples.

Learning disabilities.
Exceptionalities that involve difficulties in acquiring and using listening, speaking, reading, writing, reasoning, or mathematical abilities.

Communication disorders.
Exceptionalities that interfere with students' abilities to receive and understand information from others and to express their own ideas or questions.

Speech disorders (or *expressive disorders*).
Problems in forming and sequencing sounds.

TABLE 3.4   Kinds of Speech Disorders

Disorder	Description	Example
Articulation disorders	Difficulty in producing certain sounds, including substituting, distorting, and omitting	"Wabbit" for *rabbit* "Thit" for *sit* "Only" for *lonely*
Fluency disorders	Repetition of the first sound of a word (stuttering) and other problems in producing "smooth" speech	"Y, Y, Y, Yes"
Voice disorders	Problems with the larynx or air passageways in the nose or throat	High-pitched or nasal voice

As shown in Table 3.4, there are three kinds of speech disorders: articulation, fluency, and voice. If they are chronic, a therapist is usually required, but sensitive teachers can help students cope with the emotional and social problems that are often associated with them.

Language disorders (also called *receptive disorders*) include problems with understanding language or using language to express ideas. Language disorders are often connected to other problems, such as a hearing impairment, learning disabilities, or mental retardation (Turnbull et al., 2007). Symptoms of a language disorder include

- Seldom speaking, even during play
- Using few words or very short sentences
- Overrelying on gestures to communicate

Because they affect learning, language disorders are more serious. The vast majority of students learn to communicate quite well by the time they start school, but a small percentage (less than 1 percent) continue to experience problems expressing themselves verbally (Hardman et al., 2005; Heward, 2006).

If teachers suspect a speech or language disorder, they should keep cultural diversity in mind. As you saw earlier in the chapter, English is not the primary language for many students. The difficulties these students encounter in learning both content and a second language should not be confused with communication disorders. English language learners will respond to an enriched language environment and teacher patience and understanding. Students with communication disorders require the help of a speech and language specialist who not only works individually with the student but also assists the classroom teacher in adapting instruction.

Mental Retardation

Students with **mental retardation** have an exceptionality that includes limitations in intellectual functioning, as indicated by difficulties in learning, and problems with adaptive skills, such as communication, self-care, and social ability (Turnbull et al., 2007). Before the 1960s, definitions of mental retardation were based primarily on below-average scores on intelligence tests, but this approach had three problems. First, errors in testing sometimes resulted in misdiagnoses, and second, disproportionate numbers of minorities and non-English-speaking students were identified as mentally retarded (Hallahan & Kauffman, 2003; Hardman, Drew, & Egan, 2005). Third, individuals with the same intelligence test scores varied widely in their ability to cope with the real world, and these differences couldn't be explained based on the tests alone (Heward, 2006). Because of these limitations, adaptive functioning was added to the definition.

Language disorders (or *receptive disorders*). Problems with understanding language or using language to express ideas.

Mental retardation. An exceptionality that includes limitations in intellectual functioning, as indicated by difficulties in learning, and problems with adaptive skills, such as communication, self-care, and social ability.

Adaptive functioning is important because it determines how the student will be integrated into the regular classroom. Only about 10 percent of students with mental retardation are served in separate facilities, which means that the other 90 percent have some type of access to regular classrooms (Turnbull et al., 2007). The key to successful classroom interventions is increased instructional supports that make learning possible and prevent the frustrations of failure. These include shorter assignments, modified assignments, help from other students, as well as assistance from the resource teacher.

Behavior Disorders

Students with **behavior disorders** have exceptionalities involving the display of serious and persistent age-inappropriate behaviors that result in social conflict, personal unhappiness, and school failure. The IDEA uses the term *emotional disturbance,* but educators more commonly use the term *behavior disorder.* In the definition, the words *serious* and *persistent* are important. Many children occasionally fight with their peers, and all children go through periods when they want to be alone. When these patterns are chronic and interfere with normal development and school performance, however, a behavior disorder may exist.

Estimates of the frequency of behavior disorders vary (Hardman et al., 2005). Some suggest that about 1 percent of the total school population and about 9 percent of the special education population have these disorders (U.S. Department of Education, 2004b), whereas others suggest that the percentage is closer to 6 to 10 percent of the total population (Hallahan & Kauffman, 2003). Identification is a problem because the characteristics are elusive, making diagnosis difficult (Turnbull et al., 2007).

Because the line between typical school-age behavioral problems and a behavior disorder is a fine one, the teacher plays a crucial role in identifying this problem. Experts suggest that the following problems may be key indicators:

- Inability to build and maintain satisfactory interpersonal relationships
- Aggressive behaviors
- Pervasive presence of unhappiness or depression (Turnbull et al., 2007)

Teacher observations are important for both identifying a problem and suggesting productive ways for dealing with it. Behavioral approaches that use systematic applications of reinforcement combined with modeling are often effective. For example, if a first grader has difficulties making friends on the playground, the teacher might model how to approach a playmate with a toy and ask to play. Praise and feedback after a successful attempt reinforces this newly learned behavior.

Students Who Are Gifted and Talented

Although we don't typically think of gifted and talented students as having exceptionalities, they often have learning needs not met by the regular education curriculum. **Gifted and talented** is a designation given to students at the upper end of the ability continuum who need special services to reach their full potential. At one time, the term *gifted* was used to identify these students, but the category has been enlarged to include both students who do well on intelligence tests and those who demonstrate above-average talents in a variety of areas such as math, creative writing, and music (G. Davis & Rimm, 2004).

The first step in meeting the needs of students who are gifted and talented is early identification. Experts recommend using a variety of methods for identification, including standardized test scores, teacher nominations, creativity measures, and peer and parent nominations (Cross, 2005; G. Davis & Rimm, 2004). Because teacher nomination is one of the methods used for identification, you will play an important role in this process. Although the majority of states require that schools identify students who are gifted and talented, in 2003 only 27 had laws requiring that schools provide services for them (Shaunessy, 2003). Nine states, however, require that schools prepare an IEP, such as that used for students in special education, detailing specific goals for meeting a gifted student's educational needs.

Behavior disorders. Exceptionalities involving the display of serious and persistent age-inappropriate behaviors that result in social conflict, personal unhappiness, and school failure.

Gifted and talented. A designation given to students at the upper end of the ability continuum who need special services to reach their full potential.

TABLE 3.5 Acceleration and Enrichment Options for Students Who Are Gifted and Talented

Enrichment Options	Acceleration Options
1. Independent study and independent projects	1. Early admission to kindergarten and first grade
2. Learning centers	2. Grade skipping
3. Field trips	3. Subject skipping
4. Saturday and summer programs	4. Credit by exam
5. Simulations and games	5. College courses in high school
6. Small-group inquiry and investigations	6. Correspondence courses
7. Academic competitions	7. Early admission to college

The regular classroom teacher may be responsible for adapting instruction for students who are gifted and talented, or students may attend special programs. These programs are typically based on either **acceleration**, which keeps the curriculum the same but allows students to move through it more quickly, or **enrichment**, which provides richer and varied content through strategies that supplement usual grade-level work (Schiever & Maker, 2003). Table 3.5 lists some acceleration and enrichment options. Failure to address the needs of these students can result in gifted underachievers, with social and emotional problems linked to boredom and lack of motivation (Cross, 2005).

Students With Exceptionalities: Implications for Teachers

Initially, inclusion meant additional services to help students with exceptionalities function in regular school settings (Turnbull et al., 2007). Gradually, the concept of collaboration replaced this additive approach. **Collaboration** involves joint communication and decision making among educational professionals to create an optimal learning environment for students with exceptionalities. In collaboration, special and regular education teachers work closely to ensure that learning experiences are integrated into the regular classroom curriculum. For example, rather than pulling a student with special needs out of the classroom for supplementary instruction in math, a special education teacher coordinates instruction with the classroom teacher and then works with the student in the regular classroom on tasks linked to the standard math curriculum, as the following example illustrates:

Sharon Snow noticed that Joey Sanchez was having difficulties with 3-digit addition problems. After checking the IEP she had helped design in collaboration with the special education team (see Figure 3.10), she found that mastering these math problems was one of Joey's goals. She met with Ken Thomas, the resource teacher, after school, and examined some recent work samples from Joey's math homework and quizzes. They discovered he was having trouble with problems that involved carrying values over to the next column like the following problem:

345
+296

During the next week when Sharon's class was working on similar problems, Ken stopped by Joey's desk to help him. At first, they went to the back of the room, and Ken reviewed place values for him. When Ken thought Joey understood how place value affected the addition problems, he sent him back to his seat to work on the next few problems. Both Sharon and Ken monitored Joey's progress

Acceleration. A program for gifted and talented students that keeps the regular curriculum but allows students to move through it more quickly.

Enrichment. A program for gifted and talented students that provides richer and varied content through strategies that supplement usual grade-level work.

Collaboration. Joint communication and decision making among educational professionals to create an optimal learning environment for students with exceptionalities.

carefully so he wouldn't get discouraged. When the number of problems seemed overwhelming to Joey, Ken broke them down into smaller blocks of five, providing feedback and encouragement after each block. Slowly, Joey started to catch on and gained confidence. Collaboration had worked.

How does collaboration change your role as a classroom teacher? You are virtually certain to have students with exceptionalities in your classroom, and you will be expected to do the following:

- Aid in the process of identifying students with exceptionalities.
- Collaborate in the creation of IEPs that will help students with exceptionalities succeed in the classroom.
- Adapt your instruction to meet the needs of students with exceptionalities, actively seeking out the help of special educators in the process.
- Maintain communication with parents, school administrators, and special educators about the progress of students in your classroom who have special needs.

This section suggests that the fifth statement in our beginning-of-chapter survey, which said, "Most students with exceptionalities require help and assistance in special classrooms designed to meet their needs," is not true. Inclusion suggests that most students with exceptionalities are best served in regular schools and classrooms. Instruction in these classrooms is individually adapted to meet the needs of each student.

Making Connections:
To deepen your **CW** understanding of the topics in this section of the chapter and integrate them with topics you've already studied, go to the *Making Connections* module for Chapter 3 at **www.prenhall.com/kauchak**. Respond to questions 14–16.

Check Your Understanding

5.1 How have schools changed the ways they deal with exceptionalities?

5.2 What are the major categories of exceptionalities found in classrooms?

For feedback, go to Check Your Understanding *at the end of this chapter.*
CW

decision making

Defining Yourself as a Professional

You've been invited to a community awards ceremony at a local church of Pacific Island immigrants that is to honor students from your school. (This invitation and the events that followed actually happened to one educator.) You gladly accept, arrive a few minutes early, and are ushered to a seat of honor on the stage. After an uncomfortable (to you) wait of over an hour, the ceremony begins, and the students proudly file to the stage to receive their awards. Each is acknowledged, given an award, and applauded. After this part of the ceremony, you have an eye-opening experience.

The children all go back and sit down in the audience again, and the meeting continues with several more items on the agenda. The kids are fine for a while, but get bored and start to fidget. Fidgeting and whispering turn into poking, prodding, and open chatting. You become a little anxious at the disruption, but none of the other adults appear to even notice, so you ignore it, too. Soon, several of the children are up and out of their seats, strolling

about the back and sides of the auditorium. All adult faces continue looking serenely up at the speaker on the stage. Then the kids start playing tag, running circles around the seating area, and yelling gleefully. No adult response—you are amazed, and struggle to resist the urge to quiet the children. Then some of the kids get up onto the stage, run around the speaker, flick the lights on and off, and open and close the curtain! Still nothing from the Islander parents who seem either unaware or unconcerned about the children's behavior! You are caught in the middle of a conflict of cultures—yours and the Pacific Islanders'. You don't know what to do. (Adapted from Winitzky, 1994.)

What would you do in this situation?

To respond to this question online and receive immediate feedback, go to the Decision Making module for Chapter 3 on the Companion Website at www.prenhall.com/kauchak. CW

Meeting Your Learning Objectives

1. Explain how cultural diversity influences learning and how effective teachers respond to this diversity.

   - As students from diverse cultural backgrounds enter our classrooms, they bring with them unique attitudes and values. Sometimes these cultural attitudes and values complement school learning; other times they don't.
   - Diversity also results in differences in the cultural interaction patterns students bring to our classrooms. Often the interaction patterns of the classroom conflict with those of the home. Teachers who recognize this problem can adapt their instruction to meet the needs of students and also teach students how to adapt to the interaction patterns of the classroom.
   - Urban areas are often called "gateway cities," as many of the immigrants to the United States first settle there. Consequently, the numbers of cultural minorities attending urban schools is large. In addition, many of these recent immigrants do not speak English as their first language.
   - Educational responses to cultural diversity have changed over time. Initially, the emphasis was on assimilation, or socializing students to adopt the dominant social norms and patterns of behavior. Multicultural education, and especially culturally responsive teaching, recognizes, accommodates, and builds on student cultural differences.

2. Describe the major approaches to dealing with language diversity.

   - Language diversity is increasing in U.S. classrooms. During the 1960s and 1970s, the federal response to this diversity was to encourage bilingual programs. Currently, the federal emphasis is on the rapid acquisition of English with little or no emphasis on preserving students' home languages.
   - Educational responses to language diversity range from recognizing and building on the home language to attempting to teach English as quickly as possible. Currently, despite research that suggests advantages for maintaining the first language, political sentiment favors teaching English as quickly as possible.
   - Teachers who have ELL students in the classroom can do several important things to help them learn. In addition to creating a warm and inviting classroom, they can also provide multiple opportunities for students to practice their developing language skills with their peers. In addition, teachers should use a variety of concrete examples and illustrations to illustrate abstract ideas and concepts.

3. Explain how gender differences influence school success and how effective teachers respond to these differences.

   - Males and females are different, and these differences reflect genetic influences as well as differences in the way society treats boys and girls. Parents also exert powerful influences on gender differences.
   - Evidence suggests that both boys and girls encounter problems in today's schools. For girls these problems focus more on achievement and career choices, especially in math, science, and computer science, whereas for boys the problems are more behavioral and connected to learning problems. Suspected causes of these problems range from societal and parental expectations to differential treatment in classrooms. Teachers play a major role in ensuring that gender differences don't become gender inequalities.

4. Explain different views of ability differences, and describe how schools respond to ability differences.

   - Ability grouping is one of the most common responses to this dimension of diversity. Despite its popularity, ability grouping is associated with a number of problems, ranging from inappropriate and rigid placements to substandard instruction in some low-ability classrooms. An alternative is heterogeneous classrooms in which teachers adapt their instruction to the learning needs of all students.
   - Learning styles emphasize differences in the ways students process information and prefer to learn in the classroom. The concept of learning styles reminds us that all students learn differently; effective teachers are sensitive to these differences and adapt their teaching accordingly.

(continued)

5. Explain how schools have changed the way they deal with exceptionalities, and describe the major categories of exceptionalities found in classrooms.
   - Initially, students with exceptionalities were segregated in special classrooms or schools. Mainstreaming did integrate students into regular classrooms but often failed to provide the necessary help and support for either the teacher or students. Inclusion is changing the way schools assist students with exceptionalities, providing them with a comprehensive, supporting network of services.
   - Students with exceptionalities require extra help to reach their full potential. The majority of students with exceptionalities fall into four major categories: students with mental retardation, learning disabilities, communication disorders, and behavior disorders. A substantial number of students with exceptionalities are also gifted and talented.
   - Regular classroom teachers collaborate with other professionals to provide individualized educational services to students with exceptionalities. This collaboration begins with helping to identify students with exceptionalities, continues during the creation of IEPs, and extends into the classroom, where teachers adapt their instruction to meet the learning needs of these students. Throughout this process, the teacher maintains continual communication with parents, school administrators, and other school professionals.

Important Concepts

ability grouping	individualized education program (IEP)
acceleration	intelligenc
assimilation	language disorders
behavior disorders	learning disabilities
between-class ability grouping	learning styles
collaboration	least restrictive environment (LRE)
communication disorders	mainstreaming
cultural diversity	maintenance language programs
culturally responsive teaching	mental retardation
culture	metacognition
disabilities	multicultural education
English as a second language (ESLs) programs	multiple intelligences
English language learners (ELLs)	single-gender classes and schools
enrichment	special education
ethnicity	speech disorders
gender-role identity	stereotype
gifted and talented	students with exceptionalities
giftedness	tracking
immersion programs	transition programs
inclusion	within-class ability grouping

Developing as a Professional

Preparing for Your Licensure Exam

This exercise provides you with practice answering questions similar to the Praxis™ Principles of Learning and Teaching exam as well as your state-specific licensure exam. Read the case study, and answer the questions that follow:

Diane Henderson, a fifth-grade teacher at Martin Luther King Elementary School, begins her language arts class by saying, "Class, look up at the overhead. What do you notice about the two sentences?"

He gave the gift to her.
John sent him the letter.

She calls on Naitia.

"The second one has a proper noun."

"Okay. What else?" Diane says, smiling . . . "Sheila?"

"Both verbs are past tense."

"Indeed they are!" Diane nods and smiles again. "What else, Kelvin?" she asks quickly.

"The first has a pronoun for the subject."

"That's true," Diane confirms. "Does everyone see that?" she asks energetically.

"Now, let's look more closely at the first sentence. What is the direct object in that sentence? . . . Kwan?" Diane asks as she walks down the aisle.

"Her?" Kwan responds.

"Hmm. What do you think, Luciano?"

"Gift?" answers Luciano, hesitating.

"Class, what do you think? Is the direct object in sentence one her or gift? I want everyone to think about this in your head. Okay, Todd, do you want to try?"

"Uh, I think it's gift."

"That's correct. But why is gift the direct object, Theresa?"

"Because that's what he gave," Theresa replies.

"Good answer, Theresa. The direct object takes the action from the verb. But now, what about her? What is her?" Diane asks, looking around the room. "Well, that's what we are going to learn about today. Her is an indirect object. An indirect object receives the action. So, in the first sentence, gift is the direct object and her is the indirect object. Every language has direct and indirect objects, so what we are learning today will help you with both English and all other languages.

"Now let's look at the second sentence. It has both a direct object and an indirect object. Who can tell us which is which? Mireya?"

"The direct object in the second sentence is letter," Mireya responds hesitantly.

"Yes, good," Diane says and smiles reassuringly.

"So what is the indirect object? Rashad?" Diane continues.

"It must be him."

"Very good, Rashad! And why is letter the direct object? . . . Laura?"

"Because that's what John sent."

"And how about him? Why is it the indirect object? . . . Jacinta?"

"'Cause that's who received the letter."

"Good! Now look at this sentence, and tell me which is the direct and indirect object."

The batter hit the shortstop a line drive.

"Katya?"

"Umm. . . ."

"Oh, I know," Tom blurts out.

"That's great, Tom, but remember what we said about giving everyone in the class a chance to answer? Go ahead, Katya."

"I think line drive is the direct object."

"Good, Katya. That's right. Now who can tell us why it's the direct object? . . . Angie?"

"Because that's what the batter hit."

"And what's the indirect object, Kareem, and why?"

"I think it's shortstop because that's who the batter hit the line drive to."

"Yes, good answer." Diane nods and then continues.

"I think we're starting to understand the difference between direct and indirect objects. Now we need to practice to make sure. I want you to get into your learning groups, and I want each of you to complete the exercise that asks you to label the direct and indirect objects in the sentences

149

BEFORE you discuss it as a group. Then, I want you to take turns explaining your answers to each other. Quickly now, into your groups, and today's group leaders should come up and pick up the exercise sheets."

Diane watches as her students quickly get into their groups and start working. A list on the bulletin board ensures that everyone in the group will have an opportunity to be a "Group Leader." In addition, she has strategically composed the groups so they are heterogeneous in terms of ability, gender, and culture. She also has paired students with limited English proficiency with other students with similar language backgrounds to provide assistance.

As the students begin working on their sentences, Diane walks up and down the rows, monitoring each student's progress. After 15 minutes, Diane discusses the exercises with the whole class, focusing on sentences students had difficulties with.

Then, Diane continues, "That's excellent. Now I want each of you to write a sentence that has in it one example of an indirect and a direct object. Underline them in each case and label them. If you are having problems getting started, raise your hand and I'll be by in a minute."

While the students write their sentences, Diane circulates among them, periodically stopping to comment on students' work and to offer suggestions. Todd, a student who receives extra help from a resource teacher, sits with his head on his desk.

"What's the problem, Todd?"

"I can't do this," Todd replies with a shrug.

"Well, getting started is often the hardest part. Why don't you write down a sentence and then raise your hand, and I'll help you with the next step."

After 5 minutes, Diane announces, "All right, everyone. Please switch your paper with the person in the next row, and let's see how you did."

1. To what extent did Diane display culturally responsive teaching in her lesson?

2. To what extent did Diane's teaching reflect sensitivity to gender issues?

3. What did Diane do to accommodate differences in learning ability and learning styles?

To receive feedback on your responses to these exercises, go to the Companion Website at www.prenhall.com/kauchak, then to the Preparing for Your Licensure Exam module for Chapter 3.

Discussion Questions

1. Is multicultural education more important at some grade levels than in others? Why? Is multicultural education more important in some content areas than in others? Why?

2. Experts debate whether teachers should adjust instruction to match student learning styles or teach students to broaden their learning repertoires. Which approach is more desirable? Why?

3. Which approach to teaching English to ELL students makes the most sense in the teaching setting in which you hope to find yourself in your first job? Why?

4. Are single-gender classrooms a good idea? Why or why not?

5. What are the advantages and disadvantages of full-time inclusion in the regular education classroom? Should it be used with all students with exceptionalities?

6. What implications does Gardner's theory of multiple intelligences have for you as a teacher? In answering this question, be sure to relate your answer to the grade level and content area(s) in which you plan to teach.

Developing as a Professional: Online Activities

Going Into Schools

Go to the Companion Website at www.prenhall.com/kauchak, and click on the Going Into Schools module for Chapter 3. You will find a number of school-based activities that will help you link chapter content to the schools in which you work.

Virtual Field Experience: Using Teacher Prep to Explore the Profession

If you would like to participate in a Virtual Field Experience, access the Teacher Prep Website at *www.prenhall.com/teacherprep*. After logging in, complete the following steps.

1. Click on "Video Classroom" on the left panel of the screen.
2. Then go to "Foundations and Introduction to Education."
3. Finally, select the following five modules:
   - "Module 1: Ethnic Identity"
   - "Module 2: What Is Diversity?"
   - "Module 3: The Multicultural Curriculum"
   - "Module 4: What Are Our Assumptions?" and
   - "Module 5: Multicultural Assumptions in Curriculum."

Each of these videos explores a different dimension of multicultural education. Answer the questions that follow each video clip.

Online Portfolio Activities

To develop your professional portfolio, further apply your understanding of chapter content, and address the INTASC standards, go the Companion Website at *www.prenhall.com/kauchak*, then to the *Online Portfolio Activities* for Chapter 3. Complete the suggested activities.

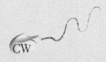

Check Your Understanding

1.1   **How do cultural attitudes, values, and interaction patterns influence learning?**

Some cultural attitudes and values complement classroom learning. For example, some cultures view success in school as an essential component of upward mobility and consequently emphasize the value of schoolwork as well as homework. At other times, cultural values can conflict with school success. This primarily occurs when success in school threatens the loss of the home culture. Language is a prime example here. Sometimes learning English is interpreted as also losing the native language.

Not all cultures have the same adult–children interaction patterns. When these interaction patterns are compatible with the question-and-answer style of most classrooms, then learning is facilitated. When the home interaction patterns differ from classroom interaction patterns, then problems can occur. Sensitive teachers are aware of this and both adapt their own interaction patterns and also help students change theirs to succeed in the classroom.

1.2   **What are three ways in which effective teachers respond to cultural diversity in their classrooms?**

Culturally responsive teaching has three essential components. First, effective teachers accept and value cultural differences and positively communicate this to students. Second, culturally responsive teachers adapt their interaction patterns to students and also teach students about successful classroom interaction practices. Finally, effective teachers build on students' cultural backgrounds, using their neighborhood and home experiences as the foundation for classroom learning.

1.3   **What is the relationship between urban schools and cultural diversity?**

Urban schools tend to have greater proportions of cultural minorities than their rural or suburban counterparts. In addition, many of these students do not speak English as their first language, requiring teachers skilled in English as a second language.

2.1   **What has been the government's response to language diversity in our nation's schools?**

Initially, Congress supported bilingual education with the passage of the Bilingual Education Act of 1968. This was reinforced in 1974 by a U.S. Supreme Court decision requiring districts to address the learning needs of non-English speakers. More recently, both federal and state governments have reversed these trends, emphasizing English-only approaches at the expense of bilingualism.

2.2   **What are the primary differences in the two major approaches schools use in working with English language learners?**

There are two very different approaches to dealing with ELL students. The bilingual approach attempts to maintain the native language, using it as the foundation for learning English. A contrasting approach focuses exclusively on learning English. For political and practical reasons, this second approach appears to be currently dominant in the United States.

2.3   **What are the major ways that teachers can adapt their instruction to meet the needs of students with varying language backgrounds?**

First, teachers should make an effort to make their classrooms welcoming places where students feel comfortable. Then, teachers should provide opportunities for students to practice their developing language skills with other students. Cooperative learning, peer tutoring, and buddy systems are all effective. Finally, teachers should illustrate their lessons with many examples to provide concrete references for new ideas and vocabulary.

3.1   **Explain how society influences gender differences in our students.**

Gender differences influence the educational experiences of boys and girls primarily through gender-role identity. Every society influences people's perceptions of the proper roles of males and females. Ours does as well, and students come into our classrooms with preconceived notions about how males and females should act, and what careers they should select.

3.2   **How should teachers respond to gender differences?**

Teachers often treat boys and girls differently based on their own stereotypical views of gender roles. Teachers should be aware of these possibilities and attempt to treat boys and girls equally in learning activities. This means that they should call on boys and girls as equally as possible, give them similar amounts of time to answer, ask the same levels of questions, and provide feedback that is similarly detailed.

4.1   **Explain the differences in current definitions of intelligence.**

The most widely held definition of intelligence says that it has three components: the capacity to acquire knowledge, the ability to think and reason in the abstract, and the ability to solve problems. A differing view of intelligence, based upon Howard Gardner's work (1983, 1999), suggests that it is composed of eight relatively independent dimensions.

4.2   **How do schools respond to differences in ability? What does research suggest about its application in classrooms?**

Ability grouping is the process of placing students with similar academic abilities in the same learning environments. While well-intentioned, it has several potential drawbacks, including lowered teacher expectations and poorer instruction for those in lower groups. Experts (Good & Brophy, 2003; Tomlinson, 2003) recommend that teachers minimize its use in classrooms and constantly be aware of potentials for adverse effects.

4.3   **What are learning styles? What are the implications of learning styles for teachers?**

Learning styles are students' preferred way of learning, problem solving, or processing information. Learning styles have at least three implications for teachers. First, to meet students' diverse learning styles, teachers should use a variety of teaching strategies. Second, learning styles remind us that each student is a unique individual. Finally, learning styles suggest the need to make students metacognitively aware of their own learning strengths and weaknesses.

5.1   How have schools changed the ways they deal with exceptionalities?

In the past, students with exceptionalities were separated from their peers in segregated schools or classrooms. Then mainstreaming was adopted, which moved students with exceptionalities from segregated settings into regular classrooms. However, adequate support and services often didn't follow the students. Currently, inclusion attempts to provide a comprehensive web of services for students with exceptionalities who are placed in regular classrooms and schools.

5.2   What are the major categories of exceptionalities found in classrooms?

In the IDEA, the federal government specifies 13 different categories of special education students; over three fourths of these fall into four categories: learning disabilities, communication disorders, mental retardation, and behavior disorders. Learning disabilities involve difficulties in acquiring and using listening, speaking, reading, writing, reasoning, or mathematical abilities. Communication disorders interfere with students' abilities to receive and understand information from others and to express their own ideas or questions. Mental retardation includes limitations in intellectual functioning, as indicated by difficulties in learning, and problems with adaptive skills, such as communication, self-care, and social interaction. Behavior disorders involve the display of serious and persistent age-inappropriate behaviors that result in social conflict, personal unhappiness, and school failure.

Governance and Finance: Regulating and Funding Schools

5

Governance and Finance: Regulating and Funding Schools

Learning Objectives

After you have completed your study of this chapter, you should be able to:

1. Describe the major educational governance structures at the state and local levels.

2. Explain the different sources and targets of educational funding.

3. Describe the major current issues in school governance and finance.

Case Studies

 Elementary

 Middle

 Secondary

Jacksonville-Courier/Clayton Statler/The Image Works

School governance and school finance may seem irrelevant to beginning teachers, but veterans know better. The way schools are run and school districts' use of money make big differences in the quality of teachers' professional lives. And reform efforts aimed at addressing funding inequalities, increasing decision making at the school level, and providing more educational choices to parents are changing the teaching profession today. To begin our discussion, let's look at the following case study.

Carla Buendia sits at her desk, looking at the pile of books and papers covering it. "I better get this one right, as it'll be our only chance," she thinks to herself. Carla is a member of Unified Metropolitan School District's Elementary Math Steering Committee. Unified Metropolitan is a large district in the Midwest, and the Steering Committee has been meeting regularly over the last 2 years to study the elementary math curriculum in the district. Test scores have been declining, especially in the areas of applications and problem solving, and the committee has been asked to make a recommendation to the district's school board. Tonight is the night.

"Don't be nervous," Carla tells herself, but her advice isn't working. She has been to school board meetings as a spectator when teacher salaries and contracts were being discussed, and she is clearly uneasy about being in front of the hundred or more people who will be in attendance. "Why did I ever say I'd do this?" she thinks. "Too late for that. I just better have my act together when it's my turn to speak."

It can be unsettling to go into two schools within a few miles of each other and see striking differences in how they look and feel. One is bright, cheerful, and clean, with student projects and works of art prominently displayed. The other is dark, depressing, and dirty, and the hallways are cluttered with trash. Some of these differences can be traced to the ways the schools are governed and financed.

School governance and finance also influence the resources available to teachers. As an example, drive across the state line from New Mexico, where the average spending per pupil in 2005 was $8,236, to Utah, where it was $5,245 (National Education Association, 2006b). Some politicians argue that money doesn't influence the quality of education, but evidence suggests otherwise (Biddle & Berliner, 2002; Flanagan & Grissmer, 2002). Money buys paper, supplies, and equipment, for example, and allows students to do science experiments rather than reading about them.

How do school governance and finance affect the lives of teachers and students? We try to answer these questions in this chapter, but before continuing, take a few minutes to respond to the following survey. We discuss each of the items as the chapter unfolds.

professional knowledge: test yourself!

For each item, circle the number that best represents your thinking. Use the following scale as a guide.

1 = Strongly disagree
2 = Disagree
3 = Agree/disagree
4 = Agree
5 = Strongly agree

1. Most states govern education in basically the same way.

    1   2   3   4   5

2. The state office of education in each state is responsible for setting rules and regulations.

    1   2   3   4   5

3. The federal government provides the largest source of educational funding.

    1   2   3   4   5

4. Most of a district's budget goes to funding instruction.

    1   2   3   4   5

5. Students across a state are provided with basically the same amount of money to fund their education.

    1   2   3   4   5

CW *This is available in a downloadable format on the Companion Website for personal portfolio use.*

Governance: How Are Schools Regulated and Run?

In a few short years, you will walk into your own classroom, look around, and think, "At last, it's all mine." That's a good feeling, and it will be all yours—sort of. Although teachers have considerable autonomy in implementing their own vision of good teaching, they also operate within a specified governance framework.

Governance: A Legal Overview

Unlike many other countries, where the federal government is responsible for schools, in the United States the Tenth Amendment to the Constitution clearly assigns legal responsibility for the education of its citizens to the 50 states.

Because the 50 states differ significantly in geography, history, economics, and politics, you might think that they would also differ in their approaches to governing education, but they don't. Each of the states has a surprisingly similar organizational structure. These structures are outlined in Figure 8.1 and described in the section that follows.

State Governance Structures

In every state a constitution outlines the roles and responsibilities of state officers with respect to education. Governors focus public attention on educational issues and attempt to solicit public support for educational funding. State legislatures meet annually to debate school finance and other issues. These legislative sessions are important to teachers because states supply almost half of a district's education budget, and legislative actions (or inactions) influence teacher salaries, class sizes, supplies, and equipment (Brimley & Garfield, 2005).

The information in this section answers the first item on our beginning-of-chapter survey, "Most states govern education in basically the same way." Despite considerable diversity with respect to views about the proper role of schools in educating children, most states govern education in much the same way.

State Board of Education

Because a governor and legislators have an entire state to run, they turn most of the responsibility for steering their state's schools to the **state board of education**, the legal governing body that exercises general control and supervision of the schools in a state. State boards are similar in purpose to district school boards and perform both regulatory and advisory functions. State boards regulate education by

- Issuing and revoking teaching licenses
- Establishing the length of the school year
- Publishing standards for approving and accrediting schools
- Developing and implementing uniform systems for gathering education data, such as standardized achievement test scores, enrollment trends, and demographics

The state board sets long- and short-term goals for its state and helps create an educational agenda for the state's governor and legislature. For example, the federal No Child Left Behind (NCLB) Act of 2001 is a pressing issue in all states, and state boards assist governors and legislatures in shaping responses to this initiative. State board members are people outside professional education. They are usually appointed by the governor, but about a fourth of the states elect these officials who typically serve without pay (National Association of State Boards of Education, 2004).

State board of education. The legal governing body that exercises general control and supervision of the schools in a state.

State Office of Education

A state board of education makes policy; the **state office of education** is responsible for implementing policy on a day-to-day basis. In contrast with state boards, which are composed of lay members who meet periodically to discharge their duties, state offices of education are

State office of education. Office responsible for implementing a state's education policy on a day-to-day basis.

Figure 8.1 State Administrative Organizational Structure

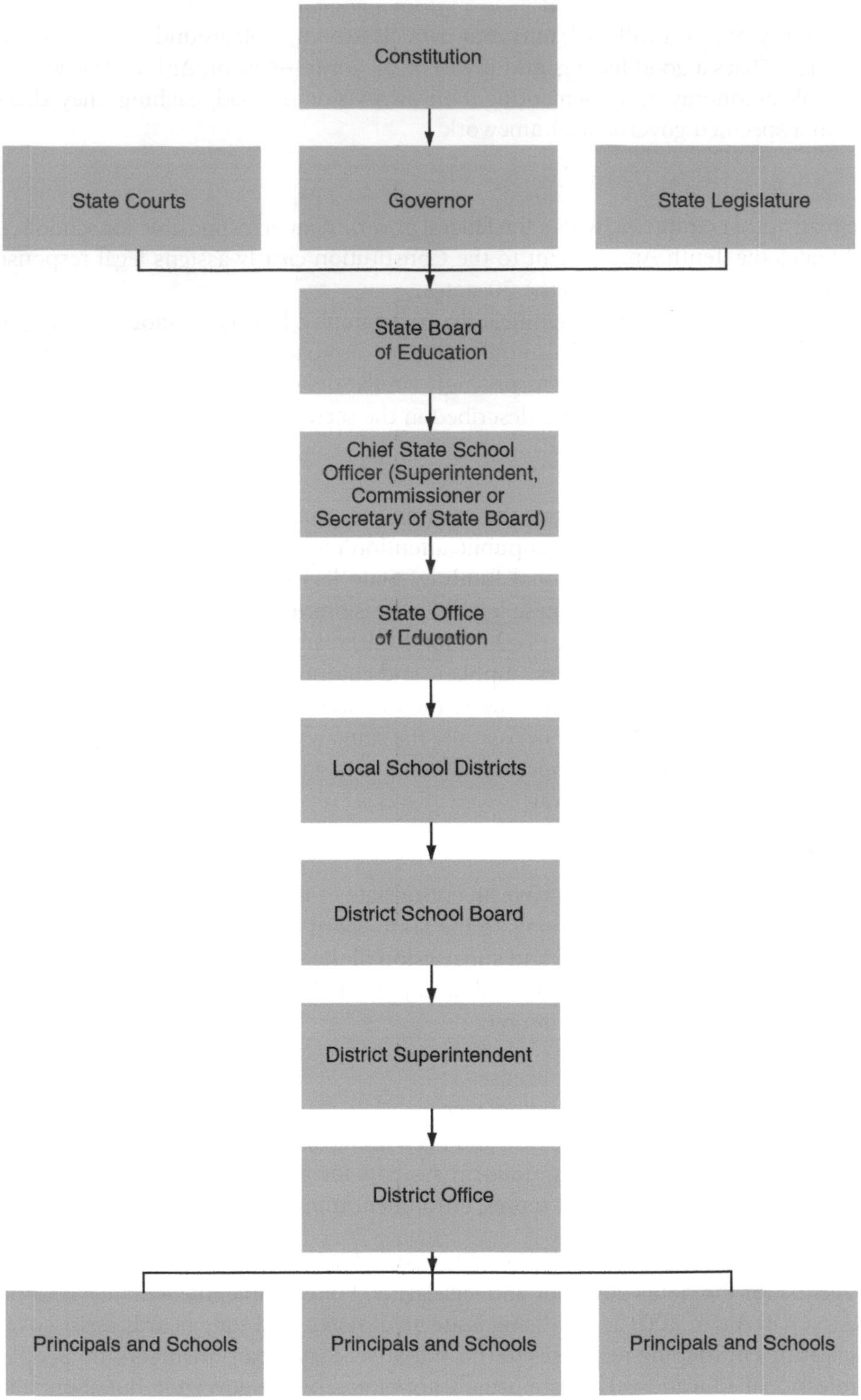

```
                    ┌──────────────────┐
                    │   Constitution   │
                    └──────────────────┘
                             │
      ┌──────────────────┐   │   ┌──────────────────┐
      │   State Courts    │  │  │ State Legislature │
      └──────────────────┘   │   └──────────────────┘
      ┌──────────────────┐   │
      │     Governor      │──┤
      └──────────────────┘   │
                    ┌──────────────────┐
                    │   State Board    │
                    │   of Education   │
                    └──────────────────┘
                    ┌──────────────────┐
                    │ Chief State School│
                    │ Officer (Superin- │
                    │ tendent,          │
                    │ Commissioner or   │
                    │ Secretary of State│
                    │ Board)            │
                    └──────────────────┘
                    ┌──────────────────┐
                    │   State Office   │
                    │   of Education   │
                    └──────────────────┘
                    ┌──────────────────┐
                    │ Local School     │
                    │ Districts        │
                    └──────────────────┘
                    ┌──────────────────┐
                    │ District School  │
                    │ Board            │
                    └──────────────────┘
                    ┌──────────────────┐
                    │ District         │
                    │ Superintendent   │
                    └──────────────────┘
                    ┌──────────────────┐
                    │ District Office  │
                    └──────────────────┘
   ┌─────────────┐  ┌─────────────┐  ┌─────────────┐
   │ Principals  │  │ Principals  │  │ Principals  │
   │ and Schools │  │ and Schools │  │ and Schools │
   └─────────────┘  └─────────────┘  └─────────────┘
```

staffed by full-time education professionals, virtually all of whom have been teachers and most of whom have advanced degrees in education.

Each state office of education is headed by a chief state officer with a title such as superintendent, commissioner, or secretary of the state board. In 2003, chief state officers were appointed by the state board of education or another board in 24 states, elected in 15 states, and appointed by the governor in 11 (Council of Chief State School Officers, 2003). The state office implements teacher and administrator licensing, supervises curriculum, approves school sites and buildings, and collects statistical data. As a new teacher, you will apply to the office of education in your state for an initial teaching license, the form and requirements of which are determined by the state board.

A state office of education influences the curriculum (what is taught) in a state in two important ways: textbook approval and state standards. Let's look at them.

Textbook Approval. The textbooks used by individual schools must be on a state-approved list. States usually offer districts a choice of several acceptable text series for a given grade level. The textbook selection process can be highly politicized and controversial when controversial topics such as evolution in science, phonics versus whole language in reading, or problem-based versus computationally oriented approaches to math are involved. In this chapter's opening case, Carla's Elementary Math Steering Committee began its search for a math series by looking at the state-approved list. The committee then conferred with the state's math specialist to evaluate the different series.

State Standards. A second way that state offices of education influence curricula is through state *standards,* which are statements specifying what students should know and what skills they should have upon completing an area of study. Currently, 49 of the 50 states have statewide standards; Iowa chose to leave that decision to local school districts (Archer, 2006b).

State offices of education are also responsible for administering statewide testing programs based on standards, and initial research suggests that establishing standards and holding students and teachers responsible for reaching them have a modest effect on student achievement (Olson, 2006a).

This section addresses the second item on our beginning-of-chapter survey, "The state office of education in each state is responsible for setting rules and regulations." Although the statement is technically false—because the state *board of education* is legally responsible for general control and supervision of the schools in a state—many decisions about implementing the rules are left to the state *office of education.*

Although state boards and state offices of education influence teaching and learning, for the most part, they do so at arm's length; the day-to-day responsibility for educating students is a district responsibility. This is why Carla's experience at a district school board meeting is relevant. Let's look at districts' roles in governing education.

School Districts

A **school district** is an administrative unit within a state that is defined by geographical boundaries and is legally responsible for the public education of children within those boundaries. With respect to educational governance, it's where the action is. School districts hire and fire teachers, and they determine the content that students learn (the curriculum) and, to a certain extent, the kinds of learning experiences (instruction) students will have in schools. That's why Carla was making her presentation to the district school board. She was involved in making decisions about the district's elementary math curriculum. Decisions such as these are usually made at the district level, and school districts also determine what books will be used and make them available to students at the beginning of the school year.

School districts differ dramatically in size. For example, in 2004 there were 14,063 school districts in the United States, and if they were divided equally among states, each state would have about 280 (Kober, 2006). But states have differing views about the ideal number and size of districts. For example, the whole state of Hawaii constitutes one school district, whereas Texas has 1,040 districts. In 2004 the New York City School District had more than 1 million students, but 4,922 of U.S. school districts had 600 or fewer students. Almost half of the districts enroll fewer than 1,000 students per year. The largest 4 percent—districts enrolling more than 10,000 students each—educated more than half the students in this country (National Center for Education Statistics, 2005c).

> **School district.** An administrative unit within a state that is defined by geographical boundaries and is legally responsible for the public education of children within those boundaries.

Historically, the trend has been toward consolidating schools into fewer and larger districts. For instance, in 1930 the United States had more than 130,000 school districts; 70 years later, it had only 14,559 (Brimley & Garfield, 2005). Efficiency is the primary reason for consolidation; larger districts can offer broader services and minimize duplication of administrative staff. For example, one medium-sized district with a superintendent and district staff of 10 people is more efficient than two small districts that require a superintendent and a staff of 6 to 8 people each. On other hand, parents often resist consolidation because of loyalty to high school athletic teams and long bus rides for their children (Richard, 2004).

Small and large districts both have advantages and disadvantages. Small districts are less bureaucratic and easier to influence, but they often lack resources and instructional support staff. For example, Carla's committee functioned in a large district. As committee members did their work, they were assisted by a district math coordinator, a testing specialist, and technology experts who helped them evaluate the claims of different commercial math programs. This type of assistance doesn't exist in small districts.

Large districts also have problems. They tend to be hierarchical and bureaucratic, and getting things done takes time. Teachers sometimes feel like nameless and faceless cogs in large, impersonal organizations. Teachers can often rely on face-to-face contacts to make things happen quickly in smaller districts; in larger districts, however, decision making is placed in the hands of large and sometimes contentious committees. The ideal district has an administrative structure that is supportive and responsive to teachers but also leaves them alone to do what they love most—work with students.

Every school district has a local school board, a superintendent, and central staff. These are the people who make the district-level decisions about teaching and learning in their district's schools. Let's see how they will influence your life as a teacher.

The Local School Board

A **local school board** is a group of elected lay citizens responsible for setting policies that determine how a school district operates. With respect to governance, what kinds of rules and regulations do school boards pass? Who are the members of these boards? How are school board members selected? Because they will influence your life as a teacher, you should know the answers to these questions.

What Do School Boards Do? The major functions of school boards occur in five areas, outlined in Figure 8.2 and discussed in the paragraphs that follow.

Working with the district budget is perhaps the most important (and contentious) school board function. School boards are responsible for raising money through taxes and disbursing funds to the schools within the district. They also make decisions about various district services, such as providing buses and maintaining lunch programs. School boards directly influence teachers by making decisions about salary increases and the benefits teachers receive. They also affect teachers indirectly by making budget decisions that impact class size and the amount of instructional materials available. Wrestling with each year's budget occupies more than a quarter of a school board's time and energy; it's a continual process that begins in the fall and ends in the spring.

Personnel responsibilities are closely aligned with financial decisions. School boards are legally responsible for hiring and firing all school personnel, including teachers, principals, custodians, and school bus drivers. Your teaching contract will be offered by a school board that has the legal authority to hire and fire teachers.

The curriculum—what teachers teach—is a third area of school board jurisdiction. School boards, assisted by district administrators, are responsible for defining the curriculum and implementing the general guidelines developed by states. In virtually all districts, teachers are consulted about the curriculum; in the better ones, teachers are directly involved in curriculum decisions. For example, in the opening case, Carla's committee helped make the decision about what math curriculum the district would adopt.

Local school board. A group of elected lay citizens responsible for setting policies that determine how a school district operates.

Figure 8.2 Functions of Local School Boards

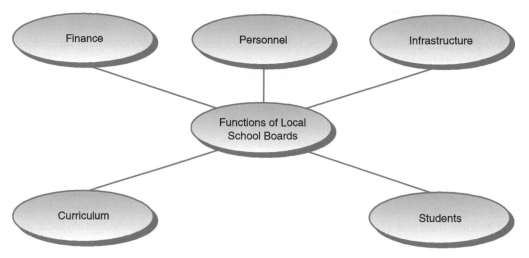

Decisions that impact students are also made by school boards. They set attendance, dress, grooming, conduct, and discipline standards for their districts. For example, the issue of school uniforms has been debated at district, state, and national levels, but the decision—sometimes after contentious debate—is ultimately made by local school boards.

School boards also determine extracurricular policies—from the mundane to the controversial. For example, some districts require students to maintain minimal grade levels to participate in sports, a policy critics contend doubly punishes struggling student athletes by failing them in the classroom and then preventing them from participating in extracurricular activities. Supporters of no-pass/no-play policies argue that they improve motivation to learn by providing incentives for academic success (Camerino, 2003). The question of whether to grant gay and lesbian clubs equal status with other school-sponsored organizations is another topic that has generated controversy at school board meetings. As you would expect, attendance at school board meetings increases when controversial issues are on their agendas, as various citizens groups attempt to influence board decisions.

Finally, school boards make decisions about district infrastructure. For example, they ensure that school buildings and school buses are maintained and safe, and they approve plans and hire contractors when new schools are built.

In recent years, given mandates such as the NCLB Act, student achievement and meeting state standards have become school board members' primary concerns, followed by issues involving budgets and decisions about curriculum and instruction (New York State School Board Association, 2006). Interestingly, student achievement wasn't even listed in school board members' top 10 concerns as recently as the late 1980s. Reform efforts and the national trend toward greater school accountability have strongly impacted the ways that school boards operate.

Members of School Boards and Their Selection. Who serves on school boards, and how do they get there? Nearly all (about 96 percent) school boards consist of members elected for 3- or 4-year terms; the remainder have members appointed by large-city mayors or city councils (D. Land, 2002). School board elections can be controversial, for two reasons. First, the voter turnout for most school board elections is embarrassingly low; as few as 5 to 10 percent of eligible voters often decide school board membership. This fact results in boards that don't represent the citizens in the district, critics contend. The second controversy involves the question of whether school board elections should be at-large or limited to specific areas within a city. At-large elections tend to favor wealthy, White-majority candidates who have either more money to run an election campaign or benefit from White-majority voting pools (D. Land, 2002). In a limited-area election, only citizens who live in a specific part of the city are allowed to vote for candidates representing that area. Area-specific elections provide greater opportunities for minority candidates to represent local, ethnic-minority neighborhoods (Howell, 2005).

Who serves on school boards? The typical school board member is male, White, older, and wealthy, although membership is slowly growing more diverse in some areas. For example, a 2004 survey found that 61 percent of board members were male and 86 percent were White (Hess, 2004a). In addition, 59 percent make more than $75,000 per year, 38 percent have graduate degrees, and another 29 percent have 4-year degrees; only 7 percent have a high school degree or less (Carr, 2003; Hess, 2004a).

Disparities exist between the characteristics of school board members and those of the people they're elected to serve. For example, only 14 percent of board members are cultural minorities, but 33 percent of the nation's students are minorities, and that figure is projected to rise to 42 percent by the year 2010 (U.S. Department of Education, 2003a). Also, 45 percent of school board members are business people or professionals, and 85 percent make more money than the average teacher (Carr, 2003; National School Boards Association, 2000). Critics contend that wealthy school board members can't empathize with the financial hardships that teachers and community members often experience. Critics also question the ability of male-dominated school boards to effectively represent the teaching force, which is almost three-fourths female.

Alternatives to Local Control. Local control by school boards is the predominant pattern in U.S. education, but what happens when local control doesn't seem to work? Several large cities answered this question by authorizing the mayor to take over the running of the city's schools. This occurred in Boston in 1991, Chicago in 1995, New York in 2002, and currently, the mayor of Los Angeles is threatening to do the same (Maxwell, 2006a). Critics call the move in Los Angeles "undemocratic," and the effort is complicated by the fact that the Los Angeles Unified School District encompasses 26 other cities in addition to Los Angeles (Gewertz, 2006b).

A second battle to wrest control of schools from local school boards is occurring in the state of Maryland (Honawar, 2006). This battle for control of schools was precipitated by the NCLB Act, which requires low-performing schools to be restructured after 3 years of subpar performance. The Maryland legislature resisted, claiming that there is little proof that state takeovers actually improve student performance. The U.S. Department of Education threatened withholding $171 million in Title I funds if the state didn't restructure the Baltimore schools. Governance battles such as these are likely to increase as more and more schools are found lacking under NCLB guidelines.

The Superintendent

The school board makes policy, and the **superintendent**, the district's head administrative officer, along with his or her staff, implements that policy in the district's schools. The division of labor between the board and the superintendent isn't simple and well-defined, however. Because most board members have little or no background in professional education, the superintendent often plays a central role in leading the board and helping set agendas.

Superintendents are hired by school boards. Most hold an advanced degree in education (National School Boards Association, 2000), but some districts are now looking outside the field of education to find superintendents. For example, in the summer of 2000, Roy Romer, a former governor of Colorado with no experience in educational administration, was picked to lead the Los Angeles schools, the nation's second largest system with an enrollment of more than 710,000 students (Richard, 2000a). The superintendents of the three largest districts in the country—New York City, Chicago, and Los Angeles—all came from outside the field of education, as school boards tend to increasingly value management experience over professional knowledge in education. Whether this trend will continue is uncertain.

Superintendent. The school district's head administrative officer, along with his or her staff, responsible for implementing that policy in the district's schools.

As on school boards, women and minorities are underrepresented as superintendents (Carr, 2003; Gewertz, 2006d). Seventy-five percent of the teaching force and 51 percent of the general population are women, but they make up only 15 percent of superintendents. Of the 15 largest districts in the country, only one, Palm Beach County in Florida, is headed by a woman. Similarly, members of cultural minorities make up 33 percent of the student population and 13 percent of teachers, but they make up only 5 percent of superintendents.

When power and authority are shared, as is the case with school boards and superintendents, conflicts are inevitable, and when they occur, the superintendent usually loses. Nationally, the average tenure for superintendents is just under 6 years; in urban districts it is less than 3 years (Borja, 2002; Snider, 2006). Accountability, in the form of student test scores, is a major reason that superintendents' tenure is so short, especially in urban districts.

Disputes with school boards, politics, and bureaucracy are major obstacles that superintendents face. When controversy flares over issues such as student drug use, school violence, desegregation, and lagging student achievement, a community looks to the superintendent for answers. Superintendents often get caught in the crossfire of politics and public opinion and, unable to quickly solve these problems, are either terminated or feel obliged to resign.

What are superintendents paid for this frustrating and insecure job? Pay varies considerably with both location and district size; the average 2005–2006 salary was $116,244, but competition for superintendents in larger districts has resulted in salaries that are considerably higher (Swanson, 2006a). For example, superintendents in large urban districts make $172,387, and in 2005, the Miami-Dade school district in Florida paid its new superintendent $480,000 plus benefits—more than the governor of the state (Bohman, 2006; Swanson, 2006a).

The District Office

The district office assists the superintendent in translating school board policies into action (see Figure 8.1). It also coordinates the myriad curricular and instructional efforts within the district (Grove, 2002). The district office is responsible for

- Ordering textbooks and supplies
- Developing programs of study
- Ordering, distributing, and analyzing standardized tests
- Evaluating teachers and assisting those with difficulties

The district office is instrumental in translating abstract state and school board mandates into reality. The manner in which it does this can give teachers a sense of empowerment or can make them feel like hired hands.

The district office also plays an important role for new teachers (Grove, 2002). It typically provides new-teacher orientations, which may include an overview of the district's curriculum, any districtwide instructional initiatives, and district assessment programs. These policies and procedures are important because they frame the district's work expectations for new teachers. In addition, the central office coordinates mentoring and assessment programs for new teachers, helping them make the transition from university students to working professionals.

The School Principal

The **school principal**, the individual given the ultimate administrative responsibility for a school's operation, is the district administrator who has the greatest impact on teachers' lives. Many larger schools have a vice principal and two or more assistant principals as part of the administrative staff. The makeup of this staff will depend on the size and organization of the school.

School principal. The individual having the ultimate administrative responsibility for a school's operation.

TABLE 8.1 Profile of School Principals

	High School Principals	Middle School Principals	Elementary School Principals
Sex			
Male	78.8%	66.8%	44.8%
Female	21.2	33.2	55.2
Ethinic Background			
White	85.9	83.0	80.8
African-American	8.4	10.5	12.0
Hispanic American	3.8	5.1	5.8
Asian-American	0.9	0.7	0.7
Native American	1.1	0.8	0.7
Other	0.7	–	0.6
Highest Degree Earned			
Bachelor's	1.4	1.8	1.8
Master's	54.8	55.5	53.9
Professioanl diploma	31.6	33.6	34.6
Doctorate	12.1	9.1	9.7
Salary (12-month) (2004–2005)	$86,938	$81,514	$76,144

Sources: Data from U.S. Department of Education (2001c); Williams (2002); and National Association of Elementary School Principals (2006).

A demographic profile of principals (see Table 8.1) mirrors that of school board members. Most are White at all levels, and males are still in the majority in secondary schools. Principals almost always have classroom experience, and most have at least a master's degree.

As the person who oversees the everyday operation of the school, the principal has wide-ranging duties; two of the most important duties are teacher selection and evaluation (Sergiovanni, 2004, 2006). His or her interview with you will be a crucial factor in whether or not you get the job, and it will give you an opportunity to learn about the person you'll be working for and the kind of school you'll be working in. During an interview, you should try to determine the principal's views about his or her role as an administrator (Cunningham & Cordeiro, 2000; Ubben et al., 2001).

The principal is also responsible for school-level curricular and instructional leadership, community relations, and the coordination of pupil services provided by school counselors, psychologists, nurses, and others. Principals also implement and monitor the school budget and ensure that the school's physical facilities are maintained.

Experienced teachers want principals who see themselves as instructional leaders and who take a hands-on ap-

Principals are crucial in creating well-run, learning-oriented schools. (Michelle D. Bridwell/PhotoEdit Inc.)

proach to the teaching–learning process (Harris & Lowery, 2002). This leadership is especially important for beginning teachers, who need support, mentoring, and feedback. However, because of their busy schedules, many principals become managers who focus primarily on the day-to-day operation of the school and forget that their most important role is to support teaching and learning (Ginsberg & Murphy, 2002).

Principals are the most important people in the district's administrative structure because they work directly with teachers and students. Effective principals can transform a mediocre school into a positive and productive learning environment, and the opposite is also true; an ineffective principal can make a school an unpleasant place in which to work.

> **Making Connections:**
> To deepen your understanding of the topics in this section of the chapter and integrate them with topics you've already studied, go to the *Making Connections* module for Chapter 8 at **www.prenhall.com/kauchak.** Respond to questions 1–4.

Check Your Understanding

1.1 Who is legally responsible for governing education in the United States?

1.2 How does each state govern education?

1.3 What role do school districts play in governing education?

For feedback, go to Check Your Understanding *at the end of this chapter.*

School Finance: How Are Schools Funded?

To begin our discussion of school finance, let's return to Carla's work on her school's Elementary Math Steering Committee.

"And based on our analysis of math programs around the country, we believe this one is best for our children. . . . Any questions?" Carla asks as she concludes her presentation to the school board.

"Let me make sure that I'm clear about this," one board member responds. "In addition to the texts themselves, students will need manipulatives. . . . I'm sorry, but I'm not sure exactly what 'manipulatives' are."

"Manipulatives are concrete objects, such as cubes that could be put in a box to help kids understand the concept of volume, and plastic squares that could be used to illustrate area. The success of this program depends on students seeing math ideas in action."

"Thank you. . . . And teachers will need additional in-service training to bring them up to speed on how to use these new materials. Is that right?"

"Yes. What we've read and heard is that teacher in-service is essential to the success of this program," Carla replies, as her fellow committee members nod in agreement.

"What seems clear to me," the chair of the school board adds, "is that this program, along with our technology initiative and the changes in our language arts program, is going to need additional funding. We need to make sure that the public understands how and why taxes are going to go up next fall. We've all got a big job ahead of us—selling, no, explaining, why our schools need additional monies."

Money is important in education. It determines teachers' salaries, professional development opportunities, and access to resources, such as computers, lab supplies, maps, and a host of other supplies. It also influences the quality of schools by allowing districts to do such things as reduce class sizes and recruit and retain qualified teachers (Biddle & Berliner, 2002). For 3 consecutive years from 2003 to 2005, national polls indicated that the general public viewed lack of financial support and funding for education as the biggest problem their local school boards face; the second biggest problem was overcrowded schools, an issue closely related to financial support (Rose & Gallup, 2005). In this section, we look at where this money comes from, how it is spent, and what can be done to make school funding more equitable.

School Funding Sources

Local, state, and federal sources all provide money for education (Brimley & Garfield, 2005; Yinger, 2004). As you can see in Figure 8.3, the state share is 48.7 percent, the local share is 42.8 percent, and both are considerably greater than the federal share, which is 8.5 percent. These facts indicate that the third statement in our beginning-of-chapter survey, "The federal government provides the largest source of educational funding," is clearly false. The federal government's share is less than 10 percent.

The share of education funding coming from local, state, and federal sources has changed over time (Brimley & Garfield, 2005). For example, from 1920 to 1980 the federal share increased from virtually nothing to a peak of nearly 10 percent, declining in the 1980s to less than 7 percent before rising to its current level of 8.5 percent. The state and local shares have remained fairly steady, hovering between 42 and 49 percent for the last fifteen years. These figures are national averages, and the federal, state, and local proportions can vary significantly from state to state. For example, none of Hawaii's 2002–2003 school budget came from local sources, whereas in Florida local funds accounted for 41 percent of school funding (Brimley & Garfield, 2005).

Shifts in education funding reflect the changing views of education throughout U.S. history. In early America, education was seen as a local responsibility with virtually no involvement by the federal government. In sharp contrast, 20th-century leaders saw a direct connection between education and the country's political and economic well-being. Quality schools and a well-educated workforce became national concerns, and the federal government's role in education increased. Similarly, states began to recognize the importance of education in attracting high-tech industries and high-paying jobs. This insight, plus efforts to equalize funding within states, has led to an increasing state role in educational funding (Biddle & Berliner, 2002).

The public is undecided about the relative amounts that local, state, and federal governments should contribute to educational funding. In a 1998 Gallup poll, 21 percent fa-

Figure 8.3   Education Revenues from Local, State, and Federal Sources

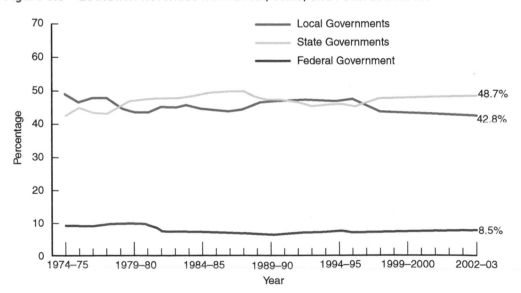

Source: Data from National Center for Education Statistics (2006).

vored local funding through property taxes, 33 percent favored state sources, and 37 percent favored federal taxes (Rose & Gallup, 1998). In a more recent poll, 49 percent said that the federal government had too much say in decisions affecting local public schools, and 43 percent said state governments also had too much control over these decisions (Rose & Gallup, 2000). The debate over the role that different levels of government should play in funding education is likely to continue.

Let's see how funds are raised at each level of government and how they make their way to classrooms.

State Revenue Sources

States are the largest source of educational funding, totaling 48.7 percent in the 2002–2003 school year (see Figure 8.3). State income taxes and sales taxes are the two largest sources of state income, each contributing about one third of all state revenues (Federation of Tax Administrators, 2006). Sales taxes are regressive, however, meaning they take proportionally more from lower-income families, who spend a larger portion of their income on necessities, such as food, clothing, and housing. Progressive states provide some relief by excluding food from items that are taxed. Personal income tax accounts for another third of state revenues. The remaining third comes from other sources such as taxes on liquor and tobacco, oil and mining revenues, and corporate income taxes.

Recently, state lotteries and gambling have also become sources of revenue, but education is often the victim of a zero-sum shell game, in which increased funding from lottery monies is balanced by decreasing monies from other sources, such as sales taxes. In 2005, 42 states had lotteries, but fewer than half allocate profits directly to education, and the percentage of income taxes going to education in these states varies considerably (Brimley & Garfield, 2005; Manzo, 2005). Also, states spend 32 cents of every lottery income dollar on expenses, and research indicates that these gambling ventures attract participants who are poor and have had little schooling (Brimley & Garfield, 2005). The long-term viability of gambling revenues for education is uncertain and highly controversial.

Local Funding

As we saw in our discussion of school governance, financing education at the local level is the responsibility of local school boards, which is why Carla made her presentation to her local board, and the need for increased funding was one of the implications of her presentation. At the local level, most funding for schools comes from **property taxes**, which are determined by the value of property in the school district (Brimley & Garfield, 2005). Other local revenue sources include income taxes, fees for building permits, traffic fines, and user fees charged to groups that hold meetings in school facilities. In collecting property taxes, local authorities first assess the value of a property and then tax the owners a small percentage of the property's value (usually less than 1 percent).

The value of property in a school district directly affects how much money schools in the district will receive from local sources.
(AP Wide World Photos)

Funding education primarily through local property taxes has disadvantages, the most glaring of which is inequities between property resources in different districts (Brimley & Garfield, 2005). Wealthier cities or districts have a higher tax base, so they're able to collect (and spend) more money for their schools. Poorer rural and urban school districts find themselves on the opposite end of this continuum, with a lower tax base, resulting in lower revenues. Property taxes also place an unfair burden on older taxpayers, whose homes may have increased in value, while their ability to pay taxes has remained constant or decreased. In

Property taxes. The major source of educational funding, determined by the assessed value of a home or property.

addition, many older taxpayers resist these charges because they no longer have children in school and don't see the immediate benefit of increased spending for schools.

The property-tax method of financing schools also has a political disadvantage (Brimley & Garfield, 2005). Unlike sales taxes, which taxpayers pay in small, continual, and almost unnoticed increments, property taxes are more visible targets for taxpayer dissatisfaction. Statements arrive once a year with a comparison to the previous year, and property-tax increases are discussed in public forums whenever school boards (e.g., Carla's in the opening case) ask their taxpayers for increased funding.

Dissatisfaction with this method of funding reached a head in California in 1978 when voters passed an initiative called Proposition 13, which limited property taxes in the state. By the 1990s, 45 other states had passed similar measures (Brimley & Garfield, 2005). The effect on educational funding has been chilling. Schools and school districts have had less to spend and have had to fight harder when requesting new funds from taxpayers.

Federal Funding for Education

The federal government is the third, smallest, and most controversial source of educational funding. As you saw earlier, federal funding for education was virtually nonexistent before 1920 but has increased over time to its present level of about 8.5 percent. Though the amount spent on education has increased in recent years to almost $67 billion in fiscal year 2005, the total still accounts for only about 2 percent of total federal expenditures (National Center for Education Statistics, 2005a). Most (46 percent) federal funds for education are channeled through the U.S. Department of Education, with the next largest proportion (20 percent) coming from the Department of Health and Human Services (Sonnenberg, 2004).

Proponents of a greater federal role in education believe that education is essential for the country's continued progress in the 21st century and that the federal government should continue to exert leadership (and provide funds) in this area. Critics warn of increased federal control over what they believe should be a local responsibility. In addition, conservatives argue against the expansion of what they consider to be an already bloated federal bureaucracy. For these critics, less is better when it comes to federal funding. Local funding, in contrast, makes schools more efficient and responsive to local needs and wishes, they say.

Although the percentage of education funds contributed by the federal government has been small, the impact has been considerable, largely because of the use of **categorical grants**, monies targeted for specific groups and designated purposes. Head Start, aimed at preschoolers, and Title I, which benefits economically disadvantaged youth, are examples of categorical aid programs targeting specific needs or populations. Because the funds must be used for specific purposes, categorical grants have strongly influenced local education practices.

During the 1980s, categorical funds were replaced by **block grants**, federal monies provided to states and school districts with few restrictions for use. Begun during the conservative Reagan administration, block grants purposely reduce the federal role in policy making, in essence giving states and districts control over how monies are spent. Proponents contend this makes sense—who knows local needs better than local educators? Critics contend that funds are often misspent or spent in areas where they aren't needed (Brimley & Garfield, 2005).

Educational Revenues: Where Do They Go?

Categorical grants. Monies targeted for specific groups and designated purposes.

Block grants. Federal monies provided to states and school districts with few restrictions for use.

In 2004–2005, the 50 states and the District of Columbia spent an average of $8,618 per pupil, but as you see in Table 8.2, spending varied considerably from state to state (National Education Association, 2006b). The District of Columbia and New Jersey spent the highest amounts ($15,073 and $13,370, respectively), while Utah spent the lowest ($5,245). The data in Table 8.2 demonstrate some regional trends. Most of the higher per-pupil expenditures are found in Northeastern and upper Midwest states, and lower expenditures are found in the South and West.

TABLE 8.2   State-by-State Spending per Student

State	2004–2005 ($)
Alabama	6,886
Alaska	10,042
Arizona	5,474
Arkansas	6,202
California	7,815
Colorado	8,337
Connecticut	11,893
Delaware	11,016
District of Columbia	15,073
Florida	7,035
Georgia	8,451
Hawaii	8,622
Idaho	6,743
Illinois	9,591
Indiana	8,723
Iowa	7,477
Kansas	7,558
Kentucky	7,906
Louisiana	7,589
Maine	10,723
Maryland	9,762
Massachusetts	11,681
Michigan	8,909
Minnesota	9,249
Mississippi	6,452
Missouri	7,451
Montana	8,025
Nebraska	7,608
Nevada	6,525
New Hampshire	9,624
New Jersey	13,370
New Mexico	8,236
New York	12,879
North Carolina	7,350
North Dakota	7,033
Ohio	9,557
Oklahoma	6,269
Oregon	7,842
Pennsylvania	9,638
Rhode Island	10,641
South Carolina	8,161
South Dakota	7,618
Tennessee	6,856
Texas	7,142
Utah	5,245
Vermont	11,608
Virginia	8,577
Washington	7,858
West Virginia	9,448
Wisconsin	9,619
Wyoming	10,198
U.S. and D.C. Average	8,618

Source: National Education Association (2006b). *Rankings and estimates.* Available at http://www.nea.org/index.html.

A significant portion of a district's budget goes to transportation, building maintenance, and food services. (Anthony Magnacca/Merrill)

It is tempting to conclude that a state's commitment to education can be judged by its per-pupil spending, but, in fact, some states are wealthier than others, and the number of children per taxpayer varies, so they have a greater capacity to fund education. Funding differences between states are also influenced by differences in the cost of living and the number of children that need to be educated. Utah, for example, which has the lowest per-student spending in the country ($5,245) also has the highest birth rate in the nation—approximately one and a half times the national average—so whatever funds are available must be divided among more children.

The effects of funding on excellence in education is a controversial topic, with early research concluding that the amount spent has little or no influence on achievement (Hanushek, 1996). However, more recent research in this area found that higher per-pupil expenditures resulted in higher achievement, mainly because of better-qualified teachers and smaller class sizes (Flanagan & Grissmer, 2002; Krueger & Whitmore, 2002). Increased expenditures seem to have their greatest effect on low-income and minority students.

The relationship between funding and learning isn't simple or precise, however. Achievement tests—the most commonly used measure of student learning—focus on core academic areas, such as math, science, and reading, and not every dollar spent on education goes to teaching these basic subjects. Some monies go to art and music, for example, which are valuable areas of the curriculum, but increased expenditures in these areas won't be directly reflected in higher test scores. Furthermore, as you see in Figure 8.4, only about 61 percent of

Figure 8.4   Educational Expenditures on Different District Programs

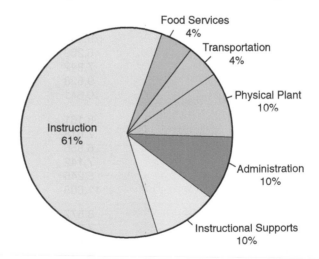

Source: Data from Odden, A., Monk, D., Nakib, Y., & Picus, L. (1995); U.S. Department of Education (2006c).

the money allocated to education is spent on instruction, most of which goes to teacher salaries (Odden et al., 1995; U.S. Department of Education, 2006). The rest is spent on areas that affect achievement only indirectly.

In addition to the 61 percent that directly supports instruction, 10 percent of school district funds goes to instructional assistance needs, such as student services, teacher professional advancement, and curriculum development (see Figure 8.4). Another 10 percent goes to administration. Approximately one third of administration funding is spent in the central district offices, and two thirds goes to schools. Maintenance of school buildings and grounds (physical plant) takes up another 10 percent of the budget. Transportation (school buses) and food services (cafeteria lunches) each account for another 4 percent.

To understand the magnitude of transportation expenditures, consider these national figures. In an average school year, 450,000 yellow school buses travel 4 billion (*billion*, not *million*) miles, providing 10 billion separate rides to nearly 24 million K–12 students (Brimley & Garfield, 2005). Student activities add 5 million trips. Schools provide transportation to 54 percent of the nation's student population at a cost of $493 per student.

Critics often decry the large amount of monies (39 percent) spent on areas other than academics and have initiated national efforts to mandate that 65 percent of education funds go to instruction (Hoff, 2005, 2006). However, school finance experts point out that expenditures for school nurses, school buses, and school lunches, for example, are all part of the total education process, and no research evidence links higher spending on instruction to increases in student achievement (Education Vital Signs, 2006a). In addition, experts note that the amounts schools spend on administration and maintenance of the physical plant compare favorably with those spent in industry (Bracey, 1999b; Odden et al., 1995).

This section provides an answer to the fourth item on our beginning-of-chapter survey, "Most of a district's budget goes to funding instruction." The answer is yes; the average U.S. district spends 61 percent of its budget on instruction.

> **Making Connections:**
> To deepen your understanding of the topics in this section of the chapter and integrate them with topics you've already studied, go to the *Making Connections* module for Chapter 8 at **www.prenhall.com/kauchak**. Respond to questions 6–9.

Check Your Understanding

2.1 What are the major sources of educational funding?

2.2 How are educational revenues spent?

 For feedback, go to Check Your Understanding *at the end of this chapter.*

Emerging Issues in School Governance and Finance

As schools confront the challenges of the 21st century, they face a number of issues in the areas of governance and finance. Some of the most important include the following:

- Equity in funding, one of the most fundamental issues facing education
- Site-based decision making, which attempts to involve teachers and parents in the running of schools
- School choice in the form of charter schools and vouchers

Let's look at these challenges.

Savage Inequalities: The Struggle for Funding Equity

Lakesha Lincoln walks into Jackson Middle School among a horde of other students. Jackson is a 72-year-old urban school in a large northeastern city. She doesn't notice that the three of the five lights down the long main hall are out, and that the hall badly needs a paint job.

She walks by the girls' bathroom, where a sign on the door says, "Bathroom out of order. Use the bathroom on the second floor." She decides she'll wait and get permission to go to the bathroom during her first-period class.

She enters her homeroom and sits down. She has barely enough room to squeeze through the rows of desks, because there are 38 students in her homeroom, and the room was built for 25. Paper is still on the floor from yesterday, and the boards haven't been cleaned from the last class of the previous day.

Students are milling around the room as the bell rings, and Mr. Jensen, her homeroom teacher, tries his best to get them to settle down. He is struggling, because he has had no professional training, and he is doing his best to feel his way through the year, since this is his first year of teaching.

Dawn Johnson walks into Forest Park Middle School, which is in the suburbs. It was built in 2001, and it is roomy, well-lit, and pleasant. Dawn walks into her homeroom, which is spotless with ample equipment and materials that support instruction. Her room is comfortable with plenty of space available for her and her 22 classmates.

The last of the students slide into their chairs as the bell rings, and Mrs. August is standing in front of the room ready to begin. She is a 10-year veteran, with a reputation for being demanding but fair. Students agree that they learn a lot from her.

As you saw earlier, research indicates that significant differences in per-pupil expenditures exist, both between and within states (Biddle & Berliner, 2002; Rothstein, 1998). Jonathan Kozol outlines this issue in his influential book, *Savage Inequalities*:

Americans abhor the notion of a social order in which economic privilege and political power are determined by hereditary class. Officially, we have a more enlightened goal in sight: namely, a society in which a family's wealth has no relation to the probability of future educational attainment and the wealth and station it affords. By this standard, education offered to poor children should be at least as good as that which is provided to the children of the upper-middle class. (1991, p. 207)

This standard of equality is not what Kozol found in his research on school funding. Instead, he found that many urban schools around the country were like Lakesha's—dirty and run down with peeling paint, broken toilets, antiquated or missing textbooks, and teachers who were uncertified or lacked experience, or both. Only miles away, suburban schools like Forest Park Middle, where Dawn goes, featured new, well-maintained buildings that were attractive and inviting learning environments. And teachers were generally seasoned, knowledgeable professionals. These stark contrasts gave Kozol's book its title.

In 1968 Demetrio Rodriguez, a sheet-metal worker in a poor suburb of San Antonio, Texas, looked at the schools his children were attending, compared them with schools in wealthier districts only 10 miles away, and found contrasts similar to those between Jackson and Forest Park middle schools. The fact that property taxes for his district produced only $37 per student compared to $412 per student for the wealthier suburb was the primary problem. These differences are not unusual. For example, in Texas during the 1980s, the 100 most affluent districts in the state spent an average of $7,233 per student, whereas the poorest 100 averaged $2,978. Faced with these inequalities, Mr. Rodriguez sued, contending that his children were being unfairly penalized by where they lived (Brimley & Garfield, 2005; Imazeki & Reschovsky, 2004).

Nationally, wealthy districts spend an average of 23 percent more on their students than do poorer districts. In Alaska, wealthier districts spend more than double the amount per pupil ($16,546 versus $7,379) than do poorer districts in the state (Biddle & Berliner, 2002). Similar patterns exist in other states (Kober, 2006).

Disparities in property tax revenues can result in dramatic differences in funding for schools that are quite close geographically. (left: Anthony Magnacca/Merrill; right: Rachel Epstein/The Image Works.

This section suggests that the fifth item in our beginning-of-chapter survey, "Students across a state are provided with basically the same amount of money to fund their education," is not true. Large disparities in the property tax base that provides funds for schools result in widely varying resources for teachers and students.

Legal challenges over funding equity have increased. The battle lines for these cases were drawn in California in 1971, when the California Supreme Court ruled in a 6–1 vote that the use of property taxes to fund education resulted in unconstitutional funding inequities in the state (*Serrano v. Priest,* 1971). In an attempt to reduce funding inequities, the state's share of education funding rose from 40 to 70 percent.

The *Serrano v. Priest* lawsuit went all the way to the U.S. Supreme Court. Many believed, based on the California decision, that the Supreme Court would find the spending patterns in Texas unconstitutional. However, in a 5–4 vote, it did just the opposite, ruling in 1973 that the U.S. Constitution does not guarantee citizens a right to an education. The Court did point out, however, that funding inequities may violate state constitutions, many of which do guarantee citizens that right.

The Supreme Court ruling on the Rodriguez case sent the issue back to state courts, and many other state suits followed. By mid-2002, courts had overturned existing systems in 21 states and upheld others in 7 states, with 10 cases still pending (Kober, 2006). Differences in state rulings are primarily the result of differences in the wording of state constitutions. Some constitutions are quite specific in guaranteeing "equal education for all," whereas others are vague in specifying that educational opportunity should be "ample" or "efficient." When rulings favored the plaintiffs, researchers found that inequities were reduced by almost 14 percent. Decreasing or eliminating reliance on the property tax was the primary reason (Flanagan & Grissmer, 2002).

The problem of funding inequalities is complicated by the fact that not all districts in a state have the same needs (Brimley & Garfield, 2005; Yinger, 2004). Some have a higher proportion of low-income children, non-native English speakers, or children who need special education services. These populations require extra resources. Reformers are calling for funding formulas that go beyond simply equalizing dollars; they want plans that meet the needs of all students (Rebell, 2004). These proposed reforms are expensive and controversial, as many parents from wealthier districts object to having their local taxes used to fund distant schools across the state. In addition, the problems involved in attempting to quantify educational needs in terms of dollars and cents is complex.

One recent change in educational funding attempts to change funding practices within districts rather than between (National Education Association, 2005). The **weighted student formula** allocates resources within a district to schools on an individual basis based on student

Weighted student formula. A means of allocating resources within a district to schools on an individual basis based on student needs.

To view this video, go to the *Becoming a Professional* DVD included with this text, click on ABC News, and then this chapter's video: *Failing Grade*.

This ABC News video examines a school district that was not only underfunded but also administratively mismanaged. The video focuses on Chester High in Pennsylvania, one of the lowest-rated schools in Pennsylvania. It has been plagued with the worst problems facing the worst schools: overcrowding, which led to a riot; a continuous turnover of staff and administrators; and even a bailout from the state just to pay the teachers' salaries.

How did it get to this stage? Chester High was part of a bold experiment in privatization in which the private sector was supposed to be able to fix all that ailed the public sector when it came to educating children. In Chester, it didn't quite work out that way. You will meet a dynamic young principal, with his own unconventional path, who tried to help these kids beat the odds. You will also meet parents who worry about their children's futures, and a school board that is at a loss.

Think About This

1. Which of Chester High's problems were due to governance? How did the multiple layers of educational governance relate to Chester High's negative situation?

2. Which of Chester High's problems were due to finance issues? How did these problems relate to Kozol's (1991) idea of "savage inequalities"?

3. Why was privatization seen as a solution to Chester High's problems? (See the *Teaching in an Era of Reform* feature in this chapter for a discussion of privatization.)

*To answer these questions online and receive immediate feedback, go to the Companion Website at **www.prenhall.com/kauchak**, then to the Video Perspectives module for Chapter 8.*

needs. Instead of every school in a district getting the same per-pupil amount, the weighted student formula provides more funds to schools that have more special education students or other students requiring additional services. Several U.S. urban school districts—Chicago, Denver, Houston, Los Angeles, and Seattle—have implemented this change. Advocates claim that it is a fairer way of distributing funds and that it decentralizes educational decision making by allowing individual schools to decide how education dollars will be spent. Comprehensive research is still needed to see if this change will work in other, smaller districts where increased funding for some schools could mean decreased, and potentially crippling, funding for others.

The role the federal government should play in reducing or eliminating funding inequities is another issue facing funding reformers. Critics of the current system point out that two thirds of funding differences occur between states rather than within states, and states receiving low levels of educational funding are clustered in the South and Southeast, areas that also have large proportions of poor and minority students. Experts estimate that it would take a minimum of $25 billion to equalize states' expenditures, a daunting figure considering current federal budget deficits (Flanagan & Grissmer, 2002).

Site-Based Decision Making

In the chapter's opening case, Carla made her proposal to her school board, which would ultimately decide which math series to use. Her recommendation came from a committee composed of other teachers in the district whose ideas and opinions were solicited and considered. Concerned parents, whose children would use the new series, were also at the meeting and had the opportunity to ask questions and influence the decision. This appears to be democracy in action, but is it? The decision would still be made at the district level, far removed from local schools.

Critics of this "top–down," district-level form of school governance contend that too many important educational decisions are made by people far removed from schools. They argue that school board members from across town may not know what is best for a particular school, for example. **Site-based decision making** is a school management reform movement that attempts to place increased responsibility for governance at the individual school level. Proponents of site-based decision making believe that the people most affected by educational decisions—teachers, parents, and even students—ought to be more directly involved in those decisions (Archer, 2006b; National Education Association, 2005). Proponents also believe that site-based decision making, in addition to being more democratic, ought to result in better-run schools. People who help make decisions about schools are more likely to support them and help them succeed.

Site-based decision making is appealing from a professional perspective. It seems sensible that professional educators should have a substantial say in how learning and teaching occur in their schools. However, in one poll, 70 percent of teachers felt they were out of the loop in their district's decision-making process (Public Agenda, 2000). Involvement in decision making creates dilemmas for teachers, however. Teachers join the profession to work with students, and the demands of extended committee work can siphon energies away from teaching (van den Berg, 2002). For example, was the effort Carla spent on the textbook selection process worth it, or would her students be better served if she had been able to devote more of her time to teaching? If decisions such as these are made at the school level, will this increase duplication of effort in the district? These questions don't have easy answers.

Site-based decision making usually exists in one of two forms. Increased community participation in advisory committees, composed of parents, teachers, community members (and sometimes students) is the most common (Archer, 2006b). School boards and building administrators maintain legal control over schools, and the advisory committees provide input in areas such as setting school goals and priorities, making curricular and extracurricular decisions, and selecting and evaluating teachers and administrators.

A more radical form of site-based decision making involves actual community control of educational decisions through an elected council. When this occurs, the district school board shares decision-making power with the council in areas such as the hiring and retention of principals and teachers, the curriculum, and budgets. Experiments in several large cities have raised thorny questions about who should serve on these community councils and whether or not decentralized decision making results in better schools for children (D. Land, 2002).

School Choice

The freedom to choose is a central American value. Americans can choose where and how they live and what occupation they work in, for example. Shouldn't they also have a choice in the kind of schools their children attend? As presently organized, public school systems are centralized and bureaucratic, and where students go to school is determined by the neighborhoods in which they live. In the name of efficiency, we've created a governance and finance system that begins in state capitals, runs through local district offices, and culminates in schools that are similar in form and function. Walk into most public schools across the country, and you'll see teachers teaching the same content in basically the same way (Cuban, 1993; Goodlad, 1984). Even the boxlike architecture of school buildings is the same.

Critics decry this uniformity and make several arguments in support of greater variety and choice. For example, we are a nation of 50 states with unique individuals and distinctive subcultures, and our schools ought to reflect this diversity. In addition, experimentation and innovation

Site-based decision making. A school management reform movement that attempts to place increased responsibility for governance at the individual school level.

Proponents of school choice believe charter schools and vouchers will provide economically disadvantaged children with better schools. (Scott Cunningham/Merrill)

have been central to our nation's progress, and conformity discourages innovation. From an economic perspective, the present system represents a monopoly that forces parents to send their children to neighborhood public schools (Betts, 2005). Critics believe that alternatives would result in healthy competition, which would ultimately result in better schools. They also argue that the public school system has become bloated, bureaucratic, and unresponsive to individual citizens' needs. In response to these criticisms, reformers call for school choice.

What does choice mean? At one level, parents already have choices, because they move to neighborhoods served by particular schools. The quality of the schools is one of the major features parents consider when choosing a neighborhood (Hassel & Hassel, 2004). If parents don't like the schools in their neighborhood, they can send their children to private schools, something that 10 percent of parents currently do (U.S. Department of Education, 2000). In addition, through open enrollment programs, districts typically allow parents who believe their local schools are subpar to send their children across town to better schools. Doing so requires greater time and expense, but parents still have choices.

But choice advocates point out that many poor, minority, and inner-city parents don't have the resources to vote with their wallets or their cars. They cannot afford to move to better neighborhoods with better schools, to send their children to private schools, or even to drive across town each day to transport their children to a non-neighborhood public school. In addition, some school districts are so bad, critics contend, that other schools in the district don't really provide viable alternatives. These parents deserve the right to choose, just as much as more wealthy parents do.

But how can parents be provided with options? The concept of school choice has resulted in two educational innovations: charter schools and vouchers.

Charter Schools

Charter schools are alternative schools that are independently operated but publicly funded. In many states, parents or others dissatisfied with the local school choices have the right to create their own alternative or specialty schools. Charter schools typically begin when a group—teachers, community members, or a private corporation—develops a plan for a school, including its curriculum, staffing, and budget. This plan, or "charter," must then be accepted by the local school board or state office of education and serves as a contract with the state.

Many school districts already have alternative schools, such as magnet schools with specialized programs as well as schools designed to meet the needs of students who can't successfully function in regular schools and classrooms (e.g., young, unwed mothers or children with serious behavior or emotional problems). Charter schools are similar to other alternative schools in that they offer a different curriculum or target special populations; they differ in that they are independently administered public schools and subject to less regulatory control from a district's central administration (Carnoy, Jacobsen, Mishel, & Rothstein, 2005).

The charter school movement began in Minnesota in 1991, when the legislature approved the creation of eight teacher-created and -operated outcome-based schools. (An outcome-based school makes curricular and instructional decisions based on student performance on specified assessments.) Since that time, 39 additional states and the District of Columbia have passed charter school legislation resulting in the creation of more than 3,600 schools with more than 1 million students, or about 2 percent of the public school student population (Kober, 2006; West & Manno, 2006). The five states with the most charters in the 2005–2006 school year were California, Arizona, Florida, Ohio, and Texas, in that order (Charter Connection, 2006).

Charter schools. Alternative schools that are independently operated but publicly funded.

178

The focus of different charter schools varies dramatically, although most attract parents seeking smaller schools and class sizes, better quality instruction, and alternatives to public school curricula and environments (Carpenter & Finn, 2006; Casey, Andreson, Yelverton, & Wedeen, 2002). Many (about one third of all charter schools) are designed by urban community leaders to meet the needs of inner-city youth (West & Manno, 2006), and, nationally, 58 percent of charter students are members of racial or ethnic minorities, compared with 41 percent for regular public schools (Viadero, 2005a). Some, for example, focus on developing students' African heritage through language instruction, literature, and the arts. Others attract parents who want a return to the basics, while still others focus on technology and the arts.

Initial research on charter school teachers has revealed greater teacher involvement in school governance issues (Gresham, Hess, Maranto, & Milliman, 2000). As Figure 8.5 shows, 62 percent of teachers in charter elementary schools reported having high levels of influence over curriculum decisions at their schools, whereas only 25 percent of teachers at regular schools reported such influence. Similar differences occurred in teachers' beliefs about their influence over selection of instructional materials and scheduling.

School philosophy, smaller size, and characteristics of the teachers themselves are all possible reasons for teachers' greater role in decision making. The best charter schools begin with the view that teachers are central to a quality education and actively attempt to involve teachers in school planning. Charter schools also tend to be smaller, which allows change to occur more rapidly. Finally, teachers who choose to work in charter schools are likely to be more adventurous and willing to experiment with their teaching. One charter school teacher commented, "Everyone who came was one of the best in the program from wherever they came from. There were no slackers in the group" (Brouillette, 2000, p. 31).

Issues of Quality in Charter Schools. Considerable variation exists in the quality of charter schools, and this uneven quality is having a negative effect on the charter school movement (Hutton, 2005). For example, in Texas—a leader in establishing charter schools—a panel of state lawmakers recommended a moratorium on new charter schools, citing poor student performance,

Figure 8.5 Perceptions of Governance Issues by Charter and Non-Charter Arizona Teachers

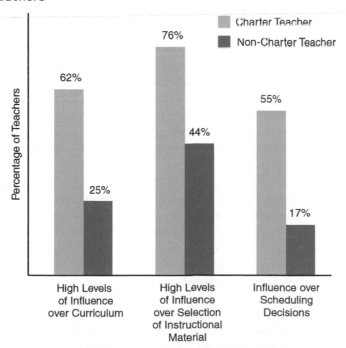

Source: Data from Gresham, A., Hess, F., Maranto, R., & Milliman, S. (2000).

179

financial troubles, and unexpected closures (Associated Press, 2000). In 1999, Texas had 193 charter schools, and the state spent $218 million on them. However, only 59 percent of charter school students passed a state skills exam in the 1998–1999 school year, compared with the state average of 78.4 percent. In reviewing existing charter schools, the state education agency gave an "unacceptable" rating to nearly one fourth of the 103 charter schools it evaluated. In 2002 Texas revoked the charters of five schools for chronically poor performance on state tests; two charter schools serving 2,000 students were at the bottom of the state's accountability rankings for 3 years in a row (Hendrie, 2002). Nationally, in 2005, about 65 charter schools closed their doors in 17 states, about 2 percent of charters in these states (Robelen, 2006b).

California, another leader in the charter school movement, has encountered similar problems. In 2004, California's Charter School Academy, which operated more than 50 schools, abruptly closed all of its schools, leaving families, teachers, and school officials scrambling (Hutton, 2005). A subsequent state audit found the charter organization had misused state and federal funds and sought the return of $23 million from the for-profit management company (Hendrie, 2005b).

The problem of quality is partially linked to the large numbers of unlicensed teachers in charter schools. One national study found that 43 percent of charter school teachers lacked appropriate licenses, compared to 9 percent in regular public schools, and this figure increased to nearly 60 percent in predominantly African-American charters (H. Brown, 2003). In a time when teacher quality is seen as central to school-improvement efforts, these figures are troubling. A major advantage of charter schools—freedom from bureaucratic oversight—also seems to be a major weakness of this reform.

Inadequate resources and facilities are also persistent problems in charter schools (Casey, Andreson, Yelverton, & Wedeen, 2002). Many lack libraries and laboratories and sometimes even basic supplies such as paper and pencils (Carnoy et al., 2005). The arrival of for-profit corporations into the charter school arena, which you'll read about in a later section, has exacerbated the problem (Hendrie, 2003a).

Charters were proposed as a more effective alternative to existing schools; however, early research failed to demonstrate a clear relationship between charter schools and increased student achievement (Bracey, 2004; Carnoy et al., 2005). More recent research has even found that charter schools actually trailed regular public schools in both reading and math achievement (Robelen, 2006d).

The charter school movement is controversial and highly politicized. Charter advocates generally adhere to a political ideology suggesting that the private sector, such as the business world in our country, is superior to the public sector—our public school system, for example. Adherents to this ideology argue that charter schools are superior to regular public schools, because they reduce the size of the existing educational bureaucracy and are more consistent with existing business models. Research data, however, don't support this contention. These data indicate that, with a few exceptions, charters are no better, and are often inferior, to our existing public schools.

Vouchers

Vouchers are a second approach to school choice. A **voucher** is a check or written document that parents can use to purchase educational services. The voucher approach is grounded in the belief that parents know what their children need and should be free to purchase the best education wherever they can find it. Some voucher plans give parents the choice of either a public or private school, whereas others limit the choice to public schools.

Vouchers are often promoted by political conservatives who argue that public schools are a monopoly, and that opening up schools to parental choice allows market forces to improve education. All schools (not just those in immediate neighborhoods) become viable alternatives. Over time, the best schools would attract more students and flourish, whereas poorer schools would be shut down by informed consumers and market forces.

Because of possible disruptive influences on public schools and issues with religious instruction, the voucher movement is highly controversial. Critics, including the National Ed-

Voucher. A check or written document that parents can use to purchase educational services.

ucation Association and the American Federation of Teachers, the two largest professional organizations in education, argue that vouchers increase segregation, split the public along socioeconomic lines, and drain students and resources from already struggling inner-city schools (American Federation of Teachers, 2003a; National Education Association, 2002a).

Some voucher advocates would also like to use them for religious schools; critics contend that this violates the principle of separation of church and state. In Cleveland and Milwaukee, two cities that have led the country in the voucher movement, religious schools have been the major beneficiaries. For example, in Cleveland, 82 percent of participating schools in a voucher program were religiously affiliated, and 96 percent of participating students attended religious schools (National Association of Elementary School Principals, 2002). Nationally, almost 80 percent of private schools have a religious affiliation (Brimley & Garfield, 2005). Supporters of voucher programs ask why parents should have to pay for a quality education twice—once when they pay public school taxes and again when they pay tuition at private schools.

In 2002 the U.S. Supreme Court, in a narrow 5–4 decision, ruled that the voucher program in Cleveland did not violate separation of church and state (Flanigan, 2003; Walsh, 2002b). The idea that voucher funds went to parents rather than directly to religious schools was central to the decision. Since the Supreme Court made its decision, the number of applicants for the Cleveland voucher program has risen 29 percent, suggesting that more parents are taking advantage of this educational option (Hendrie, 2002). However, a research study conducted by a Cleveland-based nonprofit organization, Policy Matters Ohio, concluded that Cleveland vouchers served more as a subsidy for students already attending private schools than as an "escape hatch" for students eager to leave the public schools.

Since 1990 three state legislatures have enacted voucher systems: Wisconsin, Ohio, and Florida. However, the Wisconsin and Ohio plans apply only to Milwaukee and Cleveland, respectively, and in January of 2006, the Florida Supreme Court, in a 5–2 ruling, struck down Florida's voucher system. The court ruled that "the diversion of money not only reduced public funds for a public education but also used public funds to provide an alternative education in private schools that are not subject to the 'uniformity' requirements for public schools" (Romano, 2006, p. A05). Legal battles are likely to occur in other states and may be difficult for voucher advocates because 37 state constitutions currently have language that prohibits state aid to religious schools (Gehring, 2002b).

As with charter schools, the academic benefits of vouchers are unclear. Some research suggests that voucher programs can lead to small achievement gains (Bowman, 2000a, 2000b; Goldhaber, 1999), but other research indicates no achievement gains (Robelen, 2006c) or gains in some populations (e.g., African-American) but not others (Gewertz, 2003b; National Education Association, 2002a). A curriculum emphasizing academics, more effective instruction, and greater parental involvement are explanations offered for any gains that exist. In addition, parents provided with choice are generally more satisfied with the schools their children attend (Goldhaber, 1999). However, questions about the effects of choice on school diversity are continually raised, as we'll see later in the chapter.

In general, support for vouchers comes from dissatisfaction with existing public schools, and if public schools improve, public interest in vouchers is likely to wane. In the 2000 election, voters in California and Michigan overwhelmingly (70 percent in California and 69 percent in Michigan) voted against voucher initiatives, which opponents contend sounds a death knell for the movement (Walsh, 2000b). However, Republican legislatures in Texas, Colorado, and Louisiana are considering statewide voucher plans, primarily aimed at low-income students in poor-performing schools (Richard, 2003).

State tuition tax-credit plans are a variation on school voucher programs in which parents are given tax credits for money they spend on private-school tuition. Tuition tax credits have emerged in some states as a more politically viable alternative to publicly financed school vouchers. However, research suggests that tuition tax credits primarily benefit wealthy families who are already sending their children to private schools. In Illinois, for example, tax credits cost the state more than $61 million in lost revenues in 2000 (Gehring, 2002a). Taxpayers earning more than $80,000 claimed 46 percent of that amount, whereas less than 3 percent went to households making less

State tuition tax-credit plans. A variation on school voucher programs in which parents are given tax credits for money they spend on private-school tuition.

than $20,000. A similar problem occurred in Arizona (Bracey, 2002). Households earning more than $50,000 received 81 percent of the tax credits as well as 84 percent of the $109 million state revenues spent on tuition tax credits. More equitable ways of distributing the benefits of this form of school choice need to be designed if this reform effort is to grow.

Homeschooling provides parents with the opportunity to customize a child's education to a family's specific educational goals. (Buccina Studios/Getty Images, Inc.—Photodisc)

Making Connections:
To deepen your understanding of the topics in this section of the chapter and integrate them with topics you've already studied, go to the *Making Connections* module for Chapter 8 at **www.prenhall.com/kauchak.** Respond to questions 10 and 11.

Homeschooling. An educational option in which parents educate their children at home.

Homeschooling

Homeschooling, an educational option in which parents educate their children at home, may be the ultimate form of school choice. Homeschooling has become increasingly popular in recent years, with 2003 estimates of the number of children participating at 1.1 million students, accounting for 2.2 percent of the school-age population, up almost 30 percent from 1999 (Princiotta, Bielick, & Chapman, 2004; Zehr, 2006).

Parents choose to homeschool their children for a wide variety of reasons. Most (49 percent) do so because of concerns about the moral climate of existing schools or because of religious objections to the curriculum. Others want a more positive social climate (15 percent), or seek academic excellence (14 percent), or want to design a program that meets the specific needs of their child (12 percent) (Home School Legal Defense Association, 2004). All are seeking an alternative to existing public schools.

State laws regulating homeschooling vary greatly (Fischer et al., 2006). In most states, parents must demonstrate that their instruction is equivalent to that offered in public schools. Forty-one states don't have any minimum educational qualifications for parents who homeschool their children; eight of the remaining nine states require at least a high school diploma (Zehr, 2004). Approximately half the states require homeschooled students to participate in regular standardized testing. Homeschooled students who take these tests typically do well, scoring, on average, between the 65th and 90th percentiles on various tests (Mathews, 1999).

Despite its growing popularity, homeschooling has its critics. Some wonder whether children schooled at home will learn important social interaction skills (Galley, 2003). Other critics question whether narrow courses of study will expose children to alternative views and perspectives (Reich, 2002). One troubling trend is the tendency of some homeschool learning materials to criticize specific religious beliefs or entire religions. One study found that some of the more popular religiously oriented homeschool texts describe Islam as "a false religion," blame Hinduism for India's problems, and attribute Africa's problems to the absence of non-Christian religions (Patterson, 2001/2002). These types of messages are troubling in a pluralistic society such as ours.

teaching in an era of reform

Privatization

The move toward school choice has taken an interesting turn, with one option being privately run, for-profit schools. Modeled after HMOs (health maintenance organizations), EMOs (education maintenance organizations) propose to run and manage either whole districts or specific schools within a district.

Aspects of school privatization are not new. Schools have been outsourcing contracts for support services, such as school lunches and transportation, for years. More recently, districts have hired companies such as IBM and Hewlett-Packard to provide technology support (Trotter, 2002a). What is new is the idea of handing over control of a whole school or district to a private corporation.

Estimates indicate that 70 percent of school districts currently engage in some type of business partnership (L. Alexander & Riley, 2002). At one time, school–business partnerships often consisted of corporations buying a football scoreboard or placing an ad in the school newspaper. More recently, Channel

One, a privately run school news/advertising company, offered 10 minutes of news to schools in return for 2 minutes of advertising. Incentives include free satellite disks, a schoolwide cable system, and free televisions in all classrooms. In 2001 Channel One reached 12,000 schools and 8 million students, 40 percent of the nation's 12- to 18-year-olds (Molnar & Reeves, 2001; Trotter, 2001). This is a huge advertising market.

Corporations such as Edison Schools, Inc., and Sylvan Learning Incorporated are leaders in the school privatization movement. Edison began in 1992 and made its stock public in 1998 with an initial Wall Street offering of $18 per share; optimism soon propelled share prices to $38 (Woodward, 2002). Chris Whittle, its founder, predicted that by 2020 Edison would run one in every 10 schools in America, but so far the company has grown slowly, and its stock sank to $2 in 2001. In 2005, Edison ran 136 schools across the country, serving 53,500 students (Reid, 2005). Edison's most visible challenge came when the school district of Philadelphia, a floundering system suffering from perennial low student achievement, offered Edison a 5-year, $60 million contract to manage 20 of its schools.

Nationwide, the privatization movement has received a big boost from the trend toward school choice, and the number of privately run schools grew from 285 in 2001 to 417 in 2003 (Walsh, 2003b); of these, 74 percent were charter schools. The number of for-profit companies in the educational arena also grew from 21 in 2001 to 47 in 2003.

Technology also plays a key role in the school privatization movement. William Bennett, former Secretary of Education, founded K12, a virtual school that serves both homeschoolers and charter schools embedded within public school districts (Bracey, 2004). Despite the use of technology, both its curriculum and instruction appear to be traditional, emphasizing the memorization of facts.

The Issue

As would be expected, private, for-profit schools are highly controversial. Should corporations, whose primary objective is making a profit, be entrusted with the education of children?

Critics make a number of arguments against privatization (Belfield & Bevin, 2005; Saltman, 2005). They question the ability of a corporate efficiency model to work in education and assert that corporate strategies will adversely affect both teachers and students. Further, they contend, privatized schools have a dual mission—improving test scores and making a profit—and corporate profits and education don't mix. Attention to the bottom line means that student welfare may be sacrificed in an effort to make money. Critics also claim that a narrow focus on the basics as well as neglect of non-native English speakers and students with special needs are additional problems. Teachers are treated as workers, not professionals, and are expected to implement a regimented, top-down curriculum.

Support for the critics' position can be found in Edison's efforts in Philadelphia, where controversy has existed from the beginning. Apparently, the district's call for outside help was based on an evaluation conducted by Edison itself and not sent out for competitive bids (Gewertz, 2002). In essence, the state of Pennsylvania hired Edison to conduct a study, completed in 2

months, for $2.7 million (Bracey, 2002). Not surprisingly, the Edison report concluded that external help should be sought, and the district authorized the creation of 20 Edison charter schools. After less than 1 year of operation, the Philadelphia School District, citing budget considerations, decided to shift $10 million of the next year's $20 million contract from Edison and other private companies to other reform projects (Gewertz, 2003b). One disillusioned parent commented, "I don't consider putting 15,000 students with a company that can't guarantee operations next year reform. It's not just a stock game, this is my child's life" (Saltman, 2005, p. 154).

Teacher morale and lagging student performance in Edison schools are persistent problems. For example, in an Edison-contracted San Francisco elementary school, approximately half of the teachers left in each of Edison's 2 years of operation, citing problems with long work hours, a regimented curriculum, and overemphasis on test preparation. There were also claims that students with academic or behavioral difficulties were "counseled out" of the school in hopes of raising test scores (Woodward, 2002). San Francisco cancelled its contract with Edison; under a renewed charter contract with the state of California, the Edison school's test scores remained low, ranking last among scores from San Francisco's 75 elementary schools.

Privatization advocates argue that these problems are exceptions, that Edison works in some of the most challenging schools in the country, and that the public shouldn't expect miracles overnight. They also assert that competition from the corporate sector is good because it encourages public schools to reexamine unproductive practices. In addition, advocates claim, the same business efficiencies that have made America a world leader can also work in schools, and a focus on performance (as measured by standardized tests) can provide schools with a clear mission to increase student achievement. They also claim that privatization can inject a breath of fresh air into the educational bureaucracy.

Research has found some benefits of privatized schools. They are cleaner and more efficiently run than public schools (Reid, 2005). Technology is typically emphasized, and more attention is given to individualized instruction. However, companies have not provided clear evidence that students learn more in privately run schools, a core assertion of privatization advocates. Some research shows improved achievement, but other research shows either no gain or declines (Shay & Gomez, 2002; Walsh, 2003c). Unfortunately, the research on achievement gains in privatized schools is murky, clouded by the sponsors—either privatization backers or critics—who seem to produce results that bolster their position.

You Take a Position

Now it's your turn to take a position on the issue. State in writing whether you do or do not favor the operation of schools by for-profit corporations, and provide a two-page rationale for your position.

For additional references and resources, go to the Companion Website at www.prenhall.com/kauchak, then to the Teaching in an Era of Reform *module for Chapter 8. You can respond online or submit your response to your instructor.*

School Choice and Cultural Minorities

School choice is often framed in terms of parental empowerment, or providing parents with educational alternatives. But can the process of school choice result in such unintended negative consequences as increased social and racial segregation, as some critics claim (Gill, 2005; Ross, 2005)?

Research from New Zealand, which began experimenting with school choice via a quasi voucher system in 1989, raises some cautionary flags (Fiske & Ladd, 2000). Under new choice rules, schools with more student applicants than openings could essentially choose whom they admitted and served. The better schools chose academically motivated students from affluent families, leaving less popular schools with poorer-achieving students. Researchers concluded that in New Zealand, "[c]hoice and competition are likely to polarize enrollment patterns by race, ethnicity, socioeconomic status, and students' performance" (Fiske & Ladd, 2000, p. 38). These same researchers cautioned against unregulated choice systems that could result in "polarization of enrollment patterns and exacerbation of the problems of noncompetitive schools" (Fiske & Ladd, 2000, p. 38). In other words, choice systems have the potential of encouraging social segregation and further damaging already weak inner-city schools.

The same concerns have been raised in the United States; critics contend that voucher programs and charter schools entice the best students away from poor-performing schools, leaving urban schools, in particular, in even worse shape than they are now (Ferguson, 2002). Further, offering school choice leads to segregation of students, either by income or race. One recent study supports critics' claims. Researchers found that 70 percent of African-American charter school students attend intensely segregated schools, compared with 34 percent of African-American students in regular public schools (Frankenberg & Lee, 2003). In virtually every state studied, the average African-American charter school student attended a school with a higher percentage of African-American students and a lower percentage of White students. However, a more recent study found that private, voucher-funded schools in Washington, D.C., were less racially homogeneous than their public school counterparts (Robelen, 2006a).

Problems of social and cultural polarization were also found in Arizona, a leader in the charter school movement (Schnaiberg, 2000). In 1996 two charter schools opened in the small rural school district of Safford, which had approximately 60 percent Anglo and 40 percent Hispanic students. In its first year of enrollment, the Triumphant Learning Center, a back-to-basics school with Christian overtones, enrolled 95 percent Anglo students. Los Milagros, a charter school with Catholic ties, enrolled 75 percent Hispanic students. Although neither school consciously chose to exclude certain types of students, "subtle signals" sent messages to parents. For example, the Triumphant Learning Center emphasized increased parental involvement by encouraging parents to volunteer in the school and by closing their doors every Friday to allow more family time. Poor Hispanic families, in which both parents worked—some holding more than one job—were not able to participate. As recently as 2000, 53 percent of Los Milagros' students were Hispanic and 90 percent of the students in the Triumphant Learning Center were Anglo, but both schools are making efforts to balance their enrollments.

Another area of concern connected with school choice has to do with equal opportunities for students with special needs and how those needs should be funded. In most voucher plans, the voucher amount is equal to the average per-pupil expenditure in the district or state, but the cost for educating children with special needs can be more than twice that amount (National Education Association, 2005; Odden et al., 1995). Consequently, students with exceptionalities could find themselves underfunded or even refused admittance by certain schools. This very problem occurred in Massachusetts when for-profit charter schools openly discouraged students with exceptionalities from attending (Zollars, 2000). Only 17 percent of private schools provide special education services (Ferguson, 2002), so the problem of access to choice schools may be particularly acute for students with special needs.

Supporters of school-choice programs counter that public schools are already segregated, especially in inner cities, and that choice can actually promote integration. For example, in 1999, 55 percent of all public-school twelfth graders attended classes that had either more than 90 percent or fewer than 10 percent minorities (Greene, 2000). In contrast, only 41 percent of students in choice-driven private schools were in similarly segregated classrooms. School choice, when designed strategically, can actually be an integration tool.

The effects of school choice on students from minority groups will remain controversial and is likely to significantly affect education in the future. Whether these effects will be positive or negative is unclear at this time (Goldhaber & Hyde, 2002; Ross, 2005). Ideally, school choice should encourage experimentation and innovation. As with all experiments, mistakes will occur. Whether these mistakes will adversely affect students and the teachers who work with them are important questions.

Check Your Understanding

3.1 What are the major causes of funding inequities in education? What are some proposed solutions to the problem?

3.2 What are the two major forms of school choice? How are they similar and different?

3.3 What is school privatization, and what are its pros and cons?

 For feedback, go to Check Your Understanding *at the end of this chapter.*

decision making

Defining Yourself as a Professional

You've just graduated from a local university with a bachelor's degree, and you're certified in special education. Jobs are plentiful, you've interviewed with three different districts, and each has offered you a position.

The first was in a large urban district in the city where you grew up. The interview in the central office went well, and they asked you to interview with a school principal. When you arrived at the school, you were surprised at how run-down the school and the surrounding neighborhoods were. The principal was dedicated and enthusiastic, and when she showed you around the school, you could tell she loved what she did. Her last words to you were, "Think about us. This is a school that needs you, and you can really make a difference here."

Your second interview was in a small rural district near the university you attended. The central office was small, the interview went well, and the assistant superintendent and head of personnel concluded the interview by walking you down the street to meet the principal you'd be working for. The school was a small traditional brick building with well-lit halls and high ceilings. Though the pay was not as good as in the urban school, the principal emphasized the opportunities for growth and leadership in a small district like this one. There were only two other full-time special education teachers in the district, and the head of the program would be retiring in a few years.

Your third interview was with a growing suburban district on the edge of a major metropolitan area in your state. The district office was modern and bustling. The head of personnel explained how the district would be hiring 50 new teachers that year and each would be assigned to a mentor. The school district had the highest tax base in the state, and this was evident in the school you visited. Computers and other forms of technology were everywhere. The pay scale was also the highest in the state.

What would you do in this situation?

To respond to this question online and receive immediate feedback, go to the Decision Making module for Chapter 8 on the Companion Website at www.prenhall.com/kauchak.

Meeting Your Learning Objectives

1. Describe the major educational governance structures at the state and local levels.
   - The responsibility for governing schools in the United States is given to the states by the Tenth Amendment to the U.S. Constitution. Despite geographical, historical, economic, and political differences between the states, the educational governance structure in each is surprisingly similar.

(continued)

- Within each state, the governor and state legislature are aided by the state board of education, a lay group of people that establishes educational policy for the state. This policy is implemented by the state office of education, an organization of education professionals. The state office of education is responsible for teacher licensing, curriculum supervision, approval of school sites and buildings, and collection of statistical data.
- Local control of education, a uniquely American idea, occurs through individual school districts. Each district is governed by a local school board, containing lay people from the community, and administered by a district superintendent. The superintendent is responsible for running the district office as well as overseeing the operations of the individual schools within the district. Principals play a major role in shaping the instructional agendas at the individual school level.

2. Explain the different sources and targets of educational funding.
   - Schools are funded from three different sources. Almost one half (49 percent) of school funds come from the states, which typically gather funds using use state income taxes and special taxes. Local sources provide another 43 percent of funding and typically do this through property taxes. The third and smallest source of school funding (8.5 percent) is the federal government. (See Figure 8.3.)
   - Most education monies (61 percent) go to instructional services, primarily to pay for teacher salaries. Ten percent also goes to instructional assistance needs such as student services, teacher professional development, and curriculum development. Another 10 percent goes to administration, both at the district and school level. Maintenance of school buildings and grounds takes up another 10 percent. Finally, transportation (school buses) and food services (cafeterias) each account for another 4 percent. (See Figure 8.4.)

3. Describe the major current issues in school governance and finance.
   - Controversies over inequities in school finance have focused on differences within, rather than between, states. The large number of court cases involving funding inequities has caused states to reexamine funding formulas and has resulted in increased state and decreased local funding. Current approaches to funding equity go beyond absolute dollar amounts to include student and district needs.
   - Site-based decision making has emerged as a major trend in governance reform. In site-based decision making, both parents and teachers have greater input into curricular and instructional decisions.
   - School choice in the form of charter schools and vouchers provides parents with greater control over their children's education. Charter schools, publicly funded by independent entities, target their efforts on specific educational goals or patrons. Vouchers, essentially tickets for educational services, allow parents to shop around for schools that fit their needs. Privatization, in which corporations contract for specific services within districts, is a growing but controversial practice. The impact of school-choice programs on cultural minorities and integration efforts is still unclear.

Important Concepts

block grants
categorical grants
charter schools
homeschooling
local school board
property taxes
school district
school principal

site-based decision making
state board of education
state office of education
state tuition tax-credit plans
superintendent
voucher
weighted student formula

Developing as a Professional

Preparing for Your Licensure Exam

This exercise will provide you with practice answering questions similar to the Praxis™ Principles of Learning and Teaching Exam as well as your state-specific licensure exam. Read the following case study, and answer the questions that follow.

"Hi, Tom. How's the world treating you?" Andrea Martinez asks, as she drops a load of books on the desk in the teachers' lounge.

"I think I'm in the wrong job," Tom replies, looking down at the newspaper he was reading. "We got a lousy 2 percent pay increase this year. That, combined with the 1 1/2 percent last year, puts us behind even inflation. Maybe I'll need to get a third job to make ends meet."

"I know what you mean. We're struggling, too, but the economy is tight—a lot of people are unemployed. I don't know what to do myself."

"Maybe I should run for the state legislature," Tom says. "I could tell those people what it's really like to live on a teacher's salary."

"Why the legislature? Why not our school board? They're the ones who actually decide our pay raises."

"Aw, I'm probably not cut out to be a politician anyways. I'm too honest," Tom replies with a cynical grin. "I have actually thought about going back to school and becoming a principal. Their salaries beat ours."

"But so do their headaches," Andrea counters. "If big bucks are what you're after, why stop there? Why not become a superintendent? Ours makes over $150,000."

"Yeah, I heard that. But I also heard he's looking for a new job. They can't seem to keep people in that job. This one's been with us 2 years. The other one lasted 3. Maybe my job isn't so bad after all. At least I know there'll be a job waiting for me next year."

1. How would you respond to Tom and Andrea's comments about who actually determines teachers' salaries?

2. How accurate was Tom's comment that principals' salaries "beat" teachers' salaries?

3. Is the experience of Tom and Andrea's superintendent unusual? What factors lead to superintendents' short tenures?

To receive feedback on your responses to these exercises, go to the Companion Website at www.prenhall.com/kauchak , then to the Preparing for Your Licensure Exam *module for Chapter 8.*

Discussion Questions

1. Should legislation be passed to make local school boards mirror the populations they serve? For example, if 25 percent of the population is Hispanic, should one fourth of the school board be Hispanic? What advantages and disadvantages are there to this approach to equitable representation? What other alternatives might be better?

2. Ordinarily, teachers cannot be school board members in their own districts because of potential conflicts of interest. Would teachers make good school board members in districts in which they live but don't teach? Should a certain number or percentage of school board positions be reserved for teachers? Why or why not?

3. Should the percentages of male and female principals reflect the gender composition of the teachers at the school level in which the principals work? Why or why not?

4. Should school districts in a state be funded equally? What are the advantages and disadvantages to this approach? Should every school district in the nation receive equal funds? What are the advantages and disadvantages to this approach?

5. Will school choice be a positive or negative development in education? Why?

6. Should vouchers be made available to private religious schools? Why or why not?

Developing as a Professional: Online Activities

Going Into Schools

Go to the Companion Website at *www.prenhall.com/kauchak*, and click on the *Going Into Schools* module for Chapter 8. You will find a number of school-based activities that will help you link chapter content to the schools in which you work.

Virtual Field Experience: Using the Internet to Explore the Profession

If you would like to participate in a Virtual Field Experience, access the following Website: *http://www.nea.org/issues/vouchers/index/html*. This site contains data and opinions about vouchers from the perspective of the National Education Association, the largest professional organization in education.

Online Portfolio Activities

To develop your professional portfolio, further apply your understanding of chapter content, and address the INTASC standards, go the Companion Website at *www.prenhall.com/kauchak*, then to the *Online Portfolio Activities* for Chapter 8. Complete the suggested activities.

Check Your Understanding

1.1 **Who is legally responsible for governing education in the United States?**

The Tenth Amendment to the Constitution clearly assigns legal responsibility for education to the 50 states.

1.2 **How does each state govern education?**

State governance of education begins with the governor and legislature. Though they have many other responsibilities, both influence education by focusing attention on educational issues. In addition, state legislatures supply about half of a district's education budget.

The organization directly and legally responsible for governing education is the state board of education. Primarily consisting of noneducators, the state board issues and revokes teaching licenses, establishes the length of the school year, creates standards for approving and accrediting schools, and develops and implements a system for gathering educational data.

The state office of education, composed of professional educators, implements education policy on a daily basis. The state office of education is responsible for teacher licensing, curriculum supervision, approval of school sites and buildings, and collection of statistical data.

1.3   What role do school districts play in governing education?

School districts are responsible for the day-to-day functioning of schools. They hire teachers and ensure that students have classrooms and books. They are governed by a local school board, consisting of elected citizens from the community. The school board sets policy; the district superintendent implements that policy. The district office, consisting of educational professionals, orders textbooks and supplies, develops programs of study, administers standardized tests, and evaluates teachers. Finally, the school principal is responsible for governing at the school level. The school principal is key to the quality of education at the school level.

2.1   What are the major sources of educational funding?

The largest percentages (49 and 43 percent, respectively) come from state and local sources. The remaining 8.5 percent comes from the federal government.

Local funding primarily comes from property taxes. State funds for education come from a variety of sources, the two largest being state income taxes and sales taxes. Smaller percentages of state education funds also come from taxes on liquor and tobacco, oil and mining revenues, corporate income taxes, and income from state lotteries and gambling.

2.2   How are educational revenues spent?

The largest percentage of the educational budget (61 percent) goes to instruction, including teacher salaries. Ten percent also goes to instructional assistance needs such as student services, teacher professional development, and curriculum development. Another 10 percent goes to administration, both at the district and school level. Maintenance of school buildings and grounds takes up another 10 percent. Finally, transportation (school buses) and food services (cafeterias) each account for another 4 percent.

3.1   What are the major causes of funding inequities in education? What are some proposed solutions to the problem?

Funding inequities in education result largely from unequal revenue bases. Within a state, this can result from districts that have differing property values. Because significant portions of educational funding come from property taxes, inequities between districts within a state are common. Between-state differences can also result from differences in states' tax bases. One proposed solution is a greater federal role in equalizing between-state differences. Cost and the problem of possible federal controls that might go along with the funding are two obstacles to this proposal.

3.2   What are the two major forms of school choice? How are they similar and different?

The two major forms of school choice are charter schools and vouchers. They are similar in their philosophical underpinnings. Both come from attempts to break up the perceived monopoly that exists in education by providing more alternatives or choices to parents. They differ in how they propose to do this. Vouchers are, in one sense, less radical in that they keep existing educational options as they are and provide parents with tickets or vouchers to shop around and choose an alternative to their neighborhood schools. Charter schools, by contrast, create alternative schools, with self-contained governance and instructional systems.

3.3   What is school privatization, and what are its pros and cons?

Privatization involves the outsourcing of educational services to private companies or corporations. This can involve hiring companies to provide services such as school lunches or transportation, or turning a whole school over to a private business. Advocates of privatization claim that competition from the private sector is good because it will encourage pub-

lic schools to perform better. They also contend that the same business efficiencies that work in the business world will produce similar efficiencies in education. Critics point to a narrowed curriculum in privatized schools because of teaching to the test. They also point to the deprofessionalization of teachers that occurs when they are treated like employees rather than knowledgeable professionals.

Education in the United States: Its Historical Roots

6

Education in the United States: Its Historical Roots

Chapter Outline

Learning Objectives

After you have completed your study of this chapter, you should be able to:

1. Explain how the diversity of the original colonies shaped our educational system, and describe the role of religion in colonial times.

2. Describe how the early national period defined state and federal roles for governing education.

3. Explain how the common school movement influenced the establishment of universal public schooling.

4. Describe the historical roots of contemporary secondary schools.

5. Discuss similarities and differences in different minority groups' struggles for educational equality.

6. Explain how schools became instruments for national purpose during the modern era.

Case Studies

 Elementary

 Middle

 Secondary

Education in the United States is unique. The organization of the schools, the content we teach, and our methods differ from those in other countries around the world. History has been a major cause of these differences. As you read the following case study, think about the ways that history affects our current educational system.

"Phew, I think I've had it," Dave Carlisle, a first-year teacher, says as he plops into an overstuffed chair in the teachers' lounge.

"Having a bad day?" Monica Henderson, one of Dave's colleagues at Westmont Middle School, asks.

"Bad day. You could say that," Dave replies. "We had lunch money missing again today. And I'm pretty sure there was cheating on the test I gave last week. It's like these kids have no moral compass. I think they could use a dose of religion."

"We already tried that," Monica replies, looking up from the papers she was grading.

"When? Before I got here?" Dave asks.

"No," Monica replies. "Back in our country's history, and often since then."

"Oh, no. Not more of that history of ed stuff you're learning in that class you're taking."

"Hey, can I help it if I'm learning some interesting stuff that makes me think about what we're trying to do?" Monica replies with a smile.

"Yeah, I know, 'Those that don't know history are destined to repeat it,'" Dave says, rolling his eyes, "but how can history help me with my cheating and stealing problems?"

Studying the history of our country's educational system may not give teachers direct answers to these questions, but it can provide you with a broader perspective on what you're doing and help you become more effective in your professional decision making. Understanding the role of religion in education, for example, can help teachers make professional decisions about the extent to which they can or should share deeply held religious beliefs with their students.

Before continuing, take a few minutes to respond to the following survey. We address each of the items as the chapter unfolds.

Each of the historical periods in our nation's history has influenced education and people's beliefs about what our children should learn and how they should be taught. And many of these influences, to a greater or lesser extent, remain with us today.

Dave and Monica's conversation is an example. The topic of students' moral development and the role of religion in promoting that development goes all the way back to the colonial period in our history. Let's take a look.

professional knowledge: test yourself!

For each item, circle the number that best represents your thinking. Use the following scale as a guide.

1 = Strongly disagree
2 = Disagree
3 = Agree/disagree
4 = Agree
5 = Strongly agree

1. The Constitution of the United States requires that religion and public schooling be kept separate from each other.

   1   2   3   4   5

2. A free public education for all students has historically been a cornerstone of education in the United States.

   1   2   3   4   5

3. The American high school has historically attempted to meet the needs of all students.

   1   2   3   4   5

4. As soon as slavery ended in this country, cultural and ethnic minorities were welcomed into U.S. schools.

   1   2   3   4   5

5. In recent times, the federal government has viewed the schools as an instrument to achieve national goals.

   1   2   3   4   5

This is available in a downloadable format on the Companion Website for personal portfolio use.

The Colonial Period (1607–1775)

Character education, seen as a way to provide moral guidance in a confusing world filled with drugs, sex, and violence, is receiving increased attention in schools (DeRoche & Williams, 2001; Viadero, 2003a). Educators generally agree that some form of moral education is needed in schools, but they disagree about the form and shape it should take. Some advocate linking character education closely to religious values that are normally taught in homes and churches. Others argue that this religious foundation is neither desirable nor possible, given the religious diversity in the United States (Wynne, 1997). The roots of character education, as well as controversies about the shape it should take, can be found in the colonial period of education in America.

Parents who believe schools should teach values and emphasize student discipline often send their children to private, church-supported schools. Should these schools receive federal assistance—money supported by general tax revenue? Proponents claim that parochial schools have as much right to federal education monies as do any other schools. Opponents claim that federal support of parochial schools violates our nation's Constitution. The controversy about the proper place of religious schools in the United States is also rooted in the colonial period.

Religion and schools are closely linked in many states. Some public schools, for example, allow prayers in classrooms, hold religious assemblies, and distribute Bibles to students (Fischer et al., 2006; LaMorte, 2005). Critics claim these practices also violate the Constitution. Proponents counter that schools should teach family, spiritual, and moral values and that religion promotes these values. The issue, repeatedly debated in court, reflects a continual tension in U.S. schools over the proper role of religion in public education (Fischer et al., 2006). This tension has its beginnings in the colonial period.

These controversies illustrate the important role of religion in American education. Why is it so important? The answers go back to the colonial period, when our country was first being shaped.

The beginnings of the relationship between religion and education in America extend back to the founding of Jamestown in 1607. Before that time, New World explorers were primarily interested in "gold and glory"—conquering the New World for riches and adventure. The Jamestown settlers, in contrast, brought families and wanted to start new lives. Like parents today, they believed that the family was central to helping children grow up straight and strong, but they realized they also needed help from schools. Colonial schools were formed in response to this felt need, and they laid the foundation for many of the controversies and structures in place today.

Although settlers came to the colonies for different reasons—in search of political independence, religious freedom, or simply a better life, for example—they all brought with them values and beliefs derived from their European roots. As a result, schooling in colonial America had the same class and gender distinctions common in Europe at the time. Formal education was usually reserved for wealthy White males and ignored females and those less wealthy. As in Europe, religion was an integral part of education, but the role of religion in the classroom differed by region.

Differences in Colonies

Education in America has always been a process of people adapting and creating schools to meet their unique needs. Although the original 13 colonies shared some similarities, such as their cultural links with Europe and people's desire for better lives, regional differences emerged, influenced by geography, economics, and the reasons the colonists came to America. Let's look at them.

The Southern Colonies

Life in the Southern colonies—Maryland, Virginia, the Carolinas, and Georgia—centered around agriculture, much of which existed on large plantations where African slaves and

195

indentured servants worked land owned by wealthy landlords. Poor White settlers worked small farms on the margins, barely scratching out an existence.

Life for most people in the colonial South was hard, and formal education was a luxury reserved for the wealthy (Pulliam & Van Patten, 2007). Private tutors often lived on plantations, or parents pooled their resources to hire a tutor to teach the children of several families. Private schools sponsored by the Church of England and boarding schools for the wealthy were in the larger Southern cities, such as Charleston and Williamsburg. The English tradition of education for the wealthy few made an easy leap over the Atlantic to the Southern colonies.

The Middle Colonies

The middle colonies—New York, New Jersey, Delaware, and Pennsylvania—were more diverse than the colonies in the South. Although English-speaking people were the majority, substantial pockets of Dutch in New York, Swedes in Delaware, and Germans in Pennsylvania also existed. Also, whereas most of the Southern colonists were members of the Church of England, middle colonists belonged to a number of different religious groups. They were Dutch Reformists, Quakers, Lutherans, Baptists, Roman Catholics, and Jews (Pulliam & Van Patten, 2007). Because religious freedom was a major reason for coming to America, and religion played such a central role in people's daily lives, it was difficult to create public schools that satisfied everyone.

In response to this diversity, families in the middle colonies created parochial schools. Students learned in their native languages, and local religious beliefs were an integral part of the curriculum.

The New England Colonies

The New England colonies—Massachusetts, Connecticut, and New Hampshire—differed from the other colonies in two important ways. First, they were culturally and religiously homogeneous, which made consensus about school goals easier to achieve. Second, industry and commerce encouraged the clustering of people into towns, which allowed the formation of common schools.

As an example, let's look at Massachusetts. Puritans, the followers of John Calvin, settled in Massachusetts. As with colonists in the other regions, religion played a major role in the Puritans' lives. They came to America because of conflicts resulting from their attempts to reform the Church of England. Puritans believed that humans are inherently evil, having fallen when Adam and Eve committed original sin. Education helped people follow God's commandments and resist the devil's temptations. By learning to read and write, people gained access to God's word through the Bible. In addition, religious education contributed to a person's general character by promoting industry, resourcefulness, punctuality, and thrift. Puritans believed education was important because it made people more righteous.

The Puritans' views shaped the schools they created. They saw children as savage and primitive, requiring education (religion) to become civilized and God-fearing. Puritans viewed play as idleness, considered children's talk as prattle, and commonly used corporal punishment to ensure conformity. Puritan teachers beat students with switches, forced them to kneel on hard pebbles, and made them wear heavy wooden yolks as punishments for unacceptable behavior. It's easy to see why "Idle minds are the Devil's workshop" and "Spare the rod and spoil the child" were principles of Puritan education.

Religion was a major reason the Pilgrims came to America and a major force in shaping early schools. (Library of Congress)

Religion also influenced curriculum and instruction. Reading, writing, arithmetic, and religion ("the four Rs") made up the curriculum. *The New England Primer* taught children the alphabet through religious rhymes such as the following:

A—In Adam's Fall
We Sinned all.
B—Thy Life to Mend
This Book Attend.

Instruction focused on memorization and recitation; teacher expected children to sit quietly for long periods of time, and discouraged them from expressing opinions and asking questions. Teachers had no formal preparation about how or what to teach, and curriculum materials were scarce, if not nonexistent.

Paradoxically, a landmark piece of legislation, the Massachusetts Act of 1647, arose from this grim educational landscape. Also known as the **Old Deluder Satan Act**, the law was designed to create scripture-literate citizens who would thwart Satan's trickery. It required every town of 50 or more households to hire a teacher of reading and writing. The historical significance of this act is enormous, because it provided the legal foundation for public support of education. It gave birth to the idea that the public good was enhanced by government-sponsored efforts at public education, and it became a cornerstone of American education.

European Crosscurrents

As you saw in the preceding section, American colonists brought many ideas from Europe, such as the view that education should be reserved for wealthy White males. Also, because schooling existed for religious purposes or for preparing the wealthy to be leaders, educators made few attempts to relate the curriculum to the average person's practical needs or the long-term needs of a growing nation. And teaching methods emphasized passive learning in the form of memorization and recitation.

Forces of change were altering education in Europe, however, and slowly making their way across the Atlantic. Some prominent European philosophers and their ideas are outlined in Table 5.1.

As Table 5.1 shows, though the ideas came from different places, all involved a more practical, humane, and child-centered view of education. These philosophers are important because they planted the seeds of educational change that would fundamentally alter the education of students in the United States.

TABLE 5.1   Changes in Educational Thought in Europe

Thinker	Educational Views
John Amos Comenius (1592–1670) Czech philosopher	Questioned the effectiveness of memorization and recitation, emphasizing instead the need to base teaching on children's interests and needs
John Locke (1632–1704) English philosopher	Emphasized the importance of firsthand experiences in helping children learn about the world
Jean Jacques Rousseau (1712–1778) French philosopher	Viewed children as innately good and argued that teachers should provide children with opportunities for exploration and experimentation
Johann Pestalozzi (1746–1827) Swiss philosopher	Criticized authoritarian educational practices that stifled students' playfulness and natural curiosity and recommended that teachers use concrete experiences to help students learn

Old Deluder Satan Act. Early colonial law designed to create scripture-literate citizens who would thwart Satan's trickery.

The Legacy of the Colonial Period

The colonial period shaped American education in three important ways. First, with few exceptions, poor Whites, females, and minorities such as Native Americans and African-Americans were excluded from schools (Spring, 2005). William Berkeley, the aristocratic governor of Virginia, supported this exclusion and in 1671 railed against both free public education and access to books: "I thank God, *there are no free schools nor printing*, and I hope we shall not have them these hundred years, for *learning* has brought disobedience, and heresy, and sects into the world, and *printing* has divulged them, and libels against the best government" (Pulliam & Van Patten, 2003, p. 86). European ideas of class structures and privilege did not die easily in the New World. Given attitudes such as these, it's easy to see why equality of educational opportunity wasn't a legal reality until the mid-20th century. Some present-day critics argue that today's schools are still racist and sexist (Spring, 2005).

Second, the colonial period shaped our current system of education through actions that planted the seeds for public support of education (the Old Deluder Satan Act) and local control of schools. These two ideas have become important foundations of our present educational system.

Third, and perhaps most significantly, the relationship between religion and schooling prevalent in the colonial period influenced attitudes about education for many years. Examining that history helps us understand why religion continues to be an important issue in education. Let's take a closer look at religion in schools.

Religion in Schools

The U.S. Constitution, the oldest written constitution in the world that is still in force, was written in 1787 and was officially adopted in 1789. It has had 27 amendments, the first 10 of which are known as our Bill of Rights. In response to the religious diversity that existed in the colonies, the "establishment clause" of the First Amendment prohibited the government from passing legislation to establish any one official religion over another. This created the principle widely known as *separation of church and state*, and it addresses the first statement in our beginning-of-chapter survey, "The Constitution of the United States requires that religion and public schooling be kept separate from each other." Although interpretations vary, the establishment clause suggests that the statement is true.

Considering the colonial legacy and the courts' evolving interpretation of the principle of separation of church and state, it is easy to see why controversies about religion in schools exist today. Some commonly raised questions include the following:

- Should prayer be allowed in schools?
- Should federal money be used to provide instruction in religious schools?
- What role should religion play in character education?

Let's look at these questions.

Should prayer be allowed in schools? In colonial times, prayer was an integral part of the curriculum. Today, this question has become so controversial that the issue has been thrown to the courts, and their answer has usually been no. A federal court in Alabama, for example, ruled that praying in schools, holding religious assemblies, and giving students Bibles all violate separation of church and state (Fischer et al., 2006; LaMorte, 2005). However, in a case involving graduation speeches, prayers were ruled legal, because they were voluntary and given by students. Further, some members of the House of Representatives sponsored a bill in 1998 that would have allowed organized voluntary prayers in the schools, but it fell 61 votes short of the 224 necessary for a two thirds majority (Walsh, 1998). This attempted legislation revealed that prayer in U.S. schools was not a dead issue. More recently, the U.S. Supreme Court ruled 6–3 that student-led prayers at Texas football games were unconstitutional, this time concluding that the prayers did violate separation of church and state (Walsh, 2000a).

Should federal dollars be used to provide instruction in religious schools? This wasn't an issue in the colonial period, because most schools were private and religion was an integral part of the curriculum. Today, however, the role of government funding for religious instruction is more controversial and less clear. For example, courts have generally ruled in favor of using federal monies to provide supplementary instruction for poor students or students with special needs who attend religious schools (Fischer et al., 2006). The Supreme Court also ruled that religious schools could receive federal aid in the form of computers and library books (Walsh, 2000a).

Funding vouchers for religious schools is another legally contentious matter, however. **Vouchers**, checks or written documents that parents can use to purchase educational services, have been promoted as one way to increase parental choice and involvement. Parents in Cleveland and Milwaukee, sites of two well-known voucher experiments, wanted to use vouchers (public monies) to send their children to religious schools. Opponents contended this violates separation of church and state, but the U.S. Supreme Court, in a 5–4 vote, approved the use of public school funds for vouchers to religious and private schools (Walsh, 2002b). The states will be the next battlefield for this issue, because 37 state constitutions currently forbid state aid to religious schools (Gehring, 2002b).

What role should religion play in character education? **Character education** is an approach to developing morality that suggests moral values and positive character traits, such as honesty and citizenship, should be emphasized, taught, and rewarded. In colonial times, religion and character education were synonymous, and in some cases religious training was the primary purpose of education. The link between the two is controversial today, however, and religious diversity is one reason why Although most Americans consider themselves Christian, significant numbers of Muslims, Hindus, Buddhists, and Jews as well as other smaller religious groups exist in the United States. Further, considerable religious diversity, ranging from liberal to ultraconservative denominations, exists within Christian ranks. Given these differences, it is hard to come to any consensus about the role of religion in the development of students' character.

The proper role of religion in schools continues to be a controversial issue. (Rob Crandall/The Stock Connection)

Making Connections:
To deepen your understanding of the topics in this section of the chapter and integrate them with topics you've already studied, go to the *Making Connections* module for Chapter 5 at **www.prenhall.com/kauchak.** Respond to questions 1 and 2.

Check Your Understanding

1.1 How did the diversity of the original colonies shape the educational system in the United States?

1.2 What role did religion play in colonial schools? What are the implications of this role for contemporary schools?

1.3 Explain why the Old Deluder Satan Act of Massachusetts was important for the development of our American educational system.

 For feedback, go to Check Your Understanding *at the end of this chapter.*

Vouchers. Checks or written documents that parents can use to purchase educational services.

Character education. An approach to developing morality that suggests moral values and positive character traits, such as honesty and citizenship, should be emphasized, taught, and rewarded.

The Early National Period (1775–1820)

Teresa Sanchez has moved with her family from a large urban center in the Northeast to a sprawling city in the South. Although the teenager encounters changes in climate and lifestyle, she finds her new high school surprisingly similar to the one she had previously attended. The buildings and their physical layout are similar, with long hallways lined with lockers and interspersed with classrooms. Even the central office seems the same, and the guidance counselor who works with her assures her that she won't lose credits because of the move.

But there are differences. Teresa rides a district school bus instead of using public transportation. The students, while friendly, talk differently and their interests differ from those of her friends back home. And the textbooks she receives, while covering the same basic material, do so in different ways.

Her mother, an elementary teacher, also notices both similarities and differences. She gets a new position almost immediately but is told that her teaching certificate is only temporary and that she will have to take additional coursework for it to become permanent. The textbooks she is given are different from the ones she had previously used, but the principal's emphasis on testing at the end of the year isn't. Some things never change.

The United States, at first glance, appears homogeneous. A McDonald's in California appears much like one in Ohio, for example, and television programs across the country are very similar. However, many regional and state differences exist.

The same paradox occurs in education. Although schools across the country appear similar, a closer look reveals important regional and state differences. For example, students in Texas study Texas state history and take specially constructed tests to determine grade advancement, and students in other states study their own history and take their own state-specific graduation tests (Feller, 2006). Education to assist English language learners (ELLs) exists in most states, but the form of this assistance varies considerably among them (Hinkel, 2005). Why do these differences exist? Some answers can be found in the early national period of our country.

Before 1775 the United States was a loose collection of separate colonies that looked mostly to Europe for trade and ideas. During the 45 years of the early national period (1775–1820), however, the separate colonies became the United States of America, and this country shaped its future through the Constitution and the Bill of Rights. In the previous section, you saw how the First Amendment to the Constitution established the principle of separation of church and state. Next we'll show how other laws and amendments also shaped the future of American education.

Educational Governance: Whose Responsibility?

Severing the governmental ties between religion and education raised an important question: Who would be responsible for organizing and managing education in our new country? Establishing a national education system was one suggestion (Pulliam & Van Patten, 2007). Proponents argued that, in addition to developing an enlightened citizenry, a national system would best meet the country's agricultural, industrial, and commercial needs. Opponents, in their arguments against a national system, cited the monolithic and unresponsive systems in Europe. They also argued that the beginnings of viable local and state systems, such as those in Massachusetts, already existed. Why create another level of bureaucracy and control when it wasn't needed? The Constitution's framers sidestepped the issue with the Tenth Amendment, which said that areas not explicitly assigned to the federal government would be the responsibility of each state.

The Tenth Amendment was important for two reasons. First, it implicitly removed the federal government from a central role in running and operating schools, and second, it passed this responsibility on to the individual states. To support the educational efforts of the states, Congress passed the Land Ordinance of 1785 and the Northwest Ordinance of 1787. The goal of these acts was to promote settlement of the present-day Midwest, which was then an undeveloped area of the country (K. Alexander & Alexander, 2001). These ordinances divided the land into townships, each 6 miles square and consisting of 36 sections; in each township, the income from one section was reserved for support of public education. The rationale for this financial support was contained in the text of the Northwest Ordinance: "Religion, morality, and knowledge being necessary to good government and the happiness of mankind, schools and the means of education shall forever be encouraged." This encouragement came in the form of federal land that states could use to support education. Although not directly involved in governing or operating schools, the federal government provided material support for schools and education, a tradition that persists to this day. With respect to education, the lines of responsibility between state and federal governments were already being blurred.

The Legacy of the Early National Period

The early national period shaped the schools of the future and planted the seeds of controversies to come. In addition to establishing the principle of separation of church and state, legislators established two other far-reaching effects on our educational system: (1) Lawmakers removed control of education from the federal government and gave it to the states, and (2) the federal government expressed the view that education was essential for improving the quality of people's lives and helping the nation grow.

The influence of these actions is still felt in the policies and views of education today. For example, courts have repeatedly upheld the principle of separation of church and state, and decisions about school and classroom policies are primarily made by individual states and local school districts (although public schools must adhere to federal laws and do receive federal funding).

Also, although education remains in the hands of the states, the federal government views it as a means of achieving national goals, just as it was in the early national period (Tyack & Cuban, 1995). When the economy sputters, for example, or when significant portions of the school-age population underachieve, the federal government steps in. The No Child Left Behind Act of 2001 is an example. The law requires each state to develop a comprehensive accountability plan to ensure that all students acquire basic skills in reading, math, and science. One mandated feature of each state's plan must be a comprehensive testing system tied to state standards. The testing aspects of the No Child Left Behind Act are controversial; the state of Connecticut, for example, unsuccessfully challenged the law in court, and other states considered similar actions. The high cost of testing, which they called "an unfunded federal mandate" was Connecticut's primary complaint (Archer, 2005).

> **Making Connections:**
> To deepen your understanding of the topics in this section of the chapter and integrate them with topics you've already studied, go to the *Making Connections* module for Chapter 5 at **www.prenhall.com/kauchak.** Respond to questions 3 and 4.

Check Your Understanding

2.1 What is the Tenth Amendment to the Constitution? Why is it important for education today?

2.2 Describe the role that was established for the federal government during the early national period.

2.3 What was the historical significance of the Ordinances of 1785 and 1787?

  For feedback, go to Check Your Understanding *at the end of this chapter.*

The Common School Movement: The Rise of State Support for Public Education (1820–1865)

Many of you reading this text will become teachers of elementary students and will work in public schools. Let's think for a moment about these schools. First, the children you'll teach will be required by law to be there; virtually all states require students to attend school until they are 16. Second, your salary and the salaries of other teachers and administrators, the building itself, your materials and supplies, the buses that will take kids to and from school, and even some of your students' lunches will be publicly supported, meaning a portion of federal, state, and local taxes will pay for these items.

Typically, your school will be organized into grade levels. At the elementary level, 5-year-olds will be in kindergarten, and 6-year-olds will be in the first grade; at the middle and high school levels, classes target different levels of expertise, such as freshman English or senior literature. You will have a designated grade or level to teach.

To get a teaching job, you'll be required to be licensed. You'll have to complete a specified set of university courses (which is one reason you're in this class), and you'll complete some clinical experiences in schools, including an internship. You'll probably also have to take a standardized test (the content of which will vary from state to state) to assess your competency as a teacher.

What are the origins of these policies, and what are the historical roots that shaped a free public education for all students in the United States?

Although developing a literate citizenry was a goal during the early national period, American education in the early 1800s remained a patchwork of schools designed primarily for the wealthy; the vast majority of children received little or no formal education. The common school movement changed that.

Historians commonly describe the period from 1820 to 1865 as the "Age of the Common Man." Andrew Jackson, a popular and down-to-earth person who gained fame as a general in the War of 1812, was elected president in 1828. Westward expansion provided opportunities for people and changed the social landscape; the poor and landless could start over by pulling up stakes and heading west. The land area of the United States nearly doubled between 1830 and 1865, and the population increased from 13 to 32 million, 4 million of whom were new immigrants (U.S. Government Printing Office, 1975).

This expansion presented both opportunities and challenges. Industrialization created jobs and contributed to the growth of cities such as New York and Boston, but it also resulted in pollution, crime, and the development of urban slums. Many new immigrants didn't speak English and were unaccustomed to American ways of living. The country needed a citizenry that could participate in political decisions and contribute to the nation's economy, but most people were functionally illiterate. America turned to its schools for help.

The Common School Movement: Making Education Available to All

As we showed in the previous section, the American educational system at the beginning of the 19th century was a patchwork of private and quasi-public schools. Those defined as "public" often charged partial tuition, discouraging all but the wealthiest from attending. States didn't coordinate their efforts, and the quality of education was uneven at best (Pulliam & Van Patten, 2007).

Around 1820, educational changes began to occur (Pulliam & Van Patten, 2007). These changes marked the beginning of the **common school movement**, a historical attempt to make education available to all children in the United States. The following are some of the events that occurred during this period:

Common school movement. A historical attempt to make education available to all children in the United States.

- States and local governments taxed citizens directly to support public schools. Educators attempted to increase the attendance of underrepresented groups such as the urban poor and freed slaves.

202

- States created state education departments and appointed state superintendents of instruction.
- Educators organized schools by grade level and standardized the curriculum.
- States improved teacher preparation.

The Contributions of Horace Mann

Horace Mann, a lawyer turned educator, was a key figure in the common school movement. Secretary of the Massachusetts State Board of Education from 1837 to 1848, he was an outspoken advocate for public education, believing that it was the key to developing the country and improving the quality of life for all people.

Under Mann's influence, Massachusetts moved to the cutting edge of education in America. During the common school period, Massachusetts doubled state appropriations for education, built 50 new secondary schools, increased teacher salaries by 50 percent, and passed the nation's first compulsory school attendance law in 1852. (By 1900, 32 other states had passed similar laws.) Perhaps Mann's biggest legacy, however, was the idea that public education, in the form of tax-supported elementary schools (common schools), should be a right of all citizens.

The common school movement made education accessible to the common person. (Courtesy of the Library of Congress)

Expansion of the Common School Movement

Despite some obstacles—such as business interests that feared a loss of cheap child labor, citizens who objected to increased taxes and having to pay to educate other people's children, and competition from private and parochial schools—the common school movement prospered. Reasons for its success include the following:

- Parents began viewing education as a way of improving their children's lives.
- National and local leaders saw education as the vehicle for assimilation of immigrants and improvement of national productivity.
- The growth of industry and commerce required an increasingly educated populace.

Fifty percent of U.S. children were enrolled in public schools by the beginning of the Civil War, and by 1865, 28 of 35 states had established state boards of education. During the common school movement, tax-supported public elementary schools were firmly established as a cornerstone of the U.S. educational system. (New Jersey eliminated the need for parents to pay for an elementary education in 1871; it was the last state to do so.)

This section addresses the second statement in our beginning-of-chapter survey, "A free public education for all students has historically been a cornerstone of education in the United States." In fact, early in our country's history, education was available only to a wealthy few. Later, largely because of the efforts of Horace Mann, universal free public elementary school slowly became available to all. And access to free public secondary school for all students didn't become fully available until the 1900s.

Issues of Quality and Quantity in Teacher Education

Although the common school movement dramatically increased access to education, quality was a problem. During the early to mid-1800s,

> teachers' workloads were heavy, and only the fundamentals were taught. For the most part, school buildings and equipment were very poor, even in the private schools and academies. Textbooks, blackboards, and all working materials were in extremely short supply. Buildings were not kept up, lighting

was not adequate, and quite often one poorly trained teacher was in charge not only of one school but also of an entire district. Teachers who possessed only an elementary school education were frequently hired. (Pulliam & Van Patten, 2003, pp. 133–134)

Then, as now, teachers were seen as keys to improving our schools. The creation of **normal schools**, 2-year institutions developed in the early 1800s to prepare prospective elementary teachers, was the most significant attempt to solve this problem. Before the existence of normal schools, the typical teacher was a man, either preparing for or waiting for a position in the ministry. Because these teachers had no training in education, they used primitive methods, such as memorization and recitation, and they maintained order with stern disciplinary measures, including corporal punishment. Normal schools, in contrast, targeted women as potential teachers and attempted to provide both content background and pedagogical training beyond the high school level.

School quality also increased when larger elementary schools began separating students into grade levels, which eliminated congested conditions and the overlapping curricula often found in one-room schools. Grade differentiation also resulted in more age-appropriate instruction and allowed content to be taught in greater depth for older students. Finally, as paper and printing presses became more common, more textbooks became available, and educational materials improved.

The Legacy of the Common School Movement

The common school movement was a turning point in American education. The idea of universal access to a tax-supported education was planted and took root. Although not all children attended elementary schools, the number who did increased steadily during this time, and public support for the idea grew. State governance and control of education was institutionalized with the creation of state departments of education, and teacher training and quality improved with the development of normal schools.

Despite these advances, the common school movement left at least two controversial issues that remain today. One involves the inequitable funding of education from state to state and district to district, both of which affect quality. In *Savage Inequalities* (1991), Jonathon Kozol addresses this issue:

Americans abhor the notion of a social order in which economic privilege and political power are determined by hereditary class. Officially, we have a more enlightened goal in sight: namely, a society in which a family's wealth has no relation to the probability of future educational attainment and the wealth and station it affords. By this standard, education offered to poor children should be at least as good as that which is provided to the children of the upper-middle class. (p. 207)

Making Connections: To deepen your CW understanding of the topics in this section of the chapter and integrate them with topics you've already studied, go to the *Making Connections* module for Chapter 5 at www.prenhall.com/kauchak. Respond to questions 5 and 6.

This often doesn't occur, however (Berliner, 2005; Gill, McLean, & Courville, 2004). Wide differences in funding exist between states and among districts within states. Nationally, wealthy districts spend an average of 23 percent more on their students than do poorer districts. In Alaska wealthier districts spend more than double the amount per pupil ($16,546 versus $7,379) than poorer districts in the state (Biddle & Berliner, 2002).

Teacher quality is the second contentious issue that remains from the common school movement, and the question of what constitutes a well-educated and qualified teacher continues to be debated, as evidenced in two contradictory movements in education today. The first is the increasing popularity of alternative licensure in an effort to open up entrance to the teaching profession. In contrast, the second movement is an effort to increase teacher professionalism, a theme of this text, by making entry into teaching more rigorous and demanding through increased course work and testing (Darling-Hammond & Bransford, 2005). How the issue will be resolved in the future is unclear.

Normal schools. Two-year institutions developed in the early 1800s to prepare prospective elementary teachers.

Table 5.2 provides a summary of the important events in our country's early history that have shaped education, the periods during which they occurred, and the issues that remain today.

TABLE 5.2   A Summary of Historical Periods in American Education

Period	Significant Features	Issues That Remain Today
Colonial period, 1607–1775	• Education reserved for wealthy White males • Seeds planted for public support of education • Religion at the core of education	• Whether prayer should be allowed in schools and in what circumstances • Tax support for religious schools • The relationship between religion and character education
Early national period, 1775–1820	• The principle of separation of church and state established • Control of education given to the states, rather than the federal government • Education viewed as crucial for furthering the national interest	• The role of the federal government in education • National testing of students • A national curriculum
Common school movement, 1820–1865	• Access to tax-supported education for all established • Grade levels introduced in elementary schools • Normal schools created to prepare teachers	• Inequities in funding among states and school districts • Teacher quality and alternative routes to teacher certification

Check Your Understanding

3.1   How was the common school movement linked to the growing number of immigrants coming to the United States?

3.2   Who was Horace Mann, and what was his contribution to education in the United States?

3.3   What were normal schools, and why are they important today?

 For feedback, go to Check Your Understanding *at the end of this chapter.*

The Evolution of the American High School

 Kareem and Antonio walk to high school together, have lockers that are side by side, and even have the same homeroom period. But that is where their contact ends. Kareem is in a college-preparation track, along with about a third of the other students in his school. As he goes from class to class, he sees many of the same students. Antonio is in a vocational track, and many of his classes are designed to introduce him to specific career options. A technology class focuses on business applications of computers and introduces him to jobs in the computer field. A metalworking class includes welding and even allows him to work on his family's car as a class project. Once Kareem and Antonio leave homeroom, they often don't see each other until football practice at the end of the day.

Think about your own experience in high school. Most of you probably attended a unique American invention, the **comprehensive high school**, a secondary school that attempts to meet the needs of all students by housing them together and providing curricular options (e.g., vocational or college-preparatory programs) geared toward a variety of student ability levels and interests (Hammack, 2004). For example, some of you took honors classes in English, history, chemistry, or biology. Others were in "standard" classes, designed for students of average ability.

> **Comprehensive high school.** A secondary school that attempts to meet the needs of all students by housing them together and providing curricular options (e.g., vocational or college-preparatory programs) geared toward a variety of student ability levels and interests.

Figure 5.1 The Evolution of the American High School

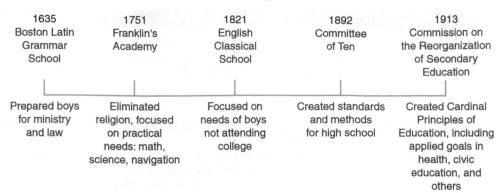

1635 Boston Latin Grammar School	1751 Franklin's Academy	1821 English Classical School	1892 Committee of Ten	1913 Commission on the Reorganization of Secondary Education
Prepared boys for ministry and law	Eliminated religion, focused on practical needs: math, science, navigation	Focused on needs of boys not attending college	Created standards and methods for high school	Created Cardinal Principles of Education, including applied goals in health, civic education, and others

Today's modern comprehensive high school can be traced back to academies, such as Franklin's Academy of Philadelphia, and English classical schools, such as the English High School in Boston. (Bohden Hrynewych/Stock Boston Inc./Jupiter Images)

Latin grammar school. A college-preparatory school originally designed to help boys prepare for the ministry or, later, for a career in law.

Academy. A secondary school that focused on the practical needs of colonial America as a growing nation.

Perhaps you enrolled in some vocational courses, such as word processing or woodworking, designed to provide you with immediately marketable skills. You may have even taken driver's training or other "life management" courses. All of these are part of a comprehensive American high school. How did the modern, comprehensive high school evolve?

Today, a high school education is seen as essential to success in life, because it prepares students for a job or entrance to college. This wasn't always the case. Before the turn of the 20th century, less than 10 percent of the population went beyond elementary school (U.S. Department of Education, 1995). By contrast, in the year 2000, 96 percent of all teenagers attended high school (National Center for Education Statistics, 2005b). A high school education has evolved from a luxury, to a right, to a necessity.

Historical Roots of the Comprehensive High School

The American high school as it exists today is the result of a long evolutionary history. A time line illustrating this development appears in Figure 5.1 and is discussed in this section.

The first American high school was a decidedly European institution aimed at the colonial elite. The Boston Latin School, established in 1635, was a **Latin grammar school**, a college-preparatory school originally designed to help boys prepare for the ministry or, later, for a career in law. Women didn't attend, because they could be neither ministers nor lawyers. The narrow curriculum and high cost made Latin grammar schools largely unattainable and irrelevant for the vast majority of Americans.

In reaction to this narrow academic orientation, Benjamin Franklin opened the Academy of Philadelphia, in 1751. Free of religious orientation and uniquely American, an **academy** was a secondary school that focused on the practical needs of colonial America as a growing nation. Math, navigation, astronomy, bookkeeping, logic, and rhetoric were all taught, and both boys and girls attended. The students selected courses from this menu, which set the precedent for electives and alternative programs at the secondary level that exist today.

Merchants and craftsmen, who had questioned the emphasis on Latin and Greek in the Latin grammar schools, enthusiastically supported this broader, more applied curriculum. By 1860 a quarter of a million students were enrolled in 6,000 tuition-charging academies, and they were the most common type of high school that existed until about 1890 (Butts & Cremin, 1953).

The academies were a significant addition to American education for three reasons. First, they emphasized a practical curriculum, suggesting that schools should continuously adapt to changes in society. Second, they eliminated religion from the curriculum, further widening the division between church and state, and third, they were partially supported by public funds, which established a trend that flourished in the common school movement. These characteristics—practical, secular, and public—were themes that would be revisited again and again in American education.

In addition to the academies, another uniquely American educational institution appeared. In 1821 Boston established the first **English classical school**, a free secondary school designed to meet the needs of boys not planning to attend college. The English Classical School offered studies in English, math, history, science, geography, bookkeeping, and surveying and, to reflect this practical emphasis, changed its name to the English High School in 1824.

Schools modeled after the English High School spread slowly because of competition from the academies and public opposition to taxes needed to support the schools. Taxpayers did not think secondary schools should be free, natural extensions of elementary education. In addition, the schools were uncertain about their role. Unable to decide whether their mission was practical or college preparatory, the schools responded by offering both types of classes. This uncertainty also affected students; in 1900 only one tenth of the students said they expected to attend college, but the majority took a college-preparatory curriculum. As we'll see in the next section, this confusion about the American high school's role and mission continued into the 20th century and persists even today.

This section answers the third statement in our beginning-of-chapter survey, "The American high school has historically attempted to meet the needs of all students." This statement isn't true; originally, high schools were oriented toward preparing students for ministry or law careers. As we'll see in the next section, it wasn't until the 1900s that educators developed comprehensive high schools to meet the needs of all students.

Redefining the High School

The American high school near the end of the 19th century was an institution in search of an identity. Begun as an elitist, college-preparatory institution, its curriculum evolved into a disorganized mix of college-preparatory, terminal, and vocational courses. Educational leaders recognized that something needed to be done.

In 1892, in response to this need, the National Education Association (NEA) appointed a group called The Committee of Ten to examine the high school curriculum and make recommendations about standards, programs, and methods. The committee concluded that students who planned to go no further than high school needed content and teaching methods that were the same as those who were college bound, an idea that has lost favor today.

Three factors contributed to the committee's conclusions (Spring, 2005). First, no high school teachers or parents were included on the committee. It was composed of college professors and administrators only, so the bias toward a college-preparatory curriculum wasn't surprising. Second, the committee members believed in *faculty psychology*, the view that exercising the powers of the mind promoted learning. Proponents of this view held that everyone, regardless of where they were heading in life, could practice mental discipline to achieve a "stronger" mind.

A third factor influencing the committee was the large number of non-English-speaking immigrants and a growing lower class that threatened to create divisions in American society. The committee felt that a different curriculum for college and non–college-bound students might create a class-based system of education and damage national unity.

The committee recognized, however, that the college-preparatory curriculum wasn't providing prospective workers with the occupational skills needed for increasingly complex jobs. In an attempt to resolve this dilemma, the NEA appointed a second committee, called The Commission on the Reorganization of Secondary Education (Pulliam & Van Patten, 2007). In 1918 this commission issued a report, *The Cardinal Principles of Secondary Education*, which included goals in basic skills such as reading and math, vocational education, personal health, worthy home membership, civic education, effective use of leisure time, and ethical character. To accommodate these more applied goals, the commission proposed the idea of comprehensive high schools with different tracks for different students. The hope was

English classical school. A free secondary school designed to meet the needs of boys not planning to attend college.

that the diverse student body, separated into different tracks, would be integrated by sports and other extracurricular activities (Spring, 2005).

Efforts to solve the problems of intellectual and other forms of diversity persist today. Although the practice of tracking was designed to provide a customized education for all students, it has had some unintended negative consequences. The curriculum in the non–college-bound tracks often offers little intellectual challenge; teachers tend to have low expectations for students; and they often use primitive and ineffective teaching methods, such as lecture and seat work (Good & Brophy, 2003).

The Challenge of Teaching in Large Urban High Schools

The move to make high schools comprehensive also had large size as an additional negative side effect. As the size of urban high schools increases, students find it harder to identify with their school, and teachers have difficulty establishing personal relationships with students (Kincheloe, 2004; Schutz, 2004). More than 70 percent of U.S. high schools have 1,000 students or more, and a number of urban districts have high schools of over 5,000 students. Historically, the largest high school on record, DeWitt Clinton High School in the Bronx, had 12,000 students in 1934 (Allen, 2002). (Can you imagine what it must have been like to be a freshman walking into that school on the first day of the school year?)

How can teachers respond to this problem? One way is to create the feeling that students and the teacher are "in this together" and "we'll work together to adapt to the size of the school." Effective urban teachers in large high schools make a special effort to get to know students as people by quickly learning their names, learning about their hopes and fears, and spending out-of-class time with them (Wilson & Corbett, 2001). They model courtesy and respect for all students and expect similar courtesy in return. And they create clear standards for behavior that require students to treat each other the same way. This creates a sense of safety and attachment to their classrooms that can help assuage the impersonal feel of large high schools.

In addition, effective urban teachers make personal and inviting statements to their students that motivate and communicate understanding (Manouchehri, 2004). For instance, a comment such as, "This has been hard for me, too. I often try to do it this way," is a personal statement; "I know this is hard, and I can feel that you're frustrated," communicates that the teacher understands students' experiences and feelings; and statements like, "*We're* going to be working on fractions this week," is more motivating than "*You're* going to be working on. . . ." These seemingly minor differences help create a classroom community and the feeling "we're all in this together" that we described earlier (Honora, 2003).

Effective urban teachers create warm, caring learning communities in their classrooms. (Michael Newman/PhotoEdit Inc.)

Junior High and Middle Schools

While groups such as the Committee of Ten and The Commission on the Reorganization of Secondary Education wrestled with curricular issues, other educators questioned the effectiveness of the 8–4 organizational pattern (8 years of elementary, 4 of high school). Critics of the pattern argued that too much emphasis was being placed on basic skills in the upper elementary grades, a time that could be better spent learning content such as science and social studies in depth. Developmental psychologists pointed out that early adolescence is a time of intellectual, emotional, and physical transition, and students undergoing these transitions require a different kind of school. In response to these arguments, educators created

junior high schools, which provide a unique academic curriculum for early adolescent youth. The first junior high, which encompassed grades 7, 8, and 9, opened in Columbus, Ohio, in 1909. The concept spread quickly, and by 1926, junior highs had been set up in 800 school systems (Gruhn & Douglass, 1971).

The 6–3–3 organizational pattern (6 years of elementary school, 3 of junior high, and 3 of high school) was more a change in form than substance, however. Most "junior" highs were exactly that—imitations of high schools with a fragmented curriculum, emphasis on academic disciplines, and little attention to the developing needs of adolescents.

In spite of these weaknesses, junior highs remained popular until the 1970s, when continued criticisms caused fundamental change. The creation of **middle schools**, schools typically for grades 6–8 and specifically designed to help students through the rapid social, emotional, and intellectual changes characteristic of early adolescence, was the response to these criticisms (Manning, 2000). Middle schools provided opportunities for teachers to get to know students by creating student and teacher teams. Working together on teams, teachers could share information about learner progress and problems as well as design interdisciplinary units that explored connections between different content areas. The curriculum became more applied and more focused on adolescents' emotional development. In addition, educational psychologists encouraged teachers to move away from the lecture-dominated instruction so common in high schools and toward more student-centered instruction, such as guided discovery and cooperative learning.

The middle school philosophy has grown in popularity. The number of junior highs decreased from 7,200 in 1968 to 1,000 in 1996 (Viadero, 1996), with an accompanying increase in middle schools.

American Secondary Schools: Future Directions

The history of American secondary schools helps us understand some of the questions facing educators today. Begun as college-preparatory institutions, high schools became comprehensive in an effort to meet the needs of a diverse student body. To help adolescents make the transition from elementary to high school, junior highs were created; when those schools failed to fulfill that mission, educators created middle schools. The academic pendulum has now swung back, however, and some leaders are calling for a redesign of middle schools to make them more academic and rigorous (Yecke, 2006).

Have American secondary schools been too trendy and overly responsive to changing conditions in society, first zigging one way and then zagging another? Or have they been too traditional and conservative, hanging onto outmoded academics in the face of dramatic changes in society? These questions are reexamined later when we discuss the modern era in American education.

> **Making Connections:**
> To deepen your understanding of the topics in this section of the chapter and integrate them with topics you've already studied, go to the *Making Connections* module for Chapter 5 at **www.prenhall.com/kauchak**. Respond to questions 7 and 8.

Check Your Understanding

4.1 What is a comprehensive high school, and why is it important for a democratic society such as ours?

4.2 How have the goals of high school education changed over time?

4.3 How are junior highs and middle schools different?

For feedback, go to Check Your Understanding *at the end of this chapter.*

> **Junior high schools.** Schools that were originally designed in the early 1900s to provide a unique academic curriculum for early adolescent youth.
>
> **Middle schools.** Schools, typically for grades 6–8, specifically designed to help students through the rapid social, emotional, and intellectual changes characteristic of early adolescence.

Searching for Equality: The Education of Cultural Minorities

The first thing to do was to clean them [Native Americans] thoroughly and to dress them in their new [military] attire. . . . [Then] everything except swallowing, walking, and sleeping had to be taught; the care of person, clothing, furniture, the usages of the table, the carriage of the body, civility, all those things which white children usually learn from their childhood by mere imitation, had to be painfully inculcated and strenuously insisted on. In addition to this, they were to be taught the rudiments of an English school course and the practical use of tools. (U.S. Bureau of Indian Affairs, 1974, p. 1749)

To this point our history of American education has been generally positive. Despite lurches and false starts, education improved in quality and became more accessible to our nation's young people. The story isn't so positive for cultural minorities, however. In this section, we outline the evolution of education for cultural minorities as we consider the experiences of Native Americans, African-Americans, Hispanic Americans, and Asian-Americans.

Two themes have been pervasive in the education of cultural minorities: the concept of assimilation and the policy "separate but equal." We define **assimilation** as a process of socializing people to adopt dominant social norms and patterns of behavior. For much of history, educators sought to bring minorities into the mainstream of American life—to assimilate them—by teaching basic skills and instilling White, middle-class values. In promoting assimilation, educators also asked minorities to reject important aspects of their own histories and cultures; this rejection is apparent in the quote about Native Americans that introduces this section.

The second theme, **separate but equal**, was a policy of segregating minorities in education, transportation, housing, and other areas of public life if opportunities and facilities were considered equal to those of nonminorities. In education, the policy was implemented by creating separate schools with different curricula, teaching methods, teachers, and resources. The policy was particularly applied to the education of African-American students. Some historians believe that these efforts were well intentioned but misguided, whereas others argue that they were inherently racist (Spring, 2005).

Let's look now at the history of education of specific minority groups.

Education of Native Americans

The history of Native American education is a story of generally unsuccessful attempts to assimilate different tribes into the American mainstream. To achieve assimilation, Native Americans were expected to exchange their tribal customs and values for mainstream American values. The process left Native American students asking the question, "Who am I?" It was a difficult question to answer.

Like American education in general, the education of Native Americans began with a religious orientation. During the 1700s and 1800s, mission schools run by various religious groups provided a common school curriculum that focused on basic skills, agriculture, vocational education, and religion. Although they provided instruction in the native language, mission schools attempted to help Native Americans bridge the gap between tribal, communal life and one in which individuals owned land, had jobs, and followed the dominant culture's way of life (Spring, 2005).

From 1890 to 1930, the federal government became involved in Native American education through boarding schools run by the Bureau of Indian Affairs. Children were forced to live at the schools, English was spoken and taught, and native languages and customs were forbidden. The best way to "Americanize" the children, leaders thought, was to remove them from tribal settings and provide them with a strict program of cultural transformation (Adams, 1995).

The failure of the boarding schools was evidenced by low participation rates (only 300 of a possible 4,000 to 5,000 eligible Navajo children attended these schools in 1901), high dropout rates (many children ran away), and a tendency for students to return to the reservation after graduation because the curriculum wasn't applicable to Native American culture or interests (Button & Provenzo, 1989).

Assimilation. A process of socializing people so that they adopt dominant social norms and patterns of behavior.

Separate but equal. A policy of segregating minorities in education, transportation, housing, and other areas of public life if opportunities and facilities were considered equal to those of nonminorities. In education, the policy was evidenced by separate schools with different curricula, teaching methods, teachers, and resources.

210

Despite the failure of boarding schools, federal control of Native American education continued through the 1960s. Tribal schools, which included Native American culture in the curriculum, opened in 1965, but financial dependence on the federal government, limited instructional materials, and poorly paid teachers were difficult problems to overcome.

More recently, the federal government shifted responsibility for Native American education from the Bureau of Indian Affairs and tribal schools to public schools. In the 1990s, 91 percent of Native Americans attended public schools (National Center for Education Statistics, 1997). Despite this shift, and increased involvement by tribal governments, the problems in Native American education persist. Underachievement, high dropout rates, low rates of college attendance and completion, as well as high rates of poverty indicate that current educational practices remain unsuccessful (Flanagan & Park, 2005).

Education of African-Americans: Up From Slavery to . . .

The first African-Americans arrived in the United States in the early 1600s, shortly after the founding of Jamestown. Brought as slaves, they had few educational opportunities before the Civil War. In 1850 fewer than 2 percent of African-Americans attended schools (about 4,000 in slave states and 23,000 in free states), and the literacy rate was low, ranging between 5 and 10 percent (U.S. Government Printing Office, 1975; West, 1972).

Educational accessibility improved after the Civil War. As a result of religious, philanthropic, and governmental efforts, school participation rates increased from 2 percent of the African American population in 1850 to 10 percent in 1870 and 35 percent in 1890 (U.S. Government Printing Office, 1975). Literacy rates increased from the 5 to 10 percent at the time of the Civil War to 40 percent by 1890 and 70 percent by 1910 (U.S. Bureau of the Census, 1990).

Near the end of the 1870s, events took a negative turn, however. After the Reconstruction period following the Civil War, the federal government shifted the responsibility for educating African-Americans back to state and local governments, par-

Early efforts at educating African-Americans were often substandard due to inadequate funding and resources. (Courtesy of the Library of Congress)

ticularly in the South, where the vast majority still lived. Segregated and substandard schools were predominant, and funding for African-American schools was consistently lower than for White schools. In 1877, for example, expenditures for African-American students in the South were less than half those for Whites; by the 1940s they had dropped to a fifth (J. Anderson, 1988). In 1907 White teachers in Alabama were paid five times more than African-American ones. In Georgia in the late 1920s, 99 percent of the money budgeted for teaching equipment went to White schools, even though African-Americans made up 34 percent of the state's student population (Bond, 1934). In 1952 Arkansas spent $102 to educate each White child but only $67 for each African-American child (Pulliam & Van Patten, 2007). Schools for African-Americans were clearly not separate but equal, more accurately described as *separate and unequal*.

Proposed Solutions to the Problem

The education of African-Americans was clearly inferior to that of Whites, but a clear solution to the problem remained elusive. Finally, two leaders, with sharply different perspectives, emerged.

Booker T. Washington (1856–1915) was born a slave and taught himself to read. Educated at Hampton Institute, a vocational school for African-Americans, he gained prominence for successfully establishing the Tuskegee Institute in 1881. Short of supplies and resources, he had his students build the school themselves. This hands-on approach to learning exemplified his strategy for bettering the education and lives of African-Americans in the South. He believed that hard work, practical training, and economic cooperation with Whites were the keys to success. His philosophy became popular, and he was often invited to address White audiences on the topic of African-American education. At one of these appearances, he summarized his philosophy in this way: "In all things that are purely social we can be as separate as the finger, yet one as the hand in all things essential to mutual progress" (Washington, 1932). Washington encouraged his students to become teachers; he felt that attempting to enter other professions or politics was premature and would lead to conflict with the White power structure in the South.

Although Washington was accepted by many African-Americans and popular with Whites, his policy of accommodating segregation angered other African-American leaders. W. E. B. Dubois (1868–1963) was an important opponent whose resistance to Washington's stance was predictable, given the differences in their backgrounds. Dubois was born in Massachusetts and educated in integrated schools. He attended colleges and universities in the United States and Europe and was the first African-American to receive a Ph.D. in the United States (Spring, 2005; Watkins, 2001).

Dubois was committed to changing the status of African-Americans and advocated a determined stand against segregation and racism. He focused his educational energies on students' achieving in the top 10 percent, believing that these students would provide leadership and create opportunities for the rest of the African-American population. He also felt that this group could take their place among the business, professional, and intellectual leaders of the White population. Dubois believed that Washington's separatist approach implied inferiority and, while expedient in the short term, would retard the educational progress of African-Americans in the long run. He advocated social activism and was a leader in helping establish the National Association for the Advancement of Colored People (NAACP). This organization played a major role in the advancement of African-Americans in the 20th century.

The Courts Examine "Separate But Equal"

Before the Civil War, African-Americans lived apart from the White majority because of slavery, legal restrictions, or de facto (not stipulated by law) segregation. Segregation continued after the Civil War because of the policy of "separate but equal." The policy justified segregation by claiming that African-Americans were receiving different but equal treatment under the law. The principle was first legally challenged in Massachusetts in 1850 when an African-American student wasn't allowed to attend a White school. At that time, the state court ruled that having separate but equal facilities was legal (Spring, 2005).

A federal challenge to the policy of "separate but equal" came in Louisiana in 1896 in a court case involving segregated railroads. In *Plessy v. Ferguson*, the U.S. Supreme Court ruled that separate but equal railroad facilities did not violate the Constitution (Spring, 2005). This decision was also applied to education, and "separate but equal" stood for almost 50 years. (We examine the federal government's response to the "separate but equal" policy in education in the Exploring Diversity section later in the chapter.)

Education of Hispanic Americans

Hispanic is a label that refers to a diverse group of people who are of Latin American or Caribbean heritage or who speak Spanish (Banks, 2006b; Nieto, 2004). Mexican-Americans in the Southwest, Puerto Rican Americans in the Northeast, and Cuban Americans in Florida are all included in this group. The term *Hispanic* is more popular in the Northeast, with groups in the Southwest preferring *Latino* (*Latina*, female). The term *Chicano* (*Chicana*, female) refers to Hispanics of Mexican-American heritage.

Hispanics are the fastest growing minority group in the United States. At the turn of the 21st century, they made up more than 15 percent of the nation's school-age children and are the largest minority group in California, Texas, and Florida (U.S. Bureau of Census, 2003). By the year 2025, 1 in 4 children in U.S. elementary schools is predicted to be of Hispanic origin.

Hispanic education in America began with Catholic mission schools in the Southwest, but it shifted to public schools after the Mexican–American War in 1848. Unlike African-American segregation, segregation of Hispanics was not mandated by law, but it occurred nevertheless. Hispanic students were often taught in separate schools or classes, with poorer facilities, fewer well-trained teachers, and smaller budgets. Migrant work, where farm laborers followed the crops, also contributed to educational problems, and attendance at school often suffered because of family work demands that led to transience.

Initially, the education of Hispanics focused on assimilation. Classes were taught in English, Spanish was forbidden, and students' own Hispanic heritage was ignored (Banks, 2006b; Spring, 2005). Apathy and resistance to school, as occurred with Native Americans, were pervasive, and dropping out was common. In 2003, 44 percent of the Hispanic school-age population left school before graduation, compared to 24 percent of White students (Olson, 2006a). Also, only 12 percent of 22-year-old Hispanics have a bachelor's degree, compared to 30 percent of Whites and 15 percent of African-Americans (Bowman, 2000c). When Hispanics go to college, they are much more likely to attend a 2-year institution than other groups (Pew Hispanic Foundation, 2003).

Language differences have been the source of many problems in the education of Hispanics. Language symbolizes differences between Hispanics and the dominant culture, and instruction in English interferes with students' learning. Some experts argue that language barriers explain why Hispanic students have historically scored lower on both intelligence and achievement tests, which are usually language based (Abedi, Hofstetter, & Lord, 2004; Popham, 2004b).

Education of Asian-Americans

Like Hispanics, Asian-Americans are a diverse group of people with varied histories (Banks, 2006b). The first Asian-Americans were Chinese who came to the United States to work in the California gold mines and on the first transcontinental railroad. Japanese immigrants came to California and Hawaii in the late 1800s as agricultural workers. More recently, Korean and Southeast Asian immigrants came to the United States seeking a better life and an escape from the Korean and Vietnam Wars.

Asian immigrants were initially welcomed because they relieved an acute labor shortage in the West. However, competition for jobs, together with racism, resulted in a series of changes in immigration laws that prevented further Chinese immigration in 1882 and then Japanese immigration in 1924 (Spring, 2005). A dark page in Asian-American history came during World War II, when more than 100,000 Japanese Americans were forced out of their homes near the Pacific coast and into internment camps in barren areas of the West.

Like other minority groups, Asian-Americans experienced discrimination. For example, in 1906 San Francisco established segregated schools for Asian-Americans. Instruction was in English, which resulted in problems similar to those that Native Americans and Hispanics encountered. A federal court ruled in 1974 (*Lau v. Nichols*) that the San Francisco school system had violated the rights of Chinese American students and that students who find their educational experience "wholly incomprehensible" must be taught in the first language if that language is not English.

As a group, Asian-Americans have fared better than other cultural minority groups in the American educational system. For example, Asian-Americans typically score higher on achievement tests and have higher rates of college attendance and completion than other groups, including White students (National Center for Education Statistics, 2005d), and the proportion of Asian-Americans in colleges and universities is higher than the proportion in

213

the general population. This success has led some educators to label this group "the model minority," a stereotypic term that some Asian-Americans reject (Asian-Nation, 2005). Stereotyping, which often results in lowered expectations for members of cultural minorities, can also work in the opposite direction, blinding us to problems that our students encounter (Steele, Spencer, & Aronson, 2002). For example, many Asian-American students have problems in school, and language and poverty remain obstacles for them (Lei, 2003; Lew, 2004). We need to remember that exclusive focus on group differences can result in inappropriate expectations for and unjust treatment of individual members of those groups.

The Search for Equality: Where Are We Now?

As you saw earlier, two themes—assimilation and "separate but equal"—have been central to the education of minorities in the United States. The policy of "separate but equal" has been banned by the courts, but where does assimilation now stand?

Assimilation has always required that ethnic groups sacrifice a portion of their cultural identity to become "American." At the extreme, success meant creating a "melting pot" in which the diverse cultures of America blended into a uniform and homogeneous society. This uniform society has never been achieved, as indicated, for example, in the present-day diversity of religions in America and holidays such as Kwanzaa, St. Patrick's Day, and the Jewish and Muslim religious holidays.

In educational circles, a "tossed salad" metaphor has replaced the melting pot; in this "salad," different ethnic and cultural groups contribute unique tastes and perspectives. The extent to which Americans should share common values and beliefs is still controversial, with some arguing for greater uniformity (Schlesinger, 1992) and others advocating an America built around diversity and shared values (Spring, 2005).

VIDEO PERSPECTIVES

The Reunion

To view this video, go to the *Becoming a Professional* DVD included with this text, click on ABC News, and then this chapter's video: *The Reunion*. This ABC News documentary examines the lasting effects of school integration during the civil rights struggle in the 1960s by doing something that has never been done before—gathering together the first wave of students who went through it themselves in Shaker Heights, Ohio. This group was at the center of the storm when their parents, at the height of the civil rights movement, carried out a bold and controversial social experiment in one of America's wealthiest suburbs. Now these 1960 kindergarten classmates reunite to see where the years and education have taken them from their then-new frontier—an integrated American suburb.

Think About This

1. How does school integration relate to the idea of "separate but equal"?
2. What were the goals of integration? Why was it necessary to bus students to achieve integration?
3. How is economic integration similar to and different from racial integration?

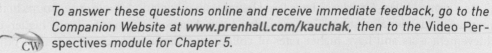

To answer these questions online and receive immediate feedback, go to the Companion Website at www.prenhall.com/kauchak, then to the Video Perspectives module for Chapter 5.

The federal government's role in the education of cultural minorities remains poorly defined. In the past, federal courts have played a major role in desegregation, but in recent times, they have been increasingly reluctant to impose busing and other legal mechanisms to achieve integration (Caldas & Bankston, 2005). During the 1960s, the commendable goal of integration, which sought to provide opportunities for cultural minorities and White majority students to attend school together and learn about each other, often became synonymous with forced busing (Pulliam & Van Patten, 2007). Busing was especially resisted by parents wanting their children to walk to and attend neighborhood schools. Public support for integration waned, and the result has been increased segregation of cultural minorities in inner-city schools (Caldas & Bankston, 2005; Kozol, 2005).

The same is true in the legislative branch; senators and members of the House of Representatives can't decide what role the federal government should play in the quest for equity and equality. Once an advocate for cultural diversity, the U.S. Senate in 2006 voted 63 to 34 to designate English as the national language (Hulse, 2006). We examine this changing federal role in education in the next section.

This section clearly indicates that the fourth item on our beginning-of-chapter survey—"As soon as slavery ended in this country, cultural and ethnic minorities were welcomed into U.S. schools"—is not true. Historically, our schools did not welcome minorities, and U.S. schools were inhospitable places for them. In fact, many minorities didn't attend U.S. schools, and when they did, their dropout rates were high. Only in the 1900s did this condition begin to change.

> **Making Connections:**
> To deepen your understanding of the topics in this section of the chapter and integrate them with topics you've already studied, go to the *Making Connections* module for Chapter 5 at www.prenhall.com/kauchak. Respond to questions 9 and 10.

Check Your Understanding

5.1   How does the concept of assimilation relate to Native American boarding schools?

5.2   How does "separate but equal" relate to African-Americans' educational experience in the United States?

5.3   How did the process of assimilation relate to Hispanic Americans and their native languages?

 For feedback, go to Check Your Understanding *at the end of this chapter.*

The Modern Era: Schools as Instruments for National Purpose and Social Change

The modern era in education began after World War II and continues to the present. It is characterized by an increased emphasis on education, which is now viewed as the key to both individual success and the progress of the nation. Given this perspective, it isn't surprising to see the federal government more actively involved in education than it was in the past. This increased involvement occurred in three areas:

- The government's response to the Cold War
- The government's War on Poverty and search for the "Great Society"
- The government's role in equity issues

Next, we look at these areas.

The Cold War: Enlisting America's Schools

After World War II, the United States became involved in a Cold War with communist countries, particularly the Soviet Union, with ever more powerful weapons being stockpiled on both sides.

It was called a Cold War because no shots were actually fired, but a struggle for world leadership evolved, nevertheless. This Cold War also significantly affected education in the United States.

The Russian launching of the satellite *Sputnik* in 1957 was a key event of the period. Believing the United States was losing the technology war, our government responded by authorizing a fivefold increase in the funding of the National Science Foundation, which had been created in 1950 to support research and improve science education. Congress also passed the National Defense Education Act (NDEA) in 1958, which was designed to enhance "the security of the nation" by improving instruction in math, science, and foreign languages. The NDEA provided funds for teacher training, new equipment, and the establishment of centers for research and dissemination of new teaching methods. During this period, Admiral Rickover, the father of the American nuclear navy, called education, "our first line of defense."

The War on Poverty and the Great Society

During the 1960s, leaders began to realize that despite the economic boom following World War II, many Americans were living in poverty. America was becoming a nation of "haves" and "have nots," and the problem was exacerbated by an economy that required ever-increasing skills from its workers.

For the unfortunate, a cycle of poverty began with inadequate education, which decreased employment opportunities, leading to a poorer quality of life that resulted in lowered achievement in the next generation (Macionis, 2006). To break this cycle and create a "Great Society" in which all could participate and benefit, President Lyndon Johnson, in his 1964 State of the Union address, stated that "this administration today, here and now, declares unconditional war on poverty in America."

Emphasis on education was a major thrust in the **War on Poverty**, a general term for federal programs designed to eradicate poverty during the 1960s. During this period, the federal government's involvement increased significantly. Initiatives included

- *Increased federal funding.* Federal funds for K–12 education went from $900 million and about 4.4 percent of the total spent on education in 1964 (before Johnson's initiatives) to $3 billion and 8.8 percent of the total educational budget by 1968.
- *The development of the Job Corps.* Modeled after the Civilian Conservation Corps of the 1930s, the Job Corps created rural and urban vocational training centers, which helped young people learn marketable skills while working in government projects.
- *The creation of the Department of Education in 1979.* Originally part of the Department of Health, Education and Welfare, education was considered so important that it was elevated to its own cabinet-level position during President Carter's administration.
- *Support for learners with exceptionalities.* The federal government passed Public Law 94-142, the Individuals with Disabilities Education Act (IDEA), in 1975. In 1976–1977, just after the law's passage, the nation educated about 3.3 million children with exceptionalities; presently the schools serve more than 6 million, an increase of nearly 82 percent (Heward, 2006).
- *The creation of national compensatory education programs.*

Let's look at compensatory programs in more detail.

Compensatory Education Programs

Compensatory education programs are government attempts to create more equal educational opportunities for disadvantaged youth. These programs provide supplementary instruction and attempt to prevent learning problems before they occur. The two best known are Head Start and Title I.

Head Start. Part of the Economic Opportunity Act of 1964, **Head Start** is a federal compensatory education program designed to help 3- to 5-year-old disadvantaged children enter school ready to learn. It has two goals: (1) to stimulate the development and academic achievement of low-income preschoolers and (2) to educate and involve parents in the edu-

War on Poverty. A general term for federal programs designed to eradicate poverty during the 1960s.

Compensatory education programs. Government attempts to create more equal educational opportunities for disadvantaged youth.

Head Start. A federal compensatory education program designed to help 3- to 5-year-old disadvantaged children enter school ready to learn.

cation of their children. In 2003, for example, 909,608 children were served in the program, which had a budget of $6.7 billion (Henry, Gordon, & Rickman, 2006). Head Start has served almost 17 million children since its inception.

The Head Start curriculum focuses on basic skills such as counting, naming colors, and prereading skills, as well as social skills such as turn-taking and following directions. Parenting goals include helping parents develop their children's literacy skills by encouraging parents to read and talk to their children and provide experiences that increase their readiness for school, such as trips to zoos, libraries, and museums.

In general, Head Start 4-year-olds perform better than comparable 4-year-olds who haven't participated in the program. In the more effective Head Start programs, such as the Perry Preschool Program in Ypsilanti, Michigan, researchers have found long-term positive effects ranging from fewer special education placements to higher numbers of high school graduates and lower crime and teen pregnancy rates (Jacobson, 2004; Lewis, 2005).

Not all Head Start programs are effective, however, and some programs have had little impact on children's readiness to learn. Poor program quality and inadequate budgets are the most commonly cited reasons (Merrow, 2002).

Title I. Title I is a federal compensatory education program that funds supplemental education services for low-income students in elementary and secondary schools. Between 1965 and 2000, more than $185 billion was spent on Title I, and these funds reached almost all of our nation's school districts. Presently funded at $14 billion per year, Title I serves 15 million low-income children in 47,600 schools (U.S. Department of Education, 2006a). Two thirds of the money goes to elementary schools, and 15 percent of the highest poverty schools receive 46 percent of Title I funds. Title I currently serves 100,000 homeless and 2.5 million English language learners. Approximately 35 percent of the recipients are White, 31 percent are Hispanic American, and 27 percent African-American.

As with Head Start, the outcomes of Title I programs have been uneven. Part of Title I's ineffectiveness resulted from initial design problems (Borman, 2002/2003). Because the funds were initially restricted to only low-income students, "pull-out" programs—where students were taken out of their regular classrooms for supplementary instruction—prevailed. During the late 1990s, 60 percent of the instruction in these pull-out programs was conducted by unlicensed aides, or paraprofessionals, and more than 40 percent of these Title I aides spent half or more of their time without the supervision of a licensed teacher (U.S. Department of Education, 1999a). The recent No Child Left Behind Act attempts to address this problem by specifying qualifications for Title I paraprofessionals. By 2005–2006, current paraprofessionals were to have finished 2 years of college or demonstrated competence through passing a rigorous test; newly hired paraprofessionals must meet this standard at the time of hire (Honawar, 2006).

Pull-out Title I programs have had other problems as well. Removing students from their classrooms causes logistical problems; the students who are pulled out miss regular instruction, and teachers have trouble helping them catch up. Also, pull-out instruction often focuses on low-level skills with few links to the regular curriculum.

In response to these criticisms, Title I programs have been redesigned to focus on total school improvement, rather than instruction in pull-out programs (Borman, 2002/2003). Newer programs attempt to achieve schoolwide improvement in a variety of ways. For example, James Comer's School Development Program focuses on involving parents and providing improved family services such as counseling and social services (Comer et al., 2004). Another program, Success for All, attempts to prevent school failure by emphasizing family involvement and by laying a strong foundation in reading, writing, and math during the early grades (Slavin & Cheung, 2004).

Putting Compensatory Education Programs Into Perspective. Critics hope to do away with compensatory education programs and point to their uneven quality. This criticism underscores the general dilemma of federal aid to education. This aid is usually given with only broad guidelines that allow schools and districts to spend the money essentially as they see fit. This necessary flexibility also results in uneven quality.

Title I. A federal compensatory education program that funds supplemental education services for low-income students in elementary and secondary schools.

exploring diversity

The Federal Government's Role in Pursuing Equality

Consider the following statistics. The average 12th-grade low-income student of color reads at the same level as the average eighth-grade middle-class White student (Kahlenberg, 2000). As a group, African-Americans have the lowest achievement test scores of any minority, and they are over-represented in special education classes (National Center for Education Statistics, 2006b). Close to 30 percent of Hispanics live at or below the poverty line, and college attendance and graduation rates are substantially below the general population (U.S. Bureau of Census, 2000).

The struggle for equality in education is an important area in which the federal government's role has increased. Civil rights and equity for women are two areas where the federal role has made an important difference.

The Civil Rights Movement

Linda Brown was an 8-year-old African-American student in Topeka, Kansas, in 1951. Instead of walking 5 blocks to an all-White elementary school, she was forced to cross unguarded and potentially dangerous railroad tracks to catch a bus to a school for African-Americans 21 blocks away. In addition to objecting to the distance, her father believed that the African-American school had substandard resources and programs. With the help of the NAACP, he went to court to change this.

We mentioned earlier in the chapter that the policy "separate but equal" was put into place after the Civil War. It remained a guiding principle in education until 1954, when Thurgood Marshall, who later became the first African-American on the U.S. Supreme Court, represented the NAACP in arguing against the "separate but equal" doctrine that forced Linda Brown to attend a segregated school. In a unanimous decision, the Supreme Court ruled in the famous watershed case, *Brown v. Board of Education of Topeka* (1954), that separate educational facilities are inherently unequal and that racially segregated schools generated "a feeling of inferiority." The days of segregated education for African-American students were supposed to be over.

In some school districts, however, Whites so strongly resisted integration that it had to be forced. For example, in 1957 President Eisenhower sent federal troops to an all-White high school in Little Rock, Arkansas, to enforce the Supreme Court's antisegregation decision and allow nine African-American students to attend the school in safety. In spite of these efforts, discrimination remained widespread because the responsibility for desegregation was left to individual school districts, many of which resisted change.

Congress responded with the Civil Rights Act of 1964, which prohibited discrimination against students on the basis of race, color, or national origin in all institutions receiving federal funds. The federal government now had a mechanism to both encourage and enforce integration efforts.

Equity for Women

As we mentioned at the beginning of the chapter, in the early periods of U.S. history, women were generally excluded from education, and historically, they have been underserved by our nation's schools. The federal government became involved in gender-equity issues by enacting Title IX of the Education Amendments of 1972. The purpose of this legislation was to eliminate gender bias in the schools and states:

No person in the United States shall, on the basis of sex, be excluded from participation in, be denied benefits of, or be subjected to discrimination under any education program or activity receiving federal financial assistance.

Federal efforts through legislation such as Title IX have increased funding and participation in girls' athletics. (Sean Justice/Getty Images Inc.–Image Bank)

The law has had its largest impact on physical education and sports: The number of girls participating in high school athletics increased from 294,000 in 1971 to more than 2.7 million in 2001 (U.S. Department of Education, 2002). Participation is still well below that of boys (3.8 million in 1998–1999), however, and in most schools, women's teams still do not receive comparable funding, facilities, equipment, publicity, travel budgets, or practice opportunities.

Title IX has become controversial at the college and university level. Critics of Title IX argue that in order to achieve an equal number of male and female athletes, schools have had to eliminate many of the "minor" men's sports, such as wrestling, swimming, gymnastics, and tennis (M. Davis, 2003). Supporters of Title IX argue that the extraordinary cost of college football skews the issue, and a modest cut in football expenditures would allow for a greater investment in women's sports with no cuts to other men's sports.

Putting Federal Efforts Into Perspective

So, how has federal intervention affected the struggle for equality in education? With respect to integration, progress is uncertain. For example, in the South in 1988, nearly 44 percent of African-American students attended integrated schools, up from virtually none in 1954. However, by 1996 the figure had shrunk to about 35 percent (Hendrie, 1999). In the North, segregated housing patterns led to de facto segregated schools. This problem has been exacerbated in urban areas by "White flight" to the suburbs. Consider these statistics:

In Chicago, by the academic year 2000–2001, 87 percent of public school enrollment was black or Hispanic; less than 10 percent of children in the schools were white. In Washington, D.C., 94 percent of children were black or Hispanic; less than 5 percent were white. In St. Louis, 82 percent of the student population was black or Hispanic by this point, in Philadelphia and Cleveland 78 percent, in Los Angeles 84 percent, in Detroit 95 percent, in Baltimore 88 percent. In New York City, nearly three quarters of the students were black or Hispanic in 2001. (Kozol, 2005, p. 8)

Currently, more than three fourths of Hispanic students attend schools populated predominantly by members of cultural minorities, and nearly 4 in 10 attend schools that are 90 to 100 percent minority (Borman, 2002/2003).

Various strategies have been proposed to achieve greater racial diversity in schools. Compensatory education, school boundary realignments, and mandatory busing are some. In the 1970s, **magnet schools**, public schools that provide innovative or specialized programs and accept enrollment from students in all parts of a district, were developed to aid in the integration of White and minority students. Magnet schools organize their curricula around high-interest or high-need areas such as math, science, and computers, or around general, high-quality programs designed to prepare students for college. Magnet schools are most common in large cities and today number about 4,000 schools, serving more than 2 million students, or about 3 percent of the K–12 student population (Kober, 2006). The federal government encouraged magnet schools' growth by allocating $108 million in fiscal year 2005 to encourage growth in more than 100 school districts (Magnet Schools of America, 2006; U.S. Department of Education, 2006b).

In spite of strong governmental support ($739 million for experimentation with magnet programs), magnet schools haven't always met their original goals. For instance, they tend to attract the highest-achieving minority students, which robs other students of role models. When they succeed in attracting bright students from cultural minority groups, they sometimes cannot attract high-performing White students into the same schools. Social class differences between wealthier and poorer students and cultural differences within magnet schools also work to minimize true integration and the development of cohesive learning communities (Dickinson, Holtfield, Holtfield, & Creer, 2000).

Civil rights and women's equity efforts also continue to be highly controversial. Some minority leaders and women's groups assert that progress for cultural minorities and women has been too slow, and the government should do more. On the other hand, conservative leaders contend that civil rights efforts have gone too far. They charge that women and minorities are receiving inappropriately preferential treatment, which amounts to reverse discrimination. These debates are likely to continue in the future as critics on various sides become increasingly vocal and polar in their positions.

> **Magnet schools.** Public schools that provide innovative or specialized programs that attempt to attract students from all parts of a district.

teaching in an era of reform

Federal Government Reform

Reforms result from various sources, such as professional organizations, states, local districts, and the federal government, with the federal government being one of the most powerful. As you saw earlier in the chapter, the federal government expanded its role in influencing education during the 20th century in three primary ways:

- Setting standards
- Creating testing programs
- Offering financial incentives

The issue in this debate about educational reform is whether reform should originate at the federal level or whether it is best done at the state or even local levels (DeBray, McDermott, & Wohlstetter, 2005).

Setting Standards

One way for the federal government to influence education is to encourage states to set standards, which provide common goals for educational efforts. The No Child Left Behind (NCLB) Act of 2001, requires each state to establish its own standards and create tests to assess the extent to which its students meet those standards. An important component of this act is the requirement that each state guarantee that 100 percent of its students are proficient in reading, math, and science by the year 2014.

Testing Programs

Begun in 1969, the National Assessment of Educational Progress (NAEP) testing program, also known as "the Nation's Report Card," was designed to provide an objective, external measure of how students in the United States are performing (Popham, 2005). The program conducts periodic assessments of students in fourth, eighth, and twelfth grades in math, science, reading, writing, and the arts, and in the social studies areas of civics, geography, and U.S. history. Because of concerns about undue federal influence and the confidentiality of scores, testing is voluntary, and only group scores are reported. In 2003, all 50 states participated in some aspect of the program. In addition to providing a nationwide snapshot of the competence of U.S. students, NAEP also provides state profiles and comparisons of test scores.

Financial Incentives

If national goals are worth pursuing, and tests can measure progress toward these goals, rewarding districts that make significant progress and punishing those that don't are logical next steps. This is exactly what President George W. Bush recommended during his presidential campaign and what Congress enacted in NCLB (DeBray et al., 2005). Low-performing schools that receive federal funds can be put on a 5-year schedule of remediation, and if scores don't improve, the schools could be taken over by the state or reconstituted. In addition, states that fail to comply with NCLB provisions could lose federal educational funds.

The Issue

Setting standards seems sensible. For instance, who would oppose the idea of every student in the nation reaching proficiency in reading and math by 2014? Also, supporters of nationwide testing argue that knowing how our students are doing and how states compare to one another is sensible, and they ask, "How can we improve our education systems if we don't know what our students are learning or how much they are learning" (Ravitch, 2006)?

Financial incentives also make sense intuitively. Why shouldn't teachers and schools be rewarded for increasing the amount their students learn (or punished when learning doesn't occur)?

However, national standards have been criticized by both political conservatives and liberals, although for different reasons (Gordon, 2006). As Chester Finn, former Assistant Secretary of Education under President Reagan, observed, "Republicans oppose any proposal with the word 'national' in it; Democrats oppose anything with the word 'standards' in it" (quoted in D. Doyle, 1999, p. 56). NCLB partially dodges this issue by making individual states responsible for setting proficiency levels in different content areas.

National testing is also controversial. Critics contend it creates a national curriculum and that it causes teachers to "teach to the test," which narrows the curriculum and detracts from an overall education (Nichols & Berliner, 2005).

Critics also charge that financial incentives will further encourage teachers to teach to tests, and states and districts will align their curricula with the content being tested—in essence, creating a de facto national curriculum (Newman, 2006).

You Take a Position

Now it's your turn to take a position on the issue. State in writing whether you favor an increased federal role in school reform that includes requiring states to set standards, creating testing programs, and offering financial incentives, and provide a two-page rationale for your position.

For additional references and resources, go to the Companion Website at www.prenhall.com/kauchak, then to the Teaching in an Era of Reform module for Chapter 5. You can respond online or submit your response to your instructor.

Critics also argue that the programs have failed to eliminate achievement differences between participants and other students. This criticism is more debatable. Expecting schools, alone, to solve the social problems associated with poverty, such as drug use, violence, unstable families, and unhealthy neighborhoods, is unrealistic (Berliner, 2005). And a long history of research consistently demonstrates that these factors adversely affect learning (Macionis, 2006).

As this section has demonstrated, the fifth item from our survey—"In recent times, the federal government has viewed the schools as an instrument to achieve national goals"—is true. As the link between an educated workforce and national prosperity became clearer, the federal government increasingly viewed the schools as essential for achieving national goals. This emphasis was most pronounced in 1983 with the publication of *A Nation at Risk* (U.S. Department of Education, 1983), and more recently with No Child Left Behind legislation.

Making Connections:
To deepen your understanding of the topics in this section of the chapter and integrate them with topics you've already studied, go to the *Making Connections* module for Chapter 5 at **www.prenhall.com/kauchak.** Respond to questions 11–13.

Check Your Understanding

6.1 How was the federal government's educational response to the Cold War similar to its actions in the War on Poverty and the Great Society?

6.2 What are magnet schools, and how do they relate to attempts to achieve equality in our schools?

6.3 What is Title IX, and how is it related to the concept of equality?

For feedback, go to Check Your Understanding *at the end of this chapter.*

decision making

Defining Yourself as a Professional

You're a first-year teacher in a large suburban district in the Midwest. When you interviewed for the job, the principal explained that the district was experiencing demographic changes, and parents were concerned about declining test scores. The fourth grade, where you have a self-contained classroom, is particularly important, because your students take the Stanford Achievement Test, a standardized test widely used to gauge individual student progress. In addition, they participate in the NAEP, the national test designed to assess the progress of students across the country.

During the weeks before school, the principal met with teams of teachers at each grade level, going over the district curriculum and explaining how it has been aligned to cover content measured on the standardized tests. You design your unit and lesson plans around these goals and feel fairly confident as the school year begins.

After 2 or 3 weeks, you see that something is wrong. You have some classroom management problems, and a number of your students don't seem motivated. In addition, many of your students can't

do the work you assign. Some have transferred from other districts where the curriculum was different, some are struggling with English as a second language, and others just don't seem to get it.

After a number of troubled evenings, you approach one of your colleagues, an experienced teacher next door, and explain how you're considering dumping the planned curriculum, assessing your students, and starting over.

"You really think that would work?" your colleague asks after hearing your plan.

"I'm not sure, but I know what I'm doing now isn't."

"And what are you going to tell Mr. Livingston when he comes around to evaluate your teaching?"

What would you do in this situation?

To respond to this question online and receive immediate feedback, go to the Decision Making module for Chapter 5 on the Companion Website at *www.prenhall.com/kauchak.*

Meeting Your Learning Objectives

1. Explain how the diversity of the original colonies shaped our educational system, and describe the role of religion in colonial schools.
   - Major geographic, economic, and cultural differences existed in the original 13 colonies. These differences spilled over into religious differences, which strongly influenced the decision to separate church and state.
   - Early colonial educational practices were largely negative and repressive. Over time European philosophies that were more humane and child-centered made their way across the Atlantic.
   - The colonial period resulted in three historical legacies. First, early schools were elitist, catering to wealthy, white males. Second, the foundation of public support for education was established by the Old Deluder Satan Act. Finally, the tangled relationship between religion and education began.

2. Describe how the early national period defined state and federal roles for governing education.
   - During the early national period, the framers of the Constitution used the First Amendment to separate religion from government.
   - The Tenth Amendment to the Constitution placed the primary responsibility for funding and governing education in the hands of state and local governments.
   - During this period, the federal government separated church and government, relegated educational responsibility to the states, and established the idea that schools were essential for improving the quality of life and helping the nation grow.

3. Explain how the common school movement influenced the establishment of universal public schooling.
   - During the years leading up to the Civil War, states laid the foundations of universal access to tax-supported schools. States established state departments of education to govern schools and built normal schools to advance the idea of professional training for teachers.
   - The common school movement was a turning point in American education because it planted the idea of universal access to a tax-supported education for all. Though this ideal was not achieved in practice, establishing the principle was important. Also during this period, states addressed the central issue of teacher quality by creating normal schools.

4. Describe the historical roots of contemporary secondary schools.
   - The history of the comprehensive American high school began with the Boston Latin School, the first secondary school in the colonies. This college-preparatory institution focused on the classics. Benjamin Franklin's Academy of Philadelphia introduced the idea of a practical curriculum. The English High School targeted non–college-bound students and was supported by public funds.
   - The comprehensive American high school evolved as a compromise out of a tug-of-war between committee reports that advocated either academic or applied orientations. The comprehensive high school attempts to meet the needs of all students—general education, vocational, and college preparatory—under one roof.
   - Current middle schools began as more traditional junior highs created in the early 1900s. Junior high schools were more academically oriented and were often "mini" versions of high schools. Middle schools were created to meet the unique developmental needs of young adolescents.

5. Discuss similarities and differences in different minority groups' struggles for educational equality.
   - The education of cultural minorities in the United States, aimed at assimilation, attempted to create schools that were separate but equal but generally failed. Native American education efforts attempted to assimilate students through boarding schools.
   - The education of African-Americans in the United States had a long history of separate but unequal treatment that was finally challenged in the Supreme Court in 1954.

- Education for Hispanic Americans had a similar uneven history, with both segregation and unequal funding. Bilingual education has been a central controversy in the education of Hispanics, and its status is currently in question.
- Asian-Americans experienced educational problems similar to other cultural minorities. In attempts to assimilate them quickly, schools often ignored Asian-Americans' native languages.
- The concepts of assimilation and melting pot have been replaced with metaphors such as "mosaic" or "tossed salad," which emphasize the importance of students' retaining their home cultures. In addition, the federal government's role in achieving educational equity is still being debated.

6. Explain how schools became instruments for national purpose during the modern era.
- During the modern era, the federal government took a more active role in education, using it as an instrument of national purpose. During the Cold War with the Soviet Union, the federal government spent large amounts of money improving math, science, and foreign language education.
- During the War on Poverty and the Great Society, the federal government also used courts and federal spending to battle poverty and inequalities in the schools.
- Currently, consensus is lacking about the federal government's role in achieving education equity. The No Child Left Behind Act is the latest federal effort in this regard.

Important Concepts

academy
assimilation
character education
common school movement
compensatory education programs
comprehensive high school
English classical school
Head Start
junior high schools

Latin grammar school
magnet schools
middle schools
normal schools
Old Deluder Satan Act
separate but equal
Title I
vouchers
War on Poverty

Developing as a Professional

Preparing for Your Licensure Exam

This exercise will provide you with practice answering questions similar to the Praxis™ Principles of Learning and Teaching Exam as well as your state-specific licensure exam.

Think about the history of American education and how the teachers' comments in the following case study reflect trends in this history. Then read the case study, and answer the questions that follow.

"Oh, my aching feet!" Dave Carlisle (the first-year middle school teacher from the opening case for this chapter) moans as he sinks onto the sofa.

"Out late dancing again?" his colleague Monica asks, looking up from the lesson plans she is working on.

"Yeah, right. Don't I wish. I've been on my feet all morning lecturing on Newton's laws of motion."

"Newton's laws of motion? Isn't that stuff they'll get in high school physics?" Monica asked.

"Yeah, but I just want to be sure that they'll be ready for it when they get there. About half of the kids in my morning class are really sharp and should go on to college. They'll need this stuff," Dave replies.

"How come you're lecturing so much? I thought we agreed we'd try more problem-based learning to get the kids involved. Lecturing is not only hard on you, it's difficult for them—especially the ones struggling in science."

"Yeah, I know that, but I'm torn. Science is really important. Especially for those going on to college. Do I aim for the average student and punish my high achievers, or teach to the college bound and hope the others come along for the ride? Any ideas?"

"Sounds like we better talk about this in our next team meeting," Monica replies with a frown.

1. Analyze Dave's comments in terms of the history of the middle school and junior high school. Where would Dave's teaching more clearly fit?

2. In which type of earlier school—Latin grammar school, academy, or English classical school—would Dave's teaching fit the best? least?

3. Which report, the report from the Committee of Ten or the Cardinal Principles of Secondary Education, would Dave agree with more? Why?

To receive feedback on your responses to these exercises, go to the Companion Website at www.prenhall.com/kauchak, then to the Preparing for Your Licensure Exam module for Chapter 5.

Discussion Questions

1. What is the proper relationship between education and religion? Is the connection between religion and education likely to become closer or more distant over the next 10 years? Why do you think so?

2. Will trends that emphasize choice, such as the use of school vouchers and enrollment in magnet schools, likely increase or decrease in the future? Why do you think so? Will choice positively or negatively influence education?

3. What is your position on bilingual education? Should it be generally banned as it has been in some states, or was this a mistake? Explain your position.

4. How would you attempt to solve the problems with Native American education?

5. Do you believe that racial discrimination remains a major problem for society? What could or should schools do to alleviate this problem?

6. Would our educational system be better if control were at the national level instead of the local and state levels? Why or why not?

Developing as a Professional: Online Activities

Going Into Schools

Go to the Companion Website at *www.prenhall.com/kauchak,* and click on the *Going Into Schools* module for Chapter 5. You will find a number of school-based activities that will help you link chapter content to the schools in which you work.

Virtual Field Experience: Using the Internet to Explore the Profession

If you would like to participate in a Virtual Field Experience, access the following Website: *http//:www.library.gcsu.edu/~sc/magepages/magelink.html.* This site provides a comprehensive overview of the history of education in the United States.

Online Portfolio Activities

To develop your professional portfolio, further apply your understanding of chapter content, and address the INTASC standards, go the Companion Website at *www.prenhall.com/kauchak*, then to the *Online Portfolio Activities* for Chapter 5. Complete the suggested activities.

Check Your Understanding

1.1 How did the diversity of the original colonies shape the educational system in the United States?

Because of cultural, geographic, economic, and religious differences in the original colonies, it was not possible to create a uniform, monolithic school system that would satisfy everyone. This led to regional or state control of education, a system that survives today.

1.2 What role did religion play in colonial schools? What are the implications of this role for contemporary schools?

Religion was often the reason that many colonists came to North America, and it played a central role in colonial life. The colonists therefore included religion as a central part of the school curriculum. The proper role of religion in schools is a contentious issue today because of differing views of the purposes of schools and schooling.

1.3 Explain why the Old Deluder Satan Act of Massachusetts was important for the development of our American educational system.

The Old Deluder Satan Act required every town of 50 or more households to hire a teacher to instruct the children in that town. This provided the legal foundation for the public support of education.

2.1 What is the Tenth Amendment to the Constitution? Why is it important for education today?

The Tenth Amendment to the Constitution mandated that responsibilities for education not explicitly assigned to the federal government would be the responsibility of each state. This put the responsibility for funding and governing education in the hands of the states. This system of state-controlled education exists today and is unique to the United States.

2.2 Describe the role that was established for the federal government during the early national period.

During the early national period, legislators established federal funding for public schools and introduced the idea that schools were instruments of national purpose.

2.3 What was the historical significance of the Ordinances of 1785 and 1787?

These ordinances were designed to encourage people to settle in frontier areas. Part of this legislation set aside a section of land for public education. These laws set the precedent of involving the federal government in supporting public education and established a historical framework for viewing public schools as instruments of national purpose. In other words, schools could be used to shape our country's goals and purposes.

3.1 How was the common school movement linked to the growing number of immigrants coming to the United States?

Immigrants brought with them different cultures and languages. Our government needed ways to make them productive citizens and assimilate them into the increasingly industrialized U.S. economy. Governmentally supported and run schools were seen as a major way to do this.

3.2   **Who was Horace Mann, and what was his contribution to education in the United States?**

Horace Mann was an outspoken advocate for universal public education. He was the Secretary of the Massachusetts State Board of Education from 1837 to 1848. Because of his influence, Massachusetts doubled state appropriations for education, built 50 new secondary schools, increased teacher salaries by 50 percent, and passed the nation's first compulsory school attendance law in 1852. He was a powerful and effective advocate for the importance of public education for everyone.

3.3   **What were normal schools, and why are they important today**

Normal schools were special schools created for the preparation of teachers. They were important because they addressed the whole issue of teacher preparation and quality, an issue that is currently being debated with fast-track and alternative certification programs.

4.1   **What is a comprehensive high school, and why is it important for a democratic society such as ours?**

A comprehensive high school attempts to educate all students—general education, vocational education, and college preparatory students—under one roof. Advocates of the comprehensive high school assert that this integration and mixing of students is important so that students of all ability levels can learn about each other.

4.2   **How have the goals of high school education changed over time?**

Initially, the predecessors of the contemporary high school were elitist and oriented primarily to preparation for college; institutions such as the Latin Grammar School were strictly college preparatory. Later, schools such as Benjamin Franklin's Academy or the English Classical School reoriented themselves to more practical subjects such as bookkeeping and surveying. Initial participation in these schools was still limited to the very wealthy or talented. The idea of a universal high school education didn't really take root until the 1900s.

4.3   **How are junior highs and middle schools different?**

Junior highs were designed to prepare students for high school. Consequently, they focused primarily on academics and, for the most part, ignored the social and emotional needs of young adolescents. Middle schools evolved out of growing recognition that the developmental needs of early adolescents were unique and were not being met by junior high schools. Middle school adaptations for developing adolescents included a more applied and integrated curriculum, more learner-centered instruction, and classes that allowed teachers and students to interact and get to know each other.

5.1   **How does the concept of assimilation relate to Native American boarding schools?**

Assimilation is the process of socializing cultural minorities so they adopt the social norms and behaviors of the dominant culture, or Whites. Boarding schools attempt to speed up the process by taking Native American youth away from their families and instructing them in residential facilities. These efforts were mainly ineffective.

5.2   **How does "separate but equal" relate to African-Americans' educational experience in the United States?**

Early attempts to educate African-Americans placed them in segregated schools that purported to be separate but equal. Unfortunately, they were separate but unequal in terms of resources and quality.

5.3 **How did the process of assimilation relate to Hispanic Americans and their native languages?**

In hopes of assimilating Hispanic Americans quickly, schools frequently taught classes in English only, and Spanish was forbidden. This practice not only caused the loss of the first language but also resulted in conflicts between home and school. Bilingual education attempted to retain and build on students' first language skills, but the status of bilingual education is currently in doubt because of restrictive legislation in a number of states.

6.1 **How was the federal government's educational response to the Cold War similar to its actions in the War on Poverty and the Great Society?**

Both federal initiatives viewed education as a tool for national progress. In the case of the Cold War, education was enlisted as a means to improve science and technology, to combat against the perceived growing threat of Communism. In the War on Poverty, education was seen as a tool to eliminate poverty and the economic disparities in our country.

6.2 **What are magnet schools, and how do they relate to attempts to achieve equality in our schools?**

Magnet schools were created as an alternative to forced busing and integration. Magnet schools attempt to achieve integration by attracting bright students from all cultural groups. The results on magnet schools are mixed. While they do achieve integration, critics charge that they tend to steal bright minority students from their home schools and that social integration within magnet schools often doesn't occur.

6.3 **What is Title IX, and how is it related to the concept of equality?**

Title IX was federal legislation enacted in 1972 to eliminate gender bias in the United States. It's most dramatic influence in education has been in the area of sports, where gender-equity advocates have used it to gain equity in facilities and expenditures.

Creating Productive Learning Environments

7

Creating Productive Learning Environments

Chapter Outline

Characteristics of Productive Learning Environments
A Focus on Learning • A Focus on Learners

The Human Dimension of Productive Learning Environments
Caring: An Essential Element in Teaching • Personal Teaching Efficacy • Positive Teacher Expectations • Modeling and Enthusiasm

Classroom Management: Creating Safe and Supportive Learning Environments
Classroom Management: A National Concern • Classroom Management Goals • Preventing Problems Through Planning • Intervening Effectively • Handling Serious Management Problems: Violence and Aggression • Effective Classroom Management in Urban Schools

Creating Productive Learning Environments: Involving Parents
Benefits of Parental Involvement • Strategies for Involving Parents

Learning Objectives

After you have completed your study of this chapter, you should be able to:

1. Describe the essential characteristics of a productive learning environment.

2. Explain how teachers' personal characteristics contribute to a productive learning environment.

3. Describe how classroom management contributes to a productive learning environment.

4. Explain how involving parents contributes to a productive learning environment.

Case Studies

 Elementary   *Middle*   *Secondary*

Creating productive learning environments is one of teachers' most important roles. As you read the following case study, ask yourself what a productive learning environment looks like and how Shannon Brinkman, the teacher, helps create one in her classroom.

Shannon, a fifth-grade teacher, is in her third year of teaching in an urban elementary school in the Southwest. As she anticipates the new year, she spends several days preparing her room. She tapes posters and pictures on the walls and labels the clock, windows, door, and other common objects with signs in both Spanish and English.

As her students enter her classroom on the first day, she greets them at the door and tells them to find the desk with their name on it. As soon as the students are settled, she asks them to introduce themselves and say a few words about themselves, their favorite activities, and anything else they think might be interesting.

After students have introduced themselves, Shannon comments, "We are going to have a great year this year. I asked you to introduce yourselves, because we all want to get to know each other and work together to help each other learn and grow as much as possible. This classroom is like a family, and in families people help each other. So, that's what we will do throughout this year.

"So, to be sure we all can help each other and learn as much as possible, we need some guidelines that will help our classroom run as smoothly as possible," she continues and then asks the students to make suggestions that will help them all be comfortable and keep the classroom safe and orderly. They discuss the suggestions, and Shannon makes notes about rules and procedures, which she plans to post the next morning.

After the discussion, she then takes a picture of each student with her digital camera and then turns to her planned math topic. She prints the pictures that evening and has them displayed on the bulletin board under a large sign saying, "Our Class," when the students come in the next day.

During language arts that day, she divides students into pairs and has them interview each other about things like family, hobbies, and favorite foods. The next day she teaches them a standard format and has each write a paragraph about the other student that they would put on the bulletin board next to the pictures. Students take turns using the two computers in the back of the room to enter their paragraphs into the computer. When students encounter difficulties, she has several students who are more familiar with computers help out.

Think about some of your past experiences in classrooms. Why were some comfortable and inviting, whereas others seemed cold and impersonal? This question is important, because the classroom environment you create will significantly influence the amount your students learn and how much they enjoy school. In this chapter, we examine the characteristics of productive learning environments and how teachers can create them.

Before proceeding on with this chapter, take a few minutes to complete the questionnaire on the following page. We address each of the items in the chapter.

Characteristics of Productive Learning Environments

Classrooms are complex places where teachers make an enormous number of decisions. One of the first, and most important, is deciding how to create a **productive learning environment**, a classroom that is orderly and focuses on learning. *Orderly* doesn't mean rigid or punitive; rather, it means safe, relaxed, and inviting. In an orderly environment, students are respectful and accept responsibility for their actions, teachers rarely raise their voices, and the focus is on helping everyone learn. How can teachers create this type of environment in their classroom? Research provides some answers.

A Focus on Learning

Learning is the central purpose of schooling. While this simple statement may seem self-evident, keeping it in mind is important because it helps simplify our decision making. For example, we try to create an environment that is comfortable and inviting because it contributes to student learning. We emphasize respect and personal responsibility because this emphasis helps students develop personally, socially, and morally. We avoid criticizing students because criticism decreases learning. We create systems of procedures and rules because students learn more in environments that are safe and predictable.

This focus on learning guides our actions as teachers and helps answer the question, Why are productive learning environments so important? They are important because they promote learning for all students.

A Focus on Learners

Productive environments are also *learner* centered. What does this mean? Learner-centered classrooms have three characteristics. They emphasize

- Classrooms as learning communities
- Personal and social development
- A positive classroom climate

Let's look at each of these.

professional knowledge: test yourself!

For each item, circle the number that best represents your thinking. Use the following scale as a guide.

1 = Strongly disagree
2 = Disagree
3 = Agree/disagree
4 = Agree
5 = Strongly agree

1. Teacher caring is most important in the lower elementary grades, and its importance diminishes as students grow older.

   1   2   3   4   5

2. Teachers who have the most orderly classrooms are those who can quickly and effectively respond to student misbehavior.

   1   2   3   4   5

3. The most effective way to increase the amount students learn about a content area, such as math, is to allocate more time to the study of the content area.

   1   2   3   4   5

4. Teachers are legally required to intervene if students in their classrooms become involved in a fight or a scuffle.

   1   2   3   4   5

5. Involving parents in their children's education can actually increase student achievement.

   1   2   3   4   5

This is available in a downloadable format on the Companion Website for personal portfolio use.

Classrooms as Learning Communities

Learner-centered classrooms create **learning communities**, classrooms in which the teacher and all the students work together to help everyone learn (Haberman, 2004; LePage et al., 2005).

A learning community is characterized by the following:

- *Inclusiveness.* All students—high and low achievers, members of cultural minorities, students with and without exceptionalities, boys and girls—participate in learning activities and believe they can succeed. Each feels that they belong in the classroom. Shannon began this process by having her students interview each other so that they could get to know each other and feel part of the classroom. Teachers also make it a point to involve all students in learning activities, such as calling on them as equally as possible.

> **Learning communities.** Classrooms in which the teacher and all the students work together to help everyone learn.

- *Respect for others.* We said earlier that teachers avoid criticizing students because criticism decreases learning. Avoiding criticism doesn't mean that students are allowed to do as they please, nor does it mean that teachers lower expectations for their students. Rather, it means that teachers respond to students with courtesy and respect, and expect the same courtesy and respect in return. For example, when the teacher speaks, students show respect by listening. When a student has the floor, he or she deserves the same respect from others. When students learn to be respectful, they grow as human beings, and this growth is part of the total learning process.
- *Safety and security.* In a learning community, students must be safe, not only from physical harm but also from name-calling, bullying, and other forms of hurtful interactions. The teacher again sets the tone with the classroom rules and procedures that he or she introduces the first day of school and reinforces throughout the year. One middle school teacher has her cardinal rule, "No Put-Downs," realizing that middle schoolers sometimes forget about the feelings of others and that sarcasm and biting humor can get laughs. When this happens, students become reluctant to share ideas, and they learn less. (We examine rules and procedures in detail later in the chapter.)
- *Trust and connectedness.* In learning communities, students learn to trust and depend on each other for assistance. Shannon promoted this support when she had students who knew more about word processing help others. When students know they can depend on each other, connectedness and trust develop.

Classrooms that share these characteristics increase student learning, and they are also pleasant environments in which to teach and learn (LePage et al., 2005; Zins et al., 2004).

Personal and Social Development

A second important dimension of learner-centered classrooms is that they provide opportunities for students to learn about themselves and others. Learning involves more than understanding how to add fractions, explain the causes of the Revolutionary War, or write an effective essay. In addition to developing cognitive abilities, it also includes developing students' personal and social development. Increasing awareness of their own strengths and weaknesses, and learning to get along with others are important dimensions of learning that will influence students' happiness and success later in life (Berk, 2005, 2007; Zins et al., 2004). Educators understand the importance of this development, as evidenced by statements such as "Works and plays well with others," "Accepts responsibility," and "Is courteous and considerate," on elementary and middle school report cards.

Personal development refers to the growth of enduring personality traits that influence the way individuals interact with their physical and social environments. Students' personalities are determined in part by genetics, but peers, parents, and other adults, especially teachers, are also influential (Berk, 2005, 2007). Some important aspects of personal development include (Zins et al., 2004):

- Self-discipline and motivation to learn
- Organizational skills and goal setting
- Personal and moral responsibility
- Control of personal impulses
- Self-awareness in terms of personal strengths, needs, and values

Personal development. The growth of enduring personality traits that influence the way individuals interact with their physical and social environments.

Teachers promote personal development by discussing these traits, explaining why they're important, modeling them in their teaching, and providing opportunities for students to practice them. For example, when Shannon gave her biography writing assignment, she explained its purpose, gave students a due date, and emphasized that each student was responsible for producing a usable product for the bulletin board. When students met this goal, they not only increased their writing skills but also developed personally.

Social development refers to the advances students make in their ability to interact with and get along with others. Healthy social development affects both learning and students' satisfaction with school. In a review of research in this area, experts concluded, "there is a growing body of scientifically based research supporting the strong impact that enhanced social and emotional behaviors can have on success in school and ultimately in life" (Zins et al., 2004, p. 19). Researchers have linked healthy social development to a number of important outcomes including increased academic achievement and motivation to learn, greater satisfaction with school, and reduced dropout and substance abuse rates (LePage et al., 2005; Zins et al., 2004).

To illustrate how teachers and classrooms influence social development, let's return to Shannon's classroom, where her students are working in small groups on social studies projects.

Small-group work provides students with opportunities to develop socially and personally. (Hope Madden/Merrill)

Rolando, Katrina, Meagan, and Bill are involved in a social studies project on the American West. They've been working as a group for 3 days and are preparing a report to be delivered to the class. There is some disagreement about who gets to research which topics and present them to the class.

"So what should we do?" Katrina asks, looking at the others. "Rolando, Meagan, and Bill all want to report on the Pony Express."

"I thought of it first," Rolando argues.

"But everyone knows I like horses," Meagan counters.

"Why don't we compromise?" Katrina asks, "Rolando, didn't you say that you were kind of interested in railroads because your grandfather worked on them? Couldn't you talk to him and get some information for the report? And Meagan, I know you like horses. Couldn't you report on horses and the Plains Indians? . . . And Bill, what about you?"

"I don't care . . . whatever," Bill replies, folding his arms and peering belligerently at the group.

At just that moment, Shannon approaches the group.

"How are we doing?" she asks. Seeing that they appear uneasy, she continues, "Does everyone want to report on the same topic?" At once she hears these comments,

"Nobody listens to me."

"She's always so bossy."

"Who cares?"

"Hmm," Shannon replies. "You know other groups are having similar problems. Maybe we ought to talk about this as a class."

Shannon's students were at different points in their social development. Katrina, for example, demonstrated **perspective taking**, the ability to understand the thoughts and feelings of others, when she suggested that Rolando and Meagan switch assignments because of their interest in different topics. She understood that the reason they were balking was because each was interested in the Pony Express.

Perspective taking develops slowly and with practice (Berk, 2005, 2007). Children up to about age 8 typically don't understand responses such as Bill's angry reaction or why Rolando might be happy reporting on railroads. As they develop, their ability to see the world from others' perspectives grows. Perspective taking is important because it helps people handle difficult social situations and feel empathy and compassion for others.

Students skilled in perspective taking are better liked and respected by their peers (Berk, 2005; Schult, 2002). Students who haven't developed this ability tend to be mistrusting and

Social development. The advances students make in their ability to interact with and get along with others.

Perspective taking. The ability to understand the thoughts and feelings of others.

often interpret the intentions of others as hostile, which can lead to arguing, fighting, and other antisocial acts. They also tend to feel less guilt or remorse when they make mistakes and hurt other people's feelings (Crick et al., 2002; Dodge et al., 2003).

Teachers can promote perspective taking by making students aware of others' feelings, providing opportunities to interact with one another as Shannon did with her group project, and intervening when problems arise (Berk, 2007).

Productive learning environments also help students develop **social problem-solving skills,** the ability to resolve conflicts in ways that are beneficial to all involved. Katrina demonstrated social problem-solving skills when she suggested a compromise that would satisfy everyone.

Social problem solving occurs in four sequential steps (Berk, 2005, 2007):

1. Observe and interpret social cues. ("Bill seems upset, probably because he isn't getting his first choice.")
2. Identify social goals. ("If we are going to finish this project, everyone must contribute.")
3. Generate strategies. ("Can we find different topics that will satisfy everyone?")
4. Implement and evaluate the strategies. ("This will work if everyone agrees to shift their topic slightly.")

Social problem solving is a powerful tool. Students who are good at it have more friends, fight less, and work more effectively in groups (Johnson & Johnson, 2004; Patrick et al., 2002).

Like perspective taking, social problem-solving skills develop gradually (Berk, 2007). Young children, for example, are not adept at reading social cues, and they tend to create simplistic solutions that satisfy themselves but not others. Older children realize that persuasion and compromise can benefit everyone, and they're better at adapting when initial efforts aren't successful.

As with perspective taking, teachers can promote social problem-solving skills by making students aware of their importance, modeling the skills, and giving students opportunities to practice, as Shannon did by guiding her groups.

In addition to perspective taking and social problem solving, productive learning environments also develop other social skills such as

- Respect for others
- Working cooperatively with classmates
- Empathy and compassion
- Appreciation of diversity (Zins et al., 2004)

Personal and social development also grow in classrooms where the classroom climate is positive and supportive. Let's see what this means and how it might be achieved.

Positive Classroom Climate

Classroom climate refers to the emotional and psychological environment of a classroom, and a positive classroom climate is essential to a productive learning environment (D. Brown, 2004). When classroom climate is positive, the teacher and students demonstrate mutual respect and courtesy, and everyone feels safe to express thoughts and opinions and ask questions without fear of embarrassment or ridicule. It is virtually impossible for students to develop personal traits, such as self-awareness and motivation to learn, or social skills, such as respect for others and empathy and compassion, if the classroom climate is negative or threatening.

Shannon attempted to promote a positive classroom climate in several ways. Before the school year began, she created displays and placed pictures on her classroom walls in an attempt to make her room physically attractive. Then, because she knew that a number of native Spanish-speaking students were in her class, she labeled objects around the room in both English and Spanish. As the students entered the first day, she greeted them at the door, had them introduce themselves, and displayed their pictures on the bulletin board. She immedi-

Social problem-solving skills. The ability to resolve conflicts in ways that are beneficial to all involved.

Classroom climate. The emotional and psychological environment of a classroom.

236

ately initiated a discussion of the procedures that they would follow to keep their classroom safe and orderly. Each of these moves was an attempt to make her classroom inviting.

What else can teachers do to promote a positive classroom climate? Let's see what Mr. Appleby, an English teacher in a rural high school in the South, says about making his classroom a place where students want to be.

 If you pay attention to these kids and do some things for them they appreciate it [Mr. Appleby explained,] . . . I think it's more important for a kid to feel he's got somebody at school—an adult—somebody he can trust or can talk to or who can cheer him up when he's feeling raunchy . . . . they need to know that when they walk into your classroom that you'll say something nice to them or that they can talk to you if things are bad 'cause there's nobody else they can go to . . . kids need to feel they can open up and share some of their feelings which they may not ever do because they may be in a family situation where they get slapped for it or put down for it . . . as they frequently are, you know. . . . (Dillon, 1989, p. 238)

How do students react to teachers' attempts to create this type of climate? Let's see what two of Mr. Appleby's students have to say.

> Melinda: *I act differently in his class—I guess because of the type of teacher he is. . . . He is hisself—he acts natural—not tryin' to be what somebody wants him to be . . . he makes sure that nobody makes fun of anybody if they mess up when they read out loud.*
>
> Bernard: *I like him just by the way he'd talk, he were good to you . . . he don't be afraid to tell you how he feels—he don't talk mean to you, he just speak right to you . . . some teachers only likes the smart people—and Coach Appleby don't do that. (Dillon, 1989, pp. 241–242).*

Shannon and Mr. Appleby both recognized that their professional commitment is first to their students and not to the content they're teaching. This doesn't imply that content isn't important or that teachers should lower their academic expectations but, rather, that students learn more when they feel cared about and the classroom climate is positive (Raider-Roth, 2005).

Making Connections:
To deepen your understanding of the topics in this section of the chapter and integrate them with topics you've already studied, go to the *Making Connections* module for Chapter 11 at **www.prenhall.com/kauchak.** Respond to questions 1 and 2.

Check Your Understanding

1.1 Describe the essential characteristics of a productive learning environment.

1.2 How do productive learning environments help promote personal and social development?

1.3 In this section, we said that learning is the primary purpose of schooling, but we also emphasized a positive classroom climate. How are the two related?

For feedback, go to Check Your Understanding *at the end of this chapter.*

The Human Dimension of Productive Learning Environments

Teachers are essential to creating productive learning environments; they set the emotional tone for the classroom, creating either an inviting or a threatening environment. (As a student, one of your authors entered his high school biology class and was greeted with, "My name is Isabel Wilharm, and the name means exactly what it says. Step out of line and I *will harm*.") Then, they design learning experiences that can engage, ignore, or even distance students. They interact with students during instruction in ways that motivate, interest, or possibly bore them.

Think about some of the best teachers you've had. What comes to mind? If you're typical, the first thing you remember is that you believed that they cared about you as a person, were committed to your learning, and were enthusiastic about the topics they taught. We examine the human dimension of creating productive learning environments as we discuss the following teacher characteristics:

- Caring
- Personal teaching efficacy
- Positive expectations
- Modeling and enthusiasm

Caring: An Essential Element in Teaching

Caring refers to a teacher's investment in the protection and development of the young people in his or her classes (Noddings, 2001), and a caring teacher is at the heart of a productive learning environment. The importance of caring is captured by one fourth grader's comment: "If a teacher doesn't care about you, it affects your mind. You feel like you're a nobody, and it makes you want to drop out of school" (Noblit, Rogers, & McCadden, 1995, p. 683).

Students are more motivated to learn and achieve higher in classrooms where they believe their teachers like, understand, and empathize with them (Furrer & Skinner, 2003). Students who feel they are welcome and who receive personal support from their teachers also demonstrate more interest in their class work and describe it as more important than students whose teachers are distant. A supportive classroom environment, where each student is valued regardless of academic ability or performance, is essential for both learning and motivation for all students (Stipek, 2002).

This section answers the first "Professional Knowledge: Test Yourself!" item, "Teacher caring is most important in the lower elementary grades, and its importance diminishes as students grow older." Teacher caring is, in fact, essential at *all* levels, and its importance *does not* diminish as students grow older.

Caring, an essential component of a productive learning environment, connects teachers with students on a human level. (Anthony Magnacca/Merrill)

Communicating Caring

How do teachers communicate that they care about their students? Some ways include

- Learning students' names quickly and calling on students by their first name
- Greeting them daily and getting to know them as individuals
- Using effective nonverbal communication such as making eye contact and smiling
- Using "we" and "our" in reference to class activities and assignments
- Spending time with students
- Demonstrating respect for students as individuals

Caring. A teacher's investment in the protection and development of the young people in his or her classes.

The last two items on the list deserve special emphasis. We all have 24 hours in our days—no more, no less—and the way we choose to allocate our time is the truest measure of our priorities. Choosing to allocate time to an individual student communicates caring better than any other single factor. Helping students who have problems with an assignment or calling a parent after school hours communicates that teachers care about students and whether or not they are learning. Spending a moment to ask a question about a baby brother or compliment a new hairstyle communicates caring about a student as a human being.

Showing respect is also essential. Teachers show respect in subtle ways, such as the way they look at students and how long they wait for students to answer questions. Interestingly, maintaining high standards is one of the most powerful ways to show respect. One school motivation expert observed,

> One of the best ways to show respect for students is to hold them to high standards—by not accepting sloppy, thoughtless, or incomplete work, by pressing them to clarify vague comments, by encouraging them not to give up, and by not praising work that does not reflect genuine effort. Ironically, reactions that are often intended to protect students' self-esteem— such as accepting low quality work—convey a lack of interest, patience, or caring. (Stipek, 2002, p. 157)

This view is corroborated by research. When junior high students were asked, "How do you know when a teacher cares about you?" they responded that paying attention to them as human beings was important, but more striking was their belief that teachers who care are committed to their learning and hold them to high standards (Wilson & Corbett, 2001).

Respect, of course, is a two-way street. Teachers should model respect for students, and in turn they have the right to expect students to respect them and one another. "Treat everyone with respect" is a rule that should be universally posted and enforced. An occasional minor incident of rudeness can be overlooked, but teachers should clearly communicate that chronic disrespect for themselves or the students in their classes will not be tolerated.

Personal Teaching Efficacy

In addition to caring, teachers who create productive learning environments believe in their ability to help students learn and grow. To illustrate this important idea, let's look at a brief conversation between Shannon and Jim Fantini, one of her colleagues.

"My students didn't score as well as I would have liked on the math part of the Stanford Achievement Test last year, and I promised myself they were going to do better this year," Shannon comments as she glances through a set of math quizzes.

"But you said your students aren't as sharp this year," Jim responds.

"That doesn't matter. I need to push them harder. I think I can do a better job than I did last year. They're going to be so good at doing decimals and percentages that they'll be able to do the problems in their sleep."

"You never give up, do you?" Jim smiles, shaking his head.

Shannon's comments illustrate **personal teaching efficacy**, a teacher's belief in his or her ability to promote learning in all students regardless of their prior knowledge or experiences (Bruning et al., 2004). Shannon's comments "I think I can do a better job than I did last year" and "They're going to be so good at doing decimals and percentages . . ." reflect her belief in her ability to help all her students learn and her decision to take responsibility for the success or failure of her own instruction. This characterizes teachers with high personal teaching efficacy.

When students aren't learning, high-efficacy teachers don't blame it on lack of intelligence, poor home environments, uncooperative administrators, or some other external cause. Instead, they redouble their efforts. They emphasize praise rather than criticism, persevere with low achievers, and maximize the time available for instruction. Low-efficacy teachers, in contrast, are less student centered, spend less time on learning activities, "give up" on low achievers, and are more critical when students fail. Not surprisingly, students taught by high-efficacy teachers learn more than those taught by low-efficacy teachers (Tschannen-Moran, Woolfolk-Hoy, & Hoy, 1998).

Personal teaching efficacy. A teacher's belief in his or her ability to promote learning in all students regardless of their prior knowledge or experiences.

Positive Teacher Expectations

Teachers who create productive learning environments have faith not only in their own capabilities but also in the capabilities of their students. **Positive teacher expectations** are teachers' beliefs in students' capabilities to learn.

To illustrate the importance of teacher expectations, let's analyze two short interactions between a teacher and her students.

Mrs. Davis:	*What kind of triangle is this? . . . Lisa?*
Lisa:	*I . . . don't know.*
Mrs. Davis:	*What do you notice about the lengths of these three sides?*
Lisa:	*They're . . . equal. It's an equilateral triangle.*

Now compare what you've just read with the following:

Mrs. Davis:	*What kind of triangle is this? . . . Jessica?*
Jessica:	*I . . . I don't know.*
Mrs. Davis:	*Can you help her out, Gena?*

The difference in the way Mrs. Davis communicated with the two students is subtle but important. By prompting Lisa, she demonstrated that she expected Lisa to be able to answer, but turning the question to another student suggested that she didn't have the same expectations for Jessica. A single incident isn't significant, but if Mrs. Davis's interactions with the two girls represent a pattern, long-term and substantial differences in achievement can result (Good & Brophy, 2003; R. Weinstein, 2002).

Teacher expectations about students' learning can have profound implications for what students actually learn. Expectations affect the content and pace of the curriculum, the organization of instruction, evaluation, instructional interactions with individual students, and many subtle and not-so-subtle behaviors that affect students' own expectations for learning and their behavior. (*Stipek, 2002, p. 210*).

Research indicates that teachers treat students for whom they have high expectations differently than those for whom they have low expectations. High-expectation students receive differential treatment in the following areas (Good & Brophy, 2003):

- *Emotional support:* Teachers interact more with perceived high achievers; their interactions are more positive; they make more eye contact, stand closer, and orient their bodies more directly toward the students; and they seat these students closer to the front of the class.
- *Teacher effort and demands:* Teachers give perceived high achievers more thorough explanations, their instruction is more enthusiastic, they ask more follow-up questions, and they require more complete and accurate student answers.
- *Questioning:* Teachers call on perceived high achievers more often, they allow the students more time to answer, and they provide more encouragement and prompt perceived high achievers more often.
- *Feedback and evaluation:* Teachers praise perceived high achievers more and criticize them less. They offer perceived high achievers more complete and lengthier feedback and more conceptual evaluations.

Students are sensitive to these differences, and even early elementary children are aware of differential treatment (Stipek, 2002). In one study, researchers concluded, "After ten seconds of seeing and/or hearing a teacher, even very young students (third grade) could detect whether the teacher talked about, or to, an excellent or a weak student and could determine the extent to which that student was loved by the teacher" (Babad, Bernieri, & Rosenthal, 1991, p. 230). This

Positive teacher expectations. Teachers' beliefs in students' capabilities to learn.

is both amazing and disquieting; it challenges teachers to communicate caring and high expectations to all students.

Expectations can be self-fulfilling; when we treat students as if they are low achievers, they don't try as hard. Reduced effort results in less learning, and a downward spiral begins (R. Weinstein, 2002). Unfortunately, teachers often aren't aware of their lowered expectations. When introduced to this research and encouraged to analyze their own classrooms with this framework, teachers can learn to treat all students as potential learners, and as a result, the learning environment becomes more productive.

Modeling and Enthusiasm

"Actions speak louder than words" is a cliché, but it is often true, and it is particularly important in productive learning environments.

Teacher modeling of enthusiasm can motivate students about the topics they are learning. [Tony Freeman/PhotoEdit Inc.]

Think about times that you have become excited about a class or topic you were studying. Often, your excitement was the result of **teacher modeling**, the tendency of people to observe and imitate others' behaviors and attitudes (Bandura, 2001, 2004). Your teacher demonstrated his or her own genuine interest in the topic, and as a result your interest also increased. Like all people, students tend to imitate behaviors and attitudes, and teachers who are enthusiastic about the topics they teach increase the likelihood that students will feel the same way.

The impact of modeling has important implications for teachers because students constantly observe their actions. For example, imagine how you would feel if one of your instructors said, "I know this stuff is boring, but we have to learn it" compared to, "Now this topic is exciting; it will help us understand how our students think." Obviously, you're more likely to be interested in the second topic.

The impact of modeling goes farther. If you want your students to be courteous and respectful to you and each other, for instance, you must treat them with courtesy and respect. If you want them to be responsible and conscientious, you must model these same characteristics in ways such as returning their papers promptly, having your instructional materials organized and ready to use, and using your instructional time effectively.

As we said at the beginning of this section, creating productive learning environments begins with the teacher, and caring, high personal teaching efficacy, positive expectations, and teacher modeling are essential elements of effective classrooms.

Making Connections:
To deepen your understanding of the topics in this section of the chapter and integrate them with topics you've already studied, go to the *Making Connections* module for Chapter 11 at **www.prenhall.com/kauchak**. Respond to questions 3 and 4.

Check Your Understanding

2.1 Why is caring important for a productive learning environment? What can teachers do to show they care?

2.2 What are personal teacher efficacy and positive teacher expectations? How are they related?

2.3 What is teacher modeling? How is it related to teacher enthusiasm?

For feedback, go to Check Your Understanding *at the end of this chapter.*

Teacher modeling. The tendency of people to observe and imitate others' behaviors and attitudes.

Classroom Management: Creating Safe and Supportive Learning Environments

To begin this section, let's revisit Shannon's classroom, where she is involved in a math lesson reviewing decimals and percentages during the second marking period of the school year.

"What kind of problem is this, . . . Gabriel?" she asks as she walks down the aisle and points to a problem on the overhead.

". . . It's . . . a percentage problem," Gabriel responds after thinking for a few seconds.

As soon as Shannon walks past him, Kevin sticks his foot across the aisle, tapping Alison on the leg with his shoe while he watches Shannon's back. "Stop it, Kevin," Alison mutters, swiping at him with her hand.

Shannon turns, comes back up the aisle, and continues, "Good, Gabriel," and standing next to Kevin, asks, "And how do we know it's a percentage problem, . . . Kevin?" looking directly at him.

"Uhhh . . ."

"What words in the problem give us a clue that it's a percentage problem, Kevin?"

". . . 'Which is the better buy?'" Kevin answers, pointing at the sales numbers from the two different stores. "We have to figure out which store sale saved us more. That's a percentage problem."

"Good," Shannon replies, and she then moves over to the overhead and displays additional word problems involving percentages.

"Go ahead and do the first problem," Shannon directs. Be sure you're able to explain your answers."

She watches as the students work on the problem and then moves over to Sondra, who has been whispering and passing notes to Nicole across the aisle. "Move up here," she says quietly, nodding to a desk at the front of the room.

"What did I do?" Sondra protests.

"When we talked about our rules at the beginning of the year, we agreed that it was important to listen when other people are talking and to be quiet when others are working," Shannon whispers.

She watches as Sondra changes seats. Then, tapping her knuckle on the overhead, Shannon says, "Okay, let's see how we did on the problem. Explain what you did first, . . . Juanita."

Shannon's experience illustrates why classroom management can be a vexing problem for teachers. She had carefully planned her lesson and was conducting it effectively, but she still had to respond to Kevin's and Sondra's disruptions. Incidents like these are common in many classrooms, and, if left unattended, they can seriously disrupt learning.

Classroom Management: A National Concern

From the 1960s until the present, national polls have identified classroom management as one of the most challenging problems teachers face. In 2003 and 2004, the public viewed it as the second greatest problem facing schools, and in 2005 it ranked third after lack of financial support and overcrowded schools (Rose & Gallup, 2005). It has historically been the primary concern of beginning teachers, and disruptive students are an important source of stress for beginners and veterans alike (Bohn, Roehrig, & Pressley, 2004; Public Agenda, 2004). It is a major reason that teachers leave the profession during their first 3 years; it's also a primary cause of teachers leaving urban classrooms (L. Weiner, 2002); and colleges of education are being asked to address the issue more carefully (J. Johnson, 2005).

Classroom management has become a major concern of policy makers, parents, and the public at large, particularly in the wake of highly publicized incidents of school violence such as the shootings at Columbine High School in Colorado in 1999 that left 14 students and a teacher dead, and Red Lake, Minnesota, in 2005 resulting in the deaths of 7 people including a teacher and security guard. Although incidents of school violence cause fear and concern in both parents and students, they are extremely rare (National Center for Education

Statistics, 2005); establishing and maintaining orderly, learning-focused classrooms is the major challenge teachers face.

The importance of classroom management in creating productive learning environments is well documented. One group of researchers concluded, "Effective classroom management has been shown to increase student engagement, decrease disruptive behaviors, and enhance use of instructional time, all of which result in improved student achievement" (Wang et al., 1993, p. 262).

Classroom Management Goals

Some of the earliest research on classroom management was done by a researcher named Jacob Kounin (1970), who found that the key to orderly classrooms is the teacher's ability to prevent problems from occurring in the first place, rather than handling misbehavior once it occurs. This research has been consistently corroborated over the years (Emmer, Evertson, & Worsham, 2006; Evertson, Emmer, & Worsham, 2006; Good & Brophy, 2003). Experts estimate that anticipation and prevention make up 80 percent of an effective management system (Freiberg, 1999b).

This research was important because it helped teachers understand the difference between **classroom management**, teachers' strategies that create and maintain an orderly learning environment, and **discipline**, teachers' responses to student misbehavior. Expert teachers place primary emphasis on management, which reduces their need for discipline.

We now have an answer to the second item on our introductory "Professional Knowledge" survey, "Teachers who have the most orderly classrooms are those who can quickly and effectively respond to student misbehavior." Though it is important to respond to management problems quickly, the most important aspect of effective classroom managers is that they are proactive and prevent problems before they occur through careful planning.

Effective classroom managers have three primary goals:

- Develop learner responsibility.
- Create a positive classroom climate.
- Maximize time and opportunities for learning.

Let's look at them.

Developing Learner Responsibility

Earlier in the chapter, we said that productive learning environments are learner centered, where teachers emphasize personal and social development. As conceptions of classroom management move away from discipline and toward prevention, educators place increased emphasis on helping students take responsibility for their own behaviors and their own roles in creating productive learning environments. Both contribute to personal and social development.

Student understanding is essential for developing responsibility (Emmer & Stough, 2001; Jones, 2005). Students need to understand *why* an orderly environment is necessary and their role in creating one. Students obey rules because the rules make sense, instead of obeying rules simply because they exist or because they will be punished for breaking one. Teachers promote this orientation by emphasizing the reasons for rules and procedures and explicitly teaching responsibility.

Let's see how one middle school teacher, Doug Ramsey, does this.

Allen, a rambunctious seventh grader, runs down the hall toward the lunchroom. As he rounds the corner, he bumps into Alyssia, causing her to drop her books.

"Oops," he replies, continuing his race to the lunchroom.

"Hold it, Allen," Doug, who is monitoring the hall, commands. "Go back and help her pick up her books and apologize."

"Aww."

"Go on," Doug says firmly.

Classroom management. Teachers' strategies that create and maintain an orderly learning environment.

Discipline. Teachers' responses to student misbehavior.

Allen walks back to Alyssia, helps her pick up her books, mumbles an apology, and then returns. As he approaches, Doug again stops him.

"Now, why did I make you do that?" Doug asks.

"Cuz we're not supposed to run."

"Sure," Doug says evenly, "but more important, if people are running in the halls, what might happen?"

"Somebody might get hurt," Allen responds sheepishly.

"Exactly, and we don't want that to happen. . . . That's why we have a rule saying, don't run in the hallways. Remember that you're responsible for your actions. Think about not wanting to hurt yourself or anybody else, and the next time you'll walk whether a teacher is here or not. . . . Now, go on to lunch."

By emphasizing the reason for the rule prohibiting running in the hallways, Doug helped Allen understand his behavior and its effect on other people. Research indicates that children who understand the effects of their actions on others become more altruistic and are more likely to take actions to make up for their misbehavior (Berk, 2007).

Developing student responsibility is both sensible and practical. Learners are more likely to obey rules when they understand the reasons for them, one of which is to protect their rights and the rights of others (Good & Brophy, 2003). This responsibility orientation can also contribute to ethical thinking and character development (Berk, 2007). For instance, in time, students may learn not to call each other insulting names, because name calling not only is unacceptable but it also hurts other people's feelings. By promoting student understanding and responsibility, teachers find that classroom management becomes easier and students develop personally. Such development takes time, but with effort it can be accomplished.

Creating a Positive Classroom Climate

We emphasized the importance of positive classroom climate earlier in the chapter, and an effective classroom management system contributes to this climate (D. Brown, 2004). Students are more likely to feel safe, secure, and welcome when their classroom environment is orderly and predictable. And students are more likely to be courteous and respectful in an orderly classroom. It is virtually impossible to create a positive classroom climate if students are disruptive or disrespectful (Certo, Cauley, & Chafen, 2002; Davis, 2003).

Maximizing Time and Opportunities for Learning

Throughout the chapter we have emphasized that learning is the central purpose of schooling. To optimize learning, teachers must use their available time efficiently. Maximizing the amount of time available for learning is the third goal of classroom management. To meet this goal, some reformers have suggested lengthening the school year, school day, and even the amount of time devoted to certain subjects. Improving learning by increasing study time isn't as simple as it appears on the surface, however, because just allocating more time to a topic may not result in significant increases in learning (C. Weinstein & Mignano, 2003).

Classroom time exists at four different levels:

- Allocated time
- Instructional time
- Engaged time
- Academic learning time

The levels can be viewed as the area of a series of concentric circles, and the correlation with learning becomes stronger as the areas of the circles get smaller. This relationship is illustrated in Figure 11.1 and discussed in the following paragraphs.

Figure 11.1 Levels of Time

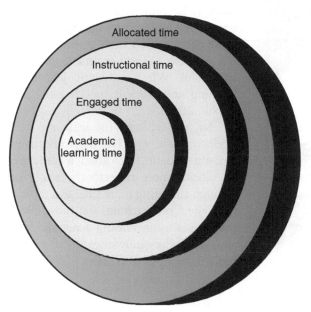

Allocated time is the amount of time a teacher designates for a particular content area or topic. For example, teachers in elementary schools typically allocate much of their time to reading, language arts, and math, with much less allocated to science, social studies, and other subjects. Although middle, junior high, and high school teachers appear to have less control over time allocations because of their fixed schedules and bells signaling the beginning and end of class periods, all teachers have considerable flexibility. A 10th-grade English teacher, for example, could choose to emphasize writing rather than grammar or literature by simply spending more time on it.

Instructional time is the amount left for teaching after teachers have completed routine management and administrative tasks, such as taking roll, returning papers, and making announcements. Teachers also lose instructional time when they respond to student disruptions and make transitions from one activity to another. Some lost time is out of a teachers' control, but they are often unaware of time as a valuable resource, thinking of it instead as something to be filled, used up, or even "killed." For example, compare two teachers. One has a warm-up exercise on the board when students enter the classroom, and takes roll and completes routine tasks while they finish it. She then moves immediately to her lesson, and when finished, gives an assignment, and monitors the class while they work on it. A second teacher takes roll and completes routine tasks while her students sit talking. After a few minutes, she begins her lesson and finishes it with 10 minutes left in the period, during which she lets students talk quietly. If these differences represent patterns, the second teacher loses nearly 40 hours of instructional time over the course of a school year! The obvious result is less student learning.

Imagine going into a classroom to observe a teacher. Intuitively, one of the first things you would look for is whether students are paying attention and thinking about the current topic. This describes **engaged time** or time-on-task, which is the time students actually spend actively involved in learning activities. The correlation between engaged time and learning is much higher than the correlation between learning and either allocated or instructional time.

Teachers influence the engagement rates of their students with the instructional strategies they use. Interactive strategies, such as questioning and group work, which place students in active roles, result in more engaged time than strategies such as lecture, which places students in passive roles (Eggen & Kauchak, 2007).

Allocated time. The amount of time a teacher designates for a particular content area or topic.

Instructional time. The amount left for teaching after routine management and administrative tasks are completed.

Engaged time The time students actually spend actively involved in learning activities. Also called *time on task.*

Student frustration also influences engaged time. If work is beyond students' capabilities, they become frustrated, give up, and go off task. *Success* is a key variable in these cases, which leads to the concept of **academic learning time**: the amount of time students are both engaged and successful. When academic learning time is high, both learning and student motivation increase (Brophy, 2004; Stipek, 2002).

So, now we know the answer to the third item on our introductory survey, "The most effective way to increase the amount students learn about a content area, such as math, is to allocate more time to the study of the content area." Though allocating more time to a topic can have a weak positive effect on learning, the most effective way to increase learning is by increasing academic learning time. Students who are successfully engaged in a topic learn significantly more than those who aren't.

Academic learning time combines student engagement with success to produce learning. (Michael Newman/PhotoEdit Inc.)

Preventing Problems Through Planning

In productive classroom environments, management is nearly invisible. The atmosphere is calm but not rigid, movement around the classroom and interaction in lessons are comfortable, and students work quietly. Learning is taking place. Teachers give few directions that focus on behavior, they reprimand students infrequently, and reprimands rarely intrude on learning. This was the case in Shannon's lesson; she stopped Kevin's and Sondra's disruptions without interrupting the flow of the lesson.

The cornerstone of an effective management system is a clearly understood and consistently monitored set of rules and procedures that prevents management problems before they occur (Emmer et al., 2006; Evertson et al., 2006). Obviously, some classes are tougher to manage than others, but an orderly classroom is possible in most instances. It doesn't happen by accident, however. It requires careful planning, and beginning teachers often underestimate the amount of time and energy it takes.

In planning rules and procedures, effective teachers consider the developmental levels of their students. For example, first graders are usually compliant and eager to please their teachers, but they also have short attention spans and tire easily (Evertson et al., 2006). In comparison, middle schoolers often attempt to test their developing independence, and they're sometimes rebellious and capricious. They need rules that are clearly stated and administered (Emmer et al., 2006). If you're a first-grade teacher, you will make different planning decisions than if you're a middle school teacher. For first-grade students, you'll need to carefully teach rules and procedures through modeling and examples and systematically reinforce them over time. Middle schoolers understand rules and procedures but need firm and consistent application of them combined with caring and positive expectations for good behavior (C. Weinstein, 2007).

Preparing Procedures and Rules

Having considered your students' developmental characteristics, you also need to make decisions about procedures and rules you will implement in your classroom. **Procedures** are the routines students follow in their daily learning activities, such as how they turn in papers, sharpen pencils, and make transitions from one activity to another. For instance, Shannon's students turn in their papers from the ends of the rows, with each student putting his or her paper on the top of the stack as it moves forward. This allows Shannon to collect the stacks from the students in the front, and when she returns the papers, she simply gives the stacks to the first students in each row, they take their papers and pass the stacks back to the students behind them. Simple procedures such as these both create a sense of order for students and save teachers time and energy.

Academic learning time. Combining engagement and success, this is the amount of time students are successful while engaged.

Procedures. Management routines students follow in their daily learning activities.

Effective teachers create procedures for activities such as

- Entering and leaving the classroom
- Handing in and returning papers
- Accessing materials such as scissors and paper
- Sharpening pencils
- Making trips to the bathroom
- Making up work after an absence

After planning and teaching students about procedures, expert teachers have students practice until the procedures become routines that students follow virtually without thinking about them.

Rules (e.g., "Listen when someone else is talking") are guidelines that provide standards for acceptable classroom behavior, and research confirms their value in creating productive learning environments (Emmer et al., 2006; Evertson et al., 2006). When consistently enforced, clear, reasonable rules not only reduce behavior problems that interfere with learning but also promote a feeling of pride and responsibility in the classroom community. Perhaps surprisingly, students also see the enforcement of rules as evidence of caring: "Students also say that they want teachers to articulate and enforce clear standards of behavior. They view this not just as part of the teacher's job but as evidence that the teacher cares about them" (Brophy, 1998, p. 23).

Some examples of rules at different grade levels are found in Table 11.1. Note that some rules occur at all levels, such as students staying in their seats and waiting for permission to speak. Other rules are specific to a grade level and reflect the developmental characteristics of students at that level.

Deciding on rules for your classroom is the first step; actually implementing and making them work is the next. Guidelines for implementing rules include:

- State rules positively.
- Emphasize rationales for rules.
- Minimize the number of rules.
- Monitor rules throughout the school year.

Each of these guidelines is intended to help students understand rules and the reasons for them, and this understanding helps students begin to accept responsibility for their

Classroom rules and procedures establish standards for behaviors that allow learning to take place. (David Young-Wolff/PhotoEdit Inc.)

Rules. Guidelines that provide standards or norms for acceptable classroom behavior.

TABLE 11.1 Examples of Classroom Rules

First-Grade Teacher	Seventh-Grade Teacher	Tenth-Grade Teacher
• We raise our hands before speaking.	• Be in your seat and quiet when the bell rings.	• Do all grooming outside class.
• We leave our seats only when given permission by the teacher.	• Follow directions the first time they're given.	• Be in your seat before the bell rings.
• We stand politely in line at all times.	• Bring covered textbooks, notebook, pen, pencils, and planner to class every day.	• Stay in your seat at all times.
• We keep our hands to ourselves.	• Raise your hand for permission to speak or to leave your seat.	• Bring all materials daily. This includes your book, notebook, pen/pencil, and paper.
• We listen when someone else is talking.	• Keep hands, feet, and objects to yourself.	• Give your full attention to others in discussions, and wait your turn to speak.
	• Leave class only when dismissed by the teacher.	• Leave when I dismiss you, not when the bell rings.

Source: Eggen, P., & Kauchak, D. (2007). *Educational psychology: Windows on classrooms* (7th ed., p. 379). Upper Saddle River, NJ: Merrill/Prentice Hall.

own behavior. Stating rules positively communicates desirable expectations for students. Providing rationales for rules is perhaps the most essential guideline. Students are much more likely to accept responsibility for their own behavior and obey rules when they understand the reasons for them. Keeping the number small helps prevent students from breaking rules simply because they forget. Finally, in spite of teachers' best efforts during planning and the initial teaching of rules, students will need periodic reminders throughout the year.

Intervening Effectively

Even when teachers have planned carefully, disruptions inevitably occur, as we saw in Shannon's lesson. Dealing with off-task or potentially disruptive behavior requires immediate and

IN TODAY'S CLASSROOMS: VIDEO

Establishing Rules and Procedures at the Beginning of the School Year

Having seen how important rules and procedures are for an effective classroom management system, you now can see how one teacher implements these in her classroom.

The episode focuses on a middle school teacher who takes the time at the beginning of the school year to describe and explain the rules and procedures for the school year. As she describes each rule, she helps students understand how it contributes to a productive learning environment. In addition, she also includes a community-building exercise in which students in the class get to know each other better.

To complete this activity, go to the *Becoming a Professional* DVD, and view the video episode "Establishing Rules and Procedures at the Beginning of the School Year."

*To answer questions about the video online and receive immediate feedback, go to the Companion Website at **www.prenhall.com/kauchak**, then to the* In Today's Classroom *module for Chapter 11.*

CW

judicious decision making. If a misbehavior is brief and minor, such as a student asking another student a quick question, it often can be ignored. However, if the behavior has the potential to disrupt the learning activity, you must intervene. Some guidelines to help you intervene effectively include the following:

- Intervene immediately.
- Direct the intervention at the correct student(s).
- Use the least intrusive intervention.

Let's see how Shannon implemented these guidelines. First, after concluding that Kevin's and Sondra's behaviors could distract others and detract from learning, she intervened immediately. Second, she identified the correct students. She recognized that Alison's muttering was a response to Kevin tapping her, so she said nothing to Alison; instead, she quickly moved to where Kevin was seated to address his behavior. Third, she used the least intrusive intervention possible. She stopped Kevin's misbehavior by looking him in the eye and calling on him, and she briefly whispered her direction to Sondra and reminded her of an agreed-upon classroom rule. Her actions simultaneously stopped the misbehaviors without disrupting the flow of her lesson.

During the episode, Shannon demonstrated a concept called **withitness**, a teacher's awareness of what is going on in all parts of the classroom at all times and the communication of this awareness to students both verbally and nonverbally (Kounin, 1970). Withit teachers seem to have eyes in the backs of their heads, and they use this awareness to monitor and direct student behavior. For instance, had Shannon admonished Alison for her muttering instead of Kevin, she would have "caught the wrong one," and in doing so, communicate that she didn't know what was going on in her classroom.

Keeping a lesson moving while simultaneously intervening requires sophisticated skills, but expert teachers do it virtually without thinking. In some cases, teachers may need to use a more intrusive intervention, such as reprimanding a student, talking to a student in the hallway, or even removing the student from the classroom if the disruption is severe. However, with effective instruction and careful planning, most disruptions can be handled as Shannon did.

Handling Serious Management Problems: Violence and Aggression

Tyrone, one of your students, has difficulty maintaining his attention and staying on task. He frequently makes loud and inappropriate comments in class and disrupts learning activities. You warn him, reminding him that being disruptive is unacceptable, and blurting out another comment will result in time-out.

Within a minute, Tyrone blurts out again. "Please go to the time-out area," you say evenly. "I'm not going and you can't make me," he says defiantly. He remains seated as his desk.

How do you react?

As you work with a small group of your fourth graders, a fight suddenly breaks out between Trey and Neil, who are supposed to be working on a group project together. You look up to the sounds of shouting and see Trey flailing at Neil, who is essentially attempting to fend off Trey's blows. Trey is often verbally aggressive and sometimes threatens other students.

What do you do?

We have emphasized repeatedly that productive learning environments are safe and inviting; the threat of violence obviously disrupts this feeling. Earlier we said that incidents

> **Withitness.** A teacher's awareness of what is going on in all parts of the classroom at all times and the communication of this awareness to students both verbally and nonverbally.

teaching in an era of reform

Assertive Discipline

In their work with teachers, Lee and Marlene Canter (Canter & Canter, 1976, 2001) observed many classrooms that were chaotic, with students out of control. In response they developed a classroom management system called Assertive Discipline, which was designed to address this problem.

What Is Assertive Discipline?

Assertive discipline is a comprehensive approach to classroom management that clearly specifies both teachers' and students' rights and responsibilities (Charles, 2005; Manning & Bucher, 2003). According to assertive discipline advocates, teachers have the right to teach in classrooms that are free from disruptions, and students have the right to learn in classrooms that are orderly and free from interruptions. Teachers create an orderly classroom by clearly communicating classroom rules and consistently enforcing the rules, with consequences specified in advance. For example, if talking without being given permission is against classroom rules, the first instance of talking results in a consequence, such as the student's name on the board; a second infraction results in a check by the student's name, and a third leads to detention. The specific rules and consequences depend on the teacher's judgment, but consistent enforcement is essential. In the case of chronic or severe misbehavior, the teacher may send a student to the principal or call parents.

In addition to a system of rules and consequences, the Canters advocate being assertive, rather than hostile or nonassertive, in their interactions with students. For example,

compare the following teacher responses to a student who is talking instead of beginning an in-class assignment.

Assertive: John, you need to stop talking and begin your assignment, NOW. That's a check by your name. One more and you stay in for recess.

Hostile: John, how many times do I have to tell you to stop talking and get to work? Your misbehavior is driving me crazy!

Nonassertive: John, I don't know what I'm going to do with you. Please stop talking.

The assertive response clearly identifies the misbehavior and communicates the consequences for misbehaving. The other two don't clearly address the misbehavior, nor do they describe consequences for continuing to misbehave.

The Issue

Assertive discipline is a successful but controversial approach to classroom management. Advocates laud the clear definition of teacher and student roles and responsibilities. Teachers are there to teach and students are there to learn, they argue, and the teacher has the right to establish and implement a management system that allows learning to take place.

Proponents also contend that its emphasis on the combination of positive reinforcement together with appropriate sanctions is extremely effective (Canter, 1988). One classroom management expert observes, "A great many teachers are very enthusiastic about Assertive Discipline because it helps them deal with students positively and teach with little interruption. It

of school violence are rare. As part of school wide safety programs, most schools have created prevention programs, taken security measures, and established detailed procedures to protect students and teachers from violent acts such as those that make national headlines (National Center for Education Statistics, 2005). When serious problems do arise, teachers are most likely to encounter verbal aggression or student fighting. These incidents are also quite rare, but teachers must be prepared for them. Once you know what options are available, you will feel more confident about your ability to deal with these problems.

When students are verbally aggressive, your goal is to keep the problem from escalating. Responding to Tyrone in a calm and unemotional tone of voice is a first step. Once the student has calmed down, you can arrange to talk to him after school, send him to a school counselor, or ask for additional support. In the case involving fighting, you should follow also preserves instructional time and helps relieve the annoyance of verbal confrontations" (Charles, 2005, p. 51).

Assertive discipline is especially popular with beginning teachers because it is relatively easy to understand and implement, and it has been proven effective in addressing the myriad of minor infractions that virtually "drive some teachers crazy." Even the original title, *Assertive Discipline: A Take-Charge Approach for Today's Educator* (Canter & Canter, 1976), was designed to instill confidence in teachers who are apprehensive about managing a classroom.

However, critics argue that the use of rewards and punishers to maintain an orderly classroom overemphasizes control and obedience at the expense of personal development (Freiberg, 1999c; Kohn, 1993b). By focusing on changing behavior instead of emphasizing the reasons for rules and by failing to teach students that they are responsible for their actions, assertive discipline works in the short run, critics claim, but doesn't contribute to students' long-term personal and social development.

One parent had this experience with her daughter's first week of kindergarten:

> After each of the first four days of school, the mother asked her daughter what she had learned. The child's answers were succinct: On the first day she learned "to sit still"; on the second day she learned "to walk in a straight line"; on the third day she learned "to raise her hand"; and on the fourth day she learned "to be quiet." On the fifth day, the mother decided not to ask any more questions! (C. Weinstein & Mignano, 2003, p. 78)

Critics argue that preoccupation with order and control can send the wrong message to students about classrooms and learning.

Critics further contend that assertive discipline treats symptoms, such as talking without permission, as the problem instead of examining possible causes, such as ineffective instruction or not understanding why it is important to give everyone a chance to speak.

Despite the controversy, the program is enormously popular and widespread. It is difficult to find a school district in the country that hasn't had at least some exposure to assertive discipline, and probably more than a million teachers have been trained in at least some aspects of the program.

You Take a Position

Now it's your turn to take a position on the issue. State in writing whether you feel that assertive discipline will contribute to a productive learning environment or detract from it, and provide a two-page rationale for your position.

For additional references and resources, go to the Companion Website at www.prenhall.com/kauchak, then to the Teaching in an Era of Reform module for Chapter 11. You can respond online or submit your response to your instructor.

CW

---

three steps: (1) Stop the incident (if possible), (2) protect the victim, and (3) get help. For instance, a loud noise, such as shouting, clapping, or slamming a chair against the floor will often surprise the students enough so they'll stop. At that point, you can begin to talk to them, check to see if anyone is hurt, and then take the students to the main office, where help is available. If your interventions don't stop the scuffle, you should immediately rush an uninvolved student to the office for help. Unless you're sure that you can separate the students without danger to yourself, or them, attempting to do so is unwise.

You are legally required to intervene in the case of a fight. If you ignore a fight, even on the playground, parents can sue for negligence on the grounds that you failed to protect a student from injury (Fischer et al., 2006). However, the law doesn't say that you're required to physically break up the fight; immediately reporting it to administrators is an acceptable form of intervention.

Serious management problems require both short- and long-term strategies. [Elena Rooraid/PhotoEdit Inc.]

So, now we know the answer to the fourth item on our introductory survey, "Teachers are legally required to intervene if students in their classrooms become involved in a fight or a scuffle." Teachers *are* legally required to intervene if a fight or scuffle occurs in their classroom. To ignore would place students' safety in jeopardy and could result in a liability lawsuit.

Breaking up a scuffle is, of course, only a short-term solution. Whenever students are aggressive or violent, experts recommend involving parents and other school personnel (Burstyn et al., 2001). Parents want to be notified immediately if school problems occur. In addition, school counselors, school psychologists, social workers, and principals have all been trained to deal with these problems and can provide advice and assistance. Experienced teachers can also provide a wealth of information about how they've handled similar problems. No teacher should face serious problems of violence or aggression alone. Further, excellent programs are available to teach conflict resolution and to help troubled students (D. Johnson & Johnson, 2006). If teachers can get help when they first suspect a problem, many incidents can be prevented.

To conclude this section, we want to put violence and aggression into perspective. Although they are possibilities—and you should understand options for dealing with them—the vast majority of your management problems will involve issues of cooperation and motivation. Many problems can be prevented, others can be dealt with quickly, while some require individual attention. We have all heard about students carrying guns to school and incidents of assault on teachers. Statistically, however, considering the huge numbers of students who pass through schools each day, these incidents remain very infrequent.

Effective Classroom Management in Urban Schools

Urban schools provide unique challenges to teachers attempting to create productive learning environments. Consider the case of Mary Gregg, a first-grade teacher in an urban school in the San Francisco Bay Area.

Mary's classroom is a small portable room with a low ceiling and very loud air fans. The room has one teacher table and six rectangular student tables with six chairs at each. Mary has 32 first graders (14 girls and 18 boys). Twenty-five of the children are children of color; a majority are recent immigrants from Southeast Asia, with some African Americans and Latinos, and seven European Americans. (LePage et al., 2005)

Research on teaching in urban contexts reveals three themes. First, students in urban environments come from very diverse backgrounds (Noguera, 2003a; Macionis & Parillo, 2007). As a result of this diversity, their prior knowledge and experiences vary, and what they view as acceptable patterns of behavior also varies, sometimes dramatically. Second, urban classes are often large; Mary had 32 first graders in a room built for 25. Third, and perhaps most pernicious, negative stereotypes about urban environments create the perception that creating a productive learning environment through classroom management is difficult if not impossible. Two of the most common stereotypes are, "Students can't control themselves," and "Students don't know how to behave because the parents don't care" (Goldstein, 2004, p. 43). In response to this stereotype, urban teachers often "teach defensively," "choosing methods of presentation and evaluation that simplify content and reduce demands on students in return for classroom order and minimal student compliance on assignments" (LePage et al., 2005, p. 331).

This defensive approach to classroom management and instruction results in lowered expectations and decreased student motivation. Students who are not motivated to learn are more likely to be disruptive because they don't see the point in what they're being asked to do, a downward spiral of motivation and learning occurs, and management issues become increasingly troublesome.

However, it doesn't have to be this way. In spite of diversity and large numbers of students in a small classroom, effective urban teachers can create active and orderly learning environments. Let's look at Mary Gregg's classroom management during a lesson on buoyancy.

Once into the science activity, management appears to be invisible. There is, of course, some splashing and throwing things into the water, but as the lesson progresses, the teacher engages in on-the-spot logistical management decisions. For instance, everyone is supposed to get a chance to go to the table to choose objects to be placed in cups. After choosing the first one to go, Mary sets them to the task. Very quickly, it is the second person's turn and the students do not know how to choose who should get the next turn. At first she says "you choose," then foresees an "It's my turn. No it's my turn" problem and redirects them with a counterclockwise motion to go around the table. (LePage et al., 2005, pp. 328–329)

This example demonstrates that, while challenging, classroom management in an urban environment doesn't have to be overly restrictive or punitive. How is this accomplished? Research suggests four important factors:

- Caring and supportive teachers
- Clear standards for acceptable behavior
- Structure
- Effective instruction

Caring and Supportive Teachers

We have emphasized the need for caring and supportive teachers throughout this chapter. Teachers who care are important in all schools but are critical in urban environments. When students perceive their teachers as uncaring, disengagement from school life occurs, and students are much more likely to display disruptive behaviors than their more involved peers (Charles, 2005; Jones & Jones, 2004).

Clear Standards for Acceptable Behavior

Because they bring diverse experiences to class, urban students' views of acceptable behaviors often vary. As a result, being clear about what behaviors are and are not acceptable is essential in urban classrooms (D. Brown, 2004). As we saw earlier in the chapter, students see clear standards of behavior as evidence that the teacher cares about them. One urban student had this to say about clear behavioral expectations:

She's probably the strictest teacher I've ever had because she doesn't let you slide by if you've made a mistake. She going [sic] to let you know. If you've made a mistake, she's going to let you know it. And, if you're getting bad marks, she's going to let you know it. She's one of my strictest teachers, and that's what makes me think she cares about us the most. (Alder, 2002, pp. 251–252).

The line between clear standards for behavior and an overemphasis on control is not cut and dried. One major difference is that in productive urban classrooms, order is created through "the ethical use of power" (Alder, 2002, p. 245). Effective teachers are demanding but also helpful; they model and emphasize personal responsibility, respect, and cooperation; and they are willing to take the time to ensure that students understand the reasons for rules

(C. Weinstein & Mignano, 2003). Further, in responding to the inevitable incidents of students failing to bring needed materials to class, talking, or otherwise being disruptive, effective teachers in urban schools enforce rules but provide rationales for them and remind students that completing assigned tasks is essential because it helps develop the skills needed for more advanced work (D. Brown, 2004). In contrast, less-effective teachers tend to focus on negative consequences, such as, "If you don't finish this work, you won't pass the class" (Manouchehri, 2004).

Structure

Students in urban schools sometimes come from environments where stability and structure may not be a regular part of everyday life. This makes order, structure, and predictability even more important in urban classrooms. Procedures that lead to well-established routines are important, and predictable consequences for behaviors are essential. A predictable environment leads to an atmosphere of order and safety, which is crucial for developing the sense of attachment to school that is essential for learning and motivation.

Effective Instruction

If students aren't learning and aren't actively involved in classroom life, management problems are inevitable. Classroom management and instruction are interdependent, and, unfortunately, students in urban classrooms are often involved in low-level activities such as listening to lectures and doing seat work that isn't challenging. This type of instruction contributes to low motivation and feelings of disengagement, which further increases the likelihood of management problems.

> **Making Connections:**
> CW To deepen your understanding of the topics in this section of the chapter and integrate them with topics you've already studied, go to the *Making Connections* module for Chapter 11 at **www.prenhall.com/kauchak**. Respond to questions 5 and 6.

Check Your Understanding

3.1 Why has classroom management become a national concern?

3.2 What are the major goals of classroom management? How do they contribute to a productive learning environment?

3.3 How are classroom management and discipline different? How can teachers prevent management problems through planning?

3.4 What are the characteristics of effective interventions?

3.5 What actions—both short- and long-term—should teachers take when encountering incidents of violence and aggression?

3.6 What makes urban classrooms unique in terms of classroom management?

For feedback, go to Check Your Understanding *at the end of this chapter.*

Creating Productive Learning Environments: Involving Parents

Learning is a cooperative venture; teachers, students, and parents are in it together. Students must be cooperative and motivated to learn if a learning environment is to be productive, and parental support is essential for promoting this cooperation and motivation.

Benefits of Parental Involvement

Students benefit from parental involvement in several ways:

- Greater willingness to do homework
- Higher long-term achievement
- More positive attitudes and behaviors
- Better attendance and graduation rates
- Greater enrollment in postsecondary education (Garcia, 2004; Hong & Ho, 2005)

These outcomes result from parents' increased participation in school activities, higher expectations for their children's achievement, and teachers' increased understanding of learners' home environments. Deciding how to respond to a student's disruptive behavior is easier, for example, when his teacher knows that his mother or father has lost a job, his parents are going through a divorce, or a family member is ill.

Parents can also help reinforce classroom management plans. One teacher reported:

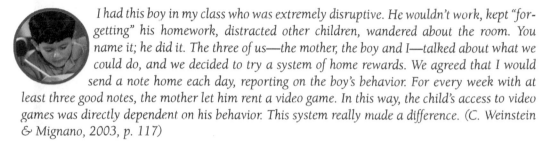

I had this boy in my class who was extremely disruptive. He wouldn't work, kept "forgetting" his homework, distracted other children, wandered about the room. You name it; he did it. The three of us—the mother, the boy and I—talked about what we could do, and we decided to try a system of home rewards. We agreed that I would send a note home each day, reporting on the boy's behavior. For every week with at least three good notes, the mother let him rent a video game. In this way, the child's access to video games was directly dependent on his behavior. This system really made a difference. (C. Weinstein & Mignano, 2003, p. 117)

Parent–teacher collaboration can have long-term benefits for teachers. For example, teachers who encourage parental involvement report more positive feelings about teaching and their school. They also have higher expectations for parents and rate them as being more helpful (Epstein, 2001).

This section answers the fifth question on our "Professional Knowledge: Test Yourself" questionnaire. Involving parents in their children's education can have a number of beneficial results, including even increased student achievement.

Strategies for Involving Parents

Virtually all schools have formal communication channels, such as open houses (usually occurring within the first 2 weeks of the year, when teachers introduce themselves and describe general guidelines); interim progress reports, which tell parents about their youngsters' achievements at the midpoint of each grading period; parent–teacher conferences; and, of course, report cards. Although these processes are schoolwide and necessary, you can do more, such as the following:

- Send a letter home to parents within the first week of school that expresses positive expectations for students and solicits parents' help (see Figure 11.2).
- Maintain communication by sending home packets of student work, descriptions of new units, and other information about academic work.
- Emphasize students' accomplishments through newsletters, e-mails, or individual notes.

It is important to note that all forms of communication with parents need to be carefully proofread to ensure that they are free of spelling, grammatical, and punctuation errors. First impressions are important and lasting. Your communications create perceptions of your competence, and errors detract from your credibility.

One of the most effective ways to involve parents is to call them. Earlier in the chapter, we said that *time* is the best indicator of caring that exists. When you allocate some of your

Figure 11.2   Letter to Parents

August 22, 2007

Dear Parents,

I am looking forward to a productive and exciting year, and I am writing this letter to encourage your involvement and support. You always have been, and still are, the most important people in your child's education. We cannot do the job without you.

For us to work together most effectively, some guidelines are necessary. With the students' help, we prepared the ones listed here. Please read this information carefully, and sign where indicated. If you have any questions, please call me at Southside Elementary School (555-5935) or at home (555-8403) in the evenings.

Sincerely,

Shannon Brinkman

Shannon Brinkman

AS A PARENT, I WILL TRY MY BEST TO DO THE FOLLOWING:

1. I will ask my child about school every day (evening meal is a good time). I will ask about what he or she is studying and try to learn about it.
2. I will provide a quiet time and place each evening for homework. I will set an example by also working at that time or reading while my child is working.
3. Instead of asking if homework is finished, I will ask to see it. I will ask my child to explain some of the information to me to check for understanding.

Parent's Signature _____

STUDENT SURVIVAL GUIDELINES

1. I will be in class and seated when the bell rings.
2. I will follow directions the first time they are given.
3. I will bring homework, notebook, paper, and a sharp pencil to class each day.
4. I will raise my hand for permission to speak or leave my seat.
5. I will keep my hands, feet, and objects to myself.

HOMEWORK GUIDELINES

1. Our motto is I WILL ALWAYS TRY. I WILL NEVER GIVE UP.
2. I will complete all assignments. If an assignment is not finished or ready when called for, I understand that I get no credit for it.
3. If I miss work because of an absence, it is my responsibility to come in before school (8:15–8:45) to make it up.
4. I know that I get one day to make up a quiz or test or turn in my work for each day I'm absent.
5. I understand that extra credit work is not given. If I do all the required work, extra credit isn't necessary.

Student's Signature _____

Home–school partnerships create effective communication channels with parents and promote higher achievement and motivation. (Michelle Bridwell/PhotoEdit Inc.)

personal time to call parents, this communicates your commitment to their child better than any other way. Also, talking to a parent allows you to be specific in describing a student's needs and gives you a chance to again solicit support. If a student is missing assignments, for example, you can alert the parent, ask for possible causes or explanations, and encourage the parents to more closely monitor their child's study habits.

When we talk to parents, we need to establish a positive, cooperative tone that lays the foundation for joint efforts. Consider the following:

"Hello, Mrs. Hansen? This is Connie Lichter, Jared's math teacher."

"Oh, uh, is something wrong?"

"Not really. I just wanted to call to share with you some information about your son. He's a bright, energetic boy, and I enjoy seeing him in class every day. But he's been having some problems handing in his homework assignments in my class."

"I didn't know he had math homework. He never brings any home."

"That might be part of the problem. He just might forget that he has any to do. I have a suggestion. Why don't we set up a system that will help him remember. I'll ask the class to write down their math homework in their folders every day. Please ask Jared to share that with you every night, and make sure that it's done. When it's done, why don't you initial it so I know you and he talked? I think that will help a lot. How does that sound?"

"Sure. I'll try that."

"Good. We don't want him to fall behind. If he has problems with the homework, have him come to my room before or after school, and I'll help him. Is there anything else I can do? . . . If not, I look forward to meeting you soon."

This phone conversation was positive and created a partnership between home and school. In addition, it created a specific plan of action.

Making Connections:
To deepen your understanding of the topics in this section of the chapter and integrate them with topics you've already studied, go to the *Making Connections* module for Chapter 11 at **www.prenhall.com/kauchak**. Respond to questions 7 and 8.

As it continues to expand, technology provides an additional channel for improving communication. For example, as they become more accessible, both voice mail and e-mail can be used to connect with busy parents. In many schools, newsletters and other communications are offered in electronic, as well as paper, form.

Check Your Understanding

4.1   Explain how involving parents contributes to a productive learning environment.

4.2   What strategies do effective teachers use to communicate with parents?

 For feedback, go to Check Your Understanding *at the end of this chapter.*

exploring diversity

Communicating With Parents

Classrooms with large numbers of students from diverse backgrounds present unique communication challenges. Lower parent participation in school activities is often associated with families that are members of cultural minorities, are lower socioeconomic status (SES), and have a child enrolled in either special education or English-as-a-second-language programs (Tiedt & Tiedt, 2005; C. Weinstein & Mignano, 2003). Each factor makes communication between home and school more challenging, both for parents and teachers.

Economic, Cultural, and Language Barriers

Economics, culture, and language can all create barriers that limit the involvement of minority and low-SES parents in school activities (Barton et al., 2004; Gollnick & Chinn, 2006). Low-SES parents frequently lack resources—such as child care, transportation, Internet access, and even telephones—that allow them to engage in school activities. Multiple jobs often prevent parents from helping their children with homework. In addition, high rates of family mobility can create obstacles to effective parent–school communication (Nakagawa et al., 2002).

Cultural differences can sometimes be misinterpreted. Because of their respect for teachers, for example, some Asian and Latino parents hesitate to become involved in matters they believe are best handled by the school, but teachers sometimes misinterpret this deference to authority as apathy (C. Weinstein & Mignano, 2003).

Language can be another barrier. Parents of bilingual students may not speak English, which leaves the child responsible for interpreting communications sent home by teachers. Homework also poses a special problem because parents cannot interpret assignments or provide help, and schools sometimes compound the difficulty by using educational jargon when they send letters home.

Involving Minority Parents

Teachers can narrow the home–school gap by offering parents specific strategies for working with their children (Epstein, 2001). Let's see how one teacher does this:

Nancy Collins, a middle school English teacher, has students who speak five different native languages in her class. During the first 2 days of school, she prepares a letter to parents, and with the help of her students, translates it into their native languages. The letter begins by describing how pleased she was to

258

have students from varying backgrounds in her class, saying that they enrich all her students' educations.

She continues with a short list of procedures and encourages the parents to support their children's efforts by

1. *Asking their children about school each night*
2. *Providing a quiet place to study for at least 90 minutes a day*
3. *Limiting television until homework is finished*
4. *Asking to see samples of their children's work and grades they've received*

She tells them that the school is having an open house and the class with the highest attendance will win a contest. She concludes the letter by reemphasizing that she is pleased to have so much diversity in her class. She asks parents to sign and return the letter.

The day before the open house, Nancy has each of her students compose a handwritten letter to their parents in their native languages, asking them to attend. Nancy writes "Hoping to see you there" at the bottom of each note and signs it.

Nancy's letter was effective in three ways. First, writing it in students' native languages communicated sensitivity and caring. Second, the letter included specific suggestions; these are important because they provide parents with concrete suggestions for helping their children. Even parents who cannot read a homework assignment are more involved if they ask their children to explain their schoolwork. The suggestions also let parents know they are needed. Third, by encouraging parents to attend the school's open house, Nancy increased the likelihood that they would do so. If they did, and the experience was positive, their involvement would likely increase.

The process of involving parents begins with awareness. As we more fully realize that parents from cultural minorities and low-SES backgrounds are often reluctant to become involved in school activities, we can redouble our efforts. We can also try to be as clear and specific as possible in our suggestions for parents as they work with their youngsters.

Finally, if parents speak English, phone calls are as effective with them as they are with nonminority parents. Experts suggest calling parents at work, where they are easier to reach, and scheduling conferences around their work schedules (Lindeman, 2001). Some teachers even conduct home visits (Bullough, 2001). Although home visits are demanding and time consuming, nothing communicates a stronger commitment to a young person's education.

decision making

Defining Yourself as a Professional

You're a first-year, sixth-grade world history teacher in an urban middle school, and you're having a difficult time maintaining order in your classroom. You're beginning the study of factors leading up to World War I, and you explain that one of the factors was increased nationalism—loyalty to a country's language and culture. As you're explaining, some of the students talk openly to each other, and a few even get out of their seats and sharpen pencils in the middle of your presentation. You point to the rules on the bulletin board, but this only seems to work for a while. You threaten them with referrals and other punishments, which work briefly, but the disruptions soon recur.

Other students seem listless and make no effort to pay attention; several even put their heads down on the desk during the lesson. You try walking around the room as you talk, and you stand near the inattentive students, but neither strategy works well. So you decide to address the issue directly. You walk up to the front of the room and say in a loud voice, "Class, this content is really important. It will help you understand why we continue to have wars in eastern Europe." As you conclude, you hear a barely audible, "Who cares?" from one of the students.

What would you do in this situation, both long-term and immediately? Why?

To respond to this question online and receive immediate feedback, go to the Decision Making Module for Chapter 11 on the Companion Website at www.prenhall.com/kauchak.

Meeting Your Learning Objectives

1. Describe the essential characteristics of a productive learning environment.
   - A productive learning environment is a place that is learning centered. In learning-centered classrooms, the primary focus is on students acquiring essential knowledge and skills. Teacher decision making is driven by the question, "How will my actions contribute to student learning?"
   - A second characteristic of a productive learning environment is that it is learner centered—a place where students can learn about themselves and others. Productive learning environments provide opportunities for students to develop social skills such as problem solving and perspective taking. They also provide opportunities for students to learn about their own strengths and weaknesses.

2. Explain how teachers' personal characteristics contribute to a productive learning environment.
   - Teacher caring is a crucial element of any productive classroom learning environment. It creates a foundation of trust for teacher–student relationships.
   - *Personal teaching efficacy* refers to a teacher's belief that he or she can affect student learning. It results in better quality instruction and increased student–teacher interactions.
   - Positive teacher expectations refer to teacher beliefs about students' ability to learn. Like personal teaching efficacy, it results in improved instruction and more effective teacher–student interactions.
   - Teacher modeling is a major way that teachers influence students' attitudes and beliefs. Teachers also model enthusiasm for the topics they teach, which can influence students' attitudes toward the subject matter.

3. Describe how classroom management contributes to a productive learning environment.
   - Classroom management is a national concern because of two major factors. First, the public often associates school violence with ineffective classroom management. Second, the public also believes, and rightly so, that there is a link between effective classroom management and increased learning.
   - Classroom management helps develop learner responsibility, it contributes to a positive classroom climate, and it maximizes time and opportunities for learning.
   - Effective classroom management depends upon a system of rules and procedures that provide guidelines for student behavior.
   - Effective interventions are immediate, target the correct student(s), and interfere with instruction and learning as little as possible.
   - Serious management problems, while rare and infrequent, can occur in classrooms. Teachers should understand procedures for dealing with these both immediately and long term.
   - Urban schools present unique management challenges. Effective urban teachers are caring and supportive, have clear standards for behavior, provide structure in their classrooms, and use effective instruction to complement their management.

4. Explain how involving parents contributes to a productive learning environment.
   - Students whose parents are involved in their education have better attitudes toward school, achieve higher, and are more likely to attend postsecondary education.
   - Teachers who encourage parental involvement also feel more positive about teaching and their school, and they have higher expectations for parents.
   - Teachers can involve parents by sending samples of student work home, emphasizing student accomplishments, and calling parents when necessary.

Important Concepts

academic learning time
allocated time
caring
classroom climate
classroom management
discipline
engaged time
instructional time
learning communities
personal development

personal teaching efficacy
perspective taking
positive teacher expectations
procedures
productive learning environment
rules
social development
social problem-solving skills
teacher modeling
withitness

Developing as a Professional

Preparing for Your Licensure Exam

This exercise will provide you with practice answering questions similar to the Praxis II exam as well as your state-specific licensure exam. Read the case study, and answer the questions that follow.

Nick Giardo is excited about the beginning of his first year of teaching at Sandalwood Junior High. Student teaching was a little rocky, but he is sure that most of his problems were due to his taking over another teacher's class in mid-year. As he sits at his desk planning for the new year, he thinks, "This has got to be better than student teaching"; then with a half smile mumbles audibly, "How could it be any worse?"

As students file into his first-period class, he is in the back of the room putting the final touches on a bulletin board. After the bell rings, he walks to the front of the room and says, "Welcome to U.S. History 101. I'm Mr. Giardo, and I'll be your teacher for the year. I see you've all found seats, so why don't we begin."

At this point, two confused students straggle in, looking for their classrooms. One of these students belongs there, the other does not. Mr. Giardo directs the one to sit down while he escorts the other into the hallway to help him find his class. As he returns to the room, there is a general buzz of student talk. Beginning again, he says, "Okay, class. Let's get started. This is American History, and I'm really excited about the year. I expect all of you to learn a lot about U.S. history and to become as excited about the topic as I am. Since you've all been in school before, I'm not going to waste a lot of time with rules. You all know how to play the game. The rules are up on the board, and I expect you to follow them . . . or else," he concluded with a stern look around the room, attempting to make eye contact with each student.

"Instead, I'd like to jump right into the content. I want this course to be important to you, so I'd like to get some idea of the kinds of things you'd like to learn about in here. I'd like you to break up into groups of four or five, and make a list of the kinds of things you'd like to learn this year. Then we'll come back together and discuss our lists."

As the students begin to talk in their groups, one student raises his hand. Nick pulls up a chair and sits down to talk with the student. As he does so, students in back of him start throwing spitballs and erasers.

The year is off to a rocky start.

1. Analyze Nick's classroom based on the characteristics of a productive learning environment.

2. Assess Nick's actions based on the human dimension of productive learning environments.

3. Assess Nick's application of research that describes the role of rules and procedures in creating an orderly classroom.

To receive feedback on your responses to these exercises, go to the Companion Website at www.prenhall.com/kauchak, and then to the Preparing for Your Licensure Exam *module for Chapter 11.*

Discussion Questions

1. Almost any teacher would agree that it is important to be a good role model. Given that belief, why do you suppose some teachers don't model the behaviors they expect their students to imitate?

2. Why is assertive discipline so popular in many schools? What are the advantages and disadvantages of this approach to management?

3. How can a teacher tell if students have developed responsibility? How might the definition of responsibility change with grade level? What types of instructional and managerial strategies promote responsibility? What types discourage the development of responsibility?

4. How do the following factors influence the optimal number of procedures in a classroom?
   a. Grade level
   b. Subject matter
   c. Type of student (e.g., high versus low achiever)
   d. Type of instruction (e.g., large group versus small group)

5. What advantages are there to seeking student input on rules? Disadvantages? Is this practice more important with younger or older students? Why?

6. If you were a substitute teacher (or a student teacher) and were going to take over a class mid-year, what kinds of things would you need to know and do in terms of classroom management?

Developing as a Professional: Online Activities

Going into Schools

Go to the Companion Website at *www.prenhall.com/kauchak*, and click on the *Going into Schools* module for Chapter 11. You will find a number of school-based activities that will help you link chapter content to the schools in which you work.

Virtual Field Experience: Using Teacher Prep to Explore the Profession

If you would like to participate in a Virtual Field Experience, access the Teacher Prep Website at *www.prenhall.com/teacherprep*. After logging in, complete the following steps:

1. Click on "Video Classroom" on the left panel of the screen.

2. Go to "General Methods."

3. Finally, select "Module 4: Classroom Management." This video focuses on low-profile management strategies that minimize interruptions to instruction. Answer the questions that follow the video clip.

Online Portfolio Activities

To develop your professional portfolio, further apply your understanding of chapter content, and address the INTASC standards, go the Companion Website at www.prenhall.com/kauchak, then to the *Online Portfolio Activities* for Chapter 11. Complete the suggested activities.

Check Your Understanding

1.1 **Describe the essential characteristics of a productive learning environment.**

Productive learning environments are orderly and focus on learning. Orderly environments are safe and inviting rather then rigid and punitive. In them, students feel free to share their thinking without fear of embarrassment or ridicule.

Learning is the central purpose of schooling. In productive learning environments, students not only learn content, they also learn about themselves and how to get along with others.

1.2 **How do productive learning environments help promote personal and social development?**

Classrooms are social places that provide opportunities for students to learn both personal and social skills. In terms of personal knowledge, productive learning environments provide opportunities for students to learn to recognize their personal strengths, needs, and values, as well as to develop self-motivation and discipline, goal-setting and organizational skills, impulse control and self-management, and personal and moral responsibility. In terms of social development, productive learning environments provide opportunities for students to learn perspective taking and social problem solving along with how to work cooperatively with others, respect for others, empathy for others, and appreciation for diversity.

1.3 **In this section, we said that learning is the primary purpose of schooling, but we also emphasized a positive classroom climate. How are the two related?**

Promoting learning and emphasizing a positive classroom climate are related in two ways. First, learning includes the knowledge and skills that schools emphasize as well as learning about ourselves and how we relate to our peers. A positive classroom climate provides opportunities for students to learn about themselves and each other.

Second, students learn more knowledge and skills, as well as more about themselves and relating to their peers, when the emotional climate in a classroom is positive.

2.1 **Why is caring important for a productive learning environment? What can teachers do to show they care?**

Caring refers to teachers' investment in the protection and development of the young people in their classes. Caring provides an emotional foundation for all teacher–student interactions and meets students' basic needs for safety and belonging. Teachers communicate caring by treating students as unique individuals and giving them their time.

2.2 **What are personal teacher efficacy and positive teacher expectations? How are they related?**

Personal teacher efficacy is a teacher's belief that he or she can promote learning in all students regardless of their backgrounds. As opposed to personal teacher efficacy, which focuses on the teacher, the term positive teacher expectations refers to teachers' beliefs in their students' ability to learn. The focus of personal teacher efficacy is on teachers' ability to produce learning, while the focus of positive teacher expectations is on students' ability to learn. These attitudes are related in that both influence teachers' actions in the classroom.

2.3   What is teacher modeling? How is it related to teacher enthusiasm?

Teacher modeling *refers to the tendency of students to observe and imitate teachers' attitudes and beliefs. Much of what teachers teach in classrooms occurs through modeling. One important dimension of teacher modeling is enthusiasm, both for learning in general as well as learning a particular subject. When teachers are enthusiastic about the topics they are teaching, this motivates students, increasing their enthusiasm for learning.*

3.1   Why has classroom management become a national concern?

The public views classroom management as important for several reasons. Perhaps most prominently, the public associates failed classroom management with reports of school violence. In addition, the public correctly links orderly classrooms and schools with increased learning.

3.2   What are the major goals of classroom management? How do they contribute to a productive learning environment?

The major goals of classroom management are to teach students self-responsibility, create a safe and orderly place where students can live and learn, and maximize opportunities for learning. They each contribute to a productive learning environment in different ways. Teaching students to be responsible for their own actions is a long-term goal that, if successful, shifts focus from the teacher as enforcer to the student as a responsible citizen. Creating a safe and orderly classroom is a precondition for all other activities; students need to feel that their classroom is a place that is safe and free from external threats. Finally, maximizing opportunities for learning creates a learning-focused classroom where students are actively engaged in acquiring new knowledge and skills.

3.3   How are classroom management and discipline different? How can teachers prevent management problems through planning?

Classroom management is the process of creating a productive learning environment through strategies that create and maintain classroom order. Discipline, by contrast, focuses on teachers' responses to student misbehavior. The differences between the two are important because research shows that effective managers emphasize management over discipline. Ineffective managers, by contrast, are continually reacting to student misbehavior because they don't have a comprehensive and effective management system in place.

Major tools to prevent management problems are rules and procedures. Rules specify standards for acceptable classroom behavior. When linked to the reasons for them, they provide guidelines for ethical student behavior. For example, the rule, "Listen when someone else is speaking," not only creates an orderly classroom but it also hopefully teaches students how to treat each other outside the classroom. Courtesy in conversation requires that we take turns listening and speaking.

Procedures, by contrast, describe efficient ways of performing classroom tasks. They don't have a moral or ethical component; instead, they contribute to a smooth and orderly classroom.

3.4   What are the characteristics of effective interventions?

Effective interventions are short and unobtrusive, interfering with instruction and learning as little as possible. Effective interventions are also immediate, nipping potential problems in the bud. Finally, and perhaps most important, interventions should target the correct student(s).

3.5   What actions—both short- and long-term—should teachers take when encountering incidents of violence and aggression?

Short-term, the teacher should intervene immediately to address the problem. This might consist of a personal intervention, or, if this is not possible, the teacher should send for help immediately. Long-term, teachers should involve parents and other school personnel in addressing the problems. Parents should be notified, and the expertise and guidance of experienced school personnel should be sought.

3.6   What makes urban classrooms unique in terms of classroom management?

First, because urban classrooms tend to be diverse, teachers need to make sure that all students understand classroom rules and procedures and how they contribute to learning. Second, urban classrooms tend to be large, making classroom management more challenging. Third, negative stereotypes often exist about urban students, resulting in teachers teaching defensively rather than positively.

4.1   Explain how involving parents contributes to a productive learning environment.

Productive learning environments are orderly and focus on learning. Research indicates that when parents are involved, students are more willing to do homework, their long-term achievement is higher, their attitudes are more positive, and they behave more responsibly. In addition their attendance and graduation rates are higher. Each contributes to a safe, orderly, learning-focused environment.

4.2   What strategies do effective teachers use to communicate with parents?

Effective teachers use a variety of strategies to communicate with parents. In addition to open houses, interim progress reports, and report cards, effective teachers also send letters home; periodically send home packets of student work; and use newsletters, e-mails, and individual notes. In addition, phone calls and home visits are also effective.

Effective Instruction in American Schools

8

Effective Instruction in American Schools

Chapter Outline

Learning and Teaching in Today's Classrooms
- Principles of Learning
- The Relationships Between Teaching and Learning

Planning for Effective Teaching
- Select Topics
- Specify Learning Objectives
- Prepare and Organize Learning Activities
- Plan for Assessment
- Ensure Instructional Alignment
- Planning in a Standards-Based Environment

Implementing Instruction: Essential Teaching Skills
- Organization
- Clear Communication
- Focus: Attracting and Maintaining Attention
- Questioning
- Feedback
- Review and Closure

Models of Instruction
- Direct Instruction
- Lecture-Discussion
- Guided Discovery
- Cooperative Learning

Learning Objectives

After you have completed your study of this chapter, you should be able to:

1. Describe the principles of cognitive learning theory, and identify examples of the principles in practice.

2. Describe essential steps in planning for instruction.

3. Explain how essential teaching skills contribute to learning.

4. Explain the relationships between principles of learning and different phases of models of instruction.

Case Studies

 Elementary

 Middle

 Secondary

A major reason you're taking this and other courses in your teacher-preparation program is to help you develop your professional knowledge and skills, with the ultimate goal of becoming an expert teacher. Understanding how to plan and conduct effective lessons is perhaps the most important professional knowledge you will acquire in your teacher-education program. Helping you begin the process of developing that understanding is the goal of this chapter.

Let's begin by looking at one elementary teacher's thinking as she plans for her next week's math instruction.

 "What are you doing?" Jim Barton asks his wife, Shirley, a fourth-grade teacher, as he sees her hard at work on a Saturday afternoon cutting and drawing on cardboard pieces.

"Working on a unit on equivalent fractions and adding fractions with unlike denominators. . . . What do you think? . . . Do they look like pizzas and cakes?" she asks, holding up the pieces of cardboard.

"They really do," he smiles, a bit impressed.

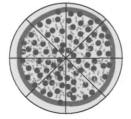 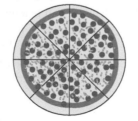

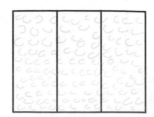

"My students had trouble with the equivalency standard on the state test last year, so I'm going to try to use more concrete, real-world examples. I want them to thoroughly understand equivalent fractions, so they'll be able to add fractions with unlike denominators."

"Equivalency standard?"

"Yeah. . . . See here," Shirley says, pointing to a document on her desk. "It says, 'Knows that two numbers in different forms are equivalent or nonequivalent, using whole numbers, decimals, fractions, and mixed numbers.' . . . For instance, ⅓ and ⅔ are equivalent forms of the same fraction. . . . Next, I want them to be able to convert fractions with unlike denominators to have common denominators, so they can add them."

"I see," Jim says, genuinely interested.

"Well, you know how kids are," Shirley continues. "They like to take the easy way out, and they often have misconceptions. . . . Like, this problem," Shirley continues, writing ½ + ⅓ on a piece of paper. "What's the answer?"

"Five-sixths," Jim answers, after a second or two.

"Wrong. . . . It's two-fifths."

Shirley grins at Jim's puzzled look at her response of " two-fifths" and then continues, "The kids see that we're adding, so they just add the top numbers and get 2 and add the bottom numbers and get 5. . . . The real answer is, of course, five-sixths, just as you said, but initially that isn't as sensible to them as two-fifths. So, that's the kind of thing I'm working on."

"Okay," Shirley thinks to herself as Jim leaves the room, "I'll use the pizzas for review, and then I'll use the cakes to help them understand equivalent fractions."

She then prepares a worksheet with additional geometric figures that students will complete for additional practice on finding equivalent fractions. "If they do okay on the worksheet, I'll give them some problems in a quiz Friday, so I can see how well they really understand both equivalent fractions and adding fractions with unlike denominators," she mumbles out loud. "If they don't do well, I'll give them some more practice. . . . I think I'm ready."

We'll examine Shirley's planning in detail in the next section, but before we do, please respond to the following survey that will introduce you to your study of this chapter. We examine each of these items as the chapter unfolds.

Learning and Teaching in Today's Classrooms

Cognitive theories of learning emphasize that students are mentally active as they attempt to understand the world. [Alan Oddie/PhotoEdit Inc.]

If we look closely at Shirley's planning, we see that her understanding of the ways that kids think and learn were important in guiding her decisions during planning. And this understanding will also guide her instruction, as we'll see later in the chapter. Let's take a closer look at several basic principles that support our understanding of the way students think and learn.

Principles of Learning

The cognitive revolution, an important change in the way educators think about learning, began about the middle of the 20th century and continues to this day. This revolution marked a major shift in educators' understanding of the way students learn and now provides the foundation on which school leaders and teachers base their approaches to instruction.

Cognitive learning theories explain learning by focusing on changes in the ways people think that result from their efforts to make sense of the world. These theories help us explain tasks as simple as remembering a phone number and as complex as solving math and chemistry problems.

professional knowledge: test yourself!

For each item, circle the number that best represents your thinking. Use the following scale as a guide.

1 = Strongly disagree
2 = Disagree
3 = Uncertain
4 = Agree
5 = Strongly agree

1. Students tend to retain ideas that make sense to them, even if the ideas are inconsistent with teachers' explanations.

      1   2   3   4   5

2. Because assessing students, such as giving quizzes and tests, uses instructional time, students who are frequently assessed learn less than those who are assessed less frequently.

      1   2   3   4   5

3. Effective planning primarily involves identifying the important topics students should learn.

      1   2   3   4   5

4. The most effective teachers in today's schools are those who are best able to clearly explain the content they are teaching to their students.

      1   2   3   4   5

5. Rather than exclusively using one particular teaching strategy, effective teachers vary their instruction.

      1   2   3   4   5

 This is available in a downloadable format on the Companion Website for personal portfolio use.

Cognitive learning theories are grounded in the following principles:

- Learning depends on experiences.
- Learners *construct*—they do not record—knowledge in an attempt to make sense of their experiences.
- Knowledge that is constructed depends on and builds on knowledge that learners already possess.
- Learning is enhanced by social interaction.
- Learning requires practice and feedback.

Learning Depends on Experiences

You have learned to drive a car, but your only experience has been with cars that have automatic transmissions. Then, you take a part-time job as a delivery truck driver, but all the trucks have standard transmissions. You initially struggle, but now you're very comfortable driving vehicles with standard transmissions.

Cognitive learning theories. Explanations for learning that focus on changes in the ways people think that result from their efforts to make sense of the world.

This simple example illustrates the importance of experience in learning. Your initial experiences with automatic transmissions helped you learn to drive, and because of additional experience, you have now learned to drive vehicles with standard transmissions.

This principle applies to schools as well. Everything that occurs in schools provides students with experiences that contribute to their learning. Shirley planned experiences intended to help her fifth graders understand equivalent fractions. This course provides you with experiences that are designed to increase your understanding of teaching and help you develop as a professional. The same is true for all learning. Experiences provide the raw material that people use to construct ideas.

Learners Construct Knowledge in an Attempt to Make Sense of Their Experiences

When our students learn, they don't behave like tape recorders, passively recording ideas in their memories in the form in which they are presented. Instead, they are cognitively active, and in an attempt to understand how the world works, they construct knowledge and understanding that makes sense to them.

Shirley's students are examples. To them, it made more sense to add both the top and bottom numbers in fractions than it did to add only the top numbers. Research has uncovered a number of misconceptions that students bring to class and that teachers must battle before more accurate understanding can occur (Crockett, 2004). For example, many students believe that people are warmer in the summer, because the earth is closer to the sun during that season. This makes intuitive sense to students who become warmer the closer they stand to a fire or heater. Unfortunately, this misconception then competes with teachers' attempts to help students see that the tilting of the earth's axis toward and away from the sun is a more accurate explanation, because it also helps us understand why the seasons in the southern hemisphere are the opposite of ours in the north. Again, it is important to remember that students' learning, both accurate and inaccurate, results from experience, and subsequent experiences are usually necessary to change students' ideas.

This section suggests that the first item on our survey, "Students tend to retain ideas that make sense to them, even if the ideas are inconsistent with teachers' explanations" is true. In fact, students' misconceptions can be difficult to dispel, and simply offering them a correct explanation is often ineffective.

Knowledge That Is Constructed Depends on and Builds on Learners' Prior Knowledge

People don't construct knowledge in a vacuum; new knowledge builds on what they already know. For instance, Shirley's students had a great deal of practice with addition. At no time in finding a sum did they add some numbers but not others. So—to them—adding both the top and bottom numbers in a fraction was sensible, more sensible than adding only the numbers on top and essentially ignoring those on the bottom.

Prior knowledge can also help us understand why students sometimes struggle with grammar rules. For example, they learn that when one boy meets another boy, we have two *boys*. The same applies to *girls*. However, when we see one body of water and then a second body of water, we don't have two *bodys* of water; we have two *bodies* of water.

Knowing that people attempt to make sense of the world and realizing that they will use what they already know in the process help us understand why students have so many misconceptions and why they sometimes have "off-the-wall" ideas. Based on their existing knowledge and experiences, the misconceptions and ideas make sense to them.

Learning Is Enhanced by Social Interaction

Social interaction helps students create and refine new ideas (Bruning et al., 2004). Experts estimate that 25 percent of what students learn in classrooms results from their interactions with fellow students (Brophy, 2006). We can see how this principle applies to Shirley's students. Without a discussion of why we add only the top numbers when finding the sums of fractions, they are likely to retain the misconception. Also, social interaction is a form of experience, and, as with experience in general, it influences all forms of learning.

272

Learning Requires Practice and Feedback

People learn to do well what they practice—an idea captured by the saying, "Practice makes perfect" (Schunk, 2004). This principle explains why true learning takes so much time and effort and is also supported by neurological studies (Craig, 2003). To become proficient at word processing, we practice at the computer; to become skilled writers, we practice writing; to solve problems effectively, we solve many problems. Shirley understood this principle when she prepared a worksheet designed to provide her students with additional practice in finding equivalent fractions.

For practice to be effective, we need to receive feedback about our performance. **Feedback** is information about existing understanding that we use to increase future understanding. As learners construct knowledge, they use additional information to determine the extent to which their understanding is valid. For instance, feedback on the screen provides us with immediate feedback about our word processing. In a similar way, feedback from students, fellow teachers, and principals provides teachers with information about their teaching performance. Much of our learning, in life and in the classroom, is influenced by the feedback we receive from the world (Nietfeld, Cao, & Osborne, 2004).

One of our most important roles as teachers is to provide students with feedback that can help them arrive at more accurate and sophisticated understandings of the world around them. In this regard, feedback is additional experience that students use to increase their learning.

The Relationships Between Teaching and Learning

Effective instruction builds on the principles of learning discussed in the previous section to maximize learning in the classroom. Simply, it is instruction based on principles of learning that maximizes learning for all students. Effective teachers are those who systematically apply the principles of learning in their planning and teaching.

As people have experiences, they continue to construct knowledge throughout their lifetimes, and they continue to learn and develop. However, schools as social institutions are designed to promote certain goals; they can't simple say, "Have experiences and learn and develop." Some experiences are more beneficial for learning than others. Effective teachers plan for and provide specific experiences for students, guide the social interaction that supports their knowledge construction, and design forms of practice and feedback that will help confirm or refine students' developing understanding. Effective instruction involves teachers' systematic attempts to help their students reach predetermined goals. This is particularly important now that standards and accountability are facts of teachers' lives.

> **Making Connections:**
> To deepen your understanding of the topics in this section of the chapter and integrate them with topics you've already studied, go to the *Making Connections* module for Chapter 12 at **www.prenhall.com/kauchak**. Respond to questions 1 and 2.

Check Your Understanding

1.1 Describe the principles on which cognitive learning theories are based.

1.2 You and a friend are trying to install a sound card in your computer, but you're a little uncertain about how to do it. You open the cabinet, look inside, and as you talk about how to proceed, she suggests looking to see where the speakers are attached. "Good idea," you say, and you easily install the card. Which principle of learning is best illustrated by this example?

1.3 Research indicates that properly designed homework increases learning (Kohn, 2006; H. Cooper, Robinson, & Patall, 2006). To which principle of learning is this research most closely related?

 For feedback, go to Check Your Understanding *at the end of this chapter.*

> **Feedback.** Information about existing understanding that we use to enhance future understanding.
>
> **Effective instruction.** Instruction that builds on principles of learning to maximize learning in the classroom.

Planning for Effective Teaching

Effective teaching doesn't just happen; it must be planned for and designed in a systematic way. Through careful planning, teachers provide students with experiences that allow them to construct new ideas and understanding. In the opening case, Shirley made decisions about the following strategies during her planning:

- Select topics that are important for students to study.
- Specify learning objectives related to the topics.
- Prepare and organize learning activities to help students reach the objectives.
- Plan assessments to measure the amount students have learned.
- Ensure that instruction and assessments are aligned with her learning objectives (L. Anderson & Krathwohl, 2001).

These planning decisions are outlined in Figure 12.1 and discussed in the sections that follow.

Careful planning helps teachers define their goals and make sure that instructional activities are aligned with these goals. [Mary Kate Denny/ PhotoEdit Inc.]

Select Topics

"What is important for students to learn?" is one of the most fundamental questions that teachers face as they plan (L. Anderson & Krathwohl, 2001). Standards—such as the one Shirley showed her husband, Jim—textbooks, and curriculum guides are all sources teachers commonly use to help answer this question (Reys, Reys, & Chavez, 2004). Their personal philosophies, students' interest in the topic, and real-world applications also influence the answer to this question. Teachers' knowledge of content is particularly important in helping decide which topics are important enough to allocate valuable teaching time to them, because there simply isn't time to teach everything. Effective teachers know their content well enough to identify key content ideas to target and emphasize.

Specify Learning Objectives

Although deciding what is important to study is an essential first step, teachers must also answer a second question: What do I want my students to know or be able to do with respect to the topic? The answer to this question is a **learning objective**. Clear learning objectives are essential because they guide the rest of the decisions teachers make during both planning and instruction. Without clear objectives, teachers won't know how to design their learning activities, nor can they create accurate assessments. Objectives also guide teachers as they implement their learning activities. When learning activities are unsuccessful, it can often be traced back to teachers' not being clear about their objectives.

Figure 12.1 Planning for Instruction

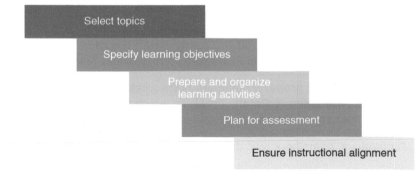

Learning objectives. Statements that specify what students should know or be able to do with respect to a topic or course of study.

TABLE 12.1 Objectives Using Mager's Approach

Objective	Condition	Performance	Criteria
Given 3 pairs of fractions, fourth graders wil will determine if each pair is or is not equivalent.	Given 3 pairs of fractions	Determine	Each
Given pairs of fractions with unlike denominators, fourth graders will create equivalent fractions for each pair.	Given pairs of fractions with unlike denominators	Create	Each
Given word problems involving the addition of fractions with unlike denominators, fourth graders will correctly add the fractions in each.	Given word problems with unlike denominators	Add	Each correctly

Different approaches to writing objectives exist, and we'll briefly introduce two of the most popular here. (You will study these approaches in detail later in your methods classes.) One approach was pioneered in 1962 by Robert Mager in his highly readable book *Preparing Instructional Objectives*. Mager's work strongly influenced teaching and remains widely used today (Mager, 1998). If Shirley wrote objectives using Mager's approach, they might appear as you see in Table 12.1.

Norman Gronlund (2004) offered a popular alternative to Mager's approach; he suggested that teachers state a general objective, such as *know, understand,* or *apply,* followed by specific learning outcomes that operationally define what students will be able to do. Table 12.2 includes examples of objectives written according to Gronlund's suggestions. Note that in both approaches, the emphasis is on what students are learning, not what the teacher is doing. Effective planning begins with a focus on students' learning; teacher actions follow logically afterward.

To assist teachers in planning learning activities for their students, researchers developed a classification system based on principles of learning (L. Anderson & Krathwohl, 2001). A revision of the famous "Bloom's Taxonomy," first published in 1956 (Bloom, Englehart, Furst, Hill, & Krathwohl, 1956), the new system uses a matrix with 24 cells that represent the intersection of four types of knowledge with six cognitive processes (see Figure 12.2).

Teachers use the taxonomy to think about and clarify their learning objectives. For instance, one of Shirley's objectives was for students to be able to convert unequivalent into equivalent fractions. The objective involves applying a procedure, so it would be placed in the cell where *procedural knowledge* intersects with the cognitive process *apply*. In order to convert unequivalent fractions to equivalent fractions, students first need to understand the concept *equivalent fractions*. That objective would be placed in the cell where *conceptual knowledge* intersects with the cognitive process *understand*. Using the taxonomy during planning allows teachers to see what types of knowledge and cognitive processes they are emphasizing in their teaching.

TABLE 12.2 Objectives Using Gronlund's Approach

General Objective	Specific Learning Outcome
Understands *equivalent fractions*	1. Identifies pairs of fractions that are and are not equivalent. 2. Creates equivalent fractions
Understands the addition of fractions with unlike denominators	1. Recognizes need for creating equivalent fractions 2. Performs operations 3. Solves problems

Source: Gronlund (2004).

275

Figure 12.2 A Taxonomy for Learning, Teaching, and Assessing

The Knowledge Dimension	The Cognitive Process Dimension					
	1. Remember	2. Understand	3. Apply	4. Analyze	5. Evaluate	6. Create
A. Factual knowledge						
B. Conceptual knowledge						
C. Procedural knowledge						
D. Metacognitive knowledge						

Source: From Lorin W. Anderson & David R. Krathwohl, *A Taxonomy for Learning, Teaching and Assessing: A Revision of Bloom's Objectives*, p. 28. Copyright 2001. Published by Allyn and Bacon, Boston, MA. Copyright © by Pearson Education. Reprinted by permission of the publisher.

The taxonomy reminds us that teaching and learning are complex processes with many possible outcomes. It also helps us remember that we want our students to do much more than just "remember" "factual knowledge," one of the cells in the taxonomy. Unfortunately, a great deal of schooling focuses as much on this most basic objective as it does on the other 23 combined. Moving to the other forms of knowledge and more advanced cognitive processes is even more important in the 21st century, as student thinking, decision making, and problem solving are increasingly emphasized (van Gelder, 2005).

Prepare and Organize Learning Activities

Once Shirley identified her learning objectives—what she wanted her students to learn and know—she then prepared and organized her learning activities. This process primarily involved finding or creating high-quality examples or problems that illustrated the topic and then sequencing them so that they would be most meaningful to her students.

High-quality examples are representations of content that ideally have all the information in them that the students need to reach teachers' learning objectives, and their importance in promoting learning is crucial. They provide the basic experiences that students need for learning; examples are what learners use to construct their knowledge (Haas, 2005; J. Freeman, McPhail, & Berndt, 2002). Examples are also important in classrooms with diverse learners, because they contain information that students need in order to reach teachers' learning objectives, accommodating differences in students' prior knowledge. High-quality examples are important to all topics at all grade levels and are especially valuable for limited-English-proficiency learners because their prior experiences may not match those of other students (Bae, 2003; Echevarria & Graves, 2007).

Shirley used cardboard "pizzas" and "cakes" as examples to provide concrete learning experiences for her students. For example, she divided her "pizzas" into eight equal parts to illustrate equivalent fractions with similar denominators. She used the cake examples to build

Effective instructional activities provide students with opportunities to construct ideas. [©Ellen B. Senisi/Ellen Senisi]

High-quality examples. Representations of content that ideally have all the information in them that students need in order to reach teachers' learning objectives.

on this knowledge and to help her students learn how to convert unequivalent into equivalent fractions. (We'll see how Shirley used them in the next section of the chapter when we discuss implementing instruction.)

Examples are also important in language arts. Teachers often use actual student writing samples to provide concrete examples of good organization, grammar, and punctuation. Middle and high school teachers often use specific examples taken from literature to teach concepts such as metaphor, simile, and irony. Elementary teachers frequently use words embedded in sentences as examples to teach the different parts of speech. All of these abstract ideas would be difficult to teach and learn without the use of examples

The importance of high-quality examples in teaching can't be overstated, and research documents their powerful role in learning in the classroom. Effective teachers use examples to illustrate topics in ways that are understandable to students, whereas less effective teachers tend to rely on verbal explanations (Cassady, 1999; Haas, 2005).

Plan for Assessment

Assessment, which is the process of gathering information about students' learning progress, is an integral part of effective teaching, and expert teachers continually think about assessment during planning. Effective assessments not only answer the question, "How can I determine if my students have reached the learning objectives?" but also, "How can I use assessment to facilitate learning?"

We saw thinking about assessment in Shirley's planning. She said to herself, "I'll give them some problems in a quiz Friday, so I can see how well they really understand both equivalent fractions and adding fractions with unlike denominators. . . . If they don't do well, I'll give them some more practice." Let's look at some of the items that Shirley used to assess her students' learning.

Part I.
Look at the drawings of pairs of fractions below. Circle the pairs that are equivalent, and explain why they are equivalent in each case.

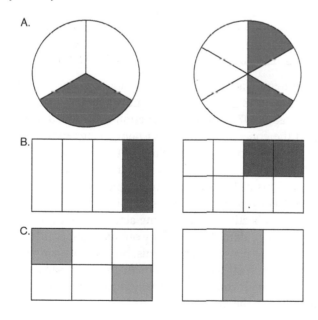

Part II.
Add the following fractions.

$$\frac{1}{5} + \frac{2}{5} = \underline{\hspace{1cm}} \qquad \frac{2}{7} + \frac{4}{7} = \underline{\hspace{1cm}}$$

$$\frac{1}{3} + \frac{1}{2} = \underline{\hspace{1cm}} \qquad \frac{3}{4} + \frac{1}{8} = \underline{\hspace{1cm}}$$

> Assessment. How student understanding is measured.

277

Shirley designed these assessment items to provide both Shirley and her students with valuable information about their learning progress. If students succeed with these items, Shirley can proceed to other topics, building on her students' developing understanding of fractions. If students do not succeed, Shirley can use their responses to redesign her instruction to address learning problems.

Research supports the crucial role of assessment in learning:

Weekly or even more frequent classroom tests provide teachers with information useful in planning their lessons. . . . Frequent tests encourage students to be prepared for classes. Even in themselves, tests can be a powerful source of learning: Regular essays and feedback, for example, help students not only comprehend subject matter but become better writers. (Walberg, 2003, p. 42)

Research also shows that expert teachers, like Shirley, assess frequently during instruction, using both verbal questions and frequent exercises to provide students and themselves with continual information about learning progress during a lesson (Ciofalo & Wylie, 2006).

This section also indicates that the second item on our beginning-of-chapter survey, "Because assessing students, such as giving quizzes and tests, uses instructional time, students who are frequently assessed learn less than those who are assessed less frequently" is clearly not true. While the process of assessment does take time, it makes a major contribution to learning and is one of the most valuable uses of instructional time.

Assessment decisions are also essential during planning because they help teachers align their instruction with important standards and objectives. Let's see how teachers do that.

Ensure Instructional Alignment

Thinking about assessment during planning helped Shirley answer an additional question, "How do I know that my instruction and assessments are logically connected to my objectives?" **Instructional alignment** is the match between learning objectives, learning activities, and assessments, and it is an essential component of effective instruction (Bransford et al., 2000; L. Anderson & Krathwohl, 2001).

Without this alignment, it is difficult to know what is being learned. Students may be learning valuable information, but one cannot tell unless there is alignment between what they are learning and the assessment of that learning. Similarly, students may be learning things that others don't value unless curricula and assessments are aligned with . . . learning goals. (Bransford et al., 2000, pp. 51–52)

Instructional alignment helps teachers match instructional strategies and assessments to learning objectives and also helps students identify and understand what is important to learn (Morrison, Kemp, & Ross, 2007). Shirley's instruction was aligned. Her objectives were for students to understand the concept *equivalent fractions,* create equivalent fractions, and add fractions with unlike denominators. She then planned to give a quiz with "problems similar to my cake example." On the quiz, the students were asked to solve problems similar to those they practiced in class. This is the essence of instructional alignment.

Maintaining alignment isn't as easy as it appears. For instance, if a teacher's objective is for students to be able to write effectively, yet learning activities focus on isolated grammar skills, the instruction is out of alignment. It is similarly out of alignment if the objective is for students to apply math concepts to real-world problems, but learning activities have students practicing computation problems. Instructional alignment encourages teachers to ask, "What does my objective (e.g., 'apply math concepts') actually mean, and do my learning and assessment activities actually lead to the objective?"

Planning in a Standards-Based Environment

Instructional alignment. The match between learning objectives, learning activities, and assessments.

Standards influence teaching in a number of ways. *Standards* specify what students should know and what skills they should have after completing an area of study and are an essential part of accountability. Standards also influence the curriculum; Shirley referred to her state standard in her planning.

Unfortunately, standards are often written with varying degrees of specificity, so teachers have to interpret the meaning of the standard, as did both Suzanne and Shirley (Hamilton, Berends, & Stecher, 2005). Once they had made their interpretation, they were then able to make important decisions about learning activities and assessments. Careful planning ensured that they would help students meet the standards and that they had aligned their objectives, learning activities, and assessments.

This section provides us with an answer to the third statement in our introductory survey, "Effective planning primarily involves identifying the important topics students should learn." This statement is false. Though planning involves identifying topics for students to learn, it is much broader and includes other components to ensure that instructional activities result in productive student learning.

Making Connections:
To deepen your understanding of the topics in this section of the chapter and integrate them with topics you've already studied, go to the *Making Connections* module for Chapter 12 at www.prenhall.com/kauchak. Respond to questions 3–6.

Check Your Understanding

2.1 What are the five essential steps in planning for instruction?

2.2 Planning in a standards-based environment involves one additional step beyond the planning steps described in this section of the chapter. What is that additional step?

2.3 Classify the following objectives into one of the cells of the taxonomy table in Figure 12.2, and explain your classification: (1) Students will identify examples of figures of speech such as similes, metaphors, and personifications in written paragraphs. (2) students will write original paragraphs that include those figures of speech.

For feedback, go to Check Your Understanding *at the end of this chapter.*

Implementing Instruction: Essential Teaching Skills

Effective teaching is based on **essential teaching skills**, abilities that all teachers, including those in their first year of teaching, should have in order to maximize student learning. To see what these are, let's return to Shirley's work. We join her on Monday morning just before math, which she schedules each day from 10:00 to 11:00.

Shirley walks up and down the aisles, placing sheets of paper on each student's desk as students finish their writing assignment in language arts.

"Quickly turn in your writing, and get out your math books," she directs. Students stop writing and pass their papers forward, each putting his or her paper on top of the stack. Shirley places the papers into a folder and at 10:01 pulls out her cardboard pizzas. "Let's see what we remember about adding fractions. Look at these pizzas. We need to find out, What fraction of one whole pizza did we eat?"

After giving students time to think, she continues, "How many pieces of the first pizza did we eat? . . . Dean?" she asks as she displays the pizzas, which now have some pieces removed, as we see here.

Essential teaching skills. Abilities that all teachers, including those in their first year, should have in order to maximize student learning.

"Three."

"And how about this pizza? How many pieces did we eat? . . . Kathy?"

"Two."

She then writes $\frac{3}{8} + \frac{2}{8}$ on the board and, pointing to these numbers, asks, "Why did I write $\frac{3}{8}$ here and $\frac{2}{8}$ there? . . . Omar?"

"You have . . . 8 pieces in each pizza . . . and you ate 3 of them," Omar responds hesitantly, pointing to the one on the left.

"Good," Shirley smiles. "And what about the second one? How many pieces of that pizza did we eat? . . . Selina?"

"Two."

"So what fraction of a total pizza did we eat altogether? . . . Gabriel?"

"Five . . . eighths of a pizza?" Gabriel responds after thinking for a few seconds.

"Good, Gabriel. . . . And, why is it $\frac{5}{8}$ . . . Kevin?"

"Uhhh. . ."

"How many pieces altogether in each pizza?"

"Eight," Kevin answers.

"Good, . . . and how many did we eat, altogether?"

"Five."

"Yes," she smiles at Kevin, "so we ate $\frac{5}{8}$ of one pizza."

Shirley then writes some additional problems on the board, such as $\frac{3}{7} + \frac{4}{7} = ?$ and $\frac{2}{5} + \frac{1}{5} = ?$ and writes $\frac{4}{8} + \frac{2}{8}$ and reviews them as she did with her pizzas.

"Now remember," she emphasizes, "in each of these problems, the two fractions have the same denominator. . . . Be sure to keep that in mind as we continue our study of fractions.

"Now, we're going to shift gears because I've got another, different kind of problem," Shirley continues, pulling out the two cardboard cakes.

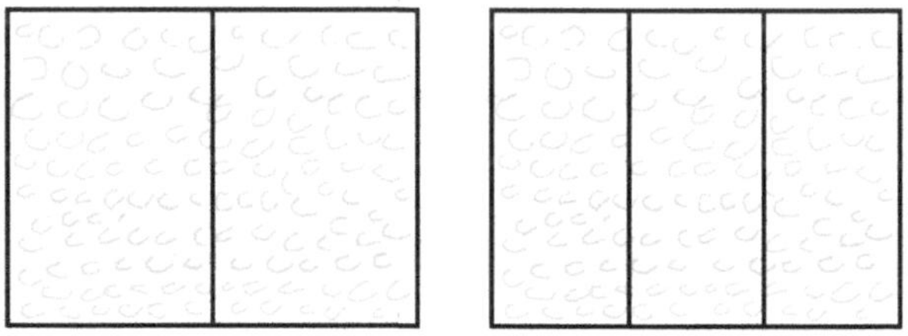

"Now, we have cakes instead of pizza, . . . and I'm still hungry, so I eat this piece," she said, pointing to a third. "Then I go sort of wild and eat this piece too," she adds, pointing to one of the halves. "How much cake have I eaten?"

"A third of one and a half of the other," Tenisha volunteers.

"Makes sense, . . .but is that more than a whole cake, a whole cake, or part of a cake?"

". . . I think less," Adam offers.

"How do you think we could find out for sure?" Shirley wonders. She pauses and then says, "To help us, take two of the sheets of paper that I put on your desks, and carefully fold them like our cakes here."

The students begin, and Shirley helps some of them who have trouble folding their papers into thirds.

"Now we have two whole cakes. Let's think about our problem again. If we eat a third of one and a half of the other one, how much have we eaten altogether? . . . How can we figure that out?"

". . . Let's lay one on top of the other," Jan suggests, after thinking for several seconds.

"Good idea. . . . Go ahead and try it."

"It's less than a whole cake," Tanya offers after peering carefully at the papers.

"How much less?"

The students offer a few uncertain suggestions, and Shirley then asks, "Let's think about the work we've been doing. What did we just review?" She points at the chalkboard.

"Adding up the pizzas," Juan offers.

"And what do we know about them?"

"They have the same-size parts, and these are different," he says, pointing to the cakes.

"Maybe we need to cut them different so they're the same," Enrico suggested.

"Good idea, Enrico. . . . Let me make a suggestion about how we can get them to be the same, using Enrico's idea. . . . Go ahead and shade one part of each of your papers, so you have a third shaded on this one and a half shaded on the other one," Shirley says, pointing to the papers.

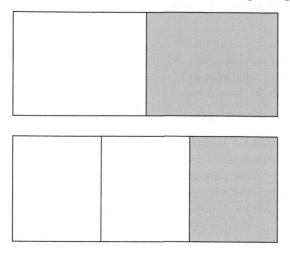

She continues, "How much cake do we have here? . . . Tim?"

"A third."

"Fine," Shirley smiles. "Now, let's all fold our cakes this way." She folds the three-piece cake in half horizontally as she watches the students. "How many pieces do I have altogether now? . . . Karen?"

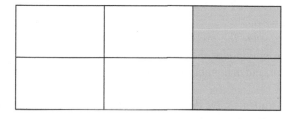

". . . It looks like six."

"Yes. Good, Karen. I saw you actually counting them," Shirley notes and then counts the six squares again out loud. "So what portion is now shaded? . . . Jon?"

"Two sixths."

"Excellent, Jon!" She moves to the chalkboard and writes ⅓ = ⅔.

"Now, how do we know that the ⅓ and the ⅔ are equal?"

"It's the same amount of cake," Dan shrugs.

"Exactly," Shirley smiles.

Shirley continues by having the students divide the two-piece cake in thirds, horizontally, so it appears as follows:

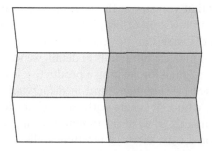

"What do we see here?"

". . . They both have the same number of pieces," Lorraine notes.

"And all the pieces are the same size," Crystal adds.

"Ooh, ooh, I know!" Adam said excitedly. "We've eaten ⅚ of the cake."

"That's an interesting thought, Adam. Would you explain that for us please?"

"It's like the pizza. We have two pieces there, and three pieces there, so it's ⅚ of the pizza, . . . uh cake."

Shirley then models a process for finding equivalent fractions by multiplying the numerator and denominator by the same number, guides the students through two more problems, and then asks, "So, what is the purpose in doing what we've done here? . . . Kelly?"

"To get fractions with the same denominators so we can add them."

"Exactly," Shirley smiles. "Now I'm going to give you the name. They're called EQUIVALENT FRACTIONS."

"Now let's see what we have. What have we been doing here? . . . Toni?"

". . . We're finding equivalent fractions."

"Good, Toni, and why do we want to find them? . . . Gary?"

". . . So we can add fractions when the denominators are not the same."

Shirley praises the class for their good work and then gives them an assignment that involves finding equivalent fractions. "Everyone, do the first one on your sheet, and tell me how much you get when you add ⅔ and ¼."

As the students work the first problem, Shirley walks up and down the rows, checking each student's progress as she goes. Periodically, she stops to point something out to an individual, then moves on.

"Let's see how we did," Shirley suggests when everyone has completed the problem. "What's the first thing you noticed? . . . Michelle?"

". . . The denominators aren't the same."

"Good! So what did we do?"

Some of the students solve the problem without difficulty, but others struggle. With Shirley's guidance they realize that multiplying the numerator and denominator of ⅔ by 4 gives them 8/12, and multiplying the numerator and denominator of ¼ by 3 gives them 3/12, so they can add the 8/12 and the 3/12 to get 11/12.

Shirley then has the students solve the second problem and guides the class through an analysis of it as she did with the first problem. She repeats the process with a third problem.

After reviewing the third problem, she has them work independently on additional fractions problems for the remainder of their time in math. As they do their seat work, she walks up and down the aisles looking over the children's shoulders, offering a few seconds of assistance to different individuals.

Finally, seeing it is 10:59, Shirley says, "It's nearly time for our break. As soon as you've cleaned up around your desks, we'll go."

Shirley demonstrated several essential teaching skills in her instruction. Understanding these essential teaching skills is important for your development as a teacher, because you'll be expected to demonstrate them when you have your own classrooms. In addition, hopefully you will see teachers demonstrating these teaching skills in their classrooms when you go into different classrooms to observe as part of your teacher education program. Grounded in the principles of learning that you saw at the beginning of the chapter, and derived from a long line of classroom research (Good & Brophy, 2003), these essential teaching skills are outlined in Figure 12.3 and discussed in the sections that follow.

Before we discuss the essential teaching skills in detail, we want to emphasize that the personal teacher characteristics essential for creating a productive learning environment—*caring, personal teaching efficacy, positive expectations,* and *modeling and enthusiasm*—also provide a foundation for effective instruction. Teachers with these characteristics create classroom climates that are positive and inviting, they also promote learning, and they use these personal characteristics as a foundation for the essential teaching skills.

Let's turn now to these essential teaching skills.

Figure 12.3 Essential Teaching Skills

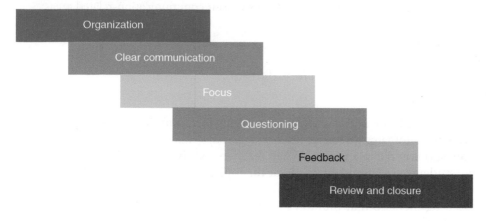

Organization

To understand the role of organization in learning, let's look back at Shirley's lesson. She scheduled math from 10:00 to 11:00 and made the transition from language arts to math in 3 minutes, starting her math lesson at 10:01. She continued the lesson until 10:59; so, of a possible 60 minutes of time allocated to math, she used 58 minutes for instruction. In addition, she had her cardboard pizzas and cakes placed where she could easily access them and distributed the sheets of paper on the students' desks as they turned in their language arts papers. Further, Shirley had taught her students time-saving routines; for instance, they placed their papers on the top of the stacks as they were passed forward, without being reminded to do so.

These examples illustrate **organization,** the set of teacher actions that maximizes the amount of time available for instruction. Teacher actions that promote organization are outlined in Table 12.3.

Less-effective teachers are less well organized, and this detracts from student learning. They spend more time in transitions from one activity to another, failing to start lessons when they're scheduled; they spend valuable class time accessing materials; and their routines are not well established. The result is fewer minutes available for instruction and, ultimately, reduced student learning.

Clear Communication

Effective teaching requires clear communication. The link between effective teacher communication and student achievement is well established (Good & Brophy, 2003; I. Weiss & Pasley, 2004). In addition, the way teachers interact with students influences their motivation, their

TABLE 12.3 Teacher Actions That Promote Organization

Teacher Action	Example
Starting on time	Shirley's students had their math books out and were waiting at 10:01.
Making smooth transitions	Shirley made the transition from language arts to math in 3 minutes.
Preparing materials in advance	Shirley had her cardboard pizzas and cakes easily accessible.
Establishing routines	At Shirley's signal, the students put their paper on the top of the stack without being told specifically to do so.

> **Organization.** The set of teacher actions that maximizes the amount of time available for instruction.

satisfaction with instruction, and their attitudes toward school (Pintrich & Schunk, 2002). Effective and less-effective teachers exhibit differences in four communication-related areas:

- Language clarity
- Thematic lessons
- Transition signals
- Emphasis

Effective teachers think about what they are trying to communicate and say it clearly. **Language clarity** eliminates vague terms (e.g., *perhaps, maybe, might, and so on,* and *usually*) in questions and explanations. When teachers use these terms in their classroom interactions, students are left uncertain about the topics they're studying, and this uncertainty detracts from learning (Shuell, 1996). For example, suppose you ask, "What do well-organized teachers do that promotes learning?" One instructor responds, "Usually, they use their time somewhat better and so on." Another responds, "They use their time well; they begin lessons on time, they have their materials ready, and they have well-established routines." The first response is muddled and uncertain, whereas the second is clear and precise.

Effective teachers also create lessons that are thematic. **Thematic lessons** lead to a specific point, and all parts of a teacher's instruction are related. If the point of the lesson isn't clear, if it is sequenced inappropriately, or if incidental information is interjected without indicating how it relates to the topic, the lesson becomes disconnected and less meaningful for students. Effective teachers keep their lessons on track, minimizing time on matters unrelated to the topic (Leinhardt, 2001).

Effective teachers also use transition signals to connect different parts of their lesson. **Transition signals** are verbal statements within a lesson that indicate to students that one idea is ending and another is beginning and that suggest connections between the two ideas. Shirley signaled a transition when she said, "Now, we're going to shift gears because I've got another, different kind of problem," as she pulled out her cardboard cakes. As another example, an American government teacher might signal a transition by saying, "We've been talking about the Senate, which is one house of Congress. Now we'll turn to the House of Representatives, the second part of Congress." Because students may be at a different place mentally, a transition signal alerts them that the lesson is making a conceptual shift—a move to a new topic—and allows them to adjust and prepare for it.

Not all information in a lesson is equally important; effective teachers use **emphasis**, verbal and vocal cues, and repetition to alert students to important information in a lesson (Jetton & Alexander, 1997). Shirley, for example, used emphasis when she said, "In each of these problems, the two fractions have the same denominator. . . . Be sure to keep that in mind as we continue our study of fractions." When teachers say, "This is very important," or "Listen carefully now," they're using verbal emphasis. Teachers can also give vocal cues—by enunciating certain words or speaking more loudly, for instance—to draw attention to important points.

Teachers' knowledge of content is an important factor in clear communication. When teachers are confident of their own understanding of the topics they teach, communication tends to be clear and precise. When they are less certain, clear communication decreases. They use more vague terms in their questions and explanations, their lessons are less thematic, and they fail to emphasize the most important points in the lesson. If you're uncertain about a topic, you should spend extra time studying, which will then be reflected in clearer language (Eggen & Kauchak, 2007).

Each of the factors in effective communication is grounded in the learning principle, "Learners construct knowledge in an attempt to make sense of their experiences." When teachers use clear language, teach thematic lessons, signal transitions, and emphasize important points, it is easier for students to make sense of lessons and remember the content in a meaningful way.

Language clarity. Teacher talk that omits vague terms in questions and explanations.

Thematic lessons. Lessons in which all parts of a teacher's instruction are related, so that the lesson leads to a specific point.

Transition signals. Verbal statements within a lesson that indicate one idea is ending and another is beginning, and suggest connections between the two ideas.

Emphasis. Verbal and vocal cues and repetition used to alert students to important information in a lesson.

✳ Focus: Attracting and Maintaining Attention

Learning begins with attention; students can't learn lesson content if they aren't paying attention. So, effective teachers plan activities that attract and maintain students' attention.

Shirley's "pizzas," "cakes," and folded pieces of paper acted as a form of **focus**—concrete objects, pictures, models, materials displayed on the overhead, or even information written on the chalkboard that attract and maintain attention during learning activities. High-quality examples, such as those Shirley used in her lesson, are a very effective form of focus. Building lessons around high-quality examples provides students with experiences that they can use to construct their understanding, so, in addition to helping maintain attention, they also serve as the raw material for constructing ideas.

Examples provide a focal point for the lesson and illustrate concrete characteristics of abstract ideas. [Scott Teven/The Stock Connection]

Questioning

In the last 20 years, a major shift in classroom instruction has occurred. In the past, teachers explained topics and students were expected to listen quietly and then work independently at their desks. However, as you saw in our discussion of learning principles, and as expert teachers know, learners are, by nature, cognitively active. To maximize learning, teachers should actively involve students in learning activities, and one of the most effective ways of doing this is through questioning.

Being able to ask effective questions is the most important ability teachers have for guiding student learning (J. Olson & Clough, 2004; Leinhardt & Steele, 2005). A teacher skilled in questioning can determine how much students already know about a topic, encourage learners to rethink their ideas, help them form relationships, involve shy or reticent students, recapture students' wandering attention, promote success, and enhance self-esteem.

With respect to questioning, effective and less-effective teachers differ in four areas:

- Frequency
- Equitable distribution
- Wait-time
- Prompting

Frequency

Questioning frequency refers to the number of questions a teacher asks during a given period of instructional time. Effective teachers ask many more questions than do less-effective teachers, and Shirley's lesson illustrates this point. Instead of relying on explaining and telling as a strategy, Shirley developed her entire lesson through questioning. Students involved in question-and-answer sessions are more attentive than those who listen passively to teacher explanations, and as a result, achievement increases (J. Finn et al., 2003; Leinhardt & Steele, 2005).

Equitable Distribution

Whom should teachers call on during a lesson? One answer might be, "whomever has a hand up." But this might not be the best answer. To begin to investigate this question, let's look again at some dialogue from Shirley's lesson.

Questioning allows teachers to guide student learning while also gauging learning progress. [Richard Hutchings/PhotoEdit Inc.]

> **Focus.** Activities or materials used to attract and maintain attention during lessons.
>
> **Questioning frequency.** Refers to the number of times a teacher asks questions during a given period of instructional time.

Shirley:	*Let's see what we remember about adding fractions. Look at these pizzas. What fraction of one whole pizza did we eat?"* After giving students time to think, she continues, *"How many pieces of the first pizza did we eat? . . . Dean?* (as she displayed the cardboard pizzas).
Dean:	*Three.*
Shirley:	*And how about this pizza? How many pieces did we eat? . . . Kathy?*
Kathy:	*Two.*
Shirley:	*Why did I write ⅜ here and ⅔ there? . . . Omar?* (as she pointed to the fractions she had written on the board).
Omar:	*You have . . . 8 pieces altogether . . . and you ate 3 of them.*
Shirley:	*Good. And what about the second one? How many pieces of that pizza did we eat? . . . Selina?*
Selina:	*Two.*
Shirley:	*So what fraction of a total pizza did we eat altogether? . . . Gabriel?*

In this dialogue, we see that Shirley directed each of her questions to a different student, and in each case, she addressed the student by name. This pattern illustrates **equitable distribution**, the practice of calling on all students—both volunteers and nonvolunteers—as equally as possible (Kerman, 1979). This practice sends an important message to students. By treating students equally, the teacher is saying, "I don't care whether you're a boy or girl, minority or nonminority, high achiever or low achiever, I want you in my classroom, and I want you actively involved. I believe you're capable of learning, and I will do whatever it takes to ensure that you're successful."

When a teacher practices equitable distribution, students believe that the teacher expects them to participate and learn. Perhaps even more important, because the teacher is making this effort, students believe the teacher is genuinely committed to their learning.

Equitable distribution is a powerful tool for promoting both achievement and student motivation (Stipek, 2002). In classrooms where it is practiced, student achievement rises, classroom management problems decrease, and attendance rates go up (Good & Brophy, 2003; Kerman, 1979). Equitable distribution also works at the college level; students who expect to be called on prepare more fully for class, retain more information, and have greater confidence in what they learn (McDougall & Granby, 1996).

Less-effective teachers spend more time lecturing and explaining than do effective teachers, and when they do question, they either call on volunteers or the highest achievers in their classes (S. M. Jones & Dindia, 2004). This subtly communicates that they have lower expectations for nonparticipants and also communicates that they care less about these students (Stipek, 2002).

Wait-Time

Look again at the dialogue between Shirley and her students. In each case, after asking a question, Shirley paused briefly and gave students a few seconds to think before she called on someone. This period of silence after a question is asked and after a student responds is called **wait-time**. Giving students a few seconds to think about their answers makes sense, but in most classrooms, wait-times are very short, often one second or less (Rowe, 1986; R. Stahl et al., 2005). Increasing wait-time to about 3 to 5 seconds positively influences learning in three ways (Rowe, 1986; Tobin, 1987):

- The length and quality of student responses improve.
- Failures to respond are reduced.
- Student participation in general, as well as participation from minority students, improves.

Equitable distribution. The practice of calling on all students—both volunteers and nonvolunteers—as equally as possible.

Wait-time. The amount of time a teacher pauses after asking a question both before and after calling on a student to answer.

Prompting

Equitable distribution is fine, you may be thinking, but what do I do if a student is unable to respond? Prompting provides one alternative. To understand how prompting works, let's look at some additional dialogue from Shirley's lesson.

> Shirley: Why is it [the fraction of the pizza they ate] ⅝? . . . Kevin?
> Kevin: . . .
> Shirley: How many pieces altogether in each pizza?
> Kevin: Eight.
> Shirley: Good, . . . and how many did we eat, altogether?
> Kevin: Five.

Kevin was initially unable to answer correctly, so Shirley provided him with a **prompt**, a teacher question or directive that elicits a student response after the student has failed to answer or has given an incorrect or incomplete answer. The importance of prompting is well documented by research (Good & Brophy, 2003; Shuell, 1996). As with equitable distribution, it communicates that the teacher believes the student is capable and that he or she expects the student to answer.

Less-effective teachers, instead of prompting, tend to turn the question to another student, asking, for instance, "Can someone help Kevin out here?" This communicates that the teacher doesn't believe Kevin is capable of answering and doesn't expect him to do so. This is not a message we want to send students.

This section addresses the fourth item on our beginning-of-chapter survey, "The most effective teachers in today's schools are those who are best able to clearly explain the content they are teaching their students." In fact, quite the opposite is true. The most effective teachers are those best able to involve their students in the learning process through questioning. This doesn't imply that teachers shouldn't be good at explaining; rather, it suggests that teachers' being able to guide students' developing understanding is the essence of effective instruction.

Feedback

Feedback is an important principle of learning; it is also an essential teaching skill. Have you ever been in a class where you had to wait until the midterm exam to find out how you were doing? Have you handed in assignments and had to wait weeks before they were scored and returned? In both instances, you were left uncertain about your learning progress because of the absence of feedback. Effective feedback is immediate and specific, and provides corrective information about the extent to which students' understanding of a topic is valid.

One of the most effective ways of providing feedback is through our interactions with learners. Shirley did this in her prompting of Kevin. She used questioning—and particularly prompting—to provide feedback. This kind of interactive feedback is very effective for promoting learning. It applies the learning principles that we discussed at the beginning of the chapter because it places students in cognitively active roles and guides students' construction (or reconstruction) of understanding.

Review and Closure

Effective teachers communicate lesson themes in a number of ways. One of the most effective of these is through review. **Review** is a summary that helps students link what they have already learned to what will follow in the next learning activity. It can occur at any point in a lesson, although it is most common at the beginning and end.

Beginning reviews help students activate the prior knowledge needed to understand the content of the current lesson. Shirley, for example, reviewed adding fractions with like denominators

Prompt. A teacher question or directive that elicits a student response after the student has failed to answer or has given an incorrect or incomplete answer

Review. A summary that helps students link what they have already learned to what will follow in the next learning activity.

before she began her discussion of equivalent fractions, and this review helped ensure that every-one was on the same page cognitively. Providing students with concrete examples during review increases its effectiveness by providing additional links to what students already know.

Closure is a form of review occurring at the end of a lesson. The purpose of closure is to help students organize what they've learned into a meaningful idea; it pulls the different aspects of the topic together and signals the end of a lesson. To illustrate how Shirley brought her lesson to closure, let's look again at some of the dialogue.

Shirley:	*So, what is the purpose in doing what we've done here? . . . Kelly?*
Kelly:	*To get fractions with the same denominators so we can add them.*
Shirley:	*Exactly. . . . Now I'm going to give you the name. They're called EQUIVALENT FRACTIONS. . . . Now let's see what we have. What have we been doing here? . . . Toni?*
Toni:	*. . . We're finding equivalent fractions.*
Shirley:	*Good, Toni, and why do we want to find them? . . . Gary?*
Gary:	*. . . So we can add fractions when the denominators are not the same.*

Closure. A form of review occurring at the end of a lesson.

Closure summarizes ideas and reminds students of the major goal of the lesson.

exploring diversity

Effective Instruction in Urban Classrooms

In our discussions of urban contexts in earlier chapters, several themes emerged. First, urban students are diverse, with backgrounds from a number of countries and cultures (R. A. Goldstein, 2004; Rosenshine, 2006). Second, many urban learners struggle in school, the result of a number of factors including large schools and crowded classrooms, less-experienced teachers, and inadequate funding and facilities (Armour-Thomas, 2004). These themes have several implications for effective instruction in urban classrooms.

The Need for Examples

As we saw earlier in the chapter, the need for high-quality examples is important for all learners, regardless of context. However, because of the diversity of urban students' prior experiences, high-quality examples are critical when teaching in urban classrooms. These examples help minimize differences in urban students' backgrounds by providing a concrete and common frame of reference for classroom discussions. For example, a science teacher explaining the concept of density might use the following examples:

- A clear plastic glass filled with cotton that can be compressed
- Several different pieces of screening that are the same size but have different numbers of meshes in them
- Bringing several different-sized groups of students to stand in the same area of the classroom.

By using examples such as these in the classroom, the teacher minimizes the need for background experiences and provides a common frame of reference to explore the concept of density. In addition to examples, graphs, models, visuals, and concrete objects are es-pecially valuable for English Language Learners who struggle with both content and language (Echevarria, Powers, & Short, 2006).

Effective urban teachers also attempt to connect their examples to situations with which their students can identify. For example, a world history teacher in an urban high school was discussing the rise of nationalism as an important factor in the events leading up to World War I. The concept was defined in students' textbooks as a feeling of loyalty and devotion to one's country, language, and culture. This definition is both abstract and distant from the world in which these urban students lived. In an attempt to personalize the concept and connect it to students' lives, the teacher related nationalism to the rivalries their athletic teams had with other urban high schools in the area, emphasizing both loyalties within their school as well as competition with other schools. Students started nodding as they began to understand how nationalism could be both a uniting and divisive force. Urban students, like students in general, sometimes wonder how abstract ideas relate to their lives; making explicit links between new content and their day-to-day experiences increases not only learning but also motivation (Rosenshine, 2006).

The Need for Interactive Instruction

When working in challenging environments, teachers have a tendency to revert to instructional strategies that afford them the most control. This often results in the use of an inordinate amount of passive learning activities like lecture and seat work (Duke, 2000; Eggen, 1998). One urban high school student complained,

In my chemistry class, the teacher just keeps going and going and writing on the board. She never stops to ask the class, "Is every-

IN TODAY'S CLASSROOMS: VIDEO

Essential Teaching Skills in an Urban Classroom

To view this video, go to the *Becoming a Professional* DVD included with this text, click on *In Today's Classrooms,* and then this chapter's video: *Essential Teaching Skills in an Urban Classroom.* Answer the questions you'll find on the DVD.

In this video episode, Scott Sowell, a middle school teacher in an urban classroom, demonstrates essential teaching skills in a science lesson.

To answer questions about the video online and receive immediate feedback, go to the Companion Website at www.prenhall.com/kauchak, then to the In Today's Classrooms *module for Chapter 12.* CW

one with me?" She's in her own little world. She never turns around, she just talks to the board, not to us. (Cushman, 2003, p. 8)

Exactly the opposite is needed. "A great deal of classroom research suggests that students need active instruction from their teachers, not solitary work with instructional materials, in order to make good achievement progress" (Brophy, 2004, p. 155).

In a comparison of more- and less-effective urban elementary teachers, researchers found that less-effective teachers interacted with students only 47 percent of the time versus 70 percent of the time for their more-effective counterparts (Waxman, Huang, Anderson, & Welnstein, 1997). Interactive teaching is characteristic of good instruction in general; its importance with urban students is crucial (Barr & Parrett, 2001; Rosenshine, 2006).

A common teacher lament is, "I tried calling on students but they either couldn't or wouldn't answer." This is why concrete examples and questioning skills such as prompting are so important. The examples provide a common focal point and frame of reference for all students; teacher questions help students use those examples to construct meaning. With teacher support and encouragement, urban students can learn to construct and connect ideas, and improved motivation and increased learning will result.

Equitable distribution is also essential in urban classrooms. Nothing better communicates that you expect all students to achieve and that you're holding them accountable for learning than developing lessons with questioning, calling on all students, and prompting them when necessary to ensure that all participate. Making equitable distribution the prevailing pattern in your classroom can do more than anything else to communicate that you believe that all your students can learn and you expect them to do so.

The Need for Practice and Feedback

Effective teaching also provides urban students opportunities to actively try out their developing ideas and receive feedback about them. You saw both at the beginning of the chapter and in our discussion of essential teaching skills that feedback is an essential learning principle, and, as with high-quality examples and interactive questioning, it is even more important when working with urban students. The knowledge different urban students construct is likely to vary considerably because their background experiences tend to be very diverse. This means that detailed discussions of assignments, homework, and quiz and test results are essential when working with urban students. Time spent providing detailed feedback about student work provides a tangible link between you and your students and assists them in constructing new knowledge.

Student success is critical in the process (Brophy, 2004). Because urban students may not have a history of successful school experiences, lack of success can result in frustration for them and can further detract from motivation that may already be low.

By now you might be saying to yourself, "Wait a minute. Aren't these procedures for urban students just good teaching?" If you did, you're absolutely correct. Effective instructional practices for urban students are not qualitatively different from those for "regular" students. The same principles of good teaching that work in the regular classroom also work with urban students. It is, however, all the more critical that teachers apply effective instructional practices conscientiously and thoroughly with urban students. Collectively, these practices provide an instructional safety net that minimizes the possibility for frustration and failure, two factors that are especially damaging for urban students.

Check Your Understanding

3.1 As middle schoolers walk into their geography class, they see a large matrix comparing the climate, geography, and economy of the northern and southern states before the Civil War. As soon as the bell stops ringing, the teacher says, "Write a minimum of two differences each in the geography, climate, and economy columns of the chart." The students begin, and as they're writing, the teacher takes roll. Which of the essential teaching skills does this example best illustrate? Explain.

3.2 Shirley used her cardboard pizzas in her review, and she used her cakes to introduce the topic of *equivalent fractions*. Which essential teaching skill did the use of these materials best illustrate? Explain.

3.3 Identify at least two essential teaching skills that are illustrated in each of the chapters of this book.

For feedback, go to Check Your Understanding *at the end of this chapter.*

> **Making Connections:**
> To deepen your understanding of the topics in this section of the chapter and integrate them with topics you've already studied, go to the *Making Connections* module for Chapter 12 at **www.prenhall.com/kauchak.** Respond to questions 7–10.

Models of Instruction

In addition to essential teaching skills, effective teachers also employ a number of alternate teaching strategies or models in their classrooms. **Models of instruction** are prescriptive approaches to teaching designed to help students acquire a deep understanding of specific forms of knowledge. They are grounded in the principles of learning you saw at the beginning of the chapter, are supported by research, and include sets of steps designed to help students reach specified learning objectives.

Research indicates that no single instructional model is most effective for all students or for helping students reach all learning objectives (Kroesbergen & van Luit, 2002; Marzano, 2003). This research indicates that the final item on our beginning-of-chapter survey, "Rather than exclusively using one particular teaching strategy, effective teachers vary their instruction" is true. Effective teachers use a variety of instructional strategies, depending on the content and students they are teaching (Eggen & Kauchak, 2006). In this section, we examine four instructional models, the first two of which are teacher directed, and the third and fourth, more learner centered. They are:

- Direct instruction
- Lecture-discussion
- Guided discovery
- Cooperative learning

Direct Instruction

Direct instruction is an instructional strategy designed to teach essential knowledge and skills that are needed for later learning (Eggen & Kauchak, 2006), and its effectiveness is well documented by research (Carnine, Silbert, Kame'enui, Tarver, & Jongjohann, 2006; Kroesbergen, van Luit, & Maas, 2004). Understanding equivalent fractions and adding fractions with both like and unlike denominators, which were the focus of Shirley's lesson, are examples of essential knowledge and skills, as are students' acquiring specific writing strategies, chemistry students' learning to balance equations, and geography students' using longitude and latitude to pinpoint locations. Direct instruction is useful when skills can be broken down into specific steps and has

> **Models of instruction.** Prescriptive approaches to teaching designed to help students acquire a deep understanding of specific forms of knowledge.
>
> **Direct instruction.** An instructional strategy designed to teach well-defined knowledge and skills that are needed for later learning.

been found to be particularly effective in working with low achievers and students with exceptionalities (Kroesbergen et al., 2004; Turnbull, Turnbull, Shank, Smith, & Leal, 2007).

Direct instruction ranges from a highly structured, nearly scripted approach (Carnine et al., 2006) to one that is more flexible in its implementation (Eggen & Kauchak, 2006). We discuss the latter here, which typically occurs in four phases, outlined in Table 12.4 and discussed in the following sections.

Shirley used direct instruction in her lesson. Let's see how she implemented each of the phases.

Introduction and Review

Shirley introduced her lesson using her cardboard pizzas as examples. The purpose in using the pizzas was to attract students' attention and pull them into the lesson. She then had students solve problems involving the addition of fractions with like denominators. This review served as the springboard for her lesson on finding equivalent fractions.

The value of introduction and review is well established by research, and although its importance seems obvious, the majority of teacher lessons begin with little or no attempt to attract attention or activate relevant prior knowledge (Brophy, 2004).

Direct instruction provides students with opportunities to practice new knowledge and skills. [Scott Cunningham/Merrill]

Developing Understanding

In the developing understanding phase of the direct instruction model, the teacher models and explains the skill being taught. Developing understanding is perhaps the most important phase of direct instruction, and ironically, it is the one teachers often perform least well. Instead of working to develop student understanding, they often emphasize memorization, fail to ask enough questions, or move too quickly to practice (Rittle-Johnson & Alibali, 1999).

Shirley's lesson was very effective in this phase. She began with her "cakes" and, in the process, asked a great many questions to ensure that her students engaged with and understood the new ideas she presented. She continued providing examples and modeled the

TABLE 12.4 The Phases of Direct Instruction

Phase	Purpose
Introduction and review: Teachers begin with a review of previous work.	• Attract students' attention. • Access learners' prior knowledge.
Developing understanding: Teachers describe and model the skill or guide students to an understanding of the concept. Teachers use many examples and emphasize high levels of student involvement.	• Develop students' understanding of the concept or skill.
Guided practice: Students practice the skill or identify additional examples of the concept, and the teacher provides guidance and detailed feedback.	• Increase students' expertise with the concept or skill.
Independent practice: Students practice on their own.	• Develop students' understanding to the point where they can identify examples of the concept or perform the skill with little effort.

process for finding equivalent fractions by multiplying the numerator and denominator by the same number. She didn't move to guided practice until she was confident that most of her students had a thorough understanding of the process. This is essential for the success of the next phase, guided practice (Kauchak & Eggen, 2007; Kroesbergen et al., 2004).

Guided Practice

Guided practice provides students with opportunities to try out the new skill and for teachers to provide feedback about learning progress. Once Shirley felt most students understood the concept of equivalent fractions and knew how to create them, she assigned three problems that required students to find equivalent fractions and asked them to solve the first one. As they worked, she carefully monitored their progress and then provided detailed feedback about the first problem before asking the students to solve the second one. She repeated this process with both the second and third problems. Had students struggled, she would have had them solve additional problems under her guidance until she believed they were ready to practice independently on their own.

Independent Practice

In the final phase of direct instruction, independent practice, Shirley helped students make the transition from working under her guidance to working on their own. The goal in this phase is for students' understanding to be developed to the point that they can perform the operation with little conscious effort. During independent practice, the teacher reduces the amount of support she gives and shifts responsibility to the students.

Teacher monitoring continues to be important, however. Effective teachers carefully monitor students to assess their developing understanding (Safer & Fleischman, 2005); less-effective teachers are more likely to merely check to see that students are on task (e.g., on the right page and following directions).

Homework is one type of independent practice, and when properly used, it can reinforce students' developing understanding and skills (H. Cooper et al., 2006; Kohn, 2006). *Properly used* means that teachers assign homework that is an extension of what students have studied and practiced in class; that is, it is aligned with learning objectives and learning activities (Bransford et al., 2000). Although grading homework can be time-consuming, teachers should have some mechanism for giving students credit and providing feedback if they are to take it seriously and use it as a learning tool.

Lecture-Discussion

Lecture-discussion is an instructional strategy designed to help students acquire **organized bodies of knowledge**, topics that connect facts, concepts, and principles, and make the relationships among them explicit (Eggen & Kauchak, 2006). For example, when students examine relationships among plot, character, and symbolism in a novel such as *Moby Dick* in literature; study landforms, climate, and economy in different regions of the world in geography; or compare parasitic and nonparasitic worms and how differences between them are reflected in their body structures in biology, they are acquiring organized bodies of knowledge.

Lecture-discussions are designed to overcome the weaknesses of traditional lectures, which include the following:

- Lectures place learners in passive roles. This is inconsistent with the principles of learning that you saw at the beginning of the chapter and is arguably the primary disadvantage of the strategy. Because of the large amounts of teacher talk and passive student roles, lectures are ineffective for attracting and maintaining student attention. We have all sat through mind-numbing lectures with the goal of simply getting the time to pass more quickly.
- Lectures involve one-way communication and don't allow teachers to determine whether or not students are interpreting or learning information accurately.
- Teachers often present too much information in lectures, so much of it is lost before students can make sense of it.

Lecture-discussion. An instructional model designed to help students acquire organized bodies of knowledge and understand the relationships of ideas within them.

Organized bodies of knowledge. Topics that connect facts, concepts, generalizations, and principles, and make the relationships among them explicit.

TABLE 12.5   The Phases of Lecture-Discussions

Phase	Purpose
Introduction and review: The teacher begins with a form of introductory focus and reviews previous work.	• Attract attention. • Access prior knowledge from long-term memory.
Presenting information: The teacher presents information. Presentations are kept short to prevent overloading learners' working memories.	• Acquire knowledge about the topic.
Comprehension monitoring: The teacher asks a series of questions to check learners' understanding.	• Check students' ongoing knowledge constructions. • Put students in active roles. • Begin constructing integrated ideas.
Integration: The teacher asks additional questions to help learners integrate new and prior knowledge.	• Construct integrated ideas that connect concepts, both old and new.

Lecture-discussions help overcome the weaknesses of lectures by interspersing short periods of presenting information with systematic teacher questioning.

As with direct instruction, lecture-discussions exist in four phases, which are outlined in Table 12.5 and discussed in the sections that follow.

Let's see how a 10th-grade American history teacher implements these phases with her students.

Diane Anderson is discussing the events leading up to the American Revolutionary War in her American history high school class. She begins with a review by saying, "About where are we now in our progress?" as she points to a time line above the chalkboard.

"About there," Adam responds, pointing to the middle of the 1700s.

"Yes, good," Diane smiles. "We're almost to the Revolutionary War. However, I would like for us to understand important events that lead up to that war, so we're going to back up a ways, actually, all the way to the early 1600s. When we're finished today, we'll see that the Revolutionary War didn't just happen; there were events that led up to it that made it almost inevitable. . . . That's the important part of history . . . to see how events that happen at one time affect events at other times, and all the way to today.

"For instance," Diane continues, "the conflicts between the British and the French in America became so costly for the British that they began policies in the colonies that ultimately led to the Revolution. That's what we want to begin looking at today. . . . Here we go."

She then begins, "We know that the British established Jamestown in 1607, but we haven't really looked at French expansion into the New World. Let's look again at the map. Here we see Jamestown, but at about the same time, a French explorer named Champlain came down the St. Lawrence River and formed Quebec City, here." She points again to the map. "Over the years, at least 35 of the 50 states were discovered or mapped by the French, and they founded several of our big cities, such as Detroit, St. Louis, New Orleans, and Des Moines." She continues pointing to a series of locations she had marked on the map.

"Now, what do you notice about the location of the two groups?"

After thinking a few seconds, Alfredo offers, "The French had a lot of Canada, . . . and it looks like this country, too," pointing to the north and west on the map.

"It looks like the east was . . . British, and the west was French," Troy adds.

"Yes, and remember, this was all happening at about the same time," Diane continues. "Also, the French were more friendly with the American Indians than the British were. Also, the French had what they called a seigniorial *system, where the settlers were given land if they would serve in the military. So, . . . what does this suggest about the military power of the French?"*

"Probably powerful," Josh suggests. "The people got land if they went in the army."

"And the American Indians probably helped, because they were friendly with the French," Tenisha adds.

"Now, what else do you notice here?" Diane asks, moving her hand back and forth across the width of the map.

"Mountains?" Danielle answers uncertainly.

"Yes, exactly," Diane smiles. "Why are they important? What do mountains do?"

". . . The British were sort of fenced in, and the French could expand and do as they pleased."

"Good. And now the plot thickens. The British needed land and wanted to expand. So they headed west over the mountains and guess who they ran into? . . . Sarah?"

"The French?" Sarah responded.

"Right! And conflict broke out. Now, when the French and British were fighting, why do you suppose the French were initially more successful than the British? . . . Dan?"

"Well, they had that sig . . . seigniorial system, so they were more eager to fight, because of the land and everything."

"Other thoughts? . . . Bette?"

"I think that the American Indians were part of it. The French got along better with them, so they helped the French."

"Okay, good thinking everyone, now let's think about the British. . . . Let's look at some of their advantages." (Adapted from Eggen & Kauchak, 2007)

Let's look now at Diane's efforts to help her students understand events leading up to the Revolutionary War, an organized body of knowledge. She introduced the lesson with a review and attempted to capture students' *attention* by explaining how events in the past influence the way we live today. Then, she *presented information* about Jamestown, Quebec, and French settlements in the present-day United States. After this brief presentation, she used questioning to involve her students in the *comprehension-monitoring* phase. To illustrate this phase, let's look at some of the dialogue from the lesson.

> Diane: Now, what do you notice about the location of the two groups?
> Alfredo: The French had a lot of Canada, . . . and it looks like this country, too (pointing to the north and west on the map).
> Troy: It looks like the east was . . . British, and the west was French.

Diane's questions were intended to actively involve students, check their level of understanding, and help them construct understanding of the body of knowledge. Satisfied with their level of understanding, she returned to presenting information when she said, "Yes, and remember, this was all happening at about the same time." She continued by briefly describing the French seigniorial system and pointing out the friendly relations between the French and American Indians.

Then she again turned back to the students.

> Diane: So, . . . what does this suggest about the military power of the French?
> Josh: Probably powerful. The people got land if they went in the army.
> Tenisha: And the American Indians probably helped, because they were friendly with the French.

The two segments appear similar, but there is an important distinction. In the first, Diane was *monitoring comprehension;* students' responses to the question, "Now, what do you notice about the location of the two groups?" helped her assess their perceptions of what she had presented in the first segment. In the second, she encouraged students to *integrate* different ideas, including the seigniorial system, the relationship between the French and the American Indians, and French military power.

After completing this cycle of *presenting information, monitoring comprehension,* and *integration,* she would repeat the process, with the second integration being broader than the first. Diane's goal for the entire lesson was for her students to understand a complex body of knowledge that represented the cause–effect relationships between the French and Indian Wars and the American Revolutionary War.

The effectiveness of lecture-discussions depends on the quality of discussions during the lesson. As you saw in the discussion of learning principles at the beginning of the chapter, students construct understanding that makes sense to them, so the understanding they construct won't necessarily mirror the way the teacher has organized the body of knowledge. The question-driven discussions allow the teacher to assess the process of knowledge construction and help students reconstruct their understanding when necessary. This is the primary reason lecture-discussion is a more effective instructional model than traditional lecture.

Guided Discovery

Guided discovery is an instructional model designed to teach concepts and relationships among them (Eggen & Kauchak, 2006; Mayer, 2004). When using this strategy, teachers present students with examples, guide them as they attempt to find patterns in the examples, and come to closure when students can describe the idea that the teacher is attempting to teach (Clark & Mayer, 2003; Moreno, 2004). It is often contrasted with "pure" or unstructured discovery, where learners identify patterns and relationships without guidance from a teacher. Research indicates that unstructured discovery is less effective than guided approaches because students don't use time efficiently; without help, students often become lost and frustrated; and this confusion can lead to misconceptions (Clark & Mayer, 2003; Mayer, 2002, 2004). As a result, unstructured discovery is rarely seen in today's classrooms, except in student projects and investigations.

When done well, guided discovery's effectiveness is supported by research: "Guided discovery may take more or less time than expository instruction, depending on the task, but tends to result in better long-term retention and transfer than expository instruction" (Mayer, 2002, p. 68). When using guided discovery, teachers spend less time explaining and more time asking questions, so students tend to be more cognitively active than they are in more teacher-centered approaches (Bay, Staver, Bryan, & Hale, 1992; Moreno & Duran, 2004).

As with direct instruction and lecture-discussion, guided discovery exists in four phases, which are outlined in Table 12.6.

Essential Teaching Skills in an Urban Classroom, which is the *In Today's Classrooms* episode on the DVD that accompanies this text, illustrates a guided discovery lesson. In that episode, Scott's goal is for students to understand Bernoulli's principle, the principle that helps explain how airplanes are able to fly, why shower curtains wrap around people's legs when they're taking a shower, and why cars feel a slight tug when a large truck whisks past them. If you haven't seen the episode, we urge you to watch it before continuing with your reading here so that you'll have a concrete frame of reference for our discussion

Let's look at Scott's lesson in more detail.

> **Guided discovery.** An instructional model designed to teach concepts and relationships among them through the use of examples.

TABLE 12.6 Phases of Guided Discovery

Phase	Learning Component
Introduction and review: The teacher begins with a review and introduction to the topic.	• Attract attention • Activate students' prior knowledge
Developing understanding: The teacher provides examples and guides the students as they identify patterns in the examples.	• Provide experiences from which knowledge will be constructed • Promote social interaction
Closure: The teacher guides the students as they describe the pattern they've identified in the examples.	• Complete construction of understanding of the topic
Application: Students identify additional examples of the concept, or they explain a real-world event on the basis of the rule or principle.	• Apply understanding to the real world

Introduction and Review

Scott began his lesson by reviewing the concept of force and the principle, "Objects move in the direction of a greater force." As with Shirley Barton in her review of adding fractions, his was very effective because in reviewing the concept *force*, he used examples to illustrate force, such as pushing on the board, tugging on the stapler, and blowing on a walkie talkie. Then, he used additional examples to illustrate the principle "Objects move in the direction of the greater force."

Developing Understanding

Scott then had students blow over pieces of paper, between the papers, and through the necks of funnels; each was an example that illustrated Bernoulli's principle. After students worked with each example, Scott asked for observations, such as, "What did you notice when we blew over the top?" The open-ended questions promoted active involvement and helped students begin to develop their understanding.

Scott then drew sketches on the board and had students restate the essential observations and conclusions. Let's look at some dialogue from the lesson that illustrates this process.

> Scott: Was I blowing on the top or the bottom? . . . Rachel? (Referring to the first sketch on the board where students blew over the top of paper)
> Rachel: The top.
> Scott: And what happened there? . . . Heather?
> Heather: The paper rose up.

He did a similar analysis with the second and third examples and then guided students as they formed conclusions.

> Scott: Let's think about the forces acting on these [turning back to the first sketch]. What forces are acting on the paper? . . . Colin?
> Colin: Gravity.
> Scott: And which direction is gravity pulling?
> Colin: Down.
> Scott: What other force is acting on the paper? . . . William?
> William: Air [pointing up].
> Scott: How do you know it's pushing up?
> William: The paper moved up.

Through questioning, teachers help students analyze patterns in the examples they encounter to form abstractions, such as concepts, generalizations, and principles. This occurs in the closure phase of the model.

Closure

Scott then moved the lesson to closure, beginning the process by saying, "Now let's look at the forces and where we blew. Study the drawings carefully, and see what kind of relationship exists between the two," and he continued to use questioning to guide students' developing understanding. Teacher questioning in this phase continues to be essential (Moreno, 2004; Moreno & Duran, 2004).

Closure is particularly important when using guided discovery because the instruction is less explicit and the direction the lesson is taking is less obvious than it is with either direct instruction or lecture-discussion. Articulating the definition of a concept or stating the principle, as was the case in Scott's lesson, helps eliminate any uncertainty that may remain in students' thinking about the specific content focus of the lesson.

Application

Applying understanding to new and real-world situations is the final phase of a guided discovery lesson. For example, Scott could ask the students to explain how Bernoulli's principle helps us understand why airplanes can fly. He would then guide them to conclude that the force the air exerts on the top of the wing is less than on the bottom, since the air is moving more rapidly over the top. This causes the wing to lift and the airplane to fly.

The application phase in guided discovery serves a function similar to independent practice in direct instruction and to integration in lecture-discussion. In all three cases, the goal is for the students to develop a deeper understanding of the topic they've studied.

Cooperative Learning

A kindergarten teacher is teaching her students basic shapes. After explaining and illustrating each with cardboard shapes, she divides the class into groups of two and asks each group to find examples of circles, squares, and triangles in their own classroom. When the class comes back together, students share their examples.

A middle school math teacher is teaching how to solve word problems involving areas of different geometric shapes. She divides the class into teams of four students and asks each team to solve the next few problems. Students in each team take turns explaining their solutions to the problems. Later, the teams take turns at the board explaining how they solved the different problems.

A senior high English teacher is reviewing literary devices such as simile, metaphor, personification, and alliteration. He assigns a scene from Shakespeare's Julius Caesar *and asks students in groups of two to identify as many of these devices as they can. The whole class compares their findings after 15 minutes.*

What do these lessons have in common? They are all examples of cooperative learning strategies being employed at different grade levels. **Cooperative learning** is a set of instructional strategies used to help learners meet specific learning and social interaction objectives in structured groups. As its name implies, it relies on cooperative social interaction to facilitate knowledge construction, so it is based on the learning principle "Learning is enhanced by social interaction." It has become one of the most popular instructional models in schools today; one study found that 93 percent of elementary teachers used some form of cooperative learning in their classrooms (Antil, Jenkins, Wayne, & Vadasy, 1998).

When implemented effectively, cooperative learning involves all students, which can be difficult in large groups. In whole-class discussions, less-confident students may get few chances to participate, so they often drift off.

Cooperative learning can also be effective for teaching students to collaborate in learning (Payton, Munro, O'Brien, & Weissberg, 2006). By participating in cooperative learning activities, students learn to understand the needs and feelings of others as well as how to build on the ideas of others in constructing knowledge. Advocates also argue that groups of learners co-construct more powerful understandings than individuals do alone, affirming the maxim "Two heads are better than one" (Summers, Woodruff, Tomberlin, Williams, & Svinicki, 2001). This external, co-constructed knowledge can then be internalized by individual students, facilitating learning (Brenner, 2001).

Though the specific form varies with the specific model being used, most researchers agree that cooperative learning consists of students working together in groups small enough (typically two to five) so that everyone can participate in a clearly assigned task

Cooperative learning activities encourage knowledge construction through social interaction. [Will Hart/PhotoEdit Inc.]

Cooperative learning. A set of instructional strategies used to help learners meet specific learning and social interaction objectives in structured groups.

(D. Johnson & Johnson, 2006). They also agree that cooperative learning shares at least four other features:

- Learning objectives direct the groups' activities.
- Social interaction is emphasized.
- Students are held individually accountable for their understanding.
- Learners depend on one another to reach objectives.

The last characteristic is important because it emphasizes the crucial role that peer cooperation plays in learning (D. Johnson & Johnson, 2006). Accountability is also essential because it keeps students focused on the objectives and reminds them that learning is the purpose of the activity.

Unlike the first three models we discussed, cooperative learning activities don't follow a specific set of steps or phases. However, successful implementation of cooperative learning activities requires careful teacher thought and planning. We examine factors influencing its success in the following sections.

Introducing Cooperative Learning

Introducing students to cooperative learning requires careful planning (Gillies, 2000; Terwel et al., 2001). Poorly organized activities can result in less learning than whole-group lessons (Brophy, 2006).

Suggestions for initially organizing cooperative learning activities include the following:

- Seat group members together, so they can move back and forth from group work to whole-class activities with little disruption.
- Have learning materials ready for easy distribution to each group.
- Introduce students to cooperative learning with short, simple tasks, and make objectives and directions clear.
- Specify the amount of time students have to accomplish the task (and keep it relatively short).
- Monitor groups while they work.
- Require that students produce a product as a result of the cooperative learning activity (e.g., written answers to specific questions).

These characteristics maximize the time available for learning and provide a focal point for students' cooperative learning efforts.

Cooperative Learning Strategies

Different models of cooperative learning are all grounded in the learning principle "Learning is enhanced by social interaction," but each is designed to accomplish different objectives. Different models are outlined in Table 12.7. Other cooperative learning strategies exist, and although they differ in format, all are grounded in this basic principle.

As we said at the beginning of the chapter, our goal in writing it is for you to see examples of effective planning and implementation of instruction. We realize that you won't be able to implement the essential teaching skills or the teaching models described in this chapter after one reading. These are sophisticated abilities that require time and effort to learn. They are intended, instead, to introduce you to effective instruction, so you have ideals for which you can look when you observe in classrooms and toward which you can strive as you move toward becoming a true professional.

Making Connections
To deepen your understanding of the topics in this section of the chapter and integrate them with topics you've already studied, go to the *Making Connections* module for Chapter 12 at **www.prenhall.com/kauchak**. Respond to questions 11–13.

TABLE 12.7 Cooperative Learning Models

Model	Description	Example
Reciprocal Questioning	Pairs work together to ask and answer questions about a lesson or text	Teacher provides question stems, such as "Summarize . . ." or "Why was . . . important?" and students use the stems to create specific questions about the topic.
Scripted Cooperation	Pairs work together to elaborate on each other's thinking	*Math:* First member of a pair offers a problem solution. The second member then elaborates, and the process is repeated. *Reading:* Pairs read a passage and the first member offers a summary. The second elaborates, and the process continues.
Jigsaw II	Individuals become expert on subsections of a topic and teach it to others in their group	One student studies the geography of a region; another, the economy; a third, the climate. Each attends "expert" meetings, and the "experts" then teach their content to others in their group.
Student Teams Achievement Divisions (STADs)	Social interaction is used to help students learn facts, concepts, and skills	The independent-practice phase of direct instruction is replaced with team study, during which team members check and compare their answers. Team study is followed by quizzes, and individual improvement points lead to team awards.

teaching in an era of reform

Teacher-Centered Versus Learner-Centered Instruction

How active a role should teachers play in directing student learning? As we saw in the previous section, different instructional models suggest different roles for teachers as they guide and assist student learning. Historically, classroom instruction was *teacher centered*, which means that teachers carefully specify goals, present the content to be learned, and then direct learning activities (Shuell, 1996). Lecture is an example, as are traditional forms of direct instruction. Both define a central teacher role in presenting information and monitoring learning progress.

Criticisms of teacher-centered instruction led to a wave of reform, resulting in what is commonly called *learner-centered instruction*, in which teachers guide learners toward an understanding of the topics they study, rather than telling or lecturing. This was the approach that Scott Sowell employed in using guided discovery to teach Bernoulli's principle. Prominent professional publications emphasizing this approach to instruction include *How Students Learn: Reforming Our Schools Through Learner-Centered Education*, published by the American Psychological Association in 1998, and *The Right to Learn*, which was written by well-known Columbia University educator Linda Darling-Hammond and published in 1997.

The Issue

Critics of teacher-centered instruction argue that it is based on outdated views of learning that emphasize teacher actions rather than student understanding (S. Lee, 2006; Pogrow, 2006). The following episode, in which a teacher is attempting to help her third graders understand place value, illustrates this criticism:

The teacher, based on the directions given in the teacher's manual, begins by putting 45 tally marks on the chalkboard and circles four groups of 10.

Teacher: *How many groups of 10 do we have there, boys and girls?*
Children: *4.*
Teacher: *We have 4 groups of 10, and how many left over?*
Children: *5.*
Teacher: *We had 4 tens and how many left over?*
Beth: *4 tens.*
Sarah: *5.*

(continued)

Teacher:	*5. Now, can anybody tell me what number that could be? We have 4 tens and 5 ones. What is that number? Ann?*
Ann:	*(Remains silent)*
Teacher:	*If we have 4 tens and 5 ones, what is that number?*
Ann:	*9.*
Teacher:	*Look at how many we have there (points to the 4 groups of ten) and 5 ones. If we have 4 tens and 5 ones we have? (slight pause) 45.*
Children:	*45.*
Teacher:	*Very good. (T. Wood, Cobb, & Yackel, 1992, p. 180)*

As the dialogue suggests, Ann and probably many others in the class didn't understand place value, but the teacher did little to increase their understanding. Once students gave the desired response, they were reinforced with "Very good," and the lesson moved on, despite the fact that students didn't really understand the point of the lesson. This happens all too often in teacher-centered instruction that fails to actively engage students' minds.

Critics also point to research indicating that student verbalization or overt performance at the expense of understanding occurs in many classrooms (Goodlad, 1984; Opdenakker & Van Damme, 2006). Critics contend that all too often teacher-centered approaches to instruction make learners passive observers during instruction (J. Wallace & Wildly, 2004) and that "the most effective learning takes place when students . . . play an active role in making sense of ideas" (Kohn, 1999, p. 43).

Learner-centered instruction proponents argue further that this approach focuses on learning and individual learners to a greater extent than does teacher-centered instruction (S. Lee, 2006), and they point to research indicating that a learner-centered teaching style is particularly effective with low-ability students (Opdenakker & Van Damme, 2006). In addition, learner-centered instruction not only teaches content but also develops critical thinking skills that students can use in their lives (Kuhn, 2005; I. Winn, 2005).

Critics of learner-centered instruction counter by saying that the approach is one more example of widespread "dumbing down" of the curriculum, that learning basic skills is abandoned in favor of fuzzy thinking, and self-esteem is emphasized instead of understanding (Battista, 1999; Schoen, Fey, Hirsch, & Coxford, 1999). They defend teacher-centered instruction by asserting that the lack of understanding so prominent in classrooms is not the result of teacher-centered instruction per se; it is with teachers' inability to implement it effectively. When teacher-centered instruction is done effectively, they argue, none of the criticisms is valid, and they point to research indicating that teacher-centered approaches, such as direct instruction, can be effective in a variety of situations (Carnine et al., 2006). Because of these criticisms, as well as pressures to help students meet accountability standards, a pendulum shift back in the direction of teacher-centered instruction is currently occurring (Pogrow, 2006). Whether this pendulum shift will result in increased student learning is currently unclear.

You Take a Position

Now it's your turn to take a position on the issue. State in writing whether you favor learner-centered instruction or teacher-centered instruction, and provide a two-page rationale for your position.

For additional references and resources, go to the Companion Website at **www.prenhall.com/kauchak**, *then to the* Teaching in an Era of Reform *module for Chapter 12. You can respond online or submit your response to your instructor.*

Check Your Understanding

4.1 Using the principles of learning presented at the beginning of the chapter as a basis, explain why the introduction phase is important in direct instruction, lecture-discussion, and guided discovery.

4.2 Which phase of direct instruction is most important for ensuring successful independent practice? Explain.

4.3 We said, "When guided discovery is done well, research supports its effectiveness." What is necessary in order for instruction to be "done well"? Explain.

4.4 A teacher places her third graders in groups of three and gives each group magnets and a packet including a dime, spoon, aluminum foil, rubber band, wooden pencil, paper clip, and nails. She tells the groups to experiment with the magnets and items for 10 minutes and write their observations on paper. As they work, she answers questions and makes comments. The class as a whole group discusses the results. How effectively did the teacher begin this cooperative learning activity with her students? Cite evidence from the example to support your conclusion.

 For feedback, go to Check Your Understanding *at the end of this chapter.*

decision making

Defining Yourself as a Professional

You're a middle school life science teacher beginning a unit on the different body systems, such as the skeletal, the circulatory, the digestive, and the muscular systems. You plan to begin with the skeletal system, and you want your students to understand the relationship between the structures and the functions of the different parts of the skeleton, such as understanding that the skull is essentially solid because it protects the brain, which is the most important organ in the body; the rib cage exists to protect other important organs, such as the heart and lungs; and the leg bones are the size and shape they are because they support the body as we stand and move.

What models of instruction could you use to help you reach your goals? Explain why you would use those models.

To respond to this question online and receive immediate feedback, go to the Decision Making module for Chapter 12 on the Companion Website at www.prenhall.com/kauchak.

Meeting Your Learning Objectives

1. **Describe the principles of cognitive learning theory, and identify examples of the principles in practice.**
   * Cognitive learning theory suggests that learning depends on experiences; people construct knowledge in an attempt to make sense of those experiences; knowledge that is constructed depends on and builds on what learners already know; social interaction enhances learning; and learning requires practice and feedback.
   * Teachers apply these learning principles when they use high-quality examples in their teaching, promote high levels of teacher–student and student–student interaction, give students a chance to practice their newly acquired knowledge and skills, and make assessment an integral part of the teaching–learning process.

2. **Describe essential steps in planning for instruction.**
   * Planning for instruction involves identifying topics, specifying learning objectives; preparing and organizing learning activities; designing assessments; and ensuring that instruction is aligned, that is, ensuring that learning activities and assessments are consistent with objectives.
   * Finding or creating high-quality examples or problems is the most important part of preparing and organizing learning activities, and this is a major reason that specifying clear learning objectives is so important. If objectives are clear, then teachers know what information the examples should contain, and they can then attempt to find or create them.
   * Planning in a standards-based environment often requires teachers to first interpret the standard. Once the standard is clearly understood, the teacher can construct learning objectives and design learning activities.

3. **Explain how essential teaching skills contribute to learning.**
   * Effective teachers are well organized, which means they begin their lessons on time, have their materials prepared and ready, and have well-established routines in their classrooms.
   * Effective teachers communicate clearly, use focus to attract students' attention, involve students through questioning, provide informative feedback, and use reviews to activate students' prior knowledge.

(continued)

4. Explain relationships between principles of learning and different phases of models of instruction.
   - Each of the models of instruction begins with an introduction and review. This phase activates students' prior knowledge and is based on the learning principle "Knowledge that is constructed depends and builds on knowledge that learners already possess."
   - In the *developing-understanding* phases of the models, learners acquire experiences that they use as a basis for constructing the knowledge about the topic being taught.
   - Each of the models strongly emphasizes social interaction between the teacher and students and the students with each other, which is grounded in the learning principle "Learning is enhanced by social interaction."

Important Concepts

assessment	instructional alignment
closure	language clarity
cognitive learning theories	learning objective
cooperative learning	lecture-discussion
direct instruction	models of instruction
effective instruction	organization
emphasis	organized bodies of knowledge
equitable distribution	prompt
essential teaching skills	questioning frequency
feedback	review
focus	thematic lessons
guided discovery	transition signals
high-quality examples	wait-time

Developing as a Professional

Preparing for Your Licensure Exam

This exercise will provide you with practice answering questions similar to the Praxis™ Principles of Learning and Teaching Exam as well as your state-specific licensure exam. Read the following case study, and answer the questions that follow.

Diane Smith, a fifth-grade teacher at Oneida Elementary, is beginning a language arts lesson on comparative and superlative adjectives. She wants her students to understand and to be able to use comparative and superlative adjectives correctly in their writing.

She begins by providing students with a written paragraph in which several adjectives are embedded. She has the students identify the adjectives and the nouns they modify, and then turns to her lesson for the day by having two of her students hold their pencils up, so everyone can see them.

Diane: Candice and Daniel, hold your pencils up high, so everyone can see. What do you notice about the pencils? . . . Mary?

Mary: Candice's is red and Daniel's is blue.

Diane: OK, what else? . . . Sheila?

Sheila: You write with them.
Diane: Indeed you do! What else, Kevin?
Kevin: Candice's is longer.
Diane: That's true. Does everyone see that? Hold them up again.

Candice and Daniel hold their pencils up again, and Diane moves to the chalkboard and writes:

*Candice has a long pencil.   Candice has a longer pencil than
Daniel has.*

Diane: Now, let's look at Matt and Aaron. What do you notice about their hair? . . .
          Maddie?
Maddie: Matt's is longer than Aaron's.
Diane: Good, Maddie. What else? What about the color? . . . Nicholas?
Nicholas: Aaron's is brown, and Matt's is blond.
Diane: Okay, good, Nicholas. So which one has darker hair?
The Class: Aaron!

Diane then writes five more sentences on the board:

*Candice has a long pencil.   Candice has a longer pencil than Daniel
has.*

Aaron has brown hair.   Aaron has darker hair than Matt has.

Matt has blond hair.

Diane: Now let's look at the adjectives in the sentences on the left compared to
          the adjectives in the sentences on the right. How do they compare?
          Heather?
Heather: The adjectives in the sentences on the right have an "er" on the end of
          them.

Diane guides the students to the conclusion that comparative adjectives have an "er" on the end of them and then repeats the process for superlative adjectives. Next, she gives the students an assignment in which they are to write a paragraph that includes at least two examples of comparative adjectives and two examples of superlative adjectives. The students complete their paragraphs by the end of their language arts time. Diane collects the paragraphs and discusses them with the class the next day. At the end of the week, Diane gives a quiz in which the students have to identify examples of comparative and superlative adjectives embedded in a written paragraph and also write a paragraph of their own that includes examples of each. (Adapted from Eggen & Kauchak, 2007, p. 124)

1. Was Diane's instruction aligned? Explain why it was or was not.

2. Which model of teaching is best illustrated in Diane's instruction? Explain.

3. Assess Diane's questioning. Support your assessment with information taken directly from the case study.

4. Explain how Diane applied each of the learning principles presented at the beginning of the chapter in her lesson.

To receive feedback on your responses to these exercises, go to the Companion Website at www.prenhall.com/kauchak, then to the Preparing for Your Licensure Exam *module for Chapter 12.*

Discussion Questions

1. Why is the practice of calling on volunteers to answer a question so prevalent? What are its advantages? What are its disadvantages?

2. How does the importance of the following essential teaching skills vary with grade level or content area: focus, questioning, feedback, and review and closure?

3. Many teachers lecture instead of guiding their students to their goals using questioning. Why do you think this is the case?

4. Which of the four instructional models is easiest to implement? Why? Most difficult or challenging?

5. How does the effectiveness of the four instructional models vary with grade level? Are some of these more effective or useful for certain content areas? Which and why?

Developing as a Professional: Online Activities

Going Into Schools

Go to the Companion Website at *www.prenhall.com/kauchak*, and click on the *Going Into Schools* module for Chapter 12. You will find a number of school-based activities that will help you link chapter content to the schools in which you work.

Virtual Field Experience: Using Teacher Prep to Explore the Profession

If you would like to participate in a Virtual Field Experience, access the Teacher Prep Website at *www.prenhall.com/teacherprep*. After logging in, complete the following steps:

1. Click on "Video Classroom" on the left panel of the screen.

2. Go to "General Methods."

3. Finally, select "Module 9: Cooperative Learning and the Collaborative Process." This video provides you with a concrete example of a cooperative learning model being used in an elementary math class. Answer the questions that follow the video clip.

Online Portfolio Activities

To develop your professional portfolio, further apply your understanding of chapter content, and address the INTASC standards, go to the Companion Website at *www.prenhall.com/kauchak*, then to the *Online Portfolio Activities* for Chapter 12. Complete the suggested activities.

Check Your Understanding

1.1 **Describe the principles on which cognitive learning theories are based.**

The principles on which cognitive learning theory is based are
- *Learning depends on experiences.* This principle is evident in our everyday lives. Learning to drive is a simple example. If our experience with driving involves only vehicles with automatic transmissions, our ability to drive is less fully developed than it would be if we have experiences driving cars with both automatic and standard transmissions.
- *Learners construct—they do not record—knowledge in an attempt to make sense of those experiences.* Learners don't behave like tape recorders, keeping an exact copy of what they hear or read in their memories. Instead, they mentally modify the experiences to make sense of them.

- *Knowledge that is constructed depends on and builds on knowledge that learners already possess.* People construct understanding based on what they already know. For example, many people believe our summers (in the northern hemisphere) are warmer than our winters because we are closer to the sun in the summer. (We, in fact, are slightly farther away, but the sun's rays are more direct.) This idea is based on knowing that as we move closer to an open fire or a hot stove burner, we get warmer.
- *Learning is enhanced by social interaction.* As people discuss ideas, understanding that they wouldn't have acquired on their own is constructed. This is consistent with the old adage "Two heads are better than one."
- *Learning requires practice and feedback.* People learn to do well only what they practice doing. Learning also requires feedback that gives them information about the validity of their understanding.

1.2 **You and a friend are trying to install a sound card in your computer, but you're a little uncertain about how to do it. You open the cabinet, look inside, and as you talk about how to proceed, she suggests looking to see where the speakers are attached. "Good idea," you say, and you easily install the card. Which principle of learning is best illustrated by this example?**

This illustrates the principle "Learning is enhanced by social interaction" You have a problem, discuss it, and solve it during the course of the discussion.

1.3 **Research indicates that properly designed homework increases learning (Cooper, Robinson, & Patall, 2006; Kohn, 2006). To which principle of learning is this research most closely related?**

Homework is a form of practice, so it most closely relates to the principle "Learning requires practice and feedback." Properly designed homework means that the homework is directly related to teachers' learning objectives and learning activities.

2.1 **What are the five essential steps in planning for instruction?**

The five steps involved in planning for instruction consist of the following:
1. *Select topics.* Standards, curriculum guides, textbooks, and the teacher's professional knowledge are sources that help guide this decision.
2. *Specify learning objectives.* Though the format for preparing learning objectives varies, the important aspect of preparing learning objectives is being clear about what you want students to know, to understand, or to be able to do.
3. *Prepare and organize learning activities.* Finding or creating examples, as Shirley Barton did with her "pizzas" and "cakes," and then sequencing the examples is the primary process involved in preparing and organizing learning activities.
4. *Prepare assessments.* Assessments should be created during planning instead of after learning activities have been completed.
5. *Ensure instructional alignment.* Instructional alignment means that teachers are careful to ensure that their learning activities and assessments are consistent with their objectives.

2.2 **Planning in a standards-based environment involves one additional step beyond the planning steps described in this section of the chapter. What is that additional step?**

When teachers' planning involves standards, the first step is to interpret the standard. Descriptions of standards vary; some are very specific, whereas others are quite general. When working with a standard described in general terms, teachers must first make a decision about what the standard means, then follow the rest of the planning steps—that is, plan learning activities and assessments.

2.3 **Classify the following objectives into one of the cells of the taxonomy table in Figure 12.2, and explain your classification: (1) Students will identify examples of figures of speech such as similes, metaphors, and personifications in written paragraphs. (2) Students will write original paragraphs that include those figures of speech.**

Because figures of speech are concepts, and being able to identify examples of them indicates understanding, the first objective would be classified in the cell where conceptual knowledge *intersects with* understand.

Writing paragraphs involves a procedure, and the fact that they must be original involves the cognitive process create, *so the second objective would be classified in the cell where* procedural knowledge *intersects with* create.

3.1 **As middle schoolers walk into their geography class, they see a large matrix comparing the climate, geography, and economy of the northern and southern states before the Civil War. As soon as the bell stops ringing, the teacher says, "Write a minimum of two differences each in the geography, climate, and economy columns of the chart." The students begin, and as they're writing, the teacher takes roll. Which of the essential teaching skills does this example best illustrate? Explain.**

Organization is the essential teaching skill best illustrated in this example. The teacher began her class right on time, and her chart was prepared and waiting when the students walked into the room.

3.2 **Shirley used her cardboard pizzas in her review, and she used her cakes to introduce the topic of *equivalent fractions*. Which essential teaching skill did the use of these materials best illustrate? Explain.**

Focus is the essential teaching skill best illustrated by Shirley's use of the pizzas and cakes. Each was an example that Shirley used to attract and maintain students' attention.

3.3 **Identify at least two essential teaching skills that are illustrated in each of the chapters of this book.**

The two essential teaching skills that are best illustrated in each chapter are feedback and review and closure. For example, when you go to Appendix A, we provide you with feedback for all of the "Check Your Understanding" questions, and when you go to the book's Companion Website, you have feedback for the "Making Connections" questions and the "Preparing for Your Licensure Exam" questions that appear at the end of the chapter.

In the "Meeting Your Learning Objectives" section of each chapter, we provide you with a review of the chapter's contents, which is aligned with the learning objectives.

We also attempt to model effective communication in our writing. We try to use clear language; emphasize important points with figures, tables, bulleted lists, and marginal definitions; and develop the chapters in thematic ways.

4.1 **Using the principles of learning presented at the beginning of the chapter as a basis, explain why the introduction phase is important in direct instruction, lecture-discussion, and guided discovery.**

One of the learning principles says, "Knowledge that is constructed depends on and builds on knowledge that learners already possess." The introduction phase activates students' prior knowledge, which then serves as a springboard for understanding the topic being taught.

4.2 **Which phase of direct instruction is most important for ensuring successful independent practice? Explain.**

The developing-understanding phase is most important for ensuring successful independent practice, and it is in this phase that we see the most difference between effective and ineffective teachers. If the developing-understanding phase is ineffective, both guided practice and independent practice will be difficult and confusing. Remember, independent practice strengthens earlier understanding; it does not teach the skill. If teachers have to provide a great deal of explanation during independent practice, error rates increase and student achievement decreases.

4.3   **We said, "When guided discovery is done well, research supports its effectiveness." What is necessary in order for instruction to be "done well"? Explain.**

If instruction is done well, the teacher's objectives are clear, and the learning activity is aligned with the objectives. Also, the teacher carefully monitors students' thinking throughout and intervenes early enough to prevent misconceptions, but not so soon as to reduce opportunities for constructing understanding.

4.4   **A teacher places her third graders in groups of three, gives each group magnets and a packet including a dime, spoon, aluminum foil, rubber band, wooden pencil, paper clip, and nails. She tells the groups to experiment with the magnets and items for 10 minutes and write their observations on paper. As they work, she answers questions and makes comments. The class as a whole group discusses the results. How effectively did the teacher begin this cooperative learning activity with her students? Cite evidence from the example to support your conclusion.**

She introduced cooperative learning quite effectively. Her task was short and simple, it was clear and specific (write observations on paper), the written observations provided a product, and she monitored the students' work. We have no evidence about them moving into and out of the groups or about the amount of time they had to work.

School Law: Ethical and Legal Influences on Teaching

9

School Law: Ethical and Legal Influences on Teaching

Chapter Outline

Law, Ethics, and Teacher Professionalism
Limitations of Laws
Ethical Dimensions of Teaching

The U.S. Legal System
Federal Influences
State and Local Influences
The Overlapping Legal System

Teachers' Rights and Responsibilities
Teacher Employment and the Law
Academic Freedom
Copyright Laws
Teacher Liability
Child Abuse
Teachers' Private Lives

Religion and the Law
Prayer in Schools
Religious Clubs and Organizations
Religion in the Curriculum
Teaching About Religion in the Schools

Students' Rights and Responsibilities
Students' Freedom of Speech
Permissible Search and Seizure
Student Records and Privacy
Corporal Punishment
Students' Rights in Disciplinary Actions
Students With AIDS

Learning Objectives

After you have completed your study of this chapter you should be able to:

1. Explain the differences between legal and ethical influences on the teaching profession.

2. Describe the U.S. legal system in terms of federal, state, and local influences on teaching.

3. Describe teachers' legal rights and responsibilities.

4. Discuss the legal implications of religion in the schools.

5. Explain students' legal rights and responsibilities.

Case Studies

 Elementary

 Middle

 Secondary

At this point in your teacher-preparation program, legal issues may seem distant, unrelated to your life as a beginning teacher, and perhaps not very interesting. Imagine, however, that you're an elementary teacher and are called to the main office to talk with a parent. Can you leave your class unsupervised? Or you're a high school teacher and you find a poem that strikes you as a powerful and moving commentary on love. Do you dare share it with your students without their parents' approval? Perhaps you're a science teacher, and you've discovered a program on the Internet that you would like to use in your classes. Can you legally download and duplicate the information? As you read the following case studies, think about the different ways that legal issues influence the lives of teachers.

Jason Taylor is a science teacher in a suburban school in the Pacific Northwest. The town in which he teaches is considering an open-space initiative that will limit urban growth. Environmentalists support the law because they believe it will help to preserve local farms and wildlife habitat in the area; business concerns in the town oppose it because of its potential to curtail economic growth. Jason talks about the initiative in class, explaining how it will help the environment. At the end of his presentation, he mentions that he is head of a local action committee and that interested students can receive extra credit for passing out fliers after school.

Some parents complain to the principal, claiming that school time shouldn't be devoted to political activity. When the principal calls in Jason to talk about the problem, Jason is adamant about his right to involve students in local politics, claiming that a part of every course ought to be devoted to civic awareness and action. The principal, unconvinced, points out that Jason was hired to teach science, not social studies, and warns that persisting on this path could cause Jason to lose his job.

 Sasha Brown looks at the two folders in front of her and frowns. Her job is to recommend one of two students from her school for a prestigious science and math scholarship to the state university. Although the decision will ultimately be made by a committee she'll be on, she knows that her recommendation will carry a lot of weight because she is chair of the math department.

One of the candidates, Brandon, is a bright, conscientious student who always scores at the top of his class. The son of a local engineer, he has a good grasp of mathematical concepts. The other candidate, Sonia, is probably not as strong conceptually but often solves problems in creative and innovative ways. She's also a female—and a female hasn't won this award in its 6-year history. In addition, Sasha knows that Sonia comes from a single-parent family and really needs the scholarship.

What would you do in Jason's position? How about Sasha's? What external guidelines exist to guide you, and how do these dilemmas relate to teacher professionalism? We address these and other questions in this chapter.

Before continuing with your study of the chapter, take a few minutes to respond to the following survey. We address each of the items as the chapter unfolds.

professional knowledge: test yourself!

For each item, circle the number that best represents your thinking. Use the following scale as a guide.

1 = Strongly disagree
2 = Disagree
3 = Agree/disagree
4 = Agree
5 = Strongly agree

1. Teachers have the legal right to determine what is taught in their classroom.

    1   2   3   4   5

2. Teachers are responsible for the safety of the students in their classroom.

    1   2   3   4   5

3. Teachers are held to the same moral standards as other citizens.

    1   2   3   4   5

4. The law prohibits any form of prayer in the schools.

    1   2   3   4   5

5. Corporal punishment in schools is prohibited by law.

    1   2   3   4   5

This is available in a downloadable format on the Companion Website for personal portfolio use.

Law, Ethics, and Teacher Professionalism

Professionals are responsible for making decisions in ill-defined situations, they have the autonomy to do so, and they use their professional knowledge as a basis for making the decisions. Understanding the legal and ethical aspects of their profession and their professional rights and responsibilities is an important part of this professional knowledge. However, research indicates that teachers' knowledge in this area is often weak, and as a result, they are ill-equipped to deal with the legal issues involving their roles in schools (Mayes & Ferrin, 2001; Stefkovich & O'Brien, 2001). Not surprisingly, students are also unaware of their constitutional rights and responsibilities (Tonn, 2005a). This chapter examines the law and how it can influence your professional decision making. We begin by putting the legal aspects of teaching into a larger perspective.

Limitations of Laws

You're working in a middle school, and you see a fight between two students on the playground. Does the law address a teacher's responsibilities in a situation like this? The answer is yes. You can't ignore the fight, because you're responsible for the safety of the children; in fact, parents have the right to sue a teacher if they can demonstrate that the teacher failed to protect students from injury, a problem labeled negligence. Should you physically break up the fight, or can you simply report it to the administration? As with many other situations, the law is vague and does not specify a particular correct response.

Laws regulate the rights and responsibilities of teachers, but two limitations of laws affect the extent to which they guide our professional decisions. The first limitation is that laws are purposely general, so they can apply to a variety of specific situations. For example, in terms of protecting their students from injury, teachers not only have to break up fights on a playground, they also need to supervise chemistry experiments, maintain order at school assemblies, and stop horseplay in locker rooms.

Jason's dilemma is another case. The law generally protects a teacher's freedom of speech, but does it allow him to campaign politically in the classroom and present issues that may not be part of the assigned curriculum? The answers to these questions are not explicitly described in laws, so professional decision making is necessary.

A second limitation of laws is that they were created in response to problems that existed in the past, so they don't provide specific guidelines for future decisions. New situations often raise new legal questions. For example, what are the rights of students and teachers who have AIDS? (We answer this question later in the chapter.) The use of technology raises additional questions, such as, What kinds of materials can we legally borrow from the Internet? What are the legal limitations to software use in schools? What can be legally copied? Experts are wrestling with these issues, and preliminary guidelines have appeared, but educators must often make decisions based on their knowledge of the law and their own professional judgment. This again illustrates why professional knowledge is so important.

Ethical Dimensions of Teaching

The law tells teachers what they can do (their rights) and what they must do (their responsibilities). However, laws don't tell teachers what they should do. For information on appropriate conduct, teachers must turn to ethics. Ethics is the discipline that examines values and offers principles that can be used to decide whether or not acts are right or wrong (Gladding, 2007).

Professional ethics provide broad guidelines for teachers as they make decisions in complex situations. [© Ellen B. Senesi/Ellen Senesi]

Professional ethics are a set of moral standards for acceptable professional behavior. For example, the Hippocratic Oath is a code of ethics that guides the medical profession. In taking the oath, physicians pledge to do their best to benefit their patients (with both curative methods and kindness), to tell the truth, and to maintain patients' confidences. Other professions have similar ethical codes, which are designed to both guide practitioners and protect clients.

The National Education Association's (NEA) code of ethics provides guidance to teachers in ambiguous professional situations such as those described at the beginning of the chapter.

As with the law, codes of ethics are limited; they provide only general guidelines for professional behavior. Let's look again at Jason's dilemma to see why this is so. Under Principle I of the NEA Code of Ethics, Item 2 states that "the educator . . . shall not unreasonably deny the student access to varying points of view." Has Jason been balanced and fair in presenting both sides of the environmental and political issue? A code of ethics isn't, and never can be, specific enough to provide a definitive answer. Jason must answer the question for himself based on his personal philosophy of education and, within it, his personal code of ethics.

The limitations of the NEA code are also apparent in Sasha's case. Item 6 of Principle I cautions teachers not to discriminate "on the basis of race, color, creed, [or] sex," but it doesn't tell Sasha which student to choose. Judged strictly on academics, Brandon appears to be the better candidate. If Sasha believes that Sonia is less talented than Brandon, choosing her because she is female would be granting her an unfair advantage. On the other hand, Sasha may believe that Sonia's math talents are equal to (even if different from) Brandon's and that it is ethically valid to consider her financial need and the good that might result from giving recognition to a female in a male-dominated area of the curriculum.

In response to these complexities, teachers are often encouraged to "treat all students equally." However, even this edict isn't as simple as it appears on the surface. Effective teachers purposefully call on shy students to involve them in lessons, sometimes avoid calling on assertive students who tend to dominate discussions, and give students who have difficulty with English more time to answer questions and finish tests. Teachers treat students differently depending on their individual needs; professional ethics help teachers treat all students equitably, but not always equally.

These examples illustrate why developing your personal philosophy of education is so important. A philosophy of education provides a framework for thinking about educational issues and guides professional practice. Your personal philosophy will guide you as you make decisions about what is important and what is fair. Because the law and professional codes of ethics can provide only general guidelines, a personal philosophy is essential in helping you make specific decisions each day.

Making Connections:
To deepen your understanding of the topics in this section of the chapter and integrate them with topics you've already studied, go to the *Making Connections* module for Chapter 9 at **www.prenhall.com/kauchak**. Respond to questions 1 and 2.

Check Your Understanding

1.1 What are two limitations of using existing laws as the basis for professional decision making?

1.2 How are laws different from ethics in terms of teacher decision making?

For feedback, go to Check Your Understanding *at the end of this chapter.*

Professional ethics. A set of moral standards for acceptable professional behavior.

The U.S. Legal System

Having briefly examined the law, ethics, and their limitations, we now look more closely at the legal system in the United States. Laws regulating schools and teachers are part of a larger, complex legal system, which exists at three interconnected levels: federal, state, and local (Underwood & Webb, 2006). This system attempts to use peoples' rights and responsibilities to each other as the basis for defining fairness.

Federal Influences

Through amendments to the Constitution and specific laws enacted by Congress, the federal government plays a central role in defining the rights and responsibilities of teachers and students.

Constitutional Amendments

Think about the following questions:

- As a teacher, how much freedom do you have in selecting topics to teach? Are you limited in what books and articles you can ask your students to read?
- Can you publicly criticize the administrators and school boards for whom you work?
- How much freedom do students have in running their school newspapers and yearbooks?

The First Amendment to the Constitution guarantees freedom of speech to all citizens of the United States (and the Constitution also established the principle of separation of church and state), but where do we draw the line with respect to the preceding questions? You certainly can't have your students read *Playboy* magazine, but how about *Catcher in the Rye*, a classic coming-of-age novel with explicit sexual references? Considering the second and third questions leaves similar uncertainties.

The Fourth Amendment protects citizens from unreasonable searches and seizures. To what extent does this amendment protect teachers and students? For instance:

- Can school officials search students' backpacks and purses when they're on school property?
- Are students' lockers considered to be personal property, or can they be searched if school officials suspect drugs or weapons are in them?

The Fourth Amendment provides general guidelines about search and seizure but doesn't specifically answer these two questions.

The Fourteenth Amendment states, "nor shall any State deprive any person of life, liberty, or property without due process of law." What does "due process" mean in the context of schools? For example:

- Can teachers be fired without a formal hearing?
- Can students be expelled from class without formal proceedings?
- How long can a student be suspended from school, and what kinds of deliberations need to precede such a suspension?

Again, the Constitution provides general guidelines about due process, but specific decisions are left to teachers and other educators. These examples further illustrate why an understanding of legal issues is so important for beginning teachers.

Federal Laws

The federal laws passed in Congress also influence education. For example, the Civil Rights Act of 1964 states, "No person in the United States shall on the grounds of race, color, or national origin, be excluded from participation in or be denied the benefits of, or be subjected to discrimination under any program or activity receiving federal financial assistance." This law was influential in ending segregation in schools in this country. Similarly, Title IX, passed in 1972, prohibits discrimination on the basis of gender and has been instrumental in helping equalize the amount of money spent on boys' and girls' sports.

State and Local Influences

States influence education by passing laws regulating teachers' qualifications, working conditions, and legal rights. For example, most states require a bachelor's degree to teach, and many are now requiring a major in an academic area.

States also create departments of education with a variety of responsibilities, such as determining the length of the school year and approving textbooks. They also pass laws creating local school districts, which are then legally responsible for the day-to-day functioning of schools.

This section addresses the first item on our beginning-of-chapter survey, "Teachers have the legal right to determine what is taught in their classroom." They *do* have the legal right to determine what is taught, but within limits; their rights and responsibilities are influenced by both federal and state laws. This has two implications for you as a beginning teacher. First, you should be familiar with constitutional amendments and laws that apply to all 50 states. Second, you need to know the laws that operate in the specific state where you work. For example, as you'll see in the next section, teacher strikes are illegal in about half of the states. Knowing the law that applies in your state can help you make a decision if collective bargaining between a district and professional organization reaches a stalemate.

The Overlapping Legal System

Overlapping levels of the legal system have been created to correspond to different levels of responsibility, but conflicts sometimes occur. When they do, the legal system attempts to solve problems and disputes at a lower level before sending them to a higher one. Let's look at two examples.

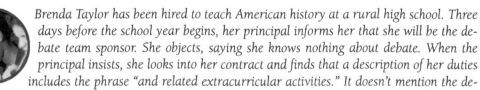

Brenda Taylor has been hired to teach American history at a rural high school. Three days before the school year begins, her principal informs her that she will be the debate team sponsor. She objects, saying she knows nothing about debate. When the principal insists, she looks into her contract and finds that a description of her duties includes the phrase "and related extracurricular activities." It doesn't mention the debate team. She complains again to the principal, but he is adamant. She writes a letter to the school board, which appoints a grievance committee. The committee rules in the district's favor. Brenda, not willing to back down, hires a lawyer, and her case goes to a state court.

Henry Ipsinger likes his job in a suburban middle school but disagrees with the school's priorities. In college he had learned that middle schools are supposed to be for all kids, not just the academically and athletically talented. He especially objects to his school's participation in Academic Olympics, an interschool academic competition, and the school's emphasis on competitive football and basketball.

Henry isn't afraid to express his opinions, and he does so frequently at faculty meetings, to the consternation of his principal. When his concerns aren't addressed, he takes his complaints to school board meetings. His complaints fall on deaf ears, though they do raise a number of eyebrows. He then tries politics, openly backing opposition candidates to the school board. Finally he goes too far; at the end of the school year, he is cited for insubordination, and his contract isn't renewed.

Henry is livid. He hires a lawyer, claiming his First Amendment right to freedom of speech has been violated. The case works its way through the court system all the way to the U.S. Supreme Court.

Can teachers be asked to perform duties in addition to their teaching responsibilities? Can their professional opinions cause them to be fired from their jobs? Both of these questions fall into a gray area called school law and are addressed by different court systems.

Because Brenda's and Henry's issues were different, the school and legal system dealt with their cases in different ways and at different levels. Both cases started at the local level. Brenda's complaint involved conditions of employment, so her case moved to state courts because employment issues are state responsibilities. Henry's case went to federal courts because freedom of speech is a right guaranteed by the U.S. Constitution.

In the next section, we examine teachers' rights and responsibilities, probably the most important dimensions of school law for teachers.

Making Connections:
To deepen your understanding of the topics in this section of the chapter and integrate them with topics you've already studied, go to the *Making Connections* module for Chapter 9 at **www.prenhall.com/kauchak**. Respond to questions 3 and 4.

Check Your Understanding

2.1 How do federal laws influence education?

2.2 How do state laws influence education policies and practices?

2.3 What is the educational significance of the overlapping legal system in the United States?

 For feedback, go to Check Your Understanding *at the end of this chapter.*

Teachers' Rights and Responsibilities

As citizens, teachers enjoy the same legal safeguards as all Americans, including freedom of speech and the right to due process. But because they are professionals entrusted with the care of children, they have responsibilities beyond those of other citizens, such as protecting their students from physical and emotional harm. In this section, we examine five areas in which the law influences teachers' rights and responsibilities. They're outlined in Figure 9.1. Let's look at them.

Teacher Employment and the Law

One of the first things you will think about as you join the teaching profession is how to get and keep a job. Legal guidelines influence the process.

Figure 9.1 Teachers' Rights and Responsibilities

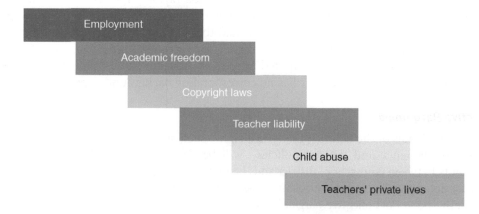

Licensure

Licensure is the process by which a state evaluates the credentials of prospective teachers to ensure that they have achieved satisfactory levels of teaching competence and are morally fit to work with youth. Every state has licensure requirements, which typically include a bachelor's degree from an accredited college or university with a minimum number of credit hours in specified areas (e.g., those required for a teaching major or minor). In addition, prospective teachers are screened for felony arrests or a history of abusing or molesting children. Applicants who fail these screens usually have the right to petition before a state professional practices board that considers each case individually.

Teachers are increasingly being asked to pass competency tests that measure their ability to perform basic skills (reading, writing, and mathematics), their background in an academic area (e.g., biology, history, or English), and their understanding of learning and teaching. These tests are controversial, but when properly developed and validated, they have been upheld in courts (Fischer et al., 2006; Underwood & Webb, 2006). Individuals who meet these requirements receive a teaching license that makes them eligible to teach but doesn't ensure employment.

Contracts

A **teaching contract** is a legal employment agreement between a teacher and a local school board. In issuing contracts, school boards must comply with laws that prohibit discrimination on the basis of sex, race, religion, or age. Contracts are legally binding for both parties. School boards can be sued for breaking one without due cause, and teachers must honor contracts they have signed. Many states permit a teacher's certificate to be revoked for breach of contract, a practice growing more common as the competition for teachers increases (Archer, 2000b).

Teachers should carefully read their contracts and any district policies and procedures manuals covered by the contract. Extracurricular assignments, such as sponsoring school clubs or monitoring sports events, may not be specified in detail in an initial contract but can be required later. This is what happened to Brenda Taylor when her contract said "and

Collective bargaining between professional organizations and school districts determines teachers' salaries and working conditions. [Abigail Bobrow/AP Wide World Photos]

related extracurricular activities." Courts have generally upheld districts' rights to require these additional responsibilities but have also said that a reasonable connection must exist between additional assignments and a teacher's regular classroom duties. So, for example, a speech or English teacher may be required to sponsor a debate club but might not have to coach an athletic team if the teacher has no corresponding background experience.

Collective Bargaining

Many of the details of the contract that you'll sign—such as working conditions, class size, salaries and benefits, and transfer policies—will be determined by collective bargaining agreements between your school district and the local professional organization. Most teachers either belong to the National Education Association or the American Federation of Teachers, and the power of collective bargaining is a major reason they do.

Licensure. The process by which a state evaluates the credentials of prospective teachers to ensure that they have achieved satisfactory levels of teaching competence and are morally fit to work with youth.

Teaching contract. A legal employment agreement between a teacher and a local school board.

Collective bargaining occurs when a local chapter of a professional organization negotiates with a school district over the rights of the teachers and the conditions of employment. Legally, teachers have a constitutional right to join a professional organization but cannot be forced to do so (Essex, 2006; Fischer et al., 2006). In most states, the law requires the local school board to negotiate with whatever professional organization represents the largest number of teachers in that district. The final agreement applies to all teachers in that district.

If teachers believe that a school district is not meeting the terms of the contract they signed or believe that they are given unreasonable responsibilities or work conditions, they can file a grievance (Imber & van Geel, 2005). A **grievance** is a formal complaint against an employer alleging unsatisfactory working conditions. When a teacher files a grievance, he or she is usually arguing that a working condition, such as class size or a teaching assignment, is in violation of the teacher's contract. A teacher cannot be dismissed for filing a grievance, and the professional organization that negotiated the contract with the district will usually provide legal counsel.

Teachers also have a limited right to strike in about half of the states. In the others, legislators group teachers with other employees such as police officers and firefighters, believing that the public welfare would suffer from a strike. Because of the variability between states in terms of issues such as strikes and items covered by collective bargaining, beginning teachers should become familiar with the educational laws governing these issues. Professional organizations in your area can be very helpful in this regard.

Tenure

Tenure is a legal safeguard that provides job security by preventing teacher dismissal without cause. Tenure is designed to protect teachers from political or personal abuses and to ensure the stability of the teaching force. It is grounded in the principle that teachers should be hired and fired on their professional merits and not because of personal connections or political views. Tenured teachers can be dismissed only for causes such as incompetence, immoral behavior, insubordination, or unprofessional conduct.

When any of these charges are filed, due process must be observed. The teacher must be provided with the following:

- Notification of the list of charges
- Adequate time to prepare a rebuttal to the charges
- Access to evidence and the names of witnesses
- A hearing, which must be conducted before an impartial decision maker
- The right to representation by legal counsel
- Opportunities to introduce evidence and cross-examine witnesses
- A school board decision based on evidence and findings of the hearing
- A transcript or record of the hearing
- The right to appeal an adverse decision

These safeguards, guaranteed by the Fourteenth Amendment, provide teachers with the same constitutional protections enjoyed by the population at large.

Dismissal

You'll work hard to become licensed and perhaps even harder to get a teaching position. Obviously, you won't want to lose your job; therefore, it's important to understand your rights so you'll be prepared should this possibility occur.

Most districts require a probationary period before tenure is granted (commonly 3 years). During this time, teachers have a yearly contract and can be dismissed for a variety of reasons, such as believed incompetence, overstaffing, or reduced school enrollments. Although some states require districts to provide a formal hearing on demand when a nontenured teacher is dismissed, this isn't common. Teachers uncertain about their rights during this period should check with their district, state office of education, or professional organization.

Collective bargaining. Process that occurs when a local chapter of a professional organization negotiates with a school district over the rights of the teachers and the conditions of employment.

Grievance. A formal complaint against an employer alleging unsatisfactory working conditions.

Tenure. A legal safeguard that provides job security by preventing teacher dismissal without cause.

Dishonesty on the initial job application can also cause a new teacher to be dismissed. Students close to obtaining their degrees are sometimes offered positions during their internships. They agree but, due to unforeseen circumstances, are then unable to graduate or obtain a license. When districts discover the problem, they can either dismiss the teacher or lower his or her status to substitute teacher, resulting in lower pay and loss of benefits.

Reduction in Force. Because of declining student numbers, budget cuts, or course or program cancellations, districts are sometimes forced to dismiss teachers. **Reduction in force** (or "riffing" as it's called in industry) is the elimination of teaching positions because of declining student enrollment or school funds. Typically, the district dismisses teachers with the least seniority—in other words, the last in are first out. Fortunately, "riffing" occurs infrequently and, as increasing numbers of students enter the educational system, should be even less common in the future.

Reduction in force can involve both tenured and nontenured teachers and is regulated either by state law or by collective bargaining agreements between districts and professional organizations (Fischer et al., 2006). Teachers faced with this possibility should consult representatives from their local professional organization.

Academic Freedom

Academic freedom refers to the right of teachers to choose both content and teaching methods based on their professional judgment. Although freedom of speech is protected by the First Amendment, professional academic freedom has limits. What are they? Consider these actual cases:

In an attempt to motivate his students, a teacher organized his classroom around a sports-competition theme called "Learnball." Dividing his students into teams, the teacher instituted a system of rewards that included playing the radio and shooting foam basketballs. His principal objected, and when the teacher refused to change his methods, he was fired. He sued to get his job back, claiming his freedom of speech had been violated. (Bradley v. Pittsburgh Board of Education, 1990)

An eleventh-grade English teacher was leading a discussion on taboo words. To illustrate his point, he wrote the four-letter slang word for sexual intercourse on the board. Parents complained and the teacher was dismissed. He sued to get his job back, claiming his freedom of speech had been curtailed. (Mailloux v. Kiley, 1971)

Academic freedom protects teachers' rights to choose both content and teaching methods. [Spencer Grant/PhotoEdit Inc.]

Reduction in force. The elimination of teaching positions because of declining student enrollment or school funds. Also known as "riffing."

Academic freedom. The right of teachers to choose both content and teaching methods based on their professional judgment.

320

Teachers are hired to teach a specific curriculum, such as first-grade math, middle school life science, or high school English. State and district curriculum frameworks exist to guide teachers, and they often identify required textbooks. Within this general framework, teachers are free to teach topics as they see fit. Sometimes these topics and methods are controversial and may result in a teacher being disciplined or dismissed, as in the cases just mentioned.

In resolving disputes about academic freedom, the courts consider the following:

- The teacher's goal in discussing a topic or using a method
- The age of the students involved
- The relevance of the materials to the course
- The quality or general acceptance of the questioned material or methods
- The existence of policies related to the issue

In the case of the teacher using the Learnball format, the courts upheld the district's dismissal. The court based its decision on the fact that this teaching strategy was not widely accepted and the teacher had been warned repeatedly by the administration to stop using it.

The case of the high school English teacher resulted in the opposite outcome. The teacher's job was reinstated because the court upheld the importance of two kinds of academic freedom: (1) the "substantive" right to use a teaching method that serves a "demonstrated" purpose and (2) the procedural right not to be discharged for the use of a teaching method not prohibited by clear regulations. The teacher's goal was for his students to understand taboo words and how they influenced literature, a topic that fell under the broad umbrella of the English curriculum. Had this not been the case, or if the teacher had been clearly warned against using this strategy, the outcome probably would have been different.

When considering the discussion of controversial topics or the use of controversial methods, teachers should try to decide if they fall within the scope of the assigned curriculum. If teachers choose to move forward, they should have clear educational goals in mind and be able to defend them if objections arise. Academic freedom protects knowledgeable, well-intentioned teachers working within their assigned responsibilities. If, as a beginning teacher, you're uncertain about an issue that could involve academic freedom, you should check with your principal or other school administrator.

Copyright Laws

As teachers, we want to share the most up-to-date information with our students. This can involve copying information from newspapers, magazines, books, and even television programs. Sometimes, however, our desire to bring this information into the classroom can violate copyright laws (Underwood & Webb, 2006).

Copyright laws are federal laws designed to protect the intellectual property of authors, which includes printed matter, videos, computer software, and various other types of original work. Just as patents protect the intellectual work of inventors, copyright laws protect the work of print writers, filmmakers, software creators, songwriters, graphic artists, and

Copyright laws provide guidelines for teachers when they use technology in their teaching. [Anthony Magnacca/Merrill]

Copyright laws. Federal laws designed to protect the intellectual property of authors, including printed matter, videos, computer software, and various other types of original work.

many others. To balance the rights of authors with the legitimate needs of teachers and learners, federal guidelines have been developed.

Fair-use guidelines are policies that specify limitations in the use of copyrighted materials for educational purposes. For example, teachers may make a single copy of a book chapter, newspaper or magazine article, short story, essay, or poem for planning purposes, and they may copy short works (poems that are less than 250 words or prose that is less than 2,500 words) for one-time use in the classroom. However, they may not create class anthologies by copying material from several sources or charge students more than it cost them to copy the materials. In addition, pages from workbooks or other consumable materials may not be copied.

Videotapes and computer software pose unique challenges. They too were created by and belong to someone, and fair-use guidelines also apply to them. For example, teachers may tape a television program, but they must use it within 10 days of taping. They may show it again for reinforcement but must erase the tape after 45 days. One copy, and no more, of software may be made as a "backup." Materials on the Internet may not be copied unless specific permission is given or unless the document is published by the federal government.

These guidelines restrict teachers, but the restrictions are not usually a major handicap. Teachers should share the principle of fair use with students to help them understand its purpose and the ways that copyright laws help protect people.

Teacher Liability

An elementary teacher on playground duty was mingling with students, watching them as they ran around. After the teacher passed one group of students, a boy picked up and threw a rock that hit another boy in the eye, causing serious injury. The injured boy's parents sued the teacher for negligence. (Fagen v. Summers, 1972)

A teacher was taking a group of first graders on a school-sponsored field trip to the Oregon coast. While some of the students were wading in the water, a big wave rolled in, bringing a big log with it, and one of the children was seriously injured. The parents sued the teacher for negligence. (Morris v. Douglas County School District, 1965)

We don't often think of schools as dangerous places, but the combination of large numbers of children, small places, and youthful exuberance and energy can result in falls, scrapes, and accidents. In addition, field trips, science laboratories, woodworking shops, and physical education classes pose special risks.

Teachers are legally responsible for the safety of children under their supervision. The courts employ the idea of *in loco parentis,* which means "in place of the parents," in gauging the limits of teacher responsibility. *In loco parentis* is a principle that requires teachers to use the same judgment and care as parents in protecting the children under their supervision. **Negligence** is a teacher's or other school employee's failure to exercise sufficient care in protecting students from injury. If negligence occurs, parents may bring a liability suit against a teacher or school district. Liability suits are a major concern of experienced teachers, influencing their day-to-day professional decision making (Public Agenda, 2004).

In attempting to define the limits of teachers' responsibilities in liability cases, the courts consider whether teachers:

- Make a reasonable attempt to anticipate dangerous conditions.
- Take proper precautions and establish rules and procedures to prevent injuries.
- Warn students of possible dangerous situations.
- Provide proper supervision.

In applying these principles to the rock-throwing incident, the courts found no direct connection between the teacher's actions and the child's injury. The teacher was

Fair-use guidelines. Policies that specify limitations in the use of copyrighted materials for educational purposes.

In loco parentis. A principle meaning "in place of the parents" that requires teachers to use the same judgment and care as parents in protecting the children under their supervision.

Negligence. A teacher's or other school employee's failure to exercise sufficient care in protecting students from injury.

properly supervising the children, and events happened so quickly that she was unable to prevent the accident. Had she witnessed, and failed to stop, a similar incident, or had she left the playground for personal reasons, the court's decision would probably have been different.

Field trips pose special safety and legal challenges because of the dangers of transportation and the increased possibility of injury in unfamiliar surroundings. Many school districts ask parents to sign a consent form to inform them of the trip and release school personnel from liability in case of injury. These forms don't do the latter, however; even with signed forms, teachers are still responsible for the safety of the children in their care. The courts ruled in favor of the parents in the Oregon case, because this type of accident is fairly common on beaches along the Oregon coast. The teacher, they ruled, should have anticipated the accident and acted accordingly.

As they supervise, teachers need to consider the ages and developmental levels of students, as well as the type of classroom activity. Young children need more direction and supervision, for example, as do some students with special needs. Science labs, cooking classes, use of certain equipment, and physical education classes pose special safety hazards. Professional organizations, such as the National Science Teachers Association, provide guidelines to help teachers avoid liability-causing situations in their classroom (D. Hoff, 2003b), and beginning teachers should be familiar with their guidelines. In addition, teachers should carefully plan ahead, anticipate potential dangers, and teach safety rules and procedures to all students.

In spite of conscientious planning, accidents can and do happen. Beginning teachers should consider the liability insurance offered by professional organizations. These organizations also often provide legal assistance to members who are sued. In addition, for a small amount per year, teachers can purchase a personal liability policy good for $1 million in damages (Portner, 2000).

This section addresses the second item on our beginning-of-chapter survey, "Teachers are responsible for the safety of the students in their classroom." According to the legal principle of *in loco parentis,* teachers are indeed legally responsible for the students in their care. Factors such as the age and intelligence of the students, as well as dangers inherent in a particular situation, should guide your actions as you attempt to protect the welfare of your students.

Child Abuse

Jimmy is a quiet, shy fourth-grader. He rarely volunteers in class and seems to withdraw from interactions with the rest of the children. He is skinny, and efforts to sign him up for federally financed lunches have been rebuffed by his parents, who assert they don't need help from anyone.

One day you notice a bruise on Jimmy's face. When you talk to him at lunch break, he says he fell while playing, but there aren't any scrapes or abrasions typically associated with a fall. You ask him how things are at home, and his eyes fill with tears. You ask him if he wants to talk about it; he just shakes his head no. When you ask him if someone hit him, he blurts out, "Please don't say anything, or I'll get in trouble."

What are your responsibilities in this situation? The student begged you to say nothing. Do you honor his request? The answer is no. All 50 states and the District of Columbia have laws requiring educators to report suspected child abuse (Fischer et al., 2006). In addition, teachers are protected from legal action if they act in "good faith" and "without malice." Teachers suspecting child abuse should immediately report the matter to school counselors or administrators. Schools generally have an established process for dealing with suspected child abuse cases, and these guidelines help new teachers understand their role in the process.

Teachers' Private Lives

Gary Hansen had lived with the same male roommate for several years. They were often seen shopping together in the local community, and they even went to social events together. Students and other faculty "talked," but Gary ignored the hints that he was homosexual until the principal called him into his office, confronted him with the charge, and threatened dismissal.

Mary Evans had taught in Chicago for more than 8 years and didn't mind the long commute from the suburbs because it gave her an opportunity to "clear her head." She had been living with her boyfriend for several years, and everything seemed fine until one day she found she was pregnant. After lengthy discussions with her partner, she decided to keep the baby but not get married. When her pregnancy became noticeable, her principal called her in. She affirmed that she wasn't married and didn't intend to be. He asked for her resignation, suggesting she was a poor role model for her students.

Teachers have a right to their own private lives but must meet community standards of acceptable conduct. [Michael Newman/PhotoEdit Inc.]

An individual's right to "life, liberty, and the pursuit of happiness" is one of our country's founding principles. What happens, however, when teachers' lifestyles conflict with those of the community in which they work? Are teachers' private lives really "private," or can teachers be dismissed for what they do in their free time?

In answering these questions, the courts have relied on a definition of teaching that is broader than classroom instruction. Teachers do more than help students understand English and history, for example; they also serve as role models. As a result, teachers are scrutinized more closely than are people in general. Other professionals, such as attorneys or physicians, might be able to lead lifestyles at odds with community values, but teachers might not. What are teachers' rights with respect to their private lives?

Clear answers in this area don't exist. Morality and what constitutes a good role model are contextual. For example, in the 1800s, women's teaching contracts required them to

- Abstain from marriage
- Be home between the hours of 8:00 PM and 6:00 AM unless attending school functions
- Wear dresses no more than 2 inches above the ankle

More recently, pregnant teachers were required (even if married) to take a leave of absence once their condition became noticeable. Obviously, views of morality change. As the California Supreme Court noted, "Today's morals may be tomorrow's ancient and absurd customs" (Fischer et al., 2003, p. 265).

Moral standards also vary among communities. What is acceptable in large cities may not be in the suburbs or rural areas. Cities also provide a measure of anonymity, and *notoriety* is one criterion courts use to decide if a teacher's private activities damage their credibility as role models. **Notoriety** is the extent to which a teacher's behavior becomes known and is controversial. For example, many young people are choosing to live together as an alternative to marriage, and this lifestyle is obviously less noticeable in a large city than in smaller communities.

Notoriety. The extent to which a teacher's behavior becomes known and controversial.

324

Where does this leave teachers? Generalizations such as "Consider the community in which you live and teach" provide some guidance, as do representative court cases. However, the law isn't clear and specific with respect to teachers' private behavior.

The issue of homosexuality illustrates how schools can become legal battlegrounds for people's differing beliefs. Some people believe that homosexuality is morally wrong and that people who are homosexual shouldn't be allowed to work with young people. Others believe that whether or not a person is homosexual is irrelevant to schools and teaching. When the issue has gone to courts, they have generally ruled in favor of homosexual teachers.

In a landmark California case, a teacher's homosexual relationship was reported to the state board of education, which revoked his license. The board argued that state law required teachers to be models of good conduct, and that homosexual behavior is inconsistent with the moral standards of the people of California (*Morrison v. State Board of Education,* 1969). The California Supreme Court disagreed, concluding that "immoral" was broad enough to be interpreted in a number of ways and stating that no evidence existed indicating that Morrison's behavior adversely affected his teaching effectiveness.

In other cases involving criminal or public sexual behavior (e.g., soliciting sex in a park), courts have ruled against teachers (Fischer et al., 2006). Notoriety was a key element in these cases.

The case involving the unwed mother further illustrates the murkiness of school law. A case in Nebraska in 1976 resulted in the dismissal of an unwed mother because the school board claimed there was "a rational connection between the plaintiff's pregnancy out of wedlock and the school board's interest in conserving marital values" (*Brown v. Bathhe,* 1976). In other cases, however, courts have ruled in favor of pregnant unwed teachers, including one in Ohio who became pregnant through artificial insemination (Fischer et al., 2006).

Although the law is ambiguous with respect to teachers' private sexual lives, it is clear regarding sexual relations with students (Hendrie, 2003b). Teachers are in a position of authority and trust, and any breach of this trust will result in dismissal. When teachers take sexual advantage of their students, they violate both legal and ethical standards.

Other teacher behaviors can also jeopardize their jobs. Drug offenses, excessive drinking, driving under the influence of alcohol, felony arrests, and even a misdemeanor, such as shoplifting, can result in dismissal (Fischer et al., 2006). The message is clear: Teachers are legally and ethically required to be good role models for their students.

This section also addresses the third item on our beginning-of-chapter survey, "Teachers are held to the same moral standards as other citizens." In fact, they are held to higher moral standards because they serve as role models for their students.

Teachers With AIDS

In determining the rights of teachers with AIDS (acquired immune deficiency syndrome) or HIV (human immunodeficiency virus) infection, the courts have generally used nondiscrimination as the legal principle guiding their decisions. The legal foundation for this principle was established in 1987 in a case involving a Florida teacher with tuberculosis (*School Board of Nassau County, Florida v. Arline,* 1987). The courts' dilemma involved weighing the rights of the individual against the public's concern about the possible spread of disease. The U.S. Supreme Court ruled in favor of the teacher, considering the disease a handicap and protecting the teacher from discrimination because of it.

The Florida decision set a precedent for a California case involving a teacher with AIDS who had been removed from the classroom and reassigned to administrative duties (*Chalk v. U.S. District Court Cent. Dist. of California,* 1988). The court ruled in favor of the teacher, using medical opinion to argue that the teacher's right to employment outweighed the minor risk of communicating the AIDS virus to children.

> **Making Connections:**
> To deepen your understanding of the topics in this section of the chapter and integrate them with topics you've already studied, go to the *Making Connections* module for Chapter 9 at **www.prenhall.com/kauchak.** Respond to questions 5–8.

Teacher Tenure

As you saw earlier in our discussion of teachers' rights and responsibilities, tenure is designed to protect teachers from political or personal abuses and to ensure the stability of the teaching force. Recently, however, tenure has been under fire by some educational reformers, who believe it is holding back the progress of the teaching profession (M. Bernstein, 2006). In 1997 lawmakers in Oregon eliminated tenure for teachers, replacing it with 2-year contracts (A. Bradley, 1999). Georgia followed suit in 2000 by eliminating tenure for new teachers, and attempted to pass legislation that would shorten the amount of time it takes to fire incompetent teachers (J. Reeves, 2004). Talk of similar measures has been heard in other states and districts across the country.

The Issue

Critics of tenure contend that it is outdated and unfair, providing teachers with protections that other professionals don't have. Further, they argue, it is unnecessary, because the existing system provides legal recourse to teachers who feel they have been wrongly dismissed (J. Johnson, 2004).

Most importantly, critics assert, it is virtually impossible to remove a tenured teacher, regardless of ability, which means that tenure protects incompetent teachers. For example, one study of 30 school districts found that only slightly more than one tenth of 1 percent of teachers believed to be incompetent were either dismissed or persuaded to resign (A. Bradley, 1999). Another study, focusing on five urban districts, found that during 1 year only four teachers out of a total of 70,000 tenured teachers were formally terminated (Rhee & Levin, 2006). Districts typically respond to the issue by moving incompetent teachers from school to school instead of taking them out of classrooms.

On the other hand, supporters of tenure argue that it was created to protect teachers from political or personal pressure and

that it continues to serve that function (Fischer et al., 2003). Teachers who have tenure are more likely to address controversial issues in class without fear of retribution. In addition, tenured teachers are more likely to become politically active, especially in school-related issues such as school board elections and bond issues.

Supporters also contend that teachers need protection from the potential abuse of power that can exist if a principal or other district leader conducts a personal vendetta against a teacher for unprofessional reasons. In addition, during times of teacher shortages, the job security that tenure provides is an incentive for teachers to go into or remain in teaching.

Not surprisingly, administrators and teachers differ dramatically on the issue in some polls (J. Johnson, 2004). Both superintendents (80 percent) and principals (65 percent) believe that good teachers don't have to worry about tenure and think it is hard to justify. Fifty-eight percent of teachers, by contrast, believe that tenure is an important safeguard, protecting teachers from politics, favoritism, and losing their jobs to newcomers who could work for less.

You Take a Position

Now it's your turn to take a position on the issue. State in writing whether or not you feel that teacher tenure should be abolished, and provide a two-page rationale for your position.

For additional references and resources, go to the Companion Website at www.prenhall.com/kauchak, then to the Teaching in an Era of Reform module for Chapter 9. You can respond online or submit your response to your instructor.

Check Your Understanding

3.1 How are teacher employment issues influenced by the law?

3.2 What is academic freedom, and why is it important to teachers?

3.3 How do copyright laws influence teachers' practices?

3.4 What is teacher liability, and how does it influence teachers?

3.5 How are teachers' rights in terms of their own private lives similar to and different from those of the general public?

For feedback, go to Check Your Understanding *at the end of this chapter.*

Religion and the Law

Religion provides fertile ground for helping us understand how conflicting views of education can result in legal challenges. The role of religion in U.S. schools is and always has been controversial, and teachers are often caught in the crossfire.

The First Amendment to the Constitution provides for the principle of separation of church and state. The amendment reads:

Congress shall make no law respecting an establishment of religion, or prohibiting the free exercise thereof; or abridging the freedom of speech, or of the press; or the right of the people peaceably to assemble, and to petition the Government for a redress of grievances.

Each of the six clauses, or sections, of the amendment presents an important legal principle. The amendment begins with the **establishment clause**, the clause that prohibits the establishment of a national religion. The words "or prohibiting the free exercise thereof" is the **free exercise clause**, the clause that prohibits the government from interfering with individuals' rights to hold religious beliefs and freely practice religion.

Because religion plays an important role in many people's lives, the issue of religion in schools has become legally contentious, and teachers and administrators are often caught in the crossfire. Some of the questions that have arisen include the following:

- Are students and teachers allowed to pray in schools?
- Can religion be included in the school curriculum?
- Are religious clubs allowed access to public school facilities?

We answer these questions in the sections that follow.

Prayer in Schools

In the past, prayer and scripture reading were common in many, if not most, schools. In fact, they were required by law in some states. For example, Pennsylvania passed legislation in 1959 that required daily Bible reading in the schools (but exempted children whose parents did not want them to participate). The law was challenged, and the U.S. Supreme Court ruled that it violated the First Amendment's establishment clause (*Abington School District v. Schempp,* 1963). Nondenominational or generic prayers designed to skirt the issue of promoting a specific religion have also been outlawed. In a New York case, the Supreme Court held that generic prayers violated the establishment clause as well (*Engle v. Vitale,* 1962). Neither schools nor teachers can officially encourage student prayer; however, prayer is permissible when student initiated and when it doesn't interfere with other students or the functioning of the school (Underwood & Webb, 2006).

The law also forbids the official use of religious symbols in schools. For example, the courts ruled that a 2-by-3-foot portrait of Jesus Christ displayed in the hallway next to the principal's office was unconstitutional (Fischer et al., 2006). Also, the U.S. Supreme Court

Although the Constitution forbids the establishment of any particular religion in schools, a number of complex issues make this a controversial topic. [©Jim Young/Corbis; All Rights Reserved]

Establishment clause. The clause of the First Amendment that prohibits the establishment of a national religion.

Free exercise clause. The clause of the First Amendment that prohibits the government from interfering with individuals' rights to hold religious beliefs and freely practice religion.

struck down a Kentucky law requiring that the Ten Commandments be posted in school classrooms (*Stone v. Graham,* 1981).

These cases illustrate a legal trend: Officially sanctioned prayer and religious symbols—whether they come from school boards, principals, or teachers—are not allowed in public schools. They violate the principle of separation of church and state, which acknowledges religious diversity. Students may be Christians, Jews, Muslims, Buddhists, Hindus, or members of other religions. Imposing a particular form of prayer or religion on children in a school can be both illegal and unethical, because it can exclude children on the basis of religion.

Although the courts have been clear about denying prayer as a regular part of schools' opening ceremonies, the issue of prayer at graduation and other school activities is less clear. In a landmark case, a high school principal asked a clergyman to provide the graduation invocation and also suggested the content of the prayer. This was ruled a violation of separation of church and state by the U.S. Supreme Court (*Lee v. Weismann,* 1992). The school's involvement in the prayer was the key point; whether or not the Court would have banned the prayer if it had been initiated by students or parents is uncertain. In a more recent decision, the Supreme Court voted 6–3 against student-led prayers at football games in Texas (Walsh, 2000a). The Court concluded that students would perceive the pregame prayer as "stamped with the school's seal of approval," thus violating separation of church and state.

This section addresses the fourth item on our beginning-of-chapter survey, "The law prohibits any form of prayer in the schools." The law does not prohibit prayer in the school per se. Students can legally pray in school, but neither school officials nor teachers can lead or sanction organized prayer in schools.

Religious Clubs and Organizations

Organized prayer in schools is illegal, but it may be legal for extracurricular religious clubs to meet on school grounds. In one instance, a student in Omaha, Nebraska, requested permission to meet with her Bible study group before school. Officials refused, concerned about the possibility of undesirable groups, such as the Ku Klux Klan, using the case as precedent. The U.S. Supreme Court ruled in the student's favor, stating that schools must allow religious, philosophical, and political groups to use school facilities in the same ways as other extracurricular organizations (*Board of Education of the Westside Community School v. Mergens,* 1990). The fact that the club was not school sponsored or initiated was central to the Court's argument.

A link between church and state may also be permissible in some situations involving religious organization: For instance, the Supreme Court recently approved the use of federally funded computers and library books for Catholic schools in Louisiana (Walsh, 2000a). The principle of separation of church and state will likely be revisited in future educational court cases.

Religion in the Curriculum

A high school biology teacher prefaces his presentation on evolution with a warning, stating that it is only a "theory" and that many theories have been proven wrong in the past. He encourages students to keep an open mind and offers creationism, or the Biblical version of the origin of the world, as an alternate theory. As part of his presentation, he holds up a pamphlet, published by a religious organization; the pamphlet refutes evolution and argues that creationism provides a more valid explanation. He offers the pamphlets to interested students.

Where does religion fit in the school curriculum? Can a well-intentioned teacher use the classroom to promote his or her religious views? Given court decisions on school prayer, simplistic answers might be "no" or "never." But considering the enormous influence that religion has had on human history—as evidenced in art and literature—the issue becomes more complex.

Evolution is one point of tension. Concern over this issue dates back to the famous 1925 "Scopes Monkey Trial," in which a high school teacher (John Scopes) was prosecuted for violating a Tennessee state law that made it illegal to teach "any theory which denies the story of the Divine Creation of man as taught in the Bible and to teach instead that man is descended from a lower order of animals." Scopes argued that the law violated his academic freedom, contending that the theory of evolution had scientific merit and should be shared with his high school biology students. Scopes was found guilty of violating the state law and fined $100, but the decision was later reversed on a technicality.

Several states have since attempted to use legislation to resolve the evolution issue. In the 1960s, the Arkansas legislature passed a law banning the teaching of evolution in that state. The U.S. Supreme Court declared the law unconstitutional, because it violated the establishment clause of the First Amendment. In 1982 the Louisiana legislature, trying to create a middle ground, passed a "Balanced Treatment Act," requiring that evolution and creationism be given equal treatment in the curriculum. The U.S. Supreme Court threw this law out, arguing that, instead of being balanced, it was designed to promote a particular religious viewpoint.

In a more recent case involving religion in the public schools, a federal judge in Pennsylvania ruled that intelligent design did not qualify as a scientific theory (Cavanagh, 2006b; Whitson, 2006). Intelligent design is the belief that the complexity we see in living things, including humans, is the result of some unnamed guiding force. The Dover, Pennsylvania, school board voted to require that intelligent design be taught as an alternative to evolution. Parents in the district sued, claiming that intelligent design was an attempt to interject religion into the public schools. The judge agreed, concluding, "The overwhelming evidence at trial established that ID [intelligent design] is a religious view, a mere relabeling of creationism, and not a scientific theory" (Cavanagh, 2006b, p. 10). While the court's ruling only has legal standing in the U.S. District Court for the Middle District of Pennsylvania, legal experts predict that this ruling will carry considerable weight in any future cases involving intelligent design.

The broader issue of religion in the curriculum has also surfaced in several other court cases. In Tennessee, fundamentalist parents objected to including literature such as *The Wizard of Oz, Rumpelstiltskin,* and *Macbeth* in the curriculum, arguing that these works exposed children to feminism, witchcraft, pacifism, and vegetarianism. A lower court supported the parents, but a higher federal court reversed the decision, asserting that accommodating every parent's religious claims would "leave public education goals in shreds." It supported the right of districts to use religiously controversial materials if they were useful in achieving important educational goals (*Mozert v. Hawkins County Public Schools,* 1987, 1988). Comparable cases in Alabama (*Smith v. Board of School Commissioners of Mobile County,* 1987) and Illinois (*Fleischfresser v. Directors of School District No. 200,* 1994) resulted in similar outcomes. When schools can show that learning materials have a clear purpose, such as exposing students to time-honored literature, parental objections are usually overridden.

Teaching About Religion in the Schools

Legal controversies have had a dampening effect on teaching about religion in the schools. Here we emphasize the difference between teaching *about* different religions and *advocating* a particular one. Religion has had an enormous impact on history (e.g., the Crusades, New World exploration) as well as art and literature. Avoiding the study of religion leaves students in a cultural vacuum that is both inaccurate and potentially dangerous (Kunzman, 2006).

But how can schools teach about religion without provoking religious controversies? The U.S. Department of Education wrestled with this problem and developed the following guidelines (U.S. Department of Education, 1999b):

- Teachers and administrators in public schools should not advocate any religion.
- Public schools should not interfere with or intrude on a student's religious beliefs.
- Public schools may teach about the history of religion, comparative religions, the Bible as literature, and the role of religion in the history of the United States and other countries.

VIDEO PERSPECTIVES

A Battle Between Faith and Science

To view this video, go to the *Becoming a Professional* DVD included with this text, click on ABC News, and then this chapter's video: *A Battle Between Faith and Science.*

This ABC News video examines the controversies surrounding the teaching of evolution and intelligent design in Dover, Pennsylvania. In this small town in central Pennsylvania, the debate turned into a kind of war, a war of words between people with deeply held convictions on both sides of the argument—those who believe in creationism and those who fight for evolution. And there is no middle ground, no compromise. A lawsuit against the school board focused on the board's introduction of a book into the curriculum called *Of Pandas and People*. The book argues that Darwin's treatise on the origin of life is only a theory, while introducing readers to the study of intelligent design, a different theory that argues an "intelligent designer" created humankind. The textbook doesn't mention God, but the theory is supported by many Christians in the Dover community, and to them, creationism is a fact.

Think About This

1. What are some reasons that religion is such a hotly debated topic in American education?

2. What areas of the curriculum are most likely to encounter problems with religious issues?

3. What are the advantages and disadvantages of including religion in our schools?

To answer these questions online and receive immediate feedback, go to the Companion Website *at www.prenhall.com/kauchak, then to the* Video Perspectives *module for Chapter 9.*

Making Connections:
To deepen your understanding of the topics in this section of the chapter and integrate them with topics you've already studied, go to the *Making Connections* module for Chapter 9 at **www.prenhall.com/kauchak.** Respond to questions 9 and 10.

Critics caution that the Bible should not be used as a history textbook, should not be framed and taught strictly from a Christian perspective, and should not be used to promote the Christian faith or religious values (Gehring, 2000). The First Amendment Center (1999), a national organization promoting free speech, published the guidelines, *The Bible and Public Schools: A First Amendment Guide,* to address this issue. The guidelines, endorsed by the National Education Association, the American Federation of Teachers, and the National School Boards Association, recommend using secondary sources to provide additional scholarly perspectives with respect to the Bible as a historical document (Gehring, 1999b). These guidelines seem straightforward, but future legal battles over this emotion-laden issue are likely.

Check Your Understanding

4.1 What federal law influences the discussion of religion in the schools?

4.2 What is the legal status of prayer in schools?

4.3 Can a school allow religious clubs or organizations to meet on school grounds?

4.4 What is the legal status of religion in the curriculum?

For feedback, go to Check Your Understanding *at the end of this chapter.*

Students' Rights and Responsibilities

As it does for teachers, the law also helps define students' rights and responsibilities. Understanding these rights and responsibilities can guide teachers and others in their treatment of students. Sharing this understanding with students allows teachers to teach them about the legal system and their rights and responsibilities as future adult citizens.

Students' rights and responsibilities fall into several general areas, which we outline in Figure 9.2 and discuss in the sections that follow.

Students' Freedom of Speech

 Many parents in an urban middle school are advocating mandatory school uniforms. They believe that having students wear uniforms would reduce classroom management problems, discourage the display of gang colors, and minimize social comparisons between wealthy and less wealthy students. The school administration has voiced support for the proposal.

The student editors of the school newspaper hear of this proposal and conduct an informal poll of students, which indicates that a majority of students are opposed to uniforms. The editors want to publish these results along with an editorial arguing for student choice in what to wear. The principal refuses to let them print the article. What are students' rights in this matter?

As you've seen at several points in this chapter, the First Amendment guarantees U.S. citizens freedom of speech, and we want our students to understand and appreciate this right as they prepare to be responsible citizens. Do they retain this right when they enter our schools? The answer is yes, but within limits. They do have the right to express themselves in schools, provided doing so doesn't interfere with learning.

The landmark case in this area occurred in the late 1960s during the peak of the Vietnam War. As a protest against the war, three high school students wore black arm bands to school, despite the school's ban on such protests (*Tinker v. Des Moines Community School District*, 1969). When the students were suspended, they sued the school district, arguing that the suspensions violated their freedom of speech. The case went all the way to the U.S. Supreme Court, which ruled in favor of the students. The Court ruled that freedom of speech is an essential right for all citizens and that students' freedom of expression should not be curtailed if it isn't disruptive and doesn't interfere with the educational mission of the schools (Zirkel, 2001/2002).

Students' freedom of speech was tested again in 1986. During a high school assembly to nominate student government leaders, a student made a speech that contained a graphic and explicit metaphor comparing a candidate to a male sex organ. Not surprisingly, students in

Figure 9.2 Students' Rights and Responsibilities

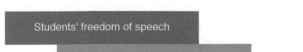

Students' freedom of speech

Permissible search and seizure

Students' records and privacy

Corporal punishment

Students' rights in disciplinary actions

Students With AIDS

the audience hooted, made sexual gestures, and became disruptive. The student was reprimanded, and he sued, claiming his freedom of speech had been curtailed. This case also went to the U.S. Supreme Court, which ruled that "schools . . . may determine that the essential lessons of civil, mature conduct cannot be conveyed in a school that tolerates lewd, indecent or offensive speech" (*Bethel School District No. 403 v. Fraser,* 1986). In this instance, freedom of speech *did* interfere with learning and could therefore be limited.

With respect to freedom of speech, school newspapers pose a special problem. Court rulings have reflected the idea that a school newspaper is an integral part of a school's extracurricular activities and should reflect a school's goals (Zirkel, 2001/2002). In a pivotal case, students working on a newspaper wanted to print two articles, one detailing the personal stories of three anonymous, pregnant teenage students, and the other dealing with the effects of divorce on children. The principal objected, arguing that the students in the first story might be identified because of the details in the articles. The newspaper authors sued, but the U.S. Supreme Court decided that school newspapers could be regulated in cases of "legitimate pedagogical concerns" (*Hazelwood School District v. Kuhlmeier,* 1988).

More recently, the issue of students' freedom of speech has resurfaced over the issue of messages and images on T-shirts (Hendrie, 2005c). In one case, a Virginia middle school banned a T-shirt with a National Rifle Association Shooting Sports Camp logo on the back containing 3 figures holding or shooting guns. The parents of the student objected, and the courts agreed, saying there was no link between the T-shirt and the district's ability to run safe and manageable schools (Galley, 2004). In a second case, schools banned a student from wearing a T-shirt with the message "Homosexuality is shameful." A federal court upheld the ban, saying that schools can limit a student's right to free speech when the content of that speech is injurious to other students (Trotter, 2006b). Courts and schools have a responsibility to protect students' freedom of speech but must weigh this right against the rights of others and the efficient operation of the schools.

What should teachers communicate to students about freedom of speech? Whether publishing a newspaper, writing an essay, or giving a speech, students should be encouraged to express their views and opinions, both because ownership of ideas promotes learning and because it prepares them to take stands and express personal opinions later in life. However, students also need to learn that individual freedoms have limits; for example, these freedoms may not impinge on the rights of others. By encouraging the open exchange of ideas, while reminding students of their responsibilities to one another, teachers can create classrooms that become democratic models. This is a worthwhile ideal.

Permissible Search and Seizure

The Fourth Amendment to the Constitution protects U.S. citizens from unlawful searches and seizures, and warrants are normally required before a person or that person's property can be searched. How do these protections apply to students? Again, educators face dilemmas. We don't want to run our schools like prisons or teach students that personal privacy is not a right. However, as drug and alcohol use and violence on school campuses remain persistent problems, many school leaders feel compelled to conduct searches of students and their property or even use entryway metal detectors to maintain the safety of the schools. Where do the courts draw the line on the issue?

School officials may search student lockers if they have probable cause to believe they contain something illegal or dangerous.
[David Young-Wolff/PhotoEdit Inc.]

Student freedom from unlawful search and seizure became an issue when a teacher discovered two girls smoking cigarettes in a restroom in a high school in New Jersey in the

1980s. When questioned by the vice principal, one student admitted smoking and the other (T.L.O.) denied the charge. The vice principal opened T.L.O.'s purse and found rolling papers in addition to cigarettes, which prompted him to empty the purse. Inside were marijuana, a pipe, empty plastic bags, a number of dollar bills, and a list titled "People who owe me money" (*New Jersey v. T.L.O.*, 1985). T.L.O. confessed that she had been selling marijuana at school and was sentenced to a year's probation by the juvenile court.

T.L.O. appealed the ruling, claiming that she was the victim of an illegal search. The U.S. Supreme Court reviewed the evidence and upheld both the verdict and the legality of the search, concluding that school searches are legal if they are targeted at a problem. Schools must have probable cause to conduct the search; that is, they must have a reasonable suspicion that the student being searched deserves the treatment (Zirkel, 2001/2002).

In addition to probable cause, the nature of the search is important. Does it involve passing through a metal detector or opening a school bag, or is it more intrusive? The courts have consistently upheld the legality of metal detectors at school entrances, asserting that such searches are nonintrusive (Zirkel, 1999). However, more intrusive strip searches are generally considered illegal. In one case, a high school student was strip-searched for drugs after a police dog mistakenly identified her as carrying drugs. (Authorities later found that the dog was drawn to the young girl because she had been playing earlier that day with her dog, which was in heat.) The school district was required to pay damages to the girl's family (*Doe v. Renfrow*, 1980). In a more recent case, high school students were required to strip to their underwear in an attempt to recover missing money ($364) (Hendrie, 2005a). A federal circuit court found the search unconstitutional, concluding that the missing money did not justify the intrusiveness of the search. While condoning searches for probable cause, the courts remain sensitive to the rights of students (Ehlenberger, 2001/2002). School lockers, however, are considered school property and may be searched if reasonable cause (e.g., suspicion of drug or weapon possession) exists.

The use of urine tests to detect drug use illustrates how legal issues can become convoluted. In one case, the Supreme Court held that random drug testing for student athletes was legal, arguing that the safety of students and the importance of a drug-free school environment outweighed the privacy rights of student athletes who were participating voluntarily (*Board of Education of Independent School District No. 92 of Pottawatomie County v. Earls*, 2002). Another case involved an Indiana youth suspended for fighting (Zirkel, 1999). The school required the student to undergo a urine test for drugs before being readmitted after a 5-day suspension. In this case, the courts ruled in favor of the student, defending the boy's right to privacy and the lack of solid reasons for the urine tests. The courts have been unanimous in prohibiting school-wide drug testing (Underwood & Webb, 2006).

Student Records and Privacy

Students' records—grades, standardized test scores, teacher comments, and letters of recommendation—can determine whether or not students are admitted to special programs or colleges of their choice. They also influence students' abilities to get jobs. What legal safeguards guide the creation and use of these potentially life- and career-influencing records?

In 1974 Congress passed the Family Educational Rights and Privacy Act (FERPA) as an amendment to the Elementary and Secondary Education Act of 1965. Also called the **Buckley Amendment**, FERPA is a federal act that makes school records open and accessible to students and their parents. Under this act, schools must do the following:

1. Inform parents of their rights regarding their child's records.
2. Provide parents access to their child's records.
3. Maintain procedures that allow parents to challenge and possibly amend information that they believe is inaccurate.
4. Protect parents from disclosure of confidential information to third parties without their consent.

Buckley Amendment. A federal act that makes school records open and accessible to students and their parents.

333

The law doesn't guarantee access to all student records, however. Teachers may jot down notes during a busy school day, such as reminders about a student's behavior that will help the teacher decide whether to refer the child for special education testing. These notes cannot be made public without the teacher's consent. Also, a teacher's letter of recommendation may remain confidential if students waive their rights to access. To protect teachers in these situations, the Buckley Amendment excludes teachers' private notes, grade books, or correspondence with administrators.

A recent court case further defined the types of information protected by the Buckley Amendment (Walsh, 2002c). A mother in Oklahoma objected to the practice of having her children's papers graded by other students and the results called out in class. She claimed this violated her children's rights to privacy, and a federal circuit court agreed. However, in a unanimous decision, the U.S. Supreme Court overturned the lower court's decision. The Supreme Court concluded that the term *education records* did not cover student homework or classroom work.

Administrators and teachers have mixed feelings about the Buckley Amendment because of the extra effort and paperwork required to put these procedural safeguards into place and because of potential encroachments into teachers' private records. However, the law has improved parents' access to information as they try to make sound decisions about their children, and it has made school officials more sensitive to the importance of confidentiality for students' and parents' needs for information.

Corporal Punishment

In one Pennsylvania elementary school, a 36-year-old, 6-foot-tall, 210-pound school principal paddled a 45-pound first-grade boy four different times during one school day for a total of 60 to 70 swats. After the incident, the boy needed psychological counseling, cried frequently, and had nightmares and trouble sleeping (Commonwealth of Pennsylvania v. Douglass, 1991).

The Fayette County Board of Education in Tennessee specified in 1994 that any paddles used to discipline students must be

- *Not less than ⅜ inch or more than ½ inch thick*
- *Free of splinters*
- *Constructed of quality white ash*
- *Three inches wide (except the handle) and not more than 15 inches long for grades K–5*
- *Three and a half inches wide (except the handle) and not more than 18 inches long for grades 6–12*

Students can receive a maximum of three swats with these district-approved paddles (R. Johnston, 1994).

Corporal punishment—the use of physical, punitive disciplinary actions to correct student misbehavior—is highly controversial, both because of the legal issues involved and because using physical punishment as a disciplinary tool is questionable. In a 1977 landmark case, the U.S. Supreme Court ruled that corporal punishment in schools is not a violation of the Eighth Amendment to the Constitution (which prohibits cruel and unusual punishment). The Court further ruled that states may authorize corporal punishment without prior hearing and without the prior permission of parents (*Ingraham v. Wright*, 1977). In the 2002–2003 school year, more than 300,000 students were disciplined with corporal punishment, and corporal punishment is much more common in the rural south and the lower midwest (Lyman, 2006). As of 2004, it was prohibited in 28 states and the District of Columbia, which means the door is left open for the use of corporal punishment in the remaining 22 states. So where does that leave prospective teachers?

In states where corporal punishment is permitted, legal guidelines suggest teachers may use corporal punishment under the following conditions:

- The punishment is intended to correct misbehavior.
- Administering the punishment doesn't involve anger or malice.
- The punishment is neither cruel nor excessive and doesn't result in lasting injury.

Corporal punishment. The use of physical, punitive disciplinary actions to correct student misbehavior.

Teachers considering this disciplinary option should also ask themselves several questions:

- Is this the best way to teach students about inappropriate behavior?
- Would other options be more effective in encouraging students to consider their behaviors and the effects of those behaviors on others?
- What does corporal punishment teach children about the use of force to solve problems?

Psychologists generally disapprove of the use of corporal punishment, not only because of the possibilities that negative side effects can occur, such as modeled aggression, but also because more effective alternatives exist (Berk, 2005). Because of both legal and psychological issues, corporal punishment should be avoided in all but the most extreme conditions.

This section addresses the last item on our beginning-of-chapter survey, "Corporal punishment in schools is prohibited by law." As you saw above, the majority of states (28) prohibit the use of corporal punishment, but it is legal in 22 others. Despite its legality, experts suggest that corporal punishment should be avoided in all but the most extreme circumstances.

Students' Rights in Disciplinary Actions

Jessie Tynes, a sixth-grade teacher, turns around just in time to see Billy punch Jared. "Billy, what did I tell you about keeping your hands to yourself?" the teacher demands. "This school and my classroom have no room for this kind of nonsense! You're out of this class until I meet with your parents. Come with me to the principal's office where you'll sit until we can solve this problem of keeping your hands to yourself."

Sean, a high school junior, is walking to his locker when someone reaches in from behind to knock his books on the floor. When he turns around, he sees Dave standing behind him with a smirk on his face. Losing his temper, Sean pushes Dave. A scuffle begins, but it is broken up by Mr. Higgins, the vice principal. Both students receive 10-day suspensions from school.

How are the problems similar? How are they different? What legal guidelines assist educators as they try to deal fairly and effectively with school discipline problems? Both incidents involve infractions of school rules, but they differ in the severity of the problem and resulting actions. These differences are important when the courts consider due process, a central issue with respect to students' rights.

Students have a right to an education, and the courts specify that limiting this right can occur only when due process is followed. However, the courts also acknowledge the rights of schools to discipline students in the day-to-day running of schools.

Suspending Billy from class, for example, would be considered an internal affair best resolved by his teacher, parents, and himself. Unless a suspension lasts longer than 10 days or results in expulsion from school, teachers and administrators are generally free to discipline as they see fit, assuming the punishment is fair and administered equitably.

Actions that lead to out-of-school expulsion, such as the incident between Sean and Dave, entry on a student's record, or permanent expulsion require more formalized safeguards, especially if they last longer than 10 days. These include the following:

1. A written notice specifying charges and the time and place of a fair, impartial hearing
2. A description of the procedures to be used, including the nature of evidence and names of witnesses
3. The right of students to legal counsel and to cross-examine and present their own evidence
4. A written or taped record of the proceedings as well as the findings and recommendations
5. The right of appeal

As this list shows, the procedures involved in long-term (longer than 10 days) suspensions and expulsions are quite detailed and formal. Whether due process means that students have a right to a lawyer during suspension proceedings remains unclear, however. A current court case in North Carolina involving this issue could set a national precedent (Bowman, 2003). Due process rights exist to safeguard students' rights to an education, an economic necessity in today's modern world. Since long-term suspensions or expulsion consume considerable amounts of time and energy, schools generally use them only as a last resort.

Disciplinary Actions and Students With Exceptionalities

Students with exceptionalities are provided with additional legal safeguards under the Individuals with Disabilities Education Acts (IDEA) of 1997 and 2004. These laws were passed to ensure students with exceptionalities access to an education while still safeguarding the rights of other students (Hardman, Drew, & Egan, 2006; Heward, 2006). IDEA 1997 enabled school administrators to discipline students with disabilities in the same way as students without disabilities but required them to review a change of placement, suspension, or expulsion in excess of 10 days. The purpose of this special review was to determine if the student's behavior was related to a disability, such as a behavior disorder. If the review determined that the student's behavior was not related to the disability, the same disciplinary procedures used with other students could be imposed, but the school must still continue to provide educational services in the alternative placement.

The Individuals with Disabilities Education Act of 2004 revised these discipline procedures to make it easier to remove a student with disabilities under special circumstances (e.g., the student brings a weapon to school; possesses, uses, or sells illegal drugs at school; or inflicts serious injury to someone at school). Under these circumstances, school officials can remove a student with disabilities to an interim alternative educational setting for up to 45 school days, regardless of whether the misconduct was related to the child's disability. This latter provision was designed to ensure the safety of other students and teachers.

Students With AIDS

AIDS became a major health and legal issue in the schools in the 1980s. Previously thought to be limited to sexually active gay men and drug users who shared hypodermic needles, AIDS entered the school-age population through contaminated blood transfusions.

Battle lines were quickly drawn. Concerned parents worried that the AIDS virus would be spread in school through either casual contact or the sometimes rough-and-tumble world of children on playgrounds. Parents of children with AIDS wanted their children to have access to as normal an education as possible. The courts were soon drawn into the fray.

A landmark and precedent-setting case occurred in St. Petersburg, Florida, in 1987 and involved 7-year-old Randy Ray, a hemophiliac infected with the AIDS virus through a blood transfusion. Because of his condition and fears about possible spread of the disease, school officials refused to allow Randy and his two brothers, who also were infected, to attend school. His parents first reacted by moving elsewhere, but when that failed to open school doors, they moved back to St. Petersburg and sued the school district.

A U.S. district court ruled that the boys should be allowed to attend school with special safeguards, including special attention to the potential hazards of blood spills (*Ray v. School District of DeSoto County,* 1987). Subsequent cases involving other students with HIV/AIDS have been similarly resolved, with courts holding that these children are protected by the Individuals with Disabilities Act of 1991 as well as Section 504 of the Rehabilitation Act of 1973, laws that prohibit discrimination against individuals with disabilities. Central to the courts' decisions has been the potential negative effects of exclusion on the social and emotional well-being of the child. The courts have been clear in rejecting exclusion as the automatic solution to the problem of dealing with HIV-infected students and instead have required schools to address the specific risk factors involved in each case.

Making Connections:
To deepen your
CW understanding of the
topics in this section of the
chapter and integrate them
with topics you've already
studied, go to the *Making
Connections* module for
Chapter 9 at
www.prenhall.com/kauchak.
Respond to questions 11–14.

Affirmative Action

Affirmative action—a collection of policies and procedures designed to overcome past racial, ethnic, gender, and disability discrimination—was one outcome of the civil rights movement of the 1960s. Affirmative action was based on the belief that merely outlawing discrimination was not enough; to correct past discriminatory practices, society should take steps to ensure racial and gender equity and balance in all aspects of society, including schools. Currently, advocates of some forms of affirmative action emphasize the educational benefits of racial diversity for all students.

The legal basis for affirmative action comes from three sources. The Fourteenth Amendment to the Constitution guarantees equal protection under the law. Titles VI and VII of the Civil Rights Act of 1964 specifically prohibit discrimination in federally assisted educational programs with respect to race, color, religion, sex, or national origin. The Americans with Disabilities Act of 1990 extends similar protection to persons with disabilities.

Affirmative action affects schools in two important areas: hiring policies for teachers and admission policies for students. In an attempt to remedy past discriminatory hiring practices, courts required a number of school districts under affirmative action guidelines to hire more minority teachers. Higher courts have generally upheld this practice if affirmative action is deemed necessary to reverse past discriminatory practices (Fischer et al., 2003).

However, in cases where discrimination was not evident as a problem in past instances, courts discourage preferential hiring practices for minorities on criteria other than merit or qualifications. For example, because of declining enrollments, a school district in New Jersey was forced to reduce the teaching staff in the business department of a high school by one teacher. Two teachers, one White and one African-American, had equal seniority and were considered to be of equal quality. The school board decided to retain the African-American, using affirmative action as a rationale. The White teacher sued, claiming she was being discriminated against, and the courts agreed, arguing that minorities had not been underrepresented in the district's teaching force in the past (*Taxman v. Board of Education of Township of Piscataway*, 1996). Subsequently, higher federal courts ruled in her favor, deciding that for affirmative action to be legal, a logical basis for its use must be present (Fischer et al., 2003).

Affirmative action affects K–12 students in two ways (Walsh, 2002a). A number of districts nationwide attempt to achieve racially balanced schools through voluntary transfers across schools. In these cases, a student from a poor-performing school would have the option to transfer to a better school elsewhere in the district. In addition, magnet schools, designed to provide diversity by attracting talented students, use race as one selection criteria.

Affirmative action cases have resulted in charges of reverse discrimination, with critics alleging that minorities and women have been given unfair preferential treatment in hiring and admission decisions. One such claim was made in 1974 by Alan Bakke, a White student denied admission to medical school. Bakke sued the school because minority candidates with grades and test scores lower than his had been admitted. The case reached the U.S. Supreme Court, which ruled in a 5–4 vote that Bakke should be admitted. However, in making its decision, the Court did not rule out other forms of race-conscious admission procedures (*Regents of the University of California v. Bakke*, 1978). Recently, the Supreme Court heard an affirmative action case involving the University of Michigan. In a close 5–4 vote, the Court upheld the practice of considering race in admissions decisions (Walsh, 2003a). The benefits of a diverse student body were central to the Court's decision. Experts predict that this decision will influence not only colleges and universities but also future efforts to achieve racial balance in K–12 schools.

The issue of affirmative action is likely to remain controversial in the future. Toward the end of the 1990s, voters in California and Washington supported legislation eliminating preferential admission policies in higher education (Dworkin, 1998). In addition, court cases have raised questions about the legality of racial quotas for magnet schools (Dowling-Sendor, 1999). Legal experts in this area conclude, "In sum, the Supreme Court, like the country as a whole, is deeply divided on the question of the constitutionality and desirability of affirmative action (Fischer et al., 2003, p. 316).

A court case currently before the Supreme Court could provide some insights into the future of affirmative action. While not directly involving affirmative action, the court case, brought by parents in both Jefferson County, Kentucky, and Seattle, Washington, questions the legality of using race to assign students to schools (Trotter, 2006a). District administrators support this practice, believing that racial diversity has both educational and social benefits and is one powerful tool to battle segregation in housing that then leads to segregated schools. Parents opposing this practice believe that their children suffer because of lack of access to certain schools and having to travel long distances to help the district attain racial diversity.

> **Affirmative action.** A collection of policies and procedures designed to overcome past racial, ethnic, gender, and disability discrimination.

Check Your Understanding

5.1 What are students' rights in terms of freedom of speech?

5.2 Can students be searched? What about their lockers and other possessions?

5.3 What is the Buckley Amendment? Why is it important to both schools and teachers?

5.4 Is corporal punishment legal in schools?

5.5 What are students' rights in terms of disciplinary actions?

5.6 What are the legal rights of students with AIDS?

 For feedback, go to Check Your Understanding, *at the end of this chapter.*

decision making

Defining Yourself as a Professional

You are an elementary teacher in a self-contained classroom. You have a class of 29 lively sixth graders, and you've been struggling all year with classroom management. Damien, a larger than average boy, seems to resist your efforts at every turn.

You like science and have tried to provide concrete, hands-on science activities whenever you can. You've been debating about a fun activity on chemical changes where students actually test different mystery powders (e.g., sugar, salt, baking soda) with different liquids such as water and vinegar. You decide to go ahead with it and strategically place Damien up toward the front of the room where you can watch him, and have paired him with Katie, one of your more responsible female students.

Everything is going well until you go to the back of the room to answer a question and hear a student shriek, "Damien!" As you rush to the front of the room, you see Katie holding her eye, with a mixture of vinegar and baking soda dripping down her cheek. Damien is sitting there with a guilty look on his face. As you rush the crying Katie to the office, you wonder if there isn't something you should have done differently.

What would you do in this situation?

To respond to this question online and receive immediate feedback, go to the Decision Making *module for Chapter 9 on the Companion Website at* www.prenhall.com/kauchak.

Meeting Your Learning Objectives

1. Explain the differences between legal and ethical influences on the teaching profession.
   - Laws and ethical codes provide guidelines as teachers make professional decisions. Laws specify what teachers must and can do. Codes of ethics provide guidelines for what teachers should do as conscientious and caring professionals. Professional organizations such as the National Education Association and American Federation of Teachers publish codes of ethics for teachers.
   - Two major drawbacks to using both laws and ethical codes to guide professional decisions are (1) they are general, lacking in specificity, and (2) they are created to address problems in the past and, consequently, may not be relevant to current issues and topics.

2. Describe the U.S. legal system in terms of federal, state, and local influences on teaching.
   - The U.S. legal system is a complex web of interconnected bodies. At the federal level the U.S. Constitution provides broad guidelines for legal issues, and Congress passes laws that impact education.
   - Most of the direct legal responsibility for running schools belongs to states and local school districts. The U.S. Constitution gives states the legal rights to govern education, and many day-to-day responsibilities are passed on to districts.
   - The overlapping U.S. legal system places the legal responsibility for specific issues or cases at different levels depending on the particular issue involved.

3. Describe teachers' legal rights and responsibilities.
   - Teachers have rights and responsibilities as professional educators. Licensure provides them with the right to teach; a teaching contract specifies the legal conditions for employment. Most new teachers are hired on probationary status. Once granted tenure, teachers cannot be dismissed without due process.
   - Teachers' academic freedom is guaranteed by the First Amendment to the Constitution. However, in deciding on issues of academic freedom, the courts examine the educational relevance of the content or method involved and the age of the students.
   - Copyright laws, designed to protect the property rights of authors, provide restrictions on teachers' use of others' original materials. New questions about fair use are being raised by the increased use of videotape and DVDs and material presented on the Internet.
   - Liability poses unique challenges to teachers. The courts hold that teachers act *in loco parentis,* and when they fail to protect the children under their charge, they can be sued for negligence. When deciding on issues of liability, the courts take into account the age and developmental level of students as well as the kinds of risks involved in an activity.
   - Teachers' private lives are not as private as some would wish. Teachers are expected to be role models to students, so their activities in their hours away from school are often scrutinized and, if illegal, can result in dismissal.

4. Discuss the legal implications of religion in the schools.
   - Because of differing beliefs about the proper role of religion in education, religion provides a legal battleground in the schools. Organized or school sponsored prayer is banned in schools, but students' rights to pray in school is protected by law.
   - Courts have approved religious clubs and organizations and private expressions of student religious beliefs. Religious clubs are provided the same legal safeguards as other extracurricular organizations.
   - Although the courts disapprove of religious advocacy, teaching about religion is legal when it can be justified educationally.

5. Explain students' legal rights and responsibilities.
   - Many of the same issues of rights involving freedom of speech and due process that affect teachers also pertain to students. Students' right to freedom of speech are protected by the courts, but the expression of free speech must not interfere with the school's or teacher's instructional agenda.
   - Students are protected from unreasonable search and seizure by the U.S. Constitution. However, lockers are considered school property, and students' and their belongings may be searched if school officials have a reasonable suspicion about the possession of drugs or dangerous weapons.
   - Students' education records are protected by federal legislation called the Buckley Amendment. The main thrust of this law is to protect the privacy rights of students' educational records.
   - Corporal punishment is legally allowed in a number of states. Those laws contain safeguards against injury and anger or malice.
   - Because the courts view attending public schools as a legal right, school officials must conduct student suspension or expulsion from school in a prescribed manner that makes the process transparent to parents or guardians.
   - The educational rights of students with AIDS are protected by law. School officials must address specific risk factors to other students when excluding children with AIDS from educational activities.

Important Concepts

academic freedom
affirmative action
Buckley Amendment
collective bargaining
copyright laws
corporal punishment
establishment clause
fair use guidelines
free exercise clause

grievance
in loco parentis
licensure
negligence
notoriety
professional ethics
reduction in force
teaching contract
tenure

Developing as a Professional

Preparing for Your Licensure Exam

This exercise will provide you with practice answering questions similar to the Praxis™ Principles of Learning and Teaching Exam as well as your state-specific licensure exam. Read the following case study, and answer the questions that follow.

"Hi, Kyle. What are you working on?" Jan Trefino asks, as she returns the borrowed overhead projector to her neighbor's high school classroom.

"Oh, just trying to plan for next week. You know, try to stay a day or two ahead of the students. How did it work?"

"Great! Thanks a lot. It was a real life-saver. I had all these transparencies and. . . . While I have you here, can I ask you a question? Since you're a veteran, you seem to know everything."

"Yeah, right. Teaching for 4 years will do that to you," Kyle says, laughing. "What's the question?"

"Well, the unit coming up is on the labor movement in the United States, and I'd like to connect it with some of the controversies we've been reading about in the local papers. I'd like to talk about the unionization of the migrant farm workers, but I'm a little nervous about getting into hot water. Any advice?"

"I'd say go for it. Students need to see how abstract ideas from the past relate to their everyday lives," Kyle responds. "Let me tell you about something that happened to me in my English class. We were reading a short story about a young runaway girl who was in trouble. The story hinted at, but didn't say explicitly, that she might be pregnant. So as we were discussing the story, I mentioned that there were agencies around like adoption agencies and Planned Parenthood to help people in that situation."

"Yikes, you're brave. Any fallout?"

"Not yet, though I may have overstepped my bounds when one student started preaching about morality and religion. I cut him off, saying, 'We can't talk about religion in school.' He gave me a funny look but didn't say anything more."

"So, you think it's okay to bring in clippings from the local newspaper about the union controversy?" Jan asks.

"Sure, if it's in the newspaper, why couldn't you?"

1. What professional legal issue were Jan and Kyle wrestling with, and what legal safeguards influence this issue?

2. How did the two teachers differ in terms of work experience, and how might this influence their curricular decisions?

3. Comment on Kyle's statement, "We can't talk about religion in school," from a legal perspective.

4. From a professional ethics perspective, what advice do you have for Jan about her discussion of local union controversies?

To receive feedback on your responses to these exercises, go to the Companion Website at www.prenhall.com/kauchak, then to the Preparing for Your Licensure Exam *module for Chapter 9.*

Discussion Questions

1. What are the advantages and disadvantages of teacher tenure? What arguments might there be for a longer period of probation before granting a teacher tenure? A shorter period? Should teachers be reviewed periodically after tenure is granted?

2. What is the proper role of religion in the schools? In what areas of the curriculum should religion enter? Should teachers reveal their religious beliefs to students? What should a teacher do if a student shares his or her religious beliefs with the class?

3. Touching can be a powerful way of expressing caring or concern. Should teachers touch their students? How and under what circumstances? How might circumstances differ depending on the age and gender of students and the age and gender of the teacher?

4. What place should corporal punishment have in schools? How might the use of corporal punishment be influenced by the following factors: age of student, type of misbehavior, and age and gender of teacher?

5. Should teachers' private lives be placed under any more public examination than the lives of other professionals, such as doctors or lawyers? Why or why not?

Developing as a Professional: Online Activities

Going Into Schools

Go to the Companion Website at *www.prenhall.com/kauchak*, and click on the *Going Into Schools* module for Chapter 9. You will find a number of school-based activities that will help you link chapter content to the schools in which you work.

Virtual Field Experience: Using the Internet to Explore the Profession

If you would like to participate in a Virtual Field Experience, access the following Website: *http://www.nea.org/he/tenure.html*. This site provides data and opinions about teacher tenure from the perspective of the National Education Association, the largest professional organization in education.

Online Portfolio Activities

To develop your professional portfolio, further apply your understanding of chapter content, and address the INTASC standards, go the Companion Website at *www.prenhall.com/kauchak*, then to the *Online Portfolio Activities* for Chapter 9. Complete the suggested activities.

Check Your Understanding

1.1   **What are two limitations of using existing laws as the basis for professional decision making?**

One limitation is that laws are left purposefully abstract and general so they can apply to a large number of bases. This makes laws vague in terms of specific instances requiring decision making. A second limitation of using laws is that they were created in response to problems that existed in the past and may not provide specific guidelines for future professional decisions.

1.2   **How are laws different from ethics in terms of teacher decision making?**

Laws tell teachers what they can do (their rights) as well as what they must do (their responsibilities), but they don't tell teachers what they should do. This is the role of professional ethics, which attempts to provide guidelines for professional conduct.

2.1   **How do federal laws influence education?**

Federal laws primarily influence education through three amendments to the Constitution. The First Amendment to the Constitution guarantees all citizens freedom of speech. This amendment forms the basis for academic freedom in the classroom. The Fourth Amendment protects citizens from unreasonable searches and seizures. This amendment protects students from unwarranted or unreasonable searches while they are on school grounds. The Fourteenth Amendment to the Constitution guarantees due process in issues involving deprivation of life, liberty, or property. This amendment not only protects teachers from dismissal without a formal hearing, it also protects students from expulsion or suspension from school without due process.

2.2   **How do state laws influence education policies and practices?**

States are legally entrusted with the education of children. States influence education by passing laws regulating teachers' qualifications, working conditions, and legal rights. States also create departments of education, which are given responsibilities for formulating educational policies in the state.

2.3   **What is the educational significance of the overlapping legal system in the United States?**

Because different laws influencing education are created at different levels, legal issues and problems that arise from these different levels need to be resolved at the level at which the law was formed. For example, if a legal dispute involves a teacher's qualifications for being a teacher, this would go to a state court because the laws regulating teacher qualifications are formed at that level.

3.1   **How are teacher employment issues influenced by the law?**

Teacher employment issues are influenced in several ways by legal considerations. First, licensure is a state responsibility, and rules and regulations passed by each state determine licensure policies and procedures. Local school boards are given the legal responsibility for issuing contracts, which specify the legal conditions for a teacher's employment. Teacher tenure, which is a legal safeguard that provides job security for teachers, is determined at the state level and protects teachers from dismissal without cause. Because of these overlapping spheres of influence, teacher dismissal is a gray area that may be influenced both by state as well as district legal regulations.

3.2   **What is academic freedom, and why is it important to teachers?**

Academic freedom, which is based on the First Amendment to the Constitution, protects the right of teachers to choose both content and teaching methods based on their professional judgment. It protects teachers from undue external influences on their classroom instruction.

3.3   How do copyright laws influence teachers' practices?

Copyright laws are federal laws designed to protect the intellectual property of authors. Fair-use guidelines specify limitations on the number of copies of books that teachers can reproduce for their classrooms. They also place restrictions on the use of videotaped programs and computer software.

3.4   What is teacher liability, and how does it influence teachers?

Teachers are legally responsible for the safety of children under their case. The term in loco parentis means that teachers are legally expected to act in the place of parents. Failure to do so can result in negligence and a legal suit involving liability for the teacher.

3.5   How are teachers' rights in terms of their own private lives similar to and different from those of the general public?

All citizens of the United States are guaranteed the right to "life, liberty, and the pursuit of happiness." However, because teachers, as professionals, are expected to be role models for the children they teach, their rights as private individuals may be curtailed.

4.1   What federal law influences the discussion of religion in the schools?

The First Amendment to the Constitution states, "Congress shall make no law respecting an establishment of religion, or prohibiting the free exercise thereof." This law explicitly forbids the teaching of religion in the schools, but it also prohibits the government from interfering with individuals' rights to hold religious beliefs and freely practice religion.

4.2   What is the legal status of prayer in schools?

Neither schools nor teachers can officially encourage school prayer; however, prayer is permissible when student initiated and when it doesn't interfere with other students or the school. For example, an individual student or students saying grace before lunch in a cafeteria would be permissible under the law.

4.3   Can a school allow religious clubs or organizations to meet on school grounds?

If the school does not specifically sponsor the religious club or organization, the U.S. Supreme Court has ruled that it is legal for schools to allow religious, philosophical, and political groups to use school facilities in the same way as other extracurricular organizations.

4.4   What is the legal status of religion in the curriculum?

Advocacy of religion in the schools is legally forbidden. However, teachers may discuss how religion has influenced history or culture.

5.1   What are students' rights in terms of freedom of speech?

The First Amendment to the Constitution guarantees all U.S. citizens freedom of speech. Students in school have this same right, provided that doing so doesn't interfere with learning. So, for example, students can't get up in a social studies class and make a speech about their political beliefs. This doesn't mean they can't express their beliefs briefly if the context is appropriate, but in exercising free speech, they can't interfere with the teacher's (and the class's) academic agenda.

5.2   Can students be searched? What about their lockers and other possessions?

If school authorities believe there is probable cause in terms of a student possessing drugs or a dangerous weapon, the school may conduct a nonobtrusive search of the student and his or her possessions (nonobtrusive does not include a strip search). School lockers are considered school property and may be searched if reasonable cause of a drug or weapons violation exists.

343

5.3   What is the Buckley Amendment? Why is it important to both schools and teachers?

The Buckley Amendment protects a family's rights to privacy in terms of school records. It requires schools to (1) inform parents of their rights regarding their child's records, (2) provide parents access to their child's records, (3) maintain procedures that allow parents to challenge those records, and (4) protect parents from disclosure of confidential information. Since teachers are legal extensions of schools, they are legally bound by the same safeguards.

5.4   Is corporal punishment legal in schools?

Corporal punishment is a state-by-state legal issue. In those states that do allow corporal punishment, it must be administered to correct misbehavior, can't involve anger or malice, and can't be cruel or excessive or result in lasting injury.

5.5   What are students' rights in terms of disciplinary actions?

Students have a right to an education, and this right can only be abridged or changed through due process. If school administrators must suspend a student for an extended period of time, they must notify the student in writing of the reasons or charges, share the legal procedures and evidence, guarantee the student access to legal counsel, and record proceedings and findings, and the student must have a right to appeal.

5.6   What are the legal rights of students with AIDS?

Because they have a right to an education, students with AIDS cannot be automatically excluded from school activities. Schools must address specific risk factors to other students when they change the instructional activities or opportunities for a student with AIDS.

References

AAUW Education Foundation Commission on Technology, Gender, and Teacher Education. (2000). *Tech-savvy: Educating girls in the new computer age*. Washington, DC: Author.

Abedi, J., Hofstetter, C., & Lord, C. (2004). Assessment accommodations for English language learners: Implications for policy-based empirical research. *Review of Educational Research, 74*(1), 1–28.

Abington School District v. Schempp, 374 U.S. 203 (1963).

Abowitz, K. (2000). A pragmatist revisioning of resistance theory. *American Educational Research Journal, 39*, 877–907.

Adams, D. (1995). *Education for extinction: American Indians in the boarding school experience, 1875–1928*. Lawrence: University Press of Kansas.

Adler, M. (1982). *The Paideia proposal: An educational manifesto*. New York: Macmillan.

Adler, M. (1998). *The Paideia proposal: An educational manifesto*. (Reprint.) New York: Simon & Schuster.

Alan Guttmacher Institute. (2004). *Teen pregnancy: Trends and lessons learned*. Retrieved June 13, 2006, from *http://www.agi-us.org/pubs/ib_1_02.pdf*

Alder, N. (2002). Interpretations of the meaning of care: Creating caring relationship in urban middle school classrooms. *Urban Education, 37*(2), 241–266.

Alexander, K., & Alexander, M. D. (2001). *American public school law*. Belmont, CA: Wadsworth.

Alexander, L., & Riley, R. (2002). A compass in the storm. *Education Week, 22*(6), 36–37, 48.

Alexander, P. (2006). *Psychology in learning and instruction*. Upper Saddle River, NJ: Merrill/Prentice Hall.

Allen, R. (2002). Big schools: The way we are. *Educational Leadership, 59*(5), 36–41.

Allington, R. L., & McGill-Franzen, A. (2003). The impact of summer setback on the reading achievement gap. *Phi Delta Kappan, 85*(1), 68–71.

Alperstein, J. F. (2005). Commentary on girls, boys, test scores and more. *Teachers College Record*. Date Published: May 16, 2005. Retrieved June 21, 2005, from *http://tcrecord.org* ID Number: 11874

American Association for the Advancement of Science. (1989). *Project 2061: Science for all Americans*. Washington, DC: Author.

American Association of University Women. (1992). *How schools shortchange girls*. Annapolis Junction, MD: Author.

American Association of University Women. (1998). *Gender gaps: Where schools still fail our children*. Annapolis Junction, MD: Author.

American Association of University Women. (2006). *Drawing the line: Sexual harassment on campus*. New York: Harris Interactive.

American Association of University Women Educational Foundation. (2001). *Hostile hallways: Bullying, teasing, and sexual harassment in school*. New York: Harris Interactive.

American Council of Trustees and Alumni. (2000). *Losing America's memory: Historical illiteracy in the 21st century*. Washington, DC: Author.

American Educational Research Association. (2006). Retrieved September 6, 2006, from *http://www.aera.net*

American Federation of Teachers. (2003). *Voucher home page*. Retrieved February 3, 2004, from *http://www.aft.org/research/vouchers*

American Federation of Teachers. (2004). *Survey and analysis of teacher salary trends 2004*. Retrieved February 2004, from *http://www.aft.org/research/survey02/SalarySurvey02.pdf*

American Federation of Teachers. (2006). Retrieved August 16, 2006, from *http://www.aft.org*

American Psychological Association. (1998). *How students learn: Reforming our schools through learner-centered education*. Washington, DC: Author.

American Psychological Association. (2006). Retrieved September 6, 2006, from *http://www.apa.org*

Amrein, A., & Berliner, D. (2003). The effects of high-stakes testing on student motivation and learning. *Educational Leadership, 60*(5), 32–38.

Anagnostopoulos, D. (2006). "Real students" and "true demotes": Ending social promotion and the moral ordering of urban high schools. *American Educational Research Journal, 43*(1), 5–42.

Anderson, G., Jimerson, S., & Whipple, A. (2002). *Student's ratings of stressful experiences at home and school: Loss of a parent and grade retention as superlative stressors.* Manuscript prepared for publication, available from authors at the University of California, Santa Barbara, CA.

Anderson, J. (1988). *The education of Blacks in the South.* Chapel Hill: University of North Carolina Press.

Anderson, L., & Krathwohl, D. (Eds.). (2001). *A taxonomy for learning, teaching, and assessing: A revision of Bloom's taxonomy of educational objectives.* New York: Addison Wesley Longman.

Ansell, S., & McCabe, M. (2003). Off target. *Education Week, 22*(17), 57–58.

Ansell, S., & Park, J. (2003). Tracking tech trends. *Education Week, 22*(35), 43–49.

Antil, L., Jenkins, J., Wayne, S., & Vadasy, P. (1998). Cooperative learning: Prevalence, conceptualizations, and the relation between research and practice. *American Educational Research Journal, 35*(3), 419–454.

Apple, M. (1995). *Education and power* (2nd ed.). New York: Rutledge.

Archer, J. (2000a). Competition fierce for minority teachers. *Education Week, 19*(18), 32–33.

Archer, J. (2000b). Teachers warned against teaching contracts. *Education Week, 20*(15), 30.

Archer, J. (2003). Increasing the odds. *Education Week, 22*(17), 52–56.

Archer, J. (2005). Connecticut files court challenge to NCLB. *Education Week, 25*(1), 23, 27.

Archer, J. (2006a). Building capacity. *Supplement to Education Week, 26*(3), S3–S12.

Archer, J. (2006b). The road less traveled. *Education Week, 25*(17), 34–37.

Armour-Thomas, E. (2004). What is the nature of evaluation and assessment in an urban context? In S. R. Steinberg & J. L. Kincheloe (Eds.), *19 Urban questions: Teaching in the city* (pp. 109–118). New York: Peter Lang.

Armstrong, D. (2003). *Curriculum today.* Upper Saddle River, NJ: Merrill/Prentice Hall.

Aronson, E., Wilson, T., & Akert, R. (2005). *Social psychology* (5th ed.). Upper Saddle River, NJ: Pearson.

Asian-Nation. (2005). Retrieved February 17, 2005, from *http://www.asian-nation.org/model-minority.shtml*

Associated Press. (2000). Texas legislative panel calls for charter schools moratorium. *Boston Globe,* December 29, A13.

Attewell, P. (2001). The first and second digital divides. *Sociology of Education, 74*(July), 252–259.

Attiel, A., Sober, S., Numbers, R., Amasino, R., Cox, B., Berceau, B., Powell, T., & Cox, M. (2006). Defending science education against intelligent design: A call to action. *Journal of Clinical Investigation, 116,* 1134–1138.

Ayers, W., Dohrn, B. & Ayers, R. (Eds.). (2001). *Zero tolerance.* New York: New Press.

Azevedo, R. (2005). Computer environments as metacognitive tools for enhancing learning. *Educational Psychologist, 40*(4), 193–197.

Babad, E., Bernieri, F., & Rosenthal, R. (1991). Students as judges of teachers' verbal and nonverbal behavior. *American Educational Research Journal, 28*(1), 211–234.

Bae, G. (2003, April). *Rethinking constructivism in multicultural contexts: Does constructivism in education take the issue of diversity into consideration?* Paper presented at the annual meeting of the American Educational Research Association, Chicago.

Baker, D. (2006, July 3). For Navajo, science and tradition intertwine. *Salt Lake Tribune,* pp. D1, D5.

Baker, P., & Slevin, P. (2005, August 3). Bush remarks on "Intelligent Design" Theory fuel debate. *The Washington Post.* Retrieved October 1, 2006, from *http://www.washingtonpost.com/wp-dyn/content/article/2005/08/02/AR2005080201686.html*

Bali, V., Anagnostopoulos, D., & Roberts, R. (2005). Toward a political explanation of grade retention. *Educational Evaluation and Policy Analysis, 27*(2), 133–155.

Bandura, A. (2001). *Social cognitive theory. Annual Review of Psychology.* Palo Alto, CA: Annual Review.

Bandura, A. (2004, May). *Toward a psychology of human agency.* Paper presented at the meeting of the American Psychological Society, Chicago.

Bangert-Drowns, R. (1993). The word processor as an instructional tool: A meta-analysis of word processing in writing instruction. *Review of Educational Research, 63,* 69–93.

Banks, J. (2006a). *An introduction to multicultural education* (4th ed.). Boston: Allyn & Bacon.

Banks, J. (2006b). *Cultural diversity and education* (6th ed.). Boston: Allyn & Bacon.

Bardige, B. (2005). *At a loss for words: How America is failing our children and what we can do about it.* Philadelphia: Temple University Press.

Barnoski, L. (2005). My purpose. *Education Week, 25*(13), 37.

Barone, M. (2000). In plain English: Bilingual education flunks out of schools in California. *U.S. News & World Report, 128*(21), 37.

Barr, R., & Parrett, W. (2001). *Hope fulfilled for at-risk and violent youth* (2nd ed.). Boston: Allyn & Bacon.

Bartell, C. (2005). *Cultivating high-quality teaching through induction and mentoring.* Thousand Oaks, CA: Corwin Press.

Barton, A., Drake, C., Perez, J. G., St. Louis, K., & George, M. (2004). Ecologies of parental engagement in urban education. *Educational Researcher, 33*(4), 3–12.

Barton, P. (2004). Why does the gap persist? *Educational Leadership, 62*(3), 9–13.

Barton, P. (2006). The dropout problem: Losing ground. *Educational Leadership, 63*(5), 14–18.

Battista, M. (1999). The mathematical miseducation of America's youth: Ignoring research and scientific study in education. *Phi Delta Kappan, 80,* 425–433.

Bauman, S., & Del Rio, A. (2006). Preservice teachers' responses to bullying scenarios: Comparing physical, verbal, and relational bullying. *Journal of Educational Psychology, 98*(1), 219–231.

Bay, M., Staver, J., Bryan, T., & Hale, J. (1992). Science instruction for the mildly handicapped: Direct instruction versus discovery teaching. *Journal of Research in Science Teaching, 29,* 555–570.

Belfield, C., & Levin, H. (2005). *The privatization of school choice: Consequences for parents, schools, and public policy.* Boulder, CO: Paradigm Publishers.

Benard, B. (1994). *Fostering resilience in urban schools.* San Francisco: Far West Laboratory.

Bennett, C. (1999). *Comprehensive multicultural education: Theory and practice* (4th ed.). Boston: Allyn & Bacon.

Bennett, C. (2007). *Multicultural education* (6th ed.). Boston: Allyn & Bacon.

Bennett, S. (1978). Recent research on teaching: A dream, a belief, and a model. *British Journal of Educational Psychology, 48,* 27–147.

Bergin, M. (2006). Junk science. *World Magazine, 21*(8), 317–345.

Berk, L. (2005). *Infants & children* (5th ed.). Boston: Allyn & Bacon.

Berk, L. (2006). *Child development* (7th ed.). Boston: Allyn & Bacon.

Berk, L. (2007). *Development through the lifespan* (4th ed.). Boston: Allyn & Bacon.

Berliner, D. (2004). If the underlying premise for No Child Left Behind is false, how can that act solve our problems? In K. Goodman, P. Shannon, Y. Goodman, & R. Rapoport (Eds.), *Saving our schools.* Berkeley, CA: RDR Books.

Berliner, D. (2005a). *Our impoverished view of educational reform.* Paper presented at the annual meeting of the American Educational Research Association, Montreal.

Berliner, D. (2005b). The near impossibility of testing for teacher quality. *Journal of Teacher Education, 56*(3), 205–213.

Bernstein, D., & Tiegerman-Farber, E. (2002). *Language and communication disorders in children* (5th ed.). Boston: Allyn & Bacon.

Bernstein, M. (2006). Is tenure an anachronism? *Education Week, 25*(28), 34.

Berry, B., Hoke, M., & Hirsch, E. (2004). The search for highly qualified teachers. *Phi Delta Kappan, 85*(9), 684–689.

Bertman, S. (2000). *Cultural amnesia: America's future and the crisis of memory.* Westport, CT: Praeger.

Bethel School District No. 403 v. Fraser, 106 S. Ct. 3159 (1986).

Betts, J. (2005). The economic theory of school choice. In J. Betts & T. Loveless (Eds.), *Getting choice right: Ensuring equity and efficiency in education policy* (pp. 14–39). Washington, DC: Brookings Institution Press.

Biddle, B. (2001). Poverty, ethnicity, and achievement in American schools. In B. J. Biddle (Ed.), *Social class, poverty, and education* (pp. 1–30). New York: Routlege Falmer.

Biddle, B., & Berliner, D. (2002). Unequal school: Funding in the United States. *Education Leadership, 59*(8), 48–59.

Billings, L., & Fitzgerald, J. (2002). Dialogic discussion and the Paideia Seminar. *American Educational Research Journal, 39,* 907–942.

Black, S. (2002). The well-rounded student. *American School Board Journal, 189*(6), 33–35.

Blair, J. (2000). AFT urges new tests, expanded training for teachers. *Education Week, 19*(32), 11.

Blair, J. (2003). Skirting tradition. *Education Week, 22*(17), 35–38.

Blatchford, P., Bassett, P., & Brown, P. (2005). Teachers' and pupils' behavior in large and small classes: A systematic observation study of pupils aged 10 and 11 years. *Journal of Educational Psychology, 97*(3), 454–467.

Bloom, B., Englehart, M., Furst, E., Hill, W., & Krathwohl, O. (1956). *Taxonomy of educational objectives: The classification of educational goals: Handbook 1. The cognitive domain.* White Plains, NY: Longman.

Bloomfield, D. (2006). Come clean on small schools. *Education Week, 25*(20), 34, 35.

Board of Education of Independent School District No. 92 of Pottawatomie County v. Earls 536 U.S. 822, 1225. Ct. 2559 (2002).

Board of Education of the Westside Community School v. Mergens, 496 U.S. 226 (1990).

Bohman, D. (2006). *School superintendent pay*. Retrieved March 7, 2006, from *http://www.tampabays10.com/news. aspx?storyied=25049*

Bohn, C. M., Roehrig, A. D., & Pressley, M. (2004). The first days of school in the classrooms of two more effective and four less effective primary-grades teachers. *Elementary School Journal, 104*(4), 269–288.

Bolkan, J. V., Roland, J., & Smith, D. N. (2006). Designing the new school. *Learning and Leading With Technology, 33*(7), 10–14.

Bond, H. (1934). *The education of the Negro in the American social order*. New York: Prentice Hall.

Borja, R. (2002). Study: Urban school chiefs' tenure is 4.6 years. *Education Week, 21*(21), 5.

Borja, R. (2003). Prepping for the big test. *Education Week, 22*(35), 23–26.

Borko, H., & Putnam, R. (1996). Learning to teach. In D. Berliner, & R. Calfee (Eds.), *Handbook of educational psychology* (pp. 673–708). New York: Simon & Schuster Macmillan.

Borman, G. (2002/2003). How can Title I improve achievement? *Educational Leadership, 60*(4), 49, 53.

Borman, G., & Kimball, S. (2005). Teacher quality and educational inequality: Do teachers with higher standards-based evaluation ratings close student achievement gaps? *The Elementary School Journal, 106*(1), 3–20.

Borman, G., & Overman, L. (2004). Academic resilience in mathematics among poor and minority students. *Elementary School Journal, 104*(3), 177–196.

Botstein, L. (2006). The trouble with high school. *School Administrator, 63*(1), 16–19.

Bowman, D. (2000a). Arizona poised to revisit graduation exam. *Education Week, 20*(13), 16, 18.

Bowman, D. (2000b). Charters, vouchers earning mixed report card. *Education Week, 19*(34), 1, 19–21.

Bowman, D. (2000c). White House proposes goals for improving Hispanic education. *Education Week, 19*(41), 9.

Bowman, D. (2002). Researchers see promising signs in DARE's new drug ed. program. *Education Week, 22*(11), 6–7.

Bowman, D. (2003). Student drug testing gathers prominent support. *Education Week, 23*(3), 1, 16, 17.

Bowman, D. (2004). Spending on anti-smoking education slips. *Education Week, 23*(43), 18–20.

Bracey, G. (1999). Top-heavy. *Phi Delta Kappan, 80*, 472–473.

Bracey, G. (2002). The 12th Bracey report on the condition of public education. *Phi Delta Kappan, 84*, 135–150.

Bracey, G. (2003a). Investing in preschool. *American School Board Journal, 90*(1), 32–35.

Bracey, G. (2003b). Not all alike. *Phi Delta Kappan, 84*, 717–718.

Bracey, G. (2004). The 14th Bracy Report on the condition of public education. *Phi Delta Kappan, 86*(2), 149–167.

Bracey, G. (2005a). A nation of cheats. *Phi Delta Kappan, 86*(5), 412–413.

Bracey, G. (2005b). And now, the Indian spelling gene. *Phi Delta Kappan, 87*(1), 91–93.

Bracey, G. (2005c). Dropouts to the fore. *Phi Delta Kappan, 86*(8), 711–712.

Bracey, G. (2005d). Plus ca change. *Phi Delta Kappan, 86*(6), 476–478.

Bradley v. Pittsburgh Board of Education, 913 F.2d 1064 (3d Cir. 1990).

Bradley, A. (1999). Confronting a tough issue: Teacher tenure. *Education Week, 18*(17), 48–52.

Bransford, J., Brown, A., & Cocking, R. (Eds.). (2000). *How people learn: Brain, mind, experience, and school*. Washington, DC: National Academy Press.

Bransford, J., Darling-Hammond, L., & LePage, P. (2005). Introduction. In L. Darling-Hammond & J. Bransford (Eds.), *Preparing teachers for a changing world: What teachers should learn and be able to do* (pp. 1–39). San Francisco: Jossey-Bass/Wiley.

Bransford, J., Derry, S., Berliner, D., Hammerness, K. (2005). Theories of learning and their roles in teaching. In L. Darling-Hammond & J. Bransford (Eds.), *Preparing teachers for a changing world: What teachers should learn and be able to do* (pp. 40–87). San Francisco: Jossey-Bass.

Brenner, D. (2001, April). *Translating social constructivism into methodology for documenting learning*. Paper presented at the annual meeting of the American Educational Research Association, Seattle, WA.

Brimley, V., & Garfield, R. (2005). *Financing education* (9th ed.). Boston: Allyn & Bacon.

Broh, B. (2002). Linking extracurricular programming to academic achievement: Who benefits and why? *Sociology of Education, 75*, 69–91.

Brooke, R. (Ed.). (2003). *Rural voices: Place-conscious education and the teaching of writing*. New York: Teachers College Press.

Brophy, J. (1998). *Motivating students to learn*. Boston: McGraw-Hill.

Brophy, J. (2004). *Motivating students to learn* (2nd ed.). Boston: McGraw-Hill.

Brophy, J. (2006). Graham Nuthall and social constructivist teaching: Research-based cautions and qualifications. *Teaching and Teacher Education, 22,* 529–537.

Brouillette, L. (2000, April). *What is behind all that rhetoric? A case study of the creation of a charter school.* Paper presented at the annual meeting of the American Educational Research Association, New Orleans, LA.

Brown, D. (2004). Urban teachers' professed classroom management strategies: Reflections of culturally responsive teaching. *Urban Education, 39*(3), 266–289.

Brown, D. F. (2006). It's the curriculum, stupid: There's something wrong with it. *Phi Delta Kappan, 87*(10), 777–783.

Brown, H. (2003). Charter schools found lacking resources. *Education Week, 22*(31), 30.

Brown, K., Anfara, V., & Roney, K. (2004). Student achievement in high performing, suburban middle schools and low performing, urban middle schools: Plausible explanations for the differences. *Education and Urban Society, 36*(4), 428–456.

Brown, R., & Evans, W. (2002). Extracurricular activity and ethnicity: Creating greater school connections among diverse student populations. *Urban Education, 37*(1), 41–58.

Brown v. Bathhe, 416 F. Supp. 1194 (D. Neb. 1976).

Brown v. Board of Education of Topeka, 347 U.S. 483 (1954).

Bruning, R., Schraw, G., Norby, M., & Ronning, R. (2004). *Cognitive psychology and instruction* (4th ed.). Upper Saddle River, NJ: Prentice Hall.

Brunner, C., & Tally, W. (1999). *The new media literacy handbook: An educator's guide to bringing new media into the classroom.* New York: Anchor Books.

Bryan, L. (2005). Once upon a time: A Grimm approach to character education. *Journal of Social Studies Research, 29*(1), 3–6.

Buckley, J., Schneider, M., & Shang, Y. (2005). Fix it and they might stay: School facility quality and teacher retention in Washington, D.C. *Teachers College Record, 107*(5), 1107–1123.

Buhi, E., & Goodson, P. (2006). Abstinence education: Research and practice—a reaction to Young and Penhollow. *American Journal of Health Education, 37*(4), 253–254.

Bullock, A., & Hawk, P. (2005). *Developing a teaching portfolio: A guide for preservice and practicing teachers* (2nd ed.). Upper Saddle River, NJ: Merrill/Prentice Hall.

Bullough, R., Jr. (1989). *First-year teacher: A case study.* New York: Teachers College Press.

Bullough, R., Jr. (1999, April). *In praise of children at-risk: Life on the other side of the teacher's desk.* Paper presented at the annual meeting of the American Educational Research, Association, Montreal.

Bullough, R., Jr. (2001). *Uncertain lives: Children of promise, teachers of hope.* New York: Teachers College Press.

Burns, M. (2005/2006). Tools for the mind. *Educational Leadership, 63*(4), 48–53.

Burstyn, J., Bender, G., Casalla, R., Gordon, H., Guerra, D., Luschen, K., Steven, R., & William, K. (2001). *Preventing violence in schools: A challenge to American democracy.* Mahwah, NJ: Lawrence Erlbaum.

Butin, D. (2003). Of what use is it? Multiple conceptualizations of service learning within education. *Teachers College Record, 105*(9), 1674–1692. Retrieved June 2, 2005, from *http://www.tcrecord.org* ID Number 11561

Button, H., & Provenzo, E. (1989). *History of education in American culture.* New York: Holt, Rinehart & Winston.

Butts, R., & Cremin, L. (1953). *A history of education in America.* New York: Holt, Rinehart & Winston.

Byrnes, J. (2003). Factors predictive of mathematics achievement in White, Black, and Hispanic 12th graders. *Journal of Educational Psychology, 95,* 316–326.

Caldas, S., & Bankston, C. (2005). *Forced to fail: The paradox of school desegregation.* Westport, CT: Praeger.

Callister, T., & Burbules, N. (2004). Just give it to me straight: A case against filtering the Internet. *Phi Delta Kappan, 85*(9), 649–655.

Camerino, C. (2003). Pay to play? *Education Week, 22*(23), 32, 34.

Campbell, D., Cignetti, P., Melenyzer, B., Nettles, D., & Wyman, R. (2007). *How to develop a professional portfolio: A manual for teachers* (4th ed.). Boston: Allyn & Bacon.

Campbell, J., & Beaudry, J. (1998). Gender gap linked to differential socialization for high achieving senior mathematics students. *Journal of Educational Research, 91,* 140–147.

Canter, L. (1988). Let the educator beware: A response to Curwin and Mendler. *Educational Leadership, 46*(2), 71–73.

Canter, L., & Canter, M. (1976). *Assertive discipline: A take-charge approach for today's educators.* Santa Monica, CA: Canter.

Canter, L., & Canter, M. (2001). *Assertive discipline: Positive behavior management for today's classroom.* Bloomington, IN: Solution Tree.

Carbo, M. (1997). Reading styles times twenty. *Educational Leadership, 54,* 38–42.

Carnegie Forum on Education and the Economy. (1986). *A nation prepared: Teachers for the 21st century.* Washington,

DC: Author. (ERIC Document Reproduction Service No. ED268120)

Carnegie Learning. (2005). *Success stories and case studies.* Retrieved March 16, 2005, from *http://www.carnegielearning.com*

Carnine, D., Silbert, J., Kameenui, E., Tarver, S., & Jongjohann, K. (2006). *Teaching struggling and at-risk readers: A direct instruction approach.* Upper Saddle River, NJ: Merrill/ Prentice Hall.

Carnoy, M., Jacobsen, R., Mishel, L., & Rothstein, R. (2005). *The charter school dust-up: Examining the evidence on enrollment and achievement.* New York: Teachers College Press.

Carpenter, D., & Finn, C. (2006). *Playing to type.* Washington, DC: Thomas Fordham Foundation. Retrieved June 22, 2006, from *www.edexcellence.net*

Carr, N. (2003). The toughest job in America. Education vital signs [Supplement.]. *American School Board Journal, 190*(2), 14–19.

Casey, J., Andreson, K., Yelverton, B., & Wedeen, L. (2002). A status report on charter schools in New Mexico. *Phi Delta Kappan, 83,* 518–524.

Cassady, J. (1999, April). *The effects of examples as elaboration in text on memory and learning.* Paper presented at the annual meeting of the American Educational Research Association, Montreal.

Cavanagh, S. (2004). Online teacher training courses win converts. *Education Week, 23*(23), 20.

Cavanagh, S. (2006a). Perkins bill is approved by Congress. *Education Week, 25*(44), 1, 27.

Cavanagh, S. (2006b). Possible road map seen in Dover case. *Education Week, 25*(10), 1, 10, 11.

CDW Government. (2005). *Teachers talk tech.* Retrieved December 21, 2005, from *www.cdwg.com/ttt*

Center on Addiction and Substance Abuse. (2001). *Malignant neglect: Substance abuse and America's schools.* New York: Columbia University.

Certo, J., Cauley, K., & Chafen, C. (2002, April). *Students' perspectives on their high school experience.* Paper presented at the annual meeting of the American Educational Research Association, New Orleans, LA.

Chalk v. U.S. District Court Cent. Dist. of California, 840 F.2d. 701 (9th Cir. 1988).

Chance, P. (1997). Speaking of differences. *Phi Delta Kappan, 78*(7), 506–507.

Charles, C. M. (2005). *Building classroom discipline* (8th ed). Boston: Allyn and Bacon.

Charner-Laird, M., Watson, D., Szczesuil, S., Kirkpatrick C., & Gordon, P. (2004, April). *Navigating the "Culture Gap": New teachers experience the urban context.* Paper presented at the annual meeting of the American Educational Research Association, San Diego, CA.

Charter Connection. (2006). *Charter school facts.* Center for Education Reform. Retrieved June 22, 2006, from *http://edreform.com/charter_schools*

Chekles, K. (1997). The first seven . . . and the eighth: A conversation with Howard Gardner. *Educational Leadership, 55*(1), 8–13.

Christie, K. (2005). Providing the facts. *Phi Delta Kappan, 86*(5), 341–342.

Ciofalo, J., & Wylie, C. (2006). Using diagnostic classroom assessment: One question at a time. *Teachers College Record.* Retrieved March 20, 2006, from *http://www.tcrecord.org* ID Number: 12285.

Clandinin, J., & Connelly, M. (1996). Teacher as curriculum maker. In P. Jackson (Ed.), *Handbook of research on curriculum* (pp. 363–401). New York: Macmillan.

Clark, R. C., & Mayer, R. E. (2003). *E-learning and the science of instruction: Proven guidelines for consumers and designers of multimedia learning.* San Francisco: Pfeiffer/Wiley.

Cochran-Smith, M. (2005). The new teacher education: For better or for worse? *Educational Researcher, 34*(6), 1–17.

Cognition and Technology Group at Vanderbilt. (1992). The Jasper Series as an example of anchored instruction: Theory, program description, and assessment data. *Educational Psychologist, 27,* 291–315.

Cognition and Technology Group at Vanderbilt. (1997). *The Jasper Project: Lessons in curriculum, instruction, assessment, and professional development.* Mahwah, NJ: Erlbaum.

Cohen, J. (2006). Social, emotional, ethical, and academic education: Creating a climate for learning, participation in democracy, and well-being. *Harvard Educational Review, 76*(2), 201–237.

Coleman, J. (2005, November 15). California Latinos to reach parity with Anglos by 2010. *Salt Lake Tribune,* p. C5.

Coleman, J., Campbell, E., Hobson, D., McPortland, J. Mood. A., Weinfield, F., & York, R. (1966). *Equality of educational opportunity.* Washington, DC: U.S. Department of Health, Education and Welfare.

Coley, R. (2001). *Differences in the gender gap: Comparisons across racial/ethnic groups in education and work.* Princeton, NJ: Educational Testing Service.

Colgan, C. (2004). The controversy over charter school scores reinforces a partisan split. *The American School Board Journal, 191*(10), 6–8.

Colgan, C. (2005). The new look of school safety. *The American School Board Journal, 192*(3), 11–13.

Collis, B., Peters, O., & Pals, N. (2001). A model for predicting the educational use of information and communication technologies. *Instructional Science, 29*, 95–125.

Comer, J., Joyner, E., & Ben-Avie, M. (Eds.) (2004). *Six pathways to healthy child development and academic success.* Thousand Oaks, CA: Corwin Press.

Commonwealth of Pennsylvania v. Douglass, 588 A.2d 53 (Pa. Super. Ct. 1991).

Compayre, G. (1888). *History of pedagogy* (W. Payne, Trans.). Boston: Heath.

Conant, J. (1959). *The American high school.* New York: McGraw-Hill.

Conoley, J., & Goldstein, A. (2004). *School violence intervention: A practical handbook.* New York: Guilford Press.

Cook, G. (2006). What's a teacher worth? Houston joins the push for merit pay. *The American School Board Journal, 193*(3), 4–6.

Cooper, D., & Snell, J. (2003). Bullying—not just a kid thing. *Educational Leadership, 60*(6), 22–25.

Cooper, H., Robinson, J., & Patall, E. (2006). Does homework improve academic achievement? A synthesis of research, 1987–2003. *Review of Educational Research, 76*(1), 1–62.

Cooper, H., Valentine, J., Nye, B., & Lindsay, J. (1999). Relationships between five after-school activities and academic achievement. *Journal of Educational Psychology, 91*(2), 369–378.

Cooper, L. (2001). A comparison of online and traditional computer applications classes. *T.H.E. Journal, 28*(8), 52–58.

Cooperman, S. (2003). A new order of things. *Education Week, 22*(38), 30, 32.

Coppola, E. (2004). *Powering up: Learning to teach well with technology.* New York: Teachers College Press.

Cornelius, L. (2002, April). *Legal implications of school violence.* Paper presented at the annual meeting of the American Educational Research Association, New Orleans, LA.

Corno, L., Cronbach, L. J., Kupermintz, H., Lohman, D. F., Mandinach, E. B., Porteu, A. W., & Talbert, J. E. (2002). *Remaking the concept of aptitude: Extending the legacy of Richard E. Snow.* Mahwah, NJ: Erlbaum.

Corporation for Public Broadcasting. (2003). *Connected to the future: A report on children's Internet use from the Corporation for Public Broadcasting.* Retrieved February 2004, from *http://www.cpb.org/Ed/resources/connected*

Coughlin, E. (1996, February 16). Not out of Africa. *Chronicle of Higher Education,* pp. A6–A7.

Council for Exceptional Children. (2005). Retrieved May 17, 2005, from *http://www.CEC.sped.org.IDEALaw&resources*

Council of Chief State School Officers. (2003). Chief state school officers method of selection. Retrieved February 2004, from *http://www.ccsso.org/chief_state_school_officers/method_of_selection/index.cfm*

Coyle, K., Kirby, D., & Robin, L. (2006). All4You! A randomized trial of an HIV, other STDs, and pregnancy prevention intervention for alternative school students. *AIDS Education and Prevention, 18*(3), 187–203.

Craig, D. (2003). Brain-compatible learning: Principles and applications in athletic training. *Journal of Athletic Training, 38*(4), 342–350.

Crick, N. R., Grotpeter, J. K., & Bigbee, M. A. (2002). Relationally and physically aggressive children's intent attributions and feelings of distress for relational and instructional peer provocation. *Child Development, 73*, 1134–1142.

Crockett, C. (2004). What do kids know—and misunderstand—about science? *Educational Leadership, 61*(5), 34–37.

Cross, T. (2005). *The social and emotional lives of gifted kids: Understanding and guiding their development.* Austin, TX: Prufrock Press.

Cuban, L. (1993). *How teachers taught. Constancy and change in American classrooms: 1890–1980* (2nd ed.). New York: Teachers College Press.

Cuban, L. (1996). Curriculum stability and change. In P. Jackson (Ed.), *Handbook of research on curriculum* (pp. 216–247). New York: Macmillan.

Cuban, L. (2005). *Growing instructional technology in U.S. classrooms.* J. George Jones & Velma Rife Jones Lecture: University of Utah, Salt Lake City.

Cunningham, W., & Cordeiro, P. (2000). *Education administration.* Boston: Allyn & Bacon.

Cushman, K. (2003). *Fires in the bathroom: Advice for teachers from high school students.* New York: The New Press.

Cushman, K. (2006). Help us care enough to learn. *Educational Leadership, 63*(5), 34–37.

Dance, L. J. (2002). *Tough fronts: The impact of street culture on schooling.* New York: Routledge Falmer.

Darling-Hammond, L. (1997). *The right to learn.* San Francisco: Jossey-Bass.

Darling-Hammond, L. (2000). How teacher education matters. *Journal of Teacher Education, 51*, 166–173.

Darling-Hammond, L., & Baratz-Snowdon, J. (Eds.). (2005). *A good teacher in every classroom: Preparing the highly qualified teachers our children deserve*. San Francisco: Jossey-Bass/Wiley.

Darling-Hammond, L., Berry, B., & Thoreson, A. (2001). Does teacher certification matter? Evaluating the evidence. *Educational Evaluation and Policy Analysis, 23,* 57–77.

Darling-Hammond, L., & Bransford, J. (Eds.). (2005). *Preparing teachers for a changing world: What teachers should learn and be able to do*. San Francisco: Jossey-Bass.

Darling-Hammond, L., Chung, R., & Frelow, F. (2002). Variation in teacher preparation: How well do different pathways prepare teachers to teach? *Journal of Teacher Education, 53,* 286–302.

Darling-Hammond, L., & Hammerness, K. (2005). The design of teacher education programs. In L. Darling-Hammond & J. Bransford (Eds.), *Preparing teachers for a changing world: What teachers should learn and be able to do* (pp. 390–441). San Francisco: Jossey-Bass.

Datnow, A., Hubbard, L., & Conchas, G. (2001). How context mediates policy: The implementation of single gender public schooling in California. *Teachers College Record, 103,* 184–206.

Davis, G. (2003). Identifying creative students, teaching for creative growth. In N. Colangelo & G. Davis (Eds.), *Handbook of gifted education* (3rd ed., pp. 311–324). Boston: Allyn & Bacon.

Davis, G., & Rimm, S. (2004). *Education of the gifted and talented* (5th ed.). Boston: Allyn & Bacon.

Davis, M. (2003). Title IX panel deadlocks on critical change. *Education Week, 22*(21), 24–25.

Davis, M. (2006). Drug-free-schools grants targeted by Bush. *Education Week, 25*(25), 21, 23.

DeAngelis, T. (2004). Size-based discrimination may be hardest on children. *Monitor on Psychology, 35*(1), 62.

DeBray, E., McDermott, K., & Wohlstetter, P. (2005). Introduction to the special issue on federalism reconsidered: The case of No Child Left Behind Act. *Peabody Journal of Education, 80*(2), 1–18.

DeMeulenaere, E. (2001, April). *Constructing reinventions: Black and Latino students negotiating the transformation of their academic identities and school performance*. Paper presented at the annual meeting of the American Educational Research Association, Seattle, WA.

Denig, S. J. (2003, April). *A proposed relationship between multiple intelligences and learning styles*. Paper presented at the annual meeting of the American Educational Research Association, Chicago.

DeRoche, E., & Williams, M. (2001). *Character education: A guide for school administrators*. Lanham, MD: Scarecrow Press.

Dewey, J. (1902). *The child and the curriculum*. Chicago: University of Chicago Press.

Dewey, J. (1906). *Democracy and education*. New York: Macmillan.

Dewey, J. (1923). *The school and society*. Chicago: University of Chicago Press.

Dewey, J. (1938). *Experience and education*. New York: Macmillan.

Diamond, J. (1999). *Guns, germs and steel: The fates of human societies*. New York: Norton.

Dickinson, G., Holifield, M., Holifield, G., & Creer, D. (2000). Elementary magnet school students' interracial interaction choices. *Journal of Educational Research, 93,* 391–394.

Dill, V., & Stafford-Johnson, D. (2002). A different road. *American School Board Journal, 189*(11), 44–46.

Dillon, D. (1989). Showing them that I want them to learn and that I care about who they are: A microethnography of the social organization of a secondary low-track English reading classroom. *American Educational Research Journal, 26,* 227–259.

Dillon, S. (2006, July 25). Most states fail demands set out in education law. *New York Times,* p. A14.

Dimick, A., & Apple, M. (2005). Texas and the politics of abstinence-only textbooks. *Teachers College Record.* Retrieved June 29, 2005, from *http://www.tcrecord.org* ID Number 11855.

Dodge, K. A., Lansford, J. E., Burks, V. S., Bates, J. E., Pettit, G. S., Fontaine, R., & Price, J. M. (2003). Peer rejection and social information-processing factors in the development of aggressive behavior problems in children. *Child Development, 74,* 374–393.

Doe v. Renfrow, 635 F.2d 582 (7th Cir. 1980).

Doll, B., Zucher, S., & Brehm, K. (2004). *Resilient classrooms: Creating healthy environments for learning*. New York: Guilford Press.

Donovan, M. S., & Bransford, J. D. (2005). Introduction. In M. S. Donovan & J. D. Bransford (Eds.), *How students learn: History, mathematics, and science in the classroom* (pp. 1–26). Washington, DC: National Academies Press.

Dowling-Sendor, B. (1999). Struggling with set-asides. *American School Board Journal, 186*(4), 20, 22, 63.

Doyle, D. (1999). De facto national standards. *Education Week, 18*(42), 56, 36.

Doyle, W. (1986). Classroom organization and management. In M. Wittrock (Ed.), *Handbook of research on teaching* (3rd ed., pp. 392–431). New York: Macmillan.

Drajem, L. (2002, April). *Life stories: Successful White women teachers of ethnically and racially diverse students.* Paper presented at the annual meeting of the American Educational Research Association, New Orleans, LA.

Drake, S., & Burns, R. (2004). *Meeting standards through integrated curriculum.* Alexandria, VA: Association for Supervision and Curriculum Development.

Drevitch, G. (2006). Merit pay: Good for teachers? *Instructor,* 115(5), 21–23.

Duke, N. (2000). For the rich it's richer: Print experience and environments offered to children in very low- and very high-socioeconomic status first-grade classrooms. *American Educational Research Journal,* 37, 441–478.

Dulude-Lay, C. (2000). *The confounding effect of the dimensions of classroom life on the narratives of student teachers.* Unpublished manuscript, University of Utah, Salt Lake City.

Durst, A. (2005). "The union of intellectual freedom and cooperation": Learning from the University of Chicago's Laboratory School community, 1896–1904. *Teachers College Record,* 107(5), 958–984.

Dworkin, R. (1998, October 23). Affirming affirmative action. *New York Times Review of Books,* pp. 91–102.

Dynarski, M., & Gleason, P. (1999, April). *How can we help? What we have learned from evaluations of federal dropout-prevention programs.* Paper presented at the annual meeting of the American Educational Research Association, Montreal.

Echevarria, J., & Graves, A. (2007). *Sheltered content instruction* (3rd ed.). Boston: Allyn & Bacon.

Echevarria, J., Powers, K., & Short, D. (2006). School reform and standards-based education: A model for English language learners. *Journal of Educational Research,* 99(4), 195–211.

Economic Policy Institute. (2002). *Inequality at the starting gate: Social background differences in achievement as children begin school.* Washington, DC: Author.

Economic Policy Institute. (2005). *Wage trends.* Retrieved July 14, 2006, from *http://www.epinet.org*

Education Vital Signs. (2005, February). Poverty. *American School Board Journal Supplement,* pp. 22–23.

Education Vital Signs. (2006a, February). School finance. *American School Board Journal Supplement,* pp. 20–21.

Education Vital Signs. (2006b, February). Student health. *American School Board Journal Supplement,* pp. 12–13.

Educational Testing Service. (2005). *The Praxis series 2005–2006: Information and registration bulletin.* Available online at *http://www.ets.org/praxis/prxtest.html*

Educational Testing Service. (2006). *The Praxis series 2005–2006: Information and registration bulletin.* Retrieved August 23, 2006, from *http://www.ets.org/praxis/prxtest.html*

Edwards, V. (2003). Techs answer to testing. *Education Week,* 22(35), 8, 10.

Eggen, P. (1998, April). *A comparison of urban middle school teachers' classroom practices and their expressed beliefs about learning and effective instruction.* Paper presented at the annual meeting of the American Educational Research Association, San Diego, CA.

Eggen, P., & Kauchak, D. (2006). *Strategies and models for teachers: Teaching content and thinking skills* (5th ed.). Boston: Allyn and Bacon.

Eggen, P., & Kauchak, D. (2007). *Educational psychology: Windows on classrooms* (7th ed.). Upper Saddle River, NJ: Merrill/Prentice Hall.

Ehlenberger, K. (2001/2002). The right to search students. *Educational Leadership,* 59(4), 31–35.

Eide, E. R., & Goldhaber, D. D. (2005). Grade retention: What are the costs and benefits? *Journal of Education Finance,* 31(2), 195–214.

Eisner, E. (1993). *The educational imagination: On the design and evaluation of school programs* (3rd ed.). New York: Macmillan.

Eisner, E. (2003). Questionable assumptions about schooling. *Phi Delta Kappan,* 84, 648–657.

Emmer, E., Evertson, C., & Worsham, M. (2006). *Classroom management for secondary teachers* (7th ed.). Boston: Allyn & Bacon.

Emmer, E., & Stough, L. (2001). Classroom management: A critical part of educational psychology with implications for teacher education. *Educational Psychologist,* 36, 103–112.

Engel, B., & Martin, A. (Eds.). (2005). *Holding values: What we mean by progressive education.* Portsmouth, NH: Heinemann.

Engle v. Vitale, 370 U.S. 421 (1962).

Epstein, J. (2001). *School, family, and community partnership: Preparing educators and improving schools.* Boulder, CO: Westview Press.

Ertmer, P. (2005). Teacher pedagogical beliefs: The final frontier in our quest for technology integration? *Educational Technology Research and Development,* 53(4), 25–39.

Essex, N. (2006). *A teacher's pocket guide to school law.* Boston: Allyn & Bacon.

Evans, C., Kirby, U., & Fabrigar, L. (2003). Approaches to learning, need for cognition, and strategic flexibility among university students. *The British Journal of Educational Psychology,* 73, 507–528.

Evans, G. W., & English, K. (2002). The environment of poverty: Multiple stressor exposure, psychophysiological stress, and socioemotional adjustment. *Child Development, 73*, 1238–1248.

Evertson, C., Emmer, E., & Worsham, M. (2006). *Classroom management for elementary teachers* (7th ed.). Boston: Allyn & Bacon.

Evertson, C., & Smithey, M. (2000). Mentoring effects on protégés' classroom practice: An experimental field study. *Journal of Educational Research, 93*, 294–304.

Fagen v. Summers, 498 P.2d 1227 (Wyo. 1972).

Fairchild, T. (2006). Race and class: Separate and not equal. *Education Week, 26*(3), 35, 36.

Faject, W., Bello, M., & Leftwich, S. A. (2005). Pre-service teachers' perceptions in beginning education classes. *Teaching and Teacher Education, 21*(6), 717–727.

Farkas, R. (2003). Effects of traditional versus learning-styles instructional methods on middle school students. *Journal of Educational Research, 97*(1), 42–51.

Federal Interagency Forum on Child and Family Statistics. (2005). *Family structure and children's living arrangement.* Retrieved April 23, 2006, from *http://www.childstats.gov/americaschildren/pop6.asp*

Federation of Tax Administrators. (2006). *State comparisons.* Retrieved March 21, 2006, from *http://www.taxadmin.org*

Feiman-Nemser, S. (2001). From preparation to practice: Designing a continuum to strengthen and sustain teaching. *Teachers College Record, 103*, 1013–1055.

Feinberg, W., & Soltis, J. (2004). *School and society* (4th ed.). New York: Teachers College Press.

Feldman, A., & Matjasko, J. (2005). The role of school-based extracurricular activities in adolescent development: A comprehensive review and future directions. *Review of Educational Research, 75*(2), 159–210.

Feldman, J., López, L., & Simon, K. (2006). *Choosing small: The essential guide to successful high school conversion.* San Francisco: Jossey-Bass.

Feller, B. (2006, August 17). Support for new high school graduation tests is waning, study says. *Salt Lake Tribune,* p. A4.

Ferguson, J. (2002). Vouchers—an illusion of choice. *American School Board Journal, 189*(1), 42–45, 51.

Ferrero, D. (2005). Does "research based" mean "value neutral"? *Phi Delta Kappan, 86*(6), 425–432.

Fine, L. (2002). Writing takes a digital turn for special-needs students. *Education Week, 21*(20), 8.

Finkelstein, E. (2005). Making PowerPoint quizzes. *Presentations, 19*(1), 18–20.

Finn, J., Gerber, S., & Boyd-Zaharias, J. (2005). Small classes in the early grades, academic achievement, and graduating from high school. *Journal of Educational Psychology, 97*(2), 214–223.

Finn, J., Pannozzo, G., & Achilles, C. (2003). The "why's" of class size: Student behavior in small classes. *Review of Educational Research, 72*(3), 321–368.

Finn, K., Willert, H., & Marable, M. (2003). Substance use in schools. *Educational Leadership, 60*(6), 80–85.

First Amendment Center. (1999). *The Bible and public schools: A First Amendment guide.* Nashville, TN: Author. Retrieved February 2004 from *http://www.freedomforum.org/publications/first/BibleAndPublicSchools/bibleguide_reprint.pdf*

Fischer, L., Schimmel, D., & Kelly, C. (2003). *Teachers and the law* (6th ed.). New York: Longman.

Fischer, L., Schimmel, D., & Stellman, L. (2006). *Teachers and the law* (7th ed.). New York: Longman.

Fisher, D. (2006). Keeping adolescents "alive and kickin' it": Addressing suicide in schools. *Phi Delta Kappan, 87*(10), 784–786.

Fiske, E. (2001). *Learning in deed: The power of service-learning for American schools.* Battle Creek, MI: W.K. Kellogg Foundation.

Fiske, E., & Ladd, H. (2000). A distant laboratory. *Education Week, 19*(56), 38.

Flanagan, A., & Grissmer, D. (2002). The role of federal resources in closing the achievement gap. In J. Chubb & T. Loveless (Eds.), *Bridging the achievement gap* (pp. 199–226). Washington, DC: Brookings Institution Press.

Flanagan, A., & Murray, S. (2004). A decade of reform: The impact of school reform in Kentucky. In J. Yinger (Ed.), *Helping children left behind* (pp. 195–214). Cambridge, MA: MIT Press.

Flanagan, K., & Park, J. (2005). *American Indian and Alaska Native children: Findings from the base year of the early childhood longitudinal study, Birth Cohort (ECLS-B).* Washington, DC: National Center for Education Statistics.

Flanigan, R. (2003). A challenging year for schools. Education Vital Signs [Supplement]. *American School Board Journal, 190*(2), 21–25.

Fleischfresser v. Directors of School District No. 200, 15 F.3d 680 (7th Cir. 1994).

Florida Department of Education. (2005). *Sunshine State standards, mathematics preK–2.* Retrieved June 27, 2006, from *http://www.firn.edu/doe/menu/sss.htm*

Florida Department of Education. (2007). *Florida comprehensive assessment test: Mathematics sample test book* (2007). Retrieved October 1, 2006, from *http://www.firn.edu/doe/sas/fcat/pdf/sample/0607/math/FL07_STM_G3M_TB_Cwf001.pdf*

Forcier, R., & Descy, D. (2005). *The computer as an educational tool: Productivity and problem solving* (4th ed.). Upper Saddle River, NJ: Merrill/Prentice Hall.

Francis, B., & Skelton, C. (2005). *Reassessing gender and achievement.* New York: Routledge Falmer.

Franek, M. (2005/2006). Foiling cyberbullies in the new wild west. *Educational Leadership, 63*(4), 39–43.

Frankenberg, E., & Lee, C. (2003). *Charter schools and race: A lost opportunity for integrated education.* Retrieved February 2004 from Harvard University, Civil Rights Project Website: *http://www.civilrightsproject.harvard.edu/research/deseg/Charter_Schools03.pdf*

Franklin, W. (1997, March). *African-American youth at promise.* Paper presented at the annual meeting of the American Educational Research Association, Chicago.

Fredericks, J. A., & Eccles, J. S. (2006). Is extracurricular participation associated with beneficial outcomes? Concurrent and longitudinal relations. *Developmental Psychology, 42*(4), 698–713.

Freedman, M. (2004). A tale of plagiarism and a new paradigm. *Phi Delta Kappan, 85*(7), 545–548.

Freeman, J., McPhail, J., & Berndt, J. (2002). Sixth graders' views of activities that do and do not help them learn. *Elementary School Journal, 102*(4), 335–347.

Freiberg, J. (1999a). Consistency management and cooperative discipline. In J. Freiberg (Ed.), *Beyond behaviorism: Changing the classroom management paradigm* (pp. 75–97). Boston: Allyn & Bacon.

Freiberg, J. (1999b). Sustaining the paradigm. In J. Freiberg (Ed.), *Beyond behaviorism: Changing the classroom management paradigm* (pp. 164–173). Boston: Allyn & Bacon.

Furlan, C. (1999). States tackle Internet-filter rules for schools. *Education Week, 17*(43), 22, 28.

Furlan, C. (2000). Satellite broadcasts seek to enliven study of history. *Education Week, 19*(26), 8.

Furrer, C., & Skinner, E. (2003). Sense of relatedness as a factor in children's academic engagement and performance. *Journal of Educational Psychology, 95,* 148–162.

Gall, M., Gall, J., & Borg, W. (2003). *Educational research: An introduction* (7th ed.). Boston: Allyn & Bacon.

Galley, M. (2003). Despite concerns, online elementary schools grow. *Education Week, 22*(16), 1, 12.

Galley, M. (2004). Court blocks school ban on weapons images. *Education Week, 23*(16), 6.

Garcia, D. (2004). Exploring connections between the construct of teacher efficacy and family involvement practices: Implications for urban teacher preparation. *Urban Education, 39*(3), 290–315.

Garcia, R. (2006). Language, culture, and education. In J. Banks, *Cultural diversity and education* (5th ed., pp. 266–291). Boston: Allyn & Bacon.

Gardner, H. (1983). *Frames of mind: The theory of multiple intelligences.* New York: Basic Books.

Gardner, H. (1999). The understanding pathway. *Educational Leadership, 57*(3), 12–17.

Gardner, H., & Hatch, T. (1989). Multiple intelligences go to school. *Educational Researcher, 18*(8), 4–10.

Gay, B. (2000). Educational equality for students of color. In J. Banks & C. Banks (Eds.), *Multicultural education: Issues and perspectives* (4th ed., pp. 195–228). Boston: Allyn & Bacon.

Gay, G. (2005). Politics of multicultural teacher education. *Journal of Teacher Education, 56*(3), 221–228.

Gay, Lesbian, Straight Education Network. (2005). *National school climate survey.* Retrieved July 14, 2006, from *http://www.glsen.org*

Gaziel, H. (1997). Impact of school culture on effectiveness of secondary schools with disadvantaged students. *Journal of Educational Research, 90,* 310–318.

Gee, J. P. (2005). *Learning by design: Games as learning machines.* Retrieved April 23, 2006, from *http://labweb.education.wisc.edu/room130/papers.htm*

Gehring, J. (1999a). Displays entangle Ten Commandments, First Amendment. *Education Week, 19*(15), 7.

Gehring, J. (1999b). Groups endorse guidelines on using the Bible in instruction. *Education Week, 19*(12), 7.

Gehring, J. (2000). Schools' Bible courses "taught wrong," report says. *Education Week, 19*(19), 10.

Gehring, J. (2002a). Benefit of Illinois credit misses needy, study says. *Education Week, 22*(8), 11.

Gehring, J. (2002b). Vouchers battles head to state capitols. *Education Week, 21*(42), 1, 24, 25.

Gehring, J. (2005). Researchers say girls thrive in single-sex gym classes. *Education Week, 25*(1), 13.

Gewertz, C. (2000). Wisconsin study finds benefits in classes of 15 or fewer students. *Education Week, 19*(31), 10.

Gewertz, C. (2002). Edison buffeted by probe, loss of contracts. *Education Week, 22*(1), 3.

Gewertz, C. (2003a). Study: No academic gains from vouchers for Black student. *Education Week, 22*(30), 13.

Gewertz, C. (2003b). Vallas calls for cuts to private companies. *Education Week, 22*(29), 3.

Gewertz, C. (2006a). Groups accuse Fla. districts of harsh discipline approaches. *Education Week, 25*(34), 7.

Gewertz, C. (2006b). L.A. mayor steps up bid to control schools. *Education Week, 25*(16), 3, 9.

Gewertz, C. (2006c). H.S. dropouts say lack of motivation top reason to quit. *Education Week, 25*(26), 1, 14.

Gewertz, C. (2006d). Race, gender, and the superintendency. *Education Week, 25*(24), 1, 22, 24.

Gilbert, L. (2005). What helps beginning teachers? *Educational Leadership, 62*(8), 36–39.

Gill, B. (2005). School choice and integration. In J. Betts & T. Loveless (Eds.), *Getting choice right: Ensuring equity and efficiency in education policy* (pp. 130–145). Washington, DC: Brookings Institution Press.

Gill, S., McLean, M., & Courville, M. (2004). A tale of two professions. *Phi Delta Kappan, 86*(1), 63–64.

Gillies, R. (2000). The maintenance of cooperative and helping behaviours in cooperative groups. *British Journal of Educational Psychology, 70*, 97–111.

Gilman, D., & Kiger, S. (2003). Should we try to keep class sizes small? *Educational Leadership, 60*(7), 80–85.

Ginsberg, A., Shapiro, J., & Brown, S. (2004). *Gender in urban education: Strategies for student achievement.* Portsmouth, NH: Heinemann.

Ginsberg, M., & Murphy, D. (2002). How walkthroughs open doors. *Educational Leadership, 59*(8), 34–36.

Girard, K. (2005). Lost in translation. *Edutopia, 1*(8), 36–38.

Gladden, J. E. (2003). Where have all the reading groups gone? *Education Week, 22*(36), 33.

Gladding, M. (2007). *A guide to ethical conduct for the helping professions* (2nd ed.). Upper Saddle River, NJ: Merrill/Prentice Hall.

Glanzer, P. (2004). In defense of Harry . . . but not his defenders: Beyond censorship to justice. *English Journal, 93*(4), 58–63.

Glanzer, P. (2005). Moving beyond censorship: What will educators do if a controversy over "His Dark Materials" erupts? *Phi Delta Kappan, 87*(2), 166–168.

Goddard, R., Hoy, W., & Hoy, A. (2004). Collective efficacy beliefs: Theoretical developments, empirical evidence, and future directions. *Educational Researcher, 33*(3), 3–13.

Goldhaber, D. (1999). School choice: An examination of the empirical evidence on achievement, parental decision making and equity. *Educational Researcher, 28*(9), 16–25.

Goldhaber, D., & Hyde, E. (2002). What do we know (and need to know) about the impact of school choice reforms on disadvantaged students? *Harvard Educational Review, 72*, 157–173.

Goldstein, D. (2006, May 6). Upset over anthem translation? Change your tune; it's old news. *Salt Lake Tribune*, pp. A1, A4.

Goldstein, L. (2002). Election results boost special ed. vouchers. *Education Week, 22*(14), 21, 24.

Goldstein, R. A. (2004). Who are our urban students and what makes them so different? In S. R. Steinberg & J. L. Kincheloe (Eds.), *19 Urban questions: Teaching in the city* (pp. 41–51). New York: Peter Lang.

Gollnick, D., & Chinn, P. (2006). *Multicultural education in a pluralistic society* (7th ed.). Upper Saddle River, NJ: Merrill/Prentice Hall.

Gonzales, P., Guzmán, J., Partelow, L., Pahlke, E., Jocelyn, L., Kastberg, D., & Williams, T. (2004). *Highlights from the trends in international mathematics and science study (TIMSS) 2003 (NCES 2005–005).* U.S. Department of Education. Washington, DC: National Center for Educational Statistics.

Good, T., & Brophy, J. (2003). *Looking in classrooms* (9th ed.). Boston: Allyn & Bacon.

Goodlad, J. (1984). *A place called school.* New York: McGraw-Hill.

Goodman, J. F. (2005). How bad is cheating? *Education Week, 24*(16), 32, 35.

Gordon, R. (2006). The federalism debate: Why the idea of national education standards is crossing party lines. *Education Week, 25*(27), 48, 35.

Gordon, R., Della Piana, L., & Keleher, T. (2001). Zero tolerance: A basic racial report card. In W. Ayers, B. Dohrn, & R. Ayers (Eds.), *Zero tolerance* (pp. 165–175). New York: New Press.

Grant, L. W. (2006). Persistence and self-efficacy: A key to understanding teacher turnover. *The Delta Kappa Gamma Bulletin, 72*(2), 50–54.

Gratz, D. B. (2005). Lessons from Denver: The pay for performance pilot. *Phi Delta Kappan, 86*(8), 569–581.

Gray, T., & Fleischman, S. (2005). Successful strategies for English language learners. *Educational Leadership, 62*(4), 84–85.

Greene, J. (2000). Why school choice can promote integration. *Education Week, 19*(31), 72, 52.

Greene, J. P., & Winters, M. A. (2006). Getting ahead by staying behind: An evaluation of Florida's program to end social promotion. *Education Next, 6*(2), 65–69.

Greifner, L. (2006). National PTA aims to restore time for recess. *Education Week, 25*(28).

Gresham, A., Hess, F., Maranto, R., & Milliman, S. (2000). Desert bloom: Arizona's free market in education. *Phi Delta Kappan, 81,* 751–757.

Griffith, J. (2002). A multilevel analysis of the relation of school learning and social environments to minority achievement in public elementary schools. *The Elementary School Journal, 102,* 349–366.

Gronlund, N. (2004). *Writing instructional objectives for teaching and assessment* (7th ed.). Upper Saddle River, NJ: Merrill/Prentice Hall.

Grove, K. (2002). The invisible role of the central office. *Educational Leadership, 59*(8), 45–47.

Gruhn, W., & Douglass, H. (1971). *The modern junior high school* (3rd ed.). New York: Ronald Press.

Grunbaum, J., Kann, L., Kinchen, S., Williams, B., Ross, J., Lowry, R., & Kolbe, L. (2002). Youth risk behavior surveillance: United States, 2001. *Morbidity and Mortality Weekly Report, 51*(SS-4), 1–64.

Guarino, C., Santibañez, L., & Daley, G. (2006). Teacher recruitment and retention: A review of the recent empirical literature. *Review of Educational Research, 76*(2), 173–208.

Guest, A., & Schneider, B. (2003). Adolescents' extracurricular participation in context: The mediating effects of schools, communities, and identity. *Sociology of Education, 76,* 89–109.

Gunderson, L., & Siegel, L. (2001). The evils of the use of IQ tests to define learning disabilities in first- and second-language learners. *Reading Teacher, 55*(1), 48–55.

Gurian, M., & Stevens, K. (2005). What is happening with boys in school? *Teachers College Record.* Date Published: May 02, 2005. Retrieved June 21, 2005, from *http://www.tcrecord.org* ID Number: 11854.

Gutek, G. L. (2005). *Historical and philosophical foundations of education: A biographical introduction.* Upper Saddle River, NJ: Pearson/Prentice Hall.

Gutherie, J. W., & Springer, M. G. (2006). Teacher pay for performance: Another fad or sound and lasting policy. *Education Week, 25*(30), 52, 42.

Gutiérrez, K., Asato, J., Pacheco, M., Moll, L., Olsen, K., Horng, C., Ruiz, R., Garcia, E., & McCarthy, T. (2002). "Sounding American": The consequences of new reforms on English language learners. *Reading Research Quarterly, 37,* 328–343.

Gutiérrez, R. (2002). Beyond essentialism: The complexity in teaching mathematics to Latino students. *American Educational Research Journal, 39,* 1047–1088.

Haas, M. (2005). Teaching methods for secondary algebra: A meta-analysis of findings. *NASSP Bulletin, 89*(642), 24–46.

Haberman, M. (2004). Can star teachers create learning communities? *Educational Leadership, 61*(8), 52–56.

Hallahan, D., & Kauffman, J. (2003). *Exceptional learners: Introduction to special education* (9th ed.). Needham Heights, MA: Allyn & Bacon.

Hamilton, L., Berends, M., & Stecher, B. (2005). *Teachers' response to standards-based accountability.* Paper presented at the annual meeting of the American Educational Research Association, Montreal.

Hammack, F. (Ed.). (2004). *The comprehensive high school today.* New York: Teachers College Press.

Hammack, F. (2005). High school reform, again. *Teachers College Record.* Retrieved August 30, 2005, from *http://www.tcrecord.org* ID Number 11853.

Hammerness, K., Darling-Hammond, L., & Bransford, J. (2005). How teachers learn and develop. In L. Darling-Hammond & J. Bransford (Eds.), *Preparing teachers for a changing world: What teachers should learn and be able to do* (pp. 358–389). San Francisco: Jossey-Bass.

Hanushek, E. (1996). A more complete picture of school resource policies. *Review of Educational Research, 66,* 397–410.

Hardman, M., Drew, C., & Egan, W. (2005). *Human exceptionality* (8th ed.). Needham Heights, MA: Allyn & Bacon.

Hardman, M., Drew, C., & Egan, W. (2006). *Human exceptionality: IDEA 2004 update edition* (8th ed.). Boston: Allyn & Bacon.

Hardy, L. (2002). A new federal role. *American School Board Journal, 18*(9), 20–24.

Hardy, L. (2005). A place apart: How rural schools are tackling the twin problems of isolation and poverty. *American School Board Journal, 192*(4), 18–23.

Harris, S., & Lowery, S. (2002). A view from the classroom. *Educational Leadership, 59*(8), 64–65.

Harris Interactive Inc. 2005. *Nearly two-thirds of U.S. adults believe human beings were created by God.* Retrieved November 8, 2006, from *http://www.harrisinteractive.com/harris_poll/index.asp?PID=581*

Hartman, C. (2006). Students on the move. *Educational Leadership, 63*(5), 20–24.

Hassel, B., & Hassel, E. (2004). Parents take choice driver's seat, but few have a map. *Education Week, 24*(3), 34, 36.

Hasselbring, T., & Bausch, M. (2005/2006). Assistive technologies for reading. *Educational Leadership, 63*(4), 72–75.

Haycock, K. (2001). Closing the achievement gap. *Educational Leadership, 58*(6), 6–11.

Hazelwood School District v. Kuhlmeier, 484 U.S. 260 (1988).

Heath, S. (1982). Questioning at home and at school: A comparative study. In G. Spindler (Ed.), *Doing the ethnography of schooling* (pp. 102–131). New York: Holt, Rinehart & Winston.

Heath, S. (1989). Oral and literate traditions among Black Americans living in poverty. *American Psychologist, 44*, 367–373.

Hecht, E. (2006). There is no really good definition of mass. *Physics Teacher, 44*(1), 40–45.

Hendrie, C. (1999). Harvard study finds increase in segregation. *Education Week, 18*(41), 6.

Hendrie, C. (2002). New scrutiny for sponsors of charters. *Education Week, 22*(12), 1, 18.

Hendrie, C. (2003a). California charter-funding fight hits home. *Education Week, 22*(18), 18–19.

Hendrie, C. (2003b). States target sexual abuse by educators. *Education Week, 22*(33), 1, 16–18.

Hendrie, C. (2005a). Court: Class strip searches unconstitutional. *Education Week, 24*(3), 3, 22.

Hendrie, C. (2005b). Legislation tightens fiscal oversight of California charters. *Education Week, 25*(7), 18.

Hendrie, C. (2005c). T-shirts on gay issues spur lawsuits. *Education Week, 24*(16), 1, 16.

Henry, G., Gordon, C., & Rickman, D. (2006). Early education policy alternatives: Comparing quality and outcomes of Head Start and state prekindergarten. *Educational Evaluation and Policy Analysis, 28*(1), 77–99.

Herbert, B. (2006, July 4). Minimum-wage earners suffer while the rich just get richer. *Salt Lake Tribune,* p. A9.

Herszenhorn, D. (2006, April 19). New York offers housing subsidy as teacher lure. *New York Times,* pp. A1, C15.

Hess, F. (2004a). *School boards at the dawn of the 21st century.* Alexandria, VA: National School Boards Association.

Hess, F. (2004b). The political challenges of charter school regulation. *Phi Delta Kappan, 85*(7), 508–512.

Heward, W. (2006). *Exceptional children* (8th ed.). Upper Saddle River, NJ: Merrill/Prentice Hall.

Hewitt, T. (2006). *What we teach and why.* Thousand Oaks, CA: Sage.

Hiebert, J., Gallimore, R., & Stigler, J. (2002). A knowledge base for the teaching profession: What would it look like and how can we get one? *Educational Researcher, 31*(5), 3–15.

Hinkel, E. (2005). *Handbook of research on second language teaching and learning.* Mahwah, NJ: Erlbaum.

Hirsch, E. (1987). *Cultural literacy: What every American needs to know.* Boston: Houghton Mifflin.

Hirsch, E. (2000). The tests we need and why we don't quite have them. *Education Week, 19*(21), 40–41.

Hirsch, E. (2001). Seeking breadth and depth in the curriculum. *Educational Leadership, 59*(2), 22–25.

Hirsch, E. (Ed.). (2005). What your fourth grader needs to know: Fundamentals of a good fourth-grade education. New York: Dell.

Hirsch, E. (2006). *Knowledge deficit: Closing the shocking education gap for American children.* Boston: Houghton Mifflin.

Hoff, D. (2000). Gap widens between Black and White students on NAEP. *Education Week, 20*(1), 6–7.

Hoff, D. (2003a). KERA: In midlife crisis or golden years? *Education Week, 23*(2), 18, 21.

Hoff, D. (2003b). Math education panel issues long-range plan for action. *Education Week, 22*(33), 11.

Hoff, D. (2005). Schools feel pressure of efforts to increase fiscal responsibility. *Education Week, 24*(39), 1, 24.

Hoff, D. (2006). Texas proposes classroom costs per "65 percent" plan. *Education Week, 25*(32), 23, 24.

Hoff, T. (2002). A fresh approach to sex education. *American School Board Journal, 189*(11), 60–61, 66.

Hofferth, S., & Januniene, Z. (2001). Life after school. *Educational Leadership, 58*(7), 10–23.

Hoffman, L. (2003). *Overview of public elementary and secondary schools and districts: School year 2001–02* (NCES 2003–411). U.S. Department of Education, National Center for Education Statistics. Washington, DC: U.S. Government Printing Office.

Holloway, J. (2001). Grouping students for increased achievement. *Educational Leadership, 59*(3), 84–85.

Holloway, J. (2001/2002). Research Link: The dilemma of zero tolerance. *Educational Leadership, 59*(4), 84–85.

Holloway, J. (2004). Family literacy. *Education Leadership, 61*(6), 88–89.

Holmes, C. (2006). Low test scores + high retention rates = more dropouts. *Kappa Delta Pi Record, 42*(2), 56–58.

Home School Legal Defense Association. (2004). *Survey of home schooling parents.* Retrieved June 26, 2006, from *http://www.hslda.org*

Honawar, V. (2005). Smoking in movies spurs youth to try it, Dartmouth study says. *Education Week, 25*(13), 15.

Honawar, V. (2006). Md. Lawmakers fight school takeover plan. *Education Week, 25*(31), 25, 28.

Hong, S., & Ho, H. (2005). Direct and indirect longitudinal effects of parental involvement on student achievement: Second-order latent growth modeling across ethnic groups. *Journal of Educational Psychology, 97*(1), 32–42.

Honora, D. (2003). Urban African American adolescents and school identification. *Urban Education, 38*(1), 58–76.

Hopkins, A. (2006). Evolution debate rears head again in Ohio. *Pew Forum on Religion and Public Life.* Retrieved October 1, 2006, from *http://pewforum.org/news/display.php?NewsID=11246*

Hopkins, J. (2006). All students being equal. *Technology & Learning, 26*(10), 26–28.

Horn, I. (2005). Learning on the job: A situated account of teacher learning in high school mathematics departments. *Cognition and Instruction, 23*(2), 207–236.

Howell, W. (2005). School boards besieged. *Education Week, 24*(26), 44.

Howley, C., & Howley, A. (2004). School size and the influence of socioeconomic status on student achievement: Confronting the threat of size bias in national data sets. *Education Policy Analysis Archives, 12*(52). Retrieved September 26, 2006, from *http://epaa.asu.edu/epaa/v12n52/*

Hulse, C. (2006, May 16). Senate passes a bill that favors English. *New York Times,* p. A19.

Hunsader, P. (2002). Why boys fail—and what we can do about it. *Principal, 82*(2), 52–54.

Hurst, M. (2004). School lunchrooms take digital twists and turns. *Education Week, 24*(9), 8.

Hutton, I. (2005). The charter option: 5 big questions your board should ask before authorizing a charter school. *American School Board Journal, 192*(5), 16–20.

Hyland, N., & Noffke, S. (2005). Understanding diversity through social and community inquiry: An action-research study. *Journal of Teacher Education, 56*(4), 367–381.

Ilg, T., & Massucci, J. (2003). Comprehensive urban high schools: Are there better options for poor and minority children? *Education and Urban Society, 36*(1), 63–78.

Illig, D. (1996). *Reducing class size: A review of the literature and options for consideration.* Sacramento, CA: California Research Bureau.

Imazeki, J., & Reschovsky, A. (2004). School finance reform in Texas: A never-ending story? In J. Yinger (Ed.), *Helping children left behind* (pp. 251–282). Cambridge, MA: MIT Press.

Imber, M., & van Geel, T. (2005). *A teacher's guide to education law* (3rd ed.). Mahwah, NJ: Lawrence Erlbaum.

Individuals with Disabilities Education Act of 1997. Pub. L. No. 105–17. C.F.R. 3000 (1997).

Individuals with Disabilities Education Act of 2004. Pub. L. No. 108–446. (2004).

Ingersoll, R., & Smith, T. (2003). The wrong solution to the teacher shortage. *Educational Leadership, 60*(8), 30–33.

Ingersoll, R., & Smith, T. (2004). What are the effects of induction and mentoring on beginning teacher turnover? *American Educational Research Journal, 41*(3), 681–714.

Ingraham v. Wright, 430 U.S. 651 (1977).

INTASC. Interstate New Teacher Assessment and Support Consortium. (1993). *Model standards for beginning teacher licensing and development: A resource for state dialogues.* Washington, DC: Council of Chief State School Officers.

Jackson, A., & Davis, G. (2000). *Turning points 2000: Educating adolescents in the 21st century.* New York: Teachers College Press.

Jackson, P. (1968). *Life in classrooms.* New York: Holt, Rinehart & Winston.

Jacobsen, D. (2003). *Philosophy in classroom teaching: Bridging the gap* (2nd ed.). Upper Saddle River, NJ: Prentice Hall.

Jacobsen, D., Eggen, P., & Kauchak, D. (2006). *Methods for teaching* (7th ed.). Upper Saddle River, NJ: Merrill/Prentice Hall.

Jacobson, L. (2004). Research updates lives of Perry preschoolers. *Education Week, 24*(4), 6.

Jacobson, L. (2005). E-mail opens lines of communication for teachers. *Education Week, 24*(30), 8.

Jencks, C., & Phillips, M. (Eds.). (1998). *The Black–White test score gap.* Washington, DC: Brookings Institution Press.

Jennings, M. (2000). Attendance technology easing record-keeping burden. *Education Week, 19*(35), 7.

Jetton, T., & Alexander, P. (1997). Instructional importance: What teachers value and what students learn. *Reading Research Quarterly, 32,* 290–308.

Jimerson, S., Pletcher, S., & Graydon, K. (2006). Beyond grade retention and social promotion: Promoting the social and academic competence of students. *Psychology in the Schools, 43*(1), 85–97.

Johnson, B., & Christensen, L. B. (2004). *Educational research: Quantitative and qualitative approaches* (2nd ed.) Boston: Allyn & Bacon.

Johnson, D. (2004). Plagiarism-proofing assignments. *Phi Delta Kappan, 85*(7), 549–552.

Johnson, D., & Johnson, R. (1999). The 3 C's of school and classroom management. In R. Freiberg (Ed.), *Beyond behaviorism* (pp. 119–145). Boston: Allyn & Bacon.

Johnson, D., & Johnson, R. (2004). The three Cs of promoting social and emotional learning. In J. Zins, R. Weissberg, M. Wang, & H. Walberg (Eds.), *Building academic success on social and emotional learning* (pp. 40–58). New York: Teachers College Press.

Johnson, D., & Johnson, R. (2006). *Learning together and alone: Cooperation, competition, and individualization* (8th ed.). Needham Heights, MA: Allyn & Bacon.

Johnson, J. (2004). What school leaders want. *Educational Leadership, 61*(7), 24–27.

Johnson, J. (2005). Isn't it time for schools of education to take concerns about student discipline more seriously? *Teachers College Record*. Retrieved March 22, 2005, from *http://www.tcrecord.org/* ID Number: 11739.

Johnson, L., Bachman, J., & O'Malley, P. (2001). *Monitoring the future: Questionnaire responses from the nation's high school seniors, 1997*. Ann Arbor, MI: Institute for Social Research.

Johnson, S., & Birkeland, S. (2003, April). *Pursuing a "sense of success": New teachers explain their career decisions*. Paper presented at the annual meeting of the American Educational Research Association, New Orleans, LA.

Johnson, S., & Birkeland, S. (2006). Fast track certification. *Education Week, 25*(23), 48, 37.

Johnston, J. (2004). Authority, inquiry, and education: A response to Dewey's critics. *Educational Studies, 35*(3), 230–247.

Johnston, R. (1994). Policy details who paddles students and with what. *Education Week, 14*(11), 17–18.

Jonassen, D. (2000). *Computers as mindtools for schools* (2nd ed.). Columbus, OH: Merrill/Prentice Hall.

Jonassen, D., Howland, J., Moore, J., & Marra, R. (2003). *Learning to solve problems with technology*. Upper Saddle River, NJ: Merrill/Prentice Hall.

Jones, S. (2005). More discipline? *Teachers College Record*. Retrieved March 29, 2005, from *http://www.tcrecord.org* ID Number: 11746.

Jones, S., & Dindia, K. (2004). A meta-analytic perspective on sex equity in the classroom. *Review of Educational Research, 74*(4), 443–471.

Jones, V., & Jones, L. (2004). *Comprehensive classroom management: Creating communities of support and solving problems* (7th ed.). Boston: Allyn & Bacon.

Jordan, W. (2001, April). *At-risk students during the first year of high school: Navigating treacherous waters*. Paper presented at the annual meeting of the American Educational Research Association, Seattle, WA.

Jordan, W., & Brooks, W. (2000). *Mending the safety net: A preliminary analysis of the twilight school*. Paper presented at the annual meeting of the American Educational Research Association, New Orleans, LA.

Joseph, P., & Efron, S. (2005). Seven worlds of moral education. *Phi Delta Kappan, 86*(7), 525–533.

Juvonen, J., Le, V., Kagonoff, T., Augustine, C., & Constant, L. (2004). *Focus on the wonder years: Challenges facing the American middle school*. Retrieved September 28, 2006, from *http://www.rand.org/pubs/monographs/2004/RAND_MG138.pdf*

Kahlenberg, R. (2000). *Economic school integration* (IDEA Brief No. 2). Washington, DC: The Century Foundation.

Kahlenberg, R. (2006). Integration by income. *American School Board Journal, 193*(4), 51–52.

Kain, D. (2003). *Problem-based learning*. Boston: Allyn & Bacon.

Kaiser Family Foundation. (2004a). *Sex education in America: Principals survey*. Retrieved March 20, 2005, from *http://www.npr.org/programs/morning*

Kaiser Family Foundation. (2004b). *Survey snapshot: The digital divide*. Retrieved June 19, 2006, from *www.kff.org*

Karten, T. (2005). *Inclusion strategies that work: Research-based methods for the classroom*. Thousand Oaks, CA: Corwin Press.

Kauchak, D., & Eggen, P. (2007). *Learning and teaching: Research-based methods* (5th ed.). Needham Heights, MA: Allyn & Bacon.

Kaufman, F. (2005). Diabesity. In P. Menzel, *Hungry planet: What the world eats* (pp. 242–243). Napa, CA: Material World Press.

Kedar-Voivodas, G. (1983). The impact of elementary children's school roles and sex roles on teacher attitudes: An interactional analysis. *Review of Educational Research, 20*, 417–462.

Keller, B. (2002). Report urges experimentation with teacher-pay schemes. *Education Week, 21*(39), 11.

Keller, B. (2005). Teachers flocking to online sources to advance and acquire knowledge. *Education Week, 24*(43), 22, 24.

Keller, B. (2006). Study for NBPTS raises questions about credential. *Education Week, 25*(37), 1, 16.

Keller, J. (2004). Just their type. *Technology and Learning, 25*(2), 12–18.

Kennedy, M. (2006). Knowledge and vision in teaching. *Journal of Teacher Education, 57*(3), 205–211.

Kerman, S. (1979). Teacher expectations and student achievement. *Phi Delta Kappan, 60,* 70–72.

Kids Health for Parents. (2006). *About teen suicide.* Retrieved March 21, 2006, from *http://www.kidshealth.org/sui_fact.htm*

Kilbane, C., & Milman, N. (2003). *The digital teaching portfolio handbook: A how-to guide for educators.* Boston: Allyn & Bacon.

Kincheloe, J. (2004). Why a book on urban education? In Steinberg, S., & Kincheloe, J. (Eds.), *19 Urban questions: Teaching in the city* (pp. 1–27). New York: Peter Lang.

King, K. P. (2007). *Integrating the national science education standards into classroom practice.* Upper Saddle River, NJ: Pearson/Prentice Hall.

Kitzmiller et al. v. Dover Area School District, 04cv2688 (U.S. District Court for the Middle District of Pennsylvania, 2005).

Kleiman, C. (2001, October 30). Internet helps parents keep an eye on kids [Electronic version]. *Chicago Tribune.* Retrieved May 17, 2005, from *http://www.chicagotribune.co*

Klein, P. (2003). Rethinking the multiplicity of cognitive resources and curricular representations: Alternatives to "learning styles" and "multiple intelligences." *Journal of Curriculum Studies, 35,* 45–81.

Kober, N. (2006). *A public education primer: Basic (and sometimes surprising) facts about the U.S. education system.* Washington, DC: Center on Education Policy.

Kohn, A. (1993). *Punished by rewards: The trouble with gold stars, incentive plans, A's, praise, and other bribes.* Boston: Houghton Mifflin.

Kohn, A. (1997), How not to teach values. *Phi Delta Kappan, 78,* 429–439.

Kohn, A. (1999). Direct drilling. *Education Week, 18*(30), 43.

Kohn, A. (2000). Burnt at the high stakes. *Journal of Teacher Education, 51*(4), 315–327.

Kohn, A. (2006). Abusing research: The study of homework and other examples. *Phi Delta Kappan, 88*(1), 9–22.

Konheim-Kalkstein, Y. (2006). A uniform look. *American School Board Journal, 193*(8), 25–27.

Koppich, J. E. (2005). All teachers are not the same. *Education Next, 5*(1), 13–15.

Kosar, K. (2005). *Failing grades: The federal politics of education standards.* Boulder, CO: Lynne Rienner.

Kounin, J. (1970). *Discipline and group management in classrooms.* New York: Holt, Rinehart & Winston.

Kozol, J. (1991). *Savage inequalities.* New York: Crown.

Kozol, J. (2005). *The shame of the nation: The restoration of apartheid schooling in America.* New York: Crown.

Krashen, S. (1996). *Under attack: The case against bilingual education.* Culver City, CA: Language Education Associates.

Kristoff, N. (2006, May 14). The model students. *New York Times,* Sect. 4, p. 13.

Kroesbergen, E. H., & van Luit, E. H. (2002). Teaching multiplication to low math performers: Guided versus structured instruction. *Instructional Science, 30,* 361–378.

Kroesbergen, E. H., van Luit, E. H., & Maas, C. J. (2004). Effectiveness of explicit and constructivist mathematics instruction for low-achieving students in the Netherlands. *Elementary School Journal, 104,* 233–251.

Krueger, A., & Whitmore, D. (2002). Would smaller classes help close the Black–White achievement gap? In J. Chubb & T. Loveless (Eds.), *Bridging the achievement gap* (pp. 11–46). Washington, DC: Brookings Institution Press.

Kuh, D., & Vesper, N. (1999, April). *Do computers enhance or detract from student learning?* Paper presented at the annual meeting of the American Educational Research Association, Montreal

Kuhn, D. (2005). *Education for thinking.* Cambridge, MA: Harvard University Press.

Kunzman, R. (2006). *Grappling with the good.* Albany, NY: State University of New York Press.

Labaree, D. (2004). *The trouble with ed schools.* New Haven, CT: Yale University Press.

Labaree, D. (2005). Life on the margins. *Journal of Teacher Education 56*(3), 186–191.

LaChausse, R. G. (2006). Evaluation of the positive prevention HIV/STD curriculum. *American Journal of Health Education, 37*(4), 203–209.

Laczko-Kerr, I., & Berliner, D. (2003). In harm's way: How undercertified teachers hurt their students. *Educational Leaderhip, 60*(8), 34–39.

Ladson-Billings, G. (2005). Is the team all right? Diversity and teacher education. *Journal of Teacher Education, 56*(3), 229–234.

Lafee, S. (2005). Another weighty burden. *School Administrator, 62*(9), 10–16.

LaMorte, M. (2005). *School law: Cases and concepts* (8th ed.). Boston: Allyn & Bacon.

Land, D. (2002). Local school boards under review: Their role and effectiveness in relation to students' academic achievement. *Review of Educational Research, 72,* 229–278.

Lashley, C. (2001, April). *Performance-based licensure: Developing support systems for beginning teachers*. Paper presented at the annual meeting of the American Educational Research Association, Seattle, WA.

Lau v. Nichols, 414 U.S. 563 (1974).

Lee, H. (2004). Understanding and assessing preservice teachers' reflective thinking. *Teaching and Teacher Education, 21*, 699–715.

Lee, J., & Doolittle, P. (April, 2003). *Social studies teachers' uses of non-digital and digital historical resources*. Paper presented at the annual meeting of the American Educational Research Association, Chicago.

Lee, S. (2006). The learner-centered paradigm of instruction and training. *Tech Trends, 50*(2), 21–23.

Lee, V. (2000). Using hierarchical linear modeling to study social contexts: The case of school effects. *Educational Psychologist, 35*, 125–141.

Lee, V., & Smith, J. (1999). Social support and achievement for young adolescents in Chicago: The role of school academic press. *American Educational Research Journal, 36*, 907–946.

Lee v. Weismann, 112 S. Ct. 29649 (1992).

Lei, J. (2003). (Un)necessary toughness?: Those "loud Black girls" and those "quiet Asian boys." *Anthropology & Education Quarterly, 34*(2), 158–181.

Leinhardt, G. (2001). Instructional explanations: A commonplace for teaching and location for contrast. In V. Richardson (Ed.), *Handbook of research on teaching* (4th ed., pp. 333–357). Washington, DC: America Educational Research Association.

Leinhardt, G., & Steele, M. (2005). Seeing the complexity of standing to the side: Instructional dialogues. *Cognition and Instruction, 23*(1), 87–163.

Lemke, M., Sen. A., Pahlke, E., Partelow, L., Miller D., William, T., Kastberg, D., & Jocelyn, L. (2004). *International outcomes of learning in mathematics literacy and problem solving: PISA 2003 results from the U.S. perspective* (NCES 2005–003). U.S. Department of Education. Washington, DC: National Center for Education Statistics.

LePage, P., Darling-Hammond, L., Akan, H., Guitierrez, C., Jenkins-Gunn, E., & Rosebrock, K. (2005). Classroom management. In L. Darling-Hammond & J. Bransford (Eds.), *Preparing teachers for a changing world* (pp. 327–357). San Francisco: Jossey-Bass.

Lever-Duffy, J., McDonald, J., & Mizell, A. (2003). *Teaching and learning with technology*. Boston: Allyn & Bacon.

Lew, J. (2004). The "other" story of model minorities: Korean American high school dropouts in an urban context. *Anthropology and Education Quarterly, 35*(3), 303–323.

Lewin, T. (2006, July 9). At college, women are leaving men in the dust. *New York Times*, July 9, pp. A1, A18, A19.

Lewis, A. (2005). More than just cute kids. *Phi Delta Kappan, 87*(3), 179–180.

Lewis, A. C. (2006). Redefining what high school students learn. *Phi Delta Kappan, 87*(8), 564–565.

Lichter, D., & Johnson, K. (2006). Emerging rural settlement patterns and the geographic distribution of America's new immigrants. *Rural Sociology, 71*(1), 109–131.

Lindeman, B. (2001). Reaching out to immigrant parents. *Educational Leadership, 58*(6), 62–66.

Liston, D. (2004). The lure of learning in teaching. *Teachers College Record, 106*(3), 459–486.

Lou, Y., Abrami, P., & Spence, J. (2000). Effects of within-class grouping on student achievement: An exploratory model. *Journal of Educational Research, 94*, 101–112.

Louis, B., Subotnik, R., Breland, P., & Lewis, M. (2000). Establishing criteria for high ability versus selective admission to gifted programs: Implications for policy and practice. *Educational Psychology Review, 12*, 295–314.

Luekens, M., Lyter, D., & Fox, E. (2004). Teacher attrition and mobility: Results from the teacher following-up survey. *National Center for Education Statistics Quarterly, 6*(3), 40–46.

Lustick, D. (2002, April). *National Board certification as professional development: A study that identifies a framework and findings of teachers learning to manage complexity, uncertainty, and community*. Paper presented at the annual meeting of the American Educational Research Association, New Orleans, LA.

Lyman, R. (2006, September 30). In many public schools, the paddle is no relic. *New York Times*, pp. C1, C2.

Lynch, R. L. (2000). High school career and technical education for the first decade of the 21st century. *Journal of Vocational Educational Research, 25*(2). Retrieved September 3, 2006, from *http://scholar.lib.vt.edu/ejournals/JVER/v25n2/lynch.html*

Lynn, R. (2003, June 9). State fears teacher flight. *Salt Lake Tribune*, pp. D1–D2.

Ma, X. (2001). Bullying and being bullied: To what extent are bullies also victims? *American Educational Research Journal, 38*(2), 351–370.

Macionis, J. (2006). *Society: The basics* (8th ed.). Upper Saddle River, NJ: Prentice Hall.

Macionis, J., & Parillo, V. (2007). *Cities and urban life* (4th ed.). Upper Saddle River, NJ: Merrill/Prentice Hall.

Maeroff, G. (2003). The virtual school house. *Education Week, 22*(24), 40, 28.

Mager, R. (1962). *Preparing instructional objectives.* Palo Alto, CA: Featon.

Mager, R. (1998). *Preparing instructional objectives: A critical tool in the development of effective instruction* (3rd ed.). Atlanta, GA: Center for Effective Performance.

Magnet Schools of America. (2006). Retrieved June 2, 2006, from *http://www.magnet.ed*

Magnuson, K., Meyers, M., Ruhm, C., & Waldfogel, J. (2004). Inequality in preschool education and school readiness. *American Educational Research Journal, 41*(1), 115–157.

Mailloux v. Kiley, 323 F. Supp. 1387 (D. Mass 1971), 448 F.2d 1242 (lst Cir. 1971).

Mandel, S. (2006). What new teachers really need. *Educational Leadership, 63*(6), 66–69.

Manning, M. (2000). A brief history of the middle school. *The Clearing House, 72*(4), 190–195.

Manning, M., & Bucher, K. (2003). *Classroom management.* Upper Saddle River, NJ: Merrill/Prentice Hall.

Manouchehri, A. (2004). Implementing mathematics reform in urban schools: A study of the effect of teachers' motivation style. *Urban Education, 38*, 472–508.

Manzo, K. (2004). Reading programs bear similarities across the states. *Education Week, 23*(21), 1, 13.

Manzo, K. (2005). N.C. backs lottery to fund school projects. *Education Week, 25*(3), 28, 30.

Manzo, K. (2006a). Scathing report casts cloud over "Reading First." *Education Week, 26*(6), 1, 24.

Manzo, K. (2006b). Young adults don't think world knowledge is vital. *Education Week, 25*(36), 8.

Margolis, J. (2004). A response to "The National Board Hoax." *Teachers College Record.* Retrieved February 2004 from *http://www.tcrecord.org/Collection.asp?CollectionID=72*

Marsh, C., & Willis, G. (2007). *Curriculum: Alternative approaches, ongoing issues.* Upper Saddle River, NJ: Merrill/Prentice Hall.

Marsh, H., & Kleitman, S. (2005). Consequences of employment during high school: Character building, subversion of academic goals, or a threshold? *American Educational Research Journal, 42*(2), 331–369.

Marttunen, M., & Laurinen, L. (2001). Learning of argumentation skills in networked and face-to-face environments. *Instructional Science, 29*, 127–153.

Marzano, R. (2003). *What works in schools.* Alexandria, VA: Association for Supervision and Curriculum Development.

Marzano, R., & Kendall, J. (2003). *Designing standards-based districts, schools, and classrooms.* Alexandria, VA: Association for Supervision and Curriculum Development.

Maslow, A. (1968). *Toward a psychology of being* (2nd ed.). New York: Van Nostrand.

Maslow, A. (1970). *Motivation and personality* (2nd ed.). New York: Harper & Row.

Mathews, J. (1999, March 24,). A home run for home schooling. *Washington Post,* p. A11.

Mathis, W. (2005). The cost of implementing the federal No Child Left Behind Act: Different assumptions, different answers. *Peabody Journal of Education, 80*(2), 90–119.

Maxwell, L. (2006a). L.A. mayor seeks role in district. *Education Week, 25*(33), 1, 25.

Maxwell, L. (2006b). Web systems help schools screen visitors. *Education Week, 25*(32), 5, 16.

Mayer, R. (2002). *The promise of educational psychology: Volume II. Teaching for meaningful learning.* Upper Saddle River, NJ: Merrill/Prentice Hall.

Mayer, R. (2004). Should there be a three-strikes rule against pure discovery learning? *American Psychologist, 59*, 14–19.

Mayes, C., & Ferrin, S. (2001). Spiritually committed public school teachers: Their beliefs and practices concerning religious expression in the classroom. *Religion and Education, 28*(1), 75–94.

McAllister, G., & Irvine, J. (2002). The role of empathy in teaching culturally diverse students: A qualitative study of teachers' beliefs. *Journal of Teacher Education, 53*, 433–443.

McCabe, M. (2006). State of the states. *Education Week, 25*(17), 72–96.

McCaslin, M., & Good, T. (1996). The informal curriculum. In D. Berliner & R. Calfee (Eds.), *Handbook of educational psychology* (pp. 622–670). New York: Macmillan.

McCombs, B. L. (2001, April). *What do we know about learners and learning? The learner-centered framework.* Paper presented at the annual meeting of the American Educational Research Association, Seattle.

McCombs, J. (2005). *Progress in implementing standards, assessment for highly qualified teacher provisions of NCLB: Initial finding from California, Georgia, and Pennsylvania.* Paper presented at the annual meeting of the American Educational Research Association, Montreal.

McDermott, J. (1994). Buddhism. *Encarta* [CD-ROM]. Bellevue, WA: Microsoft.

McDevitt, T., & Ormrod, J. (2004). *Child development: Educating and working with children and adolescents* (2nd ed.). Upper Saddle River, NJ: Merrill/Prentice Hall.

McDevitt, T., & Ormrod, J. (2007). *Child development and education* (3rd ed.). Upper Saddle River, NJ: Merrill/Prentice Hall.

McDougall, D., & Granby, C. (1996). How expectation of questioning method affects undergraduates' preparation for class. *Journal of Experimental Education, 65,* 43–54.

McMahon, S., Rose, D., & Parks, M. (2004). Multiple intelligences and reading achievement: An examination of the Teele Inventory of Multiple Intelligences. *Journal of Experimental Education, 73*(1), 41–52.

McMillan, J. (2004). *Educational research: Fundamentals for the consumer* (4th ed.). New York: Longman.

Meier, D. (2002). Standardization versus standards. *Phi Delta Kappan, 84,* 190–198.

Merrow, J. (2002). The failure of Head Start. *Education Week, 22*(4), 52, 38.

Michener, J. A. (2006). Sex education: A success in our social-studies class. *Clearing House, 79*(5), 210–214.

Milanowski, A., & Kimball, S. (2005). *The relationship between teacher expertise and student achievement: A synthesis of three years of data.* Paper presented at the annual meeting of the American Educational Research Association, Montreal.

Mills, G. (2002, April). *Teaching and learning action research.* Paper presented at the annual meeting of the American Educational Research Association, New Orleans, LA.

Mishel, L. (2006). The exaggerated dropout crisis. *Education Week, 25*(26), 40.

Mishel, L., Bernstein, J., & Allegretto, S. (2006). *The state of working Americans, 2004/2005.* Washington, DC: Economic Policy Institute.

Molnar, A., Percy, S., Smith, P., & Zahorik, J. (1998). *1997–98 results of the Student Achievement Guarantee in Education (SAGE) program.* Milwaukee: University of Wisconsin–Milwaukee.

Molnar, A., & Reeves, J. (2001). Buy me! Buy me! *Educational Leadership, 59*(2), 74–79.

Monitoring the Future. (2006). *Teen drug use down but progress halts among youngest.* University of Michigan: Michigan Institute for Social Research.

Monke, L. (2005/2006). The overdominance of computers. *Educational Leadership, 63*(4), 20–23.

Moreno, R. (2004). Decreasing cognitive load for novice students: Effects of explanatory versus corrective feedback in discovery-based multimedia. *Instructional Science, 32,* 99–113.

Moreno, R., & Duran, R. (2004). Do multiple representations need explanations: The role of verbal guidance and individual differences in multimedia mathematics learning. *Journal of Educational Psychology, 96,* 492–503.

Morris v. Douglas County School District No. 9, 403 P.2d 775 (Or. 1965).

Morrison v. State Board of Education, 461 P.2d 375 (Cal. 1969).

Morrison, G., Kemp, J., & Ross, S. (2007). *Designing effective instruction* (5th ed.). Hoboken, NJ: John Wiley & Sons.

Morrison, G. R., & Lowther, D. L. (2002). *Integrating computer technology into the classroom* (2nd ed.). Upper Saddle River, NJ: Merrill/Prentice Hall.

Mosenthal, J., Lipson, M., Torncello, S., Russ, B., & Mekkelsen, J. (2004). Contexts and practices of six schools successful in obtaining reading achievement. *Elementary School Journal, 104*(5), 343–368.

Mostow, J. (2005). Personal website. Retrieved August 27, 2006, from *http://www-2.cs.cmu.edu/~mostow*

Mozert v. Hawkins County Public Schools, 827 F.2d 1058 (6th Cir. 1987), cert. denied, 108 S. Ct. 1029 (1988).

Mulrine, A. (2002, May 27). Risky business. *U.S. News & World Report,* pp. 42–49.

Muñoz, M., & Portes, P. (2002, April). *Voices from the field: The perceptions of teachers and principals on the class size reduction program in a large urban school district.* Paper presented at the annual meeting of the American Educational Research Association, New Orleans, LA.

Murphy, M. (2006). *History and philosophy of education: The voices of educational pioneers.* Upper Saddle River, NJ: Pearson/Prentice Hall.

Murphy, P., DeArmond, M., & Guin, K. (2003). A national crisis or localized problems? Getting perspective on the scope and scale of the teacher shortage. *Education Policy Analysis Archives, 11*(23). Retrieved September 27, 2006, from *http://epaa.asu.edu/epaa/v11n23*

Murray, F. (1986). *Necessity: The developmental component in reasoning.* Paper presented at the 16th annual meeting, Jean Piaget Society, Philadelphia.

Nakagawa, K., Stafford, M., Fisher, T., & Matthews, L. (2002). The "city migrant" dilemma: Building community at high-mobility urban schools. *Urban Education, 37*(1), 96–125.

Nathan, J. (2005). Charters "Yes!" Vouchers "No!" *Educational Horizons, 83*(2), 110–124.

National Association of Elementary School Principals. (2002). What you might not know about vouchers. *Education Week, 22*(1), 10.

National Association of Elementary School Principals. (2006). *Principal salaries 2004–2005.* Retrieved February 14, 2006, from *http://www.naesp.org*

National Association of State Boards of Education. (2004). *State education governance at-a-glance.* Retrieved February 27, 2004, from *http://www.nasbe.org/Educational_Issues/Governance/ Governance_chart.pdf*

National Board for Professional Teaching Standards. (1995). *An invitation to National Board certification.* Detroit: Author.

National Board for Professional Teaching Standards. (2006). Retrieved August 16, 2006, from *http://www.nbpts.org*

National Campaign to Prevent Teen Pregnancy. (2004). *Teen pregnancy—so what?* Retrieved July 31, 2006, from *http://www.teenpregnancy.org/whycare/sowhat.asp*

National Center for Education Information. (2000). *Alternative teacher certification: A state by state analysis.* Washington, DC: Author.

National Center for Education Statistics. (1997). *Characteristics of American Indian and Alaska native education.* Washington, DC: U.S. Department of Education.

National Center for Education Statistics. (2002). *Digest of education statistics.* Washington, DC: U.S. Department of Education.

National Center for Education Statistics. (2004). Characteristics of private schools in the United States: Results from the 2001–2002 Private School Universe survey. *National Center for Education Statistics Quarterly, 6*(4), 39–45.

National Center for Education Statistics. (2005a). *Federal expenditures for education.* Washington, DC: Author. Retrieved July 1, 2006, from *http://nces.ed.gov/ubs2005/2005074.pdf*

National Center for Education Statistics. (2005b). *Indicators of school crime and safety: 2005.* Retrieved July 27, 2006, from *http://nces.ed.gov/programs/crimeindicators/index.asp?*

National Center for Education Statistics. (2005c). *Public school enrollments.* Washington, DC: U.S. Government Printing Office.

National Center for Education Statistics. (2005d). *The condition of education 2005.* Washington, DC: U.S. Department of Education.

National Center for Education Statistics. (2006a). *Internet access in U.S. public schools and classrooms: 1994–2003.* Retrieved January 3, 2006, from *http://nces.ed.gov*

National Center for Education Statistics. (2006b). *The condition of education 2006.* Washington, DC: U.S. Department of Education.

National Commission on Excellence in Education. (1983). *A nation at risk: The imperative for educational reform.* Washington, DC: Government Printing Office.

National Council of Teachers of Mathematics. (2000–2004). *Principles and standards for school mathematics.* Retrieved October 1, 2006, from *http://standards.nctm.org/document/ appendix/numb.htm*

National Education Association. (1995). *Code of ethics of the education profession, NEA Representative Assembly.* Washington, DC: Author.

National Education Association. (1997). *Status of the American public school teacher, 1995–1996.* Washington, DC: Author. Retrieved February 3, 2004, from *http://www.nea.org/neatoday/ 9709/status.html*

National Education Association. (2002a). *Status of the American public school teacher, 1999–2000.* Washington, DC: Author.

National Education Association. (2002b). *School vouchers: The emerging track record.* Washington, DC: Author.

National Education Association. (2003). *Status of the American public school teacher, 2000–2001.* Washington, DC: Author. Retrieved March 14, 2004, from *http://www.nea.org/edstats*

National Education Association. (2005). *Weighted student formula (WSF).* Washington, DC: Author. Retrieved January 30, 2006, from *http://www.nea.org/index.html*

National Education Association. (2006a). *Rankings and estimates.* Retrieved January 30, 2006, from *http://www.nea.org/index.html*

National Education Association. (2006b). *Status of the American public school teacher, 2003–2004.* Retrieved August 16, 2006, from *http://www.nea.org*

National Joint Committee on Learning Disabilities. (1994). Learning disabilities: Issues on definition. A position paper of the National Joint Committee in Learning Disabilities. In *Collective perspectives on issues affecting learning disability: Position papers and statements.* Austin, TX: Pro-Ed.

National Law Center on Homelessness and Poverty. (2006). Retrieved June 1, 2006, from *http://www.nlchp.org*

National Research Council. (1996). *National science education standards.* Washington, DC: National Academy Press.

National School Boards Association. (2000). Education vital signs: Leadership. *American School Board Journal, 187*(2), 32–37.

Neill, M. (2003). High stakes, high risk. *American School Board Journal, 190*(2), 18–21.

Neisler, O. (2000). How does teacher education need to change to meet the needs of America's schools at the start of the 21st century? *Journal of Teacher Education, 51,* 248–255.

Neville, K., Sherman, R., & Cohen, C. (2005). *Preparing and training professionals: Comparing education to six other fields.* New York: The Finance Project.

New Jersey v. T.L.O., 105 S. Ct. 733 (1985).

New York State Board Association. (2006). *Board members top 3 concerns: Academics, academics, academics.* Retrieved February 1, 2006, from *http://222.nyssba.org*

Newby, T., Stepich, D., Lehman, J., & Russell, J. (2006). *Instructional technology and teaching and learning* (3rd ed.). Upper Saddle River, NJ: Merrill/Prentice Hall.

Newman, J. (2006). *America's teachers* (5th ed.). Boston: Allyn & Bacon.

Nichols, S., & Berliner, D. (2005). *The inevitable corruption of indicators and educators through high-stakes testing.* Tempe, AZ: Education Policy Studies Laboratory.

Nietfeld, J., Cao, L., & Osborne, J. (2004). *Effect of distributed monitoring exercises and feedback on performance and monitoring accuracy.* Paper presented at the annual meeting of the American Educational Research Association, San Diego, CA.

Nieto, S. (2004). *Affirming diversity* (4th ed.). New York: Longman.

Nikitina, S. (2006). Three strategies for interdisciplinary teaching: contextualizing, conceptualizing, and problem-centering. *Journal of Curriculum Studies, 38*(3), 251–271.

No Child Left Behind Act of 2001, Pub. L. 107–110 (8 January 2002). Washington, DC: U.S. Government Printing Office.

Noblit, G., Rogers, D., & McCadden, B. (1995). In the meantime: The possibilities of caring. *Phi Delta Kappan, 76,* 680–685.

Noddings, N. (2001). The caring teacher. In V. Richardson (Ed.), *Handbook of research on teaching* (4th ed., pp. 99–105). Washington, DC: American Educational Research Association.

Noguera, P. (2003a). *City schools and the American dream: Reclaiming the promise of public education.* New York: Teachers College Press.

Noguera, P. (2003b). The trouble with black boys: The role and influence of environmental and cultural factors on the academic performance of African American males. *Urban Education, 38*(4), 431–459.

Norris, N. (2004). *The promise and failure of progressive education.* Landham, MD: Scarecrow Press.

Nye, B., Hedges, L., & Konstantopoulos, S. (2001). Are effects of small classes cumulative? Evidence from a Tennessee experiment. *Journal of Educational Research, 94,* 336–341.

Oakes, J. (2005). Keeping track: How schools structure inequality (2nd ed.). New Haven, CT: Yale University Press.

Oakes, J., & Saunders, M. (2004). Education's most basic tools: Access to textbooks and instructional materials in California's public schools. *Teachers College Record, 106*(10), 1967–1988.

Oakes, J., & Wells, A. S. (2002). Detracking for high student achievement. In L. Abbeduto (Ed.), *Taking sides: Clashing views and controversial issues in educational psychology* (2nd ed., pp. 26–30). Guilford, CT: McGraw-Hill Duskin.

Odden, A. (2003). Leveraging teacher pay. *Education Week, 22*(43), 64.

Odden, A., Borman, G. D., & Fermanich, M. (2004). Assessing teacher, classroom, and school effects, including fiscal effects. *Peabody Journal of Education, 79*(4), 4–32.

Odden, A., Monk, D., Nakib, Y., & Picus, L. (1995). The story of the education dollar: No academy awards and no fiscal smoking guns. *Phi Delta Kappan, 77,* 161–168.

Oder, N. (2005). Oklahoma legislators urge limits on kid's books with gay themes. *Library Journal, 130*(11), 16–17.

OELA (Office of English Language Acquisition). (2004). *National clearinghouse for language acquisition and language instruction programs.* Retrieved March 2, 2006, from *www.NCLE.gwu.edu/languages*

Ogbu, J. (1992). Understanding cultural diversity and learning. *Educational Researcher, 21*(8), 5–14.

Ogbu, J. (1999). Beyond language: Ebonics, proper English, and identity in a Black-American speech community. *American Educational Research Journal, 36,* 147–184.

Ogbu, J. (2003). *Black American students in an affluent suburb: A study of academic disengagement.* Mahwah, NJ: Erlbaum.

Ogbu, J., & Simons, H. (1998). Voluntary and involuntary minorities: A cultural-ecological theory of school performance with some implications for education. *Anthropology & Education Quarterly, 29*(2), 155–188.

Olivia, P. (2005). *Developing the curriculum* (6th ed.). Boston: Allyn & Bacon.

Olson, J., & Clough, M. (2004). *What questions do you have? In defense of general questions: A response to Croom. Teachers College Record.* Retrieved August 20, 2004, from *http://www.tcrecord.org/content.asp?content* ID Number: 11366.

Olson, L. (1999a). A closer look: What makes a good report card. *Education Week, 18*(17), 29.

Olson, L. (1999b). Report cards for schools. *Education Week, 18*(17), 28–36.

Olson, L. (2000). Finding and keeping competent teachers. *Education Week, 19*(18), 12–18.

Olson, L. (2003). The great divide. *Education Week, 22*(17), 9–20.

Olson, L. (2005a). In hearing, poll, PEN finds support for the goals of NCLB. *Education Week, 24*(27), 6.

Olson, L. (2005b). Nationwide standards eyed anew. *Education Week, 25*(14), 1, 24.

Olson, L. (2005c). Impact of paper and pencil, online testing is compared. *Education Week, 25*(11), 14.

Olson, L. (2006a). A decade of effort. *Education Week, 25*(17), 8–16.

Olson, L. (2006b). The down staircase. *Education Week, 25*(41S), 5, 6, 10, 11.

Opdenakker, M. C., & Van Damme, J. (2006). Teacher characteristics and teaching styles as effectiveness enhancing factors of classroom practice. *Teaching and Teacher Education, 22*(1), 1–21.

Ormrod, J. (2006). *Educational psychology: Developing learners* (5th ed). Upper Saddle River, NJ: Merrill/Prentice Hall.

Ornstein, A., & Hunkins, F. (2004). *Curriculum: Foundations, principles, and issues* (4th ed.). Boston: Allyn & Bacon.

Orr, A. (2003). Black–white differences in achievement: The importance of wealth. *Sociology of Education, 76* (October), 281–304.

Ortiz, F. (2004). Essential learning conditions for California youth: Educational facilities. *Teachers College Record, 106*(10), 2015–2031.

Osborne, J. (1996). Beyond constructivism. *Science Education, 80,* 53–81.

Ozmon, H. A., & Craver, S. M. (2007). *Philosophical foundations of education* (8th ed.). Upper Saddle River, NJ: Pearson.

Park, C. (1997, March). *A comparative study of learning style preferences: Asian-American and Anglo students in secondary schools.* Paper presented at the annual meeting of the American Educational Research Association, Chicago.

Patrick, H., Anderman, L. H., & Ryan, A. M. (2002). Social motivation and the classroom social environment. In C. Midgley (Ed.), *Goals, goal structures, and patterns of adaptive learning* (pp. 85–108). Mahwah, NJ: Erlbaum.

Patterson, F. (2001/2002). Teaching religious intolerance. *Rethinking Schools, 16*(2), 6, 7.

Paxson, R. (2003). Don't know much about history—never did. *Phi Delta Kappan, 85,* 265–273.

Payton, J., Munro, S., O'Brien, M., & Weissberg, R. (2006). Common ground. *Edutopia, 2*(6), 53–55.

Pecheone, R. L., & Chung, R. R. (2006). Evidence in teacher education: The performance assessment for California teachers. *Journal of Teacher Education, 57*(1), 22–36.

Pedulla, J., Abrams, L., Madaus, G., Russell, M., Ramos, M., & Miao, J. (2003). *Perceived effects of state-mandated testing programs on teaching and learning: Findings from a national survey of teachers.* Boston: Boston College.

Peevely, G., Hedges, L., & Nye, B. A. (2005). The relationship of class size effects and teacher salary. *Journal of Education Finance, 31*(1), 101–109.

Peregoy, S., & Boyle, O. (2005). *Reading, writing, and learning in ESL* (4th ed.). New York: Longman.

Perkins-Gough, D. (2005a). Fixing high schools. *Educational Leadership, 62*(8), 88–89.

Perkins-Gough, D. (2005b). The perils of high school exit exams. *Educational Leadership, 63*(3), 90–91.

Petroska, J., Lindle, J., & Pankratz, R. (2000). *Executive summary: 2000 Review of research on the Kentucky Education Reform Act.* Retrieved February 17, 2004, from *http://www.kier.org/2000Research.html*

Pew Hispanic Foundation. (2003). *Latinos in higher education: Many enroll, too few graduate.* Retrieved April 27, 2004, from *http://www.pewhispanic.org/site/docs/pdf*

Piaget, J. (1952). *Origins of intelligence in children.* New York: International Universities Press.

Piaget, J. (1970). *The science of education and the psychology of the child.* New York: Orion Press.

Picciano, A. (2001). *Distance learning.* Upper Saddle River, NJ: Pearson.

Pintrich, P., & Schunk, D. (2002). *Motivation in education: Theory, research, and applications* (2nd ed.). Upper Saddle River, NJ: Merrill/Prentice Hall.

Pittman, M., & Frykholm, J. (2002). *Turning points: Curriculum materials as catalysts for change.* Paper presented at the annual meeting of the American Educational Research Association, Seattle, WA.

Pogrow, S. (2006). The Bermuda Triangle of American education: Pure traditionalism, pure progressivism, and good intentions. *Phi Delta Kappan, 88*(2), 142–150.

Popham, W. (2004a). A game without winners. *Educational Leadership, 62*(3), 46–50.

Popham, W. (2004b). *America's failing schools: How parents and teachers can cope with No Child Left Behind.* New York: Routledge Falmer.

Popham, W. (2005). NAEP: Gold standard or fool's gold? *Educational Leadership, 68*(8), 79–81.

Porter, A. (2002). Measuring the content of instruction: Uses in research and practice. *Educational Researcher, 31*(7), 3–14.

Portner, J. (2000). Fearful teachers buy insurance against liability. *Education Week, 19*(20), 1, 18.

Pressley, M., Raphael, L., & Gallagher, J. G. (2004). Prodience-St. Mel School: How a school that works for African American students works. *Journal of Educational Psychology, 96*(2), 216–235.

Princiotta, D., Bielick, S., & Chapman, C. (2004). 1.1 million homeschooled students in the United States in 2003. *National Center for Education Statistics: Education Statistics Quarterly, 6*(3), 23–26.

Probst, R., Anderson, R., Brinnin, J., Leggett, J., & Irvin, J. (1997). *Elements of literature: Second course.* Austin, TX: Holt, Rinehart & Winston.

Proefriedt, W. (1999). Sorry, John. I'm not who you thought I was. *Education Week, 29*(15), 28, 30.

Public Agenda. (2000). *Just waiting to be asked? A fresh look at attitudes on public engagement.* Retrieved July 27, 2003, from *http://www.publicagenda.org/research/research_resports_details.cfm?list=23*

Public Agenda. (2002). *Sizing things up: What parents, teachers and students think about large and small high schools.* Retrieved June 15, 2004, from *http://www.publicagenda.org/research/research_reports_details.cfm?list=21*

Public Agenda. (2003). *Stand by me: What teachers really think about unions, merit pay, and other professional matters.* Retrieved May 15, 2006, from *http://www.publicagenda.org/specials/standbyme*

Public Agenda. (2004). *Teaching interrupted.* Retrieved June 12, 2004, from *http://www.publicagenda.org*

Pulliam, J., & Van Patten, J. (2003). *History of education in America* (8th ed.). Upper Saddle River, NJ: Merrill/Prentice Hall.

Pulliam, J., & Van Patten, J. (2007). *History of education in America* (9th ed.). Upper Saddle River, NJ: Merrill/Prentice Hall.

Pullman, P. (2002). *His dark materials* (trilogy). New York: Knopf.

Quick, P., & Normore, A. (2004). Moral leadership in the 21st century: Everyone is watching—especially the students. *Educational Forum, 68*(4), 336–347.

Quinlan, T. (2004). Speech recognition technology and students with writing difficulties: Improving fluency. *Journal of Educational Psychology, 96*(2), 337–346.

Quiocho, A., & Ulanoff, S. (2002, April). *Teacher research in preservice teacher education: Asking burning questions.* Paper presented at the annual meeting of the American Educational Research Association, New Orleans, LA.

Raider-Roth, M. (2005). *Trusting what you know: The high stakes of classroom relationships.* San Francisco: Jossey-Bass.

Rainwater, L., & Smeedings, T. (2003). *Poor kids in a rich country.* New York: Russell Sage Foundation.

Ramirez, A. (2001). How merit pay undermines education. *Educational Leadership, 58*(5), 16–20.

Raths, J., & Lynman, F. (2003). Summative evaluation of student teachers. *Journal of Teacher Education, 54,* 206–216.

Ravitch, D. (1990, October 24). Multiculturalism yes, particularism, no. *Chronicle of Higher Education,* p. A44.

Ravitch, D. (2000). *Left back: A century of failed school reforms.* New York: Simon & Schuster.

Ravitch, D. (2006). National standards. *Education Week, 25*(17), 54–58.

Ray v. School District of DeSoto County, 666 F. Supp. 1524, (M.D. Fla. 1987).

Ready, D., Lee, V., & Welner, K. (2004). Educational equity and school structure: School size, overcrowding and schools-within-schools. *Teachers College Record, 106*(10), 1989–2014.

Rebell, M. (2004). Why adequacy lawsuits matter. *Education Week, 23*(44), 40.

Recruiting New Teachers. (2006). *Teacher shortage areas.* Retrieved July 3, 2006, from *http://www.recruitingteachers.org/channels/clearinghouse*

Reeves, E., & Bylund, R. (2005). Are rural schools inferior to urban schools? A multi-year analysis of school accountability trends in Kentucky. *Rural Sociology, 70*(3), 360–386.

Reeves, J. (2004, January 30). Riley proposal would eliminate tenure panel [Electronic version]. *The Decatur Daily News.*

Regents of the University of California v. Bakke, 438 U.S. 265 (1978).

Reich, R. (2002). The civic perils of home schooling. *Educational Leadership, 59*(7), 56–59.

Reid, K. (2005). Sharing the load. *Education Week, 25*(12), 27–30.

Reis, S. M., Colbert, R. D., & Hébert, T. P. (2005). Understanding resilience in diverse, talented students in an urban high school. *Roeper Review, 27*(2), 110–120.

Remillard, J. (2005). Examining key concepts in research on teachers' use of mathematics curricula. *Review of Educational Research, 75*(2), 211–246.

Reys, B., Reys, R., & Chávez, O. (2004). Why mathematics textbooks matter. *Educational Leadership, 62*(5), 61–66.

Rhee, M., & Levin, J. (2006). Staffing urban schools. *Education Week, 25*(16), 52, 30.

Richard, A. (2000a). L.A. board taps Romer for top job. *Education Week, 19*(40), 1, 12–13.

Richard, A. (2000b). Studies cite lack of diversity in top position. *Education Week, 19*(25), 3.

Richard, A. (2003). Colorado voucher measure appears certain. *Education Week, 22*(29), 24, 30.

Richard, A. (2004). W. Va. eyes softer stand on school mergers. *Education Week, 23*(21), 16, 20.

Richard, A. (2005). Fla. board seeks social-promotion ban in all grades. *Education Week, 24*(20), 22, 27.

Richardson, J., & Newby, T. (2005, April). *The role of students' cognitive engagement in online learning.* Paper presented at the annual meeting of the American Educational Research Association, Montreal.

Richardson, P., & Watt, H. (2005). "I've decided to become a teacher": Influences on career change. *Teaching and Teacher Education, 21,* 475–489.

Richardson, V. (2003, April). *Preservice teachers' beliefs.* Paper presented at the annual meeting of the American Educational Research Association, Chicago.

Riordan, C. (2004). *Equality and achievement: An introduction to the sociology of education* (2nd ed.). Upper Saddle River, NJ: Merrill/Prentice Hall.

Ritter, G. W., & Lucas, C. J. (2005). Choosing the lesser of two inequalities. *Education Week, 24*(37), 31, 33.

Rittle-Johnson, B., & Alibali, M. (1999). Conceptual and procedural knowledge of mathematics: Does one lead to the other? *Journal of Educational Psychology, 91*(1), 175–189.

Robelen, E. (2006a). D.C. schools that take vouchers found to be less racially isolated. *Education Week, 25*(20), 13.

Robelen, E. (2006b). Disputes over charter closures winding up in court. *Education Week, 25*(16), 1, 11.

Robelen, E. (2006c). No test-score edge for Cleveland voucher students. *Education Week, 25*(24), 18.

Robelen, E. (2006d). Reanalysis of NAEP scores finds charter schools lagging. *Education Week, 26*(1), 26.

Robelen, E. (2006e). Small schools' ripple effects debated. *Education Week, 25*(34), 1, 20.

Roberts, W. (2006). *Bullying from both sides.* Thousand Oaks, CA: Corwin Press.

Roblyer, M. (2006). *Integrating educational technology into teaching* (4th ed.). Upper Saddle River, NJ: Merrill/Prentice Hall.

Rocha, A. (2006, March 1). The sex education controversy. *The Palo Alto Weekly: Online Edition.* Retrieved June 13, 2006, from *http://www.paloaltoonline.com/weekly/story.php?story_id=461*

Rodgers, C. (2002). Seeing student learning: Teacher change and the role of reflection. *Harvard Educational Review, 72,* 230–253.

Roffman, D. M. (2005). Lakoff for sexuality educators: The power and magic of "framing." *SIECUS Report, 33*(4), 20–25.

Rogers, C. (1967). Learning to be free. In C. Rogers & B. Stevens (Eds.), *The problem of being human.* Lafayette, CA: Real People Press.

Rogers, J., & Oakes, J. (2005). John Dewey speaks to Brown: Research, democratic social movement strategies, and the struggle for education on equal terms. *Teachers College Record, 107*(9), 2178–2203.

Romano, L. (2006, January 6). Fla. voucher system struck down: Court's ruling could affect programs in other states. *Washington Post,* p. A05. Retrieved April 23, 2006, from *http://www.washingtonpost.com/wp-dyn/content/article/2006/01/05/AR2006010501983.html*

Romboy, D., & Kinkead, L. (2005, April 14). Surviving in America. *Deseret Morning News, 155*(303), pp. 1, 11, 12.

Rose, L., & Gallup, A. (1998). The 30th annual Phi Delta Kappa/Gallup Poll of the public's attitudes toward the public schools. *Phi Delta Kappan, 80,* 41–56.

Rose, L., & Gallup, A. (2000). The 32nd annual Phi Delta Kappa/Gallup Poll of the public's attitudes toward the public schools. *Phi Delta Kappan, 82,* 41–58.

Rose, L., & Gallup, A. (2004). *The 36th annual Phi Delta Kappa/Gallup poll of the public's attitude toward the public schools.* Online version. Retrieved February 2005 from *http://www.pdkintl.org/kappan/k0409pol.htm*

Rose, L., & Gallup, A. (2005). *The 37th annual Phi Delta Kappa/Gallup poll of the public's attitude toward the public schools.* Online version. Retrieved March 2006 from *http://www.pdkintl.org/kappan/k0409pol.htm*

Rosenshine, B. (2006). The struggles of the lower-scoring students. *Teaching and Teacher Education, 22,* 555–562.

Ross, K. (2005). Charter schools and integration: The experience in Michigan. In J. Betts & T. Loveless (Eds.), *Getting choice right: Ensuring equity and efficiency in education policy* (pp. 146–175). Washington, DC: Brookings Institution Press.

Rother, C. (2005). Teachers talk tech. *Technological Horizons in Education, 33*(3), 34–36.

Rothman, R. (1997). KERA: A tale of one school. *Phi Delta Kappan, 79,* 272–275.

Rothstein, R. (1998). What does education cost? *American School Board Journal, 85*(9), 30–33.

Rothstein, R. (2004a). *Class and schools: Using social, economic, and educational reform to close the black–white achievement gap.* New York: Teachers College Press.

Rothstein, R. (2004b). The achievement gap. *Educational Leadership, 62*(3), 40–43.

Rowe, M. (1986). Wait-time: Slowing down may be a way of speeding up. *Journal of Teacher Education, 37*(1), 43–50.

Rubinson, F. (2004). Urban dropouts: Why so many and what can be done? In S. R. Steinberg & J. L. Kincheloe (Eds.), *19 Urban questions: Teaching in the city* (pp. 53–67). New York: Peter Lang.

Rutter, M., Maughan, B., Mortimore, P., Ouston, J., & Smith, A. (1979). *Fifteen thousand hours: Secondary schools and their effects on children.* Cambridge, MA: Harvard University Press.

Ryan, K. (1992). *The roller coaster year: Essays by and for beginning teachers.* New York: HarperCollins.

Sabo, D., Miller, K., Farrell, M., Barnes, G., & Melnick, M. (1998). The women's sports foundation report: Sport and teen pregnancy. *Volleyball, 26*(3), 20–23.

Safer, N., & Fleischman, S. (2005). How student progress monitoring improves instruction. *Educational Leadership, 62*(5), 81–83.

Saha, L., & Biddle, B. (2006). The innovative principal: Research in action. *Principal, 85*(5), 28–31.

Saltman, M. (2005). *The Edison schools: Corporate schooling and the assault on public education.* New York: Routledge/Falmer.

Saltpeter, J. (2005). Telling tales with technology. *Technology & Learning, 25*(7), 18–24.

Samuels, C. (2006a). Flexibility detailed for testing students with disabilities. *Education Week, 25*(16), 20.

Samuels, C. (2006b). Stricter school soda limits offered. *Education Week, 25*(36), 1, 18.

San Antonio, D. (2006). Broadening the world of early adolescents. *Educational Leadership, 63*(7), 8–13.

Sandham, J. (2000). Home sweet school. *Education Week, 19*(20), 24–29.

Sandholtz, J., & Reilly, B. (2004). Teachers, not technicians: Rethinking technical expectations for teachers. *Teachers College Record, 106*(3), 476–512.

Sattler, J. M. (2001). *Assessment of children: Cognitive applications* (4th ed.). San Diego, CA: Jerome M. Sattler.

Sax, L. (2005). The promise and peril of single-sex public education. *Education Week, 24*(25), 48, 34.

Schibsted, E. (2006). Fighting for fitness. *Edutopia, 1*(9), 30–37.

Schiever, S., & Maker, C. J. (2003). New directions in enrichment and acceleration. In N. Colangelo & G. Davis (Eds.), *Handbook of gifted education* (3rd ed., pp. 163–173). Boston: Allyn & Bacon.

Schlesinger, A. (1992). *The disuniting of America: Reflections on a multicultural society.* New York: Norton.

Schlozman, S. (2002). The shrink in the classroom: Fighting school violence. *Educational Leadership, 60*(2), 89–90.

Schnaiberg, L. (2000). Charter schools: Choice, diversity may be at odds. *Education Week, 19*(35), 1, 18–20.

Schoen, H., Fey, J., Hirsch, C., & Coxford, A. (1999). Issues and options in the math wars. *Phi Delta Kappan, 80,* 444–453.

Schon, D. (1983). *The reflective practitioner: How professionals think in action.* New York: Basic Books.

School Board of Nassau County, Florida v. Arline, 480 U.S. 273 (1987).

Schrimpf, C. (2006). This is me. In E. Keefe, V. Moore, & F. Duff (Eds.), *Listening to the experts* (pp. 87–90). Baltimore, MD: Paul H. Brookes.

Schult, C. A. (2002). Children's understanding of the distinction between intentions and desires. *Child Development, 73,* 1737–1747.

Schunk, D. (2004). *Learning theories: An educational perspective* (4th ed.). Upper Saddle River, NJ: Merrill/Prentice Hall.

Schutz, A. (2004, April). *Home is a prison in the global city: A critical review of urban school–community relationships.* Paper presented at the annual meeting of the American Educational Research Association, San Diego, CA.

Sears, J. (1993). Responding to the sexual diversity of faculty and students: Sexual praxis and the critically reflective administrator. In C. Capper (Ed.), *Educational administration in a pluralistic society.* Albany, NY: SUNY Press.

Selingo, J. (2004). The cheating culture. *Prism, 14*(1), 24–30.

Sergiovanni, T. (2004). *Educational governance and administration* (5th ed.). Boston: Allyn & Bacon.

Sergiovanni, T. (2006). *Principalship: The reflective practitioner perspective* (5th ed.). Boston: Allyn & Bacon.

Serrano v. Priest, (1), 96 Cal. Rptr. 601, 487 P.2d 1241, Calif. (1971).

Sewall, G. (2000). History 2000: Why the older textbooks may be better than the new. *Education Week, 19*(38), 36, 52.

Shakeshaft, C., Mandel, L., Johnson, Y., Sawyer, J., Hergenrother, M., & Barber, E. (1997). Boys call me cow. *Educational Leadership, 55*(2), 22–25.

Shaunessy, E. (2003, Summer). State policies regarding gifted education. *Gifted Child Today Magazine.* Retrieved March 14, 2004, from *http://www.findarticles.com/cf_dls/m0HRV/3_26/106290404/p1/article.jhtml*

Shay, S., & Gomez, J. (2002, April). *Privatization in education: A growth curve analysis of achievement.* Paper presented at the annual meeting of the American Educational Research Association, New Orleans, LA.

Shaywitz, S. E., & Shaywitz, B. A. (2004). Reading disability and the brain. *Educational Leadership, 61*(6), 7–11.

Shelley, A. (2003). Vanishing heritage. *Education Week, 22*(38), 24–29.

Shepard, L., & Smith, M. (1990). Synthesis of research on grade retention. *Educational Leadership, 47*(8), 84–88.

Shuell, T. (1996). Teaching and learning in a classroom context. In D. Berliner & R. Calfee (Eds.), *Handbook of educational psychology* (pp. 726–764). New York: Macmillan.

Silver-Pacuilla, H., & Fleischman, S. (2006). Technology to help struggling students. *Educational Leadership, 63*(5), 84–85.

Simonson, M., Smaldino, S., Albright, M., & Zavacek, S. (2006). *Teaching and learning at a distance* (3rd ed.). Upper Saddle River, NJ: Pearson.

Sincero, P., & Woyshner, C. (2003). Writing women into the curriculum. *Social Education, 67,* 218–225.

Siris, K., & Osterman, K. (2004). Interrupting the cycle of bullying and victimization in the elementary classroom. *Phi Delta Kappan, 86*(4), 288–291.

Skiba, R., & Peterson, R. (1999). The dark side of zero tolerance. *Phi Delta Kappan, 80,* 372–376, 381–382.

Slavin, R. (2006). *Educational psychology* (8th ed.). Boston: Allyn & Bacon.

Slavin, R., & Cheung, A. (2004). *Effective reading programs for English language learners: A best-evidence synthesis.* Baltimore: Center for Research on the Education of Students Placed At Risk, Johns Hopkins University. Retrieved April 23, 2006, from *www.csos.jhu.edu/crespar/techReports/ Report66.pdf*

Slavin, R., & Cheung, A. (2005). A synthesis of research on language of reading instruction for English language learners. *Review of Educational Research, 75*(2), 247–284.

Slavin, R., Karweit, N., & Madden, N. (Eds.). (1989). *Effective programs for students at risk.* Needham Heights, MA: Allyn & Bacon.

Sleeter, C. (2005). *Un-standardizing curriculum: Multicultural teaching in the standards-based classroom.* New York: Teachers College Press.

Smally, S., & Reyes-Blanes, M. (2001). Reaching out to African American parents in an urban community: A community–university partnership. *Urban Education, 36*(4), 518–533.

Smith, F. (2005). Intensive care. *Edutopia, 1*(9), 47–49.

Smith, F. (2006). Learning by giving. *Edutopia, 2*(1), 54–57.

Smith, J., Brewer, D. M., & Heffner, T. (2003). Using portfolio assessments with young children who are at risk for school failure. *Preventing School Failure, 48*(1), 38–40.

Smith, P., Molnar, A., & Zahorik, J. (2003). Class-size reduction: A fresh look at the data. *Educational Leadership, 61*(1), 72–74.

Smith, T., Desimone, L., & Ueno, K. (2005). "Highly qualified" to do what? The relationship between NCLB teacher quality mandates and the use of reform-oriented instruction in middle school mathematics. *Educational Evaluation and Policy Analysis, 27*(1), 75–109.

Smith, T., Polloway, E., Patton, J., & Dowdy, C. (2004). *Teaching students with special needs in inclusive settings* (4th ed.). Boston: Allyn & Bacon.

Smith v. Board of School Commissioners of Mobile County, 827 F.2d 684 (llth Cir., 1987).

Snider, J. (2006). The superintendent as scapegoat. *Education Week, 25*(18), 40, 31.

Sommers, C. (2000). *The war against boys: How misguided feminism is harming our young men.* New York: Simon & Schuster.

Sonnenberg, W. (2004). Federal support for education: Fiscal years 1980 to 2003. *National Center for Education Statistics: Education Statistics Quarterly, 6*(3), 65–68.

Spring, J. (2005). *The American School 1642–2004* (6th ed.). Boston: McGraw-Hill.

Spring, J. (2006). *American education* (12th ed.). Boston: McGraw-Hill.

Stabiner, K. (2003, January 12). Where girls aren't [Electronic version]. *New York Times.* Retrieved April 15, 2005, from *http://www.nytimes.com*

Stahl, R., DeMasi, K., Gehrke, R., Guy, C., & Scown, J. (2005, April). *Perceptions, conceptions and misconceptions of wait time and wait time behaviors among pre-service and in-service teachers.* Paper presented at the annual meeting of the American Educational Research Association, Montreal.

Stahl, S. A. (1999). Why innovations come and go (and mostly go): The case of whole language. *Educational Researcher, 28*(8), 13–22.

Starnes, B. (2006). What we don't know *can* hurt them: White teachers, Indian children. *Phi Delta Kappan, 87*(5), 384–392.

Steches, B., Hamilton, L., & Scott-Naflet, S. (2005). *Introduction to first-year findings: Implementing standards-based accountability (ISBA) project.* Paper presented at the annual meeting of the American Educational Research Association, Montreal.

Steele, C., Spencer, S., & Aronson, J. (2002). Contending with group image: The psychology of stereotype and social identity threat. In M. Zanna (Ed.), *Advances in experimental social psychology* (Vol. 34, pp. 379–440). San Diego: Academic Press.

Steering Committee on Science and Creationism. (1999). Science and creationism: A view from the National Academy of Sciences (2nd ed.). Washington, DC: National Academies Press.

Stefkovich, J., & O'Brien, G. (2001, April). *The courts, school governance, and students' rights: A meta-analysis of educators' knowledge of Fourth Amendment law.* Paper presented at the annual meeting of the American Educational Research Assoication, Seattle, WA.

Stiggins, R. (2005). *Student-centered classroom assessment* (4th ed.). Upper Saddle River, NJ: Merrill/Prentice Hall.

Stigler, J., Gonzales, P., Kawanaka, T., Knoll, T., & Serrano, A. (1999). *The TIMSS videotape classroom study: Methods and finding from an exploratory research project on eighth-grade mathematics instruction in Germany, Japan, and the United States* (NCES 990074). Washington, DC: U.S. Department of Education, National Center for Educational Statistics.

Stipek, D. (2002). *Motivation to learn: Integrating theory and practice* (4th ed.). Boston: Allyn & Bacon.

Stone v. Graham, 449 U.S. 39 (1981).

Strong, J., & Hindman, J. (2003). Hiring the best teachers. *Educational Leadership, 60*(8), 48–52.

Summers, J., Woodruff, A., Tomberlin, T., Williams, N., & Svinicki, M. (2001, April). *Cognitive processes of cooperative learning: A qualitative analysis.* Paper presented at the annual meeting of the American Educational Research Association, Seattle, WA.

Swaim, S. (2004). Strength in the middle. *Education Week, 23*(32), 32.

Swanson, C. (2004). *The real truth about low graduation rates: An evidence-based commentary.* Washington, DC: Urban Institute. Retrieved March 30, 2006, from *http://www.urban.org*

Swanson, C. (2006a). Bigger district size gives superintendents earnings edge. *Education Week, 25*(43), 18–19.

Swanson, C. (2006b, May). Tracking U.S. trends. *Education Week, Technology Counts,* pp. 50–52.

Swidler, S. (2004). *Naturally small.* Greenwich, CT: Information Age Publishing.

Sykes, S. (2006, July 31). College recruitment efforts will raise tuition. *Salt Lake Tribune,* p. B5.

Szczesiul, S. (2004, April). *Urban definitions, urban differentials: Implications for how new teachers locate the urban school problem.* Paper presented at the annual meeting of the American Educational Research Association, San Diego, CA.

Tallent-Runnels, M., Thomas, J., Lan, W., Cooper, S., Ahern, T., Shaw, S., & Liu, X. (2006). Teaching courses online: A review of the research. *Review of Educational Research, 76*(1), 93–135.

Taxman v. Board of Education of Township of Piscataway, 91 F.3d 1547 (3rd Cir., 1996).

Taylor, B., Pressley, M., & Pearson, P. (2002). Research-supported characteristics of teachers and schools that promote reading achievement. In B. Taylor & D. Pearson (Eds.), *Teaching reading: Effective schools, accomplished teachers* (pp. 361–374). Mahwah, NJ: Erlbaum.

Terwel, J., Gillies, R., van den Eeden, P., & Hoek, D. (2001). Cooperative learning processes of students: A longitudinal multilevel perspective. *British Journal of Educational Psychology, 71*, 619–645.

Thiers, N. (2006). Do single-sex classes raise academic achievement? *Educational Leadership, 63*(7), 70.

Thirunarayanan, M. O. (2004). National Board certification for teachers: A billion dollar hoax. *Teachers College Record.* Retrieved May 24, 2005, from *http://www.tcrecord.org*

Thompson, G. (2000). The real deal on bilingual education: Former language-minority students discuss effective and ineffective instructional practices. *Education Horizons, 78*(2), 80–90.

Thornton, S. (2003). Silence on gays and lesbians in social studies curriculum. *Social Education, 67*, 226–230.

Thornton, S. (2005). *Teaching social studies that matters: Curriculum for active learning.* New York: Teachers College Press.

Tiedt, P., & Tiedt, I. (2005). *Multicultural teaching* (7th ed.). Boston: Allyn & Bacon.

Tinker v. Des Moines Community School District, 393 U.S. 503 (1969).

Tobin, K. (1987). Role of wait-time in higher cognitive level learning. *Review of Educational Research, 57*, 69–95.

Tomlinson, C. (2003). *Fulfilling the promise of the differentiated classroom: Strategies and tools for responsive teaching.* Alexandria, VA: Association for Supervision and Curriculum Development.

Tomlinson, C., & Callahan, C. (2001, April). *Deciding to teach them all: Middle school teachers learning to teach for academic diversity.* Paper presented at the annual meeting of the American Educational Research Association, Seattle, WA.

Tompkins, G. (2006b). *Literacy for the 21st century: A balanced approach* (4th ed.). Upper Saddle River, NJ: Merrill/Prentice Hall.

Tonn, J. (2005a). First amendment attitudes found troubling. *Education Week, 24*(21), 6.

Tonn, J. (2005b). Sexual behavior. *Education Week, 25*(9), 15.

Trotter, A. (1999a). Preparing teachers for the digital age. *Education Week, 19*(4), 37–43.

Trotter, A. (1999b). Technology and its continual rise and fall. *Education Week, 18*(36), 30–31.

Trotter, A. (2000). Home computer used primarily for learning, families say in survey. *Education Week, 19*(30), 6.

Trotter, A. (2001). Channel One drops cash-incentive plan aimed at teachers. *Education Week, 21*(2), 17.

Trotter, A. (2002). Tech firms land privatization role. *Education Week, 22*(4), 1, 11.

Trotter, A. (2003). Simulated driver's ed. takes virtual twists and turns. *Education Week, 22*(19), 8.

Trotter, A. (2004). Digital games bring entertainment into learning realm. *Education Week, 23*(44), 8.

Trotter, A. (2005). Technology turns test-prep into clicking experience. *Education Week, 24*(36), 8.

Trotter, A. (2006a). Diversity on the docket. *Education Week, 26*(6), 27.

Trotter, A. (2006b). U.S. court backs school's decision to bar student's anti-gay T-shirt. *Education Week, 25*(34), 9.

Trotter, A. (2006c). Minorities still face digital divide. *Education Week, 26*(3), 14.

Tschannen-Moran, M., Woolfolk-Hoy, A., & Hoy, W. (1998). Teacher efficacy: Its meaning and measure. *Review of Educational Research, 68*(2), 202–248.

Turnbull, A., Turnbull, R., Shank, M., Smith, S., & Leal, D. (2007). *Exceptional lives: Special education in today's schools* (5th ed.). Upper Saddle River, NJ: Merrill/Prentice Hall.

Tyack, P., & Cuban, L. (1995). *Tinkering toward utopia.* Cambridge, MA: Harvard University Press.

Tyre, P. (2006). "The trouble with boys." *Newsweek, 147*(5), 44–52.

Tyson, H. (1999). A load off the teachers' backs: Coordinated school health programs. *Phi Delta Kappan, 80*(5), K1–K8.

U.S. Bureau of Census. (1990). *Statistical abstract of the United States* (110th ed.). Washington, DC: U.S. Government Printing Office.

U.S. Bureau of Census. (2000). *Educational attainment in the United States: March 1999* (pp. 20–528). Washington, DC: U.S. Department of Commerce.

U.S. Bureau of Census. (2001). Nation's household income stable in 2000. Retrieved June 13, 2006, from *www.census.gov/Press-Release/www/2001/cb01-158.html*

U.S. Bureau of Census. (2003). *Statistical abstract of the United States* (123rd ed.). Washington, DC: U.S. Government Printing Office.

U.S. Bureau of Census. (2004). *The foreign-born population in the United States: 2003.* Washington, DC: U.S. Government Printing Office.

U.S. Bureau of Census. (2005). *Income, poverty, and health insurance coverage in the United States, 2004.* Washington, DC: U.S. Government Printing Office.

U.S. Bureau of Census. (2006). *Effects of government taxes and transfers on income and poverty: 2004.* Washington, DC: U.S. Government Printing Office.

U.S. Bureau of Indian Affairs. (1974). Government schools for Indians (1881). In S. Cohen (Ed.), *Education in the United States: A documentary history* (Vol. 3, pp. 1734–1756). New York: Random House.

U.S. Department of Education. (1995). *Digest of education statistics, 1994.* Washington, DC: U.S. Government Printing Office.

U.S. Department of Education. (1999a). *Digest of education statistics, 1998.* Washington, DC: U.S. Government Printing Office.

U.S. Department of Education. (1999b). *Teachers' guide to religion in the public schools.* Washington, DC: Author.

U.S. Department of Education. (2000). *Digest of education statistics.* Washington, DC: Author.

U.S. Department of Education. (2001). *The longitudinal evaluation of school change and performance (LESCP) in Title I schools: Final report.* Washington, DC: Author.

U.S. Department of Education. (2002). *Press release on Title IX,* June 27. Washington, DC: Author.

U.S. Department of Education. (2003a). *Digest of education statistics, 2002.* Washington, DC: U.S. Government Printing Office.

U.S. Department of Education. (2003b). Title I—Improving the academic achievement of the disadvantaged. *Federal Register, 68*(236). Washington, DC: U.S. Government Printing Office.

U.S. Department of Education. (2004a). *A guide to education and No Child Left Behind.* Washington, DC: U.S. Government Printing Office.

U.S. Department of Education. (2004b). Individuals with Disabilities Education Act (IDEA) data (Table AA3). Washington, DC: Author. Retrieved August 23, 2005, from *http://www.ideadata.org/PartBdata.asp*

U.S. Department of Education. (2005a). *Education for homeless children and youth.* Washington, DC: U.S. Printing

Office. Retrieved July 12, 2006, from *www.ed.gov//programs/homeless/index.html*

U.S. Department of Education. (2005b). *The condition of education in 2005 in brief.* Washington DC: National Center for Education Statistics.

U.S. Department of Education. (2006a). Fact sheet on Title I. Retrieved August 15, 2006, from *http://www.ed.gov/title1*

U.S. Department of Education. (2006b). Magnet schools assistance program. Retrieved June 13, 2006, from *http://www.ed.gov/programs/magnet*

U.S. Department of Education. (2006c). *Statistics of state school systems: Revenues and expenditures to public elementary and secondary education, 2001–2002.* Washington, DC: National Center for Education Statistics.

U.S. Department of Health and Human Services. (2006). *AIDS info.* Retrieved July 31, 2006, from *http://www.aidsinfo.nih.gov/*

U.S. English. (2006). Retrieved August 13, 2006, from *http://www.us-english.org*

U.S. Government Accounting Office. (2006). *No Child Left Behind Act: Additional assistance and research on effective strategies would help small rural districts.* Washington, DC: Government Printing Office.

U.S. Government Printing Office. (1975). *Historical statistics of the United States: Colonial times to 1970* (Vol. I). Washington, DC: Author.

Ubben, G., Hughes, L., & Norris, C. (2001). *The principal: Creative leadership for excellence in schools* (4th ed.). Boston: Allyn & Bacon.

Ubben, G., Hughes, L., & Norris, C. (2004). *The principal: Creative leadership for excellence in schools* (5th ed.). Boston: Allyn & Bacon.

UCLA Center for Communication Policy. (2001). *Surveying the digital future: Year two.* Retrieved March 14, 2005, from *http://www.ccp.ucla.edu*

Underwood, J., & Webb, L. (2006). *School law for teachers.* Upper Saddle River, NJ: Pearson.

Vail, K. (2002). Same-sex schools. *American School Board Journal, 189*(11), 32–35.

van den Berg, R. (2002). Teachers' meanings regarding educational practice. *Review of Educational Research, 72,* 577–625.

Vander Ark, T. (2002). It's all about size. *American School Board Journal, 89*(20), 34–35.

Vander Ark, T. (2003). America's high school crisis: Policy reforms that will make a difference. *Education Week, 22*(29), 52, 41.

van Gelder, T. (2005). Teaching critical thinking: Some lessons from cognitive science. *College Teaching, 53,* 41–46.

Vergon, C. (2001, April). *The exclusion of students of color from elementary and secondary schools: A national dilemma and some research-based suggestions for its resolution.* Paper presented at the annual meeting of the American Educational Research Association, Seattle, WA.

Viadero, D. (1996). Middle school gains over 25 years chronicled. *Education Week 16*(8), 7.

Viadero, D. (1999). Education Department is set to release its list of recommended math programs. *Education Week, 19*(6), 1, 14.

Viadero, D. (2000). Lags in minority achievement defy traditional explanations. *Education Week, 19*(28), 1, 18–19, 21.

Viadero, D. (2003a). Nice work: The growing research base for character education programs shows benefits for students' social—and academic—skills. *Education Week, 22*(33), 38–41.

Viadero, D. (2003b). Staying power. *Education Week, 22*(39), 24–27.

Viadero, D. (2003c). Tormentors. *Education Week, 22*(18), 24–27.

Viadero, D. (2003d). Two studies highlight links between violence, bullying by students. *Education Week, 22*(36), 6.

Viadero, D. (2005a). Key data on charter achievement missing as policy questions mount. *Education Week, 25*(13), 6.

Viadero, D. (2005b). Smoking-prevention programs in schools found ineffective for teens. *Education Week, 24*(26), 6.

Viadero, D. (2006a). Debate over dropouts renewed as scholars issue dueling reports. *Education Week, 25*(33), 18.

Viadero, D. (2006b). Rose reports influence felt 40 years later. *Education Week, 25*(41), 1, 21–24.

Villegas, A. (1991). *Culturally responsive pedagogy for the 1990s and beyond.* Princeton, NJ: Educational Testing Service.

Wadsworth, D. (2001). Why new teachers choose to teach. *Educational Leadership, 58*(8), 24–28.

Walberg, H. (2003). Accountability helps students at risk. *Education Week, 22*(33), 42, 44.

Wallace, J., & Wildly, H. (2004). Old questions for new schools: What are the students doing? *Teachers College Record, 106*(4), 635–650.

Wallace, R. (2004). A framework for understanding teaching with the Internet. *American Educational Research Journal, 41*(2), 447–488.

Walsh, M. (1998). Religious freedom amendment fails in house vote. *Education Week, 17*(39), 22.

Walsh, M. (2000a). Church–state rulings cut both ways. *Education Week, 19*(42), 1, 40–41.

Walsh, M. (2000b). Voucher initiatives defeated in Calif., Mich. *Education Week, 19*(11), 14, 18.

Walsh, M. (2002a). Admissions case could have impact on K–12 education. *Education Week, 20*(15), 1, 24.

Walsh, M. (2002b). Charting the new landscape of school choice. *Education Week, 21*(42), 1, 18–21.

Walsh, M. (2002c). Peer grading passes muster, justices agree. *Education Week, 21*(24), 1, 28, 29.

Walsh, M. (2003a). Justices give K–12 go-ahead to promote diversity. *Education Week, 22*(42), 1, 28, 30.

Walsh, M. (2003b). Private management of schools. *Education Week, 22*(29), 17.

Walsh, M. (2003c). Reports paint opposite pictures of Edison achievement. *Education Week, 22*(25), 5.

Walsh, M., & Hendrie, C. (2003). High court upholds law on Internet filtering in libraries. *Education Week, 24*(42), 24.

Wang, J., & Odell, S. (2002). Mentored learning to teach according to standards-based reform: A critical review. *Review of Educational Research, 72,* 481–546.

Wang, M., Haertel, G., & Walberg, H. (1993). Toward a knowledge base for school learning. *Review of Educational Research, 63,* 249–294.

Warren, J., Jenkins, K., & Kulick, R. (2006). High school exit examinations and state-level completion and GED rates, 1975 through 2002. *Educational Evaluation and Policy Analysis, 28*(2), 131–152.

Wartofsky, A. (2001, February 19). The last word: Philip Pullman's trilogy for young adults ends with God's death and remarkably few critics. *Washington Post*, p. C–1.

Washington, B. (1932). *Selected speeches of Booker T. Washington.* New York: Doubleday.

Watch Me! Read (2005). Reinventing education. Retrieved March 20, 2005, from *http://IBM.com*

Watkins, W. (2001). *The White architects of Black education: Ideology and power in America, 1860–1954.* New York: Teachers College Press.

Waxman, H., Huang, S., Anderson, L., & Weinstein, T. (1997). Classroom process differences in inner-city elementary schools. *Journal of Educational Research, 91*(1), 49–59.

Wayne, A., & Youngs, P. (2003). Teacher characteristics and student achievement gains: A review. *Review of Educational Research, 73,* 89–122.

Wayne, A., Youngs, P., & Fleischman, S. (2005). Improving teacher induction. *Educational Leadership, 62*(8), 76–77.

Weaver-Hightower, M. (2005). *Dare the school build a new education for boys?* Retrieved June 7, 2005, from *http://www.tcrecord.org/Content.asp?ContentID=11743*

Wechsler, D. (2003). *Wechsler Intelligence Scale for Children* (4th ed.) San Antonio, TX: Psychological Corporation.

Weiner, L. (2002, April). *Why is classroom management so vexing to urban teachers? New directions in theory and research about classroom management in urban schools.* Paper presented at the annual meeting of the American Educational Research Association, New Orleans, LA.

Weiner, L. (2006). *Urban teaching: The essentials.* New York: Teachers College Press.

Weinstein, C. (2007). *Middle and secondary classroom management* (3rd ed.). Boston: McGraw-Hill.

Weinstein, C., & Mignano, A., Jr. (2003). *Elementary classroom management: Lessons from research and practice* (3rd ed.). New York: McGraw-Hill.

Weinstein, C., Woolfolk, A., Dittmeier, L., & Shankar, U. (1994). Protector or prison guard? Using metaphors and media to explore student teachers' thinking about classroom management. *Action in Teacher Education, 16*(1), 41–54.

Weinstein, R. (2002). *Reaching higher: The power of expectations in schooling.* Cambridge, MA: Harvard University Press.

Weiss, C., & Kipnes, L. (2006). Reexamining middle school effects: A comparison of middle grades students in middle schools and K–8 schools. *American Journal of Education, 112,* 239–272.

Weiss, I., & Pasley, J. (2004). What is high-quality instruction? *Educational Leadership, 61*(5), 24–28.

Weiss, L. (2005). Book battle in Fayetteville, AR, rages on. *School Library Journal, 51*(11), 20.

Weiss, S., DeFalco, A. A., & Weiss, E. M. (2005). Progressive = permissive? Not according to John Dewey . . . Subjects matter! *Essays in Education, 14,* 1–21.

Wessel, K. (2005). Campus leaders: Why this gender discrepancy? *Lessons, 7*(1), 16–19.

West, E. (1972). *The Black American and education.* Upper Saddle River, NJ: Merrill/Prentice Hall.

West, M., & Manno, B. (2006). The elephant in the reform room. *Education Week, 25*(34), 44, 36.

Whalen, S. (2002). *The Polk Bros. Foundation's Full-Service Schools-Initiative: Synopsis of evaluation findings.* Retrieved June 1, 2006, from *http://www.polkbrosfdn.org/full_service_schools_initiative.htm*

Whitson, J. (2006). *The Dover (PA) evolution case: A true win for education? Teachers College Record.* Published January, 4, 2006. Retrieved January 18, 2006, from *http://www.tcrecord.org* ID Number 12271.

Wiersma, W., & Jurs, S. G (2005). *Research methods in education: An introduction* (8th ed.) Needham Heights, MA: Allyn & Bacon.

Wiggins, G., & McTighe, J. (2005). *Understanding by design* (2nd ed.). Upper Saddle River, NJ: Pearson.

Wilder, M. (2000). Increasing African American teachers' presence in American schools: Voices of students who care. *Urban Education, 35*(2), 205–220.

Wiles, J., & Bondi, J. (2007). *Curriculum development: A guide to practice* (7th ed.). Upper Saddle River, NJ: Pearson.

"Will KERA come to PA?" (2003). *Education Advocate, 4*(3), 1–2. Retrieved August 14, 2005, from *http://www.ceopa.org/documents/Page1–4_001.pdf*

Willard, N. (2006). Cyberbullying. *Education Week, 25*(30), 41, 43.

Williams, J. (2003). Why great teachers stay. *Educational Leadership, 60*(8), 71–75.

Williams, S., Bareiss, R., & Reiser, B. (1996, April). *ASK Jasper: A multimedia publishing and performance support environment for design.* Paper presented at the annual meeting of the American Educational Research Association, New York.

Wilson, B. L., & Corbett, H D. (2001). *Listening to urban kids: School reform and the teachers they want.* Albany, NY: State University of New York Press.

Wilson, H., & Donenberg, G. (2004). Quality of parent communication about sex and its relationship to risky sexual behavior among youth in psychiatric care: A pilot study. *Journal of Child Psychology and Psychiatry and Allied Disciplines, 45*(2), 387–395.

Winitzky, N. (1994). Multicultural and mainstreamed classrooms. In R. Arends (Ed.), *Learning to teach* (3rd ed., pp. 132–170). New York: McGraw-Hill.

Winn, I. (2005). *The education mirage: How teachers succeed and why the system fails.* New York: iUniverse.

Winn, W. (2002). Current trends in technology research: The study of learning environments. *Educational Psychology Review, 14,* 331–351.

Winograd, K. (1998). Rethinking theory after practice: Education professor as elementary teacher. *Journal of Teacher Education, 49,* 296–303.

Wong, H., Britton, T., & Ganser, T. (2005). What the world can teach us about new teacher induction. *Phi Delta Kappan, 86*(5), 379–384.

Wood, K. (2005). *Interdisciplinary instruction* (3rd ed.). Upper Saddle River, NJ: Pearson.

Wood, M. (2005). *High school counselors say they lack skills to assist gay, lesbian students.* Retrieved July 14, 2006, from *www.bsu.edu/news*

Wood, T., Cobb, P., & Yackel, E. (1992). Change in learning mathematics: Change in teaching mathematics. In H. Marshall (Ed.), *Redefining student learning: Roots of educational change* (pp. 177–205). Norwood, NJ: Ablex.

Woodward, T. (2002, June 20). *Edison's failing grade. Corporate Watch.* Retrieved November 23, 2005, from *http://www.corpwatch.org/issues/PID.jsp?articleid=2688*

Wynne, E. (1997, March). *Moral education and character education: A comparison/contrast.* Paper presented at the annual meeting of the American Educational Research Association, Chicago.

Yan, W., & Gong, Y. (2003, April). *Who selects teaching as a career? An analysis of Hispanic American high school students' career aspiration of teaching.* Paper presented at the annual meeting of the American Educational Research Association, Chicago.

Yecke, C. (2006). Mayhem in the middle. *Education Week, 25*(21), 44.

Yinger, J. (Ed.). (2004). *Helping children left behind.* Cambridge, MA: MIT Press.

Young, B. (2002). *Characteristics of the 100 largest public elementary and secondary school districts in the United States: 2000–01* (NCES 2002–351). U.S. Department of Education, National Center for Education Statistics. Washington, DC: U.S. Government Printing Office.

Young, M., & Penhollow, T. (2006). The impact of abstinence education: What does the research say? *American Journal of Health Education, 37*(4), 194–202.

Young, M., & Scribner, J. (1997, March). *The synergy of parental involvement and student engagement at the secondary level: Relationships of consequence in Mexican-American communities.* Paper presented at the annual meeting of the American Educational Research Association, Chicago.

Zahorik, J. (1991). Teaching style and textbooks. *Teaching and Teacher Education, 7,* 185–196.

Zehr, M. (1999). Moving teachers along a competency continuum. *Education Week, 19*(4), 41.

Zehr, M. (2000). National standards on technology education released. *Education Week, 19*(31), 18.

Zehr, M. (2002a). Early bilingual programs found to boost test scores. *Education Week, 22*(1), 6.

Zehr, M. (2002b). Voters courted in two states on bilingual ed. *Education Week, 22*(2), 1, 22.

Zehr, M. (2004). Va. plan would ease standards for home school parents. *Education Week, 23*(34), 26.

Zehr, M. (2006). More home schoolers taking Advanced Placement tests. *Education Week, 25*(33), 12.

Zeldin, A., & Pajares, F. (2000). Against the odds: Self-efficacy beliefs of women in mathematical, scientific, and technological careers. *American Educational Research Journal, 37,* 215–246.

Zhao, Y. (2002, August 5). Wave of pupils lacking English strains school [Electronic version]. *New York Times.* Retrieved March 24, 2005, from *http://www.nytimes.com*

Zins, J., Bloodworth, M., Weissberg, R., & Walberg, H. (2004). The scientific base linking social and emotional learning to school success. In J. Zins, R. Weissberg, M. Wang, & H. Walberg (Eds.), *Building academic success on social and emotional learning* (pp. 3–22). New York: Teachers College Press.

Zirkel, P. (1999). Urinalysis? *Phi Delta Kappan, 80,* 409–410.

Zirkel, P. (2001/2002). Decisions that have shaped U.S. education. *Educational Leadership, 59*(4), 6–12.

Zollars, N. (2000). Schools need rules when it comes to students with disabilities. *Education Week, 19*(25), 1, 46, 48.

Glossary

Glossary

A

Ability grouping. The practice of placing students of similar aptitude and achievement histories together in an attempt to match instruction to the needs of different groups.

Academic freedom. The right of teachers to choose both content and teaching methods based on their professional judgment.

Academic learning time. Combining engagement and success, this is the amount of time students are successful while engaged.

Academy. A secondary school that focused on the practical needs of colonial America as a growing nation.

Acceleration. A program for gifted and talented students that keeps the regular curriculum but allows students to move through it more quickly.

Accountability. The process of requiring students to demonstrate understanding of the topics they study as measured by standardized tests, as well as holding educators at all levels responsible for students' performance.

Action research. A form of applied research designed to answer a specific school- or classroom-related question.

Administrators. Individuals responsible for the day-to-day operation of a school.

Advanced placement classes. Courses taken in high school that allow students to earn college credit.

Affirmative action. A collection of policies and procedures designed to overcome past racial, ethnic, gender, and disability discrimination.

Allocated time. The amount of time a teacher designates for a particular content area or topic.

Assessment. How student understanding is measured.

Assimilation. A process of socializing people so that they adopt dominant social norms and patterns of behavior.

Assistive technology. A set of adaptive tools that support students with disabilities in learning activities and daily life tasks.

Autonomy. The capacity to control one's own professional life.

Axiology. The branch of philosophy that considers values and ethics.

B

Behavior disorders. Exceptionalities involving the display of serious and persistent age-inappropriate behaviors that result in social conflict, personal unhappiness, and school failure.

Between-class ability grouping. Grouping that divides all students in a given grade into high, medium, and low groups.

Block grants. Federal monies provided to states and school districts with few restrictions for use.

Buckley Amendment. A federal act that makes school records open and accessible to students and their parents.

Bulletin board. An electronic message center for a given topic.

C

Career technical. A term used to identify programs designed to provide students with education and job skills that will enable them to get a job immediately after graduating from high school.

Caring. A teacher's investment in the protection and development of the young people in his or her classes.

Categorical grants. Monies targeted for specific groups and designated purposes.

Censorship. The practice of prohibiting the use of objectionable materials, such as certain books used in libraries or in academic classes.

Certification. Special recognition by a professional organization indicating that an individual has met certain requirements specified by the organization.

Character education. A curriculum approach to developing student morality suggesting that moral values and positive character traits, such as honesty and citizenship, should be emphasized, taught, and rewarded.

Charter schools. Alternative schools that are independently operated but publicly funded.

Chat room. A site on the Internet where many people can simultaneously communicate in real time.

Classroom climate. The emotional and psychological environment of a classroom.

Classroom management. Teachers' strategies that create and maintain an orderly learning environment.

Closure. A form of review occurring at the end of a lesson.

Cognitive learning theories. Explanations for learning that focus on changes in the ways people think that result from their efforts to make sense of the world.

Collaboration. Joint communication and decision making among educational professionals to create an optimal learning environment for students with exceptionalities.

Collective bargaining. Process that occurs when a local chapter of a professional organization negotiates with a school district over the rights of the teachers and the conditions of employment.

Common school movement. A historical attempt to make education available to all children in the United States.

Communication disorders. Exceptionalities that interfere with students' abilities to receive and understand information from others and to express their own ideas or questions.

Compensatory education programs. Government attempts to create more equal educational opportunities for disadvantaged youth.

Comprehensive high school. A secondary school that attempts to meet the needs of all students by housing them together and providing curricular options (e.g., vocational or college-preparatory programs) geared toward a variety of student ability levels and interests.

Computer-mediated communication (CMC). Telecommunication between people via electronic mail (e-mail).

Cooperative learning. A set of instructional strategies used to help learners meet specific learning and social interaction objectives in structured groups.

Copyright laws. Federal laws designed to protect the intellectual property of authors, including printed matter, videos, computer software, and various other types of original work.

Corporal punishment. The use of physical, punitive disciplinary actions to correct student misbehavior.

Creationism. A religious view suggesting that the universe was created by God as described in the Bible.

Credentials file. A collection of important documents teachers need to submit when they apply for teaching positions.

Cultural diversity. The different cultures that you'll encounter in classrooms and how these cultural differences influence learning.

Culturally responsive teaching. Instruction that acknowledges and accommodates cultural diversity.

Culture. The knowledge, attitudes, values, customs, and behavior patterns that characterize a social group.

Curriculum. The knowledge and skills that teachers teach and students are supposed to learn.

D

Database program. A computer program that allows users to store, organize, and manipulate information, including both text and numerical data.

Decision making. Problem solving in ill-defined situations, based on professional knowledge.

Development. The physical, intellectual, and social changes in children that occur as a result of experience.

Developmental programs. Programs that accommodate differences in children's development by allowing them to acquire skills and abilities at their own pace through direct experiences.

Digital portfolio. A collection of materials contained in an electronic file that makes the information accessible to potential viewers.

Direct instruction. An instructional strategy designed to teach well-defined knowledge and skills that are needed for later learning.

Disabilities. Functional limitations or an inability to perform a certain act, such as hear or walk.

Discipline. Teachers' responses to student misbehavior.

Distance learning. Organized instructional programs in which teachers and learners, though physically separated, are connected through technology.

Drill-and-practice programs. Software designed to provide extensive practice with feedback.

E

Early childhood education. A general term encompassing a range of educational programs for young children, including infant intervention and enrichment programs, nursery schools, public and private prekindergartens and kindergartens, and federally funded Head Start programs.

Educational technology. A combination of the processes and tools involved in addressing educational needs and problems.

Effective instruction. Instruction that builds on principles of learning to maximize learning in the classroom.

Effective school. A school in which learning for all students is maximized.

Emphasis. Verbal and vocal cues and repetition used to alert students to important information in a lesson

Engaged time. The time students actually spend actively involved in learning activities. Also called *time on task*.

English as a second language (ESL) program. Language program that emphasizes rapid transition to English.

English classical school. A free secondary school designed to meet the needs of boys not planning to attend college.

English language learners (ELLs). Students whose first language is not English and who need help in learning to speak, read, and write in English.

Enrichment.   A program for gifted and talented students that provides richer and varied content through strategies that supplement usual grade-level work.

Epistemology.   The branch of philosophy that examines questions of how we come to know what we know.

Equitable distribution.   The practice of calling on all students—both volunteers and nonvolunteers—as equally as possible.

Essential teaching skills.   Abilities that all teachers, including those in their first year, should have in order to maximize student learning.

Essentialism.   An educational philosophy suggesting that a critical core of knowledge and skills exists that all people should possess.

Establishment clause.   The clause of the First Amendment that prohibits the establishment of a national religion.

Ethics.   Sets of moral standards for acceptable professional behavior.

Ethnicity.   A person's ancestry; the way individuals identify themselves with the nation from which they or their ancestors came.

Existentialism.   A traditional philosophy suggesting that humanity isn't part of an orderly universe; rather, individuals create their own realities.

Explicit curriculum.   The curriculum found in textbooks, curriculum guides, standards, as well as other planned formal educational experiences.

Extracurriculum.   Learning experiences that extend beyond the core of students' formal studies.

Extrinsic rewards.   Rewards that come from outside oneself, such as job security and vacations.

F

Fair-use guidelines.   Policies that specify limitations in the use of copyrighted materials for educational purposes.

Feedback.   Information about existing understanding that we use to enhance future understanding.

Focus.   Activities or materials used to attract and maintain attention during lessons.

Formative evaluation.   The process of gathering information and providing feedback that teachers can use to improve their practice.

Free exercise clause.   The clause of the First Amendment that prohibits the government from interfering with individuals' rights to hold religious beliefs and freely practice religion.

Full-service schools.   Schools that serve as a family resource center to provide a range of social and health services.

G

Gender-role identity.   Differences in expectations and beliefs about appropriate roles and behaviors of the two sexes.

Gifted and talented.   A designation given to students at the upper end of the ability continuum who need special services to reach their full potential.

Giftedness.   Abilities at the upper end of the continuum that require support beyond regular classroom instruction to reach full potential.

Grievance.   A formal complaint against an employer alleging unsatisfactory working conditions.

Guided discovery.   An instructional model designed to teach concepts and relationships among them through the use of examples.

H

Head Start.   A federal compensatory education program designed to help 3- to 5-year-old disadvantaged children enter school ready to learn.

High collective efficacy.   The belief by teachers that their school can make a difference in students' lives.

High-quality examples.   Representations of content that ideally have all the information in them that students need in order to reach teachers' learning objectives.

High-stakes tests.   Assessments that states and districts use to determine whether or not students will advance from one grade to another, graduate from high school, or have access to specific fields of study.

Homeschooling.   An educational option in which parents educate their children at home.

Hypermedia.   A linked form of multimedia that allows learners to make connections to different points in the program based on their background knowledge and learning progress.

I

Icons.   Pictures displayed on computer screens that act as symbols for some action or item.

Idealism.   A traditional philosophy asserting that ideas are the only reliable form of reality.

Immersion program.   Language program that emphasizes rapid transition to English.

Implicit curriculum.   The kinds of learning children acquire from the nature and organization of the classroom and school as well as the attitudes and actions of their teachers.

In loco parentis.   A principle meaning "in place of the parents" that requires teachers to use the same judgment and care as parents in protecting the children under their supervision.

Inclusion.   A comprehensive approach to educating students with exceptionalities that advocates a total, systematic, and coordinated web of services.

Individualized education program (IEP).   An individually prescribed instructional plan devised by special education and general education teachers, resource professionals, and parents (and sometimes the student).

Induction programs. Professional experiences for beginning teachers that provide systematic and sustained assistance to ease the transition into teaching.

Instruction. The strategies teachers use to help students reach learning goals in the curriculum.

Instructional alignment. The match between learning objectives, learning activities, and assessments.

Instructional time. The amount left for teaching after routine management and administrative tasks are completed.

Integrated curriculum. Curriculum in which concepts and skills from various disciplines are combined and related.

Intelligence. The capacity to acquire knowledge, the ability to think and reason in the abstract, and the ability to solve problems.

Intelligent design. A theory suggesting that certain features of the universe and of living things are so complex that their existence is best explained by an intelligent cause, rather than an undirected process such as natural selection.

Internet. The complex web of interconnections among computers that allows people to communicate and share information worldwide.

Intrinsic rewards. Rewards that come from within oneself and are personally satisfying for emotional or intellectual reasons.

J

Junior high schools. Schools that were originally designed in the early 1900s to provide a unique academic curriculum for early adolescent youth.

L

Language clarity. Teacher talk that omits vague terms in questions and explanations.

Language disorders (or **receptive disorders**). Problems with understanding language or using language to express ideas.

Latchkey children. Children who go home to empty houses after school and who are left alone until parents arrive home from work.

Latin grammar school. A college-preparatory school originally designed to help boys prepare for the ministry or, later, for a career in law.

Learning communities. Classrooms in which the teacher and all the students work together to help everyone learn.

Learning disabilities. Exceptionalities that involve difficulties in acquiring and using listening, speaking, reading, writing, reasoning, or mathematical abilities.

Learning objectives. Statements that specify what students should know or be able to do with respect to a topic or course of study.

Learning styles. Students' personal approaches to learning, problem solving, and processing information.

Least restrictive environment (LRE). The placement of students in as normal an educational setting as possible while still meeting their special academic, social, and physical needs.

Lecture-discussion. An instructional model designed to help students acquire organized bodies of knowledge and understand the relationships of ideas within them.

Licensure. The process by which a state evaluates the credentials of prospective teachers to ensure that they have achieved satisfactory levels of teaching competence and are morally fit to work with youth.

Local school board. A group of elected lay citizens responsible for setting policies that determine how a school district operates.

Logic. The branch of philosophy that examines the processes of deriving valid conclusions from basic principles.

Looping. The practice of keeping a teacher with one group of students for more than a year.

Lower class. Socioeconomic level composed of people who typically make less than $25,000 per year, have a high school education or less, and work in blue-collar jobs.

M

Magnet schools. Public schools that provide innovative or specialized programs that attempt to attract students from all parts of a district.

Mainstreaming. The practice of moving students with exceptionalities from segregated settings into regular education classrooms.

Maintenance language programs. Language programs that place the greatest emphasis on using and sustaining the first language.

Mental retardation. An exceptionality that includes limitations in intellectual functioning, as indicated by difficulties in learning, and problems with adaptive skills, such as communication, self-care, and social ability.

Mentors. Experienced teachers who provide guidance and support for beginning teachers.

Merit pay. A supplement to a teacher's base salary intended to reward superior performance or work in a high-need area.

Metacognition. Students' awareness of the ways they learn most effectively and their ability to control these factors.

Metaphysics (ontology). The branch of philosophy that considers what we know.

Middle class. Socioeconomic level composed of managers, administrators, and white-collar workers who perform nonmanual work.

Middle schools. Schools, typically for grades 6–8, specifically designed to help students through the rapid social, emotional, and intellectual changes characteristic of early adolescence.

Models of instruction. Prescriptive approaches to teaching designed to help students acquire a deep understanding of specific forms of knowledge.

Moral education. A curriculum approach to developing student morality that emphasizes students' moral reasoning.

Multicultural education. A general term that describes a variety of strategies schools use to accommodate cultural differences in teaching and learning.

Multimedia. Combinations of media, including text, graphics, pictures, audio, and video that are designed to communicate information.

Multiple intelligences. A theory that suggests that overall intelligence is composed of eight relatively independent dimensions.

N

Negligence. A teacher's or other school employee's failure to exercise sufficient care in protecting students from injury.

Normal schools. Two-year institutions developed in the early 1800s to prepare prospective elementary teachers.

Normative philosophy. A description of the way professionals ought to practice.

Notoriety. The extent to which a teacher's behavior becomes known and controversial.

Null curriculum. Topics left out of the course of study.

O

Old Deluder Satan Act. Early colonial law designed to create scripture-literate citizens who would thwart Satan's trickery.

Organization. The set of teacher actions that maximizes the amount of time available for instruction.

Organized bodies of knowledge. Topics that connect facts, concepts, generalizations, and principles, and make the relationships among them explicit.

P

Perennialism. An educational philosophy suggesting that nature—including human nature—is constant.

Personal development. The growth of enduring personality traits that influence the way individuals interact with their physical and social environments.

Personal teaching efficacy. A teacher's belief in his or her ability to promote learning in all students regardless of their prior knowledge or experiences.

Perspective taking. The ability to understand the thoughts and feelings of others.

Philosophy of education. A framework for thinking about educational issues, and a guide for professional practice.

Philosophy. The study of theories of knowledge, truth, existence, and morality.

Positive teacher expectations. Teachers' beliefs in students' capabilities to learn.

Postmodernism. An educational philosophy contending that many of the institutions in our society, including schools, are used by those in power to control and marginalize those who lack power.

Poverty thresholds. Household income levels that represent the lowest earnings needed to meet basic living needs.

Pragmatism. A traditional philosophy that rejects the idea of absolute, unchanging truth, instead asserting that truth is "what works."

Principal. The individual who has the ultimate administrative responsibility for the school's operation.

Problem-based learning. An instructional strategy that uses a problem and the data gathered in attempts to solve it as the focal point of a lesson.

Procedures. Management routines students follow in their daily learning activities.

Productive learning environment. A classroom that is orderly and focuses on learning.

Professional ethics. A set of moral standards for acceptable professional behavior.

Professional portfolio. A collection of representative work materials to document developing knowledge and skills.

Professionalism. An occupation characterized by a specialized body of knowledge with emphasis on autonomy, decision making, reflection, and ethical standards for conduct.

Progressivism. An educational philosophy emphasizing curricula that focus on real-world problem solving and individual development.

Prompt. A teacher question or directive that elicits a student response after the student has failed to answer or has given an incorrect or incomplete answer.

Property taxes. The major source of educational funding, determined by the assessed value of a home or property.

Q

Questioning frequency. Refers to the number of times a teacher asks questions during a given period of instructional time.

R

Realism. A traditional philosophy suggesting that the features of the universe exist whether or not a human being is there to perceive them.

Reduction in force. The elimination of teaching positions because of declining student enrollment or school funds. Also known as "riffing."

Reflection. The process of teachers' thinking about and analyzing their work to assess its effectiveness.

Reforms. Suggested changes in teaching and teacher preparation intended to increase the amount students learn.

Resilient students. Students placed at-risk who have been able to rise above adverse conditions to succeed in school and in other aspects of life.

Résumé. A document that provides an overview of an individual's job qualifications and work experience.

Review. A summary that helps students link what they have already learned to what will follow in the next learning activity.

Rules. Guidelines that provide standards or norms for acceptable classroom behavior.

S

School district. An administrative unit within a state, defined by geographical boundaries, and legally responsible for the public education of children within those boundaries.

School principal. The individual having the ultimate administrative responsibility for a school's operation.

Separate but equal. A policy of segregating minorities in education, transportation, housing, and other areas of public life if opportunities and facilities were considered equal to those of nonminorities. In education, the policy was evidenced by separate schools with different curricula, teaching methods, teachers, and resources.

Service learning. An approach to promoting ethical and moral development that combines service to the community with content-learning objectives.

Sexual harassment. Unwanted and/or unwelcome sexual behavior that interferes with a student's sense of well-being.

Simulations. Programs, either in software or Web-based form, that model a system or process.

Single-gender classes and schools. Classes and schools where boys and girls are segregated for part or all of the day.

Site-based decision making. A school management reform movement that attempts to place increased responsibility for governance at the individual school level.

Social development. The advances students make in their ability to interact with and get along with others.

Social institution. An organization with established structures and rules designed to promote certain goals.

Social problem-solving skills. The ability to resolve conflicts in ways that are beneficial to all involved.

Socioeconomic status (SES). The combination of family income, parents' occupations, and the level of parental education.

Special education. Instruction designed to meet the unique needs of students with exceptionalities.

Speech disorders (or expressive disorders). Problems in forming and sequencing sounds.

Spreadsheet programs. Computer programs that are used to organize and manipulate numerical data.

Standards. Statements specifying what students should know and what skills they should have upon completing an area of study.

Standards-based education. The process of focusing curricula and instruction on predetermined standards.

State board of education. The legal governing body that exercises general control and supervision of the schools in a state.

State office of education. Office responsible for implementing a state's education policy on a day-to-day basis.

State tuition tax-credit plans. A variation on school voucher programs in which parents are given tax credits for money they spend on private-school tuition.

Stereotype. A rigid, simplistic caricature of a particular group of people.

Students placed at-risk. Students in danger of failing to complete their education with the skills necessary to survive in modern society.

Students with exceptionalities. Learners who need special help and resources to reach their full potential.

Summative evaluation. The process of gathering information about a teacher's competence, often for the purpose of making administrative decisions about retention and promotion.

Superintendent. The school district's head administrative officer, along with his or her staff, responsible for implementing that policy in the district's schools.

T

Teacher modeling. The tendency of people to observe and imitate others' behaviors and attitudes.

Teaching contract. A legal employment agreement between a teacher and a local school board.

Technician. A person who uses specific skills to complete well-defined tasks.

Tenure. A legal safeguard that provides job security by preventing teacher dismissal without cause.

Thematic lessons. Lessons in which all parts of a teacher's instruction are related, so that the lesson leads to a specific point.

Theory. A set of related principles that are based on observation and are used to explain additional observations.

Title I. A federal compensatory education program that funds supplemental education services for low-income students in elementary and secondary schools.

Tracking. The practice of ability grouping that places students in a series of different classes or curricula on the basis of ability and career goals.

Transition programs. Language programs that maintain the first language until students acquire sufficient English.

Transition signals. Verbal statements within a lesson that indicate one idea is ending and another is beginning, and suggest connections between the two ideas.

Tutorial. A software program that delivers an entire integrated instructional sequence similar to a teacher's instruction on the topic.

U

Underclass. People with low incomes who continually struggle with economic problems.

Upper class. The socioeconomic class composed of highly educated (usually a college degree), highly paid (usually above $170,000) professionals who make up about 5 percent of the population.

URL (uniform resource locator). A series of letters and/or symbols that acts as an address for a site on the Internet.

V

Voucher. A check or written document that parents can use to purchase educational services.

W

Wait-time. The amount of time a teacher pauses after asking a question both before and after calling on a student to answer.

War on Poverty. A general term for federal programs designed to eradicate poverty during the 1960s.

Website. A location on the World Wide Web identified with a uniform resource locator (URL).

Weighted student formula. A means of allocating resources within a district to schools on an individual basis based on student needs.

Within-class ability grouping. Grouping that divides students within one classroom into ability groups.

Withitness. A teacher's awareness of what is going on in all parts of the classroom at all times and the communication of this awareness to students, both verbally and nonverbally.

Working class. Socioeconomic level composed of blue-collar workers who perform manual labor.

World Wide Web. A system on the Internet that allows people to access, view, and maintain documents that include text, data, sound, and video.

Z

Zero-tolerance policies. Policies that call for students to receive automatic suspensions or expulsions as punishment for certain offenses, primarily those involving weapons, threats, or drugs.

Index